EBD 11/21/90

A Nineteenth-Century
Musical Chronicle

A NINETEENTH-CENTURY MUSICAL CHRONICLE

Events 1800–1899

Compiled by
CHARLES J. HALL

Music Reference Collection, Number 21

GREENWOOD PRESS
New York • Westport, Connecticut • London

Library of Congress Cataloging-in-Publication Data

Hall, Charles J.
   A nineteenth-century musical chronicle : events, 1800-1899 /
compiled by Charles J. Hall.
     p. cm. — (Music reference collection, ISSN 0736-7740 ; no.
21)
   Includes bibliographical references.
   ISBN 0-313-26578-X (lib. bdg. : alk. paper)
   1. Music—19th century—Chronology. I. Title. II. Title: 19th-
century musical chronicle. III. Series.
ML196.H34   1989
780'.9'034—dc20   89-17201

British Library Cataloguing in Publication Data is available.

Library of Congress Catalog Card Number: 89-17201
ISBN: 0-313-26578-X
ISSN: 0736-7740

First published in 1989

Greenwood Press, Inc.
88 Post Road West, Westport, Connecticut 06881

Printed in the United States of America

The paper used in this book complies with the
Permanent Paper Standard issued by the National
Information Standards Organization (Z39.48-1984).

10 9 8 7 6 5 4 3 2 1

Contents

Preface

A Nineteenth Century Musical Chronicle is the second of three volumes chronicling musical history since 1750. This project originated in the mid-1970's as program notes for a Michigan radio show in which musical selections of a given year were accompanied by commentary on contemporaneous events. The resulting volumes present musical events year-by-year in the context of political, social, and cultural history. Emphasis is on "art" music, but some highlights in popular genres are included. Information has been gathered from myriad sources--recognized authorities, magazines, newspapers, and, when possible, primary sources. Where different sources yield conflicting information about musical events, the author has accepted, for the most part, the authority of the *New Grove Dictionary of Music and Musicians*.

Each year begins with selected World Events and Cultural Highlights. Musical Events follow, divided into nine sections:

A. Births
B. Deaths
C. Debuts
D. New Positions
E. Prizes and Honors
F. Biographical Highlights
G. Institutional Openings
H. Musical Literature
I. Musical Compositions

Category C covers three types of debuts: the original debuts (with location); a U.S. debut, if separate from the first (also with location); and the Met debut for singers and conductors. Other debuts, such as those in Paris, Vienna, or Covent Garden, may be found under Category F. Biographical Highlights. The dates given for compositions under Category I are actual completion dates rather than premieres; however, distinction is not always possible. A detailed index provides access from the name or term to the year and category letter.

A word of acknowledgment should be given to those who helped and gave encouragement, to the many students who pored over the tomes in search of obscure items and pounded the typewriter keys, and to my wife who patiently put up with me in the hectic days of getting all the resources together; and a special word of thanks is due Allyn Craig, without whose computer expertise I could not have survived.

Charles J. Hall
B.M., M.M., Ph.D.

Abbreviations

COUNTRIES

Am	United States	Fin	Finland	Pan	Panama
Arm	Armenia	Fr	France	Peru	Peru
Arg	Argentina	Ger	Germany	Phil	Philippinès
Aus	Austria	Gr	Greece	Pol	Poland
Aust	Australia	Hol	Holland	Por	Portugal
Azer	Azerbaijan	Hun	Hungary	P.R.	Puerto Rico
Bel	Belgium	Ind	India	Rom	Romania
Boh	Bohemia	Ir	Ireland	Rus	Russia
Bol	Bolivia	Iran	Iran	Scot	Scotland
Br	Great Britain	Is	Israel	Serb	Serbia
Bra	Brazil	It	Italy	S.Af.	South Africa
Bul	Bulgaria	Jp	Japan	Sp	Spain
Can	Canada	Kor	Korea	Swe	Sweden
Chi	China	Lat	Latvia	Swi	Switzerland
Chil	Chile	Leb	Lebanon	Tai	Taiwan
Cub	Cuba	Lith	Lithuania	Tur	Turkey
Cz	Czechoslovakia	Man	Manchuria	Urg	Uruguay
Den	Denmark	Mex	Mexico	Ven	Venezuela
Egypt	Egypt	Nor	Norway	Yug	Yugoslavia
Est	Estonia	N.Z.	New Zealand		

PROFESSIONS

acous	acoustics	fl.m	flute maker	org	organ
act	actor, actress	folk	folk music	org.m	organ maker
alto	contralto	gui	guitar	pat	patron of arts
arr	arranger	harm	harmonica	ped	pedagogue
au	author	hn	horn virtuoso	perc	percussion
bal	ballet	hp	harp	pop	popular artist
band	band	hp.m	harp maker	pn	piano
bar	baritone	hps	harpsichord	pt	poet
bn	bassoon	hum	humorist	pub	publisher
bs	bass	hymn	hymn writer	rec	recorder
cas	castrato	imp	impresario	rel	religion
cb	contrabass	ind	industrialist	sax	saxophone
cd	conductor	inst.m	instrument	sing	singer
cel	cello		maker	sop	soprano
clar	clarinet	inv	inventor	ten	tenor
cm	composer	lib	librettist	the	theory
cri	music critic	mez	mezzosoprano	tpt	trumpet
c.ten	countertenor	m.ed	music educator	vn	violin
ed	educator	mus	musicology or	vla	viola
film	film music		music history	voc	vocalist
fl	flute	ob	oboe	ww.m	woodwind maker

The above abbreviations are found primarily in the Births and Deaths of each year. The country given in each case is the country of birth, except in rare cases where the parents are residing temporarily in another country.

THE CHRONICLE,
1800–1899

1800

World Events:
The United States census shows a population of 5,308,000, a 35% increase in ten years; because of a tied electoral vote, the House of Representatives chooses Thomas Jefferson as President No. 3; Washington, D.C., becomes the capitol and the White House is finished; the Harrison Land Act opens the western lands to settlers; Millard Fillmore, future president is born. Internationally, the British capture the island of Malta while Napoleon Bonaparte conquers Italy and advances on Vienna; Spain secretly gives the Louisiana Territory in the New World back to France; Alessandro Volta invents the electric battery.

Cultural Highlights:
Johann F. Tischbein becomes director of the Leipzig Academy of Art; Washington Allston graduates from Harvard and goes to London to study with West; John Constable enters the Royal Academy in London; John Flaxman is voted into the Royal Academy. British poet William Cowper dies; births include British author Anna Marie Hall and Portuguese poet Antonio de Castilho and three historians, the Frenchman Jean Jacques Ampères, Britisher Thomas Macaulay and American George Bancroft, German sculptor Emil Cauer and French artist Louis Eugène Lami. Other highlights include:

Art: John James Chalon, *Banditti at Their Repast*; Jacques-Louis David, *Napoleon Crossing the Alps*; John Flaxman, *Apollo and Marpessa*; Thomas Girtin, *The White House at Chelsea*; Francisco de Goya, *The Family of Charles IV*; Jean-Auguste Ingres, *Cincinnatus Receiving the Deputies*; John Trumbull, *Mrs. Trumbull in a White Dress*; Joseph Turner, *Dolbadern Castle*

Literature: Robert Bloomfield, *The Farmer's Boy*; Charles Brown, *Arthur Merwyn*; Maria Edgeworth, *Castle Rackrent*; James Hogg, *Donald M'Donald*; Gabriel Legouvé, *Le Merite des Femmes*; Thomas Morton, *Speed the Plough*; Novalis, *Hymnen an die Nacht*; Johann Friedrich von Schiller, *Maria Stuart*; Mme. de Staël, *On Literature*; Christoph Wieland, *Aristipp I, II*

MUSICAL EVENTS

A. Births:

Jan 11	Giuseppina Ronzi (Fr-sop)	May 17	Carl Zöllner (Ger-cd-cm)
Jan 14	Ludwig Köchel (Aus-mus)	Jun 28	Philipp Wackernagel (Ger-mus)
Feb 5	F. van Campenhout (Bel-vn)	Oct 7	Christian Nohr (Ger-vn)
Mar 10	Henry Erben (Am-org.m)	Nov 6	Eduard Grell (Ger-org)
Mar 15	Raimondo Boucheron (It-cm)	Nov 17	Louis Schlösser (Ger-vn-cm)
Mar 28	Antonio Tamburini (It-bar)	Nov 24	Henry K. Oliver (Am-org-hymn)
Apr 16	Józef Stefani (Pol-cm-cd)	Dec 27	John Goss (Br-org)
Apr 24	Georg Hellmesberger (Aus-vn)		Maria Caradori-Allan (It-sop)
May 10	Nicolai A. Titov (Rus-cm)		

B. Deaths:

Jan 4	Giambattista Mancini (It-cas)	Jun 10	Johann A. Schulz (Ger-cm)
Jan 6	William Jones (Br-rel-mus)	Jun 11	Margarethe Danzi (Ger-sop)
Feb 23	Joseph Warton (Br-cri)	Aug 3	Carl F.C. Fasch (Ger-cm-cd)
Feb 25	Gaudenzio Battistini (It-cm)	Sep 9	Pierre Gaviniès (Fr-vn)
Mar 3	Johann G. Toeschi (Ger-cm)	Sep 14	Francis Linley (Br-org)
Mar 9	Dominique Della Maria (Fr-cm)	Sep 18	Francisco Solano (Por-the)
Apr 4	Christoph Breitkopf (Ger-pub)	Dec 2	Jorge Bernat-Veri (Sp-org.m)
Apr 27	Evstigney I. Fomin (Rus-cm)		Antoine Albanese (Fr-cas)
May 3	Johann C. Fischer (Ger-ob-cm)		Louis Aubert (Fr-vn-cm)
May 7	Niccolò Piccinni (It-cm)		Louis Granier (Fr-vn-cm)

C. Debuts:

Other - Carl Czerny (Vienna), Friedrich Fesca (Magdeburg), Joseph Mayseder (Vienna), Charles Neate (London)

D. New Positions:

Conductors: Mateo de Albéniz (maestro de capilla, S. María la Redonda, San Sebastián), Ernst Häusler (cantor, St. Anne's, Augsburg), Johann S. Hermstedt (kapellmeister, Sondershausen), Marcos A. Portugal (San Carlo Theater, Lisbon), Carl Zelter (Berlin Singakademie)

Educational: Jean Jacques Grasset (violin, Paris Conservatory), Pierre Monsigny (Inspector of the Paris Conservatory)

Others: Pierre Rode (court violinist, Napoleon Bonaparte), William Spark (organ, St. George's, Leeds)

E. Prizes and Honors:

Honors: David Auguste von Apell (Order of the Golden Spur)

F. Biographical Highlights:

Ludwig van Beethoven meets Czerny and presents his first concert of his own works; Luigi Boccherini enters the service of Louis Bonaparte, Napoleon's ambassador to Madrid; Franz Danzi loses his wife and decides to resign all his Munich posts; Anton Anton Diabelli continues his priesthood studies and enters the monastery at Raichenhaslach; Jan Dussek secretly leaves England to escape his creditors and goes to Hamburg; François Fétis enters the Paris Conservatory; Josephina Grassini becomes Napoleon's mistress and goes with him to Paris; Michael Haydn loses all his property when the French occupy Salzburg; Friedrich Heinrich Himmel leaves St. Petersburg after two years to return to Berlin; Samuel Holyoke moves to Salem and continues to teach music; Konradin Kreutzer, on the death of his father, returns to the study of music; Daniel Steibelt, following his pianistic defeat by Beethoven, returns to Paris; Carl Maria von Weber fails in the lithography business in Frieberg and returns to composing.

G. Institutional Openings:

Performing Groups: Euterpean Society of New York; Philharmonic Society of New York; Société du Concert (Lille)

Educational: Library of Congress (Washington, D.C.)

Other: Flight and Robinson, Organ Builders (London); Graupner Music Store and Publishing House (Boston); Hoffmeister and Kühnel's Bureau de Musique (Leipzig-- bought out in 1814 by C.F. Peters); Momigny Publishing House (Paris); *Musical Journal for the Piano Forte*; Portable Grand (Upright) Piano (by J.I. Hawkins and M. Müller, working independently); Stockholm New Music Society

H. Musical Literature:

Corfe, Joseph, *Sacred Music*
Dalberg, Johann F., *Untersuchungen über den Ursprung der Harmonie*
Gervasoni, Carlo, *La Scuola della Musica*
Holden, Oliver, *Modern Collection of Sacred Music*
    Plain Psalmody and Sacred Dirges
Holyoke, Samuel, *Instrumental Assistant I*
Kauer, Ferdinand, *Kurzegefasste Generalbass-Schule für Anfänger*
Kimball, Jacob, *The Essex Harmony*
King, Matthew P., *A General Treatise on Music*
Page, John, *Harmonia Sacra*
Swan, Timothy, *The Songster's Assistant*

I. Musical Compositions:

Beethoven, Ludwig van, *Concerto No. 3 for Piano and Orchestra, Opus 37*
 Sonata No. 11, Opus 22, for Piano
 Sonata No. 4, Opus 23, for Violin, Viola and Piano
 String Quartets, Opus 18 (Nos. 1-6)
 Christ on the Mount of Olives, Opus 85 (oratorio)
Boccherini, Luigi, *Mass, Opus 59*
 Stabat Mater, Opus 61
Boieldieu, François, *The Caliph of Bagdad* (opera)
Cherubini, Luigi, *Les deux journées* (opera)
 Epicure (opera, with Méhul)
Dalayrac, Nicolas, *Maison à vendre* (opera)
Fomin, Evstigney, *The Americans* (opera)
 The Golden Apple (opera)
Generali, Pietro, *Gli amanti ridicoli* (opera)
Haydn, Franz Joseph, *The Seasons* (oratorio)
 Te Deum in C Major
Hewitt, James, *Robin Hood* (ballad opera)
 Pizarro (ballad opera)
Holden, Oliver, *From Vernon's Mount Behold the Hero Rise* (song)
Holyoke, Samuel, *Hark from the Tombs* (song for G. Washington's funeral)
Isouard, Nicolo, *Le Petit Page* (opera)
Kreutzer, Konradin, *Die lächerliche Werbung* (operetta)
Mayr, Simon, *Il carretto del venditore d'aceto* (opera)
Méhul, Etienne, *Bion* (opera)
 La dansomanie (ballet)
 Chant National du 14 Juillet, 1800
Mount-Edgcumbe, Richard, *Zenobia* (opera)
Naumann, Johann, *Il ritorno di figliolo prodigo* (oratorio)
Reicha, Anton, *L'ouragan* (opera)
Reichardt, Johann, *Lieb' und Treue* (opera)
 Lieb und Frieden (opera)
 Der Jubel (opera)
Reinagle, Alexander, *Masonic Overture*
 The Castle Spectre (opera)
 Pizarro (opera)
Righini, Vincenzo, *Tigrane* (opera)
Salieri, Antonio, *L'Angiolina* (opera)
 Cesare di Farmacusa (opera)
Spontini, Gaspare, *La fuga in maschere* (opera)
 I quadri parlanti (opera)
 Gli elisi delusi (opera)
Stich, Jan Václav, *Twenty Trios for Three Horns*
Süssmayr, Franz, *Gülnare* (opera)
Taylor, Raynor, *Pizarro* (ballad opera)
Weber, Carl Maria von, *Das Waldmädchen* (opera)
 Six Variations, Opus 2, for Piano
Weigl, Joseph, *Alceste* (ballet)
 Die Uniform (opera)
 Zulima und Azons (ballet)
Wesley, Samuel, *Nine Organ Voluntaries, Opus 6*
Wölfl, Joseph, *3 Piano Sonatas, Opus 7*
 3 Piano Sonatas, Opus 11
Zingarelli, Nicola, *Clitennestra* (opera)
Zumsteeg, Johann, *Kleine Balladen und Lieder* I and II

1801

World Events:

In the U.S., demands from the Pirates of Tripoli for extra tribute from all U.S. ships results in Congress sending the U.S. Navy to the Mediterranean; Robert Fulton perfects the first practical submarine; John Marshall becomes Chief Justice of the U.S. Supreme Court; E.I. du Pont de Nemours and Co. is founded in Delaware; Thomas Jefferson publishes his *Manual for Parliamentary Practices*. Internationally, the Treaty of Luneville brings about a practical end to the Holy Roman Empire; the Act of Union combines Ireland and Great Britain under one government; the British drive the French out of Cairo while the Turks regain control of Egypt; Czar Paul I of Russia is assassinated and succeeded by Alexander I.

Cultural Highlights:

Jean-Auguste Ingres receives the Prix de Rome in Art; John Vanderlyn goes to Paris to study art with Vincent; Pierre Simon Ballanche publishes his *Sentiment Considered in Its Relationship to Literature and the Arts*; Friedrich Bouterwek publishes his *History of Modern Poetry*. Births include British artists Richard Bonington and Thomas Cole, American artist Henry Inman, British author Cardinal John Henry Newman, Finnish novelist Fredrika Bremer and German dramatist Christian Dietrich Grabbe. Deaths include American artist Ralph Earl, Austrian artist Johann Schmidt and German artist Daniel Nikolaus Chodowiecki, Swiss poet Johann Kaspar Lavater, Polish poet Ignace Krasicki and German poet Novalis (Baron Friedrich von Hardenberg). Other highlights include:

Art: Antonio Canova, *Perseus with the Head of Medusa*; Jacques-Louis David, *Napoleon on Grand Saint-Bernard*; Girodet-Trioson, *Ossian Receiving the Warriors*; Thomas Girtin, *Kirkstall Abbey, Yorkshire*; Jean-Auguste Ingres, *The Envoys of Agamemnon*; Benjamin Latrobe, *Bank of Pennsylvania (Philadelphia)*; Joseph Turner, *Fisherman Cleaning Fish*

Literature: Clemens Brentano, *Godwi*; François de Chateaubriand, *Atala*; André de Chénier, *La Jeune Tarentine*; Maria Edgeworth, *Moral Tales for Young People*; James Hogg, *Scottish Pastorals*; August von Kotzebue, *Die Deutschen Kleinstadter*; Amelia Opie, *Father and Daughter*; Henry J. Pye, *Alfred*; Johann Friedrich von Schiller, *Die Jungfrau von Orleans and Don Carlos*; Robert Southey, *Thalaba*

MUSICAL EVENTS

A. Births:

Jan 21	Ramón Vilanova (Sp-cm)		Jun 3	Franz Skroup (Cz-cd-cm)
Jan 29	Johannes van Bree (Hol-cm)		Jun 25	Antonio d'Antoni (It-cm)
Feb 1	Adolf F. Lindblad (Swe-cm)		Jun 29	Pietro Alfieri (It-mus)
Feb 6	Laure Cinti-Damoreau (Fr-sop)		Jul 11	John H. Hewitt (Am-jour-cm)
Feb 21	Johann W. Kalliwoda (Boh-cm)		Aug 11	Eduard Devrient (Ger-bar)
Mar 7	Joseph Mainzer (Ger-m.ed)		Aug 13	Henry Phillips (Br-bs)
Mar 19	Salvatore Cammarano (It-lib)		Sep 10	Giuseppe Concone (It-cm-ed)
Mar 25	Georges Chanot, Sr. (Fr-vn.m)		Oct 7	Adolf Müller, Sr (Hun-cm)
Mar 30	Juste de la Fage (Fr-mus)		Oct 23	Albert Lortzing (Ger-cm)
Apr 19	Gustav T. Fechner (Aus-acous)		Nov 1	Vincenzo Bellini (It-cm)
May 13	Simon A. Forster (Br-vn.m)		Nov 27	Alexander Varlamov (Rus-cm)

B. Deaths:

Jan 11	Domenico Cimarosa (It-cm)		Mar 21	Andrea Lucchesi (It-cd-cm)
Jan 22	Angelo Morigi (It-the)		Mar 29	Claude Chiquot (Fr-org.m)
Feb 8	Johann Drexel (Ger-rel-cm)		May 14	Johann Altenburg (Ger-tpt)
Feb 19	Bernardo Aliprandi (It-cel)		May 21	Nicholas Audinot (Fr-bs)
Feb 27	Theodore Aylward (Br-org)		Jun 30	Catarina Cavalieri (Aus-sop)

Aug 13 Nicola Sala (It-cm-the)
Oct 13 Johann G. Naumann (Ger-cm)
Nov 9 Karl P. Stamitz (Ger-cm-cd)

Dec 10 Jonathan Battishill (Br-org)
Dec 19 Carlo Monza (It-cm)

C. Debuts:

Other - Teresa Belloc-Giorgi (Turin), John Braham (adult debut, London), Isabella Colbran (Paris), Ignaz Schuster (Vienna), Giovanni B. Velluti (Forli)

D. New Positions:

Conductors: Antonio Bruni (Opéra-Italienne, Paris), Franz Bühler (kapellmeister, Augsburg Cathedral), Heinrich K. Ebell (kapellmeister, Breslau), Valentino Fioravanti (St. Carlo, Lisbon), August Kotzebue (German Theater, St. Petersburg), Józef Kozlowski (Imperial Theaters, St. Petersburg), Domenico Rampini (maestro di capella, Trieste), Ignaz von Seyfried (Theater an der Wien), Georg F. Wolf (kapellmeister, Wernigerode)

Educational: Bernhard Romberg (cello, Paris Conservatory)

Others: Antonio Calegari (organ, St. Antonio, Padua), Matthew Camidge (organ, St. Michael-le-Belfrey, York), Emanuel Schikaneder (manager, Theater an der Wien, Vienna), John Stafford Smith (organ, Chapel Royal, London)

F. Biographical Highlights:

Maddalena Allegranti retires from the operatic stage; Ludwig van Beethoven's deafness becomes acute and he falls in love with Giulietta Guicciardi; Teresa Bertinotti marries singer Felice Radicati and begins touring Europe with him; Angelica Catalani makes her La Scala debut; Frédéric Kalkbrenner graduates from Paris Conservatory with first prizes in piano and harmony; Niccolò Paganini retires from public performance and begins an affair with a noblewoman of Tuscany; Anton Reicha settles in Vienna and renews his friendships with Beethoven, Haydn and Salieri; Ferdinand Ries begins piano study with Beethoven; Giovanni Viotti, back in London after three years in Germany, goes into the wine-making business which ultimately fails; Carl Maria von Weber moves back to Salzburg and studies with Michael Haydn; Joseph Wölfl, after concertizing in Germany, settles in Paris.

G. Institutional Openings:

Performing Groups: Trieste Opera Co.

Educational: American Conservatorio (Boston); Bavarian Academy of Arts and Sciences (Munich)

Other: Danziger Theater (Gdansk); Michael Kelly, Music Publisher (London); Kunst-und Industrie-Comptoir (Austrian Music Publishers, Vienna); Teatro de Circo (Havana); Teatro Lentasio (Milan); Teatro Nuovo (Teatro Grande, Trieste); Theater an der Wien (Vienna)

H. Musical Literature:

Busby, Thomas, *Complete Dictionary of Music*
Clementi, Muzio, *Introduction to the Art of Playing the Piano-Forte*
Dalberg, Johann F., *Die Äolsharfe...*
Gianelli, Pietro, *Dizionario della Musica*
Hill, Uri, *The Vermont Harmony*
Kittel, Johann C., *Der angehende praktische Organist*
Klein, Johann J., *Lehrbuchs der praktischen Musik*
Kollmann, Augustus, *A Practical Guide to Thoroughbass*
Swan, Timothy, *New England Harmony*
Thiemé, Frédéric, *Nouvelle théorie sur le différs mouvemens des airs*
Vogler, Georg, *Data zur Akustik*

I. Musical Compositions:

Abeille, Ludwig, *Amor and Psyche* (opera)
Attwood, Thomas, *The Sea-Side Story* (opera)
Beethoven, Ludwig van, *The Creatures of Prometheus, Opus 43* (ballet)
    Sonatas No. 12-15, Opus 26-28, for Piano
    Sonata No. 5, Opus 24, for Violin and Piano
    String Quintet in C Major, Opus 29
    6 Easy Variations in G Major, Opus 188, for Piano
    24 Variations on Righini's "Veni amore" for Piano
Bianchi, Francesco, *Alzira* (opera)
Boccherini, Luigi, *6 String Quartets, Opus 60*
Cimarosa, Domenico, *Artemisia* (unfinished opera)
Dalayrac, Nicolas, *Léhéman* (opera)
Eberl, Anton, *Die Königin der Schwarzen Inseln* (opera)
Field, John, *3 Sonatas, Opus l, for Piano*
Grétry, André, *La casque et les colombes* (opera)
Haydn, Franz Joseph, *The Seven Last Words* (choral version)
    Missa solennis in B-flat, "Schöpfungsmesse"
Haydn, Michael, *Missa sotto il titulo di Sancte Teresia*
Himmel, Friedrich, *Vasco da Gama* (opera)
    Frohsinn und Schwärmerei (singspiel)
Hoffmann, E. T. A., *Scherz, List und Rache* (opera)
Isouard, Nicolo, *Flaminius à Corinthe* (opera)
    Le tonnelier (opera)
    L'impromtu de campagne (opera)
Kashin, Daniil, *Natalia, the Boyard's Daughter* (opera)
Lesueur, Jean-François, *Artaxerce* (opera)
Mayr, Simon, *Ginerva di Scozia* (opera)
Méhul, Etienne, *L'irato* (opera)
Naumann, Johann, *Aci e Galatea* (opera)
    Mass in A-flat Major
Paër, Ferdinando, *Achille* (opera)
Portugal, Marcos, *La morte de Semiramide* (opera)
Reichardt, Johann, *Rosamonda* (opera)
Salieri, Antonio, *Annibale in Capua* (opera)
Sarti, Giuseppe, *Oratorio for Catherine the Great*
Spontini, Gaspare, *Gli amanti in cimento* (opera)
Süssmayr, Franz, *Phasma* (opera)
Trento, Vittorio, *Quanti casi in un sol giorno* (opera
Weber, Carl Maria von, *Six Easy Pieces, Opus 3, for Piano, Four Hands*
    12 Allemandes, Opus 4, for Piano
Weigl, Joseph, *Die tänzerin von Athen* (ballet)
    Der spanier auf der insel Christina (ballet)
Weinlig, Christian, *Die Erlösung* (oratorio)
Wölfl, Joseph, *Double Concerto for Violin, Piano and Orchestra*
    Concerto in G Major, Opus 20, for Piano and Orchestra
    3 Piano Sonatas, Opus 14, on Haydn's "Creation"
Zelter, Carl F., *Te Deum*
Zumsteeg, Johann, *Kleine Balladen und Lieder III*

1802

World Events:

In the U.S., Congress repeals several unpopular laws (Judiciary Act, Naturalization Act, etc.) which were causes of considerable political problems; West Point Military Academy is established by Congressional action; Cincinnati, Ohio, is incorporated. Internationally, Napoleon, made First Consul for life by the French, annexes Parma, Piacenza and Piedmont; the Treaty of Amiens gives France and England a 14-month breathing spell from the war; the Health and Morals Act is passed by the British Parliament; Toussaint-l'Ouverture leads an unsuccessful rebellion in Santo Domingo.

Cultural Highlights:

The American Academy of Fine Art opens in New York; Joseph Turner is inducted into the Royal Academy of Art in London. In the field of art, births include British artists Richard Bonington and Edwin Landseer, architect Richard Upjohn, and German sculptor Emil Wolff; deaths include British artists Thomas Girtin and George Romney, and the Italians Giuseppe Ceracchi and Francesco Casanova. Births in the literary field include Austrian dramatist Eduard von Bauernfeld and poets Nicolaus Lenau and Johann Vogl, British poets Letitia Landon and Winthrop Praed, French novelists Alexander Dumas, père, and Victor Hugo and German author Wilhelm Hauff; deaths include British poet Richard Cambridge, French poet Marie Anne Boccage and Russian author Aleksander Radischev. Other highlights include:

Art: Antonio Canova, *Napoleon Bonaparte*; John Constable, *View of Dedham Dale*; John Flaxman, *Illustrations to the Divine Comedy*; François Gérard, *Empress Josephine*; Anne Louis Girodet-Trioson, *Fingal*; Thomas Girtin, *The Eidometropolis*; Pierre Guérin, *Phédre and Hippolyte*; Gilbert Stuart, *Mrs. Perez Morton*; Joseph Turner, *The Tenth Plague on Egypt*; Benjamin West, *Death on a Pale Horse*

Literature: François Andrieux, *Helvétius*; Joanna Baillie, *Plays on the Passions II*; Robert Bloomfield, *Rural Tales, Ballads*; François de Chateaubriand, *The Genius of Christianity*; Ugo Foscolo, *The Last Letters of Jacopo Ortis*; Charles Lamb, *John Woodvil*; Adam G. Oehlenschläger, *The Golden Horns*; Friedrich von Schelling, *Bruno*; Walter Scott, *Minstrelsy of the Scottish Border I, II*; Mme. de Staël, *Delphine*

MUSICAL EVENTS

A. Births:

Feb 20	Charles de Bériot (Bel-vn)		Aug 8	Friedrich Wieprecht (Ger-inv)
Mar 3	Adolphe Nourrit (Fr-ten)		Aug 16	Moritz Drobisch (Ger-mus)
Apr 1	Hubert Ries (Ger-vn)		Aug 23	Eugène E. Massol (Fr-bar)
Apr 27	Louis Niedermeyer (Swi-cm)		Oct	Mary Anne Paton (Scot-sop)
May 22	Joseph d'Ortigue (Fr-mus)		Oct 7	Bernhard Molique (Ger-vn)
May 31	Cesare Pugni (It-cm)		Oct 17	Eduard Rietz (Ger-vn)
Jul 3	Joseph Labitzky (Ger-cd)		Dec 19	John Ella (Br-cri)
Jul 15	John Barnett (Br-cm)			Mary Ann Wilson (Br-sop)
Jul 23	Niels Jensen (Den-org)			
Jul 30	John Templeton (Scot-ten)			

B. Deaths:

Jan 27	Johann R. Zumsteeg (Ger-cm)		Sep	Hyacinthe Jadin (Fr-pn)
Mar 20	Isidore Bertheaume (Fr-vn)		Sep 1	François Hérold (Fr-pn)
Apr 10	Charlotte Brent (Br-sop)		Oct 2	Giuseppe Millico (It-ten)
Jun 28	Johann J. Engel (Ger-the)		Oct 22	Sophie Arnould (Fr-sop)
Jul 28	Giuseppe Sarti (It-cm)		Oct 22	Samuel Arnold (Br-mus)
Aug 7	Henri Larrivée (Fr-bar)		Oct 29	Jacques Lamoninary (Fr-vn)
Aug 10	Antonio Lolli (It-vn-cm)		Nov 2	Johann Spangler (Aus-ten)
Aug 23	Corona Schröter (Ger-sop)			Carl Franz (Ger-hn)

C. Debuts:
Other - Josef Blahack (Vienna), Ludwig Maurer (Berlin), Franz Pechaczek, Jr. (Prague)

D. New Positions:
Conductors: Mathieu-Frédéric Blasius (Opéra-Comique, Paris), Franz Clement (Theater an der Wien), Johannes S. Mayr (maestro di capella, S. Maria Maggiore, Bergamo), Wenzel Müller (German Opera, Prague), Ferdinando Paër (kapellmeister, Dresden), Giovanni Paisiello (maître de chapelle, Napoleon), Alessandro Rolla (La Scala), Friedrich Witt (kapellmeister, Würzburg)

Educational: Charles N. Baudiot (cello, Paris Conservatory), Louis E. Jadin (piano, Paris Conservatory), José Mauricio (music professor, Coimbra University)

Others: Thomas Adams (organ, Carlisle Chapel, Lambeth), Nicholas T. Ayrton (organ, Ripon Cathedral), August Bergt (organ, St. Petri, Bautzen), Robert Cooke (organ, Westminster Abbey), Joseph Kemp (organ, Bristol Cathedral), Charles Knyvett, Jr. (organ, St. George's, London)

E. Prizes and Honors:
Honors: André Grétry (Legion of Honor)

F. Biographical Highlights:
Johann Ludwig Abeille begins a thirty-year term as concertmaster in the private orchestra of the Duke of Württemberg; Daniel François Auber is sent to London by his father to study commerce; Ludwig van Beethoven, in despair over his growing deafness, writes his "Heiligenstadt Testament"; François Boieldieu marries dancer Clotilde Mafleuray but leaves her within the year; Fanny Burney and her husband are forced by the war into a ten-year stay in France; Muzio Clementi goes on a third continental tour; John Field accompanies Clementi on his tour to Paris; E.T.A. Hoffmann marries Marianna Rorer; Gertrud Mara leaves London for a concert tour of France; Giovanni Paisiello goes to Paris to be a part of Napoleon's court; Gioacchino Rossini, age ten, begins singing in local churches; Louis Spohr accompanies violinist Johann Friedrich Eck on his Russian tour where he meets Clementi and Field.

G. Institutional Openings:
Performing Groups: Leipzig Singakademie; St. Petersburg Philharmonic Society; United States Marine Band (full brass band)

Other: Bamberg Theater (Germany); Claviola (by J.I. Hawkins); John Cole, Music Publisher (Baltimore); *Correspondence des Amateurs Musiciens* (Paris); Dalmas Music Publishing Co. (St. Petersburg); *Edinburgh Review*; Hacker Music Publishing Co. (Salzburg); C. Lose and Co., Music Publishers (Copenhagen); *Le Magasin de Musique* (Paris); Miniature Scores (by Ignaz Pleyel); Order of the Legion of Honor (created by Napoleon); Staffless Music Notation (by Andrew Law); Nannette Streicher Piano Co. (Vienna)

H. Musical Literature:
Albéniz, Mateo, *Instrucción melodica, especulativa y prática...*
Calegari, Antonio, *Gioco pittagorico musicale*
Catel, Charles, *Traité d'harmonie*
Chladni, Ernst, *Die Akustik*
Hewitt, James, *Collection of the Most Favorite Country Dances*
Holyoke, Samuel, *Columbian Repository*
Jones, Edward, *The Bardic Museum*
Koch, Heinrich, *Musikalisches Lexikon*
Sabbatini, Luigi, *Trattato sopra le fughe*
Vogler, Georg, *Handbuch zur Harmonielehre und für den Generalbass*

I. Musical Compositions:

Arnold, Samuel, *The Sixty Third Letter* (opera)
Asioli, Bonifazio, *Gustava al Malabar* (opera)
Beethoven, Ludwig van, *Symphony No. 2, Opus 36*
    Sonatas No. 16-18, Opus 31, for Piano
    2 Easy Sonatas, Opus 49, for Piano
    3 Sonatas, Opus 30, for Violin and Piano
    Trio, Opus 38, for Clarinet, Viola and Piano
    Serenade, Opus 25 (flute, violin, piano)
    7 Bagatelles, Opus 33, for Piano
    6 Variations, Opus 34, for Piano
    15 Variations on Prometheus Theme, Opus 35, for Piano
    7 Variations on "Bei Männern" (cello, piano)
    Opferlied, Opus 121b (soprano, chorus, orchestra)
Boccherini, Luigi, *6 String Quartets, Opus 62*
    Christmas Cantata, Opus 63
Catel, Charles S., *Sémiramis* (opera)
Clementi, Muzio, *3 Piano Sonatas, Opus 40*
Dalayrac, Nicolas, *La boucle de cheveux* (opera)
Danzi, Franz, *El Bondocani* (opera)
Destouches, André, *Turandot* (incidental music)
Fioravanti, Valentino, *La capricciosa pentita* (opera)
Haydn, Franz Joseph, *Missa solennis, "Harmoniemesse"*
Isouard, Nicolo, *Michel-Ange* (opera)
    La statue (opera)
Kreutzer, Rodolphe, *Symphonie Concertante* (violin, cello, orchestra)
Mayr, Simon, *I Misteri eleusini* (opera)
Méhul, Etienne, *Une folie* (opera)
    Joanna (opera)
    Le Trésor supposé (opera)
Paër, Ferdinando, *Ginevra degli Almieri* (opera)
Paisiello, Giovanni, *Messa pastorale in G Major*
Portugal, Marcos, *Zaira* (opera)
    Il trionfo di Clelia (opera)
Reichardt, Johann, *Die Kreutzfahrer* (incidental music)
Righini, Vincenzo, *Concerto for Flute and Orchestra*
    Concerto for Oboe and Orchestra
Salieri, Antonio, *La bella selvaggia* (opera)
Schenk, Johann, *Der Fassbinder* (operetta)
Spontini, Gaspare, *Le metamorfosi di Pasquale* (opera)
Steibelt, Daniel, *Le Retour de Zéphyre* (ballet)
Stich, Jan Václav, *Concertos No. 8-10 for Horn and Orchestra*
    Sextet, Opus 34
Titov, Alexei, *Andromeda and Perseus* (opera)
Tritto, Giacomo, *Gli Americani* (opera)
Weber, Carl Maria von, *Mass in E-flat, "Jugendmesse"*
    Six Ecossaises for Piano
Witt, Friedrich, *Der Leidende Heiland* (oratorio)
Zingarelli, Nicola, *Edipo a Colono* (opera)
    La notte dell'armicizia (opera)
Zumsteeg, Johann, *Kleine Balladen und Lieder IV-VI*
    Elbondocani (singspiel)

1803

World Events:
In the U.S., the Louisiana Territory is purchased from Napoleon for $15,000,000 thus doubling the size of the United States; Lewis and Clark begin their expedition to the Northwest Territory; Ohio becomes State No. 17; Fort Dearborn is built on the site of present-day Chicago; James Audubon begins his work on American birds; Buffalo, New York, is founded; Samuel Adams dies. Internationally, France and Great Britain return to warfare over the Malta issue; the British turn Tasmania into a penal colony and put down an Irish independence uprising; George III suffers his third bout with mental illness.

Cultural Highlights:
The Norwich Society of Artists and its accompanying School of Art are founded by Cotman and Crome; François de Chateaubriand is given an embassy post in Rome; André Marie de Chénier is inducted into the French Academy. Births in the field of Art include French artists Alexandre Decamps, Paul Huet and Eugène Isabey and Scotch artist Robert Lauder; deaths include German poet and artist Nikolai L'vov. Births in the literary field include Americans Ralph Waldo Emerson and Sarah Whitman, British novelists Edward Bulwer-Lytton, Robert Surtees and poet Thomas Beddoes, French novelist Prosper Mérimée and Irish poet James Mangan; deaths include the German philosopher Johann von Herder and poets Johann Gleim and Friedrich Klopstock, Italian poets Vittorio Alfieri and Giovanni Casti and Scottish poet James Beattie. Other highlights include:

Art: Louis Boilly, *Arrival of the Stagecoach*; Philipp Runge, *Morning*; John Trumbull, *Caerphilly Castle in South Wales* and *Worthing in Sussex*; Joseph Turner, *Calais Pier* and *Festival at Macon*; James Ward, *Fighting Bulls by the Castle*; Benjamin Ward, *Christ Healing the Sick*

Literature: Ludwig von Arnim, *Der Wintergarten*; Thomas Campbell, *Poems*; Anne Grant, *Letters from the Mountains*; Johann Hebel, *Allemannische Gedichte*; Heinrich von Kleist, *Die Familie Schroffenstein*; Jane Porter, *Thaddeus of Warsaw*; Jean Paul Richter, *The Titan*; Johann Friedrich von Schiller, *Die Braut von Messina*

MUSICAL EVENTS

A. Births:

Jan 6	Henri Herz (Ger-pn-cm)	Sep 3	Alexander Gurilyov (Rus-cm)
Feb 16	K. von Schofhäutl (Ger-acous)	Sep 23	Jean Desiré Artôt (Fr-hn)
Feb 20	Friedrich Fröhlich (Swi-cm)	Oct 15	François Durutte (Bel-the)
Apr 2	Franz Lachner (Ger-cm-cd)	Oct 28	Caroline Unger (Aus-alto)
Apr 19	Eliza Flower (Br-hymn)	Nov 3	Gustav Schilling (Ger-mus)
Apr 27	Jean Jacques Becher (Ger-cri)	Nov 4	Carlo Blasis (It-bal)
Jun 3	William Knabe (Ger-pn.m)	Dec 11	Hector Berlioz (Fr-cm)
Jul 23	J. Vesque von Püttlingen	Dec 12	Josephine Fröhlich (Aus-sop)
	(Aus-cm)	Dec 24	Karl L. Drobisch (Ger-cm)
Jul 24	Adolphe Adam (Fr-cm)		Wojciech Sowinski (Pol-pn)
Aug 25	Ferdinand Stegmayer (Aus-cd)		

B. Deaths:

Jan 26	Georg von Pasterwitz (Aus-org)	Apr 23	Angelo Baldan (Ir-rel-cm)
Feb 6	Gasparo Angiolini (It-bal-cm)	Apr 25	John Camidge (Br-org)
Feb 16	Jan V. Stich (Punto) (Cz-hn)	Jul 5	William Jackson (Br-org)
Feb 19	Pieter van den Bosch (Hol-org)	Jul 20	Joseph Saint-Sevin (Fr-vn)
Mar 17	Cándido Ruano (Sp-cm)	Sep 2	Jean B. Janson (Fr-cel)
Mar 28	Johann Danner (Ger-vn)	Sep 5	François Devienne (Fr-fl)
Mar 29	Gottfried von Swieten (Hol-pat)	Sep 8	Richard Langdon (Br-org)

Sep 17 Franz Süssmayr (Aus-cm)
Sep 21 John C. Moller (Ger-org)
Oct 7 Pierre Vachon (Fr-vn)
Nov 3 Henri Moreau (Bel-cm-the)

Gennaro Astarita (It-cm)
Peter van Hagen (Hol-cm)
Johann C. Kellner (Ger-org)

C. Debuts:
Other - Henri Etienne Dérivis (Paris), Pauline Milder-Hauptmann (Vienna), Eliza Salmon (London)

D. New Positions:
Conductors: François Boieldieu (Imperial Court, St. Petersburg), Jan Dussek (Prince Louis Ferdinand, Magdeburg), Guillaume Kennis (kapellmeister, Antwerp Cathedral), Peter Ritter (Mannheim Orchestra), Alessandro Rolla (La Scala)

Others: Thomas Bennett (organ, Chichester Cathedral) Francis Jeffrey (editor, Edinburgh Review), Allessandro Mini (organ, Padua Cathedral)

E. Prizes and Honors:
Prizes: Albert Auguste Androt (Prix de Rome)

Honors: John Andrew Stevenson (knighted)

F. Biographical Highlights:
Daniel François Auber gives up on commerce and, with the political tensions high between England and France, returns to Paris and music; William Ayrton marries Marianne, the daughter of Samuel Arnold; John Beckwith receives his doctorate from Oxford; Ludwig van Beethoven meets Carl Maria von Weber; Teresa Belloc-Giorgi makes her Paris Opera debut; François Boieldieu finally leaves his wayward wife and accepts an invitation to go to St. Petersburg for a very attractive salary; Hippolyte-André Chélard enters the Paris Conservatory; Anton Diabelli leaves the monastery when they are secularized by the Bavarian government and returns to Vienna and music; Frédéric Kalkbrenner begins counterpoint lessons with Albrechtsberger; Jacques-Pierre Rode travels to Russia with Boieldieu and begins a five-year stay; Gaspare Spontini decides to settle down in Paris but fails in his first two operatic tries; Carl Maria von Weber moves to Vienna to study with Abbé Vogler and also meets Franz Joseph Haydn.

G. Institutional Openings:
Performing Groups: Prague Tonkünstler-Societät

Educational: Prix de Rome, Music (French)

Other: Anton Böhm und Sohn, Music Publishers (Augsburg); Chemische Druckerey (Haslinger Music Publishers, Vienna); Janiewicz's Music and Musical Instrument Warehouse (Liverpool); *Répertoire des Clavecinistes* (Zurich); Teatro Carcano (Milan); Union of Musical Artists for the Support of Widows and Orphans (London); Thaddäus Weigl, Music Publisher (Vienna)

H. Musical Literature:
Bemetzrieder, Anton, *Complete Treatise on Music*
Dibdin, Charles, *The Professional Life of Mr. Dibdin*
Eberhard, Johann, *Handbuch der Aesthetik I, II*
Gunn, John, *An Introduction to Music...*
Holden, Oliver, *Charlestown Collection of Sacred Songs*
Kittel, Johann, *Neues Choralbuch*
Knecht, Justin H., *Allgemeiner musikalischer Katechismus*
Law, Andrew, *Musical Primer*
Momigny, Jérôme de, *La Premiére Année de leçons de pianoforte*
Swan, Timothy, *The Songster's Museum*

I. Musical Compositions:

Beethoven, Ludwig van, *Symphony No. 3, Opus 55, "Eroica"*
  Sonata, Opus 47, for Violin and Piano, "Kreutzer"
  12 Contradances, Opus 141, for Orchestra
  Romance, Opus 40, for Violin and Orchestra
  6 Songs, Opus 48
Berton, Henri, *Aline, Reine de Golconde* (opera)
Boieldieu, François, *Ma tante Aurora* (opera)
Cavos, Catterino, *Rusalka* (opera)
Cherubini, Luigi, *Anacréon* (opera)
Destouches, Franz von, *Die Braut von Messina* (incidental music)
  Die Jungfrau von Orleans (incidental music)
Gossec, François, *Les sabots et le cerisier* (opera)
Grétry, André, *Delphis et Mopsa* (opera)
Haydn, Franz Joseph, *String Quartet, Opus 103* (unfinished)
Haydn, Michael, *Missa sub Titulo Sancti Francisci Serephici*
  Te Deum
Hoffmann, E.T.A., *Der Renegat* (opera)
Isouard, Nicolo, *Le Baiser et la quittance* (opera)
    Les confidences (opera)
    Le Médecin (opera)
    Le déjeuner de Garçons (opera)
Mayr, Simon, *Alonso e Cora* (opera)
Méhul, Etienne, *Héléna* (opera)
    L'heureux malgré lui (opera)
    Le Baiser et la quittance (opera)
    Daphnis et Pandrone (ballet)
Paër, Ferdinando, *Sargino* (opera)
Paisiello, Giovanni, *Prosperine* (opera)
Reicha, Anton, *Concerto for Cello and Orchestra*
Reichardt, Johann, *Kunst und Liebe* (opera)
Righini, Vincenzo, *La selva incantata* (opera)
Spohr, Louis, *Concerto No. 1, Opus 1, for Violin and Orchestra*
    Concertante in C Major for Violin and Orchestra
Süssmayr, Franz, *List und Zufall* (opera)
Titov, Alexei, *Blanka* (ballet)
Trento, Vittorio, *Ines de Castro* (opera)
Weber, Carl Maria von, *Peter Schmoll* (opera)
Wölfl, Joseph, *Symphony No. 1, Opus 40*
    Concerto, Opus 26, for Piano and Orchestra
    3 Piano Trios, Opus 23
    3 Progressive Piano Sonatas, Opus 24
    3 Sonatas, Opus 25 (with Violin and Cello)
Zelter, Carl F., *Kleiner Balladen und Lieder*
Zingarelli, Nicola, *Il Beritore fortunato* (opera)
    La distruzione di Gerusalemme (opera)

1804

World Events:
In the U.S., Thomas Jefferson is re-elected President; the 12th Ammendment on a separate vote for the Vice-President is ratified; Alexander Hamilton is killed by Aaron Burr in a political rivalry duel; the Lewis and Clark Expedition reaches the Pacific; war with Tripoli is stepped up over continued piracy on U.S. ships; future President Franklin Pierce is born. Internationally, Napoleon is crowned as emperor of France; the Code Napoleon goes into effect for France and all conquered countries; Francis II of the Holy Roman Empire takes on the title of Francis I of Austria; Spain declares war on Great Britain; the Haitians defeat the French army and declare their independence; The British and Foreign Bible Society is formed; British scientist Joseph Priestley dies.

Cultural Highlights:
François de Chateaubriand resigns his embassy post as a protest; Friedrich Hölderlein recovers his sanity enough to begin library work; Jacques-Louis David is made court painter to Napoleon. Births in the art world include German artist Moritz von Schwind and sculptor Ernst Rietschel, Italian artist Francesco Coghetti, Scottish sculptor John Steel and American architect Thomas Walter; deaths include British artist George Morland and Italian artist Giovanni Tiepolo. Births in the literary field include French novelists George Sand, Marie Joseph Sue and Charles Sainte-Beuve, German philosopher Ludwig Feuerbach and poet Eduard Mörike, British politician and author Benjamin Disraeli and American novelist Nathaniel Hawthorne; deaths include German philosopher Immanuel Kant, American novelist Charlotte Lennox and Dutch author Elizabeth Bekker. Other highlights include:

Art: Washington Allston, *The Deluge*; John S. Cotman, *Viaduct*; Jacques-Louis David, *Napoleon at Hôtel de Ville*; Antoine Gros, *Napoleon at Jaffa*; Jean-Auguste Ingres, *Napoleon as First Consul*; Joseph Turner, *Great Falls at Reichenbach*; John Vanderlyn, *Death of Jane McCrea*; Antoine Vernet, *Battle of Marengo*; David Wilkie, *Pitlessie Fair*

Literature: John Quincy Adams, *Letters*; William Blake, *Jerusalem*; Maria Edgeworth, *Popular Tales*; James Grahame, *The Sabbath*; William Hayley, *Triumphs of Music*; Sydney Morgan, *St. Clair*; Amelia Opie, *Adeline Mowbray*; Jane Porter, *The Lake of Killarney*; Jean-Paul Richter, *Der Flegeljahre I, II*; Johann Friedrich von Schiller, *William Tell*

MUSICAL EVENTS

A. Births:

Jan 12	Hippolyte Mompou (Fr-cm)	Jun 21	Karl Curschmann (Ger-cm)
Jan 16	Karl A. Krebs (Ger-cd-cm)	Jul 14	Julius Schuberth (Ger-pub)
Mar 9	Alphonse Leduc (Fr-pub)	Aug 19	Théodore Devroye (Bel-mus)
Mar 14	Johann Strauss, Sr. (Aus-cm)	Sep 1	Julius Otto (Ger-cd)
May 31	Jeanne L. Farrenc (Fr-pn)	Nov 14	Heinrich Dorn (Ger-cd-cm)
Jun 1	Michael Glinka (Rus-cm)	Nov 27	Julius Benedict (Br-cm-cd)
Jun 6	Petter Boman (Swe-mus)	Dec 6	W. Schröder-Devrient (Ger-sop)

B. Deaths:

Jan 12	Benoit Andrez (Bel-pub)	Jun 3	Jean E. Pauwels (Bel-vn-cd)
Mar	John Moorehead (Ir-cm)	Jul 16	Johann A. Miller (Ger-cm)
Mar 4	Karl L. Röllig (Aus-cm)	Jul 17	Christian E. Graf (Ger-vn)
Mar 10	Louis J. Françoeur (Fr-vn)	Aug 19	Albert A. Androt (Fr-cm)
Apr 5	Johann Schwanenberger (Ger-cm)	Aug 24	Valentin Adamberger (Ger-ten)
May 19	David Tannenberg (Ger-org.m)	Nov 19	Pietro A. Guglielmi (It-cm)

Nov 23 Giovanni Giornovichi (It-vn) Franz Eck (Ger-vn)
Dec 22 Philip Barth (Ger-ob-cm)   Caterina Galli (It-mez)

C. Debuts:

Other - Filippo Galli (as a tenor, Bologna), George A. Kollmann (London), Nicholas Mori (London), Ferdinand Ries (Vienna)

D. New Positions:

Conductors: Adalbert Gyrowetz (Vienna Opera), Jean François Lesueur (maître de chapelle, Napoleon), Joseph Ignaz Schnabel (kapellmeister, Breslau Cathedral), Carl Maria von Weber (kapellmeister, Breslau), Anton Zingarelli (maestro di capella, St. Peter's, Rome)

Educational: Lorenzo Gibelli (voice, Liceo Filarmonica, Bologna), Stanislao Mattei (counterpoint and composition, Liceo Musicale, Bologna), Giovanni Zanotti (piano, Liceo Musicale, Bologna)

Others: Arthur Corfe (organ, Salsbury Cathedral), August Müller (cantor, Thomasschule, Leipzig)

E. Prizes and Honors:

Honors: Nicolas Dalayrac (Legion of Honor), François Gossec (Legion of Honor), Franz Joseph Haydn (Honorary Citizen of Vienna), Michael Haydn (Swedish Royal Academy), Etienne Méhul (Legion of Honor), Pierre A. Monsigny (Legion of Honor)

F. Biographical Highlights:

Ludwig van Beethoven, upon hearing that Napoleon crowned himself emperor, tears up the dedication of his Eroica Symphony in a fit of rage; Teresa Belloc-Giorgi makes her La Scala debut; Louise Dugazon gives her farewell performance at the Paris Opera; Dorothea von Ertmann moves to Vienna and becomes a close friend to Beethoven; Josephina Grassini begins a two year stay in London; E.T.A. Hoffmann begins a limited law practice in Poznan; Johann Hummel becomes assistant kapellmeister in the court of Prince Esterházy; Konradin Kreutzer moves to Vienna to study counterpoint with Albrechtsberger and there meets Franz Joseph Haydn; Antonio Pacini moves to Paris where he begins teaching voice; Louis Spohr makes his first official concert tour around Germany.

G. Institutional Openings:

Performing Groups: Nordsternbund (Berlin)

Educational: Liceo Filarmonico (Bologna); Würzburg Institute of Music (Royal Music School in 1820)

Other: Charles Challen Piano Co (London); Coliseo Provisional (Theater Argentina, Buenos Aires); William Goodrich, Organ Builder (Boston); Conrad Graf, Piano Builder (Vienna); Koninklijke Schouwburg (Concert Hall, The Hague); Teatro Municipale (Piacenza); Teatro Porteño (Buenos Aires)

H. Musical Literature:

Bréval, Jean-Baptiste, *Traité du Violoncelle*
Danilov, Kirsha, *Ancient Russian Poetry*
Dibdin, Charles, *Music Epitomised*
Holyoke, Samuel, *The Christian Harmonist*
Jackson, George, *David's Psalms*
Müller, August, *Klavier- und Fortepiano-Schule*
Page, John, *Festive Harmony*
Reichardt, Johann, *Vertraute Briefe aus Paris*
Richter, Franz X., *Traité d'harmonie et de composition*
Wranitzky, Anton, *Violin Fondament*

I. Musical Compositions:

Beethoven, Ludwig van, *Triple Concerto, Opus 56* (violin, cello, piano, orchestra)
    Sonatas No. 21-23, Opus 53, 54 and 57, for Piano
    14 Variations, Opus 44, for Piano Trio
    5 Variations on "Rule, Britannia" for Piano
    7 Variations on "God Save the King" for Piano
    3 Grand Marches, Opus 45 (piano, 4 hands)
Bishop, Henry, *Angelina* (opera)
Boccherini, Luigi, *2 String Quartets, Opus 64* (unfinished)
Boieldieu, François, *Aline, reine de Golconde* (opera)
Cherubini, Luigi, *Achille à Scyros* (ballet)
Dalayrac, Nicolas, *La jeune prude* (opera)
    Une heure de mariage (opera)
Danzi, Franz, *Das Freudenfest* (cantata)
Destouches, André, *Wilhelm Tell* (incidental music)
    Die Hussiten vor Naumburg (incidental music)
Eberl, Anton, *Symphony, Opus 33*
Generali, Pietro, *Pamela nubile* (opera)
Himmel, Friedrich, *Fanchon das Leiermädchen* (singspiel)
Hoffmann, E.T.A., *Die lustigen Musikanten* (opera)
Lesueur, Jean F., *Ossian* (opera)
Mayr, Simon, *Elisa* (opera)
    I due viaggiatori (opera)
    Zamori (opera)
Méhul, Etienne, *Les Hussites* (incidental music)
    Messe Solennelle
Neukomm, Sigismund von, *Alessandro nell'Indie* (opera)
Paër, Ferdinando, *I Fuorusciti* (opera)
Paisiello, Giovanni, *Mass in B-flat for Double Chorus*
Portugal, Marcos, *Argenide* (opera)
    L'oro non compra amore (opera)
Reicha, Anton, *Concerto for Piano and Orchestra*
Rossini, Gioacchino, *6 Sonata a Quattro for Strings*
Salieri, Antonio, *Die Neger* (opera)
Schmidt, Johann, *Der Onkel* (opera)
Spohr, Louis, *Concerto No. 2, Opus 2, for Violin and Orchestra*
Spontini, Gaspere, *Milton* (opera)
    La petite maison (opera)
Steibelt, Daniel, *Le jugement du berger Paris* (ballet)
Trento, Vittorio, *Ifigenia in Aulide* (opera)
Vogler, Georg "Abbe", *Samori* (opera)
Weber, Carl Maria von, *Rübezahl* (opera)
    6 Variations on Vogler's "Castor and Pollux," Opus 5 (piano)
    6 Variations on Vogler's "Samori," Opus 6 (piano trio)
Weigl, Joseph, *La passione di Gesù Cristo* (oratorio)
    La resurrezione di Gesù Cristo (oratorio)
Wölfl, Joseph, *3 Piano Sonatas, Opus 19*
    L'amour romanesque (opera)
Wranitsky, Paul, *Mitgefühl* (opera)

1805

World Events:

The United States breaks off relations with Great Britain over the West Indies trade problem; the official war with Tripoli ends, but piracy continues; the Michigan Territory is formed out of Indian territory; the Female Charitable Society of Maine, the first known women's club in the U.S., is formed. Internationally, the War of the Third Coalition begins--the battles of Ulm and Austerlitz take place and the Battle of Trafalgar establishes British naval supremacy; the Peace of Pressburg is signed by France and Austria, who gives up her Italian possessions; the Kingdoms of Bavaria and Württemberg are formed; Mohamet Ali becomes ruler of Egypt.

Cultural Highlights:

The Royal Society of Painters in Water Colours is founded in London; F.A. Brockhaus begins publishing in Amsterdam; Bertel Thorvaldsen is inducted into the Royal Academy in Copenhagen; Johann G. Schadow become rector of the Berlin Academy of Art; James Wyatt becomes President of the Royal Academy of Art in London. The art world sees the births of American sculptors Horatio Greenough and Hiram Powers, German artists Karl Desterley and Wilhelm von Kalmbach, French artist Constantin Guys, British artist Samuel Palmer and Italian sculptor Carlo Marochetti; deaths include French artists Jean-Baptiste Greuze and Louis Moreau and British sculptor Thomas Banks. The literary world sees the birth of British novelist William Ainsworth, Argentine poet Esteban Echeverría and Danish story-teller Hans Christian Andersen; deaths include Portugese poet Manuel de Bocage, British poet Christopher Anstey, Hungarian poet Mihály Vitéz and German poet Friedrich von Schiller. Other highlights include:

Art: Washington Allston, *Self-Portrait*; Antonio Canova, *Tomb of Maria Christina*; John S. Cotman, *Greta Bridge, Yorkshire*; Jean-Auguste Ingres, *Madame Rivière*; Ferdinand Jagemann, *Schiller on His Deathbed*; Joseph Koch, *Landscape with Rainbow*; Pierre-Paul Prud'hon, *Empress Josephine*; Joseph Turner, *The Shipwreck*

Literature: Jens Baggesen, *Parthenais*; Thomas Fessenden, *Democracy Unveiled*; William Hayley, *Ballads Founded on Anecdotes of Animals*; William Hazlitt, *Essay on the Principles of Human Action*; Walter Scott, *Lay of the Last Minstrel*; Étienne de Sénancour, *Obermann*; Robert Southey, *Madoc*; William Wordsworth, *The Prelude*

MUSICAL EVENTS

A. Births:

Jan 15	Ludwig Bausch (Ger-vn.m)	Jul 28	Giuditta Grisi (It-mez)
Feb 15	Louise A. Bertin (Fr-cm)	Aug 21	Auguste Bournonville (Den-bal)
Mar 5	Théodore Labarre (Fr-hp)	Sep 7	Julie Dorus-Gras (Fr-sop)
Mar 17	Manuel P. García (Sp-bar)	Oct 28	John Thomson (Scot-cm-au)
Apr 4	Prosper Guéranger (Fr-mus)	Nov 14	Fanny Mendelssohn (Ger-pn-cm)
Apr 19	Charles Coussemaker (Fr-mus)	Nov 22	Mary Anne Goward (Br-sop)
May 12	Jan N. Bobrowicz (Pol-gui)	Dec 6	Adolf Reubke (Ger-org.m)
May 14	Johan P. Hartmann (Den-cm)	Dec 17	John T. Hart (Br-vn.m)
Jun 5	Jacob N. Ahlström (Swe-cm)	Dec 24	Sebastian Lee (Ger-cel)
Jun 5	Victor Desvignes (Fr-vn-cm)		Cesare Babiali (It-bs)
Jul 6	Julius Schneider (Ger-org)		John Chatterton (Br-hp)
Jul 8	Luigi Ricci (It-cm)		

B. Deaths:

Jan 13	Franz A. Ernst (Ger-vn)	Mar 14	John Ashley (Br-bn-cd)
Feb 4	Johann G. Tromlitz (Ger-fl)	May 28	Luigi Boccherini (It-cm)
Feb 27	Giovanni Cimador (It-cm)	Aug 1	Friedrich Gestewitz (Ger-cd)

Oct 2 Anna Marie Crouch (Br-sop)   Dec 10 Friedrich Hurka (Cz-ten)
Oct 13 Johann C. Kühnau (Ger-cd-cm)

C. Debuts:
Other - Frédéric Wilhelm Kalkbrenner (Berlin), Louis Nourrit (Paris)

D. New Positions:
Conductors: Bonifazio Asioli (maestro di cappella, Milan), Felice Blangini (kapellmeister, Saxe-Coburg, Munich), James Hewitt (municipal bands, New York), Charles F. Kreube (Paris Opéra-Comique), Johann Friedrich Rochlitz (Leipzig Gewandhaus), Gaetano Valeri (maestro di cappella, Padua Cathedral)

Educational: Johann Simon Mayr (counterpoint, Bergamo Institute), Johann Rinck (organ, Darmstadt Music School)

Others: Niccolò Paganini (music director, Princess of Lucca), Christoph E. Weyse (organ, Copenhagen Cathedral)

E. Prizes and Honors:
Prizes: Victor C. Dourlen (Prix de Rome)

Honors: Joseph A. Elsner (Warsaw Society of Friends of Science)

F. Biographical Highlights:
Pierre Baillot begins three years of concertizing in Russia with the French cellist Jacques Lamare; Ludwig van Beethoven, in a fit of rage, withdraws Fidelio after three performances--meets Cherubini who is visiting in Vienna; Alexandre Etienne Choron becomes a partner in a publishing firm; Gaetano Crivelli makes his La Scala debut; Franz Joseph Haydn completes the thematic catalogue of his own works; Anthony Philip Heinrich makes his first visit to the U.S. but does not emigrate until 1810; Giacomo Meyerbeer begins the study of composition with Zelter and with Abbé Vogler at Darmstadt; after a year of serious practice, Niccolò Paganini makes a second debut causing enthusiastic responses everywhere he performs; Johann Nepomuk Poissl takes up permanent residence in Munich; Lorenzo Da Ponti emigrates to the U.S. with his mistress and their children; Gioacchino Rossini adds horn playing to singing in local theaters; Giuseppe Siboni makes his La Scala debut; Louis Spohr takes the concertmaster's position in the court orchestra in Gotha; Joseph Wölfl leaves Paris to settle in London where he becomes a fashionable teacher and performer.

G. Institutional Openings:
Educational: Lezioni Caritatevoli di Musica (Istituto Musicale G. Donizetti, Bergamo); Pennsylvania Academy of Fine Arts (Philadelphia); Tausch School for Wind Performers (Berlin); Zürcherische Singinstitut (Zurich)

Other: Carli Music Publishers (Paris); Cramer and Keys, Music Publishers (London); Kunst und Industrie Comptoir (Music Publishing Co., Pest); Melodion (by J.C. Dietz); Purday and Button, Music Publishers (London); Charles S. Richault Publishing Co. (Paris); Teatro del Corso (Bologna)

H. Musical Literature:
Corfe, Joseph, *Thorough Bass Simplified*
Grosheim, Georg, *Über den verfall der Tonkunst*
Heinse, Wilhelm, *Musical Dialogues*
Ingalls, Jeremiah, *The Christian Harmony*
Jenks, Stephen, *The Delight of Harmony*
Langlé, Honoré, *Traité de la Fugue*
La Salette, Joubert de, *Sténographie musicale*
Vierling, Johann G., *Allgemein fasslicher Unterricht in Generalbass*

Walker, Joseph, *An Historical Account and Critical Essay on the Opera*
Werner, Johann, *Orgelschule*

I. Musical Compositions:
Beethoven, Ludwig van, *Fidelio, Opus 72* (opera)
    Leonore Overture No. 2
    Concerto No. 4, Opus 58, for Piano and Orchestra
    An die Hoffnung, Opus 32 (song)
    Romance, Opus 50, for Violin and Orchestra
    8 Songs, Opus 52
    Air and Variations on "Ich denke dein" for Piano, Four Hands
Boieldieu, François, *La jeune femme Colère* (opera)
    Amour et Mystère (opera)
    Abderkan (opera)
Cavos, Catterino, *The Invisible Prince* (opera)
Czerny, Carl, *20 Variations Concertantes for Violin and Piano*
Dalayrac, Nicolas, *Gulistan* (opera)
Destouches, Franz von, *Das Missverständniss* (opera)
Eberl, Anton, *Symphony, Opus 34*
    Concerto No. 2, Opus 32, for Piano and Orchestra
Generali, Pietro, *Don Chisciotte* (opera)
Haydn, Michael, *Leopoldmesse*
Hoffmann, E.T.A., *Die ungebetenen Gäste* (opera)
Isouard, Nicolo, *L'intrigue aux fenêtres* (opera)
    Léonce (opera)
    La ruse inutile (opera)
Mayr, Simon, *Eraldo ed Emma* (opera)
    L'amor cojugale (opera)
Paër, Ferdinando, *Leonora* (opera)
    Il maniscalco (opera)
    Sofonisba (opera)
Reicha, Anton, *Overture to Maria Theresa*
Spohr, Louis, *Concerto No. 4, Opus 10, for Violin and Orchestra*
    Sonata in C Major for Harp and Violing
Spontini, Gaspare, *Julie* (opera)
Steibelt, Daniel, *La belle laitière* (ballet)
Titov, Alexei, *The Judgment of Solomon* (incidental music)
    Yam (opera)
Trento, Vittorio, *Andromeda* (opera)
Viotti, Giovanni, *Concerto No. 25 for Violin and Orchestra*
Weigl, Joseph, *Vestas Feuer* (opera)
Winter, Peter, *Der Frauenbund* (opera)
Wölfl, Joseph, *Concerto, Opus 32, for Piano and Orchestra*
    3 String Quartets, Opus 30
    Fernando (opera)
    La Surprise de Diane (ballet)
Wranitzky, Paul, *Die Erkenntlichkeit* (opera)
Zingarelli, Anton, *Saul* (oratorio)
Zumsteeg, Johann, *Kleine Balladen und Lieder VII*

1806

World Events:
In the U.S., the Lewis and Clark Expedition returns to St. Louis; another explorer, Zebulon Pike, discovers Pike's Peak in Colorado; construction begins on the Cumberland Road, the first federal highway; U.S. ships that try to trade with France are seized by the British. Internationally, Napoleon crushes Prussia and enters Berlin, bringing about the formal dissolution of the Holy Roman Empire; the Confederation of the Rhine is founded; Napoleon closes all continental ports to the British who in turn blockade the continent; Louis Napoleon is made king of Holland and Joseph Bonaparte of Naples.

Cultural Highlights:
Benjamin West begins his second term as President of the Royal Academy of Art; Johann von Langer becomes director of the Munich Academy of Art; Friedrich Hölderlein suffers his final bout of insanity; Clodion begins work on the Paris Arch of Triumph. Births in the literary world include Americans Robert Bird, Charles Hoffman and William Simms, British poet Elizabeth Browning and author John S. Mills, German dramatists Friedrich Halm and Heinrich Laube and author Johann Burgmüller; deaths include British poet Elizabeth Carter and Irish poet Carlo Gozzi. Births in the art world include Irish artist Daniel Maclise, Scotch artist William Dyce and British artist Edward Edwards; deaths include French artists Louis Carmontelle, Gabriel Doyen and Honoré Fragonard, British artists John Russell and George Stubbs, Swiss artist Hans Füseli and Irish artist James Barry. Other highlights include:

Art: Charles Bulfinch, *Gore Place* (Massachusetts); Johann von Dannecker, *Ariadne*; Antoine Gros, *The Battle of Aboukir*; Thomas Jefferson, *Monticello*; Jean-Auguste Ingres, *Napoleon as Emperor*; Charles W. Peale, *Exhumation of the Mastodon*; Henry Raeburn, *Lord Newton*; Bertel Thorvaldsen, *Hebe*; Joseph Turner, *Garden of the Hesperides*; David Wilkie, *The Village Politicians*

Literature: Ludwig von Arnim and Clemens Brentano, *Des Knaben Wunderhorn*; Maria Edgeworth, *Leonora*; Johann von Goethe, *Faust I*; Anne Grant, *Letters from the Mountains*; Heinrich von Kleist, *Der Zerbrochene Krug*; Gabriel Legouvé, *La Mort de Henri IV*; Thomas Moore, *Epistles, Odes and Other Poems*; Sydney Morgan, *The Wild Irish Girl*; Noah Webster, *A Compendius Dictionary of the English Language*

MUSICAL EVENTS

A. Births:
Jan 3	Henriette Sontag (Ger-sop)	Aug 17	Joseph K. Mertz (Hun-gui)
Jan 18	Eduard Mantius (Ger-ten)	Oct 10	Charles Barker (Br-org.m)
Jan 27	Juan C. Arriaga (Sp-cm)	Nov 7	August Pott (Ger-vn)
Mar 26	Josef Slavík (Cz-vn-cm)	Nov 15	Ossip Petrov (Rus-bs)
May 8	Johann F. Kittl (Ger-cm)		Fanny Ayton (Br-sop)
Jun 8	Pierre Scudo (It-cri)		Elizabeth Masson (Br-sop)
Jun 28	Napoléon Coste (Fr-gui)		

B. Deaths:
Jan 18	William Shrubsole (Br-org)	Jun 4	Wenzel Pichel (Cz-vn-cm)
Jan 30	V. Martín y Soler (Sp-cm)	Jun 14	Domenico Guardisoni (It-ten)
Feb	Tommaso Giordani (It-cm)	Jun 18	Antoine Lacroix (Fr-vn-pub)
Feb 14	Jean Dauberval (Fr-bal)	Jul 6	Johann G. Arnold (Ger-cel)
Feb 18	Brigida Giorgi Banti (It-sop)	Aug 10	Michael Haydn (Ger-cm)
Feb 23	John Alcock (Br-org)	Aug 10	Christian Kalkbrenner (Ger-the)
Mar 16	Giuseppe Colla (It-cm)	Oct 23	Franz Seydelmann (Ger-cm-cd)
Mar 20	Salomea Deszner (Pol-sop)	Dec 3	Richard Potter (Br-fl.m)
May 1	Karl Cannabich (Ger-vn-cm)		Jean F. Lirou (Fr-cm-the)

C. Debuts:
Other - Davidde Banderali (Milan), Johanna S. Kollmann (London), Adelaide Malanotte (Verona), Joseph A. Roeckel (Vienna)

D. New Positions:
Conductors: João José Baldi (mestre de capela, Lisbon Cathedral), Juan Bros y Bertomeu (maestro de capilla, Léon Cathedral), Ferdinand Fränzl (Munich Opera), François-Antoine Habeneck (student orchestra, Paris Conservatory), Gabriele Prota (maestro de capela, Naples), Vittorio Trento (Italian Opera, Amsterdam)

Educational: Vincenzo Camuccini (director, Academy of St. Luke, Rome)

Others: Jeremiah Clarke (organ, Worcester Cathedral), E.T.A. Hoffmann (theater director, Bamberg)

E. Prizes and Honors:
Honors: Charles Burney (government stipend), Giovanni Paisiello (Legion of Honor)

F. Biographical Highlights:
Angelica Catalani, Giuseppe Naldi and Giuseppe Siboni make their London debuts; Girolamo Crescentini is appointed by Napoleon to be voice teacher to his family; Gaetano Donizetti enters Bergamo Free School to study music despite his father's wish that he become a lawyer; François Fétis marries into a fortune which he proceeds to lose by 1811; Mauro Giuliani goes to Vienna where he becomes famous as a guitarist; Josephina Grassini returns to Paris and becomes court singer as well as mistress to Napoleon; Ferdinand Hérold enters Paris Conservatory for the serious study of music delayed by his father's opposition; E.T.A. Hoffmann abandons civil service work for music; Luigi Marchesi retires from the stage; Gioacchino Rossini enters the Liceo Musicale in Bologna; Louis Spohr marries harpist Dorette Scheidler; Václav Tomásek becomes music tutor for the family of Count Buquoy in Prague; Carl Maria von Weber resigns his Breslau post after troubles with management but fails to gain the Karlsruhe appointment.

G. Institutional Openings:
Performing Groups: Lukas-Bund (Vienna); Thubaneau Concert Society (Marseilles)

Educational: Accademia Polimniaca (Bologna); Arras Music Conservatory; Mannheim Conservatory of Music

Other: Adelphi Theater (Sans Pareil, London); Karl Bochsa Music Store (Paris); Heinrichshofen Music Publishers (Germany); *Journal des Troubadours*; *Journal of National Music* (Moscow); Jürgen Marcussen (Marcussen and Reuter), Organ Builders (Copenhagen); Moscow Imperial Theater; Antonio Pacini, Music Publisher (Paris); Johann C. Schlimbach, Organ and Piano Builder (Königshofen); Teatro dei Floridi (S. Marco); *Wiener Theatre-Zeitung*

H. Musical Literature:
Callcott, John, *A Musical Grammar*
Dalberg, Johann, *Fantasien aus dem Reich der Töne*
Graupner, Gottlieb, *Rudiments of the Art of Playing the Pianoforte*
Hill, Uri, *The Sacred Minstrel*
Jenks, Stephen, *Laus Deo*
King, Matthew P., *Introduction to Sight Singing*
Kollmann, Augustus, *A New Theory of Musical Harmony*
Mauricio, José, *Metodo di musica*
Momigny, Jérôme de, *Cours complet d'harmonie et de composition*
Schubart, Daniel, *Ideen zu einer Aesthetik der Tonkunst*

I. Musical Compositions:

Beethoven, Ludwig van, *Symphony No. 4, Opus 60*
  Concerto, Opus 61, for Violin and Orchestra
  Leonore Overture No. 3, Opus 72a
  String Quartets No. 7-9, Opus 59, "Razumovsky"
Benda, Friedrich, *Das Blumenmädchen* (opera)
Bishop, Henry, *Tamerlane et Bajazet* (opera)
Boieldieu, François, *Télémaque* (opera)
Cherubini, Luigi, *Faniska* (opera)
Corri, Domenico, *The Travelers* (opera)
Dalayrac, Nicolas, *Deux mots* (opera)
  Koulouf (opera)
Eberl, Anton, *Grand Sonata, Opus 39, for Piano*
Fioravanti, Valentino, *Le Cantatrici villane* (opera)
Haydn, Michael, *Requiem in B-flat* (unfinished)
Himmel, Friedrich, *Die Sylphen* (opera)
Isouard, Nicolo, *La prise de Passau* (opera)
  Idala (opera)
Mayr, Simon, *Adelasia e Aleramo* (opera)
Méhul, Etienne, *Les deux aveugles de Tolède* (opera)
  Gabrielle d'Estrées (opera)
  Agar dans le désert (opera)
  Uthal (opera)
Paisiello, Giovanni, *La Finta Contessa* (opera)
Poissl, Johann, *Die Opernprobe* (singspiel)
Reicha, Anton, *Argine, regina di Granata* (opera)
Rossini, Gioacchino, *Demetrio e Polibro* (opera)
Schmidt, Johann, *Eulenspiegel* (opera)
Spohr, Louis, *Concerto No. 3, Opus 7, for Violin and Orchestra*
  Sonatas for Violin and Harp, Opus 16 and Opus 113
  Die Prüfung (operetta)
Spontini, Gaspare, *Tout le monde a tort* (vaudeville)
Steibelt, Daniel, *La fête de Mars* (intermezzo)
Titov, Alexei, *The Hungarian* (opera)
Weber, Carl Maria von, *6 Variations for Viola and Orchestra*
Weigl, Joseph, *Il principe invisibile* (opera)
  Der vier Elemente (ballet)
Weinlig, Christian, *Mass in B-flat Major*
Witt, Friedrich, *Das Fischerweib* (opera)
Wölfl, Joseph, *Grand Duo, Opus 37, for Harp and Piano*
Zelter, Carl, *Die Gunst des Augenblicks* (cantata)

1807

World Events:
In the U.S., the Embargo Act forbids any trade with foreign nations, particularly France and Great Britain; the Chesapeake Affair further strains relations between the U.S. and Great Britain; Robert Fulton makes the first successful steamship voyage with the Clermont from Albany to New York, a round trip of 32 hours; the U.S. Coast and Geodetic Survey is created; Robert E. Lee, military genius of the Confederacy, is born. Internationally, the War of the Third Coalition ends with the Treaty of Tilsit between France, Russia and Prussia; the French occupy Portugal causing the royal family to flee to Brazil; Great Britain, France, Spain and Portugal all outlaw the slave trade while Prussia frees its serfs; London streets receive new gas lights.

Cultural Highlights:
Friedrich Hölderlein is confined to an asylum for the remainder of his life; Hans H. Meyer becomes director of the Weimar Academy of Design; Francis Douce publishes his *Illustrations of Shakespeare*; Births in the field of art include American artist William S. Mount and Scottish artist Thomas Duncan; deaths include British artist John Opie and Swiss artist Angelica Kauffman. The literary world sees the birth of American poets Henry Wadsworth Longfellow and John Greenleaf Whittier, French dramatist Gabriel Legouvé and poet Louis Bertrand, Polish poet Wincenty Pol, German poet Friedrich Vischer and Italian poet Giovanni Ruffini; deaths include German novelist Sophie La Roche and poet August Meissner, French poet Ponce D. Le Brun and British novelist Clara Reeve. Other highlights include:

Art: Thomas Lawrence, *Family of Sir Francis Baring*; Philipp Runge, *Night* (design); Louis Spohr, *Self-Portrait*; Bertel Thorvaldsen, *Cupid and Psyche*; John Trumbull, *Niagara Falls, Upper Bank*; Joseph Turner, *Sun Rising in the Mist* and *Windsor Castle from Salt Hill*; John Vanderlyn, *Marius in the Ruins of Carthage*

Literature: Joel Barlow, *The Columbiad*; George Lord Byron, *Hours of Idleness*; Charles Chênedollé, *La Génie de l'homme*; George Crabbe, *Poems*; James Hogg, *The Mountain Bard*; Alexander von Humboldt, *Voyage to the Equatorial Regions of the New World I*; Adam G. Oehlenschläger, *Baldur, the Good*; Robert Southey, *Letters of Don Manuel Espriella*; Mme. de Staël, *Corinne*; William Wordsworth, *Poems*

MUSICAL EVENTS

A. Births:

Jan 4	Baltasar Saldoni (Sp-cm-mus)	Jul 11	Joseph Tichatschek (Boh-ten)
Feb 25	Ignace Dobrzynski (Pol-pn)	Aug 20	Ernesto Cavallini (It-cl-cm)
Mar 7	Franz Pocci (It-cm)	Aug 27	Karl Albrecht (Ger-cd)
Mar 14	Gaetano Gaspari (It-cm-mus)	Sep 11	Ignaz Lachner (Ger-cd-cm)
Mar 15	Gottfried von Preyer (Aus-cm)	Sep 22	Julius Knorr (Ger-pn)
Apr 14	Joseph Staudigl, Sr. (Ger-bs)	Sep 29	Michel Welte (Ger-inst.m)
Apr 27	Giuseppe Rocca (It-vn)	Oct 3	Heinrich Panofka (Ger-vn)
May 15	Luigi Casamorata (It-cm)	Oct 21	Hilarión Eslava (Sp-cm)
Jun 6	Marietta Brambilla (It-alto)	Oct 21	Napoleon H. Reber (Fr-cm)
Jun 6	Adrien F.Servais (Bel-cel)		

B. Deaths:

Feb 16	Paolo Morellati (It-pn.m)	Sep 20	Honoré F. Langlé (Fr-the-cm)
Mar 11	Anton F. Eberl (Aus-pn-cm)	Dec 8	Carl F. Cramer (Ger-pn-pub)
Apr 15	John Mainwaring (Br-rel-mus)	Dec 19	Friedrich Grimm (Ger-cri)
May 4	Carl A. Grenser (Ger-ww.m)		Sabina Hitzelberger (Ger-sop)
Sep 12	Edward Miller (Br-org)		

C. Debuts:
Other - Anton Forti (Esterháza)

D. New Positions:
Conductors: Henri M. Berton (Opèra-Comique, Paris), Franz Danzi (kapellmeister, Stuttgart), Mariano Rodrigo de Ledesma (Madrid Opera), Ferdinando Paër (maître de chapelle, Napoleon and conductor, Opèra-Comique), Georg Vogler (kapellmeister, Darmstadt)

Others: Karl Adam Bader (organ, Bamberg Cathedral), Wilhelm Friedrich Riem (organ, Thomaskirche, Leipzig), Nicolas Séjan (organ, Les Invalides, Paris), Carl Maria von Weber (private secretary to Duke Louis of Württemburg), John White (organ, St. Paul's, Leeds)

E. Prizes and Honors:
Honors: Franz Joseph Haydn (Société Academique des Enfans d'Apollon)

F. Biographical Highlights:
August Böckh receives his doctorate in philology from the University of Halle; Austrian composer Joseph Drechsler moves to Vienna where he eventually conducts at the Opera; Jan Ladislav Dussek leaves the service of Prince von Ysenburg after a short term of service and moves on to Paris to enter the service of Prince Talleyrand as his Maître de Chapelle; Manuel G. García, the Spanish tenor, leaves Spain for Paris where he is a popular success at the Théâtre-Italien; the family of Jacques François Halévy changes their name officially from Levy; E. T. A. Hoffmann returns to Germany to pursue a musical career as conductor and composer; Carl Maria von Weber moves to Stuttgart where his loose life style puts him at odds with the authorities.

G. Institutional Openings:
Performing Groups: Apollonian Society (Pittsburgh); Gesellschaft für Privatkonzerte (Bremen); Massachusetts Musical Society; Musica Amici (Auroraförbundet, Uppsala)

Educational: Dreyssigsche Singakademie (Dresden); Milan Conservatory of Music; Zelter Ripienschule (Berlin)

Other: Boston Athenaeum; Friedrich Hofmeister, Music Publisher (Leipzig); Smollet Holden Music Shop (Dublin); Musik Hug (Zurich Publishing House); Penson, Robertson and Co., Music Publishers (Scotland); Pleyel Piano Factory (Paris); James Power, Music Publisher (London); *Salmagundi* (by Irving and Paulding); Teatro Diurno (Pisa); Theater of the States (German Opera, Prague); Theater Royal (Birmingham, England); Théâtre de la Porte-St.-Martin (Paris)

H. Musical Literature:
Blanchard, Henri-Louis, *Concise Introduction to...Music*
Dibdin, Charles, *The Musical Master*
Domnich, Heinrich, *Horn Method*
Gunn, John, *An Historical Inquiry respecting the Performance on the Harp in the Highlands of Scotland...*
Holden, Oliver, *Vocal Companion*
Holyoke, Samuel, *Instrumental Assistant II*
Kollmann, Augustus, *A Second Practical Guide to Thorough Bass*
Law, Andrew, *Harmonic Companion and Guide to Social Worship*
Lichtenthal, Peter, *Der musikalische Arzt*
Villoteau, Guillaume, *Recherches sur l'analogie de la musique avec les arts...*
Vogler, Georg, *Gründliche Anleitung zum Clavierstimmen*

I. Musical Compositions:
   Attwood, Thomas, *The Curfew* (opera)
   Beethoven, Ludwig von, *Symphony No. 5, Opus 67*
       Coriolanus Overture, Opus 62
       Leonore Overture No. 1, Opus 138
       Mass in C, Opus 86
       32 Variations in C Major for Piano
   Bierey, Gottlob, *Wladimir* (opera)
   Boieldieu, François, *Un tour de soubrette* (opera)
   Catel, Charles S., *L'Auberge de Bagnères* (opera)
       Les artistes par occasion (opera)
   Cavos, Catterino, *Ilya the Hero* (opera)
   Dalayrac, Nicolas, *Lina* (opera)
   Danzi, Franz, *Iphigenie in Aulis* (opera)
   Eberl, Anton, *Concerto No. 3, Opus 40, for Piano and Orchestra*
   Fioravanti, Valentino, *I Virtuosi ambulanti* (opera)
   Hoffmann, E.T.A., *Liebe und Eifersucht* (opera)
   Isouard, Nicolo, *Les créanciers* (opera)
           Un jour à Paris (opera)
           Le rendezvous bourgeois (opera)
   Lesueur, Jean, *L'inauguration du temple de la Victoire* (intermezzo)
           Le triomphe de Trajan (opera)
   Méhul, Etienne, *Joseph und seine Brüder* (opera)
       Le retour d'Ulysse (ballet)
   Morlacchi, Francesco, *Miserere for 16 Voices*
       Il ritratto (opera)
       Il Poeta spiantata (opera)
   Romberg, Bernhard, *Ulisse und Circe* (opera)
   Spohr, Louis, *Overture in C Minor, Opus 12*
       Concerto No. 5, Opus 17, for Violin and Orchestra
       2 String Quartets, Opus 4
       2 Concertantes for Harp and Violin
       String Quartet in D Minor, Opus 11
   Spontini, Gaspare, *La vestale* (opera)
   Titov, Alexei, *Nurzadakh* (opera)
   Weber, Carl Maria von, *Grand Overture, Opus 8*
       Symphonies 1 and 2
       7 Variations on a Theme of Bianchi, Opus 7, for Piano
   Weigl, Joseph, *Cleopatra* (opera)
       Kaiser Hadrian (opera)
       Adrian von Ostade (opera)
       Das fest der bacchanten (ballet)
   Wölfl, Joseph, *Concerto, Opus 36, for Piano and Orchestra, "La Calme"*
       Alzire (ballet)
       3 Piano Sonatas, Opus 34 (with flute obbligato)
       3 Piano Sonatas, Opus 35 (with flute obbligato)
   Zelter, Carl, *Die Auferstehung und Himmelfahrt Jesu* (cantata)

1808

World Events:
In the U.S., James Madison is elected as President No. 4; Congress outlaws the importation of slaves from Africa; J.J. Astor founds the American Fur Co.; the first legal journal, *American Law Journal*, begins publication; the Union Temperate Society is founded in New York; future President Andrew Johnson is born as is future Confederate President Jefferson Davis. Internationally, Napoleon occupies the Iberian peninsula, putting his brother Joseph on the Spanish throne; Britain backs Spanish guerillas against Napoleon; the Congress of Erfurt strengthens Franco-Russian ties; the Inquisition is abolished in Spain and Italy; Frederick VI becomes ruler of Denmark and Mahmud II becomes the new Turkish ruler.

Cultural Highlights:
Louis Napleon opens the Royal Museum of Amsterdam; the Carrara School of Sculpture is opened by Lorenzo Bartolini; the Evening Sketching Society begins meeting in London; Pierre Paul Prud'hon is taken into the Legion of Honor; Jean-Paul Richter is given a government pension. Births in the art field include German artists Karl Lessing and Karl Spitzweg, French artist Honoré Daumier and sculptor Antoine Étex; deaths include German architect Carl Langhans and French artist Hubert Robert. Births in the literary world include Norwegian poet Henrik Wergeland and French poet Gérard de Nerval; deaths include Swedish poet Thomas Thorild and Italian poet Melchiorre Cesarotti. Other highlights include:

Art: Antonio Canova, *Pauline Borghese as Venus*; John Cotman, *The Waterfall*; John Crome, *The Blacksmith's Shop*; Jacques-Louis David, *Coronation of Napoleon*; David Friedrich, *The Cross on the Mountains*; Antoine Gros, *Napoleon at Eylau*; Jean-Auguste Ingres, *The Bather*; Joseph Turner, *Battle of Trafalgar*

Literature: Ernst Arndt, *Geist der Zeit*; George Colman, Jr., *Heir at Large*; Anne Grant, *Memoirs of an American Lady*; Johann von Goethe, *Pandora*; Heinrich von Kleist, *Penthesilea*; Charles Maturin, *The Wild Irish Boy*; Friedrich La Motte-Fouqué, *Sigurd, the Dragon Slayer*; Adam G. Oehlenschläger, *Hakon Jarl*; Walter Scott, *Marmion*

MUSICAL EVENTS

A. Births:

Jan 19	Joseph Menter (Ger-vn)	Jul 31	Frederick Crouch (Br-cel)
Feb 4	Michael Costa (It-cd-cm)	Aug 10	Carl Weitzmann (Ger-the)
Mar 10	Napoleone Moriani (It-ten)	Aug 20	Franz J. Kunkel (Ger-the)
Mar 24	Maria Malibran (Sp-mez)	Aug 21	Francesco Schira (It-cm-cd)
Apr 10	Auguste Franchomme (Fr-cel)	Sep 15	Antoine Clapisson (Fr-vn)
May 15	Michael Balfe (Ir-cm)	Oct 1	Eduard de Sobolewski (Ger-cd)
Nay 15	Gottfried Herrmann (Ger-vn)	Oct 11	Hyacinthe Klosé (Fr-cl)
May 30	Júnior Casimiro (Por-cm-cd)	Oct 24	Ernst F. Richter (Ger-the)
Jun 15	Giuseppe Curci (It-cm)	Nov 18	Antoine Elwart (Fr-the-cm)
Jun 24	Anna Oury (Ger-pn)	Dec 6	Carlo Bignami (It-vn)
Jun 29	Wilhelm Dettmer (Ger-bs)	Dec 6	Gilbert L. Duprez (Fr-ten)
Jul 25	Karl Liebig (Ger-cd)	Dec 26	Albert Grisar (Bel-cm)

B. Deaths:

Feb 29	Carlos Baguer (Sp-org)	Aug 13	Henri Hardouin (Fr-cm)
Apr 25	Luigi Tomasini (It-vn)	Aug 30	Joseph A. Bauer (Boh-tpt)
May 22	Edmund Ayrton (Br-org)	Sep	Johann Cuypers (Hol-vn.m)
Jun 7	Johann J. Schramm (Ger-org.m)	Sep 23	Gaëtan A. Vestris (It-bal)
Jun 9	Antonio Eximeno (Sp-the)	Sep 26	Paul Wranitzky (Cz-vn-cm)
Jun 11	Giovanni B. Cirri (It-cel)	Oct 1	Regina Mingotti (It-sop)
Jul 20	François Barthélemon (Fr-cd)	Oct 13	François Cupin (Fr-cel)

Dec 1   Anton Fischer (Ger-ten)   John Avery (Br-org.m)
Dec 14   William Forster, Sr. (Br-vn.m)   Filippo Gherardeschi (It-cm)

C. Debuts:

Other - Giulio Bordogni (Milan), Giovanni Davide (Siena), Domenico Donzelli (Bergamo), Ignaz Moscheles (Prague)

D. New Positions:

Conductors: Francisco Andreví y Castellar (choir, Segorbe Cathedral), Gottlob B. Bierey (kapellmeister, Breslau), Franz Danzi (kapellmeister, Karlsruhe), José Nunes García (mestre de capela, Brazilian Court), Wenzel Müller (Prague Opera), Friedrich Seidel (Berlin Royal Orchestra), Daniel Steibelt (kapellmeister, Kassel Opera), Christian Friedrich Uber (Cassel Opera), Karl Jakob Wagner (kapellmeister, Darmstadt)

Educational: Bonifazio Asioli (director, Milan Conservatory), Konrad Berg (piano and violin, Paris Conservatory), François Habeneck (violin, Paris Conservatory), Johann C. Haeffner (music director, Uppsala University), Georg W. Hegel (rector, Nuremberg Gymnasium), Alessandro Rolla (violin, Milan Conservatory), Giuseppe Sigismondi (librarian, Naples Conservatory), Daniel Gottlob Türk (theory, Halle University)

Others: Ignaz Assmayer (organ, St. Peter's, Salzburg), John Christmas Beckwith (organ, Norwich Cathedral), Mateo Ferrer (organ, Barcelona Cathedral), Gottfried Wilhelm Fink (music critic, *Allgemeine Musikalische Zeitung*), Johann C. Haeffner (organ, Uppsala Cathedral)

E. Prizes and Honors:

Prizes: Pierre-Auguste Blondeau (Prix de Rome)

F. Biographical Highlights:

Domenico Barbaja, Italian impresario, is given the lease on the gambling tables of Naples; Nicola Benvenuti is appointed maestro di capella at Pisa Cathedral but dos not take up his work there until 1810; Ferdinando Bertoni, after 55 years of service, is retired from St. Mark's in Venice; Isabella Colbran and Giovanni Velutti make their La Scala debuts; Manuel G. García makes his Paris Opera debut; Johann Christian Graupner becomes a naturalized American citizen; Jacques-François Halévy, age 10, enters Paris Conservatory; Johannes Nepomuk Maelzel becomes court mechanician in Vienna; Giuseppe Mercadante enters the Collegio di San Sebastiano only by changing his name birth records; Ignaz Moscheles goes to Vienna to study with Albrechtsberger and Salieri; Anton Reicha moves to Paris and gains a modest success with his operas; Franz Schubert enters the Imperial Chapel School in Vienna; Daniel Steibelt flees his creditors to St. Petersburg; Carl Maria von Weber is arrested, imprisoned for 2 weeks then expelled from Stuttgart for innocent involvement is a fraud scheme.

G. Institutional Openings:

Performing Groups: Brno Philharmonic Society; Harvard College Orchestra (first in the U.S.); Liebhaberkonzerte (Cologne); Schuppanzigh (Razumovsky) String Quartet (Vienna); Schweizerische Musikgesellschaft (Lucerne)

Educational: Accademia dei Concordi (Bologna); Anschütz Vocal School (Koblenz); Koblenz Musikinstitut; Naples Conservatory of Music

Other: Belfast Harp Society; Familienkonzerte (Cologne); *Phöbus* (Dresden); Pierian Sodality (Harvard Musical Association in 1837); *Protokoll der Schweizerischen Musikgesellschaft*; Ricordi and Co., Music Publishers (Milan); St. Phillippe Theater (New Orleans); Société de Musique Helvétique; Teatro della Concordia (Cremona); Williams Music Publishers (London)

H. Musical Literature:

Albrechtsberger, Johann, *Clavierschule für Anfänger*
Choron, Alexandre, *Principes de composition des écoles d'Italie*
Dibdin, Charles, *The English Pythagoras*
Favart, Charles, *Mémoires et Correspondance littéraires, dramatiques et Anecdotiques*
Krause, Karl, *Vollständige Anweisung*
Momigny, Jérôme de, *Le nouveau Solfège*
Moore, Thomas, *Irish Melodies I*
Türk, Daniel, *Anleitung zu Temperaturberechnungen*

I. Musical Compositions:

Auber, Daniel, *Concerto for Violin and Orchestra*
Barker/Bray, *The Indian Princess* (opera)
Beethoven, Ludwig van, *Symphony No. 6, Opus 68, "Pastoral"*
    Choral Fantasia, Opus 80 (piano, chorus, orchestra)
    Sonata, Opus 69, for Cello and Piano
    2 Piano Trios, Opus 70
    Arietta, In Questa Tomba Oscura
Boieldieu, François, *La dame invisible* (opera)
    Les voitures versées (opera)
Cavos, Catterino, *Three Hunchback Brothers* (opera)
Danzi, Franz, *Abraham auf Moria* (oratorio)
Destouches, Franz von, *Wanda* (incidental music)
Generali, Pietro, *Le lagrime d'una vedova* (opera)
    L'idolo cinese (opera)
Giuliani, Mauro, *Concerto, Opus 30, for Guitar and Orchestra*
Hoffmann, E. T. A., *Der Trank der Unsterblichkeit* (opera)
Isouard, Nicolo, *Cimarosa* (opera)
Kreutzer, Konradin, *Die Nacht im Walde* (opera)
    Aesop in Phrygien (opera)
Kreutzer, Rodolphe, *Aristippe* (opera)
    Les amours d'Antoine et Cléopatre (ballet)
Kurpinski, Karol, *Pygmalion* (operetta)
Méhul, Etienne, *Symphony No. 2 in D*
Morlacchi, Francesco, *Il corradino* (melodrama)
    Oreste (opera)
Paër, Ferdinando, *Numa Pompilio* (opera)
Paisiello, Giovanni, *I pittagorici* (opera)
Reicha, Anton, *Symphonies No. 1 and 2, Opus 41 and 42*
    Requiem
Rossini, Gioacchino, *Overture in D Major*
    5 String Quartets
    Il pianto d'armonia (cantata)
Spohr, Louis, *Concerto No. 1, Opus 26, for Clarinet and Orchestra*
    Concertante No. 1, Opus 48, for 2 Violins and Orchestra
    2 String Quartets, Opus 15
    Alruna, die Eulenkönigin (opera)
Titov, Alexei, *Le caverne orientale* (opera)
    The Wedding of Filatka (opera)
Tomásek, Jaroslav, *Serafine* (opera)
Trento, Vittorio, *The Deluge* (oratorio)
Viotti, Giovanni, *Concerto No. 26 for Violin and Orchestra*
Weber, Carl Maria von, *Der erste Ton, Opus 14* (cantata)
    Grande Polonaise, Opus 21, for Piano
    7 Variations, Opus 9, for Piano
Wölfl, Joseph, *Symphony No. 2, Opus 41*

1809

World Events:

In the U.S., Congress repeals the controversial Embargo Act and passes the Non-Intercourse Act which opens trade to all but France and Great Britain; the world's first ocean-going steamship, the *Phoenix*, makes its maiden voyage; the Illinois Territory is formed in the Northwest territory; Mother Seton founds the Sisters of Charity; Abraham Lincoln and Charles Darwin are born. Internationally, Napoleon conquers Austria who loses considerable territory as a result of the Peace of Schonnbrünn; Napoleon also annexes the Papal States; Metternich becomes Chief Minister of Austria; Great Britain and Turkey sign the Treaty of the Dardanelles; the new Swedish Constitution goes into effect; Ecuador gains its independence from Spain.

Cultural Highlights:

The *Poetical Magazine* begins publication in London; Willem Bilderdijk publishes his book, *The Art of Poetry*; Lord Byron's *English Bards and Scotch Reviewers* appears; William Allen's *American Biographical and Historical Dictionary* is published; Johann Tischbein becomes court painter to the Duke of Oldenburg; David Wilkie is inducted into the Royal Academy; Friedrich von Mattison is ennobled. In the field of literature, births include American poets Oliver Wendell Holmes and Edgar Allen Poe, British poets Edward Fitzgerald and Alfred Lord Tennyson, French poet Roger de Beauvoir, Russian novelist Nikolai Gogol and Danish poet Frederik Paludan-Müller; deaths include American revolutionary writer Thomas Paine. The art world sees the birth of French sculptor Antoine Preault and the deaths of British artist Paul Sandby, German sculptor Johann Wagner, French sculptor Augustin Pajou and Danish artist Nicolai Abildgaard. Other highlights include:

Art: John Constable, *Malvern Hall*; Jacques-Louis David, *Sappho and Phaon*; John Flaxman, *Lord Nelson*; David Friedrich, *Landscape with Rainbow*; Antoine Gros, *Surrender of Madrid*; Henry Raeburn, *Mrs. Spiers*; John Trumbull, *Lamderg and Gelchossa*; Joseph Turner, *Fishing on the Blythe-Sand*

Literature: Thomas Campbell, *Gertrude of Wyoming*; François de Chateaubriand, *Les Martyrs*; Maria Edgeworth, *Tales from Fashionable Life I*; Thomas Fessenden, *Pills, Poetical, Political and Philosophical*; Philip Freneau, *Poems of the Revolutionary War*; Washington Irving, *Knickerbocker History of New York*

MUSICAL EVENTS

A. Births:

Jan 2	Friedrich Jähns (Ger-ped)	Jul 20	Francesco Chiarmonte (It-ten)
Jan 5	Félix Delhasse (Bel-mus)	Aug 19	Sabina Heinefetter (Ger-sop)
Jan 20	Eduard E. Koch (Ger-org)	Aug 30	Adolf F. Hesse (Ger-org-cd)
Feb 3	Felix Mendelssohn (Ger-cm)	Oct 2	Anton Emil Titl (Aus-cm-cd)
Feb 25	Charles L. d'Albert (Fr-bal)	Oct 22	Federico Ricci (It-cm)
Mar 19	Fredrik Pacius (Ger-cm)	Nov 26	Auguste F. Morel (Fr-cm)
Apr 7	Arthur E. Seguin (Br-bs)	Dec 8	Jean Willent-Bordogni (Fr-bn)
Apr 23	Eugène P. Prévost (Fr-cd)	Dec 23	Henry R. Allen (Ir-bar)
Jun 1	Wilhelm von Lenz (Rus-mus)		John Brownsmith (Br-org)
Jun 3	Gotthilf Körner (Ger-pub)		Frederick Gye (Br-imp)
Jul 14	Eugène Sauzay (Fr-vn)		Eugenia Tadolini (It-sop)

B. Deaths:

Jan 4	Bartolomeo Giacometti (It-bs)	Jan 29	Luigi A. Sabbatini (It-the)
Jan 6	Johann A. Eberhard (Ger-the)	Feb 26	Francisco J. Garcia (Sp-cm)

Mar 7	Johann Albrechtsberger (Aus-cm)	Jul 8	Christian Barth (Ger-ob)
		Jul 24	Johann G. Eckard (Ger-pn)
Apr 17	Johann C. Kittel (Ger-org)	Jul 31	Jean-Pierre Legrand (Fr-org)
Apr 29	Margarete Schick (Ger-sop)	Sep 17	Johann Holzhay (Ger-org.m)
May	Johann A. Stamitz (Ger-cd-cm)	Sep 21	Alexander Reinagle (Br-cd-cm)
May 31	Franz Joseph Haydn (Aus-cm)	Nov 26	Nicolas Dalayrac (Fr-cm)
Jun 3	John Beckwith (Br-org)	Dec 31	Franz I. Beck (Ger-vn)
Jul 3	Joseph Quesne (Can-pt-cm)		Jean Lebrun (Fr-hn)

C. Debuts:
Other - Charles Edward Horn (London), Jacques Émile Lavigne (Paris)

D. New Positions:
Conductors: Joseph Preindl (kapellmeister, St. Stephen's, Vienna)

Educational: Francesco Pollini (piano, Milan Conservatory), Simon Sechter (piano and organ, Vienna Institute for the Blind), Carl Zelter (professor, Berlin Singakademie)

Others: Domenico Barbaja (manager, Royal Opera House of Naples), William Gifford (editor, *Quarterly Review*)

E. Prizes and Honors:
Prizes: Louis-Joseph Daussoigne-Méhul (Prix de Rome)

F. Biographical Highlights:
Ludwig van Beethoven gains powerful supporters in the Archduke Rudolph and Princes Kinsky and Lobkowitz who are willing to overlook his boorishness in deference to his musical genius; Italian composer Francesco Bianchi commits suicide; Marie Bigot moves with her husband to Paris where she becomes a successful piano teacher; Elizabeth Billington, at the peak of her career, retires from the opera stage; Sigismund Ritter von Neukomm leaves his conducting position in Russia for Paris where he eventually becomes pianist to Talleyrand; Italian composer Giovanni Pacini continues his piano and composition study with Furlanetto in Venice; Niccolò Paganini begins his career as a free concert artist; Fernando Sor travels to London where he makes the guitar fashionable in society; Zacharias Werner begins a four-year stay in Italy.

G. Institutional Openings:
Performing Groups: Berlin Liedertafel (male chorus); Società degli Esercizi Musicale (Livorno)

Other: Covent Garden Theater II (London); William Dale, Music Publisher (London); Piano Repetitive Action (perfected by S. Érard); Psallonian Society (Providence); Robert Purdie, Music Publisher (Edinburgh); Quarterly Review (London); Schiedemayer und Söhne, Piano Manufacturers (Stuttgart); Théâtre d'Orléans (New Orleans)

H. Musical Literature:
Asioli, Bonifazio, *Principi elementari di musica*
Beaulieu, D./Méhul, E., *Cours de composition*
Bunting, Edward, *Ancient Irish Airs II*
Désargus, Xavier, *Traité général sur l'art de jouer la Harpe*
Garaudé, Alexis de, *Méthode de chant*
Law, Andrew, *The Art of Playing the Organ and Pianoforte*
Mayr, Simon, *Breve notizii istoriche della vite e delle opere di G. Haydn*
Rossi, Giuseppe, *Alli intendenti di Contrappunto*
Thomson, George, *Select Collection of Original Welsh Airs*

I. Musical Compositions:

Abeille, Ludwig, *Peter und Ännchenn* (opera)
Beethoven, Ludwig van, *Concerto No. 5, Opus 73, for Piano, "Emperor"*
  String Quartet No. 10, Opus 74, "The Harp"
  Sonatas No. 24-26, Opus 78, 79 and 81, for Piano
  Fantasia, Opus 77, for Piano
  Military March, Opus 145 (orchestra)
Berton, Henri, *Françoise de Foix* (opera)
Bishop, Henry, *The Circassian Bride* (opera)
Champein, Stanislas, *Le nouveau Don Quichotte* (opera)
Cherubini, Luigi, *Pygmalion* (opera)
  Mass in F Major
Dalayrac, Nicolas, *Le poète et le musicien* (opera)
  Le pavillon des fleurs (opera)
  Elise-Hortense (opera)
Diabelli, Anton, *Adam in der Klemme* (opera)
Eberl, Anton, *Concerto, Opus 45, for 2 Pianos and Orchestra*
Generali, Pietro, *La moglie di tre mariti* (opera)
  Amor vince lo Sdegno (opera)
Gossec, François, *Symphony in 17 parts in F Major*
Isouard, Nicolo, *L'intrigue au sérail* (opera)
Kashin, Daniil, *Fair Olga* (opera)
Lebrun, Louis-Sébatien, *Te Deum*
Lesueur, Jean-François, *La mort d'Adam* (oratorio)
Mayr, Simon, *Il matrimonio per concorso* (opera)
  Il ritorno di Ulisse (opera)
Méhul, Etienne, *Symphony No. 3*
Morlacchi, Francesco, *Rinaldo d'Asti* (opera)
  La principessa per ripiego (opera)
  La Simoncino (opera)
  La avventure di una Giornata (opera)
Paër, Ferdinando, *Agnese* (opera)
Reicha, Anton, *Symphony No. 3*
Reichardt, Johann, *Bradamante* (opera)
Rossini, Gioacchino, *6 Quartets for Woodwinds*
Spohr, Louis, *Concerto No. 6, Opus 28, for Violin and Orchestra*
  Sonata, Opus 115, for Harp and Cello
  6 German Songs, Opus 2
Spontini, Gaspare, *Fernand Cortez* (opera)
Titov, Alexei, *The Old Bachelor* (opera)
Titov, Sergei, *The Meeting* (opera)
Weber, Carl Maria von, *Turandot, Opus 37* (incidental music)
  Andante and Rondo for Viola and Orchestra
  Piano Quartet in B-flat Major
  6 Pieces, Opus 10 (piano, 4 hands)
  6 Songs, Opus 15
Weigl, Joseph, *Die Schweitzerfamilie* (opera)
  Der Verwandlungen (operetta)
Weyse, Christoph, *The Sleeping Potion* (opera)
Winter, Peter, *Colmal* (opera)
Zingarelli, Nicola, *Il ritorno di Serse* (opera)

1810

World Events:
The U.S. Census shows a population of 7,240,000, a 36.4% increase in 10 years; Macon's Bill No. 2 reopens trade with France and Great Britain, but France continues seizing U.S. ships; the Congress annexes Florida when the Floridians revolt against Spanish rule; Yale Medical School opens its doors; the Agricultural Museum begins publication. Internationally, Napoleon marries Marie Louise of Austria and annexes Holland, Hanover, Bremen and Lübeck; the Decree of Fontainbleau calls for the confiscation of all British possessions; the Spanish Viceroy is overthrown in Argentina; the Mexican Revolution begins (continues until 1821).

Cultural Highlights:
Christian Overbeck leads a group of painters to Rome to set up the Nazarene school of painting; John Flaxman begins teaching sculpture in the Royal Academy in London; Heinrich von Kleist begins editing the *Berliner Abendblätter*, Alexander Chalmers' *Works of the English Poets* appears as does Isaiah Thomas' *History of Printing in America*; Augustus Callcott is inducted into the Royal Academy and Caspar David Friedrich into the Berlin Academy. Births in the art field include Jean Bonnassieux and Clark Mills; deaths include John Hoppner, Philipp Runge, Johannes de Troostwijck and Johann Zoffany. Births in the literary field include Louise Colet, Elizabeth Gaskell, Robert Griepenkerl, Charles de Montalembert, Alfred de Musset and Eliot Warburton. Other highlights include:

Art: William Blake, *The Canterbury Pilgrims*; Antonio Canova, *Dancing Girl*; John Crome, *The Beaters*; David Friedrich, *Cloister Graveyard in the Snow*; François Gérard, *Battle of Austerlitz*; Francisco de Goya, *Disasters of War I*; Pierre Guérin, *Andromaque et Pyrrhus*; Richard Westmacott, *Fox Memorial* (Westminster Abbey)

Literature: Joanna Baillie, *The Family Legend*; Eaton Barrett, *Woman and Other Poems*; George Crabbe, *The Borough*; James Hogg, *The Forest Minstrel*; Heinrich von Kleist, *Das Käthchen von Heilbronn*; Jane Porter, *The Scottish Chiefs*; Walter Scott, *The Lady of the Lake*; Robert Southey, *Curse of Kehama*; Zacharias Werner, *Wanda*

MUSICAL EVENTS

A. Births:

Jan	Alfred Day (Br-med-the)	Jun 13	Julius Leonhard (Ger-pn)
Jan 9	Anna Bishop (Br-sop)	Jun 19	Ferdinand David (Ger-vn)
Feb 5	Ole Bull (Nor-vn)	Jul 14	Johann Seidel (Ger-org)
Feb 8	Norbert Burgmüller (Ger-cm)	Aug 6	Giorgio Ronconi (It-bar)
Feb 22	Holger S. Paulli (Den-cd)	Aug 14	Samuel S. Wesley (Br-org)
Mar 1	Frédéric Chopin (Pol-pn-cm)	Oct 17	Giovanni Mario (It-ten)
Mar 9	Jean G. Kastner (Fr-cm-the)	Oct 22	Nicola Ivanoff (Rus-ten)
May 2	Hans C. Lumbye (Den-cm-cd)	Nov 7	Franz Erkel (Hun-cm-cd)
Jun 8	Robert Schumann (Ger-cm)	Nov 16	Friedrich Kunken (Ger-cm)
Jun 9	Otto Nicolai (Ger-cm)	Dec 29	Konstantin Decker (Ger-pn)
Jun 10	Konstancja Gladkowska (Pol-sop)		Julian Fontana (Pol-pn)

B. Deaths:

Feb 7	José Aldana (Mex-vn)	Oct 22	Franz Teyber (Aus-cm)
Feb 15	Johann M. Götz (Ger-pub)	Nov 26	Nicolas Framery (Fr-the)
Feb 20	Johann F. Krantz (Ger-vn)	Nov 27	Francesco Bianchi (It-cm)
Apr 8	Venanzio Rauzzini (It-cm)	Dec 11	Samuel Porter (Br-org)
Jul 15	Jean Baptiste Rey (Fr-cd)		Francesco Gnecco (It-cm)
Oct 19	Jean G. Noverre (Fr-bal)		

C. Debuts:
Other - Joséphine Fodor-Mainville (Paris), Joachim Kackowski (Warsaw), Mary Anne Paton (Edinburgh), John Sinclair (London), Maria Agata Szymanowska (Warsaw)

D. New Positions:
Conductors: Nicola Benvenuti (maestro di cappella, Pisa Cathedral), Henry Bishop (Covent Garden), Antonio Brunetti (maestro di cappella, Urbino Cathedral), Francesco Morlacchi (Italian Opera, Dresden), August Müller (kapellmeister, Weimar), Louis Luc de Persuis (Paris Opera), Friedrich W. Pixis, Jr. (Prague Opera), Johann Schicht (kantor, Thomasschule, Leipzig), Johann Schulz (Leipzig Gewandhaus), Gaspare Spontini (Italian Opera, Paris)

Educational: Antonio Canova (director, Academy of St. Luke, Rome), Franz von Destouches (theory, Landshut University), Adam Oehlenschläger (aesthetics, Copenhagen University)

Others: Franz Teyber (organ, Vienna Court)

E. Prizes and Honors:
Prizes: Désiré Beaulieu (Prix de Rome)

Honors: Gian Francisco Fortunati (Institute of Sciences and Letters, Parma)

F. Biographical Highlights:
Teresa Bertinotti debuts in London; Muzio Clementi, finished with his years of touring, settles in London and soon begins a business man career; Anthony Heinrich emigrates to the U.S. and settles in Philadelphia; Rodolphe Kreutzer's concert career ends with a broken arm; Friedrich Kuhlau goes to Copenhagen to escape service in Napoleon's army; Karol Kurpinski settles in Warsaw as assistant to Elsner at the opera; Giacomo Meyerbeer goes to live and study with the Abbé Vogler in Darmstadt; Marcos Portugal, on the closing of the San Carlos Theater, follows the Portugese Royal Family to Brazil; Rossini's first commissioned opera, *La cambiale di matrimonio*, is staged in Venice; Fernando Sor works up to the rank of captain in the French army; Jan Vorísek enters the University of Prague to study with Tomásek; Carl Maria von Weber, failing to gain a position at Mannheim, concertizes around Germany.

G. Institutional Openings:
Performing Groups: Boston Philo-Harmonic Society; Cercle Harmonique (Lyons); Harmonischer Verein (Mannheim); Sons of Handel (Dublin); Worchester Glee Club (Massachusetts)

Festivals: Thuringian Festival (Frankenhausen)

Educational: Conservatoire Secondaire de Paris

Other: Bass Trumpet (patent by L. Frichot); Chapell and Co., Ltd. (London); Grand Ducal Theater (Karlsruhe); Harmonichord (by F. Kaufmann); Janet et Cotelle, Music Publishers (Paris); Ludwig Maisch, Music Publisher (Vienna); Musikalske Lyceum (Oslo); Schlesingersche Buch- und Musikalienhandlung (Berlin); Society for the Improvement of Musical Art in Bohemia; Teatro del Campillo (Granada); Guillaume Triebert, Woodwind Maker (Paris)

H. Musical Literature:
Choron, A./Fayolle, F., *Dictionnaire des Musiciens I*
Corfe, Joseph, *Church Music*
Corri, Domenico, *The Singer's Preceptor*
Dignum, Charles, *Vocal Music*
Hering, Karl G., *Praktische Violin-Schule*
Kreutzer, Rodolphe, *Méthode de Violon*
La Salette, Joubert de, *Considérations sur les divers systèmes de la musique...*

Nägeli, Johann, *Gesangsbildungslehre nach Pestalozzischen Grundsätzen*
Reichardt, Johann, *Briefe auf einer Reise nach Wien*

I. Musical Compositions:

Beethoven, Ludwig van, *Egmont, Opus 84* (incidental music)
    String Quartet No. 11, Opus 95, "Serioso"
    Sextet, Opus 81b, for 2 Horns and String Quartet
    Sextet, Opus 71, for Clarinets, Horns and Bassoons
    Quintet for Flute and Strings
    6 Variations, Opus 76, for Piano
    6 Songs, Opus 75
    3 Songs, Opus 83
Boieldieu, François, *Rien de trop* (opera)
Catel, Charles, *Les bayadères* (opera)
Cherubini, Luigi, *Le crescendo* (opera)
Czerny, Carl, *Sonata No. 1, Opus 7, for Piano*
Eybler, Joseph, *Die vier letzten dinge* (oratorio)
Generali, Pietro, *Adelina* (opera)
Hummel, Johann N., *Mathilde von Guise* (opera)
Isouard, Nicolo, *Cendrillon* (opera)
    La fête du village (opera)
    La Victime des arts (opera)
Kreutzer, Konradin, *Jery und Bätely* (opera)
    Panthea (opera)
Lesueur, Jean-François, *Ruth et Naomi* (oratorio)
Marschner, Heinrich, *Die stolze Bäuerin* (ballet)
Méhul, Etienne, *Symphony No. 4*
    Persée et Andromède (ballet)
    Cantata for Napoleon's Birthday
Meyerbeer, Giacomo, *Der Fischer und das Milchmädchen* (opera)
Morlacchi, Francesco, *Le Danaïdi* (opera)
    Mass No. 1
Paër, Ferdinando, *Didone abbandonata* (opera)
Reicha, Anton, *Cagliostro* (opera)
Reichardt, Johann, *Der Taucher* (opera)
    Schiller Lyrische Gedichte
Rossini, Gioacchino, *La cambiale di matrimonio* (opera)
    Variations in C Major for Clarinet and Orchestra
Schubert, Franz, *String Quartet in G Major, D. 2*
Spohr, Louis, *Concerto No. 2, Opus 57, for Clarinet and Orchestra*
    Concerto No. 10, Opus 62, for Violin and Orchestra
    Der Zweikampf mit der Geliebten (singspiel)
Steibelt, Daniel, *Cendrillon* (opera)
Vogler, George (Abbé), *Der Admiral* (opera)
Weber, Carl Maria von, *Silvana* (opera)
    Concerto No. 1, Opus 11, for Piano and Orchestra
    Andante and Variations for Cello and Orchestra
    6 Violin Sonatas, Opus 10
    5 Songs, Opus 13
Weigl, Joseph, *Der Einsiedler auf den Alpen* (opera)
Weinlig, Christian, *Dem Chaos im dunkel der nacht* (cantata)
Winter, Peter von, *Die beiden Blinden* (opera)
Wölfl, Joseph, *Concerto, Opus 49, for Piano and Orchestra*
    3 Piano Sonatas, Opus 48

1811

World Events:
In the U.S., William Henry Harrison defeats the Indian forces under Tecumseh at the Battle of Tippecanoe; the greatest earthquake in U.S. history takes place in the Mississippi Valley and covers 300,000 square miles; the steamboat, *New Orleans*, becomes the first to sail the Mississippi River; the first news agency opens in Boston; Astoria is founded in the Oregon Territory. Internationally, the French suffer losses in Portugal; the British take over the island of Java in the South Pacific; the Prince of Wales takes over as regent on the insanity of King George III in England; Paraguay in South America gains its independence from Spain.

Cultural Highlights:
The First School of Drama opens in Warsaw; François de Chateaubriand is inducted into the French Academy; Richard Westmacott and David Wilkie are taken into the Royal Academy in London; Heinrich von Kleist, in a suicide pact, kills Henriette Vogel and self. Other literary deaths include György Bessenyei, Richard Cumberland, James Grahame, John Leyden and Thomas Percy; births include Alfred Domett, Adolphe d'Ennery, Horace Greeley, Jules Sandeau, Harriet Beecher Stowe, Alfred Street and William Thackeray. Births in the art field include Americans George C. Bingham and William Page, French artists Henri Delaborde, Jules Dupré and Théophile Gautier; deaths include British artists Peter Bourgeois and James Sharples. Other highlights include:

Art: Washington Allston, *Poor Author and Rich Bookseller*; John Constable, *East Bergholt Fair*; Wilhelm von Kobell, *Horse Races at Munich*; Pierre-Paul Prud'hon, *Empress Marie-Louise*; Thomas Sully, *George Cooke as Richard III*; Bertel Thorvaldsen, *Procession of Alexander the Great*; John Trumbull, *Lady of the Lake*; Joseph Turner, *Apollo and Python*

Literature: Ludwig von Arnim, *Halle und Jerusalem*; Jane Austen, *Sense and Sensibility*; Clemens Brentano, *Gockel, Hinkel und Gackeleia*; Johann von Goethe, *Aus Meinem Leben I*; Heinrich von Kleist, *Novellen I, II*; Friedrich La Motte Fouqué, *Undine*; Hannah More, *Practical Piety*; Friedrich Müller, *Das Nusskernan*

MUSICAL EVENTS

A. Births:

Jan 15	Pierre Chevillard (Fr-cel)		Oct 13	Henri Rosellen (Fr-pn)
Mar 11	Francesco Lamperti (It-voc)		Oct 20	Oliver Ditson (Am-pub)
Mar 23	Wilhelm Taubert (Ger-cm)		Oct 22	Franz Liszt (Hun-pn-cm)
Mar 30	Angelo Catelani (It-mus)		Oct 24	Ferdinand Hiller (Ger-cm)
May 11	Filippo Coletti (It-bar)		Oct 29	Tito Ricordi (It-pub)
Jun 13	Vissarion Belinsky (Rus-cri)		Nov 14	Friedrich Truhn (Ger-cm)
Jul 19	Vincenz Lachner (Ger-org.m)		Nov 26	Karl Brendel (Ger-cri)
Jul 28	Giulia Grisi (It-sop)		Dec 1	Pierre Varnay (Fr-cm)
Aug 5	Charles A. Thomas (Fr-cm)		Dec 8	Ludwig Schindelmesser (Ger-cd)
Aug 25	August G. Ritter (Ger-org)			Jane Shirreff (Br-sop)

B. Deaths:

Jan 1	Johann Braun (Ger-vn)		Sep 3	Ignaz Fränzl (Ger-vn)
Feb 24	Johann G. Voigt (Ger-org)		Sep 6	Julien A. Mathieu (Fr-vn)
Feb 27	Ignaz Leutgeb (Aus-hn)		Sep 23	Thomas Ebdon (Br-org)
Mar 11	Jacques Tours (Hol-org)		Nov 15	Giacomo Rampini (It-org)
May 12	Louis C. Rey (Fr-cel)		Dec 11	Louis de Reigny (Fr-cm)
Jun 19	Christian Tag (Ger-cm)		Dec 17	John Antes (Am-rel-cm)
				Sarah Bates (Br-sop)

C. Debuts:
Other - Filippo Galli (Padua, as a bass), Benedetta Pisaroni (Bergamo)

D. New Positions:
Conductors: Giacomo Carcani (maestro di cappella, Piacenza Cathedral), Johann Henneberg (kapellmeister, Eisenstadt), Giuseppe Jannaconi (maestro di cappella, St. Peter's, Rome), Marcos Portugal (mestre de capela, Rio de Janeiro), Giovanni Tadolini (Italian Theater, Paris)

Educational: August Böckh (professor, University of Berlin), Karl Gottlieb Hering (music, Zittau Seminary), François Louis Perne (harmony, Paris Conservatory), Friedrich D. Weber (director, Prague Conservatory)

E. Prizes and Honors:
Prizes: Hippolyte-André Chélard (Prix de Rome)

Honors: George Thomas Smart (knighted)

F. Biographical Highlights:
François Benoist enters Paris Conservatory; François Boieldieu, despite a firm promise of a substantial pay raise, leaves Russia and returns to Paris; Gaetano Crivelli makes his Paris debut; Jacques François Halévy begins studying counterpoint with Luigi Cherubini and harmony with Henri Berton; Moritz Hauptmann begins studying violin and composition with Louis Spohr in Gotha; Johann Nepomuk Hummel leaves Eisenstadt and settles in Vienna as a piano teacher; Johann Wenzel Kalliwoda enters the Conservatory of Prague; Heinrich August Marschner begins singing in the school choir in Zittau and studies music with Karl Hering; Bohemian pianist and teacher Josef Proksch becomes completely blind; Carl Gottlieb Reissiger enters the Thomasschule in Leipzig and studies with Johann Schicht; Franz Schubert's songs attract the attention and interest of Antonio Salieri; Nicola Zingarelli is jailed for refusing to take part in a musical tribute to Napoleon's son and is sent to Paris where he is freed by Napoleon himself.

G. Institutional Openings:
Performing Groups: Birmingham Oratorio Society (England); Elberfelder Gesangverein (Wuppertal); Havana Opera Troupe; Möser String Quartet (Berlin); Orchestra of the National Guard (Krakow)

Educational: Istituto Filarmonico (Venice); Musikalische Akademie (Munich); Prague Conservatory of Music

Other: Marco Berra Publishing House and Music Shop (Prague); Chiswick Press (London); Double-Action Harp (by S. Érard); Jacques-Joseph Frey, Music Publisher (Paris); Thomas Hall, Organ Builder (Philadelphia); Novello and Co., Ltd. (London); B.G. Teubner Publishing House (Leipzig)

H. Musical Literature:
Angeloni, Luigi, *Sopra la vita le opera ed il sapere di Guido d'Arezzo...*
Böckh, August, *De metris Pindari*
Genlis, Stéphanie, *Harp Method*
Herbart, Johann F., *Psychologische Bemerkungen zur Tonlehre*
Koch, Heinrich, *Handbuch bei dem Studium der Harmonie*
Lipowsky, Felix, *Baierisches Musiklexicon*
Pelissier, Victor, *Columbian Melodies*
Pollini, Francesco, *Metodo per Clavicembalo*
Vogler, Georg, *System für den Fugenbau*
Weinlig, Christian, *Vorlesungen über Grundbasse und Composition überhaupt*

I. Musical Compositions:

Auber, Daniel, *Julie* (opera)
Beethoven, Ludwig van, *The Ruins of Athens, Opus 113* (incidental music)
    King Stephen, Opus 117 (incidental music)
    Piano Trio, Opus 97, "Archduke"
    4 Ariettas and Duets, Opus 82
Danzi, Franz, *Dido* (opera)
Generali, Pietro, *La vedova delirante* (opera)
Gyrowetz, Adalbert, *Der Augenarzt* (opera)
Hoffmann, E. T. A., *Aurora* (opera)
Isouard, Nicolo, *Le magicien sans magic* (opera)
    Le billet de loterie (opera)
Kurpinski, Karol, *Zwei hutten* (opera)
    Luzifers Palast (opera)
Lesueur, Jean F., *Ruth et Booz* (oratorio)
Mayr, Simon, *Ifigenia in Aulide* (opera)
    L'amor figliale (opera)
Méhul, Etienne, *Sesostris* (opera)
    Les amazones (opera)
Meyerbeer, Giacomo, *Gott und die Natur* (oratorio)
Morlacchi, Francesco, *Raoul de Créqui* (opera)
    La Passione (oratorio)
Reicha, Anton, *Symphony No. 4*
Rossini, Gioacchino, *L'equivoco stravagante* (opera)
    L'inganno felice (opera)
    La mort de Didone (cantata)
Schubert, Franz, *Hagar's Klage*
    String Quartet in F, D. 998
Spohr, Louis, *Symphony No. 1, Opus 20*
    Sonata, Opus 114, for Violin and Harp
Tomásek, Jaroslav, *Seraphine* (opera)
Trento, Vittorio, *Climène* (opera)
Weber, Carl Maria von, *Abu Hassan* (opera)
    Concertos No. 1 and 2, Opus 73 and 74, for Clarinet and Orchestra
    Concerto, Opus 75, for Bassoon and Orchestra
    Concertino, Opus 26, for Clarinet and Orchestra
    Overture, Der Beherrscher der Geister, Opus 8
    Adagio and Rondo for Harmonichord and Orchestra
    7 Variations, Opus 33, for Clarinet and Piano
    Scene and Aria, "Signor se padre sei"
    Scene and Aria, "Miséra me"
    3 Songs, Opus 29
    3 Duets, Opus 31
Winter, Peter, *Die Pantoffeln* (singspiel)
Zingarelli, Nicola, *Baldovino* (opera)
    Berenice, regina d'Armenia (opera)

1812

World Events:
In the U.S., James Madison is re-elected as President; Louisiana becomes the 18th state in the Union and the Missouri Territory is formed out of the remainder of the original Purchase; the U.S. goes to war with Great Britain; Columbus, Ohio, a planned community, becomes the capitol of Ohio; the American Antiquarian Society is founded; Internationally, Napoleon invades Russia but is defeated by the Russian winter and retreats from Moscow with great losses; at home, Napoleon defeats a conspiracy to put Louis XVIII on the throne; British Prime Minister Perceval is assassinated in the House of Commons; the Great Temple of Abu Simbel is discovered in Egypt.

Cultural Highlights:
Henry Raeburn becomes the President of the Edinburgh Society of Artists; François Rude wins the Prix de Rome in Art. Births include British artist William J. Müller, French artist Pierre Rousseau and German artist Johann August Tischbein; in the literary field, British poets Robert Browning and Edward Lear and novelist Charles Dickens, French poet Pierre Laprade and German author Carl Kossmaly. Deaths in the art field include German artists Johann Friedrich Tischbein and Gottlieb Schick and French artist Philippe de Loutherbourg; the literary world loses French poet and dramatist Gabriel Legouvé, American poet Joel Barlow and German novelist Berthold Auerbach. Other highlights include:

Art: Antonio Canova, *The Italian Venus*; John Constable, *Landscape with Rainbows*; Jean Géricault, *Mounted Officer, Imperial Guard*; Francisco de Goya, *Duke of Wellington*; Antoine Gros, *Napoleon and the Austrian Emperor*; William Rush, *Nymph of the Schuylkill*; Joseph Turner, *Hannibal Crossing the Alps*

Literature: Per Atterbom, *The Flowers*; William C. Bryant, *Thanatopsis*; William Comb, *Tours of Dr. Syntax I*; George Crabbe, *Tales in Verse*; Thomas DeQuincy, *Confessions of an English Opium Eater*; Maria Edgeworth, *The Absentee*; Georg W. Hegel, *Wissenschaft der Logik I*; John Nichols, *Literary Anecdotes of the Eighteenth Century*

MUSICAL EVENTS

A. Births:

Jan 8	Sigismond Thalberg (Swi-pn)	Jul 14	Johann A. Heckel (Ger-inst.m)
Jan 27	Théodore Nisard (Fr-mus)	Aug 16	L. Burbure de Wesembeek
Feb 19	Lauro Rossi (It-cm)		(Bel-mus)
Mar 6	Joseph Schad (Ger-pn-au)	Oct 4	Fanny Persiani (It-sop)
Mar 11	William Wallace (Ir-cm)	Oct 31	Johannes Bastiaans
Apr 23	Louis A. Jullien (Fr-cd)		(Hol-org-the)
Apr 26	Friedrich von Flotow (Ger-cm)	Dec 14	Isidor Dannström (Swe-bar)
May 16	Édouard L. Fétis (Bel-cri)	Dec 24	Henry Russell (Br-voc-cm)
May 31	Otto Kraushaar (Ger-the)	Dec 26	Wilhelm Volckmar (Ger-org)
Jun 21	Jean L.F. Danjou (Fr-org.m)	Dec 28	Julius Rietz (Ger-cd-cel)
Jun 22	Carl G. Roder (Ger-pub)	Dec 30	Wiktor Kazynski (Pol-cm)
Jun 27	John P. Hullah (Br-org)	Dec 31	Julian Dobrski (Pol-ten)

B. Deaths:

Jan 15	Johannes Herbst (Cz-rel-cm)	Jun 15	Anton Stadler (Aus-cl)
Jan 24	Eligio Celestino (It-vn)	Jun 25	Samuel Harrison (Br-ten)
Feb 9	Franz Hoffmeister (Ger-pub)	Jul 22	Antoinette Saint-Huberty
Mar 20	Jan L. Dussek (Boh-cm-pn)		(Fr-sop)
Mar 27	Joachim Albertini (Pol-cm)	Jul 24	Josef Schuster (Ger-cm)
Apr 25	Edmund Malone (Ir-cri)	Jul 26	Johann Dalberg (Ger-rel-cm)
May 21	Joseph Wölfl (Aus-pn-cm)	Aug 16	John Page (Br-ten)

Aug 18   Jean J. Rodolphe (Fr-hn-cm)   Oct 28   Joseph Beer (Boh-cl-cm)
Aug 19   Vincenzo Righini (It-cm)   Nov 23   Friedrich Hiller (Ger-vn-cm)
Sep 12   Johann E. Dauer (Ger-ten)   Dec 23   Michel Delalande (Fr-cm)
Sep 21   Emanuel Schikaneder (Ger-lib)

C. Debuts:
Other - Filippo Galli (Venice, as a bass), Luigi Lablache (Naples), Johann Schelble (Stuttgart)

D. New Positions:
Conductors: Ramón Félix Cuéllar y Altarriba (maestro de capilla, Saragona), Franz Danzi (kapellmeister, Karlsruhe), Konradin Kreutzer (kapellmeister, Stuttgart), Ferdinando Paër (Italian Opera, Paris)

Educational: Luigi Belloli (horn, Milan Conservatory)

Others: James Hewitt (organ, Trinity Church, Boston), Johann C.F. Schneider (organ, St. Thomas', Leipzig), Johann Gottlob Schneider, Jr. (organ, Church of SS. Peter and Paul, Gorlitz), Johann Uhland (Ministry of Justice, Stuttgart)

E. Prizes and Honors:
Prizes: Ferdinand Hérold (Prix de Rome)

F. Biographical Highlights:
Ludwig van Beethoven falls in love with Amalie Sebald and meets Goethe; Franz Adolf Berwald begins playing violin and viola in the Stockholm Court Orchestra; Joséphine Fodor marries actor Mainville; Filippo Galli, after a serious illness that leaves him a bass, debuts at La Scala; Lowell Mason goes to Savannah, Georgia, and works as a sales clerk and then becomes a bank clerk; Giacomo Meyerbeer quits his studies to embark on a performance career; Gaspare Spontini is fired from the directorship of the Italian Opera in Paris because of financial problems; Carl Maria von Weber begins several literary works and meets Goethe and Wieland.

G. Institutional Openings:
Performing Groups: Allgemeine Musikgesellschaft (Zürich); Arras Philharmonic Society; Gesellschaft der Musikfreunde (Vienna); Lausanne Musical Society; Musikalische Gesellschaft (Cologne); Musikgesellschaft und Liedertafel (Worms)

Educational: Alday Music Academy (Dublin); Brussels Conservatory of Music; Music Institute of Pest

Other: Argyll Rooms (London); Drury Lane Theater II (London); *Quarterly Music Register* (2 issues only); Roxburghe Club (London); Theater am Isartor (Munich); Town Theater (Pest); Trochléon (by J.C. Dietz)

H. Musical Literature:
Carpani, Giuseppe, *Le Haydine Ovvera Lettere sula vita e le opera del celebre Giuseppe Haydn*
Crotch, William, *Elements of Musical Composition*
Fortia de Piles, Alphonse, *Quelques Réflexions d'un Homme du Monde*
Gerber, Ernst, *Neues historisch biographisches Lexikon der Tonkünstler I, II*
Gervasoni, Carlo, *Nuova Teoria de Musica*
Minoja, Ambrogio, *Lettere sopra il canto*
Schicht, Johann G., *Grundregeln der Harmonie*
Smith, John S., *Musical Antiqua I, II*
Telemann, Georg, *Sammlung alter und neuer Kirchenmelodien*

I. Musical Compositions:

Auber, Daniel, *Mass*
    Jean de Couvin (opera)
Beethoven, Ludwig van, *Symphonies No. 7, Opus 92*
    Symphony No. 8, Opus 93
    Sonata, Opus 96, for Violin and Piano
    Piano Trio, Opus 154
Boieldieu, François, *Jean de Paris* (opera)
Catel, Charles, *Les aubergistes de qualité* (opera)
Danzi, Franz, *Camilla und Eugen* (opera)
Drieberg, Friedrich von, *Don Cocagno* (opera)
Field, John, *Sonata No. 4 for Piano*
Generali, Pietro, *Attila* (opera)
    La Vevoda stravagante (opera)
Hérold, Ferdinand, *Madamoiselle de la Vallière* (opera)
Isouard, Nicolo, *Le prince de Catane* (opera)
    Lulli et Quinault (opera)
Kreutzer, Konradin, *Konradin von Schwaben* (opera)
    Feodora (opera)
Kreutzer, Rodolphe, *L'homme sans façons* (opera)
Kuhlau, Friedrich, *Sonatas for Piano, Opus 4*
    Piano Sonata, Opus 5, in D Minor
Meyerbeer, Giacomo, *Jephtas Gelübde* (opera)
Paër, Ferdinando, *Un passo ne fa cento* (opera)
Poissl, Johann, *Merope* (opera)
    Ottaviano in Sicilia (opera)
Reichardt, Johann, *Sakuntala Overture*
Rossini, Gioacchino, *Ciro in Babilonia* (opera)
    Il Signor Bruschino (opera)
    La scala di seta (opera)
    La pietra del paragone (opera)
    L'occasione fa il ladro (opera)
    Theme and Variations for Woodwind Quartet
Schubert, Franz, *Overture, "Der Teufel als Hydraulicus"*
    3 String Quartets, D. 18, 32 and 36
    Der Spiegelritter (operetta)
    Namensfeier (cantata)
    String Quartet in B-flat (1 movement only)
Spohr, Louis, *String Quartet, Opus 27*
    Der jüngste Gericht (oratorio)
Titov, Alexei, *Credulous Folk* (opera)
    Emmerich Tekkely (opera)
Umlauf, Michael, *Der Grenadier* (opera)
Weber, Carl Maria von, *Concerto No. 2, Opus 32, for Piano and Orchestra*
    Sonata No. 1, Opus 24, for Piano
    In Seinem Ordnung schafft der Herr (cantata)
    7 Variations on a Theme of Méhul, Opus 28, for Piano
    4 Songs, Opus 23
Weigl, Joseph, *Franciska von Foix* (opera)
Weinlig, Christian, *Jesus Christus der Welterlöser* (oratorio)
Weyse, Christoph, *Faruk* (opera)
Wölfl, Joseph, *Concerto, Opus 64, for Piano and Orchestra*
Zingarelli, Nicola, *La Riedificazione di Gerusalemme* (oratorio)

1813

World Events:

In the U.S., Captain Oliver Perry breaks the British blockade on Lake Erie but the Americans fail in their attempt to invade Canada; the Northwest Indian Confederacy collapses after the death of Chief Tecumseh; the Creek War breaks out in Alabama; Congress passes legislation making vaccination a necessity; "Uncle Sam" first appears in the Troy *Post*. Internationally, Napoleon, after several victories, is decisively defeated at the Battle of the Nations; Wellington enters France; Ferdinand VII takes the Spanish throne away from Joseph Bonaparte; William of Orange returns to Holland after the French departure; in South America, Venezuela gains its independence and Simón Bolívar becomes dictator.

Cultural Highlights:

James Pradier wins the Prix de Rome in sculpture; Robert Southey is made British Poet Laureate; Leigh Hunt is sentenced to 2 years in jail for articles about the Prince Regent. Births in the art field include American artists George Healy and Tompkins Matteson and French artist Charles Jacque; deaths include French artist and critic Jean B. Lebrun, Italian artist Alessandro Longhi and Swiss artist Anton Graff. Births in the literary world include German dramatists Georg Büchner and Friedrich Hebbel and novelist Otto Ludwig, Spanish dramatist Antonio García Gutiérrez and Danish poet Carl Ploug; deaths include German author Christoph Wieland and poet Theodor Körner, French author Michel de Crèvecoeur and poet Jacques Delille and Dutch poet Jan F. Helmers. Other highlights include:

Art: Washington Allston, *Dead Man Revived by Elisha's Bones*; John Constable, *Cornfield under Heavy Clouds*; Jacques-Louis David, *Madame David*; Jean-Auguste Ingres, *Betrothal of Raphael*; Johann P. Krafft, *Departure*; Samuel Morse, *The Dying Hercules*; Henry Raeburn, *The Macnab*; Joseph Turner, *Frosty Morning*

Literature: Jane Austen, *Pride and Prejudice*; Lord Byron, *The Giaour*; George Crabbe, *The Parish Register*; James Hogg, *The Queen's Wake*; Alessandro Manzoni, *Inni Sacri*; Thomas Moore, *The Twopenny Post Bag*; Walter Scott, *Rokeby*; Percy B. Shelley, *Queen Mab*; Johann R. Wyss, *Swiss Family Robinson*

MUSICAL EVENTS

A. Births:

Jan 14	Ignazio Raimondi (It-vn)	May 15	Stephen Heller (Hun-pn)
Jan 23	Franz Commer (Ger-mus)	Jun 5	Prosper Sainton (Fr-vn)
Feb 10	Agnes Schebest (Aus-mez)	Jun 15	William Harrison (Br-ten)
Feb 14	A. Dargomijsky (Rus-cm)	Jun 16	Otto Jahn (Ger-mus)
Feb 16	S. Gulak-Artemovsky (Rus-bar)	Aug 10	William H. Fry (Am-cm)
Feb 17	Giovanni Belletti (It-ten)	Oct 5	James W. Davison (Br-cri)
Feb 27	Carl H. Bitter (Ger-mus)	Oct 5	Ernst Haberbier (Ger-pn)
Mar 2	George A. MacFarren (Br-the)	Oct 10	Giuseppe Verdi (It-cm)
Mar 20	Matthias Keller (Ger-vn)	Oct 23	Teresa Brambilla (It-sop)
Apr 13	Justin Cadaux (Fr-pn)	Oct 26	Henry Smart (Br-org)
May 13	John S. Dwight (Am-cri)	Nov 30	Charles Alkan (Fr-cm)
		Dec 2	Jacob Rosenhaim (Ger-pn)

B. Deaths:

Jan 11	Giuseppe Aprile (It-cas)	Aug 19	Johann K. Rellstab (Ger-pub)
Jan 28	Jan J. Rösler (Boh-cm)	Aug 20	Johann Vanhal (Cz-cm)
May 5	Stepan Degtyaroff (Rus-cm)	Aug 26	Daniel G. Türk (Ger-org)
Jul 13	Johann F. Peter (Hol-org)	Sep 11	Richard Bellamy (Br-bs)
Aug 1	Carl Stenborg (Swe-cm)	Sep 24	André Grétry (Bel-cm)

Oct 1	Gotthilf von Baumgarten	Nov 30	Friedrich Baumbach (Ger-cm)
	(Ger-cm)	Dec 1	Ferdinando Bertoni (It-org)
Nov 21	William Russell (Br-org)	Dec 12	Gaetano Callido (It-org.m)
Nov 22	Johann Vierling (Ger-org)	Dec 12	Johann H. Grenser (Ger-ww.m)

C. Debuts:

Other - Giuseppe de Begnis (Modena), Giovanni Bordogni (Milan), Nicholas-Prosper Levasseur (Paris), Catherine Stephens (London)

D. New Positions:

Conductors: Friedrich Kuhlau (court musician, Copenhagen), Wenzel Müller (Leopoldstadt Theater, Vienna), Carl Maria von Weber (Prague Opera)

Educational: Jean-Louis Duport (cello, Paris Conservatory), Nicola Zingarelli (director, Royal College of Music, Naples)

Others: William Ayrton (music critic, London *Morning Chronicle*), François Fétis (organ, St. Pierre, Douai), Karl Friedrich Hellwig (organ, Berlin Cathedral), Johann Rinck (organ, Darmstadt Court)

E. Prizes and Honors:

Prizes: Auguste-Mathieu Panseron (Prix de Rome)

Honors: Jean François Lesueur (French Institute), Pierre-Alexandre Monsigny (French Institute), Ferdinand Ries (Swedish Academy)

F. Biographical Highlights:

E. T. A. Hoffmann conducts performances of his operas in both Leipzig and Dresden; Johann Nepomuk Hummel marries singer Elisabeth Röckel; Albert Lortzing and his family move to Bamberg; Heinrich August Marschner goes to Leipzig to study law at the University but is encouraged to go into music by Johann Schicht at the Thomasschule; Felix Mendelssohn, at age 4, begins piano lessons with his mother; Benedetta Pisaroni contracts a serious illness which forces her voice down to the alto range; Ferdinand Ries moves to London where he concertizes and begins teaching piano; Pierre Joseph Rode arrives in Vienna and becomes associated with Beethoven; Fernando Sor, having served in the French army and worked with the French court, leaves Madrid when the French leave and goes to Paris; Karl Maria von Weber receives his first important position as conductor of German Opera in Prague.

G. Institutional Openings:

Performing Groups: French Opera Co. (New Orleans); London Philharmonic Society; Urbany String Quartet (Pest)

Other: *Neujahrsgeschenk an die Züricherische Jugend von der Allgemeine Musikgesellschaft Zürich*; Anton Paterno, Music Publisher (Vienna); Real Teatro de Sao Joao (Rio de Janeiro); Teatro Re (Milan)

H. Musical Literature:

Asioli, Bonifazio, *Trattato d'armonia e d'accompagnamento*
Busby, Thomas, *Dictionary of Music*
Choron, Alexandre, *Traité général des voix et des instruments d'orchestre*
Fortia de Piles, Alphonse, *A Bal les Masques!*
Gerber, Ernst, *Neues historisch-biographisches Lexikon der Tonkünstler III*
Mosel, Ignaz von, *Versuch einer Aesthetik des dramatischen Tonsatzes*
Natorp, Bernhard, *Anleitung zur Unterweisung im Singen für Lehrer in Volksschulen*
Vogler, Georg, *Über Choral- und Kirchengesänge*

I. Musical Compositions:

Auber, Daniel, *Le séjour militaire* (opera)

Beethoven, Ludwig van, *Wellington's Victory, Opus 91*
    Triumphal March in C, Opus 143

Boieldieu, François, *Le nouveau seigneur du village* (opera)

Cherubini, Luigi, *Les Abencérages* (opera)

Danzi, Franz, *Rübezahl* (opera)

Field, John, *Polonaise in E-flat*

Generali, Pietro, *Eginardo e Lisbetta* (opera)

Gossec, François, *Messes des Vivants*

Hérold, Ferdinand, *Hymn sur la Transfiguration*

Himmel, Friedrich, *Der Kobold* (opera)

Isouard, Nicolo, *La français à Venise* (opera)

Kreutzer, Konradin, *Die Insulanerin* (opera)
    Der Tauber (opera)

Kuhlau, Friedrich, *3 Grande Sonaten, Opus 8, for Piano*
    Concerto, Opus 7, for Piano and Orchestra
    10 German Songs, Opus 11
    6 Songs, Opus 9

Mayr, Simon, *Medea in Corinto* (opera)
    La Rosa rossa e la Rosa bianca (opera)
    Tamerlano (opera)

Méhul, Etienne, *Le prince troubadour* (opera)

Meyerbeer, Giacomo, *Wirt und Gast* (opera)
    Alimelek (opera)

Morlacchi, Francesco, *Russian Mass for Chorus a capella*

Pacini, Giovanni, *Annetta e Lucindo* (opera)

Paër, Ferdinando, *I Baccanti* (opera)

Paganini, Niccolò, *Variations, "Le Streghe," for Violin and Orchestra*

Plantade, Charles, *Le Mari de circonstances* (opera)

Poissl, Johann, *Aucassin und Nicolette* (singspiel)

Reichardt, Johann, *Grande Sonata No. 1 for Piano*

Rossini, Gioacchino, *Tancredi* (opera)
    L'italiana in Algieri (opera)
    Aureliano in Palmira (opera)

Schmidt, Johann, *Der blinde gärtner* (liederspiel)

Schubert, Franz, *Symphony No. 1, D. 82*
    4 String Quartets, D. 46, 68, 74 and 87
    Octet for Woodwinds, D. 72
    Nonet for Winds, D. 79
    20 Minuets, D. 41, for Piano

Spohr, Louis, *Faust* (opera)
    Nonet, Opus 31 (woodwind quintet and strings)

Titov, Alexei, *An Old Fashioned Christmas* (opera)

Viotti, Giovanni, *Concerto No. 27 for Violin and Orchestra*

Weber, Carl Maria von, *6 Songs, Opus 30*
    Andante and Hungarian Rondo, Opus 35, for Bassoon and Orchestra

Weigl, Joseph, *Der Bergsturz* (opera)

1814

World Events:

In the U.S., the British set fire to Washington, D.C. but are defeated in their attempt to invade New York; at the bombardment of Ft. McHenry, Francis Scott Key writes the words of the Star Spangled Banner; the Treaty of Ghent ends the War of 1812; the last Federalist Convention at Hartford marks the decline of the party. Internationally, the British invade France--Napoleon abdicates and is sent to the isle of Elba--Louis XVIII returns to the throne as king; the Congress of Vienna begins; the Pope reinstitutes the Jesuits and the Inquisition; Norway forms a united kingdom with Sweden; Cape Town, South Africa, is ceded to the British.

Cultural Highlights:

The first public gallery to be open to the public, the Dulwich College Picture Gallery, opens; William Hazlitt becomes drama critic for the London *Morning Chronicle*. Deaths in the art world include the French sculptor Clodion; in the literary field French authors Jacques Bernadin de Saint-Pierre, Louis Mercier and Charles Palissot de Montenoy, German poets Johann Jacobi and Johann Miller and Scottish poet John Hamilton. Births in the art world include American sculptors Henry Brown and Thomas Crawford, German sculptor Albert Wolff and French artist Jean François Millet; in the literary world Russian poets Mikhail Lermontov and Taras Shevchenko, Hungarian novelist Zsigmond Kemény, British novelist Charles Reade, French dramatist François Ponsard, Irish poet Aubrey de Vers and American historian and novelist John Motley. Other highlights include:

Art: William Collins, *The Bird Catchers*; John Constable, *Cart and Horses with Dog*; Jean L. Géricault, *The Wounded Cuirassier*; Francisco de Goya, *King Ferdinand of Spain*; Jean-Auguste Ingres, *Grande Odalisque*; Georg Kersting, *Girl Embroidering*; Thomas Lawrence, *The Congress of Vienna*; John Vanderlyn, *Ariadne Asleep on Naxos*

Literature: Jane Austen, *Mansfield Park*; Fanny Burney, *The Wanderer*; Lord Byron, *Le Corsair*; Adelbert von Chamisso, *Peter Schlemihls Wunderbare Geschichte*; Maria Edgeworth, *Patronage*; E.T.A. Hoffmann, *Phantasiestücke in Callots Manier*; Friedrich Rückert, *Deutsche Gedichte*; Walter Scott, *Waverley*; William Wordsworth, *The Excursion*

MUSICAL EVENTS

A. Births:

Jan 28	Marie C. Falcon (Fr-sop)		Jun 14	Alexander Ellis (Br-acous)
Mar 3	Ludwika Rivoli (Pol-sop)		Aug 21	Augustin Savard (Fr-the)
Mar 3	Charles Salaman (Br-pn)		Aug 25	August Schäffer (Ger-cm)
Mar 22	August Gemünder (Ger-vn.m)		Oct 13	Jan K. Pisek (Boh-bar)
Apr 20	Theodor Döhler (It-cm)		Nov 6	Adolphe Sax (Bel-inst.m)
Apr 22	William Pole (Br-mus)		Nov 23	Elizabeth Rainforth (Br-sop)
May	Sebastiano Ronconi (It-bar)		Dec 1	Arnold J. Blaes (Bel-cl)
May 1	Emma Albertazzi (Br-alto)		Dec 1	August Röckel (Aus-cm)
May 6	Heinrich Ernst (Cz-vn)			Karl Beck (Aus-ten)
May 9	Adolph von Henselt (Ger-pn)			Emma Romer (Br-sop)
May 10	Franz Götze (Ger-ten)			Mary Shaw (Br-alto)

B. Deaths:

Jan 5	Johann G. Krebs (Ger-org)		May 7	Franz Buttstett (Ger-org)
Feb 3	Johann Kozeluch (Boh-cm)		Jun 8	Friedrich Himmel (Ger-pn)
Apr 12	Charles Burney (Br-mus)		Jun 19	Friedrich W. Benda (Ger-vn)
Apr 15	Carl Lichnowsky (Pol-pol)		Jun 27	Johann Reichardt (Ger-cm)
May 6	Georg J. Vogler (Ger-cm-the)		Jul 25	Charles Dibdin (Br-cm-au)

Aug 19	Angelo Tarchi (It-cm)	Dec 24 J.J. Kriegk (Ger-vn)
Sep 14	Maximilian Ulbrich (Aus-cm)	Dec 26 Nicolas Guillard (Fr-lib)
Nov 19	Christoforo Babbi (It-vn)	Marianna Monti (It-sop)

C. Debuts:
Other - Eduard Genast (Weiman), Henriette Méric-Lalande (Naples), Geltrude Righetti (Bologna), Giovanni Battista Rutini (Pavia)

D. New Positions:
Conductors: Antonio Calegari (maestro di cappella, Padua), Bonaventura Furlanetto (maestro di cappella, St. Marks), Christian Friedrich Uber (kapellmeister, Mainz), Jan Vitásek (St. Stephen's, Prague), Franz Volkert (Leopoldstadt Theater, Vienna), Georg F. Wolf (kapellmeister, Wernigerode)

Educational: Vincenzo Federici (harmony, Milan Conservatory), Christian T. Weinlig (cantor, Kreuzschule, Dresden)

Others: Thomas Adams (organ, St. Paul's, Deptford), Davidde Banderali (director, Teatro dei Filodrammatici, Milan), Angelica Catalani (manager, Italian Theater, Paris), Wilhelm F. Riem (organ, Bremen Cathedral), Nicolas Séjan (organ, Royal Chapel, Paris), Thomas F. Walmisley (organ, St. Martin-in-the-Fields), George E. Williams (organ, Westminster Abbey)

E. Prizes and Honors:
Honors: Luigi Cherubini (Legion of Honor), Jean Baptiste Davaux and Charles-Henri Plantade (Legion of Honor), Gaspare Spontini (court composer to Louis XVIII), Peter von Winter (ennobled)

F. Biographical Highlights:
Bonifazio Asioli is forced to leave his conservatory post and returns to Correggio; Ludwig van Beethoven makes his final revision of *Fidelio*; Angelica Catalani moves to Paris and takes over direction of the Théâtre Italien; Giovanni Davide makes his La Scala debut; Gaetano Donizetti goes to Bologna to study composition with Padre Martini; E.T.A. Hoffmann, dismissed from his Leipzig position, settles permanently in Berlin; Johann Hummel partially retires from concertizing; Frédéric Kalkbrenner moves to London for a ten-year stay; Pierre Rode settles for a time in Berlin and gets married; Anton Schindler meets Beethoven and soon becomes his personal secretary; Franz Schubert tries teaching in his father's school, a career definitely not to his liking; Richard Wagner's mother, eight months after her husband's death, moves to Dresden and marries actor Ludwig Geyer.

G. Institutional Openings:
Performing Groups: Accademia Filarmonica (Turin); Anacreontic Society (Belfast Orchestra); Bordeaux Orchestre de Concert

Educational: Cuban Academy of Music

Other: Chiroplast (patent by J. Logier); Claviharpe (keyed harp by J.C. Dietz); August Cranz, Music Publisher (Hamburg); *Galignani's Messenger*; Clair Godefroy, Woodwind Manufacturer (Paris); Handelian Academy (N.Y.); C. F. Peters, Music Publisher (Leipzig); Michael Schnabel Piano Co. (Breslau); Society for Religious and National Music (Warsaw); Teatro Contavalli (Bologna); Theatrum Vlahicum Bucharestini

H. Musical Literature:
Apel, Johann A., *Metrik I*
Asioli, Bonifazio, *Dialoghi sul Trattato d'armonia e d'accompagnamento*
Choron, Alexandre, *Méthode élémentaire de composition*
Gerber, Ernst, *Neues historisch-biographisches Lexikon der Tonkunster IV*
Hill, Uri, *The Handelian Repository*

Law, Andrew, *Essays on Music*
Loder, John D., *General and Comprehensive Instruction Book for the Violin*
Reicha, Anton, *Traité de mélodie...*
Stendhal, *Vies de Haydn, Mozart et Métatase*

I. Musical Compositions:

Beethoven, Ludwig van, *Fidelio Overture, Opus 72b*
    Namensfeier Overture, Opus 115
    Sonata No. 27, Opus 90, for Piano
    Der Glorreiche Augenblick, Opus 136 (cantata)
    Germania, Opus 193, for Chorus and Orchestra
Bishop, Henry, *The Maid of the Mill* (opera)
Cherubini, Luigi, *Bayard à Mézières* (opera)
    String Quartet No. 1
Danzi, Franz, *Malvina* (opera)
Drieberg, Friedrich von, *Der Sänger und der Schneider* (opera)
Field, John, *Nocturnes No. 1-3 for Piano*
Generali, Pietro, *Bajazet* (opera)
Isouard, Nicolo, *Bayard à Mézières* (opera)
    Jeannot et Colin (opera)
    Joconde (opera)
Kreutzer, Konradin, *Alimon und Zaide* (opera)
    Die Nachtmütze (opera)
    Mirsile und Anteros (ballet)
    Die Sendung Mosis (oratorio)
Kuhlau, Daniel, *Die Räuberburg* (opera)
Kurpinski, Karol, *Jadwiga* (opera)
    Laska Imperatora (opera)
Mayr, Simon, *Atar* (opera)
    Elena (opera)
Méhul, Etienne, *L'oriflamme de Charles Martel* (opera)
Meyerbeer, Giacomo, *Das Brandenburger Tor* (opera)
Morlacchi, Francesco, *Mass for the King of Saxony*
Moscheles, Ignaz, *Sonata, Opus 27, "Caractéristique" for Piano*
Pacini, Giovanni, *L'ambizione delusa* (opera)
    L'escavazione del tesoro (opera)
Paër, Ferdinando, *L'oriflamme* (opera)
Poissl, Johann, *Athalia* (opera)
Reichardt, Johann, *Schlachtsymphonie*
    Overture to Vittoria
Rossini, Gioacchino, *Il turco in Italia* (opera)
    Sigismondo (opera)
Schubert, Franz, *Des teufels lustschloss* (opera)
    Mass No. 1 in D Major, D. 105
    2 String Quartets, D. 94 and 112
    Gretchen am Spinrade (opera)
Spohr, Louis, *Concerto No. 7, Opus 38, for Violin and Orchestra*
    String Quartet, Opus 30
    2 String Quintets, Opus 33
    Octet, Opus 32 (clarinet, 2 horns, strings)
Spontini, Gaspare, *Pélage* (opera)
Tadolini, Giovanni, *La fata Alcina* (opera)
Viotti, Giovanni, *Concerto No. 28 for Violin and Orchestra*
Weber, Carl Maria von, *4 Songs, Opus 41*
Weigl, Joseph, *Der jugend Peter des Gross* (opera)

1815

World Events:
In the U.S., the Battle of New Orleans takes place after the cessation of hostilities with a defeat of the British forces; the U.S. and Great Britain sign a treaty of commerce; Stephen Decatur defeats the Barbary Pirates, bringing an end to their harassment of U.S. ships; the *USS Fulton* becomes the world's first steam-powered warship. Internationally, Napoleon escapes from Elba, reassembles his troops and is defeated at the Battle of Waterloo and re-exiled to St. Helena; the Congress of Vienna ends with the creation of a Confederation of German States and the establishment of the Austrian and Prussian monarchies; the Fourth Partition of Poland greatly benefits Russia; William I becomes king of the Netherlands; Otto von Bismarck is born.

Cultural Highlights:
François de Chateaubriand is appointed Minister of the Interior in the French Cabinet; Edward Bird and Henry Raeburn are inducted into the Royal Academy in London and Thomas Lawrence is knighted. Births include French artists Thomas Couture and Ernest Meissonier, German artist Adolf von Menzel and British artist Thomas J. Barker; in the literary field, Italian poet Giovanni Prati, British novelist Anthony Trollope, French dramatist Eugène Labiche, German poet Emmanuel Geibel and American author Richard Dana, Jr. Deaths include American inventor and artist Robert Fulton and artist John Copley, British author George Ellis, Polish author Stanislaus de Boufflers and German poet Matthias Claudius. Other highlights include:

Art: Antonio Canova, *Three Graces*; John Constable, *East Bergholt Church*; Francisco de Goya, *Third of May, 1808*; Thomas Lawrence, *Prince Regent, George IV*; Gilbert Stuart, *Mrs John Adams*; Thomas Sully, *Colonel Jonathan Williams*; Joseph Turner, *Crossing the Brook*; James Ward, *Gordale Scar, Yorkshire*; Benjamin West, *Christ Rejected*

Literature: Jane Austen, *Emma*; William C. Bryant, *To a Waterfowl*; Lord Byron, *Hebrew Melodies*; Joseph von Eichendorff, *Ahnung und Gegenwart*; James S. Knowles, *Caius Gracchus*; Silvio Pellico, *Francesca da Rimini*; Walter Scott, *Guy Mannering*; Johann L. Uhland, *Vaterländische Gedichte*; William Wordsworth, *Collected Poetry*

MUSICAL EVENTS

A. Births:

Jan 25	Alexandre Artôt (Fr-vn)	Sep 8	Giuseppina Strepponi (It-sop)
Feb 13	Rosine Stoltz (Fr-mez)	Sep 17	Halfdan Kjerulf (Nor-cm)
Mar 2	Antonio Buzzolla (It-cd)	Sep 24	J. Lathrop Allen (Am-inst.m)
Mar 8	Jean D. Alard (Fr-vn)	Oct 25	Ernesto Sivori (It-vn)
Mar 14	Josephine Lang (Ger-cm)	Oct 29	Daniel Emmett (Am-pop)
Apr 6	Robert Volkmann (Ger-cm)	Dec 5	Hermann Dam (Ger-cm)
May 13	Johann Barmig (Ger-org.m)	Dec 17	Gustave H. Roger (Fr-ten)
Jun 28	Robert Franz (Ger-cm)		Alfred G. Badger (Am-fl.m)
Aug 25	Maschinka Schneider (Ger-sop)		Giovanni Bajetti (It-cm)
Sep 2	Bartholf Senff (Ger-pub)		Charlotte Birch (Br-sop)
Sep 4	Mihály Mosonyi (Hun-cm)		Giorgio Stigelli (Ger-ten)

B. Deaths:

Jan 14	Jean Mercadier (Fr-the)	Nov 17	Luigi Asioli (It-ten)
Apr 8	Jan Jakub Ryba (Cz-cm)	Nov 28	Johann Salomon (Ger-vn-imp)
Jun 22	William Reeve (Br-cm)	Dec	Franz Götz (Boh-cm-vn)
Sep 12	José Mauricio (Pol-cm-the)	Dec 19	Robert Hudson (Br-ten)
Sep 28	Frederick Reinhold (Br-bs)	Dec 19	Michel Woldemar (Fr-vn)
Nov 15	Johann Schubaur (Ger-cm)		

C. Debuts:
Other - Pierre I. Begrez (Paris), Thomas S. Cooke (London), Giuditta Pasta (Milan), Lucia Elizabeth Vestris (London)

D. New Positions:
Conductors: Karl Hellwig (kapellmeister, Berlin), Felice Alessandro Radicati (Bologna Orchestra), Bernhard Romberg (Berlin Court), Christian Rummel (Wiesbaden Court)

Educational: Carl F. Zelter (music director, Friedrich-Wilhelm University)

Others: Ludwig Abeille (organ, Württemberg Court), Charles Lafont (violinist to Louis XVIII)

E. Prizes and Honors:
Prizes: François Benoist (Prix de Rome)

Honors: Domingo Arquimbeau (Accademia Filarmonica, Bologna), Henri-Montan Berton and Charles S. Catel (French Institute), Frédéric Duvernoy (Legion of Honor), Sigismund von Neukomm (Legion of Honor)

F. Biographical Highlights:
Ludwig van Beethoven, on the death of his brother, takes over the care of his nephew; Hector Berlioz learns the rudiments of flute and guitar from his father and begins composing; Gaetano Donizetti enrolls in Bologna's Liceo Filarmonico; François Joseph Gossec, at age 90, retires to Passy, a suburb of Paris; Moritz Hauptmann becomes music teacher to the family of Prince Repnin in Russia, where he stays for five years; Ferdinand Hérold leaves Italy, visits in Vienna and returns permanently to Paris; E. T. A. Hoffmann returns to his old civil service job in Berlin; Nicholas Prosper Levasseur makes his London debut; Giacomo Meyerbeer goes to Italy and becomes enamoured of Rossini's operas and begins writing in the Italian vein; Gioacchino Rossini is engaged by the impresario Barbaia with an exclusive contract to write operas for Naples; Henriette Sontag enters the Conservatory of Prague; Fernando Sor moves to London; Carl Maria von Weber proposes to singer Caroline Brandt whom he marries.

G. Institutional Openings:
Performing Groups: Bernische Musikgesellschaft (Switzerland); Boston Handel and Haydn Society; Bremen Singakademie; Practical Musical Society (Trondheim); Styrian Music Society (Graz)

Educational: Drechsler's Music School (Vienna); Scuola Canto Corale (Parma)

Other: Backofen Instrument Factory (Darmstadt); Louis Drouet, Flute Maker (London); John Firth (Firth, Hall and Pond), Piano Maker (N.Y.); Giuseppe Girard, Music Publisher (Naples); *North American Review*; John Osborne, Piano Maker (Boston); Jean H. Pape, Piano Maker (Paris); Piston Valve (probable date of invention); Charles-Joseph Sax, Instrument Maker (Brussels); Society of the Friends of Religious and National Music (Warsaw); Teatro Fiando (Milan)

H. Musical Literature:
Bertini, Giuseppe, *Dizionario storico-critico degli scrittori di musica*
Berton, Henri, *Traité d'harmonie...*
Choron, Alexandre, *Méthode d'accompagnement...*
Cramer, Johann, *Grosses praktische Pianoforte Schule*
Dlabac, Bohumír, *Allgemeines historisches Künstler-lexicon für Böhmen I*
Gardiner, William, *Sacred Melodies*
Kotzebue, August von, *Opera Almanach*
Prony, Gaspard, *Rapport sur la nouvelle harpe à double mouvement*
Shield, William, *Rudiments of Thorough Bass*

I. **Musical Compositions:**

Beethoven, Ludwig van, *2 Cello Sonatas, Opus 102*
 Calm Sea and Prosperous Voyage, Opus 112
 12 Songs, Opus 228
Cavos, Catterino, *Ivan Sussanin* (opera)
Chélard, Hippolyte, *La casa da vendere* (opera)
Cherubini, Luigi, *Symphony in D Major*
 Concert Overture in G Major
 Hymn to Spring (cantata)
Field, John, *Concertos No. 1 and 2 for Piano and Orchestra*
Generali, Pietro, *L'impostre* (opera)
Hérold, Ferdinand, *La gioventù di Enrico quinto* (opera)
Kreutzer, Konradin, *Die Alpenhütte* (opera)
 Der Herr und sein Diener (opera)
Kurpinski, Karol, *Nadgroda* (opera)
Lebrun, Louis-Sébastien, *Missa solemnis*
Meyerbeer, Giacomo, *Le bachelier de Salamanque* (unfinished opera)
Moscheles, Ignaz, *Sextet, Opus 35*
Pacini, Giovanni, *La Rosina* (opera)
 Bettina vedova (opera)
Paër, Ferdinando, *L'eroismo in amore* (opera)
Poissl, Johann, *Der Wettkampf von Olympia* (opera)
Rossini, Gioacchino, *Elizabeth, Queen of England* (opera)
 Torvaldo e Dorliska (opera)
Schubert, Franz, *Symphony No. 2, D. 125*
 Symphony No. 3, D. 200
 String Quartet No. 10, D. 173
 Masses No. 2 and 3, D. 167 and 324
 Piano Sonatas No. 1 and 2, D. 154 and 279
 Der Vierjährige Posten (operetta)
 Der Freunde von Salamanka (singspiel)
 Claudine von Villa Bella (singspiel)
 Der Erlkönig (song)
 Heidenröslein (song)
 12 Ecossaises, D. 299, for Piano
 Adrast (unfinished opera)
Spohr, Louis, *3 String Quartets, Opus 29*
Spontini, Gaspare, *Le roi et la paix* (opera)
Tadolini, Giovanni, *Le bestie in uomini* (opera)
Uber, Christian, *Der frohe Tag* (opera)
Vaccai, Nicola, *I solitari di Scozia* (opera)
Viotti, Giovanni, *Concerto No. 29 for Violin and Orchestra*
Weber Carl Maria von, *Clarinet Quintet, Opus 34*
 Variations on a Russian Theme, Opus 40, for Piano
 Kampf und Sieg, Opus 44 (cantata)
 Concertino, Opus 45, for Horn and Orchestra
 Scene and Aria, "Non Paventar, " Opus 51
 Scene and Aria, "Ah, se Edmondo," Opus 52
Weigl, Joseph, *L'imboscata* (opera)
Wesley, Samuel S., *12 Short Pieces for Organ*

1816

World Events:
In the U.S., James Monroe is elected as President No. 5; Indiana is admitted to the Union as state No. 19; Congress passes its first protective tariff; Baltimore, Maryland, becomes the first American city to have coal gas lights; the American Bible Society is formed in New York; Buffalo, New York, is incorporated. Internationally, the first known constitution for a German state is passed by Saxe-Weimar; Louis XVIII dissolves the Chamber of Deputies; John VI becomes ruler of Portugal; the first known bicycle is invented by Karl von Sauerbronn; Argentina declares its independence from Spain.

Cultural Highlights:
John Trumbull becomes President of the American Academy of Fine Arts; Johann G. Schadow becomes director of the Berlin Academy of Art; Alfred E. Chalon is inducted into the Royal Academy; Pierre-Paul Prud'hon is taken into the French Institute; William Cullen Bryant is admitted to the bar. In the art world, births include American artists George Flagg and Richard Hubbard and sculptor William Rimmer and German artist Emmanuel Leutze. In the literary field, births include German authors Gustav Freytag and Friedrich von Hackländer and poet Wolfgang Müller, British author Charlotte Brontë and poet Philip Bailey and Swedish author Bernhard Malmström; deaths include Irish dramatist Richard Sheridan and American novelist Hugh Brackenridge. Other highlights include:

Art: Peter von Cornelius, *Joseph and His Brothers*; John Constable, *Weymouth Bay*; John Crome, *Bruges River near Ostend*; John Martin, *Joshua Commanding the Sun to Stand Still*; Pierre-Paul Prud'hon, *Assumption of the Virgin*; Thomas Rowlandson, *Dance of Death and Dance of Life*; Bertel Thorvaldsen, *Venus with the Apple*

Literature: Lord Byron, *The Siege of Corinth*; E.T.A. Hoffmann, *Die Elixiere des Teufels*; Leigh Hunt, *The Story of Rimini*; John Keats, *On First Looking into Chapman's Homer*; Charles Lamb, *Glenarron*; Giovanni B. Niccolini, *Nabucco*; Thomas L. Peacock, *Headlong Hall*; Walter Scott, *Old Mortality*; Percy B. Shelley, *Alastor*

MUSICAL EVENTS

A. Births:

Feb 1	Rudolf Hirsch (Aus-cri)	Jul 18	Antoine Marmontel (Fr-ped)
Feb 9	Karl L. Fischer (Ger-cd-cm)	Jul 19	Achille Graffigna (It-cm)
Feb 16	Gaetano Fraschini (It-ten)	Jul 23	Charlotte Cushman (Am-alto)
Feb 20	Josef Poniatowski (Pol-cm)	Aug 7	Karl J. Formes (Ger-bs)
Mar 4	Jenny Dingelstedt (Boh-sop)	Sep 1	Gustav Schmidt (Ger-cd-cm)
Mar 19	Johannes Verhulst (Hol-cd)	Sep 4	Emmanuel J. Bazin (Fr-cm)
Mar 24	Johanna Loewe (Ger-sop)	Sep 26	Marius P. Audran (Fr-ten)
Mar 27	George J. Elvey (Br-org)	Oct 6	William B. Bradbury (Am-cm)
Apr 13	William S. Bennett (Br-cm)	Oct 27	William A. Johnson (Am-org.m)
Jun 11	Karl Haslinger (Aus-pn-pub)	Nov 14	John Curwen (Br-m.ed)
Jun 13	Edward T. Rimbault (Br-mus)	Nov 17	August W. Ambros (Aus-mus)
		Nov 29	Karl Binder (Aus-cm-cd)

B. Deaths:

Jan 10	Giovanni Valesi (Ger-ten)	Jun 5	Giovanni Paisiello (It-cm)
Feb 9	Rafael Anglés (Sp-org-cm)	Jul 31	Joseph Fialo (Boh-ob-cm)
Feb 10	Jean Paul Martini (Fr-org)	Aug 6	Karl Fribert (Aus-ten-cm)
Mar 16	Giuseppe Jannaconi (It-cm)	Aug 8	Blas de Laserna (Sp-cm)
Mar 19	Heinrich C. Koch (Ger-vn-the)	Sep 22	Matteo Babbini (It-ten)
Apr 10	Antoine M. Lemoine (Fr-pub)	Oct	Joseph Arquier (Fr-cm)
May 25	Samuel Webbe, Sr. (Br-org)		

| Oct | Pierre Leduc (Fr-vn-pub) | Dec 15 | Joseph F. Lobkowitz (Cz-pol) |
| Nov 16 | Pierre Ginguené (Fr-mus) | | Anna Lucia de Amicis (It-sop) |

C. Debuts:

Other - Joseph Boehm (Vienna), Laure Cinti-Damoreau (Paris), Philip Cipriani Potter (London), Giuseppina Ronzi de Begnis (Bologna), Harriett Waylett (Bath)

D. New Positions:

Conductors: Georg F. Bischoff (kapellmeister, Hildesheim), Valentino Fioravanti (music director, St. Peter's, Rome), Joseph A. Gürrlich (kapellmeister, Berlin), Johann Hummel (kapellmeister, Stuttgart), Charles F. Kreubé (Opèra-Comique, Paris), Sigismund von Neukomm (kapellmeister, Brazilian Court), Charles-Henri Plantade (maître de chapelle, Royal Chapel, Paris), Pietro Terziani (maestro di capella, St. John Lateran), Nicola Zingarelli (maestro di cappella, Naples Cathedral)

Educational: Henri-Montan Berton (composition, Paris Conservatory), Giuseppe Blangini (voice, Paris Conservatory), Luigi Cherubini (composition, Paris Conservatory), Girolamo Crescentini (voice, Naples Conservatory), Victor Dourlen (harmony, Paris Conservatory), Alexis de Garaude (voice, Paris Conservatory), Georg W. Hegel (professor, Heidelberg), Jean-Blaise Martin (voice, Paris Conservatory), Pierre-Joseph Zimmerman (piano, Paris Conservatory)

Others: August W. Bach (organ, Marienkirche, Berlin), Dmitri Bortniansky (censor of composition, Russian Orthodox Churches), Francisco Cabo (organ, Valencia Cathedral), Kaspar Ett (organ, St. Michael's, Munich), August Klengel (organ, Dresden Catholic Court Church)

E. Prizes and Honors:

Honors: Friedrich Herschel (knighted), Francesco Morlacchi (Order of the Golden Spur)

F. Biographical Highlights:

Ludwig van Beethoven sues his brother's wife over the custody of his nephew; William Bradford begins music study with Lowell Mason; John Braham breaks with Nancy Storace and marries Frances Bolto; Frédéric Chopin begins piano study; Joséphine Fodor-Mainville makes her London debut; Jacques Halévy wins the second Prix de Rome; James Hewitt leaves Boston and returns to New York; Johann Kalliwoda graduates from Prague Conservatory; Johann N. Maelzel builds the metronome on an idea of Winkel; Heinrich Marschner begins teaching in Pressburg; Felix Mendelssohn visits Paris and studies with Marie Bigot; Giuseppe Mercadante begins composition study with Zingarelli; Giacomo Meyerbeer turns a visit into a 9-year stay in Italy; Sigismund von Neukomm travels to Rio with the Duke of Luxembourg and stays for 5 years; Giuseppina Ronzi marries bass Giuseppe de Begnis; Anton Schindler moves in with Beethoven and becomes his secretary; Franz Schubert gives up on teaching.

G. Institutional Openings:

Performing Groups: Augsburg Harmoniegesellschaft; Essener Bergkapelle; Euterpian Society (Hartford); Havana St. Cecilia Academy; Rheinischer Musikverein (Mannheim); Società Filarmonica (Cremona); The Sons of Handel (Dublin)

Educational: Fitzwilliam Collection and Museum (donated to Cambridge University by the 7th Viscount Fitzwilliam); Mees Music Academy (Brussels)

Other: Allyn and Bacon, Music Publishers (Philadelphia); William Blackwood and Sons, Publishers (Edinburgh); Thomas Boosey Publishing House (London); New San Carlo Theater (Naples)

H. Musical Literature:

Bomtempo, João D., *Piano Method*
Campbell, Alexander, *Albyn's Anthology I*
Choron, Alexandre, *Le Musicien Pratique*
Davisson, Ananias, *Kentucky Harmony*
Désargus, Xavier, *Cours Complet de Harpe*
Gérard, Henri, *Méthode de Chant*
Hastings/Warriner, *Musica Sacra*
Lichtenthal, Peter, *Harmony Treatise*
Serassi, Giuseppe, *Sugli Organi*
Thomson, George, *Select Collection of Original Irish Airs*

I. Musical Compositions:

Beethoven, Ludwig von, *Piano Sonata No. 28, Opus 101*
    An die Ferne Geliebte, Opus 98
    An die Hoffnung, Opus 94
    25 Scotch Songs, Opus 108
    75 Irish Songs, Opus 223, 224 and 225
Berwald, Franz, *Theme and Variations for Violin and Orchestra*
Bishop, Henry, *The Slave* (opera)
Cherubini, Luigi, *Messe Solemnelle in C Major*
Donizetti, Gaetano, *Il Pigmalione* (opera)
Field, John, *Concerto No. 3 for Piano and Orchestra*
    Concerto No. 4 for Piano and Orchestra
    Piano Quintet in A-flat Major
Hoffmann, E.T.A., *Undine* (opera)
Isouard, Nicolo, *Les deux maris* (opera)
    L'une pour l'autre (opera)
Kreutzer, Rudolphe, *Le Carnaval de Venise* (ballet)
Kurpinski, Karol, *Kleine Schule für Männer* (opera)
    Superstition (opera)
Loewe, Carl, *Die Alpenhütte* (opera)
Marschner, Heinrich, *Titus* (opera)
Méhul, Etienne, *La journée aux aventures* (opera)
Meyerbeer, Giacomo, *Glimori di Teolindo* (monodrama)
Morlacchi, Francesco, *Il nuovo barbiere di Siviglia* (opera)
    Il capricciosa pentita (opera)
Moscheles, Ignaz, *Piano Sonatas, Opus 41 and 47*
Reicha, Anton, *Natalie* (opera)
Rossini, Gioacchino, *Il barbiere di Siviglia* (opera)
    Othello (opera)
    La gazzetta (opera)
Schmidt, Johann, *Die Alpenhütte* (opera)
Schubert, Franz, *Symphony No. 4, D. 417, "Tragic"*
    Symphony No. 5, D. 485
    Overture in B-flat Major
    Die Burgschaft (opera)
    Mass No. 4, D. 452
    Requiem in E-flat Major, D. 453
    Piano Sonata No. 3, D. 459
    3 Violin Sonatinas, Opus 137
    String Quartet in E Major, D. 353
Spohr, Louis, *Concerto, Opus 47, for Violin and Orchestra*
Weber, Carl Maria von, *Piano Sonatas No. 2 and 3, Opus 39 and 49*
Weigl, Joseph, *Margaritta d'Anjou* (opera)

1817

World Events:
In the U.S., Mississippi becomes State No. 20; the Seminole War with the Indians in Florida begins; work begins on the Erie Canal; the American School for the Deaf is founded in Hartford, Connecticut; the University of Michigan is founded in Ann Arbor; the American Society for the Return of Negroes to Africa is founded. Internationally, Great Britain signs the Rush-Bagot Treaty with the U.S. limiting Naval forces on the Great Lakes; Liberia is founded in Africa as a home for returned slaves from the U.S.; José San Martin defeats the Spanish forces in Chile; Turkey grants partial autonomy to the Serbs.

Cultural Highlights:
The Amsterdam Rijksmuseum is opened; the *Ladies Literary Museum or Weekly Repository* begins publication in the U.S.; Clemens Brentano, suffering severe depression, enters a monastery; George Catlin begins the study of law; Charles S. Catel is taken into the Academy of Fine Arts in Paris. Births in the art world include American artist Peter Rothermel and sculptor Erastus Palmer, British artist George F. Watts, French artist Charles-François Daubigny, Belgian artist Alfred Stevens and Italian sculptor Giovanni Dupré; deaths include American artists Julius Caesar Ibbetson and Edward Savage and Italian artist Andrea Appiani. Deaths in the literary field include French novelist Mme. de Staël, British novelist Jane Austen and Spanish poet Juan Meléndez-Valdéz; births include Russian poets Alexei Tolstoy and Konstantin Aksakov, German poet Theodor Storm, French novelist Paul Féval, American poet Henry Thoreau and Hungarian poet János Arany. Other highlights include:

Art: Washington Allston, *Uriel in the Sun*; John Constable, *Flatford Mill on the Stour*; Jacques-Louis David, *Cupid and Psyche*; Jean L. Géricault, *Riderless Horse Race*; Pierre Guérin, *Enée et Didon, Ville de Troie*; Johann Krafft, *The Battle of Leipzig*; Frederick Lewis, *Herefordshire's Harvest*; Bertel Thorvaldsen, *Ganymede with the Eagle*

Literature: Ludwig von Arnim, *Die Kronenwächter*; William Cullen Bryant, *Thanatopsis*; George Lord Byron, *Manfred* and *The Lament of Tasso*; Samuel Taylor Coleridge, *Sibylline Leaves*; Maria Edgeworth, *Ormond*; Johann von Goethe, *Italienische Reise*; Franz Grillparzer, *Die Ahnfrau*; Thomas Moore, *Lalla Rookh*; Walter Scott, *Rob Roy*

MUSICAL EVENTS

A. Births:

Feb 3	Emile Prudent (Fr-pn-cm)	Sep 23	Léon Kreutzer (Fr-cm-cri)
Feb 22	Niels W. Gade (Den-cm-cd)	Oct 13	Aloys Ander (Boh-ten)
Feb 28	Robert Schaab (Ger-org)	Oct 22	Alexander Thayer (Am-mus)
Mar 24	Louis Maillart (Fr-cm)	Nov 2	Elisa Blaes (Bel-sop)
Apr 2	Teodulo Mabellini (It-cd-cm)	Nov 12	Marin Nottebohm (Ger-mus)
May 2	Anton Berlijn (Hol-cm-cd)	Nov 12	Carlo Pedrotti (It-cm-cd)
May 11	Fanny Cerrito (It-bal)	Nov 13	Henry B. Richards (Br-pn)
May 19	Theodore Heintzman (Ger-pn.m)	Nov 13	Louis Lefébure-Wély (Fr-org)
May 31	Édouard Delvedez (Fr-cd-au)	Dec 4	Eugène L. Vivier (Fr-hn)
Jul 14	Hermann Küster (Ger-mus)	Dec 19	Jean C. Dancla (Fr-vn-cm)
Jul 28	Hippolyte Seligmann (Fr-cel)		Salvatore Agnelli (It-cm)

B. Deaths:

Jan 14	Pierre Monsigny (Fr-cm)	Feb 21	Pietro C. Guglielmi (It-cm)
Jan 28	Friedrich L. Kunzen (Ger-cm)	Mar 1	Luigi Gatti (It-cm-cd)
Feb 2	Ernst Leuckart (Ger-pub)	Apr 6	Bonaventura Furlanetto (It-cm)
Feb 9	Franz Tausch (Ger-cl)	May 2	Wenzel Krumpholz (Boh-vn)

May 13 Giuseppe Serassi, Jr. (It-org.m)
Jun 23 Otto Kospoth (Ger-cm)
Jun 27 Joseph Gürrlich (Ger-cb-cm)
Aug 24 Ann S. Storace (Br-sop)
Oct 12 Johann Sterpel (Ger-org)

Oct 18 Étienne Méhul (Fr-cm)
Nov 1   Giovanni Zanotti (It-cm)
Dec 1   Justin H. Knecht (Ger-org)
Dec 3   August E. Müller (Ger-org)

C. Debuts:

Other - Carlo Angrisani (London), Luigia Boccabadati (Italy), Alberico Curioni (Milan), Christian Fischer (Leipzig), Franz Hauser (Prague), Bernhard Molique (Vienna), Giovanni Puzzi (London)

D. New Positions:

Conductors: Johannes Amon (kapellmeister, Prince of Oettingen-Wallerstein), Ramòn Félix Cuéllar y Altarriba (Ovieto Cathedral), Traugott Eberwein (kapellmeister, Rudolstadt), Pietro Generali (Barcelona Opera), Konradin Kreutzer (Donaueschingen Court), Giuseppe Mosca (maestro di cappella, Palermo), Giovanni A. Perotti (St. Mark's, Venice), Louis Spohr (Frankfurt Opera), Carl Maria von Weber (German Opera, Dresden)

Educational: François Boieldieu (composition, Paris Conservatory), Friedrich Silcher (music director, University of Tübingen)

Others: Eduard Grell (organ, Nicolaikirche, Berlin), Johann Rinck (chamber musician, Darmstadt)

E. Prizes and Honors:

Prizes: Désiré-Alexandre Batton (Prix de Rome)

Honors: François Boieldieu (French Academy), William Shield (Master of the King's Music)

F. Biographical Highlights:

Ludwig Berger has his career halted by a nervous disorder of the arm; Nicolas Bochsa, involved in forgery charges, flees England for France; Violante Camporese and Gaetano Crivelli make their London debuts; Frederic Chopin makes his first appearance at a private recital; Alexander Dargomijsky's family moves to St. Petersburg; Gaetano Donizetti goes to Bergamo and begins writing opera; Franz Gebel goes to Moscow and becomes active in its musical life; Pietro Generali goes to Spain to direct the Barcelona Opera Co.; Mikhail Glinka is sent to the Pedagogic Institute in St. Petersburg; Jacques Halévy again wins the second Prix de Rome; Anthony Heinrich moves to Kentucky; Luigi Lablache makes his La Scala debut; Heinrich Marschner marries Emilie von Cerva and meets Beethoven in Vienna; Felix Mendelssohn begins composition study with Zelter; Franz Schubert leaves home for the Bohemian life; Gaspare Spontini becomes a naturalized French citizen; Carl Maria von Weber marries singer Caroline Brandt.

G. Institutional Openings:

Performing Groups: German Opera of Dresden; Gesangverein zu Danzig; Halifax Choral Society (England); Kraków Society of Friends of Music; Städischer Singverein Barmen (Wuppertal); Warsaw Amateur Music Society

Educational: Conservatorium der Gesellschaft der Musikfreunde (Vienna); Institution Royale de Musique Classique et Religieuse (Paris)

Other: *Edinburgh Monthly Magazine* (*Blackwood's Magazine*); Franz Feller and Sons, Organ Builders (Königswald); Franklin Music Warehouse (Boston); König and Bauer, Steam Press Manufacturers (Würzburg)

H. Musical Literature:

Chladni, Ernst, *Beiträge zur praktischen Akustik*
Choron, Alexandre, *Méthode concertante de musique à plusiers parties*
Hastings, Thomas, *The Musical Reader*
Hofmeister, Friedrich, *Handbuch der musikalischen Literatur*
Jackson, George K., *The Choral Companion*
La Salette, Joubert de, *De la notation musicale en général...*
Natorp, Bernhard, *Über den Gesang in den Kirchen der Protestanten*
Umbreit, Karl G., *Die Evangelischen Kirchenmelodien...*
Weber, Gottfried, *Versuch einer geordneten Theorie der Tonsetzkunst I*

I. Musical Compositions:

Beethoven, Ludwig van, *String Quintet, Opus 104*
    Fugue in D Major, Opus 137 (string quintet)
    26 Welsh Songs, Opus 226
Berwald, Franz, *Double Concerto for 2 Violins and Orchestra*
Carafa, Michele, *Ifigenia in Tauride* (opera)
Cherubini, Luigi, *Requiem in C Minor*
Clementi, Muzio, *Gradus ad Parnassum* (piano)
Danzi, Franz, *Turandot* (opera)
    L'Abbé di l'Attaignant (opera)
Donizetti, Gaetano, *Olimpiade* (opera)
    L'ira d'Achille (opera)
Field, John, *Concerto No. 5 for Piano and Orchestra*
    Nocturnes No. 4-6 (piano)
Generali, Pietro, *Rodrigo di Valenza* (opera)
Halévy, Jacques, *La Mort d'Adonis* (cantata)
Hérold, Ferdinand, *La clochette* (opera)
    Les rosières (opera)
Kashin, Daniil, *The One-day Reign of Nourmahal* (opera)
Kuhlau, Friedrich, *Die Zauberharfe* (opera)
Kurpinski, Karol, *Jan Kochanowski* (opera)
Méhul, Etienne, *Valentine de Milan* (opera)
Meyerbeer, Giacomo, *Romilda e Costanze* (opera)
Morlacchi, Francesco, *Laodicea* (opera)
    Isaaco, Figura di Redentroe (oratorio)
Pacini, Giovanni, *Adelaide e Comingio* (opera)
Poissl, Johann, *Nittetis* (opera)
Romberg, Bernhard, *Rittertreue* (opera)
Rossini, Gioacchino, *La gazza ladra* (opera)
    Adelaide di Borgogna (opera)
    La Cenerentola (opera)
    Armida (opera)
Schubert, Franz, *Overture in the Italian Style in D* Major
    Overture in the Italian Style in C Major
    Overture in D Minor
    Piano Sonatas No. 4-11
    Sonata, Opus 162, for Violin and Piano
    String Trio in B-Flat Major
    Die Forelle (song)
    Death and the Maiden (song)
Spohr, Louis, *String Quartet, Opus 43*
    6 Songs for Male Voices, Opus 44
Weber, Carl Maria von, *Donna Diana* (incidental music)
    König Yngurd (incidental music)
    7 Variations on a Gypsy Song, Opus 55 (piano)
    L'Accoglianza (cantata)
Winter, Peter, *Maometto II* (opera)

1818

World Events:

In the U.S., Congress approves the Stars and Stripes as the official U.S. flag and passes the Flag Act which provides an additional star for each new state; General Andrew Jackson puts down the Indian uprising of the First Seminole War; Illinois becomes State No. 21; the U.S.-Canadian boundary dispute is settled on the 49th Parallel. Internationally, San Martin leads Chile to independence; the German states of Baden and Bavaria receive constitutional governments; all foreign troops are removed from France; John Ross leads an expedition to find the Northwest Passage; Charles XIII of Sweden dies and is succeeded by Charles XIV.

Cultural Highlights:

The Prado Museum of Art opens in Madrid; the National Museum opens in Prague; the Old Vic Theater opens in London; the *Literarisches Wochenblatt* begins publication in Mannheim; German poet Friedrich von Matthisson is ennobled and Thomas Lawrence knighted. Births in the literary field include Swedish poet Carl Strandberg, Italian poet Tommaso Gherardi del Testa, French poet Charles de Lisle, Russian novelist Ivan Turgenev, British novelist Emily Brontë and poet Eliza Cook; death include British novelist Matthew Lewis. Births in the art field include American artists Martin Heade, Thomas Rossiter and sculptor Thomas Gould, Irish sculptor John Henry Foley and German artist Wilhelm Camphausen; German artist Heinrich Füger dies. Other highlights include:

Art: Washington Allston, *Elijah in the Desert*; Edward Baily, *Eve at the Fountain*; John Flaxman, *The Shield of Achilles*; David Friedrich, *Traveler Overlooking a Sea of Fog*; Jean L. Géricault, *Raft of the Medusa*; Edwin Landseer, *Fighting Dogs*; John Trumbull, *The Declaration of Independence*; Joseph Turner, *Forum Romanum*

Literature: Jane Austen, *Northanger Abbey*; George Lord Byron, *Childe Harold IV*; Marceline Desbordes-Valmore, *Élégies et Romances*; Franz Grillparzer, *Sappho*; John Keats, *Endymion*; Thomas Peacock, *Nightmare Alley*; Walter Scott, *The Heart of Midlothian*; Mary Shelley, *Frankenstein*; Percy B. Shelley, *Prometheus Unbound*

MUSICAL EVENTS

A. Births:

Jan 4	Paul Mériel (Fr-cm)	Jul 15	Heinrich Esser (Ger-cd-cm)
Feb 6	Henry C. Litolff (Br-pub)	Jul 24	Félix Godefroid (Bel-hp)
Mar 11	Antonio Bazzini (It-vn-cm)	Aug 25	Jacques L. Battmann (Fr-org)
Mar 12	Georges Bousquet (Fr-cm)	Aug 30	Friedrich Ladegast (Ger-org.m)
Mar 18	Maria Dolores Nau (Am-sop)	Sep 12	Theodor Kullak (Pol-pn-cd)
Jun 10	Hubert Kufferath (Ger-vn-cd)	Sep 26	John S. Reeves (Br-ten)
Jun 10	Clara A. Novello (Br-sop)	Oct 15	Alexander Dreyschock (Boh-pn)
Jun 13	Livia Frege (Ger-sop)	Oct 26	Stefano Golinelli (It-pn-cm)
Jun 18	Charles Gounod (Fr-cm)	Nov 29	Abramo Basevi (It-cri)
Jun 30	Edward Hopkins (Br-org)	Dec 16	Moritz Deutsch (Ger-ten)
Jul 6	Carl Engel (Ger-mus)		Erminia Frezzolini (It-sop)

B. Deaths:

Jan 1	Fedele Fenaroli (It-cm)	Aug 13	Agostino Accorimboni (It-cm)
Feb 1	Giuseppe Gazzaniga (It-cm)	Aug 25	Elizabeth Billington (Ger-sop)
Feb 13	Marie-Jeanne Trial (Fr-sop)	Sep 18	Franz Gleissner (Ger-pub)
Mar 20	Johann N. Forkel (Ger-mus)	Oct 30	John Geib (Ger-pn.m)
Mar 23	Nicolo Isouard (Fr-cm)	Dec 31	Jean Pierre Duport (Fr-cel)
Mar 28	Giuseppe Capuzzi (It-vn)		Pierre Lahoussaye (Fr-vn)
May 7	Leopold Kozeluch (Boh-cm)		

C. Debuts:
U.S. -- Charles Incledon (tour), Charles Thibault (N.Y.)

Other - Jean Baptiste Chollet (as baritone), Frances Corri (London), Felix Mendelssohn (age 9, Berlin), Eduard Rietz (Berlin), Antonio Tamburini (Cento)

D. New Positions:
Conductors: Johann Kasper Aiblinger (kapellmeister, Munich), Giuseppi Baini (maestro di cappella, St. Peter's, Rome), Ramón Carnicer (Coliseo Theater, Barcelona), Konradin Kreutzer (kapellmeister, Donaueschingen), Franz Krommer (kapellmeister, Vienna), Stefano Pavesi (maestro di capella, Crema Cathedral), Jan Václav Vorísek (Gesellschaft der Musikfreunde, Vienna)

Educational: Ferdinand Gassner (music director, Gneissen University), Georg W. Hegel (professor, Berlin University), Johann August Heinroth (music director, University of Göttingen), Jean-François Lesueur (composition, Paris Conservatory), Anton Reicha (counterpoint, Paris Conservatory)

Others: Theobald Böhm (court musician, Munich), Johann Henneberg (organ, Vienna Court), Oliver Holden (South Carolina House of Representatives)

E. Prizes and Honors:
Honors: François Boieldieu (French Institute), Gaspare Spontini (State Pension by Louis XVIII)

F. Biographical Highlights:
Nicholas Bochsa, having fled to London, is sentenced in absentia to 12 years imprisonment for his forgeries; Frédéric Chopin, age 8, performs a Gyrowetz concerto at a public concert; Ferdinand David, age 8, becomes chorister at Aix-en-Provence; Gaetano Donizetti is exempted from military duty by a gift from a lady of Bergamo; François Fétis leaves his post as organist at St. Pierre in Douai and returns to Paris; Frédéric Kalkbrenner simplifies and promotes Logier's Chiroplast; Lowell Mason founds the Savannah Missionary Society; Felix Mendelssohn, age 9, makes his first public performance in chamber music in Berlin; Jeanne Saint-Aubin retires from the stage; Franz Schubert becomes music master to the Esterházy family during the summer months; Robert Schumann begins taking piano lessons from the Zwickau organist, J. G. Kuntzsch; Giovanni Viotti fails in the wine business and returns to Paris.

G. Institutional Openings:
Performing Groups: Bavarian State Opera (Munich); Bradford Harmonic Society; Frankfurt Cäcilienverein; Königsberg Singverein

Educational: Académie de Musique et de Chant (Brussels); Royal Harmonic Institution (London)

Other: Amphion (The Netherlands); Cappi and Diabelli, Music Publishers (Vienna); Dumont-Schauberg Verlag (Cologne); National Theater (Munich); Quarterly Musical Magazine and Review; Teatro Nuovo (Pesaro)

H. Musical Literature:
Burrowes, John, The Pianoforte Primer
Busby, Thomas, A Grammar of Music
Choron, Alexandre, Méthode de plain-chant
Dlabacz, Gottfried J., Allgemeines historisches Künstlerlexikon für Böhmen
Galin, Pierre, Exposition d'une nouvelle méthode pour l'enseignement de la musique
Logier, Johann B., Chiroplast Méthod de Piano
Mosel, Ignaz von, Die Tonkunst in Wien während der letzten fünf Dezennien
Reicha, Anton, Cours de composition musicale
Stevenson/Moore, National Airs

Watts, Isaac, *The Psalms of David*
Werner, Johann G., *Harmonielehre I*

I. Musical Compositions:

Beethoven, Ludwig van, *Piano Piece in B-flat Major, Opus 172*
    O Hoffnung (chorus)
Bellini, Vincenzo, *Magnificat*
Boieldieu, François, *Le petit chaperon rouge* (opera)
Carafa, Michele, *Berenice in Siria* (opera)
    Elisabetta in Derbyshire (opera)
Cavos, Catterino, *Dobrynia Nikitich* (opera)
Cherubini, Luigi, *Messe Solemnelle in E* Major
Donizetti, Gaetano, *Enrico di Borgogna* (opera)
    Una follia (opera)
Generali, Pietro, *Il servo padrone* (opera)
    La cecchina sonatrice (opera)
Gruber, Franz, *Silent Night* (Christmas song)
Hérold, Ferdinand, *Le premier venu* (opera)
Isouard, Nicolo, *Aladin* (opera)
    Une nuit de Gustave Waso (opera, finished by Gasse)
Kreutzer, Rodolphe, *La servante justifiée* (ballet)
Kurpinski, Karol, *Der Prinz Czaromysl* (opera)
Loewe, Carl, *3 Songs, Opus 1* (includes *Edward* and *The Erlking*)
Marschner, Heinrich, *Heinrich IV* (opera)
    Overture on Hungarian National Airs
Morlacchi, Francesco, *Gianni di Parigi* (opera)
    Messa a capella
Pacini, Giovanni, *Atala* (opera)
    Il barone di Dolsheim (opera)
Poissl, Johann, *Issipile* (opera)
Romberg, Bernhard, *Daphne und Agathokles* (ballet)
Rossini, Gioacchino, *Mosè in Egitto* (opera or oratorio)
    Ricciardo e Zoraide (opera)
    Adina (opera)
Salieri, Antonio, *Cyrus und Astyages* (opera)
Schmidt, Johann, *Das Fischermädchen* (opera)
Schubert, Franz, *Symphony No. 6, D. 589*
    Deutsche Trauermesse, D. 621
    Piano Sonatas No. 12 and 13, D. 613 and 625
Spohr, Louis, *3 String Quartets, Opus 45*
Tadolini, Giovanni, *Tamerlano* (opera)
Vaccai, Nicolo, *Il lupo di Ostenda* (opera)
Vorísek, Jan, *12 Rhapsodies, Opus 1, for Piano*
Weber, Karl Maria von, *Das Haus Anglade* (incidental music)
    König von Frankreich (incidental music)
    Lieb' um Liebe (incidental music)
    Jubel Overture, Opus 59
    Jubilee Cantata, Opus 58
    Missa Sancta No. 1
    Natur und Liebe (cantata)
    Scene and Aria, "Was sag ich," Opus 56
    6 Songs, Opus 54
Weigl, Joseph, *Die Nachtigall und die Rabe* (opera)
Winter, Peter, *Etelinda* (opera)

1819

World Events:
In the U.S., the Panic of 1819 brings on a four-year depression; Alabama becomes State No. 22; the Florida territory is bought from Spain for $5,000,000; the Universities of Cincinnati and Virginia are founded; Fort Snelling (Minneapolis) is built; a patent is given for the first plow with interchangeable parts. Internationally, the city of Singapore is founded by the British East India Co.; Simón Bolívar defeats the Spanish in Venezuela and is elected to the presidency of Greater Colombia; the Carlsbad Decrees attempt to bar liberalism from all European universities; the Peterloo Massacre takes place in England; future Queen Victoria is born.

Cultural Highlights:
Sir Walter Scott is given a baronet. Births in the literary field include British poets Arthur Clough, Ernest Jones and John W. Marston and novelists Georg Eliot and Charles Kingsley, German poets Friedrich Bodenstedt, Klaus Groth and Wilhelm Jordan and novelists Theodor Fontane and Gottfried Keller, American authors Julia Ward Howe and Hermann Melville and poets James R. Lowell, Thomas Parsons and Walt Whitman; deaths include German dramatist August Kotzebue and poet Friedrich Stolberg, British author John Wolcot, critic and author John Ruskin and Portugese poet Francisco Nascimento. Births in the art field include French artists Théodore Chassériau and Gustave Courbet, American sculptors Thomas Ball and William Story and British artist William Frith; deaths include Dutch artist Jurriaen Andriesson and British artist Edward Bird. Other highlights include:

Art: Washington Allston, *Moonlit Landscape*; Antonio Canova, *Stuart Monument*; John Constable, *The White Horse*; Francisco de Goya, *Last Communion of St. Joseph*; Jean-Auguste Ingres, *Nicolò Paganini*; Johann Schadow, *Blücher Monument (Rostock)*; Thomas Sully, *Passage of the Delaware*; Bertel Thorvaldsen, *Christ and the Apostles*

Literature: George Lord Byron, *Mazeppa* and *Don Juan I, II*; George Crabbe, *Tales of the Hall*; E.T.A. Hoffmann, *Serapionsbrüder I*; Washington Irving, *Rip Van Winkle*; Hannah More, *Moral Sketches*; Adam Oehlenschläger, *The Gods of the North*; Arthur Schopenhauer, *World as Will and Idea*; Walter Scott, *The Bride of Lammermoor*

MUSICAL EVENTS

A. Births:

Feb 11	Samuel P. Tuckerman (Am-org)		Sep 6	Karl F. Pohl (Ger-org-mus)
Feb 23	Heinrich Vincent (Ger-the)		Sep 13	Clara Schumann (Ger-pn)
Feb 26	Elizabeth Stirling (Br-org)		Sep 15	Jules Pasdeloup (Gr-cd)
Mar 12	Henriette Nissen (Swe-sop)		Sep 28	Karl R. Köstlin (Ger-the)
Apr 7	Hubert Léonard (Bel-vn-cm)		Oct 15	Ferdinand Laurencin (Aus-mus)
Apr 11	Charles Hallé (Br-cd-pn)		Oct 23	Isaac Woodbury (Am-cm)
Apr 18	Franz von Suppé (Aus-cm)		Dec 13	Edwain G. Monk (Br-org)
Apr 30	Susan Sunderland (Br-sop)		Dec 22	Franz W. Abt (Ger-cm)
May 5	Stanislaw Moniuszko (Pol-cm)			Sophie Thillon (Br-sop)
Jun 20	Jacques Offenbach (Ger-cm)			

B. Deaths:

Jan	Francisco Galeazzi (It-vn)		Aug 7	Josef Bähr (Aus-cl)
Mar 16	Nicolas Séjan (Fr-org)		Sep 7	Jean Louis Duport (Fr-cel)
May 5	Giacomo Morelli (It-mus)		Sep 28	Karl Haack (Ger-vn)
May 11	Casper Fürstenau (Ger-fl)		Oct 13	Giovanni Gaiani (It-org)
May 29	Simon Peter (Hol-hymn)		Nov 21	Antonio Moreira (Por-cm)
Jun 4	Carlo Gervasoni (It-the)		Dec 20	Louis de Persuis (Fr-cd-cm)
Jun 30	Ernst Gerber (Ger-mus)		Dec 29	Josepha Weber (Ger-sop)
Jul 24	Edmée Sophie Gail (Fr-cm)			Franz C. Hartig (Ger-ten)

C. Debuts:
> **Other** - Ole Bull (age 9, Bergen), Eduard Devrient (Berlin), Georg Hellmesberger (Vienna), Luigi Legnani (Milan), Ann Maria Tree (London)

D. New Positions:
> **Conductors:** Johann Aiblinger (Italian Opera, Munich), Francisco Andreví y Castellar (choirmaster, Valencia Cathedral), Johan F. Berwald (Stockholm Royal SO), Johann Hummel (kapellmeister, Weimar), Karol Kurpinski (kapellmeister, Polish Royal Chapel), Peter von Lindpainter (kapellmeister, Stuttgart), Giuseppe Niccolini (maestro di cappella, Piacenza Cathedral), Pietro Rovelli (maestro di cappella, S. Maria Maggiore, Bergamo), Giuseppe Siboni (Copenhagen Opera), Giovanni Battista Viotti (Italian Opera, Paris)

> **Educational:** François Benoist (organ, Paris Conservatory), Joseph Boehm (violin, Vienna Conservatory), Anna Fröhlich (voice, Vienna Conservatory), François Louis Perne (librarian, Paris Conservatory)

> **Others:** Zechariah Bush (organ, Norwich Cathedral), Thomas Greatorex (organ, Westminster Abbey), Hippolyte Mompou (organ, Tours Cathedral)

E. Prizes and Honors:
> **Prizes:** Jacques Halévy (Prix de Rome)

F. Biographical Highlights:
> Teresa Belloc-Giorgi makes her London debut; Giuseppe de Begnis and his wife, soprano Giuseppina Ronzi de Begnis, make their Paris Opera debuts together; Vincenzo Bellini enters Naples Conservatory for his first professional music instruction; Giulio Bordogni makes his Paris debut; Pietro Generali leaves Barcelona and returns to Italy to become Maestro di Capella at Novara Cathedral; August von Kotzebue is stabbed to death by a university student; Carl Loewe makes a concert tour of Germany before settling down in Stettin; Felix Mendelssohn, age 10, enters the Berlin Singakademie and begins composing; Franz Schubert fails to gain Goethe's approval for the setting of his poems; Louis Spohr, following the great success of his opera *Zemire und Azor*, resigns his Frankfurt directorship; Carl Maria von Weber is visited by Marschner, Mendelssohn and Spohr.

G. Institutional Openings:
> **Performing Groups:** Gotha Singverein; Hamburg Singakademie; Neue Liedertafel von Berlin; Rostocker Singakademie; Spirituel-Concerte (Vienna)

> **Educational:** Library of the Gesellschaft der Musik Freunde, Vienna; Oxford Choral Society; Pastou Singing School (Paris)

> **Other:** Beethoven Musical Society of Portland, Maine; Dubois and Stodart, Piano Manufacturers (N.Y.); Gesellschaft der Freunde Religiösen Gesanges (Hamburg); Haydn Society of Cincinnati; *The Indicator*; Irish Harp Society (Belfast); Klemm and Brother, Instrument Dealers (Philadelphia); *London Magazine*; New Darmstadt Theater; Paterson and Sons, Music Publishers (Edinburgh)

H. Musical Literature:
> Burrowes, John, *The Thorough-bass Primer*
> Busby, Thomas, *General History of Music*
> Choron, Alexandre, *Exposition élémentaire des principes de la Musique*
> Drieberg, Friedrich von, *Aufschlüss über die musik der Griechen*
> Gérard, Henri, *Considérations sur la Musique...*
> Jacob, Benjamin, *National Psalmody*
> Jousse, Jean, *Lectures on Thoroughbass*
> Kemp, Joseph, *A New System of Musical Education*
> Relfe, John, *Remarks on the Present State of Musical Instruction*

Savart, Félix, *Mémoire sur la Construction des Instruments à Cordes et Archet*
Shaw, Oliver, *Melodia Sacra*

I. Musical Compositions:
Arriaga, Juan, *Les esclavos felices* (opera)
Auber, Daniel, *Le testament et les billets-doux* (opera)
Beethoven, Ludwig van, *Piano Sonata No. 29, Opus 106, "Hammerklavier"*
  6 Easy Variations, Opus 105 (violin or flute and piano)
Carnicer, Ramón, *Adele di Lusignano* (opera)
Catel, Charles S., *L'Officier enlevé* (opera)
Clementi, Muzio, *Symphony in D, Opus 44*
Donizetti, Gaetano, *Il falegname di Livónia* (opera)
Generali, Pietro, *Adelaide di Borgogna* (opera)
Halévy, Jacques, *Herminie* (cantata)
Hérold, Ferdinand, *L'amour platonique* (opera)
  Les troquers (opera)
Hummel, Ferdinand, *Piano Sonata in F-sharp Minor, Opus 81*
Kreutzer, Konradin, *Cordelia* (opera)
Kuhlau, Daniel, *12 Songs, Opus 23*
Kurpinski, Karol, *The Castle of Czorsztyn* (opera)
Loewe, Carl, *Grande Sonate Brillante, Opus 41, for Piano*
  Grande Sonate Élégique, Opus 32, for Piano
Marschner, Heinrich, *Saidar und Zulima* (opera)
  Das stille Volk (opera)
Mercadante, Saverio, *L'apoteosi d'Ercole* (opera)
Meyerbeer, Giacomo, *Semiramide Riconosciuta* (opera)
  Emma di Resburgo (opera)
Moscheles, Ignaz, *Concerto No. 1, Opus 45, for Piano and Orchestra*
Pacini, Giovanni, *La sposa fedele* (opera)
Rossini, Gioacchino, *Ermione* (opera)
  La donna del lago (opera)
  Bianca e Falliero (opera)
  Eduardo e Cristina (opera)
  Partenope (cantata)
Schenk, Johann, *Der Mai* (cantata)
  Die Huldigung (cantata)
Schubert, Franz, *Piano Quintet, "The Trout"*
  Die Zwillingsbrüder (operetta)
  Overture in E Minor
  Piano Sonatas No. 14 and 15, D. 655 and 664
Spohr, Louis, *Zemire und Azor* (opera)
  Concert Overture in F
  String Quartet, Opus 61
  Sonata for Harp and Violin in A-flat
Spontini, Gaspare, *Olimpie* (opera)
Vertovsky, Alexei, *Grandmother's Parrot* (opera)
Weber, Carl Maria von, *Invitation to the Dance* (orchestrated 1841 by Berlioz)
  Mass in G, Opus 76
  Rondo Brillante, Opus 62, for Piano
  Trio, Opus 63 for Piano, Flute and Cello
  8 Pieces, Opus 6, for Piano, Four Hands
  14 Songs, Opus 64 and 71

1820

World Events:

The U.S. Census shows a population of 9,683,000, a 33% increase in ten years; New York is the largest city with 124,000 inhabitants; James Monroe is re-elected as President; Maine becomes State No. 23; the Missouri Compromise limits slavery in the Louisiana Purchase Territory; Indiana University is founded; the U.S. Pharmacopoeia is founded; Daniel Boone, frontiersman, dies. Internationally, King George III of England dies and is succeeded by George IV; revolutions take place in Portugal and Spain--King Ferdinand VII restores the Spanish Constitution; the Egyptians, under British instigation, invade the Sudan; the continent of Antartica is discovered; the Royal Astronomical Society is founded in London.

Cultural Highlights:

The statue of Venus de Milo is discovered; Thomas Campbell becomes editor of the *New Monthly Magazine*; Percy Bysshe Shelley moves to Pisa, Italy; Alexander Pushkin is exiled to South Russia; George Catlin begins law practice; Thomas Lawrence becomes President of the Royal Academy of Art. Births in the literary field include British author Anne Brontë, American author Margaret Preston and poet Alice Cary; deaths include American poet Joseph Drake, British poet William Hayley and Irish poet William Drennan. Deaths in the art field include German artist Ferdinand Jagemann, American artist Benjamin West and architect Benjamin Latrobe; Czech artist Josef Mánes is born. Other highlights include:

Art: John Constable, *Harwich Lighthouse*; John Crome, *Mousehold Heath, Norwich*; David Friedrich, *Landscape in Silesian Mountains*; Francisco de Goya, *The Giant*; Edwin Landseer, *Alpine Mastiffs and Traveler*; Rembrandt Peale, *The Court of Death*; Thomas Rowlandson, *Tours of Dr. Syntax II*; Benjamin West, *Franklin and the Lightning*

Literature: William Blake, *Jerusalem*; William Combe, *Tours of Dr. Syntax II*; Tommaso Grossi, *Idelgonda*; Washington Irving, *Sketch Book*; John Keats, *Lamia and Other Poems*; Alphonse de Lamartine, *Méditations Poétiques*; Alessandro Manzoni, *Il Conte di Carognola*; Alexander Pushkin, *Russlan and Ludmilla*; Walter Scott, *Ivanhoe*

MUSICAL EVENTS

A. Births:

Jan 5	Ange-Conrad Prumier (Fr-hp)		Aug 13	George Grove (Br-mus)
Jan 12	Stéphane Morelot (Fr-mus)		Aug 30	George Root (Am-cm)
Jan 23	Alexander Serov (Rus-cm)		Sep 1	Robert Burton (Br-org)
Feb 17	Henri Vieuxtemps (Bel-vn)		Sep 5	Louis Köhler (Ger-pn)
Mar 16	Enrico Tamberlik (It-ten)		Sep 21	Cesare Aria (It-cm-ed)
Mar 24	Fanny Crosby (Am-hymn)		Oct 1	Gustav Heinze (Ger-cd)
Apr 12	Johann Eschmann (Swi-pn)		Oct 6	Jenny Lind (Swe-sop)
May 3	Jules Armingaud (Fr-vn)		Nov 17	Lodovico Graziani (It-ten)
May 20	Michal Bergson (Pol-pn)		Nov 24	Friedrich Lux (Ger-cm)
May 22	Alexander Fesca (Ger-cm)		Dec 5	Hans Schläger (Aus-cm)
Jul 2	Charles L. Hanon (Fr-pn)		Dec 23	Isaac Fiske (Am-inst.m)
Jul 7	George Cooper (Br-org)			Marianna Barbieri-Nini (It-sop)
Jul 10	Louis A. Vidal (Fr-cel)			Gustave A. Besson (Fr-inv)

B. Deaths:

Jan 4	Bohumíl Dlabac (Cz-mus)		May 10	Matthaeus Stegmayer (Aus-lib)
Jan 25	Joseph Weigl, Sr. (Ger-cel-cm)		Jul 29	Joseph Corfe (Br-org)
Jan 30	Josepha Auernhammer (Aus-pn)		Aug 6	Anton Wranitzsky (Cz-vn)
Feb 7	Samuel Holyoke (Am-cm)		Aug 11	János Lavotta (Hun-vn)
Mar 19	Felice Radicati (It-vn)		Aug 28	Anton Kraft (Cz-cel)

Sep 17	Henri Hamal (Bel-cm)	Oct 17	Paolo Altieri (It-cm)
Sep 20	Marie Bigot (Fr-pn)	Dec 14	Giuseppe Naldi (It-bs)
Sep 24	Pedro Aranaz y Vides (Sp-cm)		Joseph Gehot (Bel-vn)
Oct 3	Ludwig Lachnith (Boh-hn)		Giovanni Grazioli (It-org)

C. Debuts:
Other - Aline Bertrand (Paris), Franz Liszt (age 9, Raiding)

D. New Positions:
Conductors: Ramón Carnicer (Barcelona Opera), Georg A. Schneider (Berlin Opera), Gaspare Spontini (kapellmeister, Berlin), Henri-Justin Valentino (Paris Opera)

Educational: Giovanni Bordogni (voice, Paris Conservatory), Carl Loewe (schoolmaster, Stettin)

Others: William Beale (organ, Trinity College, Cambridge), John Clarke (organ, Herford Cathedral), Lowell Mason (organ, Independent Presbyterian Church, Savannah)

E. Prizes and Honors:
Prizes: Aimé Ambroise Leborne (Prix de Rome)

Honors: Franz S. Kandler (Accademia Filarmonica, Bologna)

F. Biographical Highlights:
Ludwig van Beethoven wins his lawsuit against his sister-in-law for the custody of his nephew; Hector Berlioz, at his father's insistence, reluctantly begins the study of medicine; Ludwig Böhner suffers a nervous breakdown that destroys his piano career; James Hook decides to retire from active music life and resigns his organ position at Vauxhall Gardens; Nicholas Levasseur makes his La Scala debut; Franz Liszt begins piano study with Czerny and gives his first recital; Giovanni Pacini goes to Rome and begins an affair with Napoleon's sister; Anton Schindler begins work as Beethoven's secretary; Robert Schumann enters the Zwickau Lyceum; Louis Spohr makes the first known use of the baton in a concert in London; Gaspare Spontini leaves Paris for a new position in Berlin; Carl Maria von Weber makes a concert tour with his wife and visits Copenhagen.

G. Institutional Openings:
Performing Groups: Amateur Music Society of Warsaw; Bamberg Musikverein; Cologne Singverein; Orchestra of the Militia of the Free Town of Kraków; Philharmonic Society of Bethlehem (Pennsylvania); Quebec Harmonic Society

Educational: Musikalische Bildungsanstalt (Berlin); Toulouse Conservatory of Music

Other: Elwer and Co., Publishers (London); *Euterpeiad, or Musical Intelligencer* (U.S.); Charles F. Gand, Violin Maker (Paris); William Hall, Piano Maker (Firth, Hall and Pond, N.Y.); Musical Fund Society (Philadelphia); *National Gazette and Literary Register; New Monthly Magazine and Literary Journal; The Scottish Minstrel*; Trautwein Music Publishers (Berlin); Eberhard Walcker, Organ Builder (Ludwigsburg)

H. Musical Literature:
Aguado, Dionysio, *Estudios para la Guitarra*
Blaze, François, *De l'opéra en France*
Carden, Allen, *Missouri Harmony*
Carrell, James, *Songs of Zion*
Choron, Alexandre, *Méthode de Chant...*
Hill, Uri, *Solfeggio Americano...*
Jones, Edward, *Cambro-British Melodies*
Savart, Félix, *Sur la communication des mouvements vibratoires entre les corps solides*
Schneider, Friedrich, *Elementarbuch der Harmonie und Tonsetzkunst*

I. Musical Compositions:

André, Anton, *Grande Symphony, Opus 41*
Auber, Daniel, *La bergère châtelaine* (opera)
Balbi, Melchiore, *La notte perigliosa* (opera)
Beethoven, Ludwig von, *Piano Sonata No. 30, Opus 109*
 10 National Themes with Variations, Opus 107
Berwald, Franz A., *Concerto for Violin and Orchestra*
Clementi, Muzio, *Piano Sonata in B-flat, Opus 46*
Donizetti, Gaetano, *La nozze in Villa* (opera)
Halévy, Jacques, *Les bohémiennes* (opera)
 De Profundis
Heinrich, Anthony, *The Dawning of Music in Kentucky, Opus 1*
 The Western Minstrel, Opus 2
Hérold, Ferdinand, *L'auteur mort et vivant* (opera)
Klein, Bernhard, *Job* (oratorio)
Kreutzer, Konradin, *Scenes from Goethe's Faust*
Kreutzer, Rodolphe, *Clari* (ballet)
Kuhlau, Friedrich, *Elisa* (opera)
 3 Piano Sonatinas, Opus 20
 2 Piano Sonatas, Opus 26
Kurpinski, Karol, *Kalmora* (opera)
 Mars i Flora (ballet)
Lortzing, Albert, *Andante and Variations for Harp and Orchestra*
Mercadante, Saverio, *Violenza e costanza* (opera)
 Il gelosa ravveduto (opera)
 Scipione in Cartagine (opera)
 Anacreonte in Samo (opera)
Meyerbeer, Giacomo, *Margherita d'Anjou* (opera)
Moscheles, Ignaz, *Concerto No. 3, Opus 60, for Piano and Orchestra*
Pacini, Giovanni, *La gioventù di Enrico V* (opera)
 La schiava in Bagdad (opera)
Poissl, Johann, *La rappressaglia* (opera)
Reicha, Anton, *Rondo for Horn and Orchestra*
Rossini, Gioacchino, *Maometto II* (opera)
 Messe Solennelle
 Messe di Gloria
Schneider, Friedrich, *Der Weltgericht* (oratorio)
Schubert, Franz, *Sakuntala* (opera)
 Die Zauberharfe (opera)
 Gesang der Geister über den Wassern, Opus 167
 Quartettsatz in C Minor, D. 703
Spohr, Louis, *Symphony No. 2, Opus 49*
 Concerto No. 9, Opus 55, for Violin and Orchestra
 Mass in C Major, Opus 54
 Woodwind Quintet in C Major, Opus 52
Tadolini, Giovanni, *Il finto molinaro* (opera)
Vertovsky, Alexei, *Quarantine* (opera)
Weber, Carl Maria von, *Preciosa* (incidental music)
 Der Leuchtturm (incidental music)
 Agnus Dei (chorus and winds)
 6 Songs, Opus 80
Weigl, Joseph, *Daniel in der Löwengrube* (opera)
Winter, Peter, *Der Sänger un der Schneider* (singspiel)

1821

World Events:

In the U.S., Missouri becomes State No. 24; the U.S. begins the official settlement of the Florida Territory; Texas, a State of Mexico, is opened to settlement by Moses Austin; the first public high school, the English Classical School, opens in Boston; Congress rejects a bid to change over to the metric system. Internationally, Mexico declares its independence and Santa Anna becomes President; Guatamala, Panama and Santo Domingo also declare independence through the actions of San Martin; Greece begins a war of independence with Turkey; Faraday invents the electric motor and generator; McGill University is founded in Montreal; Napoleon Bonaparte dies in exile.

Cultural Highlights:

Henry H. Milman begins teaching poetry at Oxford; Edward Hodges Baily is inducted into the Royal Academy; François de Chateaubriand becomes ambassador to Berlin. Births in the art field include American sculptor Anne Whitney, French artist Charles Meryon, Scottish artist Joseph Paton and British artist Ford Brown; deaths include British artists Richard Cosway, John Crome, Joseph Farington and Hester Piozzi, German artist Johann Fiorillo and American artist John Krimmel. Births in the literary field include French novelists Champfleury, Octave Feuillet and Gustave Flaubert and poet Charles Baudelaire, German poet Hermann Allmers and Russian novelist Feodor Dostoyevsky; deaths include French philosopher Joseph de Maistre, Italian poet Carlo Porta, German poet Christian Stolberg and British poet John Keats. Other highlights include:

Art: Antonio Canova, *Endymion*; John Constable, *The Hay Wain*; John Flaxman, *St. Michael Overcoming Satan*; Jean L. Géricault, *The Epsom Derby*; John Martin, *Belshazzar's Feast*; Samuel Morse, *Old House of Representatives*; Thomas Rowlandson, *Tours of Dr. Syntax III*; John Trumbull, *Surrender of General Burgoyne*

Literature: John Banim, *Damon and Pythias*; William Cullen Bryant, *Poems I*; George Lord Byron, *Don Juan III, IV and V*; John Clare, *The Village Minstrel*; James F. Cooper, *The Spy*; Franz Grillparzer, *The Golden Fleece*; William Hazlitt, *Table Talk*; Walter Scott, *Kenilworth*; Percy B. Shelley, *Adonais*; Robert Southey, *Vision of Judgement*

MUSICAL EVENTS

A. Births:

Jan 1	Joseph Tagliafico (Fr-bs)	Aug 31	Hermann von Helmholtz
Jan 12	Nicolai Afanas'yev (Rus-vn)		(Ger-acous)
Mar 12	Italo Gardoni (It-ten)	Sep 3	Ernst Pasqué (Ger-bar)
Mar 24	Mathilde Marchesi (Ger-mez)	Oct 11	Angelo Mariani (It-cd-cm)
Apr 12	Carl Bergmann (Ger-cd)	Oct 13	Oscar Byström (Swe-pn-cm)
Apr 13	Hans von Milde (Aus-bar)	Oct 16	Albert Doppler (Aus-fl)
Apr 27	Henry Willis (Br-org.m)	Oct 20	Karl Mikuli (Pol-pn)
May 12	Bernard Kothe (Ger-mus)	Oct 31	Heinrich Willmers (Ger-pn)
May 17	Charlotte Sainton-Dolby	Nov 29	Jean B. Weckerlin (Fr-cm-au)
	(Br-alto)	Dec 15	Auguste Vaucorbeil (Fr-cm)
Jul 18	Pauline Viardot-García	Dec 22	Giovanni Bottesini (It-cb)
	(Fr-mez)	Dec 31	Rudolf Schachner (Ger-pn)
Aug 24	Emanuele Muzio (It-cd)		

B. Deaths:

Jan 2	F. Geissenhof (Aus-vn.m)	Mar 23	Bernhard A. Weber (Ger-pn)
Jan 25	Matthias Kasnienski (Pol-cm)	May 15	André F. Eler (Fr-cm)
Mar 19	Georg G. Müller (Ger-rel-cm)	Jun 18	John Callcott (Br-org)

Jul 13	Charles Hague (Br-vn)	Oct 28	Gasparo Pacchiarotti (It-cas)
Apr 21	Andrew Law (Am-cm)	Nov 10	Andreas Romberg (Ger-vn)
Aug 6	Antonio Bruni (It-cm-cd)	Dec 20	Gian F. Fortunati (It-cm)
Sep 22	Louise Dugazon (Fr-sop)	Dec 30	Angelo Benincori (It-vn)

C. Debuts:
Other - Charles Auguste de Bériot (Paris), Josephine Fröhlich (Vienna), Anton Haizinger (Vienna), Ferdinand Hiller (age 10), Adolphe Nourrit (Paris), Wilhemine Schröder-Devrient (Vienna), Josef Slavík (Prague), Henriette Sontag (Prague), Mary Ann Wilson (London)

D. New Positions:
Conductors: Friedrich Schneider (kapellmeister, Dessau)

Educational: Davidde Banderali (voice, Milan Conservatory), Henri François Berton (voice, Paris Conservatory), John Clarke (music professor, Cambridge), François Fétis (counterpoint, Paris Conservatory), Georg Hellmesberger, Sr. (violin, Vienna Conservatory), Joseph Sellner (oboe, Paris Conservatory)

Others: François Habeneck (director, Paris Opera), Carl Loewe (organ, St. Jacobus Cathedral)

E. Prizes and Honors:
Honors: Edward Hodges Baily (Royal Academy), François Boieldieu (Legion of Honor), Andrew Law (honorary doctorate, Allegheny College), Félix Savard (French Academy)

F. Biographical Highlights:
Giuseppe de Begnis and Giuseppina Ronzi de Begnis make their London debut together; Julius Benedict is taken to Dresden to study with Hummel and eventually with Carl Maria von Weber; Hector Berlioz is sent to a Paris medical school by his father; Alberico Curioni makes his London debut; Pietro Generali goes to Naples; Louis Ferdinand Hérold goes to Italy to recruit singers for Paris; Johann Wenzel Kalliwoda leaves Prague for a European concert tour; Italian contralto Adelaide Malanotte retires from the stage; Felix Mendelssohn travels to Weimar with Zelter and meets Goethe; Ignaz Moscheles settles in London and continues his concert tours from there; Sigismund Ritter von Neukomm arrives back in Paris following his South American visit; Carl Gottlieb Reissiger goes to Vienna and studies with Antonio Salieri; Louis Spohr settles temporarily in Dresden; Nicola Vaccai moves to Trieste for a two-year period as singing teacher; Richard Wagner loses his stepfather, Ludwig Geyer, but is given help by his brother; Carl Maria von Weber turns down a call to Kassel and establishes subscription concerts in Dresden.

G. Institutional Openings:
Performing Groups: Accademie Filarmonica Romana (Rome); Bradford Musical Friendly Society; The Diligentia Music Society and Hall (The Hague)

Festivals: Niederrheinisches Musikfest (Cologne)

Educational: Free School of Music (Marseilles)

Other: Thomas Appleton, Organ Maker (Boston); Chelard Publishing Co. (Paris); Karl Heckel, Music Publisher (Mannheim); Carl August Klemm Publishing Co. (Leipzig); Kolozavár National Theater (Hungary); Neue Schausspielhaus (Berlin); Ophecleide (patented); Ratti, Cencetti and Co., Music Publishers (Rome); Maurice Schlesinger, Music Publisher (Paris); Henry Smart, Piano Maker (England)

H. Musical Literature:
Blaze, François, *Dictionnaire de musique moderne*
Chladni, Ernst, *Beiträge zur praktische Akustik*
Davisson, Ananias, *An Introduction to Sacred Music*

Horn, Karl F., *A Treatise on Harmony*
Momigny, Jérôme de, *La seule vraie théorie de la Musique*
Mortimer, Peter, *Choralgesang zur Zeit der Reformation*
Raynouard, F., *Choix de Poésies originales des Troubadours*
Relfe, John, *Lucidus Ordo*
Stöpel, Franz, *Grundzuge der Geschichte der modernen Musik*
Telemann, Georg, *Über die wahl der melodie eines Kirchenliedes*

I. Musical Compositions:
Auber, Daniel, *Emma* (opera)
Beethoven, Ludwig van, *Piano Sonata No. 31, Opus 110*
Benoist, François, *Léonore et Félix* (opera)
Carafa, Michele, *Jeanne d'Arc a Orlèans* (opera)
Carnicer, Ramón, *Elena e Constantino* (opera)
Cherubini, Luigi, *Blanche de Provence* (opera)
Clementi, Muzio, *3 Piano Sonatas, Opus 50*
Field, John, *Nocturnes No. 7 and 8 for Piano*
    Exercice Nouveau in C
Generali, Pietro, *Elena e Olfredo* (opera)
    La festa maraviglione (opera)
Kalliwoda, Johann, *Concerto, Opus 9, for Violin and Orchestra*
Kuhlau, Friedrich, *Piano Sonata, Opus 34*
    Quartet, Opus 32, for 4 Flutes
Kurpinski, Karol, *Kasimir der Grosse* (opera)
    Der schatten des fürsten Josef Poniatowski (opera)
    Der Forster aus dem wald vor Kozienice (opera)
Lesueur, Jean F., *Alexandre à Babylone* (opera)
Lortzing, Albert, *Overture alla Turca*
Marschner, Heinrich, *Prinz Friedrich von Homburg* (incidental music)
Mendelssohn, Felix, *Piano Sonata, Opus 105*
Mercadante, Saverio, *Andronico* (opera)
    Elisa e Claudio (opera)
Meyerbeer, Giacomo, *L'Almanzore* (unfinished opera)
Morlacchi, Francesco, *Donna Aurora* (opera)
    La gioventu di Enrico V (opera)
    La morte d'Abel (oratorio)
Pacini, Giovanni, *Cesare in Egitto* (opera)
Paër, Ferdinando, *La Maître de Chapelle* (opera)
    Blanche de Provence (opera)
Reissiger, Carl G., *Overture, Das Rockenweibchen, Opus 10*
Rossini, Gioacchino, *Matilde di Shabran* (opera)
    La riconoscenza (cantata)
Schubert, Franz, *Symphony No. 7* (sketches only)
    12 Waltzes for Piano, D. 145
Spohr, Louis, *Concerto No. 3 for Clarinet and Orchestra*
Spontini, Gaspare, *Lalla Rookh* (opera)
Vorísek, Jan, *Symphony in D*
Weber, Carl Maria von, *Der Freischütz* (opera)
    Die Drei Pintos (unfinished opera)
    Konzertstücke, Opus 70, for Piano and Orchestra
Weigl, Joseph, *König Waldemar* (opera)
    Edmund und Caroline (opera)
Zelter, Carl F., *Neue Lieder* (voice and piano)

1822

World Events:
In the U.S., Boston, Massachusetts (founded in 1630) is incorporated; Florida is made into a U.S. Territory; Congress works to establish relations with the newly independent South American countries; Gardiner Lyceum becomes the first technical institute in the U.S.; future presidents Rutherford B. Hayes and Ulysses S. Grant are born; a slave rebellion in South Carolina is crushed. Internationally, Brazil and Peru win their independence from Portugal and Spain respectively; the Congress of Verona studies the Spanish rebellion problem; Turkish troops invade Greece and massacre the Greek inhabitants of Chios; the Republic of Haiti is formed; French scientist Louis Pasteur is born.

Cultural Highlights:
The first free public library in the U.S. opens in Dublin, New Hampshire; François de Chateaubriand is appointed French ambassador to London; Henry Raeburn is knighted; Louis Daguerre and Charles Bouton open the Diorama in Paris. Births in the art field include French artist Rosa Bonheur and American artists George Fuller and Thomas Read; deaths include Italian sculptor Antonio Canova, German artist Franz Kobell and British artist Arthur Devis. Births in the literary field include American authors Edward Everett Hale and Thomas Hughes, French author Edmond de Goncourt, Russian novelist Dmitri Grigorovich, German author Alfred von Meissner and British poet and critic Matthew Arnold. Other highlights include:

Art: Antonio Canova, *The Fainting Magdalen*; Eugène Delacroix, *Dante and Virgil in Hell*; David Friedrich, *Wreck of the Hope*; Wilhelm Hensel, *Felix Mendelssohn*; John Martin, *The Destruction of Herculaneum*; Charles Peale, *The Artist in His Museum*; Richard Westmacott, *Achilles* (Hyde Park); David Wilkie, *Chelsea Prisoners Reading*

Literature: George Lord Byron, *The Vision of Judgment*; Antônio Castilho, *Amor e Melancolia*; Johann von Goethe, *Trilogie der Leidenshaft*; Heinrich Heine, *Gedichte*; Washington Irving, *Bracebridge Hall*; Charles Nodler, *Trilby*; Alexander Pushkin, *Eugen Onegin*; Walter Scott, *The Fortunes of Nigel*; Percy B. Shelley, *The Triumph of Life*

MUSICAL EVENTS

A. Births:

Jan 8	Alfredo C. Piatti (It-cel)	Jul 22	Luigi Arditi (It-cm)
Jan 13	Félix Clément (Fr-the-mus)	Aug 15	Wilhelm Rust (Ger-org)
Jan 15	Salvatore Marchesi (It-bar)	Aug 17	Louis Gueymard (Fr-ten)
Feb 26	Franz Strauss (Ger-hn)	Sep 30	Charles Battaille (Fr-bs)
Feb 27	Jean Gautier (Fr-cm)	Oct 13	Karl Reinthaler (Ger-cm-cd)
Mar 7	Victor Massé (Fr-cm)	Oct 15	Kornél Abrányi (Hun-pn)
Apr 13	Gaetano Valeri (It-cm)	Dec 5	Ferdinand Sieber (Aus-bar)
May 22	Henry Wylde (Br-cm-cd)	Dec 10	Cèsar Franck (Fr-org-cm)
May 27	Joseph J. Raff (Ger-cm)	Dec 12	Hermine Rudersdorff (Rus-sop)
May 31	Rafael Hernándo (Sp-cm)	Dec 14	Baldassare Gamucci (It-cm)
Jun 17	Enrico Delle Sedie (It-bar)	Dec 16	Charles E. Horsley (Br-org)

B. Deaths:

Jan 19	Charles Knyvett (Br-c.ten)	Jul 24	E.T.A. Hoffmann (Ger-cm-au)
Feb 2	Jean Baptiste Davaux (Fr-cm)	Aug 25	William Herschel (Br-astr-cm)
Mar 2	Christian F. Uber (Ger-cm)	Sep 8	Joseph Ambrosch (Ger-ten)
Mar 29	Johann Hässler (Ger-org)	Oct 27	Christian Schwencke (Ger-cd)
Apr 20	Wilhelm Biese (Ger-pn.m)	Nov 18	George K. Jackson (Am-cm-ed)
May 9	Charles Duquesnoy (Bel-ten)	Nov 18	Anton Teyber (Aus-cm)
May 15	Christian Dieter (Ger-vn)	Nov 19	Martin Teyber (Bel-bs)
Jul 19	Johann G. Werner (Ger-org)	Nov 26	Johann Henneberg (Aus-org)

Dec 13   Franz X. Gebauer (Ger-org)   Luigi Caruso (It-cm)
Dec 29   Albert C. Dies (Ger-art-mus)

C. Debuts:
Other - Maria Caradori-Allen (London), Sabina Heinefetter (Frankfurt am Mainz), Lambert Massart (Liège), Mary Anne Paton (London)

D. New Positions:
Conductors: Pamphile L. Aimon (French Theater, Paris), José Elizaga (maestro de capilla, Mexico City), Johann Wenzel Kalliwoda (Donaueschingen), Konradin Kreutzer (Kärnthnertor Theater, Vienna), George F. Perry (Haymarket Theatre, London), Friedrich Ludwig Seidel (kapellmeister, Berlin), Louis Spohr (kapellmeister, Kassel)

Educational: Thomas Attwood (Royal Academy, London), Thomas Greatorex (organ and piano, Royal Academy), Robert Lindley (cello, Royal Academy), Philip Cipriani Potter (piano, Royal Academy, London), Carl Friedrich Zelter (director, Royal Institute for Church Music, Berlin)

Others: François-Henri Blaze (music critic, *Journal des Débats*), George T. Smart (organ, Chapel Royal, London)

E. Prizes and Honors:
Honors: Pierre N. Guérin (French Academy, Rome), François Habeneck (Legion of Honor), Niccolò Zingarelli (knighted)

F. Biographical Highlights:
Hector Berlioz abandons medicine and begins the serious study of music with Lesueur; Frédéric Chopin begins the study of piano with Elsner; Gaetano Donizetti enjoys his first real success in Rome with his *Zoraide di Granata*; Mikhail Glinka leaves school and becomes a musical dilettante; Johann Hummel travels in Russia and meets Field; Charles Incledon retires from the stage; Felix Mendelssohn meets Spohr and Hiller and travels in Switzerland; Giuseppina Ronzi de Begnis makes her Covent Garden debut; Gioacchino Rossini finally marries soprano Isabella Colbran and meets with Beethoven; Anton Schindler gives up the study of law to devote full time to music and Beethoven; Franz Schubert finally gets to meet Beethoven and Weber; Henriette Sontag makes her Vienna Opera debut; Antonio Tamburini makes his La Scala debut; Filippo Traetta settles in Philadelphia as a private music teacher; Johann Vogl retires from the stage; Jan Vorísek abandons civil service after one year when he is appointed organist of the Vienna court; Richard Wagner enters the Kreuzschule in Dresden.

G. Institutional Openings:
Performing Groups: Jubal Society (Hartford); Sociedad Filarmónica (Buenos Aires); Sociedade Philarmonica (Lisbon); Società Filarmonica (Bergamo)

Educational: Akademie für Kirchenmusik (Berlin); American Conservatorio (Philadelphia); Escuela de Música y Canto (Buenos Aires); Linz Music Academy (Bruckner Conservatorium); Royal Academy of Music (London); Trieste Academy of Music

Other: *Aurora* (Hungary); Cologne Theater; Andreas Mollenhauer, Woodwind Maker (Vienna); Theater in der Josefstadt (Vienna); P. J. Tonger, Music Publisher and Retailer (Cologne)

H. Musical Literature:
Deshayes, Prosper-Didier, *Idées générales sur l'Académie royale de musique*
Glöggl, Franz X., *Der musikalische Gottesdienst*
Hastings, Thomas, *Dissertation on Musical Tastes*
Hempel, Charles, *Introduction to the Pianoforte...*

Hering, Karl G., *Zittauer Choralbuch*
Mason, Lowell, *Handel and Haydn Society's Collection of Church Music*
Natorp, Bernhard, *Melodienbuch*
Pastou, Etienne, *École de la lyre harmonique*
Perne, François, *Cours d'harmonie et d'accompagnement*
Weber, Gottfried, *Allgemeine Musiklehre zum Selbstunterrichte*

I. Musical Compositions:

Auber, Daniel, *Leicester* (opera)
Beethoven, Ludwig von, *Consecration of the House Overture, Opus 124*
    Piano Sonata No. 32, Opus 111
    Arietta, "The Kiss," Opus 128 (piano)
Bishop, Henry, *Maid Marion* (opera)
Carafa, Michele, *Le solitaire* (opera)
Carnicer, Ramón, *Don Giovanni Tenoria* (opera)
Cavos, Catterino, *The Firebird* (opera)
Donizetti, Gaetano, *La zingara* (opera)
    Zoriada di Granata (opera)
    Chiara e Serafina (opera)
    La lettera anonima (opera)
Generali, Pietro, *Argene e Alsindo* (opera)
    La sposa indiana (opera)
Halévy, Jacques, *Marco Curzio* (opera)
Kreutzer, Konradin, *Libussa* (opera)
Kurpinski, Karol, *Die drei Grazien* (ballet)
Liszt, Franz, *Variations on a Diabelli Waltz* (piano)
Mendelssohn, Felix, *String Symphony No. 8*
    Piano Quartet No. 1, Opus 1
Mercadante, Saverio, *Amleto* (opera)
    Il posto abbandonato (opera)
    Alfonso ed Elisa (opera)
Meyerbeer, Giacomo, *L'esule di Granata* (opera)
Morlacchi, Francesco, *Tebaldo e Isolina* (opea)
Pacini, Giovanni, *Il puro omaggio* (cantata)
Perry, George, *Morning, Noon and Night* (opera)
Reicha, Anton, *Sapho* (opera)
Rossini, Gioacchino, *Zelmira* (opera)
Schubert, Franz, *Symphony No. 8, "Unfinished"*
    Alfonso und Estrella (opera)
    Piano Fantasy, "The Wanderer"
    Mass No. 5 in A-flat Major, D. 678
    Mass, D. 755, "Für meinen Bruder Ferdinand"
    Wanderer's Nachtlied
Spohr, Louis, *3 String Quartets, Opus 58*
Spontini, Gaspare, *Nurmahal* (opera)
Vertovsky, Alexei, *New Mischief* (opera)
    The Madhouse (opera)
Weber, Carl Maria von, *Den Sachsen Sohn* (incidental music)
    Piano Sonata No. 4, Opus 70
    Marcia Vivace in D (10 trumpets and orchestra)

1823

World Events:
In the U.S., President James Monroe proclaims his Monroe Doctrine warning the European nations to steer clear of the Americas; the steamboat *Virginia* becomes the first on the Mississippi River; the first teacher's training school opens in Concord, Vermont; Fort Brook, on the site of present-day Tampa, is founded in Florida. Internationally, several states unite to form the United Provinces of Central America; Ferdinand VII revokes the Spanish Constitution and, with French help, crushes the people's rebellion; the British Anti-Slavery Society is founded; a patent is given for a digital calculating machine.

Cultural Highlights:
Walter Scott founds the Bannatyne Club and becomes the first President; the *New York Mirror and Ladies Literary Gazette* begins publication. Births in the art field include American artists Jaspar F. Cropsey and William H. Powell and French artist Alexandre Cabanel; deaths include British sculptor Joseph Nollekens, Scottish artist Henry Raeburn and French artist Pierre-Paul Prud'hon. The literary world witnesses the births of American authors Thomas Higginson and Francis Parkman and poet George H. Boker, British poet and critic Coventry Patmore, French poet Théodore de Banville, German poet and novelist Oskar von Redwitz, Russian dramatist Alexander Ostrowsky, Hungarian poet Sándor Petofi and Brazilian poet Antônio Dias. Other highlights include:

Art: John Constable, *Salisbury Cathedral*; Asher Durand, *Signing of the Declaration of Independence*; Jean L. Géricault, *The Kiln*; Henry Inman, *Rip Van Winkle Awakening*; Charles Peale, *After the Bath*; Robert Smirke, *British Museum*; Joseph Turner, *Bay of Baiae*; Ferdinand Waldmüller, *Ludwig van Beethoven*; James Ward, *Deer Stealer*

Literature: George Lord Byron, *The Island*; James F. Cooper, *The Pioneers*; Victor Ducange, *Léonide*; William Hazlitt, *Liber Amoris*; Alphonse de Lamartine, *Nouvelles Méditations Poétiques*; Charles Lamb, *Essays of Elia*; Clement Moore, *The Night Before Christmas*; Friedrich Rückert, *Liebesfrühling*; Walter Scott, *Quentin Durward*

MUSICAL EVENTS

A. Births:

Jan 5	William S. Rockstro (Br-mus)		Apr 15	Theodor Hagen (Ger-cri)
Jan 17	Jean Vogt (Ger-pn-cm)		Aug 3	Francisco Barbieri (Sp-mus)
Jan 27	Edouard Lalo (Fr-cm)		Oct 5	Vincenzo Battista (It-cm)
Feb 7	Richard Genée (Ger-cm-lib)		Oct 13	Immanuel Faisst (Ger-org)
Mar 2	Julius Hesse (Ger-pn)		Oct 21	P. Arriete y Correra (Sp-cm)
Mar 10	John B. Dykes (Br-hymn)		Oct 23	Emilio Naudin (Fr-ten)
Mar 10	Theodor Wachtel (Ger-ten)		Nov 26	Thomas Tellefsen (Nor-pn)
Mar 16	William H. Monk (Br-org)		Dec 1	Louis E. Reyer (Fr-cm)
Apr 4	Otto Gumprecht (Ger-cri)		Dec 15	Friedrich Schwencke (Ger-org)
				Achille Errani (It-ten)

B. Deaths:

Jan	Matthew P. King (Br-cm)		Oct 2	Daniel Steibelt (Ger-pn)
Feb 16	Johann G. Schicht (Ger-cm)		Oct 26	Joseph Preindl (Aus-cm)
Mar	John E. Betts (Br-vn.m)		Nov 12	Emanuel Förster (Aus-cm)
Mar 1	Pierre Jean Garat (Fr-ten)		Dec 7	Johann G. Schwencke (Ger-bn)
Mar 18	Jean B. Bréval (Fr-cel)		Dec 19	François Chanot (Fr-vn.m)
Apr	Jacob Wiederkehr (Fr-cm)		Dec 19	Nicolas Hüllmandel (Fr-hp)
May 25	Auguste Leduc (Fr-mus-pub)		Dec 24	Philipp Kayser (Ger-pn)
Jun 20	Theodor von Schacht (Ger-cm)			Thomas H. Butler (Br-ten)

C. Debuts:
   Other - Michael Balfe (as violinist), Mary Anne Goward (Dublin)

D. New Positions:
   Conductors: Johan F. Berwald (kapellmeister, Stockholm), Ferdinand Fränzl (kapellmeister, Munich), Johann Gänsbacher (kapellmeister, Vienna Cathedral), Johann H. Kufferath (music director, Bielefeld), Giuseppe Mosca (Messina Opera), Friedrich Seidel (kapellmeister, Berlin), Joseph Strauss (kapellmeister, Mannheim)

   Educational: Carlo Coccia (composition, Royal Academy, London), Vicenzo Lavigna (Milan Conservatory), Joseph Merk (cello, Vienna Conservatory), Christian Theodor Weinlig (cantor, Thomasschule, Leipzig)

   Others: William Ayrton (editor, *Harmonicon*), Karl Friedrich Horn (organ, St. George's, Windsor), Jan Václav Vorísek (organ, Vienna Court)

E. Prizes and Honors:
   Honors: Józef A. Elsner (Order of St. Stanislaw)

F. Biographical Highlights:
   Violante Camporese retires from the opera stage; Heinrich Dorn is forced into the study of law by his family; Mikhail Glinka visits the Caucasus region of Russia; Josephina Grassini retires to live in Milan; Thomas Hastings moves to Uttica, New York; Franz Liszt travels with his father to Paris and plays for Beethoven and Schubert in Vienna and studies music with Salieri; Albert Lortzing marries actress Rosina Ahles; Heinrich Marschner joins Weber and Morlacchi as joint kapellmeisters in Dresden; Giacomo Meyerbeer tries unsuccessfully to have his operas performed in Berlin; Carl Proske gives up medicine for theology; Gioacchino Rossini moves to Paris and visits in London; Wilhemine Schröder marries actor Karl Devrient; Fernando Sor goes to Russia to oversee the production of his ballets; Giuseppe Verdi is sent to Busseto for music study; Alexei Vertovsky moves to Moscow; Carl Maria von Weber corresponds with Beethoven and finally gets to meet him in Baden.

G. Institutional Openings:
   Performing Groups: Freiberg Singakademie; Geneva Musical Society; Lüneburg Musikverein; New York Sacred Music Society

   Festivals: Yorkshire Music Festival (Bradford)

   Educational: Accademie di Revvivati (Pisa); Agthe-Kräger Music Academy (Dresden); American Conservatorio (Philadelphia)

   Other: Briedenstein's Musikalischer Apparet (University of Bonn); George Chanot Violin Co. (Paris); Robert Cocks and Co., Music Publishers (London); Ewer and Co. Music Publishers (London); Hibernicon (patented by J.R. Cotter); *Muse Française*; R. and W. Nunns, Piano Makers; Probst (Kistner's) Music Publishing Co. (Leipzig); Jean Savary, Bassoon Maker (Paris); Wessel and Stodart, Music Publishers (London); Zwickau Theater

H. Musical Literature:
   Asioli, Bonifazio, *Elementi di Contrabasso...*
   Elizaga, José, *Elementos de música*
   Gould, Nathaniel, *Social Harmony*
   Heinroth, Johann, *Gesangunterrichts-Methode*
   Kocher, Conrad, *Die Tonkunst in der Kirche*
   Nathan, Isaac, *An Essay on the History and Theory of Music...*
   Tritto, Giacomo, *Scuola di contrappunto*
   Urban, Christian, *Über die Musik, deren theorie und den musikunterricht*
   Werner, Johann, *Orgelschule II*

I. Musical Compositions:

Auber, Daniel, *La neige* (opera)
Beethoven, Ludwig von, *Symphony No. 9, Opus 125, "Choral"*
    Missa Solemnis, Opus 123
    Cantata, Opus 199
    Diabelli Variations, Opus 12 (piano)
    Bundeslied, Opus 122
    7 Bagatelles, Opus 126 (piano)
Berlioz, Hector, *Estelle et Nemorin* (opera)
    Le passage de la Mer rouge (oratorio)
Bishop, Henry, *Cortez* (opera)
    Clari (opera)
Boieldieu, François, *La France et l'Espagne* (opera)
Carafa, Michele, *Le valet de chambre* (opera)
Donizetti, Gaetano, *Alfredo il grande* (opera)
    Il fortunato inganno (opera)
Field, John, *Piano Concerto No. 6*
Generali, Pietro, *Chiara di Rosemberg* (opera)
    Le nozze fra Nemici (opera)
Hérold, Ferdinand, *Le muletier* (opera)
    Lasthénie (opera)
Klein, Bernhard, *Dido* (opera)
Kurpinski, Karol, *Krakauer hochzeit* (ballet)
    Concerto for Clarinet and Orchestra
Lesueur, Jean F., *Alexandre à Babylone* (opera)
Marschner, Heinrich, *Der Holzdieb* (opera)
    Schön Ella (incidental music)
    Ali Baba (incidental music)
Mason, Lowell, *Missionary Hymn* (From Greenland's Icy Mountains)
Mendelssohn, Felix, *String Symphonies No. 10-12*
    Piano Quartet No. 2, Opus 2
Mercadante, Saverio, *Didone abbandonata* (opera)
Meyerbeer, Giacomo, *Costanza ed Almeriska* (opera)
Moscheles, Ignaz, *Piano Concerto No. 4, Opus 64*
Reicha, Anton, *Grand Overture in D Major*
Ricci, Luigi, *L'impresario in angustie* (opera)
Rossini, Gioacchino, *Semiramide* (opera)
    La vera omaggio (cantata)
Schneider, Friedrich, *The Deluge* (oratorio)
Schubert, Franz, *Rosamunde* (incidental music)
    Die Schöne Müllerin (song cycle)
    Fierabras, D. 796 (opera)
    Der Häusliche Krieg (opera)
    Rüdiger (opera)
    Piano Sonata No. 16, D. 784
    12 German Dances, D. 790
Sor, Fernando, *Cendrillon* (opera)
Spohr, Louis, *Jessonda* (opera)
    String Quartet in A, Opus 68
    Double Quartet, Opus 65
Titov, Alexei, *The Mogul's Feast* (opera)
Weber, Carl Maria von, *Euryanthe* (opera)
Weigl, Joseph, *Die eiserne Pforte* (opera)

1824

World Events:

In the U.S., none of the four presidential candidates have an electoral majority, so Congress picks John Quincy Adams as President No. 6; the Bureau of Indian Affairs is created in the War Department; frontiersman Jim Bridger becomes the first white man to visit the Great Salt Lake; a frontier treaty is signed with Russia; future General "Stonewall" Jackson is born. Internationally, Colombia wins its independence in South America; the first Burmese War begins with the British taking Rangoon; Charles X begins his reign in France; Civil War breaks out in the Ottoman Empire; Joseph Aspdin patents a process for obtaining Portland Cement.

Cultural Highlights:

The London National Gallery opens; Antoine Jean Gros is given a baronet; Jean Auguste Ingres is inducted into the Legion of Honor; Kasper Friedrich begins teaching at the Dresden Art Academy; Carl Begas becomes editor of the *New York Mirror and Ladies Literary Journal*. Births in the art world include American artists William Hunt and J. Eastman Johnson, French artists Eugène Boudin and Pierre de Chavannes and German artist Heinrich Hofmann; deaths include British artist John Downman, French artists Anne-Louis Girodet-Trioson and Théodore Gèricault and German artist Johann von Langer. Births in the literary field include British novelist Wilkie Collins and poet Sidney Dobell, Irish poet William Allingham, German poet Otto Roquette, American author George Curtis and poet Phoebe Cary, French novelist Alexander Dumas, fils, Italian poet and historian Ignazio Ciampi and Russian poet Ivan Nikitin; deaths include British novelist Sophie Lee and poet Georges Lord Byron and Scottish poet Alexander Campbell. Other highlights include:

Art: Jacques-Louis David, *Mars and Venus*; Eugène Delacroix, *Massacre of Chios*; John Flaxman, *The Pastoral Apollo*; Edwin Landseer, *The Cat's Paw*; Alexander Nasmyth, *The Lawn Market*; Friedrich Overbeck, *Christ Entering Jerusalem*; William Strickland, *Second Bank of Philadelphia*; Joseph Turner, *The Lock*

Literature: George Lord Byron, *Don Juan XVI*; Susan Ferrier, *The Inheritance*; James Hogg, *Confessions of a Justified Sinner*; Washington Irving, *Tales of a Traveler*; Letitia Landon, *The Improvisatrice*; Walter Landor, *Imaginary Conversations I*; Walter Scott, *Redgauntlet*; Percy B. Shelley, *The Witch of Atlas*; Alfred de Vigny, *Éloa*

MUSICAL EVENTS

A. Births:

Jan 5	Utto Kornmüller (Ger-mus)	Jul 26	Moritz Fürstenau (Ger-fl)
Jan 9	Francesco Malipiero (It-cm)	Aug 1	Edward Fitzwilliam (Br-cm)
Jan 14	Vladimir Stasov (Rus-mus)	Aug 23	Emanuel Aguilar (Br-pn)
Jan 25	James Coward (Br-org)	Sep 4	Anton Bruckner (Aus-cm)
Feb 22	Richard Wuerst (Ger-cm)	Oct 24	Hermann Wichmann (Ger-cd)
Mar 2	Bedrich Smetana (Boh-cm)	Dec 12	Rudolf Genée (Ger-mus-cri)
Mar 5	Anne Charton-Demeur (Fr-mez)	Dec 24	Peter Cornelius (Ger-cm)
Apr 12	Joseph Barbot (Fr-ten)		Eliza Biscaccianti (Am-sop)
May 24	Carlo-Romani (It-cm)		Pasquale Brignoli (It-ten)
Jun 23	Carl Reinecke (Ger-pn-cm)		

B. Deaths:

Jan 8	Josefa Dusek (Cz-sop)	Apr 5	Francesco Benucci (It-bs)
Feb 1	Marie von Paradies (Aus-pn)	Apr 18	Edward Jones (Br-hp)
Feb 4	Franz Bühler (Ger-cd)	May 22	Joseph Kemp (Br-org)
Feb 22	John Davy (Br-cm)	Jun 24	Henry Condell (Br-vn)
Mar 3	Giovanni Viotti (It-vn)	Jul 24	William Forster, Jr. (Br-vn.m)
Mar 22	Johann Dreyer (Ger-cm)	Aug 21	Santiago Ferrer (Sp-cm)

Sep 16   Giacomo Tritto (It-cm)   Nov 30   Johann Schetky (Ger-cel)
Oct 25   Barnaba Bonesi (It-the)   Karl Baumgarten (Ger-org)
Nov 30   Luigi Mosca (It-cm)   Jacques G. Cousineau (Fr-hp.m)

C. Debuts:
Other - Matilde Palazzesi (Dresden), Henry Phillips (London), August Pott (Kassel),
Caroline Unger (Vienna)

D. New Positions:
Conductors: Henry Bishop (Drury Lane), Josef Blahack (kapellmeister, St.
Peter's, Vienna), Carlo Coccia (King's Theatre, London), Joseph Eybler (kapellmeister,
Vienna), François Habeneck (Paris Opera), Karol Kurpinski (Warsaw Opera),
Heinrich Marschner (Dresden Court), Giovanni Polledro (maestro di cappella, Turin),
Pietro Raimondi (Royal Theater, Naples), Gioacchino Rossini (Italian Theater, Paris),
Joseph Strauss (Karlsruhe Court)

Educational: John Chatterton (harp, Royal Academy, London)

Others: Thomas Adams (organ, St. George's, Camberwell), Adolf Marx (editor,
Allgemeine Musikalische Zeitung), Gottfried Weber (editor, *Cäcilia*)

E. Prizes and Honors:
Honors: Rodolphe Kreutzer (Legion of Honor), Stanislao Mattei (French Institute)

F. Biographical Highlights:
Adolphe Adam receives honorable mention in the Prix de Rome competition; Anna
(Rivière) Bishop enters the Royal Academy of Music; Frèdèric Chopin is admitted to
the Warsaw Lyceum; Isabella Colbran retires from the stage; Mikhail Glinka takes a
post in the Russian Ministry of Communications; Frèdèric Kalkbrenner becomes a
partner in the Pleyel Piano Co. in Paris; Franz Liszt, concertizing in England, plays
for King George IV; Adolf Marx receives his Ph.D. degree in law from the University
of Halle but chooses to carry on in music; Niccolò Paganini begins a liason with
Antonia Bianchi; Benedetta Pisaroni makes her La Scala debut as an alto; Anton
Schindler, accused of financial cheating, is thrown out of the house (temporarily) by
Beethoven; Václav Tomásek marries Wilhelmine Ebert and opens his own music
school; Jan Vorísek goes to Graz to find a cure for his ailments; Richard Wagner
takes some piano lessons, but finds the opera more interesting; Carl Maria von Weber
receives a commission from London for a new opera.

G. Institutional Openings:
Performing Groups: Accademia Filarmonica (Cagliari); Athenaeum Club (London);
Basler Gesangverein; Königsberg Liedertafel; Luxembourg Philharmonic Society; New
Orleans Philharmonic Society; Norwich Choral Society; Sociedad Filharmónica
(Mexico City); Stuttgarter Liederkranz

Festivals: Norfolk and Norwich Triennial Music Festival

Educational: Benvenuti Music School (Pisa); Mees Music Academy (Antwerp)

Other: *Berliner Allgemeine Musikalische Zeitung*; *Cäcilia* (Mannheim); Camp Street
Theater (New Orleans); Johann B. Cramer and Co., Ltd., Music Publishers (London);
Königstädtisches Theater (Berlin); *Westminster Review*

H. Musical Literature:
Bacon, Richard, *Elements of Vocal Science*
Campagnoli, Bartolomeo, *Nouvelle méthode de la mecanique...du jeu de violon*
Carpani, Giuseppe, *Lettere Musico-Teatrali*
Fétis, François-Joseph, *Traité du contrepoint et de la fugue*
La Salette, Joubert de, *De la fixité et de l'invariabilité des sons musicaux*
Mount-Edgcumbe, Richard, *Musical Reminiscences*

Reicha, Anton, *Traité de haute composition musicale I*
Rochlitz, Johann F., *Für Freunde der Tonkunst I*
Sainsbury, John H., *A Dictionary of Musicians*
Urban, Christian, *Theorie der Musik nach Rein Naturgemässen Grundsätzen*

I. Musical Compositions:

Auber, Daniel, *Léocadie* (opera)
    Le concert à la cour (opera)
    Les trois genres (opera, with Boieldieu)
Beethoven, Ludwig van, *String Quartet No. 12, Opus 127*
    Variations, Opus 121a (violin, cello, piano)
Carafa, Michele, *L'auberge supposée* (opera)
Chopin, Frederic, *Mazurka in A-flat Major, Opus 7, No. 4*
Donizetti, Gaetano, *Emilia di Liverpool* (opera)
Glinka, Mikhail, *Overture in G Minor*
    Overture in D Major
    Andante and Rondo in D Minor (orchestra)
    String Quartet No. 1
Hérold, Ferdinand, *Les deux Pavillons* (opera)
    Le roi René (opera)
Kreutzer, Konradin, *Erfüllte Hoffnung* (opera)
Kuhlau, Friedrich, *Lulu* (opera)
Loewe, Carl, *Piano Sonata, Opus 47, "Le Printemps"*
    3 Ballads, Opus 2
Lortzing, Albert, *Ali Pascha von Janina* (opera)
Mendelssohn, Felix, *Symphony No. 1, Opus 11*
    Overture for Winds, Opus 24
    Piano Sextet, Opus 110
Mercadante, Saverio, *Nitocri* (opera)
    Doralice (opera)
    Gli amici di Siracusa (opera)
    Le nozze di Telemaco ed Antiope (opera)
Meyerbeer, Giacomo, *Il crociato in Egitto* (opera)
Morlacchi, Francesco, *Ilda d'Avenello* (opera)
Pacini, Giovanni, *Alessandro nelle Indie* (opera)
Reicha, Anton, *Grand Overture in E-flat Major*
    Quartet for Piano and Woodwinds, Opus 104
Reissiger, Carl, *Didone abbandonata* (opera)
Schmidt, Johann, *Das verborgene fenster* (singspiel)
Schubert, Franz, *String Quartet in A Minor, D. 804*
    String Quartet, D. 810, "Death and the Maiden"
    Octet in F Major, Opus 166
    16 German Dances, D. 783 (piano)
    20 Waltzes, D. 146 (piano)
    34 Valses Sentimentales, D. 779 (piano)
Tadolini, Giovanni, *Moctar* (opera)
Thrane, Waldemar, *A Mountain Adventure* (opera)
Vaccai, Nicola, *Pietro il grande* (opera)
    La pastorella feudataria (opera)
Vertovsky, Alexei, *Who Is Brother? Who Is Sister?* (opera)
    Teacher and Pupil (opera)
    The Petitioner (opera)
Vorísek, Václav, *Mass in B-flat Major*
Weinlig, Christian, *Unser Vater in den seel'gen Höhen* (cantata)

1825

World Events:

In the U.S., the Erie Canal is opened for shipping by DeWitt Clinton, governor of New York; Congress seeks to move all Indians to reservations west of the Mississippi River; T. Kensett patents the tin can; Omaha, Nebraska, is established as a fur trading post; the community of New Harmony, Indiana, is founded. Internationally, the country of Bolivia gains its independence; trade unions are officially legalized in Europe; Nicholas I becomes Czar of Russia and crushes the Decembrists revolt; the Dutch put down revolts in Java and consolidate their control over the area; R. Keeley of England invents the farm tractor.

Cultural Highlights:

The Hudson River School of Art comes into being as does the New York Drawing Association; Emil Cauer begins teaching art in the University of Bonn and Lorenzo da Ponte Italian literature at Columbia University; Jean Auguste Ingres is inducted into the French Institute. Births in the field of art include American sculptors Benjamin P. Akers, William Rinehart and Randolph Rogers and artist George Inness; deaths include Swiss artist and author Henry Füseli and French artist Jacques-Louis David. Births in the literary field include Scottish novelist Robert Ballantyne, British authors Richard Blackmore and Thomas H. Huxley, Swiss author Conrad Meyer and Russian poet Aleksei N. Plescheyev; deaths include Italian poet Giuseppe Carpani, German poet and artist Friedrich Müller and author Jean Paul Richter. Other highlights include:

Art: John Constable, *The Leaping Horse*; Jean Corot, *Homer on the Isle of Patmos*; Thomas Lawrence, *The Red Boy*; Samuel Morse, *The Marquis de Lafayette*; Friedrich Overbeck, *Madonna and Child*; Pierre-Paul Prud'hon, *The Crucifixion*

Literature: John Banim, *Tales of the O'Hara Family I*; Samuel Taylor Coleridge, *Aids to Reflection*; Franz Grillparzer, *König Ottokars Glück und Ende*; William Hazlitt, *The Spirit of the Age*; Alphonse de Lamartine, *Le Dernier Chant du Pèlerinage d'Harold*; Alexander Pushkin, *Boris Godounov*; Walter Scott, *The Talisman*

MUSICAL EVENTS

A. Births:

Jan 1	Joseph Goldberg (Aus-vn)	Aug 12	Frederick Ouseley (Br-cm)
Jan 10	Wulf C. Fries (Ger-cel)	Sep 10	Adolf von Doss (Ger-cm)
Jan 18	Léon Carvalho (Fr-imp)	Sep 11	Eduard Hanslick (Aus-cri)
Jan 26	François de Villars (Fr-mus)	Sep 30	Joseph Dachs (Ger-pn)
Feb 7	Mary Ann Gabriel (Br-pn)	Oct 25	Catherine Hayes (Ir-sop)
Apr 17	Alexander Reichardt (Hun-ten)	Oct 25	Johann Strauss, Jr. (Aus-cm)
May 12	Giuseppe de' Filippi (It-mus)	Nov 14	August Reissmann (Ger-mus)
Jun 30	Hervé (F. Rongé)(Fr-cm-imp)	Dec 7	M. Schnorr von Carolsfeld
Jul 24	Anne de la Grange (Fr-sop)		(Dan-sop)
Aug 2	Julius Schulhoff (Cz-pn)	Dec 19	George F. Bristow (Am-cm)

B. Deaths:

Feb 5	Pierre Gaveaux (Fr-ten)	Jul 10	Ludwig Fischer (Ger-bs)
Feb 24	Johann Buchholz (Ger-org.m)	Aug 3	Ambrogio Minoja (It-cd-cm)
Mar 24	Giovanni D. Perotti (It-cm)	Aug 17	Raynor Taylor (Br-cm)
Mar 29	Johannes A. Amon (Ger-hn)	Sep 13	Luigi Bassi (It-bar)
Apr 13	Josef Gelinek (Boh-cm)	Oct 6	Bernard Lacépède (Fr-the)
May 7	Antonio Salieri (It-cm)	Oct 10	Dmitri Bortniansky (Rus-cm)
May 12	Stanislav Mattei (It-m.ed)	Oct 17	Peter Winter (Ger-cm)
May 22	Domenico Corri (It-cm-cd)	Oct 25	Ignacio de Almeida (Por-cm)
May 22	Stepan J. Davydoff (Rus-cm)		

Nov 1   R. Ferraira da Costa (Por-the)   Dec 29   Giovanni Cambini (It-vn)
Nov 19 Jan Hugo Vorísek (Boh-cm)

C. Debuts:

U.S. -- Manuel García (N.Y.), Maria Malibran (N.Y.)

Other - Ferdinand David (Leipzig), Julie Aimée Dorus-Gras (Brussels), Gilbert-Louis Duprez (Paris), Antoine de Kontski (Warsaw), Maria Malibran (London), Eugéne Massol (Paris), Giovanni Rubini (Paris)

D. New Positions:

Conductors: Henry Bishop (Drury Lane), Jonathan Blewitt (Sadler's Wells), Adolf Ganz (kapellmeister, Darmstadt), Joseph Hartmann (Munich Opera), Karol Kurpinski (Warsaw Opera), Wilhelm Mangold (Darmstadt Court), Georg Schneider (Berlin Court), Giovanni Tadolini (maestro di cappella, Bologna Cathedral)

Educational: François Naderman (harp, Paris Conservatory), Pietro Raimondi (composition, Naples Conservatory), Francesco Ruggi (counterpoint and composition, Naples Conservatory)

Others: Karl F. Becker (organ, St. Peter's, Leipzig), John D. Corfe (organ, Bristol Cathedral), Karl von Lichtenstein (director, Berlin Opera), John Lockhart (editor, *Quarterly Review*), Johann Schneider (organ, Dresden Court), Ludwig Tieck (literary advisor, Dresden Court Theater), Alexei Vertovsky (Inspector of Theaters, Moscow)

E. Prizes and Honors:

Honors: Daniel-François Auber, Charles-Simon Catel and Johann Hummel (Legion of Honor), Giovanni Tadolini (Accademia Filarmonica, Bologna)

F. Biographical Highlights:

Adolphe Adam wins the second Prix de Rome; Dionysio Aguado moves to Paris where he meets Rossini and Paganini; Michael Balfe goes to Italy to study music; Maria Caradori-Allan makes her London debut; Charles Coussemaker begins the study of law; Félicien David enters a Jesuit College; Domenico Donzelli makes his Paris Opera debut; Joséphine Fodor-Mainville loses her voice during a Paris performance and retires from the stage; John Hill Hewitt has his first songs published; Ferdinand Hiller is sent to Weimar to study with Hummel; Friedrich Kuhlau, in Vienna, meets Beethoven; Franz Liszt makes a second concert tour to London; Felix Mendelssohn visits Paris and meets Cherubini, Rossini and Meyerbeer; Ignaz Moscheles marries Charlotte Embden and settles in London; Giuseppina Ronzi de Begnis leaves her husband and returns to Italy; Johann Strauss, Sr., marries Maria Streim; Anna Maria Tree retires from the stage; Giovanni Velutti makes his London debut; Luigi Zamboni retires from the stage.

G. Institutional Openings:

Performing Groups: García Italian Opera Co. (N.Y.); Joseph Labitzky Orchestra (Karlsbad); Société Philharmonique de Beauvais

Educational: Elíazaga Conservatory of Music (Mexico City)

Other: Aibl Music Publishers (Munich); Edwin Ashdown, Ltd., Music Publisher (London); Buffet Auger Woodwind Co. (Buffet-Crampon et Cie., Paris); Hart and Sons, Violin Makers (London); Lucca Music Publishing House (Milan); J.F. Schulze and Sons, Organ Builders (Mühlhausen); Eugéne Troupenas, Music Publisher (Paris); Warsaw Grand Theater; Weimar National Theater

H. Musical Literature:

Aguado, Dionysio, *Escuela o Método de Guitarra*
Bacon, Richard, *Art of Improving the Voice and Ear*
Balbi, Melchiore, *Grammatica ragionata della musica...*

Busby, Thomas, *Concert Room and Orchestral Anecdotes*
Horsley, William, *An Explanation of the Musical Intervals*
Nägeli, Hans, *Vorlesungen über Musik*
Savart, Félix, *Sur la voix humaine*
Thibaut, Anton, *Über Reinheit der Tonkunst*
Tröstler, Bernhard, *Traité général et raisonné de Musique*
Winter, Peter, *Vollständige singschule*

I. Musical Compositions:

Auber, Daniel, *Le maçon* (opera)
Balfe, Michael, *La Pérouse* (ballet)
Beethoven, Ludwig van, *String Quartet No. 13, Opus 130*
    String Quartet No. 15, Opus 132
    Grosse Fuge, Opus 133
Bellini, Vincenzo, *Adelson e Salvina* (opera)
Berlioz, Hector, *Resurrexit*
    Messe Solennelle
Bishop, Henry, *The Fall of Algiers* (opera)
Boieldieu, François, *La dame blanche* (opera)
Cherubini, Luigi, *Coronation Mass in A Major*
Chopin, Frédéric, *Rondo in C Minor, Opus 1*
    Polonaise, Opus 71, No. 1
Glinka, Mikhail, *Symphony in B-flat Major*
Hérold, Ferdinand, *Le lapin blanc* (opera)
Loewe, Carl, *Rudolph der deutsche Herr* (opera)
    3 Ballads, Opus 3
    Poems and Ballads, Opus 4
    6 Serbian Songs, Opus 15
Mendelssohn, Felix, *Die Hochzeit des Camacho, Opus 10* (opera)
    Concerto for 2 Pianos and Orchestra
    String Octet, Opus 20
    Violin Sonata, Opus 4
    Piano Quartet No. 3, Opus 3
Mercadante, Saverio, *Ipermestra* (opera)
Meyerbeer, Giacomo, *Ines di Castro* (opera)
Moscheles, Ignaz, *Piano Concerto No. 2, Opus 56*
Niedermeyer, Louis, *La casa nel bosco* (opera)
Pacini, Giovanni, *Il felice ritorno* (cantata)
    L'ultimo giorno di Pompei (opera)
Poissl, Johann, *Die Prinzessin von Provence* (opera)
Reicha, Anton, *Grand Overture in C Major*
    Chamber Symphony No. 1
Reissiger, Carl, *Overture, Der Ahrenschatz, Opus 80*
Rossini, Gioacchino, *Il viaggio a Reims* (opera)
Schubert, Franz, *Gastein Symphony* (lost)
    Piano Sonatas No. 17-19
    Ave Maria (song)
Spohr, Louis, *Macbeth* (incidental music)
    Der Berggeist (opera)
    Violin Concerto No. 11, Opus 70
Spontini, Gaspare, *Alcidor* (opera)
Vaccai, Nicola, *Giulietta e Romeo* (opera)
Vertovsky, Alexei, *The Caliph's Amusement* (opera)
    The Miraculous Nose (opera)
Weyse, Christoph, *Floribella* (opera)

1826

World Events:
In the U.S., Congress presents a cool front to the Pan-American Conference meeting in Panama to form plans for future conferences; the Treaty of Washington is signed with the Creek Indians; Kansas City is founded as a trading post on the Missouri River; the first working reaper is built by Henry Ogle; the internal combustion engine is patented by Samuel Morey; former Presidents John Adams and Thomas Jefferson die on the same day, July 4. Internationally, Saudi Arabia is formed from the conquests of Ibn Saud; the Treaty of Yandabu ends the First Burmese War; the Russo-Persian War begins; the massacre of the Janissaries takes place in Constantinople; Pedro IV of Portugal abdicates in favor of Maria II.

Cultural Highlights:
The National Academy of Design is founded with Samuel Morse as its first President; Rembrandt Peale becomes President of the American Academy of Fine Arts; Washington Irving joins the embassy staff in Madrid; Walter Scott loses his wife and his printing firm. Births in the art world include American artist Frederick Church, French artist Gustave Moreau and Italian artist Silvestro Lega; British sculptor John Flaxman dies. Deaths in the literary field include German poets Johann P. Hebel, Siegfried Mahlmann and Johann Voss and author Johannes Falk, Russian poet Kondrati Ryleyev, Danish poet Jens Baggesen and British poets William Gifford and Edward Williams; German poet Josef von Scheffel is born. Other highlights include:

Art: William Blake, *Illustrations on Job*; Richard Bonington, *A Mountain Landscape*; Jean B. Corot, *View of the Coliseum*; Eugéne Delacroix, *Greece on the Ruins of Missolonghi*; Francisco de Goya, *The Butcher's Table*; John Martin, *The Deluge*; William Strickland, *U.S. Naval Asylum* (Philadelphia); Joseph Turner, *The Cornfield*

Literature: Giovanni Casanova, *Mémoires I*; François de Chateaubriand, *Les Adventures du Dernier des Abencérages*; James F. Cooper, *The Last of the Mohicans*; Benjamin Disraeli, *Vivian Grey*; Joseph von Eichendorff, *Aus dem Leben eines Taugenichts*; William Hazlitt, *The Plain Speaker*; Karl Nicander, *The Death of Tasso*

MUSICAL EVENTS

A. Births:

Mar 5	Hans Balatka (Cz-cd)		Jul 22	Julius Stockhausen (Ger-bar)
Mar 6	Marietta Alboni (It-alto)		Aug 9	Adelaide Borghi (It-mez)
Mar 12	Jeanne Cruvelli (Ger-sop)		Sep 6	Vladimir Kashperov (Rus-cm)
Mar 23	Alois H. Minkus (Aus-cm)		Sep 11	Francesco Cortesi (It-cd-cm)
Jun 1	Karl Bechstein (Ger-pn.m)		Sep 12	Richard Pohl (Ger-cri)
Jun 5	Ivar Hallström (Swe-pn-cm)		Dec 3	E. Van der Straetten (Bel-mus)
Jun 14	Lindsay Sloper (Br-pn)		Dec 7	Emil Buchner (Ger-cm)
Jun 24	Theodor Formes (Ger-ten)		Dec 20	Otto Dresel (Ger-pn)
Jul 3	Rudolf Westphal (Ger-mus)		Dec 21	Jenny Bürde-Ney (Aus-sop)
Jul 4	Stephen Foster (Am-cm)		Dec 21	Ernst Pauer (Aus-pn)
Jul 8	Karl Chrysander (Ger-mus)		Dec 26	Frans Coenen (Hol-vn)
				Johann Decker-Schenk (Aus-gui)

B. Deaths:

Jan 17	Juan C. Arriaga (Sp-cm)		May 6	Rosalie Levasseur (Fr-sop)
Feb 6	Jacob Kimball, Jr. (Am-m.ed)		May 24	Friedrich Fesca (Ger-vn)
Feb 18	Charles Incledon (Br-ten)		May 27	Carl D. Stegmann (Ger-ten)
Mar 11	Gervais Couperin (Fr-org)		Jun 5	Carl Maria von Weber (Ger-cm)
Apr 3	Reginald Heber (Br-hymn)		Jul 7	Friedrich Dülon (Ger-fl)
Apr 13	Franz Danzi (Ger-cm)		Jul 15	Giovanni Ansani (It-ten)

| Jul 17 | Joseph Graetz (Ger-pn-cm) | Oct 9 | Michael Kelly (Ir-ten) |
| Sep 28 | Dietrich Windel (Ger-inv) | Nov 17 | Louise Reichardt (Ger-sop) |

C. Debuts:

Other - James Bland (London), Jean Baptiste Chollet (Paris, as tenor), Giuditta Grisi (Vienna), Ossip Petrov (Elizavetgrad), Agostino Rovere (Pavia)

D. New Positions:

Conductors: Johann Aiblinger (Munich Royal Theater), Carl Eberwein (Weimar Opera), Karl A. Krebs (Vienna Opera), Carl Reissiger (German Opera, Dresden), Eduard Rietz (Berlin Philharmonic Society)

Educational: Georg Hellmesberger (violin, Vienna Conservatory), Auguste-Mathieu Panseron (solfeggio, Paris Conservatory), Jan A. Vitásek (director, Prague Organ School)

Others: Johann C. Haeffner (organ, Uppsala Cathedral), Edward Holmes (music critic, *Atlas*), Prosper C. Simon (organ, Notre Dame, Paris), Samuel Sebastien Wesley (organ, St. James', London)

E. Prizes and Honors:

Honors: Gioacchino Rossini (Composer to His Majesty and Inspector-General of Singing, Paris)

F. Biographical Highlights:

Ludwig von Beethoven's nephew attempts suicide; Hector Berlioz enters Paris Conservatory and fails in his attempt at the Prix de Rome; James Hewitt submits to a cancer operation on his face; Rodolphe Kreutzer retires from active musical life; Johannes Simon Mayr goes blind from cataracts; Saverio Mercadante begins a 5-year stay in Spain and Portugal; Giacomo Meyerbeer marries his cousin, Minna Mosson; Sigismund von Neukomm travels in Italy; Otto Nicolai runs away from home and begins music study in Berlin; Louis Nourrit retires from the opera stage; Gioacchino Rossini quits the Italian Theater in Paris leaving himself free to write for the Opera; Anton Schindler returns to care for Beethoven until his death; Franz Schubert tries for the court post in Vienna but fails; Henriette Sontag makes her Paris Opera debut; Richard Wagner, left in Dresden, begins writing *Leubald*; Carl Maria von Weber, still suffering the effects of tuberculosis, travels to England where he dies.

G. Institutional Openings:

Performing Groups: Berlin Philharmonic Society; Cäcilien-Verein (Lvov); Dublin Philharmonic Society; Gregorius Musis Sacrum (Leider Orchestra); Munich Liederkranz; Nantes Philharmonic Society; Salem Mozart Association; Sängerverein der Stadt Zurich; Johann Strauss Orchestra (Vienna)

Educational: Agthe Music Academy (Posen); Bibliographisches Institut (Gotha); Koninklijke Music School (The Hague); Carl Reissiger Conservatory of Music (The Hague); South African Academy of Music (Cape Town)

Other: *Atlas*; Bernardel Violin Shop (Paris); Elíazaga Music Publishers (Mexico City); Eruditio Musica (Rotterdam); Hachette et Cie., Publishers (Paris); Meneely and Co., Bell Foundry (N.Y.); Friedrich Pustet, Music Publisher (Regensburg); J. Schuberth and Co., Music Publishers (Hamburg); Society for the Promotion of Church Music in Bohemia (Prague)

H. Musical Literature:

Baudiot, Charles, *Méthode d'violoncelle I*
Berton, Henri, *De la musique méchanique et de la musique philosophique*
Blaze, François, *De l'opéra en France II*
Crouch, Frederick, *Complete Treatise on the Violoncello*

Kelly, Michael, *Reminiscences*
Kiesewetter, Raphael, *Die Verdienste der Niederlander um die Tonkunst*
Lichtenthal, Peter, *Dizionario e bibliografia della musica*
Loewe, Carl, *Gesang-lehre für Gymnasien, Seminarien und Bürgerschulen*
Mason, Lowell, *Address on Church Music*
Savart, Félix, *Sur la communication des mouvements vibratoires entre les corps solides*

I. Musical Compositions:

Auber, Daniel, *Fiorella* (opera)
    Le timide (opera)
Beethoven, Ludwig van, *String Quartet No. 14, Opus 131*
    String Quartet No. 16, Opus 135
    Rondo a Capriccio, Opus 129, "Rage over a Lost Penny"
Bellini, Vincenzo, *Bianca e Gernando* (opera)
Berlioz, Hector, *La Revolution Grecque* (cantata)
Bishop, Henry, *Knights of the Cross* (opera)
    Aladdin (opera)
Chopin, Frédéric, *3 Ecossaises, Opus 72, No. 3*
    2 Mazurkas (G, B-flat)
    Introduction and Variations on German National Air
Donizetti, Gaetano, *Gabriella di Vergy* (opera)
    Elvida (opera)
    Alahor di Granata (opera)
Dorn, Heinrich, *Rolands Knappen* (opera)
Glinka, Mikhail, *Memorial Cantata*
Hérold, Ferdinand, *Marie* (opera)
Kalliwoda, Johann, *Symphony No. 1, Opus 7*
Kreutzer, Konradin, *Die lustige Werbung* (opera)
Kuhlau, Friedrich, *Shakespeare* (opera)
Marschner, Heinrich, *Lucretia* (opera)
Mendelssohn, Felix, *Overture, Midsummer Night's Dream*
    Piano Sonata in E, Opus 6
    String Quintet No. 1, Opus 18
Mercadante, Saverio, *Caritea, regina di Spagna* (opera)
Moscheles, Ignaz, *Piano Concerto No. 5, Opus 87*
    Etudes, Opus 70 (piano)
Pacini, Giovanni, *Niobe* (opera)
Rossini, Gioacchino, *Le siège de Corinthe* (opera)
Schubert, Franz, *String Quintet No. 15, Opus 18*
    String Quartet in G, D. 887
    Piano Sonata No. 20, D. 894
    Piano Trio, Opus 99
    Rondo Brillant, Opus 79, for Violin and Piano
    Who Is Sylvia (song)
    Hark! Hark! the Lark (song)
Spohr, Louis, *The Last Judgment* (oratorio)
    3 String Quartets, Opus 74
    String Quintet in B Minor, Opus 69
Tadolini, Giovanni, *Mitridate* (opera)
Vaccai, Nicola, *Bianca di Messina* (opera)
    Il precipizio (opera)
Weber, Carl Maria von, *Oberon* (opera)
    March in C Major for Winds
Zelter, Carl, *6 German Songs for Bass Voice*

1827

World Events:
In the U.S., the Baltimore and Ohio becomes the first passenger and freight railroad to be chartered; the Cherokee Nation forms a constitutional government in the Georgia Territory; the first Mardi Gras celebration takes place in New Orleans; Fort Leavenworth, Kansas,is built to protect wagon trains on the Santa Fe trail. Internationally, the Greek-Turkish War continues as Russia, France and Great Britain enter the war against Turkey; the Turkish fleet is destroyed at the Battle of Navarino; the screw propellor is designed by Joseph Ressel; Argentina and Brazil battle over the Uruguayan territory; the first friction matches appear.

Cultural Highlights:
The *American Quarterly Review* begins publication; James Pradier is inducted into the Legion of Honor; Edgar Allen Poe runs away from home and joins the U.S. Army; James Audubon publishes his *Birds of North America*. Births in the art field include British artist William H. Hunt, Swiss artist Arnold Böcklin, French artist Jules A. Breton and sculptor Jean Baptiste Carpeaux; deaths include British poet and artist William Blake and artist Thomas Rowlandson and American artist Charles W. Peale. Births in the field of literature include Swiss poet Heinrich Leuthold and American novelist Lewis Wallace; deaths include Italian poet and novelist Ugo Foscolo, Mexican novelist José Fernández de Lyardi, German author Wilhelm Hauff and poet Wilhelm Müller. Other highlights include:

Art: Karl Begas, *Carl F. Zelter*; Thomas Cole, *Last of the Mohicans*; Jean B. Corot, *The Bridge at Narni*; Francisco de Goya, *Nun and Monk*; Jean-Auguste Ingres, *Apotheosis of Homer*; John Martin, *Milton's Paradise Lost*; Samuel Morse, *The Muse*; François Rude, *Neapolitan Fisher Boy*; John Vanderlyn, *View of Niagara Falls*

Literature: James F. Cooper, *The Prairie*; Richard Dana, *The Buccaneer and Other Poems*; Charles Forrester, *Absurdities in Prose and Verse*; Heinrich Heine, *Buch der Lieder*; Victor Hugo, *Cromwell*; John Keble, *The Christian Year*; Giacomo Leopardi, *Operette Morali*; Thomas Moore, *The Epicurean*; Edgar Allen Poe, *Tamerlane*

MUSICAL EVENTS

A. Births:

Jan 31	Marie Cabel (Bel-sop)	Aug 28	Teresa Milanollo (It-vn)
Feb 4	Lucien Southard (Am-cm)	Sep 8	Emil Naumann (Ger-cm)
Feb 14	Alexander Gottschalg (Ger-org	Sep 27	Hermann Wollenhaupt (Ger-pn)
Mar 11	Franz Böhme (Ger-mus)	Oct 6	Karl Reidel (Ger-cd)
Apr 15	Julius Tausch (Ger-cd)	Nov 16	Charles E. Norton (Am-ed)
Apr 26	Friedrich Ehrbar (Ger-org.m)	Nov 26	Hugo Ulrich (Ger-cm)
May 5	Johann N. Bech (Hun-bar)	Dec 24	Lisa Cristiani (Fr-cel)
Jul 30	Luigi F. Valdrighi (It-mus)	Dec 31	Marie Carvalho (Fr-sop)
Aug 11	Ellsworth Phelps (Am-org)		Fernando Bonamici (It-pn)
Aug 22	Edouard Silas (Hol-pn)		Antonio Giuglini (It-ten)

B. Deaths:

Jan 30	Johann P.G. Schulz (Ger-cd)	Jul 25	Gottfried Härtel (Ger-pub)
Feb 7	Franz Dimmler (Ger-hn-cm)	Aug 2	James Hewitt (Br-cm-pub)
Mar 9	Franz X. Gerl (Aus-bs-cm)	Sep 20	Vincenzo Federici (It-cm)
Mar 26	Ludwig van Beethoven (Ger-cm)	Oct 21	János Bihari (Hon-vn-cd)
Mar 29	Charles Dignum (Ir-ten)	Nov 7	Bartolomeo Campagnoli (It-vn)
Apr 3	Ernst Chladni (Ger-acous)	Nov 20	Carl F. Peters (Ger-pub)
Apr 24	Pierre Candeille (Fr-cm)	Nov 20	Alexei Titov (Rus-cm)
May 9	Friedrich Berner (Ger-the)		Benjamin Blake (Br-vn)
Jul 21	Archibald Constable (Scot-pub)		James Hook (Br-org)

C. Debuts:
U.S. -- Charles Edward Horn (N.Y.)

Other - Marietta Brambilla (London), Alexandrine Duprez (Paris), Heinrich Panofka (Vienna), Ernesto Sivori (Italy), Sigismond Thalberg (Vienna)

D. New Positions:
Conductors: Carlo Bignani (Cremona Opera), Ramón Carnicer (Madrid Opera), Pietro Generali (maestro di cappella, Novara Cathedral), Ferdinand Hérold (chorusmaster, Paris Opera), Karl Krebs (Hamburg Theater), Franz Lachner (Kärntnertor Theater, Vienna), Heinrich Marschner (Leipzig Theater), Giuseppe Mosca (director, Messina Theater), Christian Pohlenz (Leipzig Gewandhaus)

Educational: Francesco Basili (director, Milan Conservatory), Louis-Joseph Daussoigne-Méhul (director, Liège Conservatory), Jacques Halévy (harmony, Paris Conservatory), Johann Lübeck (director, Conservatory of the Hague)

Others: François Fétis (librarian, Paris Conservatory and editor, La Revue Musicale), Ernst Köhler (organ, Elisabethkirche, Breslau)

E. Prizes and Honors:
Prizes: Pierre Chevillard (cello, Paris Conservatory), Jean Baptiste Guiraud (Prix de Rome)

Honors: Conrad Kocher (honorary doctorate, Tübingen University), Niccolò Paganini (Knight of the Golden Spur)

F. Biographical Highlights:
Hector Berlioz falls in love with the British actress Henrietta Smithson and again fails to win the Prix de Rome; François Boieldieu loses his wife and marries singer Jenny Phillis-Bertin; Laure Cinti-Damoreau marries actor V.C. Damoreau; Alexander Dargomijsky enters the service of the Russian government; Filippo Galli makes his London debut; Anton Haizinger marries soprano Amalia Neumann; Anthony Heinrich travels to London where he plays violin in a theatre orchestra and studies some theory; Ferdinand Hiller travels with Hummel to Vienna; Lowell Mason moves to Boston and begins supervision of church music and organ work; Karl Nicander, on winning the Swedish Academy Award, travels to Italy for further music study; Ferdinando Paër, blamed for the financial loses sustained, is forced to resign his post at the Italian Theater in Paris.

G. Institutional Openings:
Performing Groups: Bonn Gesangverein; Bremen Liedertafel; Breslau Liedertafel; Hartford Choral Society; Leeds Amateur Society; Santiago SO (Chile); Società Armonica (London); Zagreb Musikverein

Educational: Académie de Chant (Strasbourg); Accademia Peloritana (Messina); Breslau Singakademie; Adolf Lindblad Music School (Sweden)

Other: Accademia Filarmonica (Casale Monferrato); Carl Baedeker, Publisher (Koblenz); Bowery Theater (N.Y.); Christiania National Theater (Oslo); Constable's Miscellany; Thomas Glen, Instrument Maker (Edinburgh); August Guicharde, Musical Instruments (Paris); Hook and Hastings, Organ Builders (Salem); Niblo's Gardens (N.Y.); La Revue Musicale; Rotary Valve (probable date); Société de Chant Sacré (Geneva); Teatro delle Muse (Ancona); Theater am Dammtor (Hamburg)

H. Musical Literature:
Alday, François, Grande méthode pour l'alto
Chladni, Ernst, Kurze Übersicht der Schall- und Klanglehre
Fétis, François, Solfège progressifs

Goss, John, *Parochial Psalmody*
Griepenkerl, Friedrich, *Lehrbuch der Aesthetik*
Krause, Karl, *Darstellung aus der geschichte der Musik*
Logier, Johann, *System der Musikwissenschaft und der musikalischen Komposition*
Preindl, Josef, *Wiener Tonschule* (posthumous publication)
Schneider, Friedrich, *Vorschule der Musik*

I. Musical Compositions:

Bellini, Vincenzo, *Il pirata* (opera)
Berlioz, Hector, *La Mort d'Orphée* (cantata)
Bertin, Louise, *Le loup-garou* (opera)
Berwald, Franz, *Concertstücke for Bassoon and Orchestra*
   Gustav Wasa (opera)
Chélard, Hippolyte, *Macbeth* (opera)
Chopin, Frédéric, *Mazurka in A Minor, Opus 68, No. 2*
   Nocturne in E Minor, Opus 72, No. 1
   Funeral March, Opus 72, No. 2
   Variations on "La ci darem"
Donizetti, Gaetano, *Olivo e Pasquale* (opera)
   Il borgomastro di Saardam (opera)
   Otto mesi in due ore (opera)
Dorn, Heinrich, *Der Zauberer* (opera)
Halévy, Jacques, *L'artisan* (opera)
Hérold, Ferdinand, *La Somnambule* (ballet)
   Astolphe et Joconde (ballet)
Kalliwoda, Johann, *Blanda* (opera)
   Prinzessin Christine (opera)
Kreutzer, Konradin, *L'eau di jouvenance* (opera)
Kuhlau, Daniel, *Hugo und Adelheid* (opera)
Loewe, Carl, *2 Ballads, Opus 8*
Mendelssohn, Felix, *String Quartet No. 2, Opus 13*
   Piano Sonata in B-flat Major, Opus 106
   Tu es Petrus, Opus 111 (cantata)
   7 Characteristic Pieces for Piano, Opus 7
Mercadante, Saverio, *Ezio* (opera)
   Il montanaro (opera)
   La testa di bronzo (opera)
Morlacchi, Francesco, *Requiem for the King of Saxony*
Moscheles, Ignaz, *50 Piano Preludes, Opus 73*
Pacini, Giovanni, *Gli arabi nelle Gallie* (opera)
Persiani, Giuseppe, *Attila* (opera)
Reicha, Anton, *Chamber Symphony No. 2*
Reissiger, Carl, *Yelva* (melodrama)
Rossini, Gioacchino, *Moïse* (opera)
Schubert, Franz, *Die Winterreise* (song cycle)
   Deutsche Messe, D. 872
   2 Piano Trios, Opus 99 and 100
   Nachtgesang in Walde, Opus 139b
   4 Impromtus, Opus 142 (piano)
Sor, Fernando, *Le Sicilien* (ballet)
Spohr, Louis, *Pietro von Abano, Opus 76* (opera)
   Double Quartet, Opus 73
Tadolini, Giovanni, *Almanzor* (opera)
   Mitridate (opera)
Vaccai, Nicola, *Giovanna d'Arco* (opera)
Weigl, Joseph, *Mass, "Conceptione B.M.V."*
Zelter, Carl, *6 German Songs for Alto Voice*

1828

World Events:

In the U.S., Andrew Jackson becomes the first candidate of the Democratic Party to be elected President and introduces the spoils system into politics; Congress passes the so-called Tariff of Abominations over southern protest; horse-drawn rail service begins on the Baltimore and Ohio Railroad. Internationally, the British Parliament repeals the laws forbidding Catholics and Nonconformists to hold public office; the Treaty of Rio de Janeiro makes Uruguay an independent state between Brazil and Argentina; Don Miguel deposes Maria II in Portugal; the Duke of Wellington becomes the British Prime Minister.

Cultural Highlights:

Several cultural magazines begins publication, *Edinburgh Literary Journal, New England Magazine, Paisley Magazine* and *Southern Review*; Noah Webster's *American Dictionary of the English Language* is published; Pierre Guérin receives a baronet and Franz Winterhalter becomes court painter at Karlsruhe. Births in the literary field include French novelist Jules Verne, British poet and artist Dante Rossetti and poets Gerald Massey and George Meredith, Norwegian dramatist Henrik Ibsen, Scotch novelist Margaret Oliphant, German poet Julius Grosse, Russian novelist Leo Tolstoy and American poet Henry Timrod; deaths include British novelist Caroline Lamb, Spanish poet L. Fernández de Moratin, Italian poet Vincenzo Monti and German philosopher Friedrich Bouterwek. Births in the art field include German sculptor Karl Cauer and artist Oscar Begas, French artists Paul Baudry and Jules Delaunay and American sculptor Leonard W. Volk; deaths include French sculptor Jean Houdon, Spanish artist Francisco de Goya, British artist Richard Bonington and American artist Gilbert Stuart. Other highlights include:

Art: Vincenzo Camuccini, *Judith*; John Constable, *Hadleigh Castle*; William Dyce, *Madonna and Child*; Charles Eastlake, *Pilgrims in Sight of Rome*; John Martin, *The Fall of Ninevah*; Samuel Palmer, *Hilly Scene*; John Quidor, *Ichabod Crane and the Headless Horseman*; William Rush, *Schuylkill Chained*; Bertel Thorvaldsen, *Amor and Anacreon*

Literature: Edward Bulwer-Lytton, *Pelham*; James F. Cooper, *The Red Rover*; Izaak Da Costa, *Feestliederen*; Robert Gilfillan, *Peter M'Craw*; Nathaniel Hawthorne, *Fanshawe*; Charles Lamb, *The Wife's Trial*; Jane Porter, *The Field of Forty Footsteps*; Jean Reboul, *L'Ange et l'Enfant*; Walter Scott, *The Fair Maid of Perth*

MUSICAL EVENTS

A. Births:

Feb 8	Antonio Cagnoni (It-cm)	Jul 1	Karl Hubay (Hun-cd-cm)
Feb 9	Arrey von Dommer (Ger-mus)	Jul 25	Karl Fischer (Ger-org)
Mar 14	Karl von Bruyck (Aus-mus)	Jul 31	François Gevaert (Bel-mus)
Apr 5	Pietro Platania (It-cm)	Aug 5	Giovanni Rossi (It-cm)
Apr 8	Mathis Lussy (Swi-pn)	Oct 19	Adolfo Fumagalli (It-pn)
Apr 26	Francesco Graziani (It-bar)	Nov 3	Joseph Hellmesberger (Aus-vn)
Jun 3	Ferdinand Poise (Fr-cm)	Nov 24	Juan F. Riaño (Sp-mus)
Jun 7	Grat-Norbert Barthe (Fr-cm)	Dec 4	Luigi Vannuccini (It-voc)

B. Deaths:

Jan 13	Elizabeth Anspach (Br-cm)	Oct 3	Josephus Fodor (Hol-vn)
Jan 15	Brizzio Petrucci (It-cm)	Nov 19	Franz Schubert (Aus-cm)
Mar 28	Luigi Luzzi (It-cm)	Dec 30	Waldemar Thrane (Nor-cd)
Jul 22	Antonio Calegari (It-cm)		

C. Debuts:
Other - Luciano Fornasari (Italy), Stephen Heller (Vienna), Antonio Oury (London), Arthur Sequin (London), Eugenia Tadolini (Florence), Henry C. Timm (Germany), Clara Wieck (Leipzig)

D. New Positions:
Conductors: Ramón Carnicer (Madrid Opera), Heinrich Dorn (Königsberg Theater), Friedrich Grund (Hamburg Philharmonic Concerts), François Habeneck (Société des Concerts du Conservatoire de Paris), Adolf Müller, Sr. (Theater an der Wien), Carl G. Reissiger (Dresden Court), Ignaz Schuppanzigh (German Opera, Vienna)

Educational: Davidde Banderali (voice, Paris Conservatory)

Others: Ramón Cuéllar y Altarriba (organ, Santiago de Compostela), Gottfried W. Fink (editor, *Allgemeine Musikalische Zeitung*), Niels Peter Jensen (organ, St. Peter's, Copenhagen)

E. Prizes and Honors:
Honors: Frédéric Kalkbrenner and Ferdinando Paër (Legion of Honor), Joseph Rastrelli (Knight of the Golden Spur)

F. Biographical Highlights:
Teresa Belloc-Giorgi retires from the stage; Hector Berlioz finally wins second prize in the Prix de Rome competition; François van Campenhout retires from the stage; Angelica Catalani retires to her home in Florence; Frédéric Chopin visits Berlin; Gaetano Donizetti marries Virginia Vasselli; Mikhail Glinka resigns his government post and begins studying composition with Zamboni; Ferdinand Hiller moves to Paris for a 7-year teaching stay; Maria Malibran makes her Paris Opera debut; Niccolò Paganini, following his Vienna debut, becomes the idol of the Viennese public; Robert Schumann begins the study of law at Leipzig University but also studies piano with his future father-in-law, Friedrich Wieck; Henriette Sontag makes her London debut; Fernando Sor settles permanently in Paris; Maria Szymanowska retires from performing and settles in St. Petersburg as a teacher; Ambroise Thomas enters the Paris Conservatory but studies privately with Kalkbrenner and Lesueur; Richard Wagner enters St. Nicholas School in Leipzig and hears his first Beethoven composition.

G. Institutional Openings:
Performing Groups: Bürgerlicher Gesangverein (Jena); Hamburg Philharmonic Concert Society; Portland Handel and Haydn Society (Maine); St. Martin's Church Music Society (Bratislava); Sociétè des Concerts du Conservatoire de Paris

Educational: Brno Music Institute

Other: Boehm Flute Co. (Munich); Bösendorfer Piano Co. (Vienna); Music Lover's Society (St. Petersburg); New York Musical Fund Society; Polyplectron (by J.C. Dietz); Teatro Carlo Felice (Genoa); Jean Vuillaume, Violin Maker (Paris)

H. Musical Literature:
Barsotti, Tommaso, *Méthode de musique*
Blatt, Frantisek, *Clarinet Method*
Busby, Thomas, *A Musical Manual*
Heinroth, Johann, *Kurze Anleitung, das Klavier oder Forte-piano spielen zu lernen*
Holmes, Edward, *A Ramble among the Musicians of Germany*
Hummel, Johann, *Anweisung zum Piano-forte Spiel*
Marx, Adolf, *Über Malerei in der Tonkunst*
Nägeli, Hans G., *Musikalisches Tabellwerk für Volksschulen...*
Schiedermayer, Johann, *Theoretisch-praktische Chorallehre...*
Weber, Friedrich D., *Allgemeine theoretisch-praktische Vorschlule der Musik*

I. Musical Compositions:

Auber, Daniel, *La muette de Portici* (opera)
Berlioz, Hector, *8 Scenes from Faust, Opus 1*
    Waverly Overture, Opus 1 bis
    Les Franc-Juges Overture, Opus 3
    Herminie (cantata)
Carafa, Michele, *La violette* (opera)
Chopin, Frédéric, *Piano Sonata in C Minor, Opus 4*
    Grand Concert Rondo in F Major (piano and orchestra)
    Grand Fantasia on Polish Airs, Opus 13 (piano and orchestra)
    Piano Trio in G Minor
    2 Polonaises, Opus 71, No. 2 and 3
Costa, Michael, *Il carcere d'Ildegonda* (opera)
Donizetti, Gaetano, *Alina, regina di Golconda* (opera)
    Gianni di Calais (opera)
    L'esule di Roma (opera)
    Inno reale (oratorio)
Dorn, Heinrich, *Die Bettlerin* (opera)
Generali, Pietro, *Il divorzio persiano* (opera)
Glinka, Mikhail, *Viola Sonata in D Minor*
Halévy, Jacques, *Clari* (opera)
    Le roi et le bâtelier (opera)
Hérold, Ferdinand, *Lydie* (ballet)
    La fille mal gardée (ballet)
Klein, Bernhard, *Jephtha* (oratorio)
Kuhlau, Friedrich, *Der Elfenhügel* (singspiel)
Loewe, Carl, *Alperfantasie, Opus 53* (piano)
Lortzing, Albert, *Die Himmelfahrt Christi* (oratorio)
    Die Hochfeuer (incidental music)
Marschner, Heinrich, *Der Vampyr* (opera)
    Alexander und Darius (incidental music)
Mercadante, Saverio, *Gabriella di Vergy* (opera)
    Francesca da Rimini (opera)
    Adriano in Siria (opera)
Morlacchi, Francesco, *Il Colombo* (opera)
    I saraceni in Sicilia (opera)
Reissiger, Karl, *Libella* (opera)
Rossini, Gioacchino, *Le Comte Ory* (opera)
Schubert, Franz, *Symphony No. 9 in C, "The Great"*
    Der Graf von Gleicher (opera)
    Mass No. 6, D. 950
    String Quintet, Opus 163
    Piano Sonatas No. 21-23, D. 958-960
    Glaube, Hoffnung und Liebe (chorus and orchestra)
    Der Hirt auf dem Felsen
    Schwanengesang (song cycle)
    4 Impromtus, Opus 90, for Piano
    Moments Musicaux, Opus 94, for Piano
Sor, Fernando, *Guitar Etudes, Opus 6, 29 and 31*
Spohr, Louis, *Symphony No. 3, Opus 78*
    Violin Concerto No. 12, Opus 79
Vaccai, Nicola, *Saladino e Clotilde* (opera)
Vertovsky, Alexei, *Pan Tsardovsky* (opera)
Zelter, Carl, *6 Songs for Male Chorus*

1829

World Events:
In the U.S., the first steam locomotive in the New World, the "Tom Thumb" goes into operation; the Working Man's Party is founded in New York; the "Kitchen Cabinet" becomes a part of Andrew Jackson's presidency; the first modern hotel, the Tremont House, opens in Boston; the Northeast Asylum for the blind opens in Boston; the typographer is patented. Internationally, Russia and Turkey sign the Peace of Adrianople; Greece, gaining her independence, becomes a republic; the Catholic Emancipation Law is passed in England; Braille printing is invented by Louis Braille; the Swiss constitution is revised for universal suffrage and freedom of the press.

Cultural Highlights:
The magazine *American Monthly* begins publication; William Cullen Bryant becomes co-editor of the New York *Evening Post*; Henry Wadsworth Longfellow begins teaching modern languages at Bowdoin College; John Constable is inducted into the Royal Academy; Robert S. Lauder is inducted into the Royal Scottish Academy; Pierre-Narcisse Guérin is given a baronet. Births in the literary field include British dramatist Thomas W. Robertson, Russian novelist Aleksei Potekhin and Swiss novelist Victor Cherbuliez; deaths include Polish dramatist Wojciech Boguslawski and German poet Karl von Schlegel. Births in the art field include American sculptor John Rogers and artist Albert Bellows, Swedish artist Johan Malmström, German artist Anselm Feuerbach and British artist John Everett Millais; German artist Johann Heinrich Tischbein, Jr., dies. Other highlights include:

Art: John Constable, *Salisbury Cathedral from the Meadows*; Eugéne Delacroix, *Death of Sardanapalus*; Antoine Etex, *Death of Hyacinthe*; Théodore Gudin, *The Devotion of Captain Desse*; Edwin Landseer, *High Life, Low Life*; Samuel Morse, *Apple Hall, Cooperstown*; Joseph Turner, *Ulysses Deriding Polyphemus*

Literature: Honoré de Balzac, *Les Dernier Chouan*; John Banim, *The Denounced*; Alexander Dumas, père, *Henry III*; Johann von Goethe, *Wilhelm Meisters Wanderjahre*; Victor Hugo, *Les Orientales*; Frances Lieber, *Encyclopedia Americana*; Alfred de Musset, *Tales of Spain and Italy*; Walter Scott, *Anne of Geierstein*; Alfred Lord Tennyson, *Timbuctoo*

MUSICAL EVENTS

A. Births:

Jan 24	William G. Mason (Am-cm)	Aug 24	Ernst Lübeck (Hol-pn-cm)
Feb 7	C. Oudrid y Segura (Sp-cm)	Aug 28	Albert Dietrich (Ger-cd)
Mar 9	Dar'ya M. Leonova (Rus-alto)	Sep 5	Henry S. Edwards (Br-mus)
Mar 24	August G. Fricke (Ger-bs)	Sep 10	Harrison Millard (Am-cm)
Apr 14	Domenico Mustafà (It-cas)	Sep 19	Gustav Schirmer (Ger-pub)
May 8	Louis M. Gottschalk (Am-pn)	Nov 28	Anton Rubinstein (Rus-cm)
Jun 9	Gaetano Braga (It-cel)	Dec 3	Delphine Ugalde (Fr-sop)
Jun 26	Domenico Bertini (It-cm-cri)	Dec 24	José Rogel (Sp-cm)
Aug 21	Otto Goldschmidt (Ger-pn)	Dec 25	Patrick Gilmore (Am-band)

B. Deaths:

Jan 8	Maurice Artôt (Fr-hn)	Feb 24	Jan Stefani (Cz-cm-cd)
Jan 12	Michael Fischer (Ger-org)	Apr 19	Augustus Kollmann (Ger-the)
Jan 25	William Shield (Br-vn)	Apr 28	Karl G. Umbreit (Ger-cm)
Jan 26	Domingo Arquimbau (Sp-cm)	May 2	Benedikt Hacker (Swi-pub)
Feb 16	François Gossec (Bel-cm)	May 8	Mauro Giuliani (It-gui)
Feb 18	Johann Kucharz (Boh-org)	May 18	Bernardo Bittoni (It-cm)

Jun 5   Jean Ancot, fils (Bel-pn)   Jun 27   Louis Lebrun (Fr-the)
Jun 11 Bernardo Porta (It-cm-cd)   Nov 9   Jean Lefèvre (Fr-cl)

C. Debuts:
Other - Emma Albertazzi (London), Giulia Grisi (Bologna), Domenico Reina (Milan), Henri Vieuxtemps (Paris)

D. New Positions:
Conductors: Carlo Bignani (Teatro Sociale, Mantua), Paolo Bonfichi (maestro di cappella, Santa Casa, Loreto), Félicien David (maître de chapelle, St. Sauveur), Juste de la Fage (maître de chapelle, St. Étienne du Mont, Paris), Georg Hellmesberger (Austrian Imperial Opera), Konradin Kreutzer (Karnthnerthor Theater, Vienna), Johann H. Lübeck (kapellmeister, The Hague), Giovanni Tadolini (Italian Theater, Paris)

Educational: Jean Louis Tulou (flute, Paris Conservatory), Johann Uhland (professor, University of Tübingen)

Others: Samuel Sebastien Wesley (organ, St. Giles)

E. Prizes and Honors:
Honors: Daniel-François Auber (French Institute), Christian Kramer (Master of the King's Music), Gioacchino Rossini and Gustave Vogt (Legion of Honor)

F. Biographical Highlights:
Charles Auguste de Bériot meets Maria Malibran and begins touring with her; Franz Berwald, on scholarship, travels to Germany; Frédéric Chopin concertizes in Vienna and begins a liason with Constantia Gladkowska; Michael Costa is sent to England where he remains for the rest of his life; Domenico Donzelli makes his London debut; Friedrich von Flotow enters the Paris Conservatory; Felix Mendelssohn conducts the revival of Bach's *St. Matthew Passion* and visits England and Scotland; Mihály Mosonyi leaves home for a church job in Magyarovar; Benedettta Pisaroni makes her London debut; Anton Reicha becomes a naturalized French citizen; Robert Schumann gives up on law study and temporarily goes to Heidelberg to study music; Henri Vieuxtemps makes his Paris debut; Richard Wagner studies some violin and theory and meets Dorn.

G. Institutional Openings:
Performing Groups: Maatschappij tot Bervordering der Toonkunst (Amsterdam Choral Society); Mannheim Musikverein; Società Filarmonico-drammatica (Trieste); Teatro Regio and Opera Co. (Parma)

Educational: Bartay-Menner Singing Academy (Pest); Paganini Music Conservatory (Genoa); Domenico Ronconi Singing School (Milan); Friedrich Schneider Music School (Dessau)

Other: Jacob Alexandre Harmonium Co. (Paris); *Allgemeiner Musikalischer Anzeiger*; Association for the Promotion of the Art of Music (Rotterdam); Concertina (by Charles Wheatstone); Asa Hopkins, Woodwind Maker (Litchfield, Connecticut); Conrad Meyer, Piano Maker (Philadelphia); *Musikalisch-litterarischer Monatsbericht* (by F. Hofmeister); *La Revue de Paris*; Pierre Silvestre, Violin Maker (Lyons)

H. Musical Literature:
Antony, Franz J., *Archäologisch-liturgisches Gesangbuch des...Kirchengesangs*
Calegari, Antonio, *Sistema Armonico* (posthumous publication)
Marx, Adolf B., *Über die Geltung Händelscher Sologesänge für unsere Zeit*
Mason, Lowell, *The Juvenile Psalmist*
Natorp, Bernhard, *Choralbuch für evangelische Kirchen*
Novello, Vincent, *Purcell's Sacred Music*

Ortigue, Joseph d', *De la Guerre des Dilettanti*
Traetta, Filippo, *Introduction to the Art and Science of Music*
Vroye, Théodore de, *Vesperal*

I. Musical Compositions:

Adam, Adolphe, *Pierre et Catherine* (opera)
Auber, Daniel, *La fiancée* (opera)
Bellini, Vincenzo, *Zaira* (opera)
    La straniera (opera)
Berlioz, Hector, *Cléopatre* (cantata)
Boieldieu, François, *Les deux nuits* (opera)
Carafa, Michele, *Jenny* (opera)
Carnicer, Ramón, *Elena e Malvina* (opera)
Cherubini, Luigi, *String Quartets No. 2 and 3*
Chopin, Frédéric, *2 Mazurkas, Opus 68*
    3 Pieces, Opus 70, for Piano
    Polonaise, Opus 3, for Cello and Piano
    Variations, "Souvenir de Paganini"
Costa, Michael, *Malvina* (opera)
Donizetti, Gaetano, *Il paria* (opera)
    Elisabetta (opera)
Generali, Pietro, *Francesca da Rimini* (opera)
Halévy, Jacques, *La dilettante d'Avignon* (opera)
Hérold, Louis, *Emmaline* (opera)
    La belle au bois dormant (ballet)
Hiller, Ferdinand, *Symphony No. 1*
Kalliwoda, Johann, *Symphony No. 2, Opus 17*
    Variations Brillantes, Opus 14, for 2 Violins and Orchestra
Kreutzer, Konradin, *Das Mädchen von Montfermeuil* (opera)
Loewe, Karl, *Die Zerstörung von Jerusalem* (oratorio)
Lortzing, Albert, *Don Juan and Faust* (dramatic poem)
Marschner, Heinrich, *Der Templer und die Jüdin* (opera)
Mendelssohn, Felix, *"Trumpet" Overture, Opus 101*
    String Quartet No. l, Opus 12
    Die Heimkehr aus der Fremde, Opus 89 (operetta)
    Variations Concertantes, Opus 17, for Cello and Piano
    3 Fantasies, Opus 16, for Piano
    12 Songs, Opus 9
Mercadante, Saverio, *Don Chisciotte* (opera)
    La rappresaglia (opera)
Moscheles, Ignaz, *Symphony No. 1, Opus 81*
Rossi, Lauro, *Le contesse villane* (opera)
Rossini, Gioacchino, *William Tell* (opera)
Schumann, Robert, *Piano Quartet in C Minor*
Sor, Fernando, *Guitar Divertissements, Opus 1, 2, 8, 13 and 23*
    Guitar Etudes, Opus 35, 44 and 60
    6 Guitar Pieces, Opus 48
Spohr, Louis, *3 String Quartets, Opus 82*
    Double String Quartet, Opus 77
Spontini, Gaspare, *Agnes von Hohenstaufen* (opera)
Traetta, Filippo, *Daughter of Zion* (oratorio)
Vaccai, Nicola, *Saul* (opera)
Weigl, Joseph, *Mass, "Purificatione B.M.V."*

1830

World Events:

In the U.S., the census shows a population of 12,866,000, a 33% increase in ten years; the Webster-Haynes debates feature the question of State's Rights; further U.S. colonization of Texas territory is forbidden by the Mexican government; Springfield, Missouri, is founded; the fountain pen is patented; future President Chester A. Arthur is born. Internationally, the July Revolution takes place in France and Charles X abdicates in favor of Louis Philippe; the French invade Algeria; Denmark is given a constitutional government; the Belgians begin a revolt against the rule of the Netherlands; England's first railway line begins operating; Ecuador and Venezuela gain their independence; British Royal Geographic Society is formed.

Cultural Highlights:

The Société des Beaux-Arts is founded in Nantes; *Godey's Lady's Book* begins publication; Stendhal is appointed French Consul to Trieste; David Wilkie becomes Painter to the King; Martin A. Shee becomes President of the Royal Academy of Art. Births in the art field include American artist William J. Hays, sculptor John Quincy Adams Ward, French artist Camille Pissarro, Belgian artist Wilhelm F. Pauwels and German artist Albert Bierstadt; deaths include British artist Thomas Lawrence and German artist Johann von Müller. Births in the literary field include American authors John E. Cooke, Paul H. Hayne, Helen H. Jackson and poet Emily Dickinson, German author Paul von Heyse, British poet Christina Rosetti, Scotch poet Alexander Smith, French novelist Jules Alfred de Goncourt and poet Frédéric Mistral; deaths include French novelist Benjamin Constant and British author and critic William Hazlitt. Other highlights include:

Art: John Constable, *Hampstead after the Storm*; Jean Corot, *Chartres Cathedral*; Eugène Delacroix, *Liberty Guiding the People*; Thomas Doughty, *The Raft*; François Gérard, *Pantheon Ceiling* (Paris); Samuel Palmer, *Coming from Evening Church*; William Rimmer, *Despair, Seated Youth*; Joseph Turner, *Old Chain Pier at Brighton*

Literature: Honoré de Balzac, *La Vendetta*; Adelbert von Chamisso, *Frauenliebe und Leben*; Théophile Gautier, *Premières Poésies*; Oliver W. Holmes, *Old Ironsides*; Victor Hugo, *Hernani*; Alphonses de Lamartine, *Harmonies Poétiques et Religieuses*; Alexander Pushkin, *Tales of Belkin*; Stendhal, *Le Rouge et le Noir*

MUSICAL EVENTS

A. Births:

Jan 8	Hans von Bülow (Ger-cd)		Jun 22	Theodor Leschetizky (Pol-ped)
Jan 13	Filippo Filippi (It-cri)		Jul 17	Ede Reményi (Hun-vn)
Jan 15	Jean Baptiste Faure (Fr-bar)		Jul 18	M. Auguste Durand (Fr-pub)
Jan 25	Theodor Steingräber (Ger-pub)		Jul 26	Karl A. Riccius (Ger-vn)
Feb 1	Adolph Schlösser (Ger-pn)		Aug 22	Angiolina Bosio (It-sop)
Feb 19	Wilhelm Tappert (Ger-mus)		Aug 31	Edmund Kretschmer (Ger-org)
Mar 10	Johann G. Bellermann (Ger-mus)		Sep 25	Karl Klindworth (Ger-ped)
			Nov 1	August Adelburg (Turk-vn)
Mar 21	Georg Arlberg (Swe-bar)		Dec 21	Albert Eilers (Ger-bs)
Apr 13	Eduard Lassen (Den-cd-cm)			Pietro Mongini (It-ten)
May 18	Karl Goldmark (Hun-cm)			

B. Deaths:

Feb 7	Marcos da Portugal (Por-cm)		Apr 18	José Nunes García (Bra-cm)
Mar 2	Ignaz Schuppanzigh (Aus-cd)		Aug 5	Karl F. Horn (Ger-org)
Apr 1	Carl Neuner (Ger-vn)		Aug 12	Franz de Paula Rose (Aus-cm)
Apr 15	Therese Teyber (Aus-sop)		Aug 16	Antonio Benelli (It-ten)

Aug 19	Peter Petersen (Ger-fl)	Nov 29	Charles S. Catel (Fr-the)
Sep 19	Stanislas Champein (Fr-cm)	Dec 28	Adrien van Helmont (Bel-cm)
Nov 25	Jacques P. Rode (Fr-vn)	Dec 31	Giacomo Davide (It-ten)

C. Debuts:
Other - Frédéric Chopin (Warsaw), Konstancja Gladkowska (Warsaw), Urban Kreutzbach (Borna), Eduard Mantius (Berlin), Ludwika Rivoli (Warsaw), Emma Romer (London), Lorenzo Salvi (Naples)

D. New Positions:
Conductors: Georg Hellmesberger (Vienna Opera), Joseph Rastrelli (Dresden Opera), Ramón Vilanova (maestro de capilla, Barcelona Cathedral),

Educational: Pedro Albéniz (piano, Madrid Conservatory), Ramón Carnicer (composition, Madrid Conservatory), Manuel García (voice, Paris Conservatory), Johann H. Kufferath (Utrecht School of Music)

Others: Henry Bishop (music director, Vauxhall), Stephen Elvey (organ, New College, Oxford), Julius Otto (cantor, Dresdner Kreuzkirche), Louis Véron (director, Paris Opera), George Webb (organ, Old South Church, Boston)

E. Prizes and Honors:
Prizes: Hector Berlioz (Prix de Rome)

F. Biographical Highlights:
Hector Berlioz becomes engaged to Camille Moke before leaving for Rome; Frédéric Chopin leaves Poland permanently; Muzio Clementi retires from the publishing business; Julie Dorus-Gras, Wilhemine Schröder-Devrient and Eugenia Tadolini all make their Paris Opera debuts; César Franck enters the Liège Conservatory; Mikhail Glinka begins a three-year stay in Italy; Antoine de Kontski studies piano with Field; Luigi Lablache makes his London debut; Jenny Lind enrolls in the Swedish Royal Opera School; Franz Liszt, in Paris, meets Chopin, Berlioz and Paganini; Felix Mendelssohn refuses the chair of music at Berlin University and visits Italy; Ferdinand Ries begins teaching in Frankfurt; Gioacchino Rossini loses his contract during the Revolution and writes his last opera; Robert Schumann leaves Heidelberg to return to Leipzig where he moves in with the Wiecks; Fanny Tacchinardi marries composer Giuseppe Persiani; Sigismond Thalberg begins his career with a successful German tour; Richard Wagner joins the Leipzig revolt and sufers a concert fiasco with his *Overture in B-flat*; George J. Webb moves to the U.S.

G. Institutional Openings:
Performing Groups: Academic Music Society (Helsinki); Alte Hannoversche Liedertafel; Buffalo Philharmonic Society; Dresdner Liedertafel; Florence Philharmonic Society; Müller String Quartet I (Braunschweig); Union Alsacienne de Music (Strasbourg); Uppsala University Choral Union

Educational: Madrid Royal Conservatory of Music; Proksch Music School (Prague); Städtische Singschule (Munich)

Other: Philipp Furtwängler, Organ Builder (Hammer-Orgelbau); Samuel Graves and Co., Instrument Makers (New Hampshire); Urban Kreutzbach, Organ Builder (Borna); Edward Moxon, Publisher (London); *Musikalisches Jugendblatt für Gesang, Clavier und Flöte* (Zittau); Telford and Telford, Organ Builders (Dublin)

H. Musical Literature:
Aubéry du Boulley, Prudent, *Grammaire Musicale*
Ferrari, Giacomo, *Studio di musica teorica pratica*
Fétis, François, *Curiosités historiques de la Musique*
Goss, John, *Piano Forte Student's Catechism*

Hastings, Thomas, *The Union Minstrel*
Kalkbrenner, Friedrich, *Méthode pour apprendre le piano-forte à l'aide du guide-mains*
Langbecker, Emanuel, *Das Deutsch-Evangelische Kirchenlied*
Schilling, Gustav, *Musikalisches Handwörterbuch*
Schneider, Friedrich, *Handbuch des Organisten*
Sor, Fernando, *Méthode pour la Guitare*
Weber, Friedrich, *Theoretisch-praktisches Lehrbuch der Harmonie I*

I. Musical Compositions:

Adam, Adolphe, *Danilowa* (opera)
Auber, Daniel, *Fra Diavolo* (opera)
   Le dieu et la bayadère (opera)
Balfe, Michael, *I Rivali di se stressi* (opera)
   Un avertimento ai gelosi (opera)
Bellini, Vincenzo, *Il Capuleti e i Montecchi* (opera)
Berlioz, Hector, *Fantastic Symphony, Opus 14*
   Sardanapale (cantata)
   9 Irish Melodies, Opus 2
Bishop, Henry, *Under the Oak* (opera)
Chopin, Frédéric, *Concertos No. 1 and 2, for Piano and Orchestra*
   Nocturne in C-sharp Minor
   4 Songs, Opus 74
Donizetti, Gaetano, *Anna Bolena* (opera)
   Il diluvio universale (opera)
   Imelda de' Lambertazzi (opera)
   I pazzi per progetto (opera)
Dorn, Heinrich, *Amor's macht* (ballet)
Glinka, Mikhail, *String Quartet No. 2 in F Major*
Halévy, Jacques, *Manon Lescaut* (ballet)
Hastings, Thomas, *Toplady* (hymn tune, "Rock of Ages")
Kalliwoda, Johann, *Symphony No. 3, Opus 32*
   Grosses Rondo, Opus 16, for Piano and Orchestra
Klein, Bernhard, *David* (oratorio)
Kreutzer, Konradin, *Baron Luft* (operetta)
Kuhlau, Friedrich, *Die Drillingsbrüder von Damaskus* (opera)
Liszt, Franz, *Malediction for Piano and Strings*
   12 Etudes for Piano
Loewe, Carl, *Mazeppa, Opus 27* (tone poem for piano)
Lortzing, Albert, *Yelva* (incidental music)
Marschner, Heinrich, *Des Falkners Braut* (opera)
Mendelssohn, Felix, *Hebrides Overture, Opus 26*
   Psalm CXV, Opus 31, "Non nobis, Domine"
   12 Songs, Opus 8
   6 Songs, Opus 19
Pacini, Giovanni, *Giovanna d'Arc* (opera)
Perry, George, *Family Jars* (opera)
   The Fall of Jerusalem (oratorio)
Rossi, Lauro, *Costanza e Oringaldo* (opera)
Schmidt, Johann, *Alfred der Grosse* (opera)
Schumann, Robert, *Abegg Variations, Opus 1, for Piano*
   Piano Sonata in A-flat Major
Spohr, Louis, *Der Alchymist* (opera)
Spontini, Gaspare, *Mignon's Lied*
Thalberg, Sigismond, *Concerto, Opus 5, for Piano and Orchestra*
Vertovsky, Alexei, *Man and Wife* (opera)
Wagner, Richard, *Overture in B-flat Major*
Weigl, Joseph, *Mass, "Annuntiatione B.M.V."*

1831

World Events:

In the U.S., Turner's Rebellion in Virginia results in 50 whites killed--Turner is captured and hanged; William Garrison begins publication of *The Liberator*; South Bend, Indiana, is founded; New York University is chartered; R. L. Stevens introduces the flanged railroad track; future President James A. Garfield is born; former President James Monroe dies. Internationally, Leopold I becomes King of an independent Belgium; Austria tries unsuccessfully to stamp out Italian nationalism; the Polish Insurrection is crushed by Russian troops; Michael Faraday discovers the principle of electro-magnetic induction; Charles Darwin begins a five-year voyage on the *H.M.S. Beagle*.

Cultural Highlights:

The Trumbull Art Gallery opens at Yale; Joseph Eichendorff becomes Minister of Culture in Berlin; Edwin Landseer is inducted into the Royal Academy of Art; John Sloan is knighted. Births in the field of art include German sculptors Robert Cauer and Reinhold Degas, French sculptor Jean A. Falguière and Belgian artist Constantin Meunier; deaths include French artist François Dumont and British artist John A. Atkinson. Births in the literary world include British novelist Amelia Barr, poet Charles Calverley, German novelist Wilhelm Raabe and French dramatist Victorien Sardou; deaths include German novelist Friedrich von Klinger, poets Achim von Arnim and Friedrich von Matthisson, Scottish novelist Henry Mackenzie, American poet John Trumbull, Hungarian author Ferenc Kazinczy, Portugese author José de Macedo and Dutch poet Willem Bilderdijk. Other highlights include:

Art: Jean Baptiste Corot, *Quarry of La Chaise à Marie*; Alexandre Decamps, *The Turkish Patrol*; Eugène Delacroix, *July 28, 1830* and *The Battle of Nancy*; Francis Grant, *Sir Walter Scott with Staghounds*; Robert Lauder, *The Bride of Lammermoor*; François Rude, *Jacques L. David* (bust); Joseph Turner, *Chichester Canal*

Literature: James F. Cooper, *The Bravo*; Benjamin Disraeli, *The Young Duke*; Johann von Goethe, *Faust II*; Nicolai Gogol, *Evenings on a Farm I*; Franz Grillparzer, *Hero and Leander*; Victor Hugo, *Notre Dame de Paris*; James Paulding, *Dutchman's Fireside*; Thomas Peacock, *Crotchet Castle*; John Greenleaf Whittier, *Legends of New England*

MUSICAL EVENTS

A. Births:

Jan 11	Georges Chanot, Jr. (Fr-vn.m)		Aug 13	Salomon Jadassohn (Ger-the)
Jan 15	Albert Niemann (Ger-ten)		Aug 22	William Cummings (Br-org)
Feb 17	Francisco Daniel (Fr-mus)		Aug 22	Marie L. Dustmann (Fr-sop)
Feb 26	Fillippo Marchetti (It-cm)		Aug 28	Frederik Norman (Swe-cm-cd)
May 24	Richard Hoffman (Br-pn)		Sep 14	Antonio Sangiovanni (It-m.ed)
Jun 13	Henry Banister (Br-the)		Nov 16	Constance Nantier-Didiée
Jun 28	Joseph Joachim (Hun-vn)			(Fr-mez)
Jul 17	Therese Tietjens (Ger-sop)		Dec 25	Johann von Herbeck (Aus-cd)
Aug 1	Antonio Cotogni (It-bar)		Dec 25	Cipriano Pontoglio (It-cm)
Aug 9	Bessie Palmer (Br-alto)		Dec 26	Charles Meerens (Bel-acous)

B. Deaths:

Jan 6	Rodolphe Kreutzer (Fr-vn-cd)		May 8	Friedrich Seidel (Ger-org)
Jan 8	Franz Krommer (Cz-vn-cm)		May 24	Benjamin Carr (Br-cm-cd)
Feb 27	Józef Kozlowski (Pol-cm-cd)		May 31	Daniel Jelensperger (Ger-the)
Mar 4	George M. Telemann (Ger-the)		May 31	Jean Pierre Porro (Fr-gui)
Mar 30	François Lays (Fr-ten)		Jun 10	Johann C. Barthiel (Ger-cd)
Apr 13	Ferdinand Kauer (Aus-cm)		Jun 23	Mateo de Albéniz (Sp-the-cm)

Jul 18	Thomas Greatorex (Be-org)	Nov 14	Ignaz J. Pleyel (Ger-cm-pub)
Jul 24	Maria Szymanowska (Pol-pn)	Nov 15	Vincenz Masek (Boh-cd-cm)
Aug 5	Sébastien Érard (Fr-pn.m)	Dec 2	Traugott Eberwein (Ger-vn)
Sep 8	John Aitken (Scot-pub)	Dec 11	J. George Schetky (Ger-pub)
Sep 18	Peter Hänsel (Aus-vn-cm)		Isaiah Thomas (Am-pub)
Sep 23	Louis Norrit (Fr-ten)		

C. Debuts:

Other - Delphin Alard (Paris), Anna de Belleville-Oury (London), Anna Bishop (London), Teresa Brambilla (Milan), Prosper Dérivis (Paris), Heinrich Ernst (Paris), Anna Maria Hasselt-Barth (Trieste), Clara Heinefetter (Vienna), Julius Knorr (Leipzig), Sebastian Lee (Hamburg), Elizabeth Masson (England), Giorgio Ronconi (Pavia), Jane Shirreff (London), John Templeton (London), Pierre-François Wartel (Paris)

D. New Positions:

Conductors: Francisco Andreví y Castellar (choirmaster, Madrid Royal Chapel), Heinrich Dorn (St. Peter's Cathedral, Riga), Ignaz Lachner (Kapellmeister, Stuttgart), Heinrich Marschner (kapellmeister, Hanover), Friedrich Müller (Rudolstadt), Lauro Rossi (Teatro Valle, Rome), Anton Schindler (choirmaster, Münster Cathedral), Henri-Justin Valentino (Paris Opéra-Comique)

Educational: Auguste Bottée de Toulmon (librarian, Paris Conservatory), Johann T. Mosewius (director, Institute for Church Music, Breslau)

Others: Henry F. Chorley (music critic, *London Athenaeum*)

E. Prizes and Honors:

Prizes: Eugène-Prosper Prévost (Prix de Rome)

Honors: Eduard Brendler and Adolf F. Lindblad (Swedish Royal Academy), Ferdinando Paër (French Academy of Fine Arts), Anton Reicha (Legion of Honor)

F. Biographical Highlights:

Emma Albertazzi, Giulia Grisi and Agostino Rovere make their La Scala debuts; Frédéric Chopin moves to Paris; Gaetano Crivelli gives his farewell performance; Alexander Dargomijsky enters the Russian Department of Justice; Félicien David leaves the Paris Conservatory and joins the Saint-Simonian cult; Julie Dorus-Gras makes her Paris Opera debut; John Field, sick from cancer, returns to England; Felix Mendelssohn meets Berlioz in Italy and Liszt in Paris; Giuseppe Mercadante returns to Italy; Niccolò Paganini makes highly successful debuts in London and Paris; Anna Rivière marries composer Henry Bishop; Giovanni Rubini makes his London debut; Robert Schumann begins studying composition with Dorn; Richard Wagner enters the University of Leipzig.

G. Institutional Openings:

Performing Groups: Ansbach Choral Society; Bradford Philharmonic Society; Bund der Nordwestdeutschen Liedertafeln; Darmstadt Musikverein; Glasgow Amateur Musical Society; Mainz Liedertafel; Newark Handel and Haydn Society

Festivals: Dublin Music Festival

Educational: Agthe Music Academy (Breslau)

Other: *Charivari* (France); Exeter Hall (London); *Figaro in London*; Grand Theater (Lyons); Johann Heckel, Instrument Maker (Wiesbaden); Meiningen Hoftheater; Tulou-Nonon Flute Co. (Paris)

H. Musical Literature:
Haeser, August F., *Chorgesangschule*
Hastings/Mason, *Spiritual Songs for Social Worship*
Lichtenthal, Peter, *Estetica*
Mainzer, Joseph, *Singschule*
Mason, Lowell, *The Juvenile Lyre*
Momigny, Jérôme-Joseph de, *A l'Académie des Beaux-Arts*
Spohr, Louis, *Violin School*
Virués y Spinola, José, *La Geneuphonia*
Vroye, Théodore de, *Graduel*
Zeuner, Charles, *Church Music*

I. Musical Compositions:
Auber, Daniel, *Le philtre* (opera)
Bellini, Vincenzo, *Norma* (opera)
　　La sonnambula (opera)
Berlioz, Hector, *King Lear Overture, Opus 4*
　　Le Corsaire Overture, Opus 21
　　Meditation, Opus 18 (chorus and orchestra)
Bertin, Louise-Angélique, *Fausto* (opera)
Carafa, Michele, *Le lure de l'hermite* (opera)
Carnicer, Ramón, *Cristoforo Colombo* (opera)
Chélard, Hippolyte, *Mitternacht* (opera)
Chopin, Frédéric, *5 Mazurkas, Opus 7*
　　5 Nocturnes, Opus 9 and 15
　　Waltz in E-flat Major, Opus 18
　　Grand Polonaise, Opus 22, for Piano and Orchestra
Costa, Michael, *Kenilworth* (ballet)
Donizetti, Gaetano, *Gianni di Parigi* (opera)
　　Francesca di Foix (opera)
Dorn, Heinrich, *Abu Kara* (opera)
Flotow, Friedrich von, *Pierre et Catherine* (opera)
Generali, Pietro, *Il Romito di Provenza* (opera)
Halévy, Jacques, *La langue musicale* (opera)
Heinrich, Anthony, *Pushmataha* (opera)
Hérold, Ferdinand, *Zampa* (opera)
Kalliwoda, Johann, *Concertante, Opus 20, for 2 Violins and Orchestra*
Kreutzer, Konradin, *Die Hochländerin* (opera)
　　La femme sanglante (opera)
Mendelssohn, Felix, *Concerto No. 1, Opus 25, for Piano and Orchestra*
　　String Quintet No. 1, Opus 18
Mercadante, Saverio, *Zaïra* (opera)
Meyerbeer, Giacomo, *Robert, le diable* (opera)
Pacini, Giovanni, *Il corsaro* (opera)
Reissiger, Carl, *Die Felsenmühle zu Estaliéres* (opera)
Ricci, Luigi, *Chiara di Rosemberg* (opera)
Rossi, Lauro, *Lo sposo al lotto* (opera)
　　La casa in vendita (opera)
Schumann, Robert, *Papillons, Opus 2* (piano)
　　Allegro for Piano, Opus 8
Taubert, Wilhelm, *Symphony No. 1*
Vertovsky, Alexei, *The Old Hussar* (opera)
Wagner, Richard, *Overture in D Minor*
　　Overture in C Major
Zelter, Carl, *10 Songs for Male Chorus*

1832

World Events:

In the U.S., Andrew Jackson is re-elected as President and proceeds to veto the National Bank Reform Bill; the Black Hawk War takes place in Wisconsin; a great cholera epidemic occurs in the east; the first clipper ship, the *Ann McKim*, is launched; Tulsa, Oklahoma, Toledo, Ohio, and Buffalo, New York, are founded. Internationally, Giuseppe Mazzini founds the Young Italy Society to promote nationalism; the British Reform Bill doubles the amount of eligible voters for seats in Parliament; the Egyptians defeat the Turks at the Battle of Konia; H. Pixil builds the first electric generator; a major cholera epidemic sweeps the world.

Cultural Highlights:

Paul Delaroche begins teaching in the École Supérieure des Beaux-Arts in Paris; Andrew Geddes is inducted into the Royal Academy; Honoré Daumier is imprisoned for his satirical prints; Ralph Waldo Emerson resigns from the ministry; William Dunlap's *History of the American Theater* is published. Births in the literary field include American author Louisa May Alcott, British poets John C. Hughes and Theodore Watts-Dunton, author Lewis Carroll, German poet Wilhelm Busch and Norwegian author Bjørnstjerne Bjornson; deaths include British novelists Anna M. Porter and Walter Scott and poet George Crabbe, German poet Johann von Goethe and American poet Philip Freneau. Births in the art field include American artist Samuel Colman, French artists Gustav Doré and Édouard Manet, Scotch artist William Orchardson and Dutch artist Maurice de Haas. Other highlights include:

Art: John Constable, *Waterloo Bridge*; Horatio Greenough, *George Washington*; Jean-Auguste Ingres, *Louis Bertin*; Samuel Morse, *The Gallery of the Louvre*; James Pradier, *12 Victories* (Invalides); Bertel Thorvaldsen, *Artist with the Statue of Hope*; Joseph Turner, *Childe Harold's Pilgrimage*; David Wilkie, *The Preaching of Knox*

Literature: Honoré de Balzac, *Louis Lambert*; William C. Bryant, *Poems* (includes *The Prairie*); Fanny Burney, *Memoires*; Victor Hugo, *Le Roi s'Amuse*; Washington Irving, *The Alhambra*; Eduard Mörike, *Maler Noten*; James R. Paulding, *Westward Ho*; Walter Scott, *Castle Dangerous*; Alfred Lord Tennyson, *Poems II*

MUSICAL EVENTS

A. Births:

Jan 19	Ferdinand Laub (Boh-vn)	Jul 23	Giovanni Sbriglia (It-ten)
Jan 28	Franz Wüllner (Ger-cm-cd)	Jul 24	Johann Lauterbach (Ger-vn)
Feb 3	William H. Doane (Am-hymn)	Aug 27	Louisa Pyne (Br-sop)
Mar 1	Friedrich Grützmacher (Ger-cel)	Sep 21	Friedrich Langhans (Ger-mus)
Mar 4	Ivan Mel'nikov (Rus-bar)	Oct 1	Henry Clay Work (Am-cm)
Mar 5	Alfred Jaëll (Aus-pn)	Oct 7	Charles Converse (Am-hymn)
Mar 10	Heinrich Bellermann (Ger-the)	Oct 22	Leopold Damrosch (Ger-cd)
Jun 3	Charles Lecocq (Fr-cm)	Oct 22	Robert Eitner (Ger-mus)

B. Deaths:

Jan 2	Eduard Rietz (Ger-vn-cd)	Jul 19	Henri Berton (Fr-pn-cm)
Jan 30	David von Apell (Ger-cm-cd)	Aug 26	Henrik Klein (Ger-cm)
Mar 10	Muzio Clementi (Ger-pn)	Aug 31	Jean Kreutzer (Fr-vn)
Mar 12	Friedrich Kuhlau (Ger-cm)	Sep 9	Bernhard Klein (Ger-cm)
Apr 15	Jean Imbault (Fr-vn-pub)	Sep 27	Karl Krause (Ger-mus)
May 15	Carl F. Zelter (Ger-cm)	Nov 3	Pietro Generali (It-cm)
May 18	Bonifazio Asioli (It-cm)	Dec 20	Charles F. Angelet (Bel-pn)
May 26	François Perne (Fr-cm-mus)	Dec 21	Francisco Cabo (Sp-org)
Jun 9	Manuel G. García (Sp-ten)		Johann S. Demar (Ger-org)
Jun 12	Nikolaus Simrock (Ger-pub)		Xavier Désargus (Fr-hp)

C. Debuts:
U.S. -- Luciano Fornasari (N.Y.)

Other - Ole Bull (Paris), Fanny Cerrito (Naples), Julian Dobrski (Warsaw), Marie-Cornélie Falcon (Paris), Livia Frege (Leipzig), Nicola Ivanov (Naples), Hubert Léonard (Liège), Henry Charles Litolff (London), Sophie Loewe (Vienna), Clara Novello (Windsor), Fanny Persiani (Livorno), Jacob Rosenhaim (Frankfurt), Maschinka S. Schubert (London), Rosine Stoltz (Brussels)

D. New Positions:
Conductors: Heinrich Dorn (Riga Opera), Hilarión Eslava (maestro de capilla, Seville Cathedral), Lauro Rossi (Theatro Valle, Rome), Alexander Varlamov (kapellmeister, Moscow Imperial Theaters)

Educational: August W. Bach (Royal Institute for Church Music, Berlin), Henri Brod (oboe, Paris Conservatory), Jean Blaise Martin (voice, Paris Conservatory), Adolph Marx (music director, University of Berlin), Johann T. Mosewius (music director, University of Breslau), Thomas Mudie (piano, Royal Academy, London)

Others: Franz Joseph Antony (organ, Münster Cathedral), Michael Costa (director, King's Theater, London), Gottfried Herrmann (organ, Marienkirche, Lübeck), Ferdinando Paër (Royal Chamber Music, Paris), Samuel Sebastian Wesley (organ, Hereford Cathedral)

E. Prizes and Honors:
Prizes: Ambroise Thomas (Prix de Rome)

Honors: Giacomo Meyerbeer (Legion of Honor)

F. Biographical Highlights:
Frédéric Chopin makes his Paris debut and meets John Field; Gaetano Donizetti breaks his contract with the Naples management to spend more time on composition; John Sullivan Dwight graduates from Harvard and continues study for the ministry; John Field returns to London from his Russian triumphs; Giulia Grisi and Sebastian Lee make their Paris Opera debuts; Thomas Hastings settles in New York and joins the Norman Institute with Lowell Mason; Anthony Heinrich, returning once more to the U.S., settles in Boston; Felix Mendelssohn meets Chopin and Field and makes his second trip to England; Niccolò Paganini returns to Italy and buys the villa Gajona with his English fortune; Gioacchino Rossini meets Olympe Pélissier who becomes his mistress; Wilhemine Schröder-Devriant makes her London debut; Robert Schumann ruins his hand with the so-called "strengthening apparatus"; Elizabeth Stevenson marries William Gaskell; Giuseppe Verdi is refused admittance to the Milan Conservatory after failing the entrance exams.

G. Institutional Openings:
Performing Groups: Adelphi Glee Club (London); Glasgow Philoharmonic Society; New Haven Musical Society (Connecticut); Sacred Harmony Society of London; Société Philharmonique (Dijon); Trotebau Male Choir (Marseilles)

Educational: Boston Academy of Music; Brussels State Academy (Conservatory) of Music

Other: Charles Barker, Organ Maker (Bath); Boehm Flute (first known); De Muzen (The Netherlands); Revue Rétrospective; San Juan Municipal Theater; J. Schuberth and Co., Leipzig Branch; Ticknor and Fields Publishing House (Boston)

H. Musical Literature:
Blaze, François, Chapelle musique des Rois de France
Dotzauer, Friedrich, Violoncellschule
Gardiner, William, The Music of Nature

Häuser, Johann, *Neue pianoforte-schule*
Hoffmann, Heinrich, *Geschichte des deutschen Kirchenlieds*
Kahlert, August, *Blätter aus der Brieftasches eines Musikers*
Mason, Lowell, *Lyra Sacra*
Seyfried, Johann, *Wiener Tonschule*
Zeuner, Charles, *The American Harp*

I. Musical Compositions:

Auber, Daniel, *Le serment* (opera)
Berlioz, Hector, *Rob Roy Overture*
    Lélio, Opus 14
    Les Nuits d'Été
    The Fifth of May, Opus 6
Chopin, Frédéric, *12 Etudes, Opus 10*
    Introduction and Rondo, Opus 16
    Allegro de Concert, Opus 46
    Scherzo in B Minor, Opus 20
Costa, Michael, *Une Heure à Naples* (ballet)
Donizetti, Gaetano, *L'elisir d'amore* (opera)
    Fausta (opera)
    Ugo, conte di Parigi (opera)
Dorn, Heinrich, *Das Schwarmermädchen* (opera)
Field, John, *Grand Pastorale in E Major for Piano and String Quartet*
    Nocturne, "The Troubadour"
Halévy, Jacques, *Yella* (opera)
Hérold, Ferdinand, *Le pré aux clercs* (opera)
    La médecine sans médecin (opera)
Loewe, Carl, *Malekadhel* (opera)
    Lieder, Romanzen und Balladen, Opous 9
    6 Gedichte von Herder
    3 Ballads, Opus 20
Lortzing, Albert, *Der Weihnachtsabend* (singspiel)
    Der Pole und sein kind (singspiel)
    Andreas Hofer (singspiel)
Mendelssohn, Felix, *Symphony No. 5, Opus 107, "Reformation"*
    Calm Sea and Prosperous Voyage Overture, Opus 27
    Capriccio Brillante, Opus 22, for Piano and Orchestra
    Te Deum (voice and organ)
Mercadante, Saverio, *I normanni a Parigi* (opera)
    Ismalia (opera)
Moscheles, Ignaz, *Grosses Septet in D Major, Opus 88*
Rossi, Lauro, *Baldorino, tiranno di Spoleto* (opera)
    Il maestro di scuola (opera)
Schumann, Robert, *Symphony in G Minor* (unpublished)
    Paganini Etudes I, Opus 3, for Piano
    6 Intermezzi, Opus 4, for Piano
Spohr, Louis, *Symphony No. 4, Opus 86, "Die Weihe der Töne"*
    3 String Quartets, Opus 84
Vertovsky, Alexei, *Vadim* (opera)
Wagner, Richard, *Die Hochzeit* (unfinished opera)
    Symphony in C Major
Weigl, Joseph, *Mass, "In Nomine B.M.V."*

1833

World Events:
In the U.S., President Andrew Jackson withdraws all public funds from the Bank of the United States; the American Anti-Slavery Society is founded in the New England States; Oberlin College becomes the first coed college in America; Chicago, Illinois, is incorporated with a population of 200; future President Benjamin Harrison is born. Internationally, the British Parliament bans slavery throughout the British Empire; the Factory Act improves the lot of children working in English factories; the Ottoman Empire concludes a treaty with Russia in order to prevent an Egyptian takeover; Isabella II becomes ruler in Spain; Antonio de Santa Anna becomes President of Mexico; Swedish inventor Alfred Nobel is born.

Cultural Highlights:
Jean A. Ingres becomes President of the École des Beaux-arts in Paris; Wilhelm von Kobell is ennobled; Heinrich Heine's *Geschichte der Neuren Schönen Literatur in Deutschland* is published. Births in the field of art include British artists Edward Burne-Jones and Philip H. Calderon, French sculptor Henri M. Chapu and Irish sculptor Launt Thompson; deaths include American sculptor William Rush and French artist Pierre-Narcisse Guérin. Births in the literary field include Spanish authors Pedro de Alarcón and José de Peroda, British poet Lewis Morris, Australian poet Adam Gordon and American author David R. Locke; deaths include French authors François Andrieux and Victor H. Ducange and poet Charles J. Chenedollé. Other highlights include:

Art: George Catlin, *The Dying Buffalo*; Thomas Cole, *The Catskill Mountains*; Eugène Delacroix, *Murals in the Palais Bourbon*; Antoine Etex, *Cain Cursed by God*; Edwin Landseer, *Jack in Office*; Thomas Sully, *Fanny Kemble as Beatrice*; Joseph Turner, *Music at Petworth*; Richard Westmacott, *The Duke of York* (Waterloo)

Literature: Honoré de Balzac, *Eugénie Grandet*; Black Hawk, *Autobiography*; Marguerite Blessington, *Grace Cassidy*; Thomas Carlyle, *Sartor Resartus*; Davy Crockett, *Autobiography*; Charles Lamb, *Last Essays of Elia*; Charles Lyell, *Principles of Geology*; Edgar A. Poe, *Manuscript Found in a Bottle*; George Sand, *Lelia*

MUSICAL EVENTS

A. Births:

Feb 12	Charles W. Bériot (Fr-pn)	Sep 14	Francis Bache (Br-pn)
Mar	Antonin Bennewitz (Boh-vn)	Sep 21	Josef Rozkosný (Cz-pn)
Mar 4	Michael Hermesdorff (Ger-mus)	Oct 14	William Cusins (Br-pn)
Apr 2	Adolph Fürstner (Ger-pub)	Oct 18	Johannes Hobert (Boh-org)
May 7	Johannes Brahms (Ger-cm)	Oct 26	Adelaide Phillipps (Br-alto)
May 11	Jean Becker (Ger-vn)	Nov 6	Wilhelm Ganz (Ger-pn)
May 18	Robert Forberg (Ger-pub)	Nov 12	Alexander Borodin (Rus-cm)
Jun 27	Alexander Ritter (Ger-vn)	Nov 14	Henry Barnabee (Am-imp)
Jul 17	Luigi Agnesi (Bel-bs)	Dec 6	Barbara Marchisio (It-alto)
Jul 26	Maria Geistinger (Aus-sop)		Giuseppe Fancelli (It-ten)
Aug 4	Robert Pflughaupt (Ger-pn)		

B. Deaths:

Jan 7	R. Cuellar y Altarriba (Sp-org)	May 14	Johann von Königslow (Ger-org)
Jan 10	António Leite (Por-cm)	May 28	Johann Haeffner (Swe-org-cd)
Jan 19	Ferdinand Hérold (Fr-cm)	May 30	Josef Slavík (Cz-vn-cm)
Jan 20	Gertrud E. Mara (Ger-sop)	Sep 15	William Goodrich (Am-pn.m)
Feb 3	Philip Cogan (Ir-org)	Oct 1	Luiza Rosa Todi (Por-mez)
Feb 4	J. de la Salette (Fr-the)	Oct 18	Michael Oginski (Pol-cm)
Apr 8	Antoni Radziwill (Ger-pol)	Oct 20	John Crosse (Br-mus)

Nov   Maria Rosa Coccia (It-cm)   Paul Alday (Fr-vn)
Nov 8   Maximilian Stadler (Aus-cm)   Maria Dickens (Br-sop)
Nov 10 Jacob Eckhard (Ger-org)   Vittorio Trento (It-cm)
Nov 19 Ferdinand Fränzl (Ger-vn)

C. Debuts:
Other - Niels Gade (Copenhagen), Ignazio Marini (Milan), Napoleone Moriani (Pavia), Otto Nicolai (Berlin)

D. New Positions:
Conductors: Carlo Bignani (Verona Opera), Konradin Kreutzer (Josephstadt Theater, Vienna), Felix Mendelssohn (Düsseldorf SO), Giuseppe Saverio Mercadante (maestro di cappella, Novara Cathedral), Carl Rungenhagen (Berlin Singakademie), Francesco Shira (San Carlos Theater, Lisbon), Richard Wagner (chorusmaster, Würzburg)

Educational: Joao Bomtempo (director, Lisbon Conservatory), Guillaume Cassel (voice, Brussels Conservatory), François Fétis (director, Brussels Conservatory), Joseph Fischhof (piano, Vienna Conservatory), Jacques Halévy (counterpoint, Paris Conservatory), Georg Hellmesberger (professor, Vienna Conservatory), Pietro Raimondi (professor, Palermo Conservatory)

Others: Eduard Passy (organ, Stockholm Court)

E. Prizes and Honors:
Honors: Friedrich Berr (Legion of Honor), Hans Nägeli (honorary doctorate, Bonn University)

F. Biographical Highlights:
Alkan (Charles Morhange) begins teaching in Paris; Michael Balfe returns to England from Italy and goes into management; Hector Berlioz marries Henriette Smithson; Giulio Bordogni retires from the opera stage; John Field spends nine months in an Italian hospital; César Franck, age eleven, makes his first tour of Belgium as a concert organist; Mikhail Glinka goes to Berlin for further music study; Louis Antoine Jullien enters the Paris Conservatory but fails in his studies; William Knabe emigrates to the U.S. and settles in Baltimore; Franz Liszt meets Mme. d'Agoult; Albert Lortzing moves to Leipzig and sings in the Opera; Alexis L'vov composes the Russian Czarist Anthem; Felix Mendelssohn makes two further visits to London; Pauline Milder-Hauptmann retires from the stage; Jacques Offenbach enters the Paris Conservatory; Niccolò Paganini commissions a viola work from Berlioz; Robert Schumann founds his "Davidsbundler"; Johann Strauss, Sr., begins touring with his orchestra; Eugenia Tadolini makes her La Scale debut; Henri Vieuxtemps begins a long German tour at the age of 13.

G. Institutional Openings:
Performing Groups: Ansbach Male Chorus; Concerts Symphoniques (Lyons); Distin Family Brass Quartet (London); Glasgow Choral Society; Kiev Philharmonic Society; Lübeck Gesangverein (Singakademie); Sociedade Beneficente Musical (Rio de Janeiro); Société Philharmonique (Rheims); Warsaw Grand Opera; York Choral Society; Zöllner-Verein (Leipzig)

Educational: Accademia Filo-Armonica di Messina

Other: Coventry and Hollier, Publishers (London); *Gazette Musicale de la Belgique*; *Magasin Pittoresque*; Mainz Stadttheater; C. J. Martin and Co., Guitar Makers (N.Y.); *Le Ménestrel*; New York Italian Opera House; The Ossolineum (Lvov); Paris Orphéon; Henry Pilcher and Sons, Organ Builders (Newark); *Régolo* (Hungary); Small Opera Theater (St. Petersburg)

H. Musical Literature:

Fétis, François, *Universal Biography of Musicians and Music I*
Gérard, Henri, *Traité methodique d'harmonie*
Gollmick, Karl, *Kritische terminologie*
Goss, John, *Introduction to Harmony and Thoroughbass*
Häuser, Johann, *Geschichte des christlichen evangelischen Kirchengesanges*
d'Ortigue, Joseph, *Le Balçon de l'Opéra*
Reicha, Anton, *L'Art du compositeur dramatique*
Weber, Gottfried, *Generalbasslehre zum selbstunterrichte*

I. Musical Compositions:

Adam, Adolphe, *Faust* (ballet)
Auber, Daniel, *Gustave III* (opera)
Balfe, Michael, *Enrico IV* (opera)
Bellini, Vincenzo, *Beatrice di Tenda* (opera)
Carafa, Michele, *La prison d'Edimbourg* (opera)
Cherubini, Luigi, *Ali Baba* (opera)
Chopin, Frédéric, *4 Mazurkas, Opus 17*
    Nocturne in G Minor, Opus 15
Costa, Michael, *Sir Huon* (ballet)
Donizetti, Gaetano, *Lucrezia Borgia* (opera)
    Torquato Tasso (opera)
    Parisina (opera)
Field, John, *Concerto No. 7 for Piano and Orchestra*
    Nocturne No. 11 in E-flat Major
    Nouvelle Fantasie in G Major for Piano
Flotow, Friedrich von, *Die Bergknappen* (opera)
    Alfred der Grosse (opera)
Halévy, Jacques, *Les souvenirs de Lafleur* (opera)
Kalliwoda, Johann, *Concertino, Opus 37, for Violin and Orchestra*
Kastner, Jean G., *Oskars Tod* (opera)
Kreutzer, Konradin, *Melusina* (opera)
Loewe, Carl, *Die sieben Schlafer* (oratorio)
    Neckereien (opera)
Marschner, Heinrich, *Hans Heiling* (opera)
Mason, Lowell, *Olivet (hymn tune, "My Faith Looks Up to Thee")*
Mendelssohn, Felix, *Symphony No. 4, Opus 90, "Italian"*
    Beautiful Melusine Overture, Opus 32
    Concertstück No. 1, Opus 113
    Sonata Ecossaise, Opus 28, for Piano
Mercadante, Saverio, *Il conte di Essex* (opera)
Moscheles, Ignaz, *Concerto No. 6, Opus 90, for Piano and Orchestra*
Pucitta, Vincenzo, *Adolfo e Chiara* (opera)
Ricci, Luigi, *I due sergenti* (opera)
Rossi, Lauro, *La fucine di Bergen* (opera)
    Saul (oratorio)
Schmidt, Johann, *Missa Solemnis in D Major*
Schumann, Robert, *Paganini Etudes II, Opus 10*
    Impromtus on a Theme of Clara Wieck, Opus 5
    Piano Toccata in C Major, Opus 7
Sobolewski, Friedrich von, *Imogen* (opera)
Spohr, Louis, *Concertante No. 2, Opus 88, for 2 Violins*
    Double Quartet, Opus 87
Thomas, Ambroise, *String Quartet*
Wagner, Richard, *Die Feen* (opera)
Weigl, Joseph, *Mass, "Nativitate B.M.V."*

1834

World Events:

In the U.S., the Whig Party is formed as an anti-Jackson political party; the Anti-Abolitionist Riots take place in the North; Cyrus McCormick patents the first practical reaper; Fort Laramie is built on the Oregon Trail; Columbus, Ohio, is incorporated; Brooklyn, New York, is chartered; the University of Louisville is founded. Internationally, Robert Peel becomes the British Prime Minister; Civil War takes place in Spain between the Constitutionalists and the Carlists; the Zollverein, the first step towards unity, is formed by several of the German States; the South Australia Act opens the country for colonization--Melbourne is founded.

Cultural Highlights:

Lithographers Currier and Ives are open in New York City; François Saint-Marc Girardin begins teaching poetry at the Sorbonne; Jean A. Ingres becomes professor at the Royal Academy of Art. Births in the art field include American artist James Whistler, French artists Edgar Degas and Frédéric Bartholdi and British author and artist William Morris; Thomas Stothard dies. Births in the literary field include American humorist Charles Browne (Artemus Ward), authors Horatio Alger and Frank R. Stockton and poet George Upton, British poet James Thomson and novelist-artist George du Maurier, German historian and poet Felix Dahn, Czech novelist and poet Jan Neruda, Finnish poet and novelist Alexis Kivi and Argentine poet Joséf Hernandez; deaths include Dutch novelist Aernout Drost, French author H. F. de Lamennais, Scotch poet Thomas Pringle and British authors William Blackwood, Alexander Chalmers and poets Samuel Taylor Coleridge and Charles Lamb. Other highlights include:

Art: George Catlin, *Commanche Village*; Alexandre Decamps, *Defeat of the Cimbri*; Eugène Delacroix, *Women of Algiers*; Jean-Auguste Ingres, *The Martyrdom of St. Symphorion*; William Strickland, *Merchant's Exchange* (Philadelphia); Joseph Turner, *The Burning of Parliament*; Emil Wolff, *Hebe and Ganymed*

Literature: Honoré de Balzac, *Le Père Goriot*; Robert Browning, *Porphyria's Lover*; Edward Bulwer-Lytton,*The Last Days of Pompeii*; Benjamin Disraeli, *The Infernal Marriage*; Maria Edgeworth, *Helen*; Adam Mickiewicz, *Pan Tadeusz*; Alexander Pushkin, *The Queen of Spades*; Charles Sainte-Beuve, *Volupté*

MUSICAL EVENTS

A. Births:

Feb 9	Charles R. Adams (Am-ten)	Jun 22	Frédéric Ritter (Ger-cd)
Feb 11	Gustav Walter (Aus-ten)	Jul 20	Wilhelm Rischbieter (Ger-the)
Feb 23	Ernest Nicolini (Fr-ten)	Aug 6	Arthur Pougin (Fr-cri)
Feb 28	Charles Santley (Br-bar)	Aug 17	Peter Benoît (Bel-cm)
Mar 15	Marietta Piccolomini (It-sop)	Aug 31	Amilcare Ponchielli (It-cm)
Mar 23	Julius Reubke (Ger-pn)	Sep 28	Charles Lamoureux (Fr-cd)
Apr 6	Hart P. Danks (Am-voc-cm)	Oct 3	Vilém Blodek (Cz-fl-cm)
Apr 23	Jan Pieter Land (Hol-mus)	Nov 15	Paul Jausions (Fr-mus)
Jun 5	Teresa Stolz (Boh-sop)	Nov 18	Henry Higginson (Am-pat)
Jun 16	Carlo Angeloni (It-cd)		

B. Deaths:

Feb 4	Julie Candeille (Fr-sop)	Sep 2	J. Beauvarlet-Charpentier
May 23	Charles Wesley (Br-org-cm)		(Fr-org)
Jun 29	Alexandre Choron (Fr-the)	Oct 8	François Boieldieu (Fr-cm)
			August Duranowski (Pol-vn)

C. Debuts:
U.S. -- Mary Anne Paton (tour), Joseph Wood (tour)

Other - Anne Childe (London), Filippo Coletti (Naples), Francilla Pixis (Karlsruhe), Elizabeth Poole (London), Mary Shaw (London), Arthur Saint-Léon (Stuttgart), Felice Varesi (Varese)

D. New Positions:
Conductors: Juan Bros y Bertomeu (maestro de capilla, Oviedo Cathedral), Franz Lachner (Mannheim Opera), Ferdinand Ries (Aix-la-Chapelle), Théophile Tilmant (Italian Theater, Paris), Richard Wagner (Magdeburg Opera)

Educational: Laure Cinti-Damoreau (voice, Paris Conservatory), Leopold Jansa (violin, University of Vienna), George MacFarren (professor, Royal Academy of Music), Jean-Henri Ravina (piano, Paris Conservatory)

Others: Pedro Albéniz y Basanta (organ, Royal Chapel, Madrid), William Ayrton (editor, *The Musical Library*), John Parry (music critic, London *Morning Post*)

E. Prizes and Honors:
Prizes: Antoine-Aimable Elwart (Prix de Rome)

Honors: Henri-Montan Berton (Legion of Honor), Heinrich Marschner (honorary doctorate, University of Leipzig), Giacomo Meyerbeer (French Institute)

F. Biographical Highlights:
Eduard Devrient loses his singing voice and turns to acting; Mikhail Glinka, on the death of his father, returns to Russia to take care of the family affairs; Giulia Grisi makes her London debut; Anthony Philip Heinrich again leaves the U.S. and returns to Europe where he has several works performed; Nicola Ivanov and Maria Malibran both make their La Scala debuts; Franz Liszt goes to Geneva and moves in with the Countess d'Agoult by whom he has three children, one of them Cosima Liszt; Niccolò Paganini, in failing health, returns to Italy and begins limiting his engagements; Gioacchino Rossini recuperates in Bologna from serious illness; Henri Vieuxtemps, with only two weeks practice, reintroduces Beethoven's *Violin Concerto*; Johann Michael Vogl gives his last public appearance; Richard Wagner, while conducting the orchestra with Bethmann's theater company in Magdeburg, meets actress Christine (Minna) Planer.

G. Institutional Openings:
Performing Groups: Antient Concerts Society (Dublin); Helsinki City Orchestra; Maglioni Chamber Concerts (Florence); Musikalischer Cirkel (Breslau); Société des Derniers Quators de Beethoven

Educational: Orleans Institut Musical

Other: A = 440 vps (decided by the Stuttgart Congress of Physicists); Alexandre Debain Instrument Co. (Paris); *Le Franc-juge*; Jacques Heugel and Co., Publishers (Paris); Maatschaplpij moor Tonkunst (Leiden music society); *Neue Zeitschrift für Musik*; Paradise Street Town Hall (Birmingham); Society of British Musicians (London)

H. Musical Literature:
Baillot, Pierre, *L'Art du violon*
Bartay, András, *Magyar Apollo*
Czerny, Carl, *Lehrbuch der...Composition*
Kiesewetter, Raphael, *Geschichte der europäisch-abendländischen, das ist unserer heutigen Musik*
Mason, Lowell, *Manual of Instruction (Pestalozzian)*
Momigny, Jérôme-Joseph de, *Cours général de musique*
Scheibler, Johann, *Der physikalische und musikalische Tonmesser*

Winterfeld, Carl von, *Johannes Gabrieli und sein zeitalter*

I. Musical Compositions:
Adam, Adolphe, *Le Châlet* (opera)
Anonymous, *Turkey in the Straw* (song)
Auber, Daniel, *Lestocq* (opera)
Barnett, John, *The Mountain Sylph* (opera)
Bennett, William S., *Symphony No. 4*
    Concerto No. 3 for Piano and Orchestra
    Parisina Overture
Berlioz, Hector, *Harold in Italy, Opus 16*
    Sara la Baigneuse, Opus 11
Bishop, Henry, *The Seventh Day* (cantata)
Cherubini, Luigi, *String Quartet No. 3 in D Minor*
Donizetti, Gaetano, *Maria Stuarda* (opera)
    Rosamonda d'Inghilterra (opera)
    Gemma di Vergy (opera)
Glinka, Mikhail, *Overture-Symphony on Russian Themes*
    Sextet for Piano and Strings
Hiller, Ferdinand, *Symphony No. 2*
Kalliwoda, Johann, *Concert Overtures No. 2-4, Opus 44, 55 and 56*
    Introduction and Rondo, Opus 51, for Horn and Orchestra
Kastner, Jean G., *Der Sarazene* (opera)
Kreutzer, Konradin, *Tom Rick* (opera)
    Das Nachtlager von Granada (opera)
    Der Verschwender (incidental music)
Liszt, Franz, *Grande Fantaisie Symphonique for Piano and Orchestra*
Loewe, Carl, *Die eherne Schlange* (oratorio)
    Die drei Wünsche (opera)
    5 Gedichte aus Goethes Nachlass
Mendelssohn, Felix, *Songs without Words, Opus 19*
    Rondo Brillant, Opus 29, for Piano
    6 Partsongs, Opus 41
    Infelice, Opus 94, for Soprano and Orchestra
Mercadante, Saverio, *Emma d'Antiochia* (opera)
    La gioventù di Enrico V (opera)
    Uggero il danese (opera)
Moniuszko, Stanislaw, *The Bureaucrats* (opera)
Neukomm, Sigismund, *David* (oratorio)
Pacini, Giovanni, *Irene* (opera)
Paër, Ferdinando, *Un caprice de femme* (opera)
Paganini, Niccolò, *Concerto for Viola and Orchestra*
Prévost, Eugène, *Cosimo* (opera)
Ricci, Luigi, *Chi dura vince* (opera)
    Un aventura di Scaramuccia (opera)
Rosenhaim, Jacob, *Der besuch im irrenhause* (opera)
Rossi, Lauro, *Amelia* (opera)
    La casa disabitata (opera)
Schumann, Robert, *Etudes Symphoniques, Opus 13, for Piano*
Scott, Lady John D., *Annie Laurie* (song)
Spohr, Louis, *String Quintet, Opus 91*
Suppé, Franz von, *Mass in F Major*
Taubert, Wilhelm, *Der Zigeuner* (opera)
Weigl, Joseph, *Mass in A Major*

1835

World Events:
In the U.S., President Andrew Jackson escapes harm when an assassin's pistol misfires; the Liberty Bell cracks during Justice Marshall's funeral; Samuel Colt patents the revolver; the Second Seminole War is fought in Florida; Philadelphia passes the first ten-hour labor law; the Texas Revolution against Mexico begins. Internationally, Haley's Comet makes its scheduled appearance; the Municipal Corporations Act attempts to regulate and standardize local Governments in England; Turkey takes over in Tripoli; Francis I of Austria dies and is succeeded by Ferdinand I; the Geological Survey of Great Britain is founded.

Cultural Highlights:
The magazine *Monde Dramatique* begins publication; Edgar Allen Poe becomes editor of the *Southern Literary Messenger*; Georg K. Nagler begins publication of his monumental *Neues Allgemeines Künstlerlexikon*; Henry Wadsworth Longfellow begins teaching modern languages at Harvard. Births in the art field include American artist John La Farge and sculptor Larkin G. Mead; French artist Antoine-Jean Gros dies. Births in the literary world include American author Samuel Clemens (Mark Twain) and poets Ellen Moulton and John J. Piatt, Czech poet Vítezslav Hálek, British poet Alfred Austin and author Samuel Butler, German poet Wilhelm Hertz and Italian poet Giosuè Carducci; deaths include Scotch poets James Hogg and William Motherwell, German author Friederike Brun, poet August Platen and Polish poet Kazimierz Brodzinski. Other highlights include:

Art: John Constable, *Valley Farm*; Jean Baptiste Corot, *Hagar in the Desert*; Thomas Doughty, *In Nature's Wonderland*; Thomas Eakins, *The Swimming Hole*; Wilhelm von Kaulbach, *Battle of the Huns*; Samuel Morse, *Niagara Falls from Table Rock*; William Mount, *Bargaining for a Horse*; William Strickland, *U.S. Mint, Charlotte*

Literature: Hans Christian Andersen, *Fairy Tales for Children I*; Robert Browning, *Paracelsus*; Georg Büchner, *Dantons Tod*; Edward Bulwer-Lytton, *Rienzi*; Théophile Gautier, *Madamoiselle de Maupin*; Micolai Gogol, *Taras Bulba*; Victor Hugo, *Songs of Twilight*; Washington Irving, *A Tour of the Prairies*; William Wordsworth, *Poems*

MUSICAL EVENTS

A. Births:

Jan 18	César Cui (Rus-cm)	Jul 21	Marguerite Artôt (Fr-mez)
Jan 26	Vassili Bezekirsky (Rus-vn)	Aug 7	Allen J. (Signor) Foli (Ir-bs)
Mar 1	Ebenezer Prout (Br-the)	Oct 7	Felix Draeseke (Ger-cm)
Mar 8	Hans von Rokitansky (Aus-bs)	Oct 9	Camille Saint-Saëns (Fr-cm)
Mar 19	Franz Betz (Ger-bar)	Oct 11	Theodore Thomas (Ger-cd)
Mar 24	August Winding (Den-pn)	Oct 30	Carlotta Patti (It-sop)
Mar 25	Franz Nachbaur (Ger-ten)	Nov 2	Jules E. Cohen (Fr-cm)
Apr 22	Guglielmo Andreoli (It-pn)	Nov 11	Isabella Galletti-Gianoli (It-sop)
Jun 2	Nicholai Rubinstein (Rus-pn)	Nov 25	Andrew Carnegie (Am-pat)
Jun 14	Adolf Stern (Ger-mus)	Dec 7	Joseph Pothier (Bel-mus)
Jul 5	Frederick Brandeis (Aus-pn)	Dec 8	Carlotta Marchisio (It-sop)
Jul 10	Henri Wieniawski (Pol-vn)	Dec 9	George Hutchings (Am-org.m)

B. Deaths:

Jan 22	Marie A. Guénin (Fr-vn)	Aug 10	Klaus Scholl (Den-cm)
Mar 13	Aline Bertrand (Fr-hp)	Aug 11	Olaf Ahlström (Swe-org)
Apr	François Tourte (Fr-bow.m)	Aug 25	Nicolas Platel (Fr-cel)
Apr 3	François Nadermann (Fr-hp)	Sep 23	Vincenzo Bellini (It-cm)
Aug 3	Wenzel Müller (Aus-cm-cd)		

C. Debuts:
U.S. -- Charlotte Cushman, Henry Christian Timm (N.Y.)

Other - Adelaide Kemble (London), Jan K. Pisek (Prague), Carl Reinecke (as violinist)

D. New Positions:
Conductors: Felix Mendelssohn (Leipzig Gewandhaus), Hubert Ries (Berlin PO), Giuseppe Verdi (maestro di musica, Busseto)

Educational: Victor F. Desvignes (director, Metz Conservatory), Gaetano Donizetti (counterpoint, Naples Music College), Lambert Meerts (violin, Brussels Conservatory), Martin J. Mengal (director, Ghent Conservatory)

Others: Hector Berlioz (music critic, *Journal des Débats*), George Elvey (organ, St. George's, Windsor), Lauro Rossi (director, Italian Opera Co., Mexico), Samuel Sebastian Wesley (organ, Exeter Cathedral)

E. Prizes and Honors:
Honors: Vincenzo Bellini (Legion of Honor), Lowell Mason (honorary doctorate, New York University), Anton Reicha (French Academy)

F. Biographical Highlights:
Julius Benedict leaves Paris and settles permanently in London; Franz Adolf Berwald opens an orthopedic institution in Berlin; Anton Bruckner begins some regular music instruction from his father and cousin; Frédéric Chopin falls in love with Marie Wodzinski and meets the Schumanns; Gaetano Donizetti visits Paris for a performance of his opera at the Italian Theater; César Franck moves with his family to Paris and begins organ lessons with Reicha; Robert Franz, with his parents reluctant approval, enters the Conservatory in Dessau; Mikhail Glinka enters into a very unhappy marriage and soon leaves his wife; Felix Mendelssohn, age 26, accepts the position as conductor of the Gewandhaus Orchestra and soon turns it into one of the best on the continent; Georg K. Nagler begins publication of the monumental *Neues Allgemeines Künstlerlexikon*; Franz von Suppé, following his father's death, moves with his mother to Vienna and studies at the Conservatory; Giuseppe Verdi decides to return to Busseto when he wins the appointment as music master; William Vincent Wallace begins his travels to Australia, New Zealand and the Americas.

G. Institutional Openings:
Performing Groups: Boston Brass Band; Carlsbad SO (Germany); Philipp Fahrbach Orchestra (Vienna); Gotha Liedertafel; Philadelphia Männerchor; Société de Musique de Chambre (Paris)

Educational: Conservatório Nacional (Lisbon); Geneva Conservatory of Music; Ghent Conservatory of Music; Metz Conservatory of Music; Whittlesey's Music School (Salem)

Other: Bass Tuba (by W. F. Wieprecht); Brinsmead Piano Co. (London); Giovanni Canti, Music Publisher (Milan); C. A. Challier and Co., Publishers (Berlin); *Deutsche Revue*; Oliver Ditson and Co. (Boston); *Gazette Musicale de Paris*; *Musical Magazine* (N.Y.); St. James Hall (Buffalo)

H. Musical Literature:
Alfieri, Pietro, *Saggio storico teorio pratico del canto gregoriano*
Ayrton, William, *Sacred Minstrelsy*
Cherubini, Luigi, *Cours de contrepoint et de la fugue*
Drieberg, Friedrich von, *Wörterbuch der grieschen Musik*
Elizaga, José, *Principios de la harmonía y de la melodia*
Hogarth, George, *Musical History, Biography and Criticism*
Mason, Lowell, *Boston Academy Collection of Church Music*
Oliphant, Thomas, *Brief Account of the Madrigal Society*

Schilling, Gustav, *Enzyklopädie der gesamten musikalischen Wissenschaften I*
Sechter, Simon, *Praktische Generalbass-Schule*
Walker, William, *Southern Harmony*
Woolhouse, Wesley, *Essay on Musical Intervals*

I. Musical Compositions:
Auber, Daniel, *Le cheval de bronze* (opera)
Balfe, Michael, *The Siege of Rochelle* (opera)
Bellini, Vincenzo, *I puritani* (opera)
Carafa, Michele, *La grande duchesse* (opera)
Chélard, Hippolyte, *Die Hermannschlacht* (opera)
Cherubini, Luigi, *String Quartets No. 4-6*
Chopin, Frédéric, *4 Mazurkas, Opus 24*
    2 Polonaises, Opus 26
    2 Nocturnes, Opus 27
    Fantasie-Impromtu, Opus 66
    Ballade in G Minor, Opus 23
Donizetti, Gaetano, *Lucia de Lammermoor* (opera)
    Marino Faliero (opera)
    Requiem Mass in Memory of Bellini
Flotow, Friedrich von, *Pierre et Catherine* (opera)
Halévy, Jacques, *La juive* (opera)
    L'eclair (opera)
Kalliwoda, Johann, *Symphony No. 4, Opus 60*
    String Quartet No. l, Opus 61
Kastner, Jean G., *Die Königin der Sarmaten* (opera)
Kreutzer, Konradin, *Der Bräutigam in der Klemme* (opera)
Lindblad, Adolf F., *Frondörerne* (opera)
Liszt, Franz, *Apparitions for Piano*
Loewe, Carl, *Die Apostel von Philippi, Opus 48* (oratorio)
    Gutenberg, Opus 48 (oratorio)
    6 Ballads, Opus 43 and 44
Lortzing, Albert, *Die beiden Schützen* (opera)
Mendelssohn, Felix, *3 Capriccios, Opus 33, for Piano*
    2 Sacred Songs, Opus 112
Mercadante, Saverio, *I due Figaro* (opera)
    Francesco Donato (opera)
Moscheles, Ignaz, *Overture, Joan of Arc, Opus 91*
Pacini, Giovanni, *Carlo di Borgogna* (opera)
Persiani, Giuseppe, *Ines de Castro* (opera)
Reissiger, Carl, *Turandot* (opera)
Ricci, Luigi, *Chiara di Montalbano* (opera)
    La donna colonello (opera)
Rossi, Lauro, *Leocadia* (opera)
Rossini, Gioacchino, *Soirées Musicales* (based on earlier works)
Schumann, Robert, *Carnaval, Opus 9, for Piano*
    Piano Sonata No. l, Opus 11
Spohr, Louis, *Concerto No. 13, Opus 92, for Violin and Orchestra*
    Des Heilands letzte Stunden (oratorio)
    String Quartet in A Major, Opus 93
Thomas, Ambroise, *String Quintet*
Truhn, Friedrich, *Trilby* (opera)
Vertovsky, Alexei, *Askold's Grave* (opera)
Wagner, Richard, *Das Liebesverbot* (opera)
    Columbus Overture

1836

World Events:
In the U.S., Martin Van Buren is elected as President No. 8; Arkansas becomes State No. 25; the Texans are defeated at the Battle of the Alamo but defeat the Mexicans at the Battle of San Jacinto; President Andrew Jackson puts out his *Specie Circular* causing a panic; Cleveland, Ohio, is incorporated; work begins on the Washington Monument; former President James Madison dies. Internationally, the People's Charter, a working class movement, begins in England; the Boers begin the "Great Trek" out of South Africa to escape British rule; the University of London is founded; settlement of Adelaide, Australia, begins; J. F. Daniell developes the voltaic cell.

Cultural Highlights:
The first printing is made of *McGuffey's Readers*; Jean Bonnassieux receives the Prix de Rome in Art; David Wilkie is knighted. Births in the literary field include American authors Thomas Aldrich and Bret Harte, British novelist Walter Besant and Spanish poet Gustavo A. Becquer; deaths include French philosopher A. Destutt de Tracy, dramatist François Raynouard and poet Rouget de Lisle, Hungarian poet Dániel Berzsenyi, British authors William Godwin and George Colman, Jr. and German dramatist Christian Grabbe. Births in the art field include American artists Winslow Homer, Homer D. Martin and Elihu Vedder, British artists Lawrence Alma-Tadema and Edward J. Poynter, French artists Ignace Fantin-Latour and James J. Tissot and German artist Franz von Lensbach; deaths include Belgian sculptor Matthieu Kessels and French artist Carle Vernet. Other highlights include:

Art: Thomas Cole, *The Course of Empire*; William Collins, *Happy as a King*; John Constable, *Stonehenge*; Jean Baptiste Corot, *Diana and Actaeon*; Edward Hicks, *The Cornell Farm*; Ernest Meissonier, *The Errand Boy*; Friedrich Overbeck, *Marriage of the Virgin*; François Rude, *La Marseillaise* (Arc de Triomphe)

Literature: Honoré de Balzac, *L'Enfant Maudit*; Georg Büchner, *Woyzeck*; Charles Dickens, *The Pickwick Papers*; Antonio García Gutiérrez, *Il Travador*; Nicolai Gogol, *The Inspector General* and *The Nose*; Oliver W. Holmes, *Poems*; Alphonse de Lamartine, *Jocelyn*; Nikolaus Lenau, *Faust*; Frederick Marryat, *Mr. Midshipman Easy*

MUSICAL EVENTS

A. Births:

Jan 4	Ilma di Murska (Yug-sop)	May 28	Friedrich Baumfelder (Ger-pn)
Jan 12	Arabella Goddard (Br-pn)	Jun 14	Frederike Grün (Ger-sop)
Jan 20	John T. Carrodus (Br-vn)	Jun 29	Thomas P. Ryder (Am-org)
Feb 16	Vincenzo Graziani (It-bar)	Jul	Thomas A. Cook (Br-bs)
Feb 21	Léo Delibes (Fr-cm)	Jul 2	Ludwig Schnoor von Carolsfeld
Feb 22	Mitrophan Belaiev (Rus-pub)		(Ger-ten)
Mar 8	Adolf Christiani (Ger-pn)	Jul 11	Antonio C. Gomes (Bra-cm)
Mar 12	Samuel David (Fr-cm)	Aug 10	Oskar Kolbe (Ger-the)
Mar 28	Arthur von Oettingen (Ger-the)	Sep 5	Myron Whitney (Am-bs)
Apr 4	Charles J. Hopkins (Am-cm)	Nov 18	William S. Gilbert (Br-lib)
May 7	Euphrosyne Parepa-Rosa	Dec 23	William Castle (Br-ten)
	(Br-sop)		Elise Hensler (Am-sop)

B. Deaths:

Jan 3	Friedrich Witt (Ger-vn-cm)	Jun 9	Supply Belcher (Am-cm-au)
Apr 16	Gottlieb Graupner (Ger-cm)	Jul 3	Cecilia Davies (Br-sop)
May 6	Christian Latrobe (Br-cm)	Jul 16	Gaetano Crivelli (It-ten)
May 7	Norbert Burgmüller (Ger-pn)	Jul 26	José M. Gomis (Sp-cm)
May 28	Anton Reicha (Boh-cm-the)	Aug 26	James Power (Ir-pub)

Sep 14 Vincenzo Lavigna (It-voc)
Sep 19 Karl F. Ebers (Ger-cm)
Sep 21 John S. Smith (Br-org)
Sep 23 Maria Malibran (Sp-mez)
Oct 16 Friedrich Fröhlich (Swi-cm)

Dec 4 Daniel Read (Am-cm)
Dec 12 Giuseppe Farinelli (It-cm)
Dec 26 Hans Nägeli (Swi-cm-au)
Dec 29 Johann Schenk (Aus-cm-cd)

C. Debuts:

Other - Nikolai Afanas'yev (Moscow), Aloys Fuchs (Vienna), Katinka Heinefetter (Frankfurt), Teresa Milanollo (Mondovi), Maria Dolores Nau (Paris), Elizabeth Rainforth (London), Edward Roeckel (London), Sebastiano Ronconi (Lucca)

D. New Positions:

Conductors: Hippolyte Chélard (kapellmeister, Weimar), Ferdinand David (Leipzig Gewandhaus), Franz Lachner (kapellmeister, Munich), Luigi Ricci (maestro di cappella, Trieste), Ferdinand Ries (Frankfurt St. Cecilia Society)

Educational: Antoine E. Batiste (solfeggio, Paris Conservatory), Antoine-Aimable Elwart (harmony, Paris Conservatory), Louis Kufferath (director, Leeuwarden Conservatory), Aimé-Ambroise Leborne (counterpoint and fugue, Paris Conservatory), Auguste-Mathieu Panseron (voice, Paris Conservatory), Etienne Pastou (voice, Paris Conservatory), Thomas Walmisley (professor, Cambridge)

Others: Thomas Attwood (organ, Royal Chapel, London)

E. Prizes and Honors:

Prizes: Xavier Boisselot (Prix de Rome)

Honors: Jacques Halévy (French Institute), Frédéric Kalkbrenner (Order of Leopold), Clara Wieck (Imperial Chamber Virtuoso, Vienna)

F. Biographical Highlights:

Luigi Arditi enters the Conservatory of Milan; John Braham returns to the stage after several poor investments deplete his finances; Ferdinand David, on the invitation of Mendelssohn, becomes concertmaster of the Leipzig Gewandhaus Orchestra; Livia Frege marries and retires from the opera stage; Charles Gounod enters the Conservatory of Paris; Charles Hallé goes to Paris for music study and joins the Chopin-Liszt circle; Ferdinand Hiller, on the death of his father, travels in Italy; Louis Jullien becomes a conductor of dance music; Franz Liszt defeats Sigismond Thalberg in a pianistic "duel"; Maria Malibran marries the violinist Charles de Bériot just six months before her death from a fall from a horse; Felix Mendelssohn becomes engaged to Cécile Sophie Jeanrenaud; Gioacchino Rossini, after winning his litigation suit against France, settles in Bologna; Louis Spohr marries pianist Marianne Pfeiffer, his second wife; Eugenia Tadolini makes her La Scala debut; Giuseppe Verdi marries Margherita Barezzi; Robert Volkmann studies music with K. F. Becker in Leipzig; Richard Wagner marries Minna Planer but loses his position when the Magdeburg Opera group fails.

G. Institutional Openings:

Performing Groups: Huddersfield Choral Society (England); Old Settler's Harmonic Society (Chicago); Portland Sacred Music Society (Maine); Purcell Club (London); Toronto Musical Society

Other: Brainard and Son, Publishers (Cleveland); Danish Musical Society (Copenhagen); J. F. Edelmann, Music Publisher (Havana); Friedrich Haas, Organ Builder (Switzerland); Luigi Lambertini, Piano Maker (Lisbon); J. B. Lippincott and Co. (Philadelphia); Mahillon Wind Instrument Co. (Brussels); *Musical World*; Pestbuda Society of Musicians; Samuel R. Warren, Organ Builder (Montreal)

H. Musical Literature:

   Asioli, Bonifazio, *Il Maestro di composizione* (posthumous publication)
   Berr, Friedrich, *Traité complet de la clarinette...*
   Calegari, Antonio, *Modi generali del canto*
   Knorr, Julius, *Neue pianoforteschule*
   Mainzer, Joseph, *Méthode de chant pour voix d'hommes*
   Mason, Lowell, *Sabbath School Songs*
   Oliphant, Thomas, *A Short Account of Madrigals*
   Tulou, Jean-Louis, *Flute Method*
   Wolle, Peter, ed., *Moravian Tune Book*

I. Musical Compositions:

   Adam, Adolphe, *Le Postillon de Longjumeau* (opera)
      La Fille du Danube (opera)
   Auber, Daniel, *Actéon* (opera)
      Les chaperons blanc (opera)
   Balfe, Michael, *The Maid of Artois* (opera)
   Bennett, William S., *The Naiads Overture*
   Bertin, Louise, *Esmeralda* (opera)
   Cherubini, Luigi, *Requiem in D Minor*
   Chopin, Frédéric, *12 Etudes, Opus 25*
      Ballade in F Major, Opus 38
      17 Polish Songs, Opus 74
   Donizetti, Gaetano, *Belisario* (opera)
      Il campanello di notte (opera)
      L'assedio di Calais (opera)
   Field, John, *Nocturnes No. 14-16 for Piano*
   Flotow, Friedrich von, *Sérafine* (opera)
   Glinka, Mikhail, *A Life for the Tsar* (opera)
   Grisar, Albert, *Sarah* (opera)
   Heinrich, Anthony, *Symphony, "Combat of the Condor"*
   Hullah, John P., *The Village Coquette* (opera)
   Liszt, Franz, *Années de Pèlerinage, Year I*
      Grande Valse de Bravura
   Loewe, Carl, *3 Ballades, Opus 56*
      Die Festizeiten (oratorio)
   Lortzing, Albert, *Die Schatzkammer des Ynka* (opera)
   Marschner, Heinrich, *Das Schloss am Aetna* (opera)
   Mendelssohn, Felix, *St. Paul, Opus 36* (oratorio)
      Trauermarsch, Opus 103, for Band
   Mercadante, Saverio, *I briganti* (opera)
   Meyerbeer, Giacomo, *Les Huguenots* (opera)
   Moscheles, Ignaz, *Concerto No. 7, Opus 93, for Piano and Orchestra*
      Characteristic Etudes for Piano, Opus 95
   Perry, George, *Belshazzar's Feast* (cantata)
   Rossi, Lauro, *Giovanni Shore* (opera)
   Schmidt, Johann, *Rinaldo* (cantata)
   Schumann, Robert, *Piano Sonata in F Minor, Opus 14*
      Fantasy in C Major, Opus 17, for Piano
   Sobolewski, Friedrich von, *Velleda* (opera)
   Strauss, Joseph, *Armiodan* (opera)
   Suppé, Franz von, *Mass in C Major*
   Thomas, Ambroise, *Fantasy for Piano and Orchestra*
   Vaccai, Nicola, *Giovanna Gray* (opera)
   Wagner, Richard, *Polonia Overture*
      Rule, Britannia Overture
   Wesley, Samuel S., *6 Organ Voluntaries, Opus 36*
   Weyse, Christoph, *Festen paa Kenilworth* (opera)

1837

World Events:
In the U.S., the Panic of 1837 takes place; Michigan becomes State No. 26; Atlanta, Georgia is founded; the Chesapeake and Ohio Railroad is chartered; the Second Seminole War comes to an end in Florida; the Power Loom is patented by W. Crompton; future President Grover Cleveland is born. Internationally, the Victorian Era begins with the accession of Queen Victoria to the British Throne; several unsuccessful rebellions against British rule take place in Canada; the American and Foreign Bible Society is founded; F. Fröbel opens the first Kindergarten in Germany.

Cultural Highlights:
The Royal College of Art opens in London as the School of Design; Augustus Callcott and Richard Westmacott are knighted; Hermann Melville runs away from home and goes to sea; Louis F. Lejeune becomes director of the École des Beaux-Arts in Paris. Births in the world of art include British artist Thomas Moran, German artist Hans von Maurées and French artist Alphonse Legros; deaths include British artist John Constable and French artist François Gérard. Births in the literary world include American authors John Burroughs, Edward Eggleston and William D. Howells, poet Cincinnatus Miller, British poet Algernon Swinburne and French dramatist Henri F. Becque; deaths include Italian poet Giacomo Leopardi, German dramatist Georg Büchner and Russian poet Alexander Pushkin. Other highlights include:

Art: Alfred Edward Chalon, *John Knox, the Reprover*; Thomas Cole, *Departure and Return*; John Constable, *Arundel Mill and Castle*; Jean Baptiste Corot, *St. Jerome*; Eugène Delacroix, *The Battle of Taillebourg*; Horatio Greenough, *The Rescue* (marble); Joseph Turner, *Interior at Petworth*; George Watts, *A Wounded Heron*

Literature: Honoré de Balzac, *Illusions Perdues*; Louis Bertrand, *Gaspard de la Nuit*; Thomas Carlyle, *The French Revolution*; Charles Dickens, *Oliver Twist*; Joseph von Eichendorff, *Poems*; Ralph W. Emerson, *The Concord Hymn*; Nathaniel Hawthorne, *Twice-Told Tales*; Alphonse de Lamartine, *Chute d'un Ange*

MUSICAL EVENTS

A. Births:

Jan 2	Mily Balakirev (Rus-cm)	May 23	Joseph Wieniawski (Pol-pn)
Feb 1	Gustave M. García (Sp-bar)	May 24	Georgina Weldon (Br-sop)
Feb 7	Gustav Mollenhauer (Ger-ww.m)	Jun 23	Ernest Guiraud (Am-cm)
Feb 27	Eugène Diaz de la Peña (Fr-cm)	Jul 20	Hans Sommer (Ger-cm)
Mar 6	Georg Unger (Ger-ten)	Aug 24	Théodore Dubois (Fr-cm)
Mar 12	Alexandre Guilmant (Fr-org)	Sep 29	Charles J. Grisart (Fr-cm)
Mar 13	Leo Koffler (Aus-voc-cm)	Nov 2	Auguste Vianesi (It-cd)
Apr 26	F. von Hausegger (Aus-the)	Dec 9	Emil Waldteufel (Ger-cm)
Apr 30	Alfred R. Gaul (Br-org)	Dec 28	Benjamin Land (Am-pn-cd)
May 8	William S. Mathews (Am-org)	Dec 30	M. Lipsius (La Mara)(Ger-cri)

B. Deaths:

Jan 7	Franz Antony (Ger-cm-mus)	Jun 16	Valentino Fioravanti (It-cm)
Jan 11	John Field (Br-pn-cm)	Jun 20	Giovanni Furno (It-the)
Feb 5	James Cervetto (Br-cel)	Aug 7	Johann Schelble (Ger-ten)
Feb 10	August Bergt (Ger-cm)	Oct 6	Jean F. Lesueur (Fr-cm)
Feb 20	Ernst Häusler (Ger-cel)	Oct 11	Samuel Wesley (Br-org)
Mar 26	Joseph Lincke (Ger-cel)	Oct 17	Johann Hummel (Aus-pn)
Mar 26	Charles Nicholson (Br-fl)	Oct 28	Jean B. Martin (Fr-ten)
May 5	Nicola Zingarelli (It-cm)		John Relfe (Br-cm-the)

C. Debuts:
Other - Jeanne Anaïs Castellan (Turin), Gaetano Fraschini (Pavia), Joseph Goldberg (as violinist), Anna R. Laidlaw (Leipzig), Alfredo Piatti (Milan), Paulina Rivoli (Warsaw), Joseph Tichatschek (Graz), Pauline Viardot-García (Brussels)

D. New Positions:
Conductors: Francesco Basili (maestro di cappella, St. Peter's, Rome), Franz Erkel (Pest Opera), Alexei L'vov (Imperial Chapel, St. Petersburg), Otto Nicolai (Kärntnerthor Theater, Vienna), Giovanni Pacini (Ducal Chapel, Lucca), Heinrich Proch (Josephstadt Theater, Vienna), Franz Skroup (Bohemian Theater, Prague), Richard Wagner (Riga Opera)

Educational: Gaetano Donizetti (director, Naples Conservatory), Antoine Marmontel (solfeggio, Paris Conservatory), Lowell Mason (superintendent of music, Boston Schools)

Others: William Ayrton (music critic, London *Examiner*), Karl F. Becker (organ, St. Nicholas', Leipzig), Konstantin J. Becker (editor, *Neue Zeitschrift für Musik*), Dieudonné Duquet (organ, Liège Cathedral)

E. Prizes and Honors:
Prizes: Louis-Désiré Besozzi (Prix de Rome)

Honors: Manuel Bretón de los Herreros (Spanish Academy), Michele Carafa de Colobrano (French Academy), Franz Cramer (Master of the King's Music); Johann Carl Loewe (Berlin Academy), Felix Mendelssohn (honorary doctorate, Leipzig University)

F. Biographical Highlights:
Franz Abt, upon his father's death, drops theology study to concentrate on music; Anton Bruckner becomes a choir-boy at St. Florian; Frédéric Chopin breaks up with Marie Wodzinska and meets Aurora Dupin, who writes under the name George Sand; Carl Czerny makes his second visit to Paris and London; Gaetano Donizetti loses his wife of nine years; César Franck enters the Conservatory of Paris and is given a prize for his sight-reading ability; Charles Gounod wins the second Prix de Rome with his cantata *Maria Stuart et Rizzio*; Anthony Heinrich leaves Europe again and settles in New York; Franz Liszt's daughter Cosima is born; Lowell Mason makes his first visit to Europe; Felix Mendelssohn marries Cécile Sophie Jeanrenaud and conducts at the Birmingham Festivals in England; Stanislaw Moniuszko leaves Warsaw for Berlin where he studies with Rungenhagen; Gioacchino Rossini leaves his wife Isabella and goes to live with Olympe Pélissier; Robert Schumann becomes engaged to Clara Wieck over her father's objections; Rosine Stoltz makes her debut at the Paris Opera; Richard Wagner separates briefly from Minna when she leaves with a rich business man in Königsberg.

G. Institutional Openings:
Performing Groups: Bristol Madrigal Society (England); Cleveland Harmonic Society; Concerts Valentino (Paris); Hanover Hofoper; Melophonic Society of London; Newark Amateur Glee Company; Prague Mozart Society; Regensburger Liederkranz; University of Dublin Choral Society

Educational: Kolozavár Music Conservatory (Hungary)

Other: *La France Musicale*; Hungarian National Theater (Pest); Knabe and Gaehle, Piano Makers (Baltimore); Tauchnitz Publishing House (Leipzig); Tiffany, Young and Ellis (New York--Tiffany and Co. by 1853)

H. Musical Literature:
Caldwell, William, *The Union Harmony*
Cherubini, Luigi, *Traité de la Fugue*

Daniel, Salvador, *Grammaire philharmonique*
Fétis, François, *Traité du chant en choeur*
Kastner, Jean G., *Traité générale d'instrumentation*
Mainzer, Joseph, *Abécédaire de chant*
Marx, Adolf B., *Die lehre von der musikalischen Komposition I, II*
Mason, Lowell, *The Sabbath School Harp*
Oliphant, Thomas, *La Musa madrigalesca*

I. Musical Compositions:

Auber, Daniel, *Le domino noir* (opera)
Balfe, Michael, *Joan of Arc* (opera)
    Catherina Grey (opera)
Berlioz, Hector, *Requiem, Opus 5*
Carnicer, Ramón, *Ismalia* (opera)
Cherubini, Luigi, *String Quartet No. 7 in E Minor*
Chopin, Frédéric, *4 Mazurkas, Opus 30*
    Scherzo in B-flat Minor, Opus 31
    2 Nocturnes, Opus 32
    Piano Sonata, Opus 35, "Funeral March"
Donizetti, Gaetano, *Robert Devereux* (opera)
    Requiem Mass for Zingarelli
Flotow, Friedrich von, *Alice* (opera)
    Rob-Roy (opera)
    Stradella (lyric piece)
Gounod, Charles, *Marie Stuart* (cantata)
    Scherzo for Orchestra
Heinrich, Anthony, *Grand American National Chivalrous Symphony*
Hullah, John P., *The Barber of Bassora* (opera)
Kreutzer, Konradin, *Fridolin* (opera)
    Die Höhle bei Waverley (opera)
Liszt, Franz, *Hexameron for Piano and Orchestra*
Lortzing, Albert, *Zar und Zimmerman* (opera)
    Le bourgmestre de Saardam (opera)
Marschner, Heinrich, *Der Bäbu* (opera)
Mendelssohn, Felix, *Concerto No. 2, Opus 40, for Piano and Orchestra*
    2 String Quartets, Opus 44
    Songs without Words II and III, Opus 30 and 38
    6 Preludes and Fugues for Piano, Opus 35
    3 Preludes and Fugues for Organ, Opus 37
    Psalm XLII, Opus 42, "As Pants the Hart"
    6 Songs, Opus 34
Mercadante, Saverio, *Il giuramento* (opera)
Niedermeyer, Louis, *Stradella* (opera)
Prévost, Eugène, *Liebeszauber* (opera)
Russell, Henry, *Woodman, Spare That Tree!* (song)
Schumann, Robert, *Die Davidsbündler, Opus 6, for Piano*
    Fantasiestücke for Piano, Opus 12
Spohr, Louis, *Symphony No. 5, Opus 102*
    6 German Songs, Opus 103
Suppé, Franz von, *Virginia* (opera)
Thomas, Ambroise, *La double échelle* (opera)
Vieuxtemps, Henri, *Concerto in F-sharp Minor, Opus 19, for Violin and Orchestra*
Webb, George J., *Webb* (hymn tune, "Stand Up for Jesus")
Weigl, Joseph, *Mass in E Major*

1838

World Events:
In the U.S., Personal Liberty Laws in the North try to offset the Fugitive Slave Law passed by Congress; the "Underground Railway" is set up to aid the runaway slaves; the Trail of Tears takes place as the Cherokee Indians are forced to move to an Oklahoma reservation; the Iowa Territory is formed; the Steam Shovel is invented by O. Evans; Samuel Morse developes the Morse Code. Internationally, the Chartist Movement in Great Britain is the first attempt at labor power; Steamship travel between the Old World and the New is inaugurated on the steamship *Great Western*; in the Battle of Blood River, the Boers defeat the Zulus in Natal; French political figure Charles M. de Talleyrand dies.

Cultural Highlights:
The London National Gallery opens as does the Grosvenor Library in Buffalo, New York; James K. Paulding is made Secretary of the U.S. Navy; John Gibson is inducted into the Royal Academy. Births in the art field include American architect Henry Richardson, French artist Charles Carolus-Durand and sculptor Aimé-Jules Dalou and British artist Valentine Prinsep; deaths include Benjamin Barker, British artist. Births in the literary world include American historian Henry Adams, politician and poet John M. Hay and novelist Albion Tourgée and Scottish poet David Gray; deaths include German author Adalbert von Chamisso and British poet and novelist Letitia E. Landon. Other highlights include:

Art: Thomas Cole, *Shroon Mountains, Adirondacks*; Jean Baptiste Corot, *View Near Volterra*; Eugène Delacroix, *The Capture of Constantinople*; Wilhelm von Kaulbach, *The Destruction of Jerusalem*; Edwin Landseer, *A Member of the Humane Society*; Ary Scheffer, *Franz Liszt*; Bertil Thorvaldsen, *Christ and the Apostles*

Literature: João Almeida-Garrett, *Auto de Gil Vicente*; Joseph Bosworth, *An Anglo-Saxon Dictionary*; Elizabeth Browning, *The Seraphim and Other Poems*; Edward Bulwer-Lytton, *The Lady of Lyons*; Victor Hugo, *Ruy Blas*; Karl Immermann, *Münchhausen I, II*; Bernhard Malmström, *Ariadne*; Eduard Mörike, *Gedichte*

MUSICAL EVENTS

A. Births:

Jan 2	Fritz A. Simrock (Ger-pub)	Jul 9	Philip P. Bliss (Am-hymn)
Jan 5	Charles Lunn (Br-ten)	Jul 23	Edouard Colonne (Fr-cd)
Jan 6	Max Bruch (Ger-cm)	Aug 12	Joseph Barnby (Br-org)
Feb 4	Tommaso Benvenuti (It-cm)	Aug 18	Angelo Neumann (Aus-ten)
Feb 18	Ernst Mach (Ger-acous)	Sep 18	Emil Scaria (Aus-bs)
Mar 13	Sebastian Bach Mills (Br-pn)	Oct 25	Georges Bizet (Fr-cm)
Mar 15	Karl Davïdov (Rus-cel)	Nov 26	Ludwig Bussler (Ger-the)
Mar 21	Wilma Neruda (Cz-vn)	Dec 4	Melesio Morales (Mex-cm)
Apr 16	Karel Bendl (Boh-cm)	Dec 16	Bernhard Pollini (Ger-ten)
May 15	Sophie Stehle (Ger-sop)	Dec 23	Friedrich Urban (Ger-cm)
Jun 13	Emil Fischer (Ger-bs)	Dec 28	Robert Lienau (Ger-pub)
Jun 16	Frederick Archer (Br-org)		Zélia Trebelli (Fr-mez)

B. Deaths:

Jan 13	Ferdinand Ries (Ger-pn)	Apr 6	Jeremiah Ingalls (Am-cm)
Jan 15	Maria Bland (Br-sop)	May 28	Thomas Busby (Br-org-cri)
Jan 20	Pierre Hus-Deforges (Fr-cel)	May 29	Pauline Milder-Hauptmann
Feb 5	Filipe Libon (Sp-vn)		(Aus-sop)
Feb 22	Friedrich J. Eck (Ger-vn)	Jul 19	Frédéric Duvernoy (Fr-hn)
Mar 2	Ludwig Abeille (Ger-org)	Jul 28	Bernhard Crusell (Fin-cm)
Mar 24	Thomas Attwood (Br-org)	Jul 31	Johann Maelzel (Ger-inv)

Aug 17 Lorenzo da Ponti (It-lib)   Nov 24 Karl F. Hellwig (Ger-org)
Sep 24 Friedrich Berr (Fr-cl-cm)   Dec 26 Franz Lessel (Pol-cm)
Oct 4 Sofia Westenholz (Ger-pn)   Andrew Ashe (Br-fl)
Oct 27 Asa Hopkins (Am-inst.m)

C. Debuts:
U.S. -- Edward Sequin, John Wilson (tour)

Other - Erminia Frezzolini (Florence), Heinrich Kotzolt (Danzig), Henry Lazarus (London), Jenny Lind (Stockholm), Giovanni Mario (Paris), John Sims Reeves (Newcastle, as baritone), Gustave Hippolyte Roger (Paris), Sophie Anne Thillon (Paris)

D. New Positions:
Conductors: Julius Benedict (Drury Lane), Luigi Palmerini (maestro di cappella, S. Petronio, Bologna), Eugène Prévost (New Orleans French Theater), August Roeckel (Weimar Theaters), Théophile Tilmant (Italian Theater, Paris)

Educational: Gottfried von Preyer (music theory, Vienna Conservatory), Edward Taylor (professor, Greshem College), Nicola Vaccai (director, Milan Conservatory)

Others: András Bartay (director, National Theater, Pest), John Goss (organ, St. Paul's, London), John B. Sale (organ, Chapel Royal, London), Franz Weber (organ, Cologne Cathedral)

E. Prizes and Honors:
Prizes: Georges Bousquet (Prix de Rome)

F. Biographical Highlights:
Alkan begins a six-year, self-imposed exile from the concert stage; Frédéric Chopin moves to Majorca with George Sand; Gaetano Donizetti, after the censor refuses his latest opera, goes to Paris; Alexander Dreyschock begins his first extended European concert tour; Stephen Heller takes up permanent residency in Paris; Adolph von Henselt goes to St. Petersburg where he becomes an important musical influence for 40 years; Louis Jullien, fleeing his creditors in France, goes to London; Felix Mendelssohn gives the premiere of Schubert's newly discovered *Great C Major Symphony*; Otto Nicolai resigns his Vienna post and returns to Italy; Niccolò Paganini belatedly pays Berlioz 20,000 francs for his *Harold in Italy*; Gioacchino Rossini returns to Bologna for a ten-year stay; Robert Schumann is responsible for the finding of the Schubert *Ninth Symphony*; Johann Strauss takes his orchestra to England; Giuseppe Verdi loses two children to illness; Henri Vieuxtemps goes on a concert tour of Russia; William V. Wallace leaves his family and his debts behind in Sydney and begins a three year stay in South America.

G. Institutional Openings:
Performing Groups: Essen Gesang-Musikverein; Königsberg Philharmonic Society; London Promenade Concerts; Norwich Madrigal Society; St. Louis Philharmonic Orchestra

Educational: Liceo Filarmónico Dramático Barcelonés de S. M. Doña Isabel II; School of Singing and Music (Krakow)

Other: Joseph Allen, Brass Instruments (Sturbridge, Massachusetts); Besson Instruments Co. (Paris); Bote and Bock, Music Publishers (Berlin); *Caricature* (Paris); Daublaine et Cie., Organ Builders (Paris); Jan Hoffman, Publisher (Prague); Gotthilf Körner, Music Publisher (Erfurt); Lambertini Piano Co. (Lisbon); Musical Fund Society (St. Louis); *Nouvelle Gazette Musicale* (Paris); The Sterling Club (London); Teatro de la Victoria (Buenos Aires)

H. Musical Literature:

Bergt, August, *Briefwechsel eines alten und jungen Schulmeisters* (posthumous publication)
Chappell, William, *National English Airs I*
Gardiner, William, *Music and Friends I*
Gassner, Ferdinand, *Ein Leitfaden zum Selbstunterricht*
Hogarth, George, *Memoirs of the Musical Drama*
Kahlert, August, *Tonleben*
Krause, Karl, *Anfangsgründe der allgemeinen Theorie der Musik* (posthumous publication)
Mason, Lowell, *The Boston Glee Book*
Schilling, Gustav, *Versuch einer Philosophie des Schönen in der Musik*
Sulzer, Salomon, *Schir Zion*

I. Musical Compositions:

Adam, Adolphe, *Le fidèle berger* (opera)
    Le Brasseur de Preston (opera)
Auber, Daniel, *Margarethe von Gent* (opera)
Balfe, Michael, *Falstaff* (opera)
    Diadeste (opera)
Benedict, Julius, *The Gypsy's Warning* (opera)
Berlioz, Hector, *Benvenuto Cellini* (opera)
Carafa, Michele, *Thérèse* (opera)
Chopin, Frédéric, *4 Mazurkas*, Opus 33
    2 Polonaises, Opus 40
David, Félicien, *Symphony No. 1*
Donizetti, Gaetano, *Maria di Rudenz* (opera)
Flotow, Friedrich von, *Lady Melvil* (opera)
    Le comte de Saint-Mégrin (opera)
Gounod, Charles, *La Vendetta* (dramatic scene)
Halévy, Jacques, *Guido et Ginevra* (opera)
Hullah, John P., *The Outpost* (opera)
Kalliwoda, Johann, *Concert Overture No. 1, Opus 38*
    Concert Overture No. 5 and 6, Opus 38, 76 (f, E-flat)
Liszt, Franz, *Grand Gallop Chromatique* (piano)
    Etudes d'Execution Transcendente d'apres Paganini (piano)
Loewe, Carl, *Three Historical Ballads, Opus 67*
Mendelssohn, Felix, *Serenade and Allegro in B Minor, Opus 43*
    String Quartet No. 5, Opus 44, No. 3
    Cello Sonata No. 1, Opus 45
Mercadante, Saverio, *Elena da Feltre* (opera)
    Le due illustri rivali (opera)
Moniuszko, Stanislaw, *A Night in the Apennines* (opera)
Moscheles, Ignaz, *Concerto No. 8, Opus 96, for Piano and Orchestra*
Nicolai, Otto, *Rosmonda d'Inghilterra* (opera)
Schumann, Robert, *Kinderszenen, Opus 15* (piano)
    Kreisleriana, Opus 16 (piano)
    Noveletten, Opus 21 (piano)
    Piano Sonata No. 2, Opus 22 (final movement)
Spohr, Louis, *String Quartet, Opus 106*
    6 Songs, Opus 105
Strauss, Joseph, *Berthold der Zähringer* (opera)
Suppé, Franz von, *Virginia* (operetta)
Thomas, Ambroise, *Le perruquier de la régence* (opera)
Vaccai, Nicola, *Marco Visconti* (opera)
Verdi, Giuseppe, *Six Romances* (voice and piano)
Vesque von Püttlingen, Johann, *Turandot* (opera)

1839

World Events:
In the U.S., the Aroostook War is averted by the settlement of the dispute over the boundary betwen Maine and Canada; Boston University and the University of Missouri are founded; Fort Sutter (Sacramento), California, is founded; Charles Goodyear accidentally discovers the process of vulcanization; Abner Doubleday supposedly builds the first baseball diamond; industrialist John D. Rockefeller is born. Internationally, the Opium War begins between China and Great Britain; Belgian independence is formally recognized by the Dutch government; the Central American Federation dissolves into the countries of Guatamala, El Salvador, Costa Rica, Nicaragua and Honduras; the Daguerreotype Process is introduced.

Cultural Highlights:
The Lico Artistico y Literario opens in Granada; Samuel C. Hall becomes editor of the *Art Journal*. Births in the field of art include French artists Paul Cézanne and Alfred Sisley and German artist Karl A. Oesterley; deaths include German artist Joseph A. Koch, British artist William Beechey and American dramatist and artist William Dunlap. Births in the literary world include Italian authors Enrico Castelnuovo and Luigi Capuana, Canadian poet Louis H. Fréchette, British author Walter Pater and American author Henry George; deaths include Swedish poets Karl A. Nicander and Johan O. Wallin and British poet Winthrop Praed. Other highlights include:

Art: Eugène Delacroix, *Jewish Wedding in Morocco*; Charles Eastlake, *Christ Blessing the Children*; Joseph Führich, *The Triumph of Christ*; Edwin Landseer, *Dignity and Impudence*; John Martin, *The Coronation of Queen Victoria*; Karl Spitzweg, *The Poor Poet*; Joseph Turner, *The Fighting Temeraire*; Richard Upjohn, *Trinity Church, N.Y.*

Literature: Edward Bulwer-Lytton, *Richelieu*; Louise Colet, *Penserosa*; Theodor Creizenach, *Dichtungen*; Charles Dickens, *Nicholas Nickleby*; Jeremias Gotthelf, *Leiden und Freuden eines Schulmeisters*; Henry W. Longfellow, *Voices of the Night*; Edgar A. Poe, *The Fall of the House of Usher*; Juliusz Slowacki, *Mazepa*

MUSICAL EVENTS

A. Births:

Jan 9	John Knowles Paine (Am-cm)	Apr 18	François Jehin (Bel-vn)
Feb 16	Riccardo Gandolfi (It-cm)	May 10	Amalie Joachim (Aus-alto)
Feb 27	Joseph A. Capoul (Fr-ten)	May 17	Henri Ghis (Fr-pn-cm)
Mar 10	Dudley Buck (Am-cm)	Aug 24	Eduard Napravnik (Boh-cd)
Mar 17	Joseph Rheinberger (Ger-org)	Oct 15	Adolf Müller, Jr. (Aus-cm)
Mar 21	Modest Mussorgsky (Rus-cm)	Oct 25	M. Peschka-Leutner (Aus-sop)
Mar 28	George Hart (Br-vn.m)	Nov 7	Hermann Levi (Ger-cd)

B. Deaths:

Jan 19	Georg Schneider (Ger-hn)	Jun 14	Nicolas Mori (Br-vn-pub)
Feb 16	Ludwig Berger (Ger-pn)	Jul 10	Fernando Sor (Sp-gui)
Mar 4	Ignaz A. Ladurner (Fr-pn)	Jul 16	Franz X. Glöggl (Aus-cd)
Mar 8	Adolphe Nourrit (Fr-ten)	Jul 29	Gaspard C. Prony (Fr-the)
Mar 20	Vincenzo Rastrelli (It-cd)	Aug 21	Heinrich Lentz (Ger-pn)
Mar 28	Giuseppe Siboni (It-ten)	Aug 23	Charles Lafont (Fr-vn)
Apr 7	Giuseppe Festa (It-vn-cd)	Aug 25	Jean J. Grasset (Fr-vn)
Apr 13	Domenico Ronconi (It-ten)	Sep 14	Giuseppe Mosca (It-cm)
Apr 23	Guillaume Villoteau (Fr-mus)	Sep 21	Gottfried Weber (Ger-the)
May 3	Ferdinando Paër (It-cm)	Nov 2	Wenzel Gallenberg (Aus-cm)
Jun 8	Aloysia Weber (Ger-sop)	Nov 13	William Carnaby (Br-org)

Dec 7   Jan A. Vitásek (Boh-pn)   Dec 19   Aloys Mooser (Swe-org.m)
Dec 9   Nikolai Kashkin (Rus-cri)   Violante Camporese (It-sop)
Dec 18   Charles H. Plantade (Fr-cel)   Jean M. Droling (Fr-pn)

C. Debuts:
U.S. -- Elizabeth Poole

Other - Alexandre-Joseph Artôt (London), Giovanni B. Belletti (Stockholm), Elisa Meerti Blaes (Leipzig), William Harrison (London), Jacques Offenbach (Paris), Fanny Salvini-Donatelli (Venice), Anna Zerr (Karlsruhe)

D. New Positions:
Conductors: Francisco Andreví y Castellar (maître de chapelle, Bordeaux Cathedral), Karl Binder (Josefstädter Theater, Vienna), Pietro A. Coppola (Lisbon Royal Opera), Vincenzo Fioravanti (maestro di cappella, Abruzzi Cathedral), Giuseppe Mercadante (maestro di cappella, Lanciano Cathedral)

Educational: Hyacinthe-Eléonore Klosé (clarinet, Paris Conservatory), Alberto Mazzucato (violin, Milan Conservatory), John Thomson (first Reid Professor, Edinburgh University)

Others: Gaetano Capocci (organ, S. Maria Maggiore, Rome), Robert Führer (organ, Prague Cathedral), Eduard A. Grell (organ, Berlin Cathedral), Jean Grosjean (organ, St. Dié Cathedral), Joseph Hanisch (organ, Regensburg Cathedral), Karl Kempter (organ, Augsburg Cathedral)

E. Prizes and Honors:
Prizes: Charles Gounod (Prix de Rome)

Honors: Gaspare Spontini (French Institute)

F. Biographical Highlights:
Adolphe Adam visits Russia in performances of his own works; August Ambros completes a doctorate in law at Prague University; Anna Bishop deserts her husband and children and elopes with Robert Bochsa; Frédéric Chopin, his health deteriorating in the wet Majorcan climate, returns to Paris; Ferdinand David visits England for the first time; Giovanni Davide retires from the stage; George Grove graduates from the Institute of Civil Engineers in London; Joseph Joachim goes to Vienna for music study; Frédéric Kalkbrenner retires from the concert stage; Edouard Lalo enters the Conservatory of Paris; Franz Liszt begins his virtuoso career; Giorgio Ronconi, Lorenzo Salvi, Mary Shaw and Giuseppina Strepponi all make their La Scala debuts; George Root begins his music teaching in Boston; Giuseppe Verdi moves his family from Busseto to Milan; Pauline Viardot-García makes her opera debut in London debut; Richard Wagner, fleeing his creditors, sails to England and France.

G. Institutional Openings:
Performing Groups: Augsburg Musikliebhaberverein; Norwich Philharmonic Society

Festivals: North German Music Festival (Lübeck)

Educational: John Reid Chair of Music (Edinburgh University); Scuola Musicale (Piacenza); Scuola Pubblica di Musica (Istituto Musicale in 1842, Lucca)

Other: Bathyphon (by Wieprecht and Skorra); Meissonier and Heugel, Music Publishers (Paris); *Musical Magazine, or Repository of Musical Science, Literature and Intelligence*; Royal Society of Female Musicians (London)

H. Musical Literature:
Elwart, Antoine, *Petit manuel d'harmonie*
Krüger, Eduard, *Grundriss der Metrik*
Mainzer, Joseph, *Esquisses musicales*

Marx, Adolf B., *Allgemeine Musiklehre*
Mason, Lowell, *The Modern Psalmist*
Masson, Elizabeth, *Original Jacobite Songs*
Mosel, Ignaz von, *Über die Originalpartitur des Requiems von W.A. Mozart*
d'Ortigue, Joseph, *De l'école musicale italienne*
Taylor, Edward, *Vocal Schools of Italy in the 16th Century*
Vroye, Théodore de, *Traité du plain-chant*

I. Musical Compositions:

Adam, Adolphe, *La reine d'un Jour* (opera)
   Le lac des fées (opera)
   La jolie fille de Gand (ballet)
Auber, Daniel, *Le lac de fées* (opera)
Barnett, John, *Farinelli* (opera)
Berlioz, Hector, *Romeo and Juliet, Dramatic Symphony, Opus 17*
   Reverie and Caprice, Opus 8, for Violin and Orchestra
Chopin, Frédéric, *3 Mazurkas, Opus 41*
   Polonaise in C Minor, Opus 40, No. 2
   Impromtu in F-sharp Minor, Opus 35 (piano)
   Scherzo in C-sharp Minor, Opus 39 (piano)
   3 Nouvelles Etudes (piano)
Dargomijsky, Alexander, *Esmeralda* (opera)
Donizetti, Gaetano, *Gabriella di Vergy II* (opera)
Flotow, Friedrich von, *L'eau merveilleuse* (opera)
   Le naufrage de la Méduse (opera)
Gade, Niels, *Aladdin* (incidental music)
Glinka, Mikhail, *Polonaise in E Major* (orchestra)
   Parting from Petersburg (song cycle)
Gounod, Charles, *Fernand* (cantata)
Halévy, Jacques, *Le shérif* (opera)
   Les treize (opera)
Hiller, Ferdinand, *Romilda* (opera)
Kalliwoda, Johann, *Concert Overture No. 7, Opus 101*
   Concertino, Opus 100, for Violin and Orchestra
Lindblad, Adolf, *Symphony in C Major*
Liszt, Franz, *Années de Pèlerinage, Year II* (piano)
   Concerto No. 2 for Piano and Orchestra
Mendelssohn, Felix, *Ruy Blas Overture, Opus 95*
   Piano Trio No. 1, Opus 49
   Psalm XCV, Opus 46, "Oh, Come Let Us Sing"
   Psalm CXIV, Opus 51, "When Israel Out of Egypt Came"
   6 Songs, Opus 47
   3 Songs, Opus 48
Mercadante, Saverio, *Il bravo* (opera)
Morlacchi, Francesco, *Francesco da Rimini* (opera)
Schumann, Robert, *Nachtstücke, Opus 23* (piano)
   Faschingsschwank aus Wien, Opus 26 (piano)
   3 Romances, Opus 28 (piano)
   4 Pieces for Piano, Opus 32
Spohr, Louis, *Der Matrose* (incidental music)
   Symphony No. 6, Opus 116, "Historische"
   Concerto No. 14, Opus 110, for Violin and Orchestra
Thomas, Ambroise, *La gypsy* (ballet)
Vaccai, Nicola, *La sposa di Messina* (opera)
Verdi, Giuseppe, *Oberto, Count of San Bonifacio* (opera)
Vertovsky, Alexei, *Homesickness* (opera)

1840

World Events:
In the U.S., the Census shows a population of 17,069,000, a 32% increase in ten years; William Henry Harrison is elected as President No. 9; Congress approves the 10-hour workday for all Federal employees; the U.S. recognizes the independence of the Republic of Texas; the *New York Tribune* is founded by Horace Greeley; the Cumberland Highway is finished. Internationally, Great Britain sets up the first postal system and the "Penny Black" becomes the first postage stamp; the Act of Union brings together Upper and Lower Canada into one; Brazil becomes an empire under Pedro I who brings order to the country; the European powers force Muhammad Ali to pull out of Syria but guarantee him hereditary rule in Egypt.

Cultural Highlights:
Carlo Conti is taken into the Naples Royal Academy of Arts; Daniel Maclise is inducted into the Royal Academy in London. Births in the art field include American artists Daniel Knight and Alfred Thompson, French artists Claude Monet and Odilon Redon and sculptor Auguste Rodin, Irish artist Thomas Hovenden and British artist Marcus Stone; deaths include Scotch artists Alexander Nasmyth and John Thomson and German artist Kasper Friedrich. Births in the literary field include British poets Wilfrid S. Blunt and Thomas Hardy, French novelists Alphonse Daudet and Émile Zola, German poet Rudolf Baumbach and Italian novelist Giovanni Verga; deaths include British novelist Fanny Burney, French poet and dramatist Louis S. Lemercier and German author Karl L. Immermann. Other highlights include:

Art: Thomas Barker, *The Bride of Death*; Augustus Callcott, *Milton Dictating to His Daughter*; Thomas Cole, *The Architect's Dream*; Joseph Dannhauser, *Liszt at the Piano*; Eugène Delacroix, *The Justice of Trajan*; Robert Lauder, *The Trial of Effie Deans*; John Martin, *The Eve of the Deluge*; Joseph Turner, *Yacht Approaching the Coast*.

Literature: Maguerite Blessington, *The Idler in Italy*; James F. Cooper, *The Pathfinder*; Richard Dana, Jr., *Two Years before the Mast*; Charles Dickens, *The Old Curiosity Shop*; Leigh Hunt, *A Legend of Florence*; Henry W. Longfollow, *The Skeleton in Armor*; Edgar A. Poe, *Tales of the Grotesque and Arabesque*; William Thackeray, *Paris Sketch Book.*

MUSICAL EVENTS

A. Births:

Jan 1	Carlo Andreoli (It-pn-cd)	Jul 30	Emil Krause (Ger-pn-cri)
Feb 22	Samuel de Lange (Hol-org)	Aug 28	Ira P. Sankey (Am-hymn)
Mar 8	Franco Faccio (It-cd)	Sep 14	George E. Whiting (Am-org)
Apr 12	Edmund Audran (Fr-cm)	Sep 30	Johan Svendsen (Nor-cm)
Apr 12	Franz X. Haberl (Ger-mus)	Oct 28	Georgine Schubert (Ger-mez)
May 7	Peter Tchaikovsky (Rus-cm)	Nov	Marie Galli-Marié (Fr-sop)
May 11	Filippo Capocci (It-org)	Nov 3	Antoine Dechevrens (Fr-mus)
Jun 6	John Stainer (Br-cm-mus)	Nov 16	Jules Danbé (Fr-cd)
Jun 24	Louis Brassin (Bel-pn)	Dec 7	Hermann Goetz (Ger-cm)
Jul 25	William Candidus (Am-ten)	Dec 11	Barrett Poznanski (Am-vn)

B. Deaths:

Jan 6	Johann Schiedermayer (Ger-org)	Jul 22	Józef Jawurek (Pol-pn-cd)
May 1	Giuditta Grisi (It-mez)	Aug 27	Johann Döring (Ger-bs)
May 5	Gottlob B. Bierey (Ger-cm)	Sep 15	Franz Pechaczek, Jr. (Boh-vn)
May 5	Matthäus Fischer (Ger-cm)	Oct 18	Pierre Gardel (Fr-bal)
May 10	Catterino Cavos (It-cm)	Nov 19	Johann M. Vogl (Aus-bar)
May 27	Niccolò Paganini (It-vn-cm)		

C. Debuts:
U.S. -- John Braham (tour), Fanny Essler (tour)

Other - Marius Pierre Audran (Paris), Marianna Barbieri-Nini (Milan), Giovanni Bottesini (Crema), Filippo Coletti (London), Italo Gardoni (Italy), Hermine Rudersdorff (Germany)

D. New Positions:
Conductors: Julius Benedict (Drury Lane), Henry Bishop (Covent Garden), Hippolyte Chélard (kapellmeister, Weimar), Francisco da Costa (mestre de capela, Oporto Cathedral, Portugal), Louis Jullien (Drury Lane), Friedrich Klingenberg (cantor, Peterskirche, Gorlitz), Konradin Kreutzer (kapellmeister, Cologne), Heinrich Proch (Vienna Opera), Pierre Varney (New Orleans Theater)

Educational: Michele Carafa (composition, Paris Conservatory), Johan P. Hartmann (director, Copenhagen Conservatory), Giuseppe Mercadante (director, Naples Conservatory), Prosper Sainton (violin, Toulouse Conservatory)

Others: Johannes Bastiaans (organ, Zuiderkerk, Amsterdam), Jean-Louis Danjou (organ, Notre Dame, Paris), Stanislaw Moniuszko (organ St. John's, Vilnius). Prosper C. Simon (organ, Chapelle Royal, St. Denis)

E. Prizes and Honors:
Prizes: François-Emmanuel Bazin (Prix de Rome)

Honors: Jenny Lind (Swedish Royal Academy)

F. Biographical Highlights:
Michal Bergson leaves Germany to studio piano in Paris; William B. Bradbury moves to New York; Anton Bruckner attends the Teacher's Preparatory School at Linz; George Elvey receives his doctorate from Oxford; César Franck takes first prize for fugue at the Paris Conservatory; Pauline García marries the manager of the Italian Theater in Paris, Louis Viardot; Franz Liszt concertizes for the Beethoven Bonn Memorial and performs for Queen Victoria; Stanislaw Moniuszko returns to Poland and settles in Vilnius as teacher and organist; Lauro Rossi becomes an impresario; Gioacchino Rossini does some teaching at the Liceo Musicale in Bologna; Robert Schumann finally gets to marry Clara Wieck; Giuseppe Verdi loses his wife; Richard Wagner spends three weeks in a Paris debtor's prison and first meets Franz Liszt.

G. Institutional Openings:
Performing Groups: Amsterdam Cecilia Society; Dortmunder Liedertafel; Liverpool Philharmonic Society; Mannheim Liedertafel; Munich Bürgersängerzunft; Musical Antiquarian Society (London); St. Cecilia Society of Prague; St. Louis Sacred Music Society

Educational: Conservatory of the Pest-Buda Society of Music (National Conservatory in 1867); Zofín Academy of Music (Prague)

Other: Aberdeen Haydn Society (Scotland); Belfast Music Hall; Cast-Iron Piano Frame (patented by Jonas Chickering); Gotha Hoftheater; *Nouvelliste* (St. Petersburg); Saxophone (by Adolph Sax); Teatro Metastasio (Assisi)

H. Musical Literature:
Becker, Carl, *Die Hausmusik in Deutschland in 16., 17. und 18. Jahrhunderts*
Dehn, Siegfried, *Theoretisch-praktische Harmonielehre*
Elwart, Antoine, *Théorie musicale*
Fétis, François, *Esquisse de l'histoire de l'harmonie*
García, Manuel G., *Traité complet de l'art du Chant*
Guéranger, Prosper, *Institutions liturgiques I*
Kist, Florentius, *Protestant Churchmusic in the Netherlands*

Schilling, Gustav, *Lehrbuch der...Musikwissenschaft*
Töpfer, Johann G., *Anleitung zur erhaltung und stimmung der Orgel*
Winterfeld, Carl von, *Martin Luthers deutsche geistliche Lieder*

I. Musical Compositions:

Auber, Daniel, *Zanetta* (opera)
Berlioz, Hector, *Funeral and Triumphant Symphony, Opus 15*
Chopin, Frédéric, *Waltz in A-flat Major, Opus 42*
    Waltz in E-flat Major, "Sostenuto"
Crouch, Frederick, *Kathleen Mavourneen* (song)
Donizetti, Gaetano, *La fille du régiment* (opera)
    La favorita (opera)
    Poliuto (opera)
    Il duc d'Alba (opera)
Gade, Neils, *Echoes from Ossian Overture, Opus 1*
Gounod, Charles, *"Roman" Mass*
Halévy, Jacques, *Le drapier* (opera)
Hiller, Ferdinand, *Der zerstörung Jerusalem, Opus 24* (oratorio)
Kalliwoda, Johann, *Symphony No. 5, Opus 106*
Knight, Joseph P., *Rocked in the Cradle of the Deep* (song)
Kreutzer, Konradin, *Die beiden Figaro* (opera)
Liszt, Franz, *3 Valse-Caprices for Piano*
Loewe, Carl, *Kleiner Hausholt, Opus 71* (lyric fantasy)
Lortzing, Albert, *Hans Sachs* (opera)
Mendelssohn, Felix, *Symphony No. 2, "Hymn of Praise"*
    Festgesang for Male Chorus and Orchestra
Mercadante, Saverio, *La vestale* (opera)
    La solitaria dell Asturie (opera)
Nicolai, Otto, *Il Templario* (opera)
Pacini, Giovanni, *Saffo* (opera)
Pedrotti, Carlo, *Lina* (opera)
    Clara di Mailand (opera)
Schumann, Robert, *Liederkreis, Opus 24* (song cycle after Heine)
    Myrthen, Opus 25 (song cycle)
    Lieder und Gesänge I, Opus 27
    3 Poems, Opus 30
    3 Ballads, Opus 31
    6 Songs for Male Chorus, Opus 33
    12 Poems, Opus 35
    6 Poems, Opus 36
    Liebesfrühling, Opus 37 (song cycle)
    Liederkreis, Opus 39 (song cycle after Eichendorff)
    5 Songs, Opus 40
    Frauenliebe und Leben, Opus 42 (song cycle)
    Dichterliebe, Opus 48 (song cycle)
Spohr, Louis, *The Fall of Babylon* (oratorio)
Strauss, Joseph, *Der Währwolf* (opera)
Thomas, Ambroise, *Carline* (opera)
Verdi, Giuseppe, *Un giorno di Regno* (opera)
Vesque von Püttlingen, Johann, *Jeanne d'Arc* (opera)
Vieuxtemps, Henri, *Concerto, Opus 10, for Violin and Orchestra*
Wagner, Richard, *Rienzi* (opera)
    A Faust Overture

1841

World Events:
In the U.S., President William Henry Harrison dies from pneumonia a month after his inauguration and John Tyler becomes President No. 10; the Whigs denounce Tyler whose cabinet resigns en masse; Brook Farm is founded in Massachusetts; Fordham University is founded; the first American advertising firm opens in Philadelphia. Internationally, the British seize the Chinese city of Hong Kong; New Zealand is made a British colony; explorer Ross claims the Antartic for Great Britain; the European Nations agree to close the Dardanelles to all countries but Turkey; David Livingstone begins the exploration of Africa.

Cultural Highlights:
The magazine *Punch* begins publication in London; George Hayter is made Painter to the Queen; Ludwig Tieck is given a lifelong pension by William IV; Friedrich Rückert begins teaching oriental languages in Berlin. Births in the art field include French artists Frédéric Bazille, Jean Charles Cazin, Berthe Morisot and Pierre-Auguste Renoir and American artist Henry Mosler; deaths include German sculptor J.H. von Dannecker and Scottish artist David Wilkie. Births in the literary field include British novelists Robert Buchanan and W.H. Hudson and French poet and novelist Catulle Mendès; deaths include German philosopher Johann F. Herbart, Danish author Peter A. Heiberg and French poet Louis Bertrand. Other highlights include:

Art: Antoine-Louis Barye, *Angelica and Roger*; Jean Baptiste Corot, *Democritus and the Abderites*; Gustave Courbet, *Mouth of the Seine*; Paul Delaroche, *Apotheosis of Art*; Charles Eastlake, *Christ Weeping over Jerusalem*; Paul Huet, *The Lake*; Karl Spitzweg, *The Sunday Walk*; Joseph Turner, *Peace: Burial at Sea* and *Rockets and Blue Lights*

Literature: Marguerite Blessington, *The Idler in France*; Robert Browning, *Pippa Passes*; James F. Cooper, *The Deerslayer*; Ralph W. Emerson, *Essays I*; Mikhail Lermontov, *The Demon*; Henry W. Longfellow, *Ballads and Other Poems*; Frederick Marryat, *Masterman Ready*; John W. Marston, *The Patrician's Daughter*

MUSICAL EVENTS

A. Births:

Jan 18	Emmanuel Chabrier (Fr-cm)	Aug 28	Bernhard Listemann (Ger-vn)
Jan 30	Giuseppe del Puente (It-bar)	Sep 8	Antonin Dvorák (Boh-cm)
Feb 10	Walter Parratt (Br-org)	Sep 18	Anna Schimon-Regan (Ger-sop)
Feb 19	Felipe Pedrell (Sp-mus)	Sep 29	Enrico Bevignani (It-cd)
Mar 10	Victor Mahillon (Bel-acous)	Oct 22	Annie L. Cary (Am-alto)
Apr 10	Alfred Volkland (Ger-pn)	Nov 4	Carl Tausig (Pol-pn)
Apr 25	Pauline Lucca (Aus-sop)	Nov 7	Daniel Filleborn (Pol-ten)
May 15	Giovanni Bolzoni (It-cd)	Dec 17	Aglaja Orgeni (Hun-sop)
May 28	Giovanni Sgambati (It-pn)	Dec 27	Julius A. Spitta (Ger-mus)
Jun 3	Edoardo Caudello (Rom-vn)		Henri Kowalski (Fr-pn)

B. Deaths:

Feb 14	Gottfried Fischer (Ger-voc)	Sep 15	Alessandro Rolla (It-vn)
Feb 17	Ferdinando Carulli (It-gui)	Oct 19	Domenico Barbaja (It-imp)
Feb 19	Elfrida Andrée (Swe-org)	Oct 28	Francesco Morlacchi (It-cm)
Mar 17	Félix Savart (Fr-acous)	Nov 18	John C. Clifton (Br-cd)
May 6	John Thomson (Scot-cm)	Nov 18	Georg C. Grosheim (Ger-cm)
Aug 10	Hippolyte Mompou (Fr-org)	Nov 25	Francis Chantrey (Fr-vn)
Aug 13	Bernhard Romberg (Ger-ce!)	Dec 18	Felice Blangini (It-ten)
Aug 24	Karl Curschmann (Ger-cm)	Dec 22	Daniil N. Kaschin (Rus-cm)
Aug 27	Ignaz X. Seyfried (Aus-cm)		Jean B. Cartier (Fr-vn)

C. Debuts:
Other - Giuseppina Brambilla (Trieste), Malvina Schnorr von Carolsfeld (Breslau), Isidor Dannström (Stockholm), Enrico Tamberlik (Naples)

D. New Positions:
Conductors: Franz W. Abt (kapellmeister, Bernburg), Karl M. Kudelski (Moscow Imperial Theater), Otto Nicolai (kapellmeister, Vienna), Carlo Pedrotti (Italian Opera, Amsterdam), Karl Taubert (Berlin Royal Opera)

Educational: Henry Bishop (professor, Edinburgh University), Carl G. Grädener (music director, Kiel University), Nicolas-Prosper Levasseur (voice, Paris Conservatory)

Others: William B. Bradbury (organ, Baptist Tabernacle, New York), Robert Franz (organ, Ulrichskirche, Halle), Edward J. Hopkins (organ, St. Luke's, London), Florentius C. Kist (editor, *Nederlandsch Musikaal Tijdschrift*)

E. Prizes and Honors:
Prizes: Louis-Aimé Maillart and Etienne Joseph Soubre (Prix de Rome)

Honors: Niels Gade (Copenhagen Musical Union)

F. Biographical Highlights:
Michael Balfe settles in London and becomes a favorite of the public; violinist Antonio Bazzini begins a four-year stay in Germany; Hector Berlioz leaves Henrietta and moves in with Marie Recio; Franz Berwald goes to Vienna before returning to Sweden and marries Mathilde Scherer; Anton Bruckner begins a career as a school teacher in Windhaag; Luigi Cherubini retires from active musical life; Karl Goldmark begins the study of music; Joseph Joachim is taken to Vienna for further music study at the Conservatory; Adelaide Kemble makes her Covent Garden debut; Jenny Lind studies with García in Paris; Clara Novello makes her operatic debut in Padua; Robert Schumann's daughter, Marie, is born; Gaspare Spontini resigns his Berlin post after problem's arise with his attitude toward the public and management; Joseph Tichatschek makes his London debut; Robert Volkmann leaves Prague and settles permanently in Budapest; William V. Wallace leaves South America and arrives in New Orleans where he stays for three years.

G. Institutional Openings:
Performing Groups: Abbey Glee Club (London); Roland de Lattre Choral Society (Mons); Maatschappij Caecilia (Amsterdam Choral Society); Mainz Instrumental-verein; The Motett Society (London); Munich Liedertafel

Educational: Hullah's Singing School for Schoolmasters (London)

Other: *Allgemeine Wiener Musik-Zeitung*; Austin Lyceum; Jacob Becker Piano Co. (St. Petersburg); Breslau Opera House; John and James Hopkinson, Piano Makers; *Iberia Musical y Literaria*; Internationale Stiftung Mozarteum (Salzburg); Kiel Stadttheater; Alphonse Leduc Publishing Co. (Paris); *La Mélomanie Revue Musicale*; *Revue Indépendante* (Paris); Royal Saxon Opera House (Dresden); Teatro Comunale Nuovo (Modena)

H. Musical Literature:
Alfieri, Pietro, *Raccolta di musica sacra I*
Chorley, Henry F., *Music and Manners in France and Germany*
Elwart, Antoine, *Feuille harmonique*
Hodges, Edward, *An Essay on the Cultivation of Church Music*
Karlovitch, Jan, *Theory of Composition*
Kiesewetter, Raphael, *Schicksale und beschaffenheit des weltlichen Gesanges*
Marx, Adolf, *Alte musiklehre im streit mit unserer Zeit*
Mason, Lowell, *Carmina Sacra*

Pond, Sylvanus, *The United States Psalmody*
Traetta, Filippo, *Rudiments of Singing I*
Wackernagel, Philipp, *Das deutsche Kirchenlied von der ältesten Zeit...*

I. Musical Compositions:
Adam, Adolphe, *Giselle* (ballet)
    La Rose de Péronne (opera)
Auber, Daniel, *Les diamants de la couronne* (opera)
Balfe, Michael, *Kéolanthe* (opera)
Bennett, William S., *The Wood Nymphs Overture*
Berlioz, Hector, *Nuits d'été for Voice and Piano*
Berwald, Franz, *Estrella de Soria* (opera)
Chopin, Frédéric, *2 Nocturnes, Opus 48*
    3 Mazurkas, Opus 50
    Polonaise in F-sharp Minor, Opus 44
    Prelude in C-sharp Minor, Opus 45
    Fantasy in F Minor, Opus 49
Donizetti, Gaetano, *Maria Padilla* (opera)
    Rita (opera)
    Adelia (opera)
Dorn, Heinrich, *Der Banner von England* (opera)
Eslava, Hilarión, *Il solitario* (opera)
Franck, César, *3 Piano Trios, Opus 1*
Fry, William H., *Aurelia, the Vestal* (opera)
Gade, Niels, *Symphony No. l, Opus 5*
Halévy, Jacques, *Le guitarrero* (opera)
    La reine de Chypre (opera)
Kalliwoda, Johann, *Symphony No. 6 in G Minor*
Kastner, Jean G., *La maschera* (opera)
Loewe, Carl, *Palestrina* (oratorio)
Lortzing, Albert, *Casanova* (opera)
    Jubel-Kantate
Mendelssohn, Felix, *Songs without Words IV, Opus 53*
    Serious Variations, Opus 54, for Piano
    Variations, Opus 82, for Piano
    Variations, Opus 83, for Piano
    Antigone, Opus 55 (incidental music)
    March in D Major, Opus 108
Mercadante, Saverio, *Il proscritto* (opera)
Moniuszko, Stanislaw, *Ideal* (opera)
    Carmagnole (opera)
Morlacchi, Francesco, *Mass No. 10*
Nicolai, Otto, *Il proscritto* (opera)
Pacini, Giovanni, *L'uomo del mistero* (opera)
Pedrotti, Carlo, *Matilde* (opera)
Rossini, Gioacchino, *Stabat Mater*
Schumann, Robert, *Symphony No. 1, Opus 38, "Spring"*
    Symphony No. 4, Opus 120
    Overture, Scherzo and Finale, Opus 52
Spohr, Louis, *Symphony No. 7, Opus 121, "Earthly and Divine"*
Thomas, Ambroise, *Le comte der Carmagnola* (opera)
Wagner, Richard, *The Flying Dutchman* (opera)

1842

World Events:

In the U.S., the Webster-Ashburton Treaty settles the dispute over the northeastern boundary between Canada and the U.S.; Massachusetts limits children's labor to 10 hours a day; Dorr's Rebellion in Rhode Island leads to universal male suffrage; ether is first used as an anesthetic; Barnum's American Museum opens in New York. Internationally, the Opium War is settled by the Treaty of Nanking in which Hong Kong is ceded to the British; the British Mining Act prohibits women and children from working in the mines; the British evacuate Afghanistan after the massacre of their troops by the natives; the Doppler Effect is first explained by experiments by C. Doppler.

Cultural Highlights:

Washington Irving is made U.S. Minister to Spain; William Allan is knighted; Hermann Melville jumps ship and lives with the cannibals in the Marquesas for a year; Edwin Landseer refuses to accept a knighthood. Births in the literary field include American philosopher William James, author Ambros Bierce, German novelist Karl May, French poet Stéphane Mallarmé and author François Coppée; deaths include the American father of the dictionary, Noah Webster, philosopher William E. Channing, Scottish poet Allan Cunningham, Irish poets John Banim and William Maginn, German poet and novelist Clemens Brentano and French novelist Marie Stendhal. Births in the art world include Russian artist Vasily Vereschagin and Italian artist Giovanni Boldini; deaths include British artist John Cotman and French artist Louise Vigée-Lebrun. Other highlights include:

Art: Thomas Cole, *Voyage of the Life*; Gustave Courbet, *Courbet with a Black Dog*; Alexandre Decamps, *Exit from the Turkish School*; Jean-Auguste Ingres, *Luigi Cherubini and the Muse of Poetry*; Clark Mills, *Treasury Building, D.C.*; Théodore Rousseau, *Under the Birches in the Evening*; Joseph Turner, *Steamer in a Snow Storm*

Literature: William C. Bryant, *The Fountain and Other Poems*; Charles Dickens, *American Notes*; Nikolai Gogol, *Dead Souls*; Nathaniel Hawthorne, *Twice-Told Tales II*; Thomas Macauley, *Lays of Ancient Rome*; Edgar A. Poe, *Murder in the Rue Morgue*; Alfred Lord Tennyson, *Poems*; Aubrey de Vere, *The Waldenses and Other Poems*

MUSICAL EVENTS

A. Births:

Jan 13	Heinrich Hofmann (Ger-pn)	Jun 12	Richard Nordraak (Nor-cm)
Jan 22	Henri Maréchal (Fr-cm)	Jun 13	Camilla Urso (Fr-vn)
Feb 3	Sidney Lanier (Am-fl-pt)	Jun 19	Walter Bache (Br-pn-cd)
Feb 17	Wilhelm Fritze (Ger-pn)	Jul 4	Gyula Erkel (Hun-pn-cd)
Feb 24	Arrigo Boito (It-cm-lib)	Jul 9	Clara L. Kellogg (Am-sop)
Mar 22	Carl Rosa (Ger-vn-imp)	Sep 9	Heinrich Wiegand (Ger-bs)
Mar 24	Gabrielle Krauss (Aus-sop)	Sep 12	Marianne Brandt (Aus-alto)
Apr 26	William Chaumet (Fr-cm)	Oct 25	Wilhelm Bäumker (Ger-mus)
May 1	Janet Patey (Scot-alto)	Oct 29	Gustav Frieman (Pol-vn)
May 5	Johann N. Fuchs (Aus-cd)	Nov 8	Eugen Gura (Ger-bar)
May 12	Jules Massenet (Fr-cm)	Nov 28	Emile Bernard (Fr-org)
May 13	Arthur Sullivan (Br-cm)	Dec 16	Melitta Otto (Ger-sop)
May 14	Alphons Czibulka (Hun-cm)	Dec 24	Jan van den Eeden (Bel-cm)
Jun 3	Albert Payne (Ger-pub)		Frank H. Celli (Br-bs)

B. Deaths:

Feb 5	Luigi Angeloni (It-mus)	Apr 6	Johann A. André (Ger-pub)
Mar 7	Christian Weinlig (Ger-org)	May 5	Jean Elleviou (Fr-ten)
Mar 15	Luigi Cherubini (It-cm)	Jun 18	Tobias Haslinger (Aus-pub)

Jun 20	Michael Umlauf (Aus-vn-cm)	Nov 15	Joseph Rastrelli (Ger-cd)
Jul 23	Timothy Swan (Ger-hymn)	Nov 24	Pehr Frigel (Swe-cm)
Aug 18	João Bomtempo (Por-pn-cm)	Dec	Giacomo Ferrari (It-the)
Aug 25	Jérôme J. Momigny (Bel-the)	Dec 5	Marie Jean Vestris (It-bal)
Sep 15	Pierre Baillot (Fr-vn)	Dec 16	Johann Rochlitz (Ger-cri)
Oct 2	José Elízaga (Mex-cm-the)	Dec 18	Manuel Doyagüe (Sp-m.ed)
Oct 8	Christoph Weyse (Den-cm)	Dec 18	Giuseppe Niccolini (It-cm)
Nov 3	Franz Clement (Aus-vn-cd)	Dec 25	Dionys Weber (Boh-the)

C. Debuts:
U.S. -- Max Bohrer (tour)

Other - Henry R. Allen (London), Anne Charton-Demeur (Bordeaux), Karl Johann Formes (Cologne), Anne de la Grange (Italy), Semyon Gulak-Artemovsky (St. Petersburg), Charlotte Sainton-Dolby (London), Willoughby H. Weiss (Liverpool)

D. New Positions:
Conductors: Gaetano Donizetti (kapellmeister, Vienna), Carl Kosmaly (Wiesbaden Opera), Ignaz Lachner (kapellmeister, Munich), Giacomo Meyerbeer (Berlin Court Opera)

Educational: Daniel-Louis Auber (director, Paris Conservatory),Gilbert-Louis Duprez (voice, Paris Conservatory), Louise Farrenc (piano, Paris Conservatory), Gottfried Wilhelm Fink (professor of music, Leipzig University), Manuel García (voice, Paris Conservatory), Moritz Hauptmann (cantor, Thomasschule, Leipzig), Henri Herz (piano, Paris Conservatory)

Others: Moritz Brosig (organ, Breslau Cathedral), Siegfried Dehn (music librarian, Royal Library, Berlin), Théodore Nisard (organ, St. Germain des Pres), Alexei Vertovsky (general manager, Moscow Opera), Samuel Sebastian Wesley (organ, Leeds' Parish Church)

E. Prizes and Honors:
Honors: Henry Bishop (knighted), Giacomo Meyerbeer (Order of Paris), Georges Onslow (Institut de France), Edward Rimbault (Swedish Academy)

F. Biographical Highlights:
J. Lathrop Allen moves his brass instrument business to Boston; Désirée Artôt marries baritone Mariano Padilla y Ramos; George Bristow becomes violinist in the newly-formed New York Philharmonic; Prosper Dérivis makes his La Scala debut; César Franck leaves the Paris Conservatory and returns to Belgium; Karl Goldmark enters the Musical Society of Sopron for music study; Louis Moreau Gottschalk goes to Paris for further music study; Charles Gounod visits Vienna; Ferdinand Hiller returns to Germany from Italy; Franz Liszt tours Russia; Felix Mendelssohn visits with Queen Victoria (her favorite *Songs without Words* were by his sister Fanny) and organizes the Leipzig Conservatory; Mihály Mosonyi moves permanently to Budapest; Edward Rimbault refuses the chair of music at Harvard; Giorgio Ronconi makes his London debut; Lauro Rossi and his wife are invited to join the New Orleans Opera Co.; François Rude moves to Italy; Robert Schumann suffers a nervous breakdown due to overwork; Mary Shaw makes her Covent Garden debut; Richard Wagner returns to Dresden and begins sketches for *Tannhauser*; Emil Waldteufel's family moves to Paris.

G. Institutional Openings:
Performing Groups: Cleveland Sacred Music Society; Cologne Männergesangverein; Dando String Quartet (London); Galitzin Boys Choir (Moscow); Mannheim Liederkranz; New York Philharmonic Orchestra; Vienna Philharmonic Orchestra

Educational: Académie du Chant (Paris); École de Musique de la Ville d'Anvers (Belgium)

Other: *Ainsworth's Magazine*; Athens Fine Arts Society; Cervený Brass Instrument Co. (Königgratz); Chicago Musical Society; Christy Minstrels; Crosby Hall (London); Escudier Publishing House (Paris); *Florentine Gazzetta Musicale*; *Gazzetta Musicale di Milano*; Harmonium (by A. Debain); Abraham Hirsch, Music Publisher (Stockholm); Elias Howe Music Store (Rhode Island); Mudie's Lending Library (London); *Musical Examiner*; *Le Musicien*; A. and S. Nordheimer, Publishers (Ontario); Thalia Theater (Hamburg); Vilnius Theater

H. Musical Literature:

Alfieri, Pietro, *Accompagnamento coll'organo de' toni ecclesiatici*
Becker, Carl F., *Harmonielehre für dilettanten*
Hoffmann, H., *Schlesische volkslieder mit melodien*
Lambillotte, Louis, *Musée des Organistes I*
Loder, John D., *The Whole Modern Art of Bowing*
Mainzer, Joseph, *The Musical Athenaeum*
Moore, John W., *Sacred Minstrel*
Schilling, Gustav, *Die musikalische Europa*
Töpfer, Johann G., *Die Scheibler'sche stimm-methode*
    Abhandlung über den saitenbezug der Pianoforte

I. Musical Compositions:

Adam, Adolphe, *Le roi d'Yvetot* (opera)
Auber, Daniel, *Le Duc d'Olonne* (opera)
Berwald, Franz, *Symphony No. 1, "Serieuse"*
    Symphony No. 2, "Capricieuse"
    Memories of the Norwegian Alps (tone poem)
Bruckner, Anton, *Mass in C Major*
Chélard, Hippolyte, *Der Scheibentoni* (incidental music)
Chopin, Frédéric, *Impromtu in G-flat Major, Opus 51*
    Ballade in F Minor, Opus 52
    Polonaise in A-flat Major, Opus 53
    Scherzo in E Major, Opus 54
Donizetti, Gaetano, *Linda di Chamounix* (opera)
Franck, César, *Piano Trio No. 4, Opus 2*
Gade, Niels, *Napoli* (ballet)
Glinka, Mikhail, *Russlan und Ludmilla* (opera)
Gounod, Charles, *Requiem Mass*
Kreutzer, Konradin, *Der Edelknecht* (opera)
Loewe, Carl, *Emmy* (opera)
    Johann Hus, Opus 82 (oratorio)
Lortzing, Albert, *Der Wildschütz* (opera)
Mendelssohn Felix, *Symphony No. 3, Opus 56, "Scotch"*
Moniuszko, Stanislaw, *The Conscription* (opera)
Mosonyi, Mihály, *Mass No. 1 in C Major*
    Overture in B Minor, Opus 15
Pacini, Giovanni, *La fidanzata corsa* (opera)
Schumann, Robert, *3 String Quartets, Opus 41*
    Piano Quintet, Opus 44
    Piano Quartet, Opus 47
Spohr, Louis, *Concert Overture in D Major, Opus 126*
    The Last Hours of the Saviour (oratorio)
Thomas, Ambroise, *La guerillero* (opera)
Verdi, Giuseppe, *Nabucco* (opera)

1843

World Events:

In the U.S., Mexican President Santa Anna warns the U.S. against the annexation of Texas; J.C. Fremont explores the Oregon Trail Territory and New Mexico; Marthasville (Atlanta), Georgia is founded; the U.S. recognizes the independence of Hawaii; Dorothea Dix begins her campaign against prison and asylum conditions; future President William McKinley is born. Internationally, the First Maori War against British rule takes place in New Zealand; Louis Napoleon becomes head of the French Republic; the Spanish dictatorship is overthrown and Isabella II is declared Queen; the British annex Natal to Cape Colony; the Thames River Tunnel is opened at Rotherhite.

Cultural Highlights:

William Wordsworth is made British Poet Laureate. Births in the art world include French artist Alexandre Regnault and Belgian sculptor Charles van der Stappen; deaths include American artists Washington Allston and John Trumbull. Births in the literary field include American novelist Henry James, Spanish novelist Benito P. Galdós and Portugese poet and critic Téofilo Braga; deaths include American lawyer and writer of the Star-Spangled Banner, Francis Scott Key, German author Friedrich La Motte-Focqué and poet Johann C. Hölderlin, British poet Robert Southey, French poet Casimir Delavigne and Austrian novelist Karoline Pichler. Other highlights include:

Art: Washington Allston, *Belshazzar's Feast*; Théodore Chassériau, *The Two Sisters*; Thomas Cole, The *Roman Campagna*; Jean Baptiste Corot, The *Destruction of Sodom*; Thomas Duncan, *Charles Edward and Flora MacDonald*; Charles Gleyre, *St. John and the Apocalypse*; William Page, *Cupid and Psyche*; Joseph Turner, *The Sun of Venice Going to Sea*

Literature: William H. Ainsworth, *Windsor Castle*; Berthold Auerbach, *Schwarzwälder Dorfgeschichten*; Charles Dickens, *A Christmas Carol*; Antonio García Gutiérrez, *Simón Bocanegra*; Friedrich Hebbel, *Maria Magdalena*; Henry W. Longfellow, *The Spanish Student*; Edgar E. Poe, *The Gold Bug*; John G. Whittier, *Lays of My Home*

MUSICAL EVENTS

A. Births:

Jan 12	Julián Gayarré (Sp-ten)		Jun 10	H. von Herzogenberg (Aus-pn)
Feb 14	Louis Diémer (Fr-pn-cm)		Jun 13	Adolf Neuendorff (Ger-cd)
Feb 19	Adelina Patti (Br-sop)		Jun 15	Edvard Grieg (Nor-cm)
Mar 28	Paul R. Ferrier (Fr-lib)		Jun 15	Feodor Stravinsky (Rus-bs)
Apr 4	Hans Richter (Hun-cd)		Jun 16	David Popper (Aus-cel)
Apr 8	Asger Hamerik (Den-cd)		Jun 19	Charles Lefebvre (Fr-cm)
Apr 9	Theodor Helm (Aus-cri)		Jul 11	Anna Mehlig (Ger-pn)
Apr 14	Gustav Huberti (Bel-cd)		Aug 20	Christine Nilsson (Swe-sop)
Apr 25	Vasily Bessel (Rus-pub)		Oct 18	Romeo Orsi (It-cl.m)
May 7	Pierre Melchissédec (Fr-bar)		Oct 24	Alexis H. Fissot (Fr-org)
May 22	Francis Hueffer (Br-cri)		Nov 23	Joseph Sucher (Ger-cd)
May 29	Émile L. Pessard (Fr-cm)		Dec 13	George Stephanescu (Rom-cd)

B. Deaths:

Jan 3	Thomas L. Bellamy (Br-bs)		May 17	Joseph Sellner (Ger-ob)
Jan 7	Franz Schoberlechner (Aus-pn)		Aug 29	Charles J. Ashley (Br-cel)
Mar	Christian Albrecht (Ger-pn.m)		Oct	Louis Pradher (Fr-pn)
Apr 11	Joseph Lanner (Aus-cd)		Oct 24	Emanuel Langbecker (Ger-mus)
May 3	Franz X. Gebel (Ger-cm)		Nov 25	Samuel Webbe, Jr. (Br-cm)

C. Debuts:

U.S. -- Ole Bull (tour), Jeanne Anaïs Castellan (N.Y.), Laure Cinti-Damoreau (tour), Henri Vieuxtemps (tour)

Other - Marietta Alboni (Milan), Joseph Goldberg (Padua, as vocalist), Alfred Jaëll (age 11, Venice), Dar'ya Leonova (St. Petersburg), Ernst Pauer (Vienna), Alexander Reichardt (Lemberg), Wilhelm Troszel (Warsaw), Marie Wieck (Leipzig)

D. New Positions:

Conductors: Heinrich Dorn (Cologne Opera), Ferdinand Hiller (Leipzig Gewandhaus), Teodulo Mabellini (Florence PO), Alessandro Nini (maestro di cappella, Novara Cathedral), August Roeckel (kapellmeister, Dresden), Richard Wagner (Dresden Opera)

Educational: Jean Delphin Alard (violin, Paris Conservatory), Jean Desiré Artôt (horn, Brussels Conservatory), Charles Auguste Bériot (violin, Brussels Conservatory), Ferdinand David (violin, Leipzig Conservatory), Johann Kittl (director, Prague Conservatory), Lambert Massart (violin, Paris Conservatory), Louis Plaidy (piano, Leipzig Conservatory), Ernst Richter (theory, Leipzig Conservatory), Ernst Wenzel (piano, Leipzig Conservatory)

Others: Johan Hartmann (organ, Copenhagen Cathedral), Edward J. Hopkins (organ, Temple Church, London), Theodor Kirchner (organ, Winterthur), Hermann Langer (organ, Leipzig University Church)

F. Biographical Highlights:

Marietta Alboni makes her Vienna debut; Hector Berlioz concertizes in Germany and meets Schumann and Mendelssohn; Ole Bull begins his first American tour; Charles Hallé begins his series of concerts in London; Joseph Joachim, age 12, goes to Leipzig where he performs with Mendelssohn accompanying and later with the Gewandhaus Orchestra; Adelaide Kemble retires from the stage following her marriage; Clara Novella marries the Count Gigliucci and temporarily retires from the stage; Amilcare Ponchielli enters the Conservatory of Milan; Joseph Joachim Raff sends some piano works to Mendelssohn who recommends them to his publisher; Carl Reinecke makes his first concert tour of Scandinavia; Gioacchino Rossini goes to Paris for an operation and returns to Bologna; Robert Schumann teaches in Leipzig and takes a hiatus from composing; Bedrich Smetana settles in Prague and teaches privately for the family of Count Thun; Caroline Unger marries and retires from the stage; Henri Vieuxtemps undertakes his first American tour; Henryk Wieniawski enters the Conservatory of Paris.

G. Institutional Openings:

Performing Groups: Adelaide Choral Society (Australia); Augsburger Liedertafel; Berlin Männergesangverein; Berlin Symphoniekapelle; Blagrove's Quartet Concerts (London); Bonn Orchesterverein; Darmstadt Mozartverein; St. Cecilia Society of Bordeaux; Société de Musique Vocale, Religieuse et Classique (Paris); Virginia Minstrels (by Dan Emmett)

Educational: Cambridge University (Peterhouse) Musical Society; Leipzig Conservatory of Music; Sinico Singing School (Trieste)

Other: Antoine Bord Piano Co. (Paris); Forster and Andrews, Organ Builders (Hull); Glasgow Musical Association; *L'Illustration*; Malmsjö Piano Co. (Göteborg); Joseph Merklin (Merklin, Schütze et Cie.), Organ Builders (Brussels); *Musikalisch-Kritisches Repertorium*; George Rogers and Sons, Piano Makers (London); *Signale für die Musikalische Welt* (Leipzig); Tivoli Gardens (Copenhagen); Carl Warmuth, Music Dealer and Publisher (Oslo)

H. Musical Literature:

Boucheron, Raimondo, *Filosofia della musica*
Fink, Gottfried, *Musikalischer hausschatz*
Hullah, John, *A Grammar of Vocal Music*
Jarmusiewicz, Jan, *A New System of Music*
Schilling, Gustav, *Musikalische dynamik*
Seidel, Johann J., *Die Orgel un ihr Bau*
Töpfer, Johann G., *Die Orgel, Zweck und beschaffenheit Teile*
Wesley, Samuel S., *The Psalter*
Winterfeld, Carl von, *Der evangelische Kirchengesang I*
Woolhouse, Wesley, *A Catechism of Music*

I. Musical Compositions:

Balfe, Michael, *Geraldine* (opera)
    The Bohemian Girl (opera)
Chopin, Frédéric, *2 Nocturnes, Opus 55*
    3 Mazurkas, Opus 56
    Berceuse In D-flat Major, Opus 57
Destouches, Franz von, *Der Teufel un der Schneider* (opera)
Donizetti, Gaetano, *Don Pasquale* (opera)
    Don Sébastien (opera)
    Maria di Rohan (opera)
Eslava, Hilarión, *Pietro il crudele* (opera)
Flotow, Friedrich von, *L'esclave de Camoëns* (opera)
Franck, César, *Grande Caprice, Opus 5, for Piano*
    Souvenirs d'Aix-la-chapelle, Opus 9, for Piano
Gade, Niels, *Symphony No. 2, Opus 10*
    9 Songs in Folkstyle, Opus 9, for Piano
Gounod, Charles, *Vienna Mass*
    Un Hymne Français
Halévy, Jacques, *Charles VI* (opera)
Kalliwoda, Johann, *Symphony No. 7 in F Major*
    Overture Pastorale, Opus 108
    Mass No. l, Opus 137
Loewe, Carl, *Der Meister von Avis* (oratorio)
Marschner, Heinrich, *Kaiser Adolf von Nassau* (opera)
Mendelssohn, Felix, *Midsummer Night's Dream, Opus 61* (incidental music)
    Cello Sonata No. 2, Opus 58
    In Grünen, Opus 59 (song cycle)
    Psalm XCVIII, Opus 91
    Hymn for Contralto, Chorus and Orchestra, Opus 96
    3 A Capella Psalms, Opus 78
Mercadante, Saverio, *Il reggente* (opera)
Meyerbeer, Giacomo, *Das Hoffest von Ferrara* (opera)
Moniuszko, Stanislaw, *The Lottery* (opera)
    The New Don Quixote (opera)
Nicolai, Otto, *Mass to Friedrich Wilhelm IV*
Pacini, Giovanni, *Medea* (opera)
Persiani, Giuseppe, *Il Fantasma* (opera)
Poissl, Johann, *Zaide* (opera)
Schumann, Robert, *Andante and Variations, Opus 46, for Two Pianos*
    Paradise and the Peri, Opus 50 (cantata)
Thomas, Ambroise, *Mina* (opera)
    Angélique et Médor (opera)
Verdi, Giuseppe, *I Lombardi* (opera)
Wagner, Richard, *The Love Feast of the Apostles* (cantata)

1844

World Events:

In the U.S., James K. Polk is elected President No. 11; the first telegraph message, "What hath God wrought?," is sent from Washington, D.C., to Baltimore; "Fifty-four Forty or Fight!" becomes the battle cry of settlers in the Oregon Territory in their dispute with Canada; the Universities of Mississippi and of Notre Dame are chartered. Internationally, the Young Men's Christian Association (YMCA) is founded in London by George Williams; the Dominican Republic succeeds in its fight for independence from Haiti; the French defeat the Moroccans in North Africa; Charles XIV of Sweden dies and is succeeded by Oscar I.

Cultural Highlights:

The Liceo Artístico y Literario opens in Havana; William Dyce is taken into the Royal Academy. Births in the art world include American artist Thomas Eakins and sculptor Moses J. Ezekiel, Irish sculptor Martin Milmore, German artist Wilhelm Leibl, French artist Henri Rousseau and Russian artist Ilya Repin; deaths include American architect Charles Bullfinch, Danish sculptor Bertel Thorvaldsen and British artist Augustus Callcott. Births in the literary field include American author George W. Cable, German philosopher Friedrich Nietzsche, British poets Robert Bridges, Gerard M. Hopkins and Arthur O'Shaughnessy, Finnish novelist Minna Canth, Italian poet Mario Rapisardi and French poets Anatole France and Paul Verlaine; deaths include Hungarian poet Sándor Kisfaludy, Scottish poet Thomas Campbell and British novelist William Beckford. Other highlights include:

Art: George Catlin, *Indian Troop*; Théodore Chassériau, *Etchings for Othello*; Thomas Cole, *American Lake Scene*; Jules Dupré, *Washington Allston*; Edward Hicks, *Calculating*; Edwin Landseer, *The Challenge*; Jean François Millet, *The Milkmaid*; Joseph Turner, *Rain, Steam and Speed*; John Vanderlyn, *The Landing of Columbus*

Literature: Honoré de Balzac, *Modeste Mignon*; Elizabeth Barrett, *Poems*; Charles Dickens, *Martin Chuzzlewit*; Benjamin Disraeli, *Coningsby*; Alexander Dumas, père, *The Three Musketeers*; Heinrich Heine, *Deutschland: Ein Wintermärchen*; James R. Lowell, *Poems*; William Thackeray, *Barry Lyndon*

MUSICAL EVENTS

A. Births:

Jan 14	Clara K. Rogers (Br-sop)	Jun 3	Emile Paladilhe (Fr-cm)
Feb 21	Charles M. Widor (Fr-org)	Jul 10	Amalie Materna (Aus-sop)
Mar 10	Pablo de Sarasate (Sp-vn)	Jul 14	Oscar Beringer (Ger-pn)
Mar 18	Nicolai Rimsky-Korsakov (Rus-cm)	Sep 11	Karl Bohm (Ger-pn)
		Oct 8	Alfred Arthur (Am-ten)
Mar 23	Eugène Gigout (Fr-org)	Nov 4	Edward Dannreuther (Ger-pn)
Apr 3	George Osgood (Am-m.ed)	Nov 12	Pierre O. Fauque (Fr-mus)
Apr 26	Enrique B. Gómez (Sp-cm)	Nov 28	Angelo Masini (It-ten)
Apr 30	Richard Hofmann (Ger-vn)	Dec 5	Frederick Bridge (Br-org)
May 3	Richard d'Oyly Carte (Br-imp)	Dec 18	Ernest Grosjean (Fr-org)

B. Deaths:

Jan 15	Joseph Mazzinghi (Br-pn)	Jul 6	François Gebauer (Fr-hn)
Jan 30	John Addison (Br-cb-cm)	Jul 13	Johann Gänsbacher (Aus-cm)
Feb 29	Thaddäus Weigl (Aus-pub)	Jul 17	André da Silva Gomes (Bra-cm)
Mar 21	Felix Lipowsky (Ger-mus)	Jul 19	Heinrich Domnich (Ger-hn)
Apr 2	Ignaz von Mosel (Aus-cm)	Sep 4	Oliver Holden (Am-cm)
Apr 22	Henri M. Berton (Fr-cm)	Sep 11	H. P. Gérard (Fr-cm-cd)
May 21	Giuseppe Baini (It-cm-mus)	Nov 1	August Haeser (Ger-cm)
Jul 2	Karl L. Blum (Ger-cm)	Nov 9	Uri Hill (Am-m.ed)

Nov 19 Johann C. Till (Am-org)   Dec 8 John Meacham, Jr. (Am-pn.m)
Nov 27 Richard M. Bacon (Br-voc)   Dec 10 Franz von Destouches (Ger-cm)

C. Debuts:
U.S. -- Henry Phillips (tour)

Other - Louis Moreau Gottschalk (Paris), Mathilde Marchesi (Frankfurt), Angelo Mariani (Messina), Louis Henri Obin (Paris), Ernst Pasqué (Mayence), Joseph Tagliafico (Paris), Fortunata Tedesco (Milan), Johanna Wagner (Dresden)

D. New Positions:
Conductors: Joseph Drechsler (kapellmeister, St. Stephen's, Vienna), Hilarión Eslava (Madrid Royal Chapel), Albert Lortzing (Leipzig Theater), Franz Mirecki (Cracow Opera), Francesco Shira (Drury Lane), Étienne Soubre (Brussels PO)

Educational: François-Emmanuel Bazin (Paris Conservatory), Arnold Blaes (clarinet, Brussels Conservatory), William Dyce (Fine Arts, King's College, London), John P. Hullah (voice, King's College), Félix Ledent (piano, Liège Conservatory), Gottfried von Preyer (director, Vienna Conservatory), George Root (voice, Abbott's School for Young Ladies, Rutgers)

Others: Ignace X. Leybach (organ, Toulouse Cathedral), August Gottfried Ritter (editor, *Urania*)

E. Prizes and Honors:
Prizes: Victor Massé and Renaud de Vilback (Prix de Rome)

Honors: William Dyce (Royal Academy, London)

F. Biographical Highlights:
Johannes Brahms, at the age of 10, plays for the first time in public with a chamber group; Alexander Dargomijsky goes on an extensive European tour; César Franck leaves Belgium to settle permanently in Paris; Niels Gade becomes assistant to Mendelssohn in Leipzig; Mikhail Glinka travels in France and Spain and meets Berlioz; Karl Goldmark is sent to Vienna for further music study; Joseph Joachim makes his London debut; Franz Liszt breaks off with Mme. d'Agoult; Carl Loewe visits Vienna; Albert Lortzing begins his conducting career; George Root moves to New York; Lauro Rossi leaves New Orleans to return to Italy; Anton and Nicolai Rubinstein settle in Berlin for music study; Robert and Clara Schumann tour Russia while Robert, suffering a second nervous breakdown, gives up his music paper; Mary Shaw, at the shock of her husband's sudden insanity, loses her voice; Sophie Thillon makes her London debut; William V. Wallace returns to Europe and tours the continent.

G. Institutional Openings:
Performing Groups: Berlin Kunstlerverein; Strauss Orchestra II (by Johann Strauss, Jr.)

Educational: Bressler's Conservatory of Music (Nantes)

Other: *Caecilia: Algemeen Musikaal Tijdschrift ver Nederlands*; G. G. Guidi, Music Publisher (Florence); *Hood's Magazine*; Josef Kroll Theater (Berlin); Macmillan and Co., Publishers (Cambridge); *Mainzer's Musical Times and Singing Circular*; *Orgel-Archiv*; Palmo's Opera House (N.Y.); Teatro de la Victoria (Santiago, Chile); Teatro del Buen Orden (Buenos Aires); *Vierteljahrsschrift für Musikwissenschaft*; Wadsworth Atheneum (Hartford)

H. Musical Literature:
Becker, Carl F., *Evangelischen choralbuch*
Berlioz, Hector, *Traité d'instrumentation*
Chevé, Emile, *Méthode élémentaire de la musique vocale*

Fétis, François, *The Theory and Practice of Harmony*
Klosé, Hyacinthe, *Grande Méthode pour la clarinette*
La Fage, Juste de, *Histoire générale de la musique*
Lobe, Johann C., *Compositionslehre*
Mason, Lowell, *The Vocalist*
d'Ortigue, Joseph, *Abécédaire du plain-chant*
Tuckerman, Samuel, *Episcopal Harp*

I. Musical Compositions:
Adam, Adolphe, *Richard in Palestine* (opera)
    Cagliostro (opera)
Auber, Daniel, *La sirène* (opera)
Balfe, Michael, *The Enchantress* (opera)
    The Castle of Aymon (opera)
Benedict, Julius, *The Brides of Venice* (opera)
Bennett, William S., *Caprice for Piano and Orchestra*
Berlioz, Hector, *Overture, Roman Carnival, Opus 9*
Bruckner, Anton, *Mass in F for A Capella Chorus*
Chopin, Frédéric, *Piano Sonata in B Minor, Opus 58*
Costa, Michael, *Don Carlos* (opera)
David, Félicien, *Le désert* (ode-symphonie)
Donizetti, Gaetano, *Catarina Cornaro* (opera)
Flotow, Friedrich von, *Allessandro Stradella* (opera)
    Lady Henrietta (ballet)
Foster, Stephen, *Open Thy Lattice, Love* (song)
Franck, César, *12 Fantasias on a Theme of Dalyrac, Opus 11 and 12, for Piano*
    Fantasie, Opus 13, for Piano
Gade, Niels, *In the Highlands Overture, Opus 7*
Halévy, Jacques, *Le lazzarone* (opera)
Kalliwoda, Johann, *Concertina, Opus 110, for Oboe and Orchestra*
    Introduction and Variations, Opus 128, for Piano and Orchestra
Loewe, Carl, *Biblische Bilder, Opus 97, for Piano*
L'vov, Alexei, *Bianca* (opera)
Massé, Victor, *Le renégat de Tanger* (opera)
Mendelssohn, Felix, *Concerto, Opus 64, for Violin and Orchestra*
    Songs without Words V, Opus 62
    10 Partsongs, Opus 88 and 100
Mercadante, Saverio, *Leonora* (opera)
Meyerbeer, Giacomo, *Ein Feldlager in Schlesien* (opera)
Mosonyi, Mihály, *Symphony No. 1*
    String Sextet
Nicolai, Otto, *Festival Overture, Ein Feste Burg*
Niedermeyer, Louis, *Marie Stuart* (opera)
Rossi, Lauro, *Il borgomastro di Schiedam* (opera)
Schumann, Robert, *Der Corsar* (opera)
Spohr, Louis, *Concerto No. 15, Opus 128, for Violin and Orchestra*
Verdi, Giuseppe, *Ernani* (opera)
Vieuxtemps, Henri, *Concerto, Opus 25, for Violin and Orchestra*
Wagner, Richard, *Trauermusik for Winds*

1845

World Events:
In the U.S., Florida and Texas become States No. 27 and 28 respectively; Mexico, due to the annexation of Texas, snubs the envoys sent to settle the Texas and California questions; the term "Manifest Destiny" first appears in local politics; the U.S. Naval Academy opens in Annapolis, Maryland; Baylor University is founded in Texas.; former President Andrew Johnson dies. Internationally, the Second Maori War takes place in New Zealand; the Sikhs battle the British in India; the Potato Blight causes the death of more than a million people in Ireland's Great Famine; the first underwater cable is laid across the English Channel; production begins on the explosive, Gun-cotton.

Cultural Highlights:
The Black Obelisk of Shalmaneser is discovered in the Near East; Henry Thoreau retires to a hut near Walden Pond. Births in the world of art include American artist Benjamin Constant and Mary Cassatt, German sculptor Karl Begas, Jr., and French sculptor Jean Antoine Injalbert; deaths include American artist Henry Sargent, French artist Louis-Léopold Boilly and sculptor François Bosio, British artist William J. Müller and Scotch artist Thomas Duncan. Births in the literary world include Swedish novelist and poet Carl Spitteler and Portugese novelist José de Eça de Queirós; deaths include American poet Maria Brooks, German poets Christian Eberhard, Friedrich Riemer and August von Schlegel, Norwegian poet Henrik Wergeland, Hungarian poet János Bacsányi and British poet Thomas Hood. Famous French actress Sarah Bernhardt is born. Other highlights include:

Art: George Bingham, *Fur Traders on the Missouri*; Thomas Cole, *L'Allegro*; William Collins, *Cromer Sands*; Jean Baptiste Corot, *Homer and the Shepherds*; David Cox, *Sun, Wind and Rain*; Charles Deas, *Death Struggle*; Adolf Menzel, *Room with a Balcony*; William Mount, *Eel Spearing at Setauket*; Joseph Turner, *Sun Setting over a Lake*

Literature: Honoré de Balzac, *Les Paysans*; Sebastian Brunner, *Der Nebeljungen Lied*; James F. Cooper, *Chainbearer and Satanstoe*; Charles Dickens, *Cricket on the Hearth*; Benjamin Disraeli, *Sybil*; Alexander Dumas, père, *The Count of Monte Cristo*; Prosper Mérimée, *Carmen*; Edgar Allen Poe, *The Raven and Other Poems*

MUSICAL EVENTS

A. Births:

Jan 15	Heinrich Vogl (Ger-ten)	Jul 6	Angela Peralta (Mex-sop)
Feb 3	Friedrich Niecks (Ger mus)	Aug 8	Thomas Korschat (Aus-bs)
Mar 14	Gustav Jacobsthal (Ger-mus)	Sep 1	Annie Curwen (Ir-pn)
Mar 22	Adolf Beyschlag (Ger-cd)	Sep 21	August Wilhelmj (Ger-vn)
Mar 30	Heinrich Gudehus (Ger-ten)	Oct 3	Charles Turban (Fr-cl)
Apr 15	T. Brambilla-Ponchielli (It-sop)	Oct 10	Anton Andersen (Nor-cel)
Apr 18	Wilhelm Gericke (Aus-cd)	Oct 13	Elizaveta Lavrovskaya (Rus-mez)
Apr 25	Karl R. Hennig (Ger-the)	Oct 22	John N. Pattison (Am-pn)
May 12	Gabriel Fauré (Fr-cm)	Oct 30	Karl G. Weber (Swi-cm)
May 25	Herman Laroche (Rus-cri)	Nov 6	Beniamino Cesi (It-pn)
Jun 7	Leopold Auer (Hun-vn-m.ed)	Nov 14	Ernst Perabo (Am-pn)
Jun 30	Italo Campanini (It-ten)	Dec 30	Mary Allitsen (Br-cm)

B. Deaths:

Jan 23	Francesco Ruggi (It-cm)	Jul 20	Alexandre Artôt (Fr-vn)
Feb 28	Charles Duvernoy (Fr-cl)	Jul 27	François Foignet (Fr-ten)
May 10	Charles Gand, père (Fr-vn.m)	Aug 2	James Hamilton (Br-the)
May 17	Thaddäus Amadé (Hun-pn-cm)	Sep 16	Karl Lichtenstein (Ger-imp)
Jul 15	Joseph A. Wade (Ir-cm)	Oct 7	Isabella Colbran (Sp-sop)

Oct 26 Carolina Nairne (Aust-pt-cm)   Dec 2 Johannes S. Mayr (Ger-cm)
Nov 2 Chrétien Urhan (Fr-vn)   Dec 25 Wilhelm F. E. Bach (Ger-pn)

C. Debuts:

U.S. -- Clara Brinkerhoff, Henri Herz (tour), Leopold von Meyer (tour), John Templeton (tour), Hermann Wollenhaupt (tour)

Other - Aloys Anders (Vienna), Édouard Gassier (Paris), Lodovico Graziani (Bologna), Catherine Hayes (Marseilles), Jesús de Monasterio (Madrid), Emilio Naudin (Cremona)

D. New Positions:

Conductors: Heinrich Esser (kapellmeister, Mainz), Aloys Kettenus (Mannheim SO), Franz von Suppé (Theater an der Wien), Karl Gottfried Taubert (kapellmeister, Berlin)

Educational: Prosper Sainton (violin, Royal Academy, London)

Others: Karl Franz Brendel (editor, *Neue Zeitschrift für Musik*), Hervé (Florimond Rongé) (organ, St. Eustache, Paris), Johann Uhland (German National Assembly)

E. Prizes and Honors:

Prizes: Adolphe Samuel (Prix de Rome)

Honors: Ambroise Thomas (Legion of Honor), Alfred Victor Vigny (French Academy)

F. Biographical Highlights:

Alkan (Charles-Henri Valentin) emerges from his self-imposed exile and resumes his concert career; Charles-Aimable Bataille turns away from his medical studies and begins music study at the Paris Conservatory; Anton Bruckner begins teaching at St. Florian; Peter Cornelius, after a poor showing as an actor, begins studying theory with Dehn in Berlin; Gaetano Donizetti suffers a paralytic stroke that ends his composing career; William Henry Fry writes what is believed to be the first American opera, *Leonora*; Theodor Leschetizky begins studying philosophy at the University of Vienna; Felix Mendelssohn resumes his teaching and conducting at Leipzig following his time in London; Carlo Pedrotti leaves Amsterdam and returns to his native Verona; Jan K. Pisek makes his London debut; Gioacchino Rossini's wife, Isabella, dies; Peter I, Tchaikovsky begins taking piano lessons at the age of 5; Theodore Thomas moves with his family to the U.S.; William V. Wallace finally returns to England.

G. Institutional Openings:

Performing Groups: Aberdeen Euterpean Society; Artisans' Glee Society (Christiana); Berner Liedertafel; Birmingham Festival Choral Society; Dortmunder Musikverein; Gloucester Choral Society; Helsinki Symphonic Society I; Jähnsscher Gesangverein (Berlin); Linz Liedertafel "Frohsinn" (Sängerbund); The Musical Union (London morning chamber series); Den Norske Studentersangforening (Norway); Toronto Philharmonic Society

Educational: Agthe School of Music (Berlin); Rheinische Musikschule (Cologne)

Other: Beethoven Memorial (Bonn); *Boose's Military Band Journal*; Casavant Frères, Organ Builders (Canada); Castle Gordon (N.Y.); Chouden's Music Publishing House (Paris); Distin and Sons, Music Dealers (London); *Jerrold's Magazine*; *Revue de la Musique Religieuse, Populaire et Classique*; Franz Rieger, Organ Builder (Jägerndorf); Sociedad Filarmónica de Cuba; *Table Book*; Teatro de la Federación (Buenos Aires); Tivoli Theater (Kiel); Henry Willis, Organ Builder (London)

H. Musical Literature:

Becker, Carl F., *Die choralsammlungen der verschiedenen Christlichen Kirchen*
Birnbach, Heinrich, *Der vollkommene Kapellmeister*

Day, Alfred, *Treatise on Harmony*
Duprez, Gilbert, *L'art du chant*
Elwart, Antoine, *Traité de contrepoint et de la fugue*
Glover, Sarah A., *Manual of the Norwich Sol-Fa System*
Hagen, Theodor, *Civilization and Music*
Kreutzer, Léon, *Essai sur l'art lyrique au théâtre*
Maier, Julius, *Klassische kirchenwerke alter Meister*
Mason, Lowell, *The Psaltery*
Töpfer, Johann G., *Theoretisch-praktische Orgelschule*
Weinlig, Theodor, *Theoretisch-praktische Anleitung zur Fuge...*

I. Musical Compositions:

Auber, Daniel, *La barcarolle* (opera)
Balfe, Michael, *L'étoile de Séville* (opera)
Berwald, Franz, *Symphony No. 3, "Singuliere"*
 Symphony No. 4 in E-flat Major
Bruckner, Anton, *Litany for Brass and Chorus*
Chopin, Frédéric, *3 Mazurkas, Opus 59*
 2 Songs, Opus 74
Dargomijsky, Alexander, *Der Triumph des Bacchus* (opera)
David, Félicien, *Les perles d'orient* (song cycle)
Elwart, Antoine, *Noé* (oratorio)
Franck, César, *Fantasia on Polish Airs for Piano*
Gade, Niels, *String Quintet, Opus 8*
Glinka, Mikhail, *Valse-Fantasie for Orchestra*
 Spanish Overture No. 1, "Jota Aragonesa"
Hiller, Ferdinand, *Ein traum in der Christnacht* (opera)
Loewe, Carl, *3 Historische Balladen*
Lortzing, Albert, *Undine* (opera)
Mendelssohn, Felix, *Songs without Words VI, VII, Opus 67 and 102*
 Athalie, Opus 74 (incidental music)
 Oedipus at Colonos, Opus 93 (incidental music)
 String Quintet, Opus 87
 Piano Trio No. 2, Opus 66
 6 Organ Sonatas, Opus 65
 6 Songs, Opus 99
Mercadante, Saverio, *Il Vascello de Gama* (opera)
Moscheles, Ignaz, *Grand Sonata Symphonique, Opus 112, for Piano*
Pacini, Giovanni, *Bondelmonte* (opera)
 Lorenzo de' Medici (opera)
Schumann, Robert, *Concerto, Opus 54, for Piano and Orchestra*
 6 Fugues on B-A-C-H, Opus 60, for Organ
 4 Fugues, Opus 72, for Piano
 6 Studies in Canonic Form, Opus 56
 Albumblätter, Opus 124, for Piano
Spohr, Louis, *Die Kreutzfahrer* (opera)
 Concerto, Opus 131, for String Quartet and Orchestra
 Clarinet Quintet, Opus 130
 String Quintet, Opus 129
Taubert, Wilhelm, *Blaubart* (incidental music)
Titl, Anton E., *Das Wolkenkind* (opera)
Vaccai, Nicola, *Virginia* (opera)
Verdi, Giuseppe, *Giovanni d'Arco* (opera)
 Alzira (opera)
 6 Romances
Wagner, Richard, *Tannhauser* (opera)
Wallace, William V., *Maritana* (opera)

1846

World Events:
In the U.S., the Mexican War breaks out over hard feelings on the annexation of Texas; the U.S. and Canada sign an agreement on the 49th Parallel as the border between Canada and the Oregon Territory; Iowa becomes State No. 29; Milwaukee, Wisconsin, is incorporated; the Pennsylvania Railroad is chartered; Elias Howe patents the sewing machine; the pneumatic tire is patented. Internationally, the Sikh War ends in India; Robert Peel is defeated as British Prime Minister; Europe's first cheap newspaper, the *London Daily News*, is founded; mathematical computation of irregularities in planetary orbits results in the discovery of the planet Neptune; H. Rawlinson succeeds in deciphering Mesopotamian cuneiform writing.

Cultural Highlights:
The Smithsonian Institution is opened in Washington, D.C.; the Semper Gallery opens in Dresden; Coventry Patmore becomes assistant librarian in the British Museum; Jean Baptiste Corot is taken into the Legion of Honor; Anton Berlijn is made a Knight of the Crown of Oak in Holland; Walt Whitman becomes editor of the *Saturday Evening Post*. In the art world American artist Henry Inman is born and British artist Benjamin Haydon dies. Births in the literary field include Italian novelist Salvatore Farina, Polish novelist Henryk Sienkiewicz, Danish poet Holger Drachmann and Irish poet Alfred P. Graves; deaths include French author Étienne Senáncour, Swedish poet Esaias Tegnér and Irish poet George Darley. Other highlights include:

Art: George Bingham, *Jolly Flatboatmen*; Thomas Cole, *The Oxbow, Connecticut River*; Eugène Delacroix, *Abduction of Rebecca*; Edwin Landseer, *Stag at Bay*; John Millais, *Pizarro and the Incas*; Jean François Millet, *Oedipus Unbound*; Moritz von Schwind, *Singing Contest at the Wartburg*; George Watts, *Paolo and Francesca*

Literature: Robert Browning, *Bells and Pomegranates*; Feodor Dostoveysky, *Poor Folk*; Ralph W. Emerson, *Poems*; Dmitri Grigorovich, *The Village*; Nathaniel Hawthorne, *Mosses from an Old Manse*; Oliver W. Holmes, *Poems*; Hermann Melville, *Typee*; Eduard Mörike, *Idylle von Bodensee*; Edgar A. Poe, *The Cask of Amontillado*

MUSICAL EVENTS

A. Births:

Jan 8	William Gilchrist (Am-cd)	Jun 30	Riccardo Drigo (It-cm-cd)
Jan 21	Albert Lavignac (Fr-mus)	Jul 9	Wilhelm M. Vogel (Ger-pn)
Feb 24	Luigi Denza (It-cm)	Jul 29	Sophie Menter (Ger-pn)
Feb 26	George Stebbins (Am-hymn)	Aug 4	Silas G. Pratt (Am-pn-cm)
Feb 27	Joaquin Valverde (Sp-cm)	Aug 17	Marie Trautmann Jaëll (Fr-pn)
Mar 2	Marie H. Roze (Fr-sop)	Sep 11	Julius Melgunov (Rus-pn)
Apr 7	Franz Ries (Ger-pub)	Oct 23	Alexander Archangelski (Rus-cm)
Apr 9	Francesco Tosti (It-cm)	Nov 7	Ignaz Brüll (Aus-pn-cm)
May 8	Oscar Hammerstein (Ger-imp)	Nov 10	Paul Kuczynski (Ger-cm)
May 22	Jacques Rensburg (Hol-cel)	Nov 10	Martin Wegelius (Fin-cd)
May 26	Arthur Coquard (Fr-cm)	Nov 23	Ernst von Schuch (Aus-cd)
Jun 24	Anton Schott (Ger-ten)		

B. Deaths:

Feb 3	Joseph Weigl (Aus-cm)	Apr 24	Girolamo Crescentini (It-cas)
Feb 18	William Hawes (Br-cd)	May 8	Giacomo Cordella (It-cm)
Feb 18	Giovanni Liverati (It-ten)	Jun 2	Johann Heinroth (Ger-the)
Feb 22	Carolus A. Fodor (Hol-pn)	Jul 19	J. B. Fourneaux (Fr-org.m)
Apr 16	Domenico Dragonetti (It-cb)	Jul 24	Joseph von Eybler (Aus-cm)
Apr 22	Josef Triebensee (Boh-ob)	Jul 27	Johann B. Logier (Ger-pn)

Aug 1	Peter Ritter (Ger-cm)	Sep 18	Johann Gabrielski (Ger-fl)
Aug 7	Johann C. Rinck (Ger-org)	Oct 19	Niels Jensen (Den-org)
Aug 10	Johann Hermstedt (Ger-cl)	Nov 1	Franz A. Ries (Ger-vn)
Aug 27	Gottfried W. Fink (Ger-cri)	Dec 12	Eliza Flower (Br-hymn)
Sep 17	Francesco Pollini (It-pn)	Dec 15	Josef Blahack (Aus-ten)

C. Debuts:

U.S. -- William Mason (Boston), Ernesto Camille Sivori (tour)

Other - Adelaide Borghi (Urbino), Angiolina Bosio (Milan), Theodor Formes (Ofen), Antonio Ghislanzoni (Lodi), Wilma Maria Neruda (age 7, Vienna), Ede Reményi (Pest), Camille Saint-Saëns (Paris), Lindsay Sloper (London)

D. New Positions:

Conductors: José Alcedo (maestro de capilla, Santiago Cathedral), Michael Balfe (Her Majesty's Theatre), Michael Costa (London PO), Eduard Tauwitz (kapellmeister, Prague)

Educational: Carlo Conti (counterpoint, Naples Conservatory), Julius Eichberg (violin, Geneva Conservatory), Auguste-Joseph Franchomme (cello, Paris Conservatory), Franz Hauser (director, Munich Conservatory), Walter C. Macfarren (piano, Royal Academy, London), Ignaz Moscheles (piano, Leipzig Conservatory), Henri Vieuxtemps (violin, St. Petersburg Conservatory)

Others: Charles W. Corfe (organ, Christ Church, Oxford), William Henry Fry (European correspondant, New York *Tribune*), George Hogarth (music critic, London *Daily News*), Johann C. Lobe (editor, *Allgemeine Musikzeitung*)

E. Prizes and Honors:

Prizes: Léon-Gustave Gastinel (Prix de Rome)

Honors: Anton Berlijn (Knight of the Crown of Oak, Holland)

F. Biographical Highlights:

Nicolai Afanas'yev decides to follow a solo career in violin playing; Carl Czerny visits in Italy; Gaetano Donizetti, now insane, is placed in a sanatorium in Ivey; Stephen Foster moves to Cincinnati to be the bookkeeper for his brother's business; Charles Gounod begins studies for the priesthood; George Grove returns from the Carribean to England and first becomes interested in music; Charles Hallé begins his concert series in Paris; Albert Lortzing, after failing as an impresario and conductor in Leipzig, moves to Vienna; Felix Mendelssohn again visits England to conduct his *Elijah*; Frederick Ouseley graduates from Oxford; John Sims Reeves makes his La Scala debut; Carl Reinecke becomes court pianist to Christian VIII in Copenhagen; Gioacchino Rossini, following the death of his wife, finally marries Olympe Pélissier; Nicholai Rubinstein returns to Moscow while his brother, Anton, stays on in Vienna for 2 more years; Henri Vieuxtemps begins a 5-year stay in Russia; Richard Wagner meets Hans von Bülow.

G. Institutional Openings:

Performing Groups: Bogota PO (Colombia); Bradford Liedertafel; Chicago Choral Union; Concordia Male Chorus (Bonn); Graz Männergesangverein; Nottingham Vocal Music Club (Sacred Harmonic Society); Oslo Philharmonic Society: Regensburger Musikverein

Educational: Munich Conservatory of Music; Zschocher'sches Musik-Institut (Leipzig)

Other: Academia Melpomenense (Lisbon); EugèneAlbert, Woodwind Maker (Brussels); Baker and Scribner, Publishers (N.Y.); Brandus Music Publishers (Paris); Carhart and Needham, Organ Builders (N.Y.); *La España Musical*; Estey Organ Co. (Vermont); August Gemünder Violin Shop (Springfield, Massachusetts); Horneman and Erslev,

Music Publishers (Copenhagen); Friedrich Ladergast, Organ Builder (Weissenfels); Peters and Co. (Peters, Field and Co.), Music Publisher (Cincinnati); Carl G. Röder, Engraver (Leipzig); Seville Amfiteatro; Carl F. W. Siegel Publishing Co. (Leipzig); Pierre Simon, Bowmaker (Paris); Teatro de Tacón (Havana); Teatro Nuovo (Verona)

H. Musical Literature:

Aikin, Jesse B., *The Christian Minstrel*
Chevé, Emile, *Méthode élémentaire d'harmonie*
Drobisch, Moritz, *Über die mathematische Bestimmung der musikalische Intervalle*
Eslava, Hilarión, *Método de solféo sin acompañamiento*
Gassner, Ferdinand S., *Dirigent und Ripienist*
Hohmann, Christian, *Lehrbuch der musikalischen Composition*
Lobe, Johann C., *Die lehre von der thematischen Arbeit*
Root, George, *The Young Ladies Choir*
Schindler, Anton, *Aesthetik der tonkunst*
Wilke, Christian, *Beiträge zur geschichte der neuen Orgelbaukunst*

I. Musical Compositions:

Balfe, Michael, *The Bondsman* (opera)
Benedict, Julius, *The Crusaders* (opera)
Berlioz, Hector, *The Damnation of Faust, Opus 24* (opera)
Chopin, Frédéric, *2 Nocturnes, Opus 62*
    3 Mazurkas, Opus 63
    Cello Sonata, Opus 65
David, Félicien, *Moses at Sinai* (oratorio)
Flotow, Friedrich von, *Lâme en peine* (opera)
Franck, César, *Ruth* (oratorio)
    The Sermon on the Mount (tone poem)
Gade, Niels, *Comala, Opus 12* (cantata)
Halévy, Jacques, *Les mousquetaires de la reine* (opera)
Kalliwoda, Johann, *Overture Solennelle (No. 9), Opus 126*
    Concert Overtures No. 10 and 11, Opus 142 and 143
Kreutzer, Konradin, *Des Sängers Fluch* (opera)
    Die Hochländerin am Kaukasus (opera)
Lortzing, Albert, *Der Waffenschmied* (opera)
Lux, Friedrich, *Die Kätchen von Heilbronn* (opera)
Macfarren, George, *Don Quixote* (opera)
Mangold, Carl, *Tannhäuser* (opera)
Mendelssohn, Felix, *Elijah* (oratorio)
    Lauda Sion, Opus 73 (cantata)
    4 Partsongs, Opus 76, for Male Voices
Mercadante, Saverio, *Orazi e Curiazi* (opera)
Meyerbeer, Giacomo, *Struensee* (incidental music)
Niedermeyer, Louis, *Robert Bruce* (opera)
Pacini, Giovanni, *La regina de Cipro* (opera)
Reissiger, Carl, *Der Schiffbruch der Medusa* (opera)
Rossi, Lauro, *La figlia di Figaro* (opera)
Schumann, Robert, *Symphony No. 2, Opus 61*
    10 Songs for Chorus, Opus 55 and 59
Smetana, Bedrich, *6 Preludes for Organ*
Spohr, Louis, *String Quartet, Opus 132*
    Piano Trio No. 4, Opus 133
Suppé, Franz von, *Poet and Peasant* (operetta)
Thomas, Ambroise, *Betty* (ballet)
Verdi, Giuseppe, *Attila* (opera)

1847

World Events:

In the U.S., peace negotiations begin with Mexico; Congress approves adhesive postage stamps; the abolitionist newspaper *North Star* begins publication; the *Chicago Tribune* begins publication; Atlanta, Georgia, is incorporated; the American Medical Association is founded; the Irish begin a giant migration into the U.S. following the Great Famine in their homeland; inventors Thomas Edison and Alexander Graham Bell are born. Internationally, the country of Liberia is founded by freed American slaves and becomes the first republic in Africa; the British Factory Act further limits working hours for women and children; the Sonderbund War in Switzerland strengthens the central government; the ophthalmoscope is invented.

Cultural Highlights:

Louis Clapisson becomes a member of the Legion of Honor; Pierre de Laprade begins teaching literature at Lyon University. Births in the art field include American artists Ralph A. Blakelock, Albert P. Ryder and sculptor Vinnie Hoxie, German artist Max Liebermann and sculptor Adolf von Hildebrand; deaths include British artists Thomas Barker and William Collins and German artist Georg F. Kersting. In the literary field Italian dramatist Giuseppe Giacosa is born; dead are Greek poet Athanasios Christopoulos and Finnish poet Frans M. Franzen. Other highlights include:

Art: George Bingham, *Raftsmen Playing Cards*; Thomas Cole, *Home in the Woods*; Gustave Courbet, *Man with a Pipe*; Thomas Couture, *Romans of the Decadence*; Honoré Daumier, *Behind in the Rent*; Adolf von Menzel, *Berlin-Potsdam Railway*; Hiram Powers, *The Greek Slave*; François Rude, *The Awakening of Napoleon*; George Watts, *King Alfred and the Saxons*

Literature: Louis Agassiz, *Introduction to Natural History*; Anne Brontë, *Agnes Grey*; Charlotte Brontë, *Jane Eyre*; Emily Brontë, *Wuthering Heights*; Leigh Hunt, *Men, Women and Books*; Henry W. Longfellow, *Evangeline*; Hermann Melville, *Omoo*; Alfred Lord Tennyson, *The Princess*; William Thackeray, *Vanity Fair*

MUSICAL EVENTS

A. Births:

Jan 2	Otakar Hostinský (Cz-mus)	Jul 14	Giuseppe Kaschmann (It-bar)
Jan 30	Joseph Maas (Br-ten)	Aug 22	Alexander Mackenzie (Scot-cm)
Jan 31	Alma Haas (Ger-pn)	Oct 3	Carl F. Glasenapp (Ger-mus)
Feb 7	Ernst Frank (Ger-cd)	Nov 1	Emma Albani (Can-sop)
Feb 8	Joseph Rubinstein (Rus-pn)	Nov 19	Lionel A. Dauriac (Fr-mus)
Feb 16	Philipp Scharwenka (Pol-cm)	Nov 30	August Klughardt (Ger-cd)
Feb 17	Mathilde Mallinger (Yug-sop)	Dec 1	Agathe Grondahl (Nor-pn)
Apr 29	Carl J. Andersen (Den-fl)	Dec 14	Jean Louis Lassalle (Fr-bar)
Jul 11	Walter W. Cobbett (Br-ed)	Dec 16	Augusta Holmès (Fr-cm)
Jul 12	Karl Barth (Ger-pn)		Emmy Fursch-Madi (Fr-sop)

B. Deaths:

Feb 19	George Baker (Br-org)	Jul 19	Jan Willem Wilms (Hol-cm)
Mar 28	Mariano Rodriguez de Ledesma	Aug 26	William T. Parke (Br-ob)
	(Sp-cm)	Nov	François J. Dizi (Bel-hp)
May 14	Fanny Mendelssohn (Ger-pn)	Nov 4	Felix Mendelssohn (Ger-cm-cd)
May 16	Kaspar Ett (Ger-cm)	Dec 25	Emma Albertazzi (Br-alto)
May 26	Ernst Köhler (Ger-pn-cm)	Dec 29	William Crotch (Br-the)
Jun 11	Heinrich Baermann (Ger-cl)		Jean L. Boisselot (Fr-pn.m)

C. Debuts:
U.S. -- Eliza Biscaccianti (N.Y.), Anna Bishop (tour), Robert N. Bochsa (tour), Giovanni Bottesini (New Orleans), Richard Hoffman (N.Y.), Caroline Richings (as pianist)

Other - Jenny Bürde-Ney (Olmütz), Jeanne Sophie Cruvelli (Venice), Inez Fabri (Kaschau), Alfred and Henry Holmes (London), Adolph Schlössser (Frankfurt), Georgina Ansell Weiss (London)

D. New Positions:
Conductors: Raimondo Boucheron (maestro di cappella, Milan Cathedral), George Bousquet (Paris Opera), Heinrich Esser (Vienna Opera), Niels Gade (Leipzig Gewandhaus), Georg Hellmesberger (Vienna PO), Ferdinand Hiller (kapellmeister, Düsseldorf), Edward Horn (Boston Handel and Haydn Society), Angelo Mariani (Copenhagen Court Theater), Otto Nicolai (Berlin Opera), Ludwig Schindelmesser (Hamburg), Eugenio Terziani (Apollo Theater, Rome)

Educational: Egide Aerts (professor, Brussels Conservatory)

Others: Manuel Bretón de los Herreros (director, Biblioteca Nacional, Spain), William Henry Fry (editor, *Philadelphia Ledger*), Louis Lefébure-Wély (organ, Madelaine, Paris)

E. Prizes and Honors:
Prizes: Pierre-Louis Deffés and François Gevaert (Prix de Rome)

Honors: Johann Friedrich Bellermann (Gold Medal of Arts and Letters, Greece), William Horsley (Swedish Royal Academy)

F. Biographical Highlights:
Adolphe Adam fails in his Opèra-National venture due to the revolution; Marietta Alboni makes both her Covent Garden and Paris debuts; Hector Berlioz concertizes successfully in Russia and visits England; William Bradbury begins a two-year study trip in Europe; Anne Charton marries flutist Jules Demeur; Frédéric Chopin breaks up with George Sand; Léo Delibe's family moves to Paris; Gaetano Fraschini makes his London debut; Mikhail Glinka leaves Spain to return to Russia; Carl Goldmark enters the Vienna Conservatory; Johann von Herbeck begins studying law and philosophy at the University of Vienna; Richard Hoffman emigrates to the U.S.; Franz Liszt gives his last concert appearance and meets the Princess Sayn-Wittgenstein; Carl Loewe visits London; Jules Massenet moves to Paris with his family; Felix Mendelssohn, broken by his sister's death, makes a last visit to England and Switzerland before his own death; Napoleone Moriani retires from the stage; Giorgio Ronconi, Agostino Rovere, Lorenzo Salví and Joseph Tagliafico all make their Covent Garden debuts; Samuel Sebastian Wesley suffers a serious injury on a fishing trip.

G. Institutional Openings:
Performing Groups: Aberdeen Harmonic Choir; Christiania Commercial Choral Society (Oslo); Deutsche Liederkranz (New York); Handelsstandens Sangforening (Norway); Mainz Philharmonische Verein; Royal Italian Opera (London); Salzburger Liedertafel; Sociedad Filarmonica (Bogota); Sternscher Gesangverein (Berlin); Stuttgarter Oratorienchor

Educational: Conservatorio Imperial de Música (Rio de Janeiro); Faiszt Organ School (Stuttgart); Salzburger Singakademie

Other: Astor Place Opera House (N.Y.); Carltheater (Vienna); Durand et Cie., Music Publishers (Paris); Flaxland Music Publishers (Paris); Gaveau Piano Co. (Paris); Gran Teatro del Liceo (Barcelona); Hals Brothers, Piano Makers (Christiana); *Italia Musicale*; Little, Brown and Co., Publishers; *Neue Berliner Musikzeitung*; Bartolf Senff, Publishers (Leipzig); Steinmeyer Organ Co. (Oettingen); Teatro de la Zarzuela (Madrid); Teatro de San Fernando (Seville); Teatro Goldoni (Livorno)

H. Musical Literature:

Aikin, Jesse B., *The Juvenile Minstrel*
Bellermann, Johann F., *Die Tonleitern und Musiknoten der Griechen*
Blondeau, Pierre, *Histoire de la musique moderne*
Brossard, Noël, *Théorie des sons musicaux*
Czerny, Carl, *Method for the Piano*
Horsley, William, *Introduction to Harmony and Modulation*
Koch, Eduard E., *Geschichte des Kirchenliedes und Kirchengesanges...*
Krüger, Eduard, *Beiträge für leben und wissenschaft der Tonkunst*
Nisard, Théodore, *La science et la pratique de plain-chant*
Singer, Peter, *Metaphysische blicke in die Tonwelt*

I. Musical Compositions:

Alkan, *Grande Sonata, Opus 73, for Piano*
Anonymous, *The Arkansas Traveler* (song)
Auber, Daniel, *Haidée* (opera)
Balfe, Michael, *The Maid of Honor* (opera)
Bottesini, Giovanni, *Cristoforo Colombo* (opera)
Bruckner, Anton, *Prelude and Fugue in C Minor for Organ*
Buzzolla, Antonio, *Amleto* (opera)
Cagnoni, Antonio, *Don Bucefalo* (opera)
Chopin, Frédéric, *3 Waltzes, Opus 64*
Conradi, August, *Rúbezahl* (opera)
David, Félicien, *Christophe Colomb* (tone poem)
Dorn, Heinrich, *Das Hallelujah der Schöpfung* (oratorio)
Flotow, Friedrich von, *Martha* (opera)
Gade, Niels, *Symphony No. 3, Opus 15*
   Siegfried und Brunhilde (symphonic fragments)
Hallström, Ivar, *The White Lady of Drottningholm* (opera)
Hiller, Ferdinand, *Konradin* (opera)
Kalliwoda, Johann, *Blonda* (opera)
Litolff, Henry C., *Die Braut von Kynast* (opera)
Lortzing, Albert, *Zum Grossadmiral* (operetta)
L'vov, Alexei, *Ondine* (opera)
Mendelssohn, Felix, *String Quartet No. 6, Opus 80*
   Songs without Words VII, Opus 85
   12 Songs, Opus 71 and 86
   3 Motets, Opus 69
   Christus, Opus 97 (unfinished oratorio)
Moniuszko, Stanislaw, *Halka* (opera)
Offenbach, Jacques, *L'alcôve* (operetta)
Ricci, Federico, *Griselda* (opera)
Ricci, Luigi, *Il birraio di Preston* (opera)
Rossi, Lauro, *Bianca Contarini* (opera)
Schumann, Robert, *Piano Trio No. 1 and 2, Opus 63 and 80*
   Zum Abschied, Opus 84 (song)
Spohr, Louis, *Symphony No. 8, Opus 137*
   Double Quartet, Opus 138
Suppé, Franz von, *Das Mädchen vom Lande* (opera)
   Die Krämer und sein Kommis (operetta)
Verdi, Giuseppe, *MacBeth* (opera)
   Jerusalem (opera)
Vogel, Charles L., *Le Siège de Leyde* (opera)
Wallace, William V., *Matilda of Hungary* (opera)

1848

World Events:
In the U.S., Zachary Taylor is elected as President No. 12; the Treaty of Guadalpe-Hidalgo ends the Mexican War and Mexico cedes most of the present-day southwestern territory to the U.S.; Wisconsin becomes State No. 30; the California Gold Rush begins; Tulsa Trading Post is established in Oklahoma; former President John Quincy Adams dies. Internationally, the "Year of Revolutions" shakes most of the European countries; Louis Napoleon becomes President of the Second French Republic; Francis Joseph becomes Emperor of Austria; the Taiping Rebellion takes place in China: I. P. Semmelweis conquers puerperal fever by the simple task of having students wash their hands before examing the women.

Cultural Highlights:
The Pre-Raphaelite Brotherhood is formed in London; Alphonse de Lamartine is made Minister of Foreign Affairs in the provisional French government; Charles Cope is admitted into the Royal Academy of Art. Births in the art world include American artists Frank Duveneck, William M. Harnett, Joseph Pickett and Louis C. Tiffany, French artists Jules Bastien-Lepage and Édouard Detaille and sculptors Paul Bartholomé and Augustus Saint-Gaudens, Spanish artist Francisco Pradilla and German artist Fritz von Uhde; deaths include British artist Thomas Cole and German sculptor Ludwig von Schwanthaler. Births in the literary field include American novelist Joel Chandler Harris and French novelist Joris K. Huysman; deaths include British novelists Emile Brontë, Isaac Disraeli and Frederick Marryat, Danish poet Steen Blicher and Italian poet Alessandro Poerio. Other highlights include:

Art: Rosa Bonheur, *Plowing in the Nivernais*; Thomas Cole, *The Vision*; George Cruikshank, *The Drunkard's Children*; William Dyce, *King Arthur Series*; Edwin Landseer, *A Random Shot*; Jean Francois Millet, *The Winnower*; William Mount, *Boys Caught Napping in the Field*; Thomas Sully, *The Student*; Richard Woodville, *War News from Mexico*

Literature: James F. Cooper, *The Oak Openings*; Theodor Creizenach, *Gedichte*; Alexander Dumas, fils, *La Dame aux Camélias*; Elizabeth Gaskell, *Mary Barton*; Charles Kingsley, *Yeast*; James R. Lowell, *Bigelow Papers I*; Marx/Engels, *A Communist Manifesto*; Richard Wagner, *Siegfried's Death*; John G. Whittier, *Poems*

MUSICAL EVENTS

A. Births:

Jan 2	Paul Runge (Ger-mus)	Jul 27	Vladimir de Pachmann (Rus-pn)
Jan 19	August Kretzschmar (Ger-mus)	Jul 31	Jean Planquette (Fr-cm)
Jan 21	Henri Duparc (Fr-cm)	Aug 1	Pierre Gailhard (Fr-bs)
Feb 27	Charles H. Parry (Br-cm)	Sep 15	Wilhelm Fitzenhagen (Ger-cel)
Apr 17	Louis C. Elson (Am-mus)	Oct 12	Alwina Valleria (Am-sop)
Apr 21	Carl Stumpf (Ger-acous)	Oct 20	Stepan Smolensky (Rus-mus)
Jun 17	Victor Maurel (Fr-bar)	Nov 13	Hans Wolzogen (Ger-mus)
Jun 18	Jacques Bouhy (Bel-bar)	Nov 24	Lilli Lehmann (Ger-sop)
Jul 3	Theodore Presser (Am-pub)	Dec 17	Frederick Gleason (Am-org)
Jul 16	Henri Viotta (Hol-cd)	Dec 18	Karl Schröder (Ger-cel)
Jul 22	Lucien Fugère (Fr-bar)	Dec 29	Camille Gurickx (Bel-pn)

B. Deaths:

Jan 24	Thomas Welsh (Br-voc-cm)	Apr 8	Gaetano Donizetti (It-cm)
Feb 26	Thomas S. Cooke (Br-ten)	Apr 24	F. von Campenhout (Bel-vn)
Feb 26	Karl Hüttenrauch (Ger-org.m)	May 21	Janiewicz Feliks (Pol-vn)
Mar 19	William H. Potter (Br-fl.m)	May 28	Vissarion Belinsky (Rus-cri)
Mar 28	Mariana de Ledesma (Sp-cm)	Jun 28	Charles Albrecht (Am-pn.m)

Jul 12	Jean Ancot, père (Bel-vn)	Aug 6	Nicola Vaccai (It-cm)
Jun 22	Karl Guhr (Ger-cd-cm)	Aug 22	Joseph Ghys (Bel-vn)
Jun 31	Christian Wilke (Ger-org.m)	Oct 27	Alexander Varlamov (Rus-cm)
Aug 1	Franz Cramer (Ger-vn)	Nov 23	Alfred Becher (Ger-cri)
Aug 2	Carlo Bignani (It-vn)	Dec 31	Oliver Shaw (Am-org-ed)

C. Debuts:

U.S. -- Otto Dresel (N.Y.), Salvator Marchesi (N.Y.)

Other - Joseph T. Barbot (Paris), Charles-Aimable Bataille (Paris), Adolfo Fumagalli (Milan), Louis Gueymard (Paris), Henryk Wieniawski (Paris)

D. New Positions:

Conductors: Vincenz Lachner (Frankfurt Opera), Franz Liszt (Weimar Orchestra), Carl Mangold (kapellmeister, Darmstadt Court), Julius Rietz (Leipzig Gewandhaus), Francesco Shira (Covent Garden), Ferdinand Stegmayer (Josephstadt Theater, Vienna)

Educational: Henry Bishop (chair of music, Oxford), Henri-Louis Duvernoy (professor, Paris Conservatory), Manuel P. García (voice, Royal Academy, London), Antoine Marmontel (piano, Paris Conservatory), Marie-Félicité Pleyel (piano, Brussels Conservatory), Adrien François Servais (cello, Brussels Conservatory)

Others: David H. Engel (organ, Merseburg), César Franck (organ, Saint Jean-Saint François, Paris), Eduard Hanslick (music critic, *Vienna Zeitung*)

E. Prizes and Honors:

Prizes: Jules-Laurent Duprato (Prix de Rome)

Honors: George F. Anderson (Master of the Queen's Music), Jakob Blumenthal (pianist to the Queen)

F. Biographical Highlights:

Georges Bizet, age 10., enters the Conservatory of Paris; Johannes Brahms gives his first public recital in Hamburg, but under an assumed name; Frédéric Chopin concertizes in England and Scotland; Jeanne Sophie Cruvelli makes her London debut; Karl Goldmark is almost shot as a rebel while performing in Raab; Charles Hallé leaves Paris and settles in Manchester; Johann Herbeck gives up on law study to begin the study of music; Franz Liszt and the Princess Sayn-Wittgenstein move to Weimar together; Sophie Loewe retires from the operatic stage; Giacomo Meyerbeer is dismissed from his Berlin post; Eduard Reményi flees to the U.S. following his revolutionary activities; August Roeckel is arrested and sentenced to death for his revolutionary activities (sentence changed to 13 years in prison); Gioacchino Rossini leaves Bologna for Florence; Camille Saint-Saëns enters Benoist's organ class; Bedrich Smetana opens his own school in Prague; Eugenia Tadolini makes her London debut; Giuseppe Verdi buys his estate at Sant' Agata; Richard Wagner joins the revolutionary Vaterlandsverein.

G. Institutional Openings:

Performing Groups: Brno Male Choral Society; Buffalo Liedertafel; Dresden Cecilia Society; Montreal Philharmonic Society I; Société Ste.-Cécile (Brussels); Verein für Choralgesang (Dresden)

Educational: Royal Irish Academy of Music (Dublin)

Other: Balmer and Weber Music House (St. Louis); Bossel Theater (Bucharest); Deichmann (Friedrich-Wilhelmstadtisches) Theater (Berlin); S. S. Griggs and Co., Music Publishers (Chicago); Holywell Hall (Oxford); Lee and Walker Publishing Co. (Philadelphia); Sasseti and Co., Music Publishers (Lisbon); Société Alard-Franchomme (Paris)

H. Musical Literature:

Andreví y Castellar, Francisco, *Traité d'harmonie et de composition*
Berlioz, Hector, *Mémoires*
Brendel, Karl F., *Grundzüge der geschichte der musik*
Devrient, Eduard, *Geschichte der deutschen Schausspielkunst*
Fétis, François J., *Les musiciens Belges*
Hagen, Theodor, *Musikalisches novellen*
Jackson, Samuel, *Sacred Harmony*
Kastner, Jean-Georges, *Manuel générale de musique militaire...*
Kiesewetter, Raphael, *Über die Octave des Pythagoras*
Mainzer, Joseph, *Music and Education*

I. Musical Compositions:

Benoist, François, *L'Apparition* (opera)
Berlioz, Hector, *Funeral March for Hamlet, Opus 18*
    La Mort d'Ophélie, Opus 18
    L'Apothéose
Bristow, George, *Symphony No. 1, Opus 10*
Chélard, Hippolyte, *La Symphonéide* (symphonic poem)
David, Félicien, *L'Eden* (oratorio)
Dorn, Heinrich, *Die musiker von Aix-la-Chapelle* (opera)
Foster, Stephen, *Oh, Susanna* (song)
    Old Uncle Ned (song)
Gade, Niels, *String Octet, Opus 17*
Gevaert, François, *Hugues de Zomerghem* (opera)
    La comédie à la ville (opera)
Glinka, Mikhail, *Kamarinskaya*
Halévy, Jacques, *Le val d'Andorre* (opera)
Kalliwoda, Johann, *Concertino, Opus 151, for Violin and Orchestra*
Liszt, Franz, *Concerto No. 1 for Piano and Orchestra*
    St. Cecilia Mass
    Sonetto 104 del Petrarco for Piano
    3 Etudes di Concert
Loewe, Carl, *Hiob* (oratorio)
Lortzing, Albert, *Regina* (opera)
Mercadante, Saverio, *La schiava saracena* (opera)
Moniuszko, Stanislaw, *Bajka* (symphonic poem)
Naumann, Emil, *Christus der Friedensbote* (oratorio)
Pacini, Giovanni, *Allan Cameron* (opera)
Raff, Joseph J., *Konzertstücke for Piano and Orchestra*
Reber, Henri, *La Nuit de Noël* (opera)
Rossini, Gioacchino, *Inno Nazionale* (cantata)
    Inno Alla Pace (cantata)
Schumann, Robert, *Manfred, Opus 115* (incidental music)
    Genoveva, Opus 81 (opera)
    Album für die Jugend, Opus 68, for Piano
    Adventlied, Opus 71
    4 Marches, Opus 76, for Piano
Smetana, Bedrich, *6 Characteristic Pieces for Piano, Opus 1*
Sobolewski, Friedrich von, *Salvator Rosa* (opera)
Spohr, Louis, *String Sextet, Opus 140*
Strauss, Johann, Jr., *Radetsky March, Opus 228*
Suppé, Franz von, *Der Bandit* (operetta)
Verdi, Giuseppe, *Il Corsaro* (opera)

1849

World Events:
In the U.S., the Department of the Interior is created by Congress; a gold rush in California earns the participants the name "'49ers"; Elizabeth Blackwell becomes the first woman to receive an M.D. degree; Memphis, Tennessee, is incorporated; W. Hunt patents the safety pin; Loyola University and Eastern Michigan University are founded; a patent is granted for the breech-loading cannon; former President James Polk dies. Internationally, Hungary declares its independence under the leadership of Kossuth but Russia steps in to help Austria crush the rebellion; the British crush the second Sikh uprising in India and annex Punjab state; Frederick IV of Prussia refuses the title, "Emperor of the Germans;" Wiliam III becomes King of the Netherlands.

Cultural Highlights:
The Brisbane School of the Arts opens in Australia; three magazines make their appearance, *Sartain's Union Magazine of Literature and Art*, the *Journal of Design and Manufactures*, and *Household Words*; Adam Oehlenschläger is acclaimed as the national poet of Denmark; Feodor Dostoyevsky is arrested and sent to Siberia. Births in the literary field include American novelists James Allen and Sarah Orne Jewett, poets Emma Lazarus and James Whitcomb Riley, British poet William Henley, Irish poet William Larminie, French author Jean Richepin, Swedish author August Strindberg and Norwegian novelist Alexander Kielland; deaths include American author Edgar Allen Poe, British authors Marguerite Blessington, Anne Brontë and Maria Edgeworth, poets Thomas Beddoes and Ebenezer Elliott, Irish poet James C. Mangan, Hungarian poet Sándor Petöfi and Polish poet Juliusz Slowacki. Births in the art world include American artists William Chase, Wyatt Eaton and Abbott H. Thayer and French artist Eugène Carrière; deaths include American artist Edward Hicks, Swiss artist Jacques-Laurent Agasse and French artists François Granet and Louis A. Lepère. Other highlights include:

Art: Gustave Courbet, *The Stonebreakers* and *Burial at Ornans*; Eugène Delacroix, *Ceiling of the Salon d'Apollon* (Louvre); Asher Durand, *Kindred Spirits*; William H. Hunt, *Rienzi*; Jean-Auguste Ingres, *The Golden Age*; John Millais, *The Disentombment of Queen Matilda*; Dante Rossetti, *Girlhood of the Virgin*; George Watts, *Life's Illusions*

Literature: Matthew Arnold, *The Strayed Reveller*; Thomas Beddoes, *Death's Jest Book*; James F. Cooper, *The Sea Lions*; Thomas DeQuincey, *The English Mail Coach*; Charles Kingsley, *Alton Locke*; Francis Parkman, *The Oregon Trail*; Edgar A. Poe, *The Bells*; Scribe/Legouvé, *Adrienne Lecouvreur*; Henry Thoreau, *Civil Disobedience*

MUSICAL EVENTS

A. Births:

Feb 19	Franz Diener (Ger-ten)	Jul 23	Mieczslaw Horbowski (Pol-bar)
Feb 23	Rosa Sucher (Ger-sop)	Aug 18	Benjamin Godard (Fr-cm)
Mar 8	Herman Winckelmann (Ger-ten)	Sep 23	Mikhail Ivanov (Rus-mus)
Mar 15	Theodor Reichmann (Ger-bar)	Sep 24	Willem De Haan (Hol-cd-cm)
Mar 20	Henri Dallier (Fr-org)	Oct 16	Charles H. Lloyd (Br-org)
May 25	"Blind Tom" Bethune (Am-pn)		Mathilde Bauermeister
May 25	Alphonse Goovaerts (Bel-mus)		(Ger-sop)
Jun 6	André Mocquereau (Fr-mus)		Emma A. Osgood (Am-sop)
Jul 18	Hugo Riemann (Ger-mus)		Eugenie Pappenheim (Aus-sop)

B. Deaths:

Jan 4	Charles S. Evans (Br-org)	Feb 13	Christian Rummel (Ger-cd)
Jan 25	Elias P. Alvars (Br-hp)	Feb 22	Alexander Fesca (Ger-pn)
Feb 8	François Habeneck (Fr-cd)	Mar 16	Dorothea von Ertmann (Ger-pn)
Feb 11	Alfred Day (Br-the)	May 11	Otto Nicolai (Ger-cm-cd)

Jun 5	Eliza Salmon (Br-sop)	Sep 26	Charles N. Baudiot (Fr-cel)
Jun 10	Frédéric Kalkbrenner (Fr-pn)	Oct 17	Frédéric Chopin (Pol-pn)
Jun 12	Angelica Catalani (It-sop)	Oct 21	Charles E. Horn (Br-cm-cd)
Jun 13	Davidde Banderali (It-ten)	Dec 14	Konradin Kreutzer (Ger-cm)
Aug	Giuseppe de Begnis (It-bs)	Dec 29	Dionysio Aguado (Sp-gui)
Sep 25	Johann Strauss, Sr. (Aus-cd)		

C. Debuts:

U.S. -- Ernst Lübeck (tour), John Rogers Thomas (N.Y.)

Other - Marie Cabel (Paris), Marie Caroline Carvalho (Paris), Wilhemine Clauss-Szarvady (Prague), William George Cushman (London), Marie Luise Dustmann (Breslau), Giacomo Galvani (Spoleto), Antonio Giuglini (Fermo), Albert Niemann (Dessau), Louisa Pyne (Bologne), Susan Sunderland (London), Therese Tietjens (Hamburg), Theodor Wachtel (Hamburg)

D. New Positions:

Conductors: Louis Dietsch (maître de chapelle, Madeleine), Heinrich Dorn (Berlin Opera), Jacopo Foroni (Stockholm Court), Charles Hallé (Gentlemen's Concerts, London), Johan P. Hartmann (kapellmeister, Copenhagen), Jacques Offenbach (Théâtres Française, Paris), Robert Schumann (Düsseldorf SO), Ferdinando Taglioni (San Carlo Theater, Naples)

Educational: Adolphe Adam (composition, Paris Conservatory), Siegfrid Dehn (professor, Berlin Royal Academy), Nicolas Jacques Lemmens (organ, Brussels Conservatory)

Others: Robert Burton (organ, Leeds Parish Church), Frederick Gye (manager, Covent Garden), Heinrich Laube (director, Vienna Hofburgtheater), Samuel Sebastian Wesley (organ, Winchester Cathedral)

E. Prizes and Honors:

Prizes: Alexandre Stadtfeldt (Prix de Rome)

Honors: Petter Boman (Swedish Academy), William Cusins (organ, Queen's Private Chapel), Ferdinand Hiller (Berlin Academy), Otto Nicolai (Royal Academy, Berlin)

F. Biographical Highlights:

Hans Balatka emigrates to the U.S. and settles in Milwaukee; András Bartay, on the collapse of the Hungarian struggle for independence, goes to Germany; Carl Bergmann, involved in revolutionary activities, emigrates to the U.S.; Hans von Bülow enters Leipzig University to study law; Michael Costa becomes director of the Birmingham Festival; Edvard Grieg begins regular piano lessons with his mother; Eduard Hanslick receives a doctorate in law from the Vienna University; Joseph Joachim becomes concertmaster in Liszt's Weimar orchestra; Charles Lecocq enters the Paris Conservatory; Jenny Lind retires from the opera stage; William Mason begins studying music in Leipzig; Modeste Mussorgsky begins piano lessons; Alexander Serov leaves his government job for music; Alexander Thayer flees Germany and settles in Zurich; Pauline Viardot makes her Paris debuts; Henryk Wieniawski re-enters Paris Conservatory to study composition.

G. Institutional Openings:

Performing Groups: Aberdeen Choral Society; Bree String Quartet (Amsterdam); Chicago Mozart Society; Cincinnati Männerchore; Detroit Harmonie; Filharmoniska Sällskapet (Uppsala); German Saengerbund of North America; Hellmesberger String Quartet (Vienna); Mendelssohn Quintette Club (Boston); Schwäbischer Sängerbund; Società Corale del Carmine (Florence); Société Ste. Cécillie (Paris); Wüppertal City Orchestra

Festivals: Norwegian Choral Festival

Educational: Istituto Musicale (Florence); National Conservatory of Music (Santiago, Chile)

Other: Liverpool Philharmonic Hall; Carl Merseburger Music Publishing Co. (Leipzig); Jakob Rieter-Biedermann, Music Publisher (Winterthur)

H. Musical Literature:
Cinti-Damoreau, Laure, *Méthode de chant*
Clément, Félix, *Rapport...sur la musique religieuse en France*
Fürstenau, Moritz, *Beiträge zur geschichte der königlich-sächsischen musikalischen Kapelle*
Hohmann, Christian, *Praktische Violin-schule*
Kalkbrenner, Frédéric, *Traité d'harmonie du pianiste*
Knorr, Julius, *Methodischer leitfaden für Klavierlehrer*
Vroye, Théodore de, *Manuale cantorum*
Wagner, Richard, *Art and Revolution*
Weitzmann, Carl F., *Geschichte der harmonie*
Wesley, Samuel S., *A Few Words on Cathedral Music*

I. Musical Compositions:
Adam, Adolphe, *Le Toréador* (opera)
Berlioz, Hector, *Te Deum, Opus 22*
Bruckner, Anton, *Requiem in D Minor*
Dorn, Heinrich, *Die Sündflut* (oratorio)
Gounod, Charles, *Messe solennelle*
Halévy, Jacques, *La fée aux roses* (opera)
  Prométhée enchaîné (incidental music)
Kalliwoda, Johann, *Concert Overture No. 13*
Kreutzer, Konradin, *Aurelia* (opera)
Liszt, Franz, *Mountain Symphony* (tone poem)
  Totentanz for Piano and Orchestra
  Festival March (Goethe Jubilee)
Lortzing, Albert, *Rolands-Knappen* (opera)
Macfarren, George A., *King Charles II* (opera)
Massé, Victor, *La Chambre gothique* (opera)
Meyerbeer, Giacomo, *Le prophète* (opera)
Mosonyi, Mihály, *Mass No. 3 in F Major*
Nicolai, Otto, *The Merry Wives of Windsor* (opera)
Pacini, Giovanni, *L'orfano svizzera* (opera)
Rossi, Lauro, *Il domino nero* (opera)
Schumann, Robert, *Concertpiece, Opus 86, for Horn and Orchestra*
  Concertpiece, Opus 92, for Piano and Orchestra
  Spanische Liebeslieder, Opus 138
  Requiem für Mignon, Opus 98b
  Nachtlied, Opus 108
  Jagdlieder, Opus 137
  12 Piano Pieces, Opus 85
  5 Pieces, Opus 102, for Cello and Piano
  Adagio and Allegro, Opus 70, for Horn and Piano
  Fantasiestücke, Opus 73 for Clarinet and Piano
  Waldscenen, Opus 82, for Piano
Smetana, Bedrich, *Overture in D Major*
Spohr, Louis, *String Quartet in C Major, Opus 141*
Thomas, Ambroise, *Le caïd* (opera)
Verdi, Giuseppe, *Luisa Miller* (opera)
  La Battaglia di Legnano (opera)

1850

World Events:

In the U.S., the Census shows a population of 31,443,000, a 31% increase in ten years; President Zachary Taylor dies and Millard Fillmore becomes President No. 13; California becomes State No. 31 while Los Angeles is incorporated; Rochester and Utah Universities are established; the Compromise of 1850 setles the slavery question in new territories. Internationally, in the Peace of Berlin, Denmark and Prussia work out a compromise on the Schleswig-Holstein question; the Taiping Rebellion continues in China while Hung Hiu-tsuen becomes emperor; the Great Kaffir War takes place in South Africa; Prussian citizens are given a new liberal constitution.

Cultural Highlights:

Harper's New Monthly Magazine begins publication; Alfred Lord Tennyson becomes Poet Laureate of Great Britain; Charles L. Eastlake and Edwin Landseer are knighted; Charles Eastlake becomes President of the Royal Academy of Art. Births in the art field include American sculptor Daniel C. French and British sculptor Hamo Thornycroft; deaths include Scottish artist William Allan, French artist Jule Auguste, German sculptor Johann-Gottfried Schadow and Italian sculptor Lorenzo Bartolini. Births in the literary field include American author Edward Bellamy and poet Eugene Field, Canadian novelist Isabella Crawford, German poet Max Kalbeck, French novelist Guy de Maupassant and poet and historian Henri Chantavoine and Scottish novelist Robert Louis Stevenson; deaths include British poets William Bowles and William Wordsworth, novelist Jane Porter, Danish dramatist and poet Adam Oehlenschläger, French novelist Honoré de Balzac and Hungarian poet Nikolaus Lenau. Other highlights include:

Art: George Bingham, *Shooting for the Beef*; Jean Baptiste Corot, *Une Matinée*; Eugène Delacroix, *Arab Attacked by a Lion*; Adolf von Menzel, *Round Table at Sans Souci*; John Millais, *Christ in His Parent's Home*; Jean-François Millet, *The Sower*; William Mount, *The Card Players*; Dante Rossetti, *The Annunciation*

Literature: Grace Aguilar, *Vale of Cedars*; Elizabeth Browning, *Sonnets from the Portugese*; Charles Dickens, *David Copperfield*; Sydney Dobell, *The Roman*; Ralph W. Emerson, *Representative Men*; Nathaniel Hawthorne, *The Scarlet Letter*; Washington Irving, *Mahomet*; John W. Whittier, *Songs of Labor and Other Poems*

MUSICAL EVENTS

A. Births:

Jan 6	Franz X. Scharwenka (Ger-cm)
Jan 14	Jean de Reszke (Pol-ten)
Jan 17	Alexander Taneiev (Rus-cm)
Jan 23	Antoinette Sterling (Am-alto)
Jan 27	Marie Fillunger (Aus-sop)
Feb 12	Clementine Schuch-Proska (Hun-sop)
Feb 17	Anton Ursprung (Ger-pn)
Feb 18	George Henschel (Ger-bar)
Mar 9	Alexandre Luigini (Fr-cd-cm)
Mar 14	Heinrich Reimann (Aus-mus)
Mar 18	Joseph Staudigl, Jr. (Br-bar)
May 7	Anton Seidl (Hun-cd)
Jun 5	Richard Barth (Ger-vn)
Oct 18	Francis Thomé (Fr-cm)
Nov 29	Sofia Scalchi (It-alto)
Dec 2	John Orth (Am-org)
Dec 9	Emma Abbott (Am-sop)
Dec 21	Zdenek Fibich (Boh-cm)
Dec 28	Francesco Tamagno (It-ten)
Dec 29	Tomás Bréton (Sp-cm-cd)
	Julia Gaylord (Am-sop)

B. Deaths:

Jan 1	Raphael Kiesewetter (Ger-mus)
Jan 3	Josephina Grassini (It-alto)
Mar 19	Adalbert Gyrowetz (Boh-cm)
Mar 22	A. Bottée de Toulmon (Fr-mus)
Mar 25	Francesco Basili (It-cm)
Apr 3	Václav Jan Tomásek (Boh-cm)
May 9	Joseph von Blumenthal (Bel-vn)
Jul 28	Stefano Pavesi (It-cm)

Sep 11	Jeanne Saint-Aubin (Fr-sop)	Oct 12	Luigia Boccabadati (It-sop)
Sep 26	Nicolas Baudiot (Fr-cel)		

C. Debuts:

U.S. -- Giovanni Belletti (tour), Ignazio Marini (N.Y.), Maria Dolores Nau (tour); Teresa Parodi, Lorenzo Salvi (N.Y.)

Other - Johann Nepomuk Beck (Budapest), Leone Giraldoni (Milan), Arabella Goddard (London), Constance Nantier-Didiée (Turin), Karoline Pruckner (Hanover)

D. New Positions:

Conductors: Hans Balatka (Milwaukee Musical Society), Pietro Coppola (Lisbon Royal Opera), Niels Gade (Copenhagen Musical Society), Charles Hallé (Gentlemen's Concerts, Manchester), Gustav A. Heinze (German Opera, Amsterdam), Ferdinand Hiller (kapellmeister, Cologne), Karl A. Krebs (kapellmeister, Dresden), Constantin Liadov (St. Petersburg Opera)

Educational: Auguste Dupont (piano, Brussels Conservatory), Jacques Dupuis (violin, Liège Conservatory), Johann Herzog (organ, Munich Conservatory), Francesco Lamperti (voice, Milan Conservatory), Lauro Rossi (director, Milan Conservatory), Adolphe Samuel (harmony, Brussels Opera)

Others: Ludwig F. Bischoff (editor, *Rheinische Review*), Samuel Sebastian Wesley (organ, Royal Academy, London)

F. Biographical Highlights:

Julius Benedict accompanies Jenny Lind on her American tour; Franz Berwald becomes manger of a glass works factory in Sweden; Alexander Borodin enters medical school in St. Petersburg; Johannes Brahms meets the violinist Reményi; Jeanne Cruvelli makes her La Scala debut; Léo Delibes enters the Paris Conservatory; Karl Formes and Enrico Tamberlik make their Covent Garden debuts; Jenny Lind appears in the U.S. under the auspices of P. T. Barnum; Adolf Marx retires from teaching to concentrate on writing; Clara Novello returns to the operatic and recital stage; Joseph Joachim Raff joins Liszt at Weimar; George Root travels to Paris for further music study; Wilhemine Schröder-Devrient marries her third husband, Herr von Bock; Peter Tchaikovsky, age 10, is left on his own in a school in St. Petersburg; Richard Wagner again visits Paris and has a brief affair with Jennie Laussot; William V. Wallace marries his second wife, Helene Stoepel, in New York.

G. Institutional Openings:

Performing Groups: Beethovenverein (Bonn); Chicago Philharmonic Society; Cleveland Mendelssohn Society; Evangelical Sacred Choral Society (Frankfurt); Leeds Madrigal and Motet Society; Washington Philharmonic Society (D.C.)

Educational: Duprez Vocal School (Paris); Musikakademie für Damen (Berlin); Stern Conservatory of Music (Berlin)

Other: Allen and Co., Music Publishers (Melbourne); Bach Gesellschaft (Germany); *The Church Musician*; Madrid Teatro Real; *Musical Review and Choral* (N.Y.); *Rheinische Musik-Zeitung für Kunstfreunde und Künstler*; Rózsavölgyi and Fárza, Music Publishers (Budapest); St. Martin's Hall (London); Tremont Music Hall (Chicago)

H. Musical Literature:

Chevillard, Pierre, *Méthode complète de violoncelle*
Glover, Sarah A., *Manual...of the Tetrachordal System*
Hastings, Thomas, *Devotional Hymns and Religious Poems*
Lobe, Johann, *Lehrbuch der musikalischen Composition*
Mason, Lowell, *Cantica Laudis*
Scudo, Pierre, *Critique et littérature musicale I*

Wagner, Richard, *Kunst und Klima*
   Das Kunstwerke der Zukunft
Winterfeld, Carl von, *Zur geschichte heiliger Tonkunst I*

I. Musical Compositions:

Adam, Adolphe, *Giralda* (opera)
Arrieta y Corera, Pascual, *La conquista de Granadas* (zarzuela)
Auber, Daniel, *L'enfant prodigue* (opera)
Barbieri, Francisco, *Gloria y peluca* (zarzuela)
Berlioz, Hector, *Fleurs der landes* (song cycle)
Bruckner, Anton, *Psalm CXIV*
David, Félicien, *La perle du Brésil* (opera)
Dorn, Heinrich, *Artaxerxes* (opera)
Flotow, Friedrich von, *Sophia Katherina* (opera)
Foster, Stephen, *Camptown Races* (song)
   Nellie Bly (song)
Gade, Niels, *Symphony No. 4, Opus 20*
   Overture, Nordische Sehnfahrt
   Mariotta (singspiel)
Gounod, Charles, *Tobie* (oratorio)
Halévy, Jacques, *La tempestà* (opera)
   La dame de pique (opera)
Liszt, Franz, *Heroïde Funèbre* (tone poem)
   Prometheus (tone poem)
   Fantasy and Fugue, "Ad nos, salutarem," for Organ
   Grand Solo de Concert for Piano
   Consolations (6 pieces for piano)
   Liebesträume (3 nocturnes for Piano)
Loewe, Carl, *4 Pianos Fantasies, Opus 137*
Lortzing, Albert, *Eine Berliner Grisette* (incidental music)
Massé, Victor, *La chanteuse voilée* (opera)
Moniuszko, Stanislaw, *Jawnuta* (opera)
   The gypsies (operetta)
   Mass in D Minor, "Funeral Mass"
Reissiger, Carl, *David* (oratorio)
Ricci, Federico, *I due ritratti* (opera)
Saint-Saëns, Camille, *Symphony in A Major*
Schumann, Robert, *Symphony No. 3, Opus 97, "Rhenish"*
   Overture, Die Braut von Messina, Opus 100
   Concertpiece, Opus 129, for Cello and Orchestra
   Neujahrslied, Opus 144
   5 Songs, Opus 77
   3 Songs, Opus 83
   6 Songs, Opus 89
   5 Songs, Opus 96
   5 Songs, Opus 127
Spohr, Louis, *Symphony No. 9, Opus 143, "Die Jahrszeiten"*
   String Quintet, Opus 144
Thomas, Ambroise, *Le songe d'une nuit d'été* (opera)
Verdi, Giuseppe, *Stiffelio* (opera)
Vieuxtemps, Henri, *Concerto, Opus 31, for Violin and Orchestra*
Wagner, Richard, *Lohengrin* (opera)
Willis, Richard S., *It Came Upon the Midnight Clear* (carol)

1851

World Events:
>In the U.S., the *New York Times* begins publication; the Illinois Central Railroad is chartered; the first American YMCA opens in Boston; Des Moines, Iowa, and Portland, Oregon, are chartered; Isaac Singer patents the Sewing Machine; the Clipper ship, *Flying Cloud*, is launched. Internationally, Louis Napoleon launches a coup-d'etat and forces a new constitution on France which paves the way for a new empire; Cuba declares its independence but is unable to resist the Spanish forces; Victoria, Australia, is given self government; the London International Industrial Exposition is the first ever held.

Cultural Highlights:
>The *Revue de Paris* begins publication with Théophile Gautier as editor; George Eliot becomes assistant editor for the *Westminster Review*; Francis Grant is taken into the Royal Academy; Joseph Paxton is knighted; Victor Hugo is exiled from France for his opposition to Louis Napoleon. In the field of art, American artist Thomas Dewing is born; deaths include American artist Thomas Birch, British artist Joseph Turner and Russian artist Alexei Egorov. Births in the literary field include Mrs. H. Ward, British novelist; deaths include American novelist James Fennimore Cooper, British authors Joanna Baillie, Harriet Lee and Mary W. Shelley, Irish dramatist Richard Sheil, Italian poet Giovanni Berchet and German author Friedrich von Heyden. Other highlights include:

>**Art:** Antoine-Louis Barye, *Jaguar Devouring a Hare*; Jean Baptiste Corot, *Dance of the Nymphs*; Gustave Courbet, *The Village Damsels*; Eastman Johnson, *Indian War Camp*; Edwin Landseer, *Monarch of the Glen*; Emanuel Leutze, *Washington Crossing the Delaware*; John Millais, *Christ in the Carpenter's Shop*

>**Literature:** Friedrich von Bodenstedt, *Lieder des Mirza-Schaffy*; Alexander Dumas, père, *Diane de Lys*; Nathaniel Hawthorne, *House of the Seven Gables*; Friedrich Hebbel, *Julia*; August Hoffmann, *Liebeslieder*; Gottfried Keller, *Der Grüne Heinrich*; Henry W. Longfellow, *The Golden Legend*; Herman Melville, *Moby Dick*; Wilhelm Müller, *Lorelei*

MUSICAL EVENTS

A. Births:

Jan 25	Jan Blockx (Bel-cm)		Aug 22	Richard Andersson (Swe-pn)
Feb 12	Anna Essipova (Rus-pn)		Aug 25	Max Josef Beer (Aus-cm)
Mar 20	Pietro Abba-Cornaglia (It-cm)		Aug 30	W. C. Brownell (Am-cri)
Mar 21	Adolf Brodsky (Rus-vn)		Sep 19	Paul E. Wachs (Fr-pn-org)
Mar 27	Vincent d'Indy (Fr-cm)		Sep 22	Julius Zimmermann (Ger-pub)
May 5	Alexander Michalowski (Pol-pn)		Oct 23	Guillaume Couture (Can-cm)
May 15	Marie Lehmann (Ger-sop)		Nov 1	André A. Wormser (Fr-cm)
May 17	Victor Bendix (Den-cm-cd)		Nov 5	Émile-Pierre Ratez (Fr-cm)
Jun 3	Theodore Baker (Am-mus)		Nov 16	Minnie Hauk (Am-mez)
Jun 12	Pol-Henri Plançon (Fr-bs)			Philippine Edwards (Br-sop)
Jun 23	Clarence Eddy (Am-org)			

B. Deaths:

Jan 17	Tomaso Albinoni (It-cm-vn)		Mar 6	Alexander Aliabiev (Rus-cm)
Jan 21	Albert Lortzing (Ger-cm)		Mar 18	Conrad Graf (Aus-pn.m)
Jan 24	Gaspare Spontini (It-cm)		Apr 9	Antoine Glachant (Fr-vn)
Jan 27	Karl Möser (Ger-vn-cd)		Jul 3	Martin Mengal (Bel-cd)
Feb 18	George Thomson (Scot-folk)		Aug 19	Gioseffo Catrufo (It-cm)
Feb 20	Josef A. Ladurner (Aus-cm)		Nov 10	Joseph Mainzer (Ger-m.ed)
Mar 4	Michael Henkel (Ger-cm)		Dec 21	Carl Rungenhagen (Ger-cm)

C. Debuts:
U.S. -- Frederick Brandeis (N.Y.), Julian Fontana, Sophie Anne Thillon (San Francisco)

Other - Enrico Delle Sedie (Florence), Francesco Graziani (Ascoli Piceno)

D. New Positions:
Conductors: Hector Berlioz (New Philharmonic), George Bristow (N.Y. Harmonic Society), Joseph Hellmesberger, Sr. (Gesellschaft der Musikfreunde, Vienna), Hervé (Palais Royal), Friedrich W. Kücken (kapellmeister, Stuttgart), Jules Pasdeloup (Société des Jeunes Artistes, Paris), Ludwig Schindelmeisser (Wiesbaden Court)

Educational: Jean Andries (director, Ghent Conservatory), Eduard Franck (piano, Cologne Conservatory), Robert Franz (music director, Halle University), Albert Löschhorn (piano, Royal Institute for Church Music, Berlin), Henri Reber (harmony, Paris Conservatory), Simon Sechter (harmony, Vienna Conservatory), Charles Steggall (professor, Royal Academy, London)

Others: Anton Bruckner (organ, St. Florian's), Karl Hennig (organ, Sophienkirche, Berlin), Henrik Ibsen (stage manager, Bergen)

E. Prizes and Honors:
Prizes: Eduard Lassen (Prix de Rome)

Honors: Ambroise Thomas (French Academy)

F. Biographical Highlights:
István Bartalus settles in Pest as concert pianist and teacher; Peter Benoit enters Brussels Conservatory to study with Fétis and conducts in the local theaters; Hans von Bülow leaves Switzerland and goes to Weimar to study with Franz Liszt; Jeanne Cruvelli makes her Paris debut; César Cui enters the Engineering Academy in St. Petersburg; Friedrich von Flotow loses his wife and new-born son; Lodovico Graziani, Constance Nantier-Didiée and Fortunato Tedesco make their Paris Opera debuts; Antoine de Kontski moves to Paris and concertizes throughout Europe; Jules Massenet, age nine, is admitted to the Paris Conservatory; Modest Mussorgsky enters the School for Cadets of the Guard; Ernst Pauer, after a successful London debut, decides to settle there; Cesare Pugni goes to St. Petersburg as ballet composer to the Imperial Theater; Joseph Rheinberger moves to Munich; Alexander Serov begins his music criticism career; Eugenia Tadolini retires from the stage; Henri Wieniawski begins his virtuoso career with 2 years in Russia.

G. Institutional Openings:
Performing Groups: Cecilia Society of Copenhagen; Choral Institute of Dublin; Classical Harmonists (Belfast); Hannoverische Männergesangverein; Milwaukee Musikverein; New York Philharmonic Society; Washington Sängerbund (D.C.)

Educational: Cologne Conservatory of Music; Grädener Vocal Academy (Hamburg); Karl Hering School of Music (Berlin); Société des Jeunes Artistes du Conservatoire de Paris; Städtische Akademie für Tonkunst (Darmstadt)

Other: Crystal Palace (London); *The Echo*; Feurich Piano Co. (Leipzig); Fireman's Hall (Detroit); Haines Brothers Piano Co. (East Rochester); Joseph Henry, Bowmaker (Paris); Henri Herz, Piano Maker (Paris); William A. Johnson, Organ Builder (Hartford); Christian Kahnt Music Publishing Co. (Leipzig); Georg Kilgen and Son, Organ Builders (N.Y.); *Revue de Paris*; St. Lawrence Hall (Toronto); Methven Simpson, Music Publisher; Teatro Sociale (Guillaume--Brescia); Théâtre-Lyrique (Paris); Trúbner and Co., Publishers (London)

H. Musical Literature:

Czerny, Carl, *Umriss der ganzen Musikgeschichte*
Gevaert, François, *Rapport sur l'état de la musique en Espagna*
Kazynski, Wiktor, *History of Italian Opera*
Lambillotte, Louis, *Clef des mélodies grégoriennes*
Lobe, Johann C., *Katechismus der musik*
Loewe, Carl, *Musikalischer Gottesdienst*
Mason, Lowell, *The Glee Hive*
Silcher, Friedrich, *Harmonie- und kompositionslehre*
Spark, William, *A Lecture on Church Music*
Wagner, Richard, *Oper und Drama*
Winterfeld, Carl von, *Musiktreiben und Musikempfindungen im 16. und 17. Jahrhundert*

I. Musical Compositions:

Auber, Daniel, *Zerline* (opera)
Berlioz, Hector, *La Menace de Francs, Opus 20*
Brahms, Johannes, *Scherzo, Opus 4, for Piano*
Bruckner, Anton, *Entsagen for Soloists and Orchestra*
Dorn, Heinrich, *Missa pro Defunctis*
Foster, Stephen, *Laura Lee*
    Old Folks at Home (song)
Gade, Niels, *String Quintet in F Minor*
    3 Pieces, Opus 22, for Organ
Gevaert, François, *Les Empiriques* (opera)
    La Feria Andaluza for Orchestra
Glinka, Mikhail, *Spanish Overture No. 2, "Summer Night in Madrid"*
Gounod, Charles, *Sapho* (opera)
Liszt, Franz, *Mazeppa* (tone poem)
    Harmonies poetiques et religieuses for Piano
    12 Études d'exécution transcendante
    Wanderer Fantasy (after Schubert)
Lortzing, Albert, *Die Opernprobe* (opera)
Macfarren, George, *Leonora Cantata*
Marschner, Heinrich, *Austin* (opera)
Mercadante, Saverio, *Medea* (opera)
Pedrotti, Carlo, *Fiorina* (opera)
Raff, Joseph J., *König Alfred* (opera)
Saint-Saëns, Camille, *Moïse sauvé des eaux* (oratorio)
Schumann, Robert, *Overture, Julius Caesar, Opus 128*
    Overture, Hermann und Dorothea, Opus 136
    Der Rose Pilgerfahrt, Opus 112
    Der Königssohn, Opus 116
    Violin Sonatas No. 1 and 2, Opus 105 and 121
    Piano Trio No. 3, Opus 110
    3 Fantasiestücke, Opus 111, for Piano
    Mädchenlieder, Opus 103
    Husarenlieder, Opus 117
    7 Songs, Opus 104
Thalberg, Sigismond, *Florinda* (opera)
Thomas, Ambroise, *Raymond* (opera)
Verdi, Giuseppe, *Rigoletto* (opera)

1852

World Events:
In the U.S., Franklin Pierce is elected as President No. 14; the Wells Fargo and Co. opens offices in San Francisco; Massachusetts passes the first compulsory school attendance law for its young people; Studebaker Co. is founded in South Bend, Indiana; the Safety Elevator is introduced by E. G. Otis; American statesman Daniel Webster dies. Internationally, Louis Napoleon declares himself Emperor of the Second French Empire; the British fight the Second Burmese War in southeast Asia; New Zealand is given a constitutional government; the Transvaal is founded in South Africa; the gyroscope is invented by Foucault.

Cultural Highlights:
Georg Nagler completes his *New General Dictionary of Artists*; William P. Frith is admitted into the Royal Academy of Art. Births in the literary field include American poet Edwin Markham, Italian novelist Alfredo Oriani, French novelist and critic Charles Bourget and Spanish novelist Emilia Pardo Bazán; deaths include Irish novelist Eliot Warburton, Argentine poet Esteban Echeverria, Irish poet Thomas Moore, Russian novelist Nikolai Gogol and poet Vasili Zhukovski, French authors Marie F. Gay and Xavier de Maistre, German poet and dramatist Ernst Raupach and Bohemian poet Frantisek Celakovsky. Births in the art world include American artists Edwin A. Abbey and Theodore Robinson, British artist George Clausen, Belgian sculptor Jef Lambeaux, Norwegian artist Christian Krohg and French artist Jean-Louis Forain; deaths include American artist John Vanderlyn and sculptor Horatio Greenough. Other highlights include:

Art: George Bingham, *County Election No. I*; Ford Brown, *Christ Washing Peter's Feet*; Anselm Feuerbach, *Hafiz at the Well*; William P. Frith, *Bedtime*; William Hunt, *The Hireling Shepherd*; John Kensett, *Cascade in the Forest*; Adolf von Menzel, *Flute Concert at Sans Souci*; John Millais, *Ophelia*; François Rude, *Jeanne d'Arc* (Paris)

Literature: Dion Boucicault, *The Corsican Brothers*; Michel Carré, *Galatée*; Alexander Dumas, fils, *Camille*; Edward Fitzgerald, *Polonius*; Nathaniel Hawthorne, *The Blithedale Romance*; Friedrich Hebbel, *Agnes Bernauer*; Charles de Lisle, *Poèmes Antiques*; Charles Reade, *Masks and Faces*; Harriet B. Stowe, *Uncle Tom's Cabin*

MUSICAL EVENTS

A. Births:

Jan 24	Max Vogrich (Aus-pn)	Jul 3	Rafael Joseffy (Hun-pn)
Jan 29	Frederic H. Cowen (Br-pn)	Jul 9	Constantin Sternberg (Rus-pn)
Feb 6	Vasili Safonov (Rus-pn)	Jul 28	Barton M'Guckin (Ir-ten)
Feb 17	Hans Bischoff (Ger-pn)	Sep 4	Edoardo Mascheroni (It-cd)
Feb 24	George Moore (Br-cri)	Sep 8	Eugenio Pirani (It-pn-cm)
Mar 6	Joseph Bayer (Aus-cd-cm)	Sep 29	Johann G. Leitert (Ger-pn)
Mar 22	Ottokar Sevcik (Boh-vn)	Sep 30	Charles V. Stanford (Ir-cm)
Mar 31	Karl Dierich (Ger-ten)	Oct 12	Max Friedlaender (Ger-mus)
May 22	Émile Sauret (Fr-vn)	Nov 7	Fritz Scheel (Ger-cd)
Jun 21	Louis Maas (Ger-pn)	Nov 21	Francisco Tárrega (Sp-gui)
Jun 23	Raoul Pugno (Fr-pn-cm)	Nov 29	Paul Hillemacher (Fr-cm)
Jun 28	Hans Huber (Swi-cm)		Augustus Harris (Br-imp)

B. Deaths:

Feb 19	Karl G. Winterfeld (Ger-mus)	Mar 25	Alexis de Garaudé (Fr-voc-cm)
Feb 27	Joseph Drechsler (Boh-cm-cd)	Mar 31	John F. Burrowes (Br-org)
Mar 12	Juan Bros (Sp-cm-cd)	May 11	Jean Baptiste Willent-Bordogni
Mar 15	Giuseppe Bertini (It-cd)		(Fr-bn)

Jun 6	Tommaso Marchesi (It-cd-cm)	Nov 22	August A. Klengel (Ger-pn)
Jun 16	Joseph Merk (Aus-cel)	Dec 2	François Fayolle (Fr-mus)
Jul 5	Johann B. Weigl (Ger-org-cm)	Dec 9	Arthur E. Sequin (Br-bs)
Sep 28	Johann F. Schwenke (Ger-org)	Dec 15	Józef Damse (Pol-cl-cm)
Nov 18	Anton B. Fürstenau (Ger-fl)	Dec 16	Henri J. Rigel (Fr-cm)

C. Debuts:

U.S. -- Marietta Alboni (tour), Alfred Jaëll (tour), Caroline Richings (as singer), Henriette Sontag (tour), Camilla Urso (tour at age 10)

Other - Antonio Cotogni (Rome), Jean Baptiste Faure (Paris), Dar'ya Leonova (St. Petersburg), Marietta Piccolomini (Florence), Amalie Weiss (Vienna)

D. New Positions:

Conductors: Julius Benedict (Her Majesty's Theater, London), Antonio Cagnoni (maestro di cappella, Cathedral of Vigevano), Karl Eckert (Italian Opera, Paris), Charles Gounod (Orphéon Choral Society), Charles Hallé (St. Cecilia Society, Manchester), Angelo Mariani (Carlo Felice Theater, Genoa), Emanuele Muzio (Italian Opera, Brussels), Pietro Raimondi (maestro di cappella, St. Peter's, Rome)

Educational: Hubert Léonard (violin, Brussels Conservatory), Julius Leonhard (piano, Munich Conservatory), Ambroise Thomas (composition, Paris Conservatory)

Others: William Henry Fry (critic, New York *Tribune*), Moritz Fürstenau (music librarian, Royal Library of Dresden), George Grove (secretary, Crystal Palace), Johann F. Schwenke (organ, Nikolaikirche, Hamburg), Robert Stewart (organ, St. Patrick's, Dublin)

E. Prizes and Honors:

Prizes: Max Bruch (Mozart), Camille Saint-Saëns (St. Cecilia, Bordeaux)

Honors: Charles Barry (knighted), Friedrich Silcher (honorary doctorate, University of Tübingen)

F. Biographical Highlights:

Michael Balfe begins a two-year tour of Russia and Austria; Joseph Barnby enters the Royal Academy of Music; Charles-Auguste de Bériot is forced to retire from his Conservatory post due to failing eyesight; Angiolina Bosio makes her Covent Garden debut; Peter Cornelius goes to Weimar where he meets Liszt; William Henry Fry returns to the U.S.; August and Georg Gemünder moves their violin-making business from Boston to New York; Mikhail Glinka returns to Paris for a second visit; Louis Moreau Gottschalk makes a very successful European concert tour; Charles Gounod decides against taking Holy Orders and marries Anna Zimmermann; Mathilde Graumann marries baritone Salvatore Marchesi in London; Nicolai Ivanov retires from the operatic stage; Otto Jadassohn begins teaching music in Leipzig; Jenny Lind marries the American conductor, Otto Goldschmidt.

G. Institutional Openings:

Performing Groups: Aachen Städtisches Orchester; Basler Liedertafel; Bonn Konzertverein; Bucharest Deutsche Liedertafel; Cleveland St. Cecilia Society; Ludwig Erk Gesangverein (Berlin); Melbourne Philharmonic Society (Australia); New Philharmonic Society (London)

Festivals: Westphalian Music Festival

Educational: Bergen Musical College; École Communale de Musique et de Déclamation (Marseilles)

Other: Boston Music Hall (Aquarius Theater); Bucharest National Theater; De Santis Music Publishers (Rome); *Dwight's Journal of Music* (Boston); *Gazzetta Musical di Napoli*; Graslin Theater (Nantes); Hanover State Opera House; H. O. Houghton and

Co. (Houghton-Mifflin Co. in 1880); Johannes Kleis, Organ Builder (Germany); *Neue Wiener Musik-Zeitung*; Weber Piano Co. (N.Y.)

H. Musical Literature:

Bellermann, Heinrich, *Die Mensuralnoten und Taktzeichen des 15. und 16. Jahrhundert*
Brendel, Karl F., *Geschichte der Musik in Italien, Deutschland und Frankreich...*
Coussemaker, Charles, *Histoire de l'harmonie au Moyen-Age*
Drobisch, Moritz, *Über musikalische Tonbestimmung und Temperatur*
Hullah, John, *A Grammar of Harmony*
Kraushaar, Otto, *Der accordliche Gegensatz und der Begründung der Scala*
Lobe, Johann C., *Musikalische Briefe eines Wohlbekannten*
Mason, Lowell, *New Carmina Sacra*
Polko, Elise, *Musikalische Märchen*
Southard, Lucien, *Union Glee Book*

I. Musical Compositions:

Adam, Adolphe, *If I Were a King* (operetta)
　　La poupée de Nuremberg (operetta)
Auber, Daniel, *Marco Spada* (opera)
Balakirev, Mily, *Grand Fantasy on Russian Folk Songs, Opus 4*
Balfe, Michael, *The Sicilian Bride* (opera)
　　The Devil's in It (opera)
Brahms, Johannes, *Sonata No. 2, Opus 2, for Piano*
Bruckner, Anton, *Psalm XXII*
　　2 Totenlieder for Chorus
　　2 Pieces in D Minor for Organ
Cornelius, Peter, *Requiem for Male Chorus*
Flotow, Friedrich von, *Rübezahl* (opera)
Foster, Stephen, *Massa's in the Cold, Cold Ground* (song)
Franck, César, *Le valet de ferme* (opera)
Gade, Niels, *Symphony No. 5, Opus 25*
　　Spring Fantasy, Opus 23 (cantata)
Glinka, Mikhail, *Ukranian Symphony* (1 movement only)
Gottschalk, Louis M., *Midnight in Seville* (piano)
Gounod, Charles, *Ulysse* (incidental music)
　　Le Bourgeois Gentilhomme (ballet)
Halévy, Jacques, *Le juif errant* (opera)
Liszt, Franz, *Hungarian Fantasy for Piano and Orchestra*
　　Fantasia on Beethoven's "Ruins of Athens" for Piano
Maillart, Louis, *La croix de Marie* (opera)
Massé, Victor, *Galathée* (opera)
Moniuszko, Stanislaw, *Bettly* (opera)
Rossi, Giovanni, *Elena di Taranto* (opera)
Rossi, Lauro, *Le sabine* (opera)
Rubinstein, Anton, *Dmitri Donskay* (opera)
Saint-Saëns, Camille, *Ode to St. Cecilia*
Schumann, Robert, *Requiem in D-flat Major, Opus 148*
　　Mass in C Major, Opus 147
　　Von Pagen und der Königstochter, Opus 140 (cantata)
　　5 Poems of Queen Mary, Opus 135
　　4 Songs, Opus 142
　　4 Ballads, Opus 141
Strauss, Johann, Jr., *Annen Polka*

1853

World Events:

In the U.S., the Gadsden Purchase from Mexico adds to the Arizona and New Mexico territories; the Washington Territory is separated from the Oregon Territory; the New York Central Railroad is chartered; "Uncle Sam" first appears in political cartoon; the first Children's Aid Society is formed. Internationally, Commodore Perry sails the fleet into Tokyo bay and opens Japan to world trade; the Crimean War begins between Turkey and Russia; Great Britain becomes the first nation to require smallpox vaccinations for its citizens; Pedro V become Portugese ruler; George Coyley tries the first known glider flight.

Cultural Highlights:

Putnam's Monthly Magazine begins publication; Nathaniel Hawthorne is made U.S. Consul to Liverpool; Prosper Merimée becomes a Senator in the French Assembly; John E. Millais is taken into the Royal Academy of Art. Births in the art world include American artists John Hamilton, Willard Metcalf, John Murphy and John Twachtman and sculptors William Couper and Frederic Ruckstull, Swiss artist Ferdinand Hodler and Dutch artist Vincent van Gogh; French artist Pierre Fontaine dies. Births in the literary field include French novelist René Bazin; deaths include German poet Johann Tieck and Italian poet Tommaso Grossi. Other highlights include:

Art: Rosa Bonheur, *The Horse Fair*; Jules Adolphe Breton, *Return of the Harvesters*; Gustave Courbet, *The Bathers*; George H. Durrie, *Going to Church*; William Frith, *Ramsgate Sands*; John Martin, *The Great Day of His Wrath*; John Millais, *The Proscribed Royalist* and *The Order of Release*; François Rude, *Marshall Ney*

Literature: Matthew Arnold, *Poems*; Charlotte Brontë, *Villette*; Charles Dickens, *Bleak House*; Alexander Dumas, père, *Ange Pitou*; Ludwig Eichrodt, *Gedichte in Allerlei Humoren*; Elizabeth Gaskell, *Cranford*; Nathaniel Hawthorne, *Tanglewood Tales*; Charles Kingsley, *Hypatia*; John Ruskin, *The Stones of Venice*

MUSICAL EVENTS

A. Births:

Jan 1	Hans Koessler (Ger-cm)	Aug 5	Richard Henneberg (Ger-cd)
Jan 3	Iwan Knorr (Ger-cm-au)	Aug 12	Jean L. Nicodé (Ger-pn)
Jan 5	Charles H. Morse (Am-org)	Aug 22	Johannes Elmblad (Swe-bs)
Jan 11	Franz Rummel (Br-pn)	Aug 28	Auguste Seidl-Kraus (Ger-sop)
Mar 5	Arthur Foote (Am-cm)	Aug 30	Percy Goetschius (Br-the)
Mar 8	Alexandre Taskin (Fr-bar)	Dec 15	Theodor von Frimmel (Aus-mus)
Apr 5	Alfonso Rendano (It-pn)	Dec 22	Teresa Carreño (Ven-pn)
Apr 21	Charles Malherbe (Fr-mus)	Dec 22	Edouard de Reszke (Pol-bs)
Apr 27	Jules Lemaître (Fr-cri)	Dec 30	André Messager (Fr-cd-cm)
Jul 15	Hedwig Reicher-Kinderman (Ger-sop)		

B. Deaths:

Jan 4	Karl G. Hering (Ger-m.ed)	Jun 3	Filippo Galli (It-bs)
Jan 7	Giuseppina Ronzi de Begnis (It-sop)	Jun 9	Egide Aerts (Bel-fl-cm)
		Aug 15	Giovanni Pelledro (It-vn)
Mar 15	Giovanni Ricordi (It-pub)	Aug 18	Peter Lichtenthal (Hun-mus)
Mar 20	Aloys Fuchs (Aus-mus)	Oct 3	Georges Onslow (Br-cm)
Apr 11	Louis E. Jadin (Fr-pn-cm)	Oct 19	Louis Duport (Fr-bal)
Apr 15	Johann L. Fuchs (Ger-pn)	Oct 29	Pierre Zimmerman (Fr-pn)
May 9	Johann Schmidt (Ger-cm)	Oct 30	Pietro Raimondi (It-cm)
May 18	Nicolaus Kraft (Hun-cel)	Nov 16	William Gardiner (Br-mus)

Nov 23   Francisco Andrevi (Sp-cm)   Dec 30   Victor Desvignes (Fr-vn)
Dec 3   Eduard Lannoy (Aus-cd-cm)   Lisa Cristiani (Fr-cel)
Dec 8   Jonas Chickering (Am-pn.m)

C. Debuts:

U.S. -- August Gockel (tour), Louis Moreau Gottschalk (tour)

Other - Amalie Joachim (Troppau), Pietro Mongini (Genoa), Hortense Schneider (Agen), Josef Strauss (Vienna)

D. New Positions:

Conductors: Karl Eckert (Vienna Opera), Franz Erkel (Budapest PO), Maurits Hagemann (kapellmeister, Groningen), Ludwig Schindelmeisser (Darmstadt Court)

Educational: Henry C. Banister (harmony, Royal Academy, London), Johannes van Bree (director, Amsterdam Conservatory), Arthur H. Clough (examiner in education, London), Johann C. Lauterbach (violin, Munich Conservatory), Karl Reinthaler (voice, Cologne Conservatory)

Others: César Franck (organ, St. Jean-St. François du Marais), Joseph Joachim (post, King of Hanover), Johann C. Lobe (editor, *Fliegende Blätter für Musik*)

E. Prizes and Honors:

Honors: Henry Bishop (honorary doctorate, Oxford), Aimé-Ambroise Leborne (Legion of Honor)

F. Biographical Highlights:

Alkan begins a 20-year withdrawal from public performance; Mily Balakirev enters the University of Kazan as a math student; Sterndale Bennett turns down the post of conductor of the Leipzig Gewandhaus; Georges Bizet begins study with Halévy; Arrigo Boito enters the Milan Conservatory; Johannes Brahms accompanies Reményi on his tour and meets the Schumanns; Hans von Bülow makes his first concert tour as pianist; Léon Carvalho marries soprano Marie Caroline Miolan; Théodore Dubois enters the Paris Conservatory; Filippo Filippi graduates from Padua University with a law degree; Stephen Foster leaves his wife and family and moves to New York; Louis Moreau Gottschalk returns to the U.S. for a long concert tour; Francesco Graziani makes his Paris debut; Jules Massenet enters the Paris Conservatory; Robert Schumann's mental illness deepens; Theodore Thomas, playing in Jullien's orchestra, gets his first taste of good music; Giuseppe Verdi decides to settle in Paris; Richard Wagner first meets the young Cosima Liszt and meets the Wesendoncks; Franz Wurlitzer emigrates to the U.S.

G. Institutional Openings:

Performing Groups: Belgrade Choral Society; Jullien's Monster Concerts for the Masses (N.Y.); London City Glee Club; London Concerti da Camera; Pest Philharmonic Society; Philharmonic Society of the Friends of Art (New Orleans); Royal Melbourne Philharmonic Society

Educational: École Spéciale de Chant (Paris, by Duprez); New York Normal Music Institute

Other: *L'Arpa*; Augener and Co., Music Publishers (London); Bechstein Piano Co. (Berlin); Berry and Gordon, Music Publishers (N.Y.); Wilhelm Biese Piano Co. (Berlin); Blüthner Piano Co. (Leipzig); *Gazzetta Musicale di Firenze*; Wilhelm Hansen Music Publishing Co. (Copenhagen); Merklin, Schütze et Cie., Organ Builders (Brussels); Miller and Beecham, Music Publishers (Baltimore); *Niederrheinische Musikzeitung* (Cologne); J. and P. Schiedmayer, Piano Makers (Stuttgart); Steinway and Sons (New York); Tonic Sol-Fa Association (London); *Tonic Sol-Fa Reporter*

H. Musical Literature:

Berlioz, Hector, *Les soirées de l'orchestre*
Hauptmann, Moritz, *Die nature der harmonik und der metrik*
Horsley, William, *The Musical Treasury*
Mason, Lowell, *Musical Letters from Abroad*
Pohl, Richard, *Akustische Briefe...*
Richter, Ernst, *Lehrbuch der harmonie*
Savard, Augustin, *Cours complet d'harmonie théorique et pratique*
Sechter, Simon, *Die Grundsätze der musikalischen Komposition I, II*
Weitzmann, Carl, *Der übermässige Dreiklang*
Wiecks, Friedrich, *Clavier und gesang*

I. Musical Compositions:

Adam, Adolphe, *Le sourd* (opera)
Bradbury, William, *Daniel* (cantata)
Brahms, Johannes, *Piano Sonatas No. 1 and 3, Opus 1 and 5*
    18 Songs, Opus 3, 6 and 7
Bristow, George, *Symphony No. 2, Opus 24, "Jullien"*
Bruckner, Anton, *Magnificat*
Foster, Stephen, *My Old Kentucky Home* (song)
    Old Dog Tray (song)
Fry, William H., *Santa Claus Symphony*
    Metropolitan Hall March
Gade, Niels, *Erlkönigs Tochter, Opus 30* (cantata)
    Chorus, Opus 26, (male chorus)
    Novelletten, Opus 29, for Violin, Cello and Piano
Gounod, Charles, *Peter, the Hermit* (oratorio)
Halévy, Jacques, *Le nabab* (opera)
Liszt, Franz, *Festklänge* (tone poem)
    Sonata in B Minor for Piano
Massé, Victor, *Les noces de Jeannette* (opera)
Mercadante, Saverio, *Violetta* (opera)
Niedermeyer, Louis, *La Fronde* (opera)
Offenbach, Jacques, *Pépito* (operetta)
Root, George, *Daniel* (cantata)
Rossi, Lauro, *L'alchimista* (opera)
Rubinstein, Anton, *Thomas, the Fool* (opera)
    The Siberian Hunters (opera)
Schumann, Robert, *Festival Overture, "Rheinweinlied," Opus 123*
    Overture to Faust
    Fantasy in C Major, Opus 131, for Violin and Orchestra
    Märchenerzählungen, Opus 132
    Introduction and Allegro, Opus 134, for Piano
    3 Piano Sonatas for the Young, Opus 118
    7 Pieces in Fughetta Form, Opus 126, for Piano
    Ballad, "Das Glück von Edenhall," Opus 143
Spohr, Louis, *Septet in A Minor, Opus 147*
Thomas, Ambroise, *La Tonelli* (opera)
Verdi, Giuseppe, *Il trovatore* (opera)
    La traviata (opera)
Vogel, Charles L., *La moissonneuse* (opera)
Wieniawski, Henri, *Concerto No. 1, Opus 14, for Violin and Orchestra*
    Polonaise No. 1, Opus 4, for Violin and Orchestra
    Souvenir de Moscow, Opus 6, for Violin and Orchestra

1854

World Events:
In the U.S., the Republican Political Party is born in Wisconsin; the Kansas-Nebraska Act is passed by Congress; the Missouri Compromise is repealed; the Ostend Manifesto on the buying or taking of Cuba is made public; the Ashmun Institute, the first black university, is founded. Internationally, the Crimean War continues with France and Great Britain declaring war on Russia; the Charge of the Light Brigade takes place; the Treaty of Kanagawa is signed by the U.S. and Japan; the Dogma of the Immaculate Conception is declared by Pope Pius IX.

Cultural Highlights:
Le Figaro begins publication as a weekly (becomes a daily in 1866); Jean Baptiste Carpeaux wins the Prix de Rome in Art; James Whistler fails chemistry and is discharged from West Point Academy. Births in the art world include Alfred Gilbert; deaths include American architect William Strickland, German artist Karl Begas and British artist John J. Chalon and John "Mad" Martin. Births in the literary world include French poet Jean Rimbaud and Irish poet and novelist Oscar Wilde; deaths include American dramatist Robert M. Bird, Italian author Silvio Pellico, Scottish poet John Wilson and novelist Susan E. Ferrier, British poet James Montgomery, German philosopher Friedrich von Schelling and Swiss authors Albert Bitzius and Jeremias Gotthelf. Other highlights include:

Art: Antoine-Louis Barye, *War, Peace, Force, Order*; George Bingham, *Stump Speaking*; Ford Brown, *English Autumn Afternoon*; Gustave Courbet, *Women Sifting Grain*; David Cox, *Beach at Rhyl*; William Hunt, *Light of the World*; Charles Méryon, *Eaux Fortes de Paris*; Jean-François Millet, *The Reaper*; Ferdinand Waldmüller, *Vienna Woods*

Literature: John Cooke, *Leather Stocking and Silk*; Maria Cummins, *The Lamplighter*; Charles Dickens, *Hard Times*; Heinrich Heine, *Neueste Gedichte*; Otto Müller, *Charlotte Ackermann*; Coventry Patmore, *The Betrothal*; William Thackeray, *The Rose and the Ring*; Henry Thoreau, *Walden*; Lev Tolstoy, *The Cossacks*

MUSICAL EVENTS

A. Births:
Jan 20	Emma Brandes (Ger-pn)
Jan 31	William Sherwood (Am-pn)
Feb 2	Adolphe Foerster (Am-cm)
Mar 5	Philip Hale (Am-cri)
Mar 10	Henry Krehbiel (Am-cri)
May 16	Louis de Wailly (Fr-cm)
Jun 19	Alfredo Catalani (It-cm)
Jul 3	Leos Janácek (Boh-cm)
Aug 2	Pavel Khokhlov (Rus-bar)
Aug 3	Alexander Vinogradsky (Rus
Aug 23	Moritz Moszkowski (Pol-pn)
Sep 1	Engelbert Humperdinck (Ger-cm)
Sep 9	Jean Lemaire (Fr-cm)
Sep 18	Hans Müller (Ger-mus)
Sep 22	Henry T. Finck (Am-cri)
Sep 25	Edmond M. Diet (Fr-cm)
Oct 23	James A. Bland (Am-cm)
Nov 6	John P. Sousa (Am-cm-cd)
Nov 9	Josef M. Weber (Boh-vn)
Nov 13	George Chadwick (Am-cm)
Nov 26	Émile X. Wambach (Lux-vn)
	Eugénie Colonne (Fr-sop)
	Maurice Devries (Am-bar)
	George Fox (Br-bar)

B. Deaths:
Feb 4	Iwan Müller (Ger-cl)
Feb 12	Teresa Bertinotti (It-sop)
Mar 3	Giovanni Rubini (It-ten)
Apr 17	Gottlob Wiedebein (Ger-org)
Apr 18	Joseph Elsner (Ger-cm-ped)
May 3	William Beale (Br-org)
May 18	Henri Lemoine (Fr-pn-pub)
Jun 15	Georges Bousquet (Fr-cm)
Jun 17	Henriette Sontag (Ger-sop)
Aug 7	Heinrich A. Praeger (Hol-vn)
Aug 20	Karl L. Drobisch (Ger-cm)
Sep 11	Johannes Pressenda (It-vn.m)
Oct 4	András Barthé (Hun-cm)

C. Debuts:
U.S. -- Louis François Drouet (tour), Giulia Grisi (tour), William Harrison (tour), Giovanni Mario (N.Y.), Louisa Pyne (N.Y.), Gustav Satter (tour)

Other - Guglielmo Andrioli (London), Albert Eilers (Dresden), Siga Garsó (Arad), Bessie Palmer (London), Adelaide Phillipps (Milan), August Wilhelmj (age 9, Wiesbaden)

D. New Positions:
Conductors: Melchiore Balbi (maestro di cappella, Basilica San Antonio), Julius Cornet (Vienna Opera), Charles Hallé (Manchester SO), Carl Reinecke (Barmen), Max Seifriz (kapellmeister, Löwenberg)

Educational: Hilarión Eslava (composition, Madrid Conservatory), Josef Hasselmans (director, Strasbourg Conservatory), Johann G. Herzog (music director, Erlangen University), Henry Lazarus (clarinet, Royal Academy, London), Mathilde Marchesi (voice, Vienna Conservatory), Antonio Sangiovanni (voice, Milan Conservatory)

Others: Antoine E. Batiste (organ, St. Eustache), Jacques Halévy (secretary, Academy of Fine Arts, Paris), Hervé (manager, Folies Concertantes), Julius Schneider (organ, Berlin Institute of Church Music)

E. Prizes and Honors:
Prizes: Grat-Norbert Barthé (Prix de Rome)

Honors: Louis Clapisson (French Academy)

F. Biographical Highlights:
Hector Berlioz, on the death of Henrietta, marries Marie Ricio; Marie Cabel makes her London debut; Gabriel Fauré enters the École Niedermeyer in Paris; Mikhail Glinka, on the outbreak of the war, returns to Russia; Antoine de Kontski moves to St. Petersburg and begins teaching; Charles Lecocq leaves the Conservatory in order to help support his parents; Carl C. Müller moves to New York and begins working in a piano factory; Frederick Ouseley receives his doctorate from Oxford; Amilcare Ponchielli graduates from Milan Conservatory; Ebenezer Prout receives his B.A. degree in education from London University; Robert Schumann is placed in an institution after attempting suicide; Arthur Sullivan enters the Chapel Royal as a chorister and a student; Richard Wagner begins a liason with Mathilde Wesendonck; Henry Work takes a printer's job in Chicago.

G. Institutional Openings:
Performing Groups: Dresdner Tonkünstlerverein; Indianapolis Männerchor; Linzer Männergesangverein (Sängerbund); Munich Oratorio Society; Neu-Weimar-Verein; Old Folks Concerts (Boston); Pittsburgh Orchestral Society; Riedelverein (Leipzig); Sociedad de Mayo (Buenos Aires); Teutonia Männerchor of Pittsburgh

Educational: Birmingham and Midland Institute (School of Music in 1859); New York Academy of Music; Strasbourg Conservatory of Music

Other: Boston Theater (New); Bradbury's Piano-Forte Warehouse (N.Y.); Conacher and Co., Organ Builders (Huddersfield); Félibrige Organization (Provençal); Mason and Hamlin Organ Co. (Boston); St. George's Hall Concert Room (Liverpool); R. S. Williams and Sons (Toronto)

H. Musical Literature:
Brendel, Karl F., *Die musik der Gegenwart und die Gesamtkunst der Zukunft*
Chorley, Henry, *Modern German Music*
Clément, Félix, *Méthode complete de plain-chant*
Hanslick, Eduard, *Vom Musikalisch-Schönen*

Hastings, Thomas, *History of Forty Choirs*
Knorr, Julius, *Erklärendes Verzeichniss der hauptsächlichsten Musikkunstwörter*
Lucas, L., *L'acoustique nouvelle*
Mason, Lowell, *Musical Notation in a Nutshell*
Moore, John, *Complete Encyclopedia of Music...*
Nisard, Théodore, *Dictionnaire litugique, historique et pratique du plain-chant*
Panofka, Heinrich, *L'art de chanter*

I. Musical Compositions:

Adam, Adolphe, *Richard en Palestine* (opera)
Balfe, Michael, *Pittore e Duca* (opera)
Berlioz, Hector, *L'enfance du Christ, Opus 25* (cantata)
Brahms, Johannes, *Concerto No. 1, Opus 15, for Piano and Orchestra*
    Piano Trio No. 1, Opus 8
    Variations on a Theme of Schumann, Opus 9, for Piano
    4 Ballades, Opus 10, for Piano
Bruckner, Anton, *Missa Solemnis in B-flat Major*
Dorn, Heinrich, *Die Nibelungen* (opera)
Foster, Stephen, *Jeannie with the Light Brown Hair* (song)
Fry, William H., *Niagara Symphony*
    Hagar, Sacred Symphony
Goldmark, Karl, *Overture*
Gottschalk, Louis M., *The Last Hope*
    El Cocoyé (piano)
Gounod, Charles, *Symphony No. 1 in D Major*
    La nonne sanglante (opera)
    The Angel and Tobias (oratorio)
Hiller, Ferdinand, *Der Advokat* (opera)
Liszt, Franz, *Orpheus* (tone poem)
    Les Preludes (tone poem)
    Hungaria (tone poem)
    Tasso (tone poem)
    A Faust Symphony
    Grande Etudes de Paganini (piano)
L'vov, Alexei, *Starosta Boris* (opera)
Massé, Victor, *La fiancée du diable* (opera)
Meyerbeer, Giacomo, *L'étoile du nord* (opera)
    Judith (unfinished opera)
Mosonyi, Mihály, *Mass No. 4*
Offenbach, Jacques, *Luc et Lucette* (operetta)
Pacini, Giovanni, *Il trionfo di Giuditta* (oratorio)
    La punizione (opera)
Pedrotti, Carlo, *Genoveffa del Brabante* (opera)
Reyer, Louis, *Maître Wolfram* (opera)
Root, George, *The Pilgrim Fathers* (cantata)
Rubinstein, Anton, *Symphony No. 2, Opus 42, "Ocean"*
Schumann, Robert, *Scenes from Faust*
    Albumblätter, Opus 124, for Piano
Smetana, Bedrich, *Triumphal Symphony in E Major*
Suppé, Franz von, *Requiem*
Wagner, Richard, *Das Rheingold* (opera)
Winner, Septimus, *Listen to the Mocking Bird* (song)

1855

World Events:

In the U.S., the Pennsylvania Rock Oil Co. becomes the first to exploit the new resource; the Court of Claims is established by Congress; Registered Mail is introduced; Northwestern Univerisity is established in Evanston, Illinois; Congress approves funds for the importation of camels to the American West. Internationally, Cyrus Field lays the first successful cable from Nova Scotia to Newfoundland; Townshend Harris becomes the first Foreign Minister to Japan; Czar Nicholas I of Russia dies and Alexander II becomes the new Czar; the Young Women's Christian Association (YWCA) is founded in England; David Livingston discovers Victoria Falls in Africa.

Cultural Highlights:

Charles L. Eastlake becomes director of the National Gallery in London; James Russell Lowell begins teaching modern languages at Harvard; Henri M. Chapu wins the Prix de Rome in Art; François Ponsard is inducted into the French Academy. Births in the art world include American sculptor James E. Kelly, Canadian artist Homer Watson, Scottish artist William Brymner and French sculptor Léonard Beguine; deaths include American architect Robert Mills, French artist Jean Baptiste Isabey, sculptor François Rude and German artist Wilhelm von Kobell. Births in the literary field include Russian author V. Mikhailovich Garshin, Belgian poet Émile Verhaeren, British dramatist Arthur Pinero and novelist Marie Corelli and Italian poet Giovanni Pascoli; deaths include British authors Mary Mitford, Charlotte Brontë and poet Samuel Rogers, French poet Gérard de Nerval, Polish poet and dramatist Adam Mickiewicz and Russian poet Konstantin Batyushkov. Other highlights include:

Art: George Bingham, *The Verdict of the People*; Frederick Church, *The Heart of the Andes*; Gustave Courbet, *The Painter's Studio*; Arthur Hughes, *April Love*; William Hunt, *The Belated Kid*; George Inness, *The Lackawanna Valley*; Ernest Meissonier, *The Gamblers*; Charles Méryon, *L'Apsis de Notre Dame*

Literature: Pedro de Alarcón, *El Final de Norma*; Robert Browning, *Men and Women*; Alexander Dumas, fils, *Le Demi Monde*; Elizabeth Gaskell, *North and South*; Paul von Heyse, *Novellen*; Charles Kingsley, *Westward Ho!*; Henry W. Longfellow, *The Song of Hiawatha*; Ivan Turgenev, *A Month in the Country*; Walt Whitman, *Leaves of Grass*

MUSICAL EVENTS

A. Births:

Jan 20	Ernest Chausson (Fr-cm)	Aug 4	Emil Mollenhauer (Am-vn)
Feb 14	Edward B. Perry (Am-pn)	Aug 29	Emil Paur (Aus-vn-cd)
Feb 27	Mary Davies (Br-mez)	Sep 19	Katharina Klafsky (Hun-sop)
Mar 13	Anton Rückauf (Ger-cm)	Sep 28	Fanny Moran-Olden (Ger-sop)
Apr 9	Joseph Hellmesberger (Aus-cm)	Oct 12	Arthur Nikisch (Hun-cd)
May 11	Anatole Liadov (Rus-cm)	Oct 25	Joseph Kotek (Rus-vn)
Jun 4	Josephine de Reszke (Pol-sop)	Oct 30	Károly Aggházy (Hun-pn)
Jun 15	Etelka Gerster (Hun-sop)	Nov 1	Guido Adler (Aus-mus)
Jun 17	Fritz Steinbach (Ger-cd)	Nov 6	Paul Kalisch (Ger-ten)
Jun 21	Therese Malten (Ger-sop)	Nov 17	Giuseppe Campanari (It-bar)
Jun 27	Bianca Bianchi (Ger-sop)	Dec 4	William Henderson (Am-cri)

B. Deaths:

Feb 22	Louis Lambillotte (Fr-mus)	Apr 30	Henry R. Bishop (Br-cm-cd)
Mar 14	Charles Hempel (Br-org)	May 4	Camille Pleyel (Fr-pn)
Mar 17	Rámon Carnicer (Sp-cm)	May 13	Teresa Belloc-Giorgi (It-alto)
Apr 10	Marie Pachler-Koschak (Aus-pn)	Jun 13	Robert Lindley (Br-cel)
Apr 12	Pedro Albéniz (Sp-org)	Jun 28	Giovanni A. Perotti (It-cm)

Oct 15   Désiré A. Batton (Fr-cm)   Jacques Lavigne (Fr-ten)

C. Debuts:

U.S. -- Pasquale Brignoli, Anna de la Grange (N.Y.), Constance Nantier-Didiée (tour), Adelaide Phillipps (Boston)

Other - Valentina Bianchi (Frankfurt), Elise Hensler (Milan), Euphrosyne Parepa-Rosa (Malta), Gustav Walter (Brünn), William Winn (London)

D. New Positions:

Conductors: Franz W. Abt (kapellmeister, Brunswick), Carl Bergmann (New York PO), Antonio Buzzolla (maestro di cappella, St. Mark's, Venice), Ferdinand Laub (Berlin Court Orchestra), Julius Tausch (Düsseldorf Concerts)

Educational: Hans von Bülow (piano, Stern-Marx Conservatory), Gaetano Gaspari (librarian, Bologna Liceo), Frederick Ouseley (professor, Oxford)

Others: W. T. Best (organ, St. George's Hall, London), Gaetano Capocci (organ, St. John Lateran, Rome), Edward Hanslick (critic, *Wiener Presse*)

E. Prizes and Honors:

Prizes: Pierre de Mol (Prix de Rome)

Honors: Henri Reber (Legion of Honor)

F. Biographical Highlights:

Mily Balakirev, encouraged by Glinka, decides on a musical career; Hector Berlioz, attending a festival of his own music at Weimar, meets Liszt; Anton Bruckner goes to Vienna to study harmony and counterpoint with Sechter; Dudley Buck begins taking piano lessons from W. J. Babcock; violinist Heinrich Ernst decides to settle in London; Francesco Graziani debuts at Covent Garden; Lodovico Graziani makes his La Scala debut; Charles Grove begins work with William Smith on the *Dictionary of the Bible*; Hermann Levi enters the Leipzig Conservatory; William Mason, after a concert tour of various American cities, settles in New York; Gioacchino Rossini moves permanently to Paris; Nicholai Rubinstein graduates with a law degree from the University of Moscow; Antonio Tamburini retires from the operatic stage; Carl Tausig begins piano study with Franz Liszt; Sigismond Thalberg begins an extended tour in South America and the U.S.; Richard Wagner conducts his music in London and meets with Queen Victoria.

G. Institutional Openings:

Performing Groups: Christopher Bach Orchestra (Milwaukee); Birmingham Amateur Harmonic Association; Buffalo Sängerbund; Crystal Palace Concerts; Detroit Philharmonic Society; Dodsworth Hall Matinee Concerts (by T. Thomas); Glasgow Choral Union; Göttingen Singakademie; Innsbruck Liedertafel; Mason-Thomas Quintet; Müller String Quartet II (Meiningen); New Orleans Classical Music Society; *L'Orphéon*; Schlosskirchenchor (Schwerin); Société de Musique de Chambre Armingaud (Armingaud-Jacquard Quartet); Stein and Buchheister Orchestra (Detroit); Teatro Ginásio Dramático (Rio de Janeiro)

Educational: Neue Akademie der Tonkunst (Berlin); Scuola Corale (Pisa)

Other: American Steam Music Co. (Worcester--by the inventor of the Calliope); Berteling Woodwind Co. (Boston-N.Y.); *Blätter für Theater, Musik und Bildene Kunst*; *Gaceta Musical de Madrid*; Holtkamp Organ Co. (Cleveland); Laryngoscope (by M. P. García); Mason Brothers Music Publishers (Boston); Melodina (by J. B. Fourneaux); Willem Paling Piano Co. (Sydney, Australia)

H. Musical Literature:

Caffi, Francesco, *Storia della musica sacra*
Duvernoy, Henri-Louis, *Solfège des chanteurs*
Kunkel, Franz J., *Kleine Musiklehre*
La Fage, Juste de, *Cours complet de plain-chant*
Marx, Adolf B., *Die Musik des 19. Jahrhundert und ihre Pflege*
Morelot, Stéphane, *Manuel de Psalmodie*
Panseron, Auguste, *Traité de l'harmonie*
Parker, James, *Manual of Harmony*
Root/Mason, *Young Men's Singing Book*
Saint-Saëns, Camille, *Harmonie et mélodie*
Southard, Lucien H., *A Course in Harmony*

I. Musical Compositions:

Auber, Daniel, *Jenny Bell* (opera)
Balakirev, Mily, *String Quartet, "Original Russian"*
Berlioz, Hector, *L'Imperiale, Opus 26* (cantata)
Berwald, Franz, *Concerto in D Major for Piano and Orchestra*
Bizet, Georges, *Symphony in C Major*
Bristow, George, *Rip Van Winkle* (opera)
Costa, Michael, *Eli* (oratorio)
Flotow, Friedrich von, *Hilda* (opera)
Foster, Stephen, *Come Where My Love Lies Dreaming* (song)
Fry, William H., *Stabat Mater*
Gevaert, François, *Les lavandières de Santarem* (opera)
Glinka, Mikhail, *The Bigamist* (operatic sketches)
Gounod, Charles, *Symphony No. 2 in E-flat Major*
　　Ste. Cecilia Mass
　　L'employ de la journée (song cycle)
Halévy, Jacques, *Jaguarita l'indienne* (opera)
　　L'inconsolable (opera)
Lalo, Edouard, *String Quartet in E-flat Major*
Liszt, Franz, *Graner Mass*
　　Prelude and Fugue on B-A-C-H (organ)
Massé, Victor, *Les saisons* (opera)
　　Miss Fauvette (opera)
Moniuszko, Stanislaw, *Mass in E Minor*
Offenbach, Jacques, *Arlequin barbier* (operetta)
　　Une nuit blanche (operetta)
　　Les deux aveugles (operetta)
　　Entrez, messieurs, mesdames (operetta)
Pacini, Giovanni, *Niccolò de' Lapi* (opera)
Reinecke, Carl, *Der vierjährige Posten* (opera)
Rossi, Lauro, *La sirena* (opera)
Rubinstein, Anton, *Das verlorene Paradies* (oratorio)
Saint-Saëns, Camille, *Symphony in E-flat Major, Opus 2*
　　Mass, Opus 4
Smetana, Bedrich, *Piano Trio, Opus 15*
　　3 Polkas for Piano, Opus 7
Southard, Lucien, *The Scarlet Letter* (opera)
Spohr, Louis, *String Quartet, Opus 152*
Thalberg, Sigismond, *Cristina de Svezia* (opera)
Thomas, Ambroise, *La cour de Célimène* (opera)
Verdi, Giuseppe, *Sicilian Vespers* (opera)

1856

World Events:

In the U.S., James Buchanan is elected as President No. 15; the first convention of the newly formed Republican party takes place; Bloody Kansas is the catch word for the Potawatomie Massacre over the slavery question; Dallas, Texas, is incorporated; the Western Union Co. is founded; future President Woodrow Wilson is born. Internationally, the Crimean War ends with Russian control of southeastern Europe broken; the Congress of Berlin settles the Eastern question and points of international law involved; Great Britain goes to war with China; the Bessemer Process revolutionizes the steel industry; psychiatrist Sigmund Freud is born.

Cultural Highlights:

The National Portrait Gallery opens in London; Théophile Gautier becomes editor of *L'Artiste*; Gabriel J. Legouvé is taken into the French Academy; Victor Massé joins the ranks of the Legion of Honor. Births in the literary field include British dramatist and critic George Bernard Shaw, novelist H. Rider Haggard, Greek poet Jean Moréas and French poet Arthur Rimbaud; deaths include German poet Heinrich Heine and American poet Thomas Doughty. Births in the art world include American artists John W. Alexander, Kenyon Cox and John Singer Sargent; deaths include French sculptor Pierre David (d'Angers), British sculptor Richard Westmacott and French artists Theodore Chasseriau and Paul Delaroche. Other highlights include:

Art: Ford Brown, *George Washington* (Union Square); Gustave Courbet, *Girls on the Bank of the Seine*; Eugène Delacroix, *The Sultan of Morocco*; Arthur Hughes, *The Eve of St. Agnes*; Jean-Auguste Ingres, *La Source*; John Millais, *The Blind Girl*; William Mount, *The Banjo Player*; Erastus Palmer, *The Indian Girl*

Literature: Charles Aïde, *Eleanore*; Sergei Aksakov, *Chronicles of a Russian Family*; Berthold Auerbach, *Barfüssele*; Heinrich Heine, *Last Poems*; Victor Hugo, *Les Contemplations*; Henrik Ibsen, *The Banquet at Solhaug*; Herman Melville, *The Piazza Tales*; Harriet B. Stowe, *Dred: A Tale of the Great Dismal Swamp*

MUSICAL EVENTS

A. Births:

Jan 2	Alma Fohstrom (Fin-sop)	Jun 8	Natalia Janotha (Pol-pn)
Jan 6	Giuseppe Martucci (It-cd-cd)	Jul 7	Marie Letta (Am-sop)
Jan 11	Christian Sinding (Nor-cm)	Jul 9	Daniel Guggenheim (Am-ind)
Jan 18	John H. Brewer (Am-org)	Jul 19	Emil Götze (Ger-ten)
Jan 25	Wilhelm Heckel (Ger-inv)	Jul 23	Arthur Bird (Am-pn)
Feb 16	Willem Kes (Hol-vn-cd)	Aug 24	Felix Mottl (Aus-cd)
Feb 27	Mattia Battistini (It-bar)	Sep 25	José Tragó (Sp-pn)
Feb 28	Marie Brema (Br-alto)	Nov 2	Oskar Fleischer (Ger-mus)
Mar 9	Frantisek Blatt (Cz-cl)	Nov 25	Sergei Taneiev (Rus-pn)
Apr 7	J. A. Fuller-Maitland (Br-mus)	Dec 2	Robert Kajanus (Fin-cm)
May 3	Max Alvary (Ger-ten)	Dec 27	André Gedalge (Fr-cm-the)

B. Deaths:

Jan 6	Robert N. Bochsa (Fr-hp)	Jun 11	F. H. van der Hagen (Ger-mus)
Feb 17	John Braham (Br-ten)	Jul 29	Robert Schumann (Ger-cm)
Feb 21	Theodor Döhler (It-cm)	Jul 31	Giulio Bordogni (It-ten)
Mar 16	Piotr Turtchaninov (Rus-cm)	Aug 5	Robert de Pearsall (Br-cm)
Apr 18	Joseph Menter (Ger-cel)	Aug 20	Philipp J. Riotte (Ger-cd)
May 3	Adolphe Adam (Fr-cm)	Aug 21	Peter von Lindpaintner (Ger-cd)
May 3	Adolfo Fumagalli (It-pn)	Oct 14	Joseph K. Mertz (Hun-gui)
May 21	Friedrich von Drieberg (Ger-cm)	Nov 17	William Knyvett (Br-c.ten)
Jun 5	Stephen Jenks (Am-cm)		

C. Debuts:
U.S. -- Charles R. Adams (Boston), Sigismond Thalberg (tour)

Other - Mily Balakirev (St. Petersburg), Franz Betz (Hanover), Thomas Cook (Manchester), August G. Fricke (Berlin), Helen Lemmens-Sherrington (London), Barbara Marchisio (Vicenza), Carlotta Marchisio (Madrid), Minna Peschka-Leutner (Breslau), Hans von Rokitansky (London), Helen Warnots (Liège)

D. New Positions:
Conductors: William Sterndale Bennett (London PO), Antonio Cognoni (maestro di cappella, Vigevano), Ludwig F. Hetsch (Mannheim SO), Alexander Ritter (Stettin Opera), Ferdinand Schulz (Berlin Cäcicienverein), Bedrich Smetana (Göteborg PO)

Educational: William Sterndale Bennett (professor, Cambridge), Edward Hanslick (music esthetics, Vienna University), Carl Reissiger (director, Dresden Conservatory), Ambroise Thomas (composition, Paris Conservatory)

Others: Anton Bruckner (organ, Linz Cathedral), George Cooper (organ, Chapel Royal, London), John Goss (composer, Chapel Royal, London), Heinrich Oberhoffer (organ, St. Michael's, Brussels), Renaud de Vilback (St. Eugène, Paris)

E. Prizes and Honors:
Prizes: Jules Delaunay (Prix de Rome), Charles Lecocq (Offenbach), Arthur Sullivan (Mendelssohn)

Honors: William Sterndale Bennett (honorary doctorate, Cambridge), Hector Berlioz (French Institute), Victor Massé (Legion of Honor)

F. Biographical Highlights:
Marianna Barbieri-Nini retires from the operatic stage; Georges Bizet wins the second Prix de Rome; Alexander Borodin graduates with honors from the Academy of Medicine in St. Petersburg and joins the staff of the medical school; Emmanuel Chabrier moves with his family to Paris; Laure Cinti-Damoreau retires; Jeanne Cruvelli retires from the operatic stage; Julius Eichberg leaves Switzerland and goes to New York; Antonio Giuglini makes his La Scala debut; Louis Moreau Gottschalk begins a five-year tour of the West Indies; Jullien loses much of his music in a Covent Garden fire; Vladimir Kashperov goes to Berlin to study music with Dehn; Modeste Mussorgsky graduates from the Cadet School and joins the regular guard; Maria Dolores Nau retires from the stage; Marietta Piccolomini makes her London debut; Nicolai Rimsky-Korsakov enters the Naval College in St. Petersburg; Pablo Sarasate is sent to Paris to study at the Conservatory; Clara Schumann moves to Berlin to be with her mother; Therese Tietjens and Gustav Walter make their Vienna Opera debuts.

G. Institutional Openings:
Performing Groups: Cincinnati PO; Coenen String Quartet (Holland); Nottingham Sacred Harmonic Society; Verein für Kirchlichen Gesang (Hanover)

Educational: Dresden Conservatory of Music; Royal Military School of Music (Twickenham)

Other: American Music Association (N.Y.); L'Armonia (Italy); Bolshoi Opera Theater II (Moscow); Casa Romero, Music Publishers (Spain); Deutsche Händelgesellschaft; École Saint Simeon (Le Havre); Free Trade Hall (Manchester); Leuckart Publishing House (Germany); A. Lundquist, Music Publisher (Stockholm); Mendelssohn Scholarship; Teatro de la Zarzuela (Madrid); Teatro Solis (Montevideo); Wurlitzer Organ Co. (Cincinnati)

H. Musical Literature:

Ambros, August, *Die Grenzen der Musik und Poesie*
Baumgartner, August, *Kurzgefasste geschichte der musikalischen Notation*
Blaze, François H., *Sur l'opéra Français*
Blaze, Henri, *Musiciens contemporains*
Boucheron, Raimondo, *La Scienza dell'armonia...*
Coussemaker, Charles, *Histoire de l'harmonie au Moyen-Age*
Hastings, Thomas, *Sacred Praise*
Köhler, Louis, *Systematische lehrmethode für Klavierspiel und Musik I*
Laurencin, Ferdinand, *Zur geschichte der Kirchenmusik bei den Italienern und Deutschen*
Morelot, Stéphane, *De la musique au XV Siècle*

I. Musical Compositions:

Adam, Adolphe, *Le Corsaire* (ballet)
Auber, Daniel, *Manon Lescaut* (opera)
Balakirev, Mily, *Concerto Movement, Opus 1, for Piano and Orchestra*
    Octet, Opus 3, for Woodwinds and Strings
Benoit, Peter, *A Mountain Village* (opera)
Bizet, Georges, *David* (cantata)
Bradbury, William, *Esther* (cantata)
Brahms, Johannes, *Variations on an Original Theme, Opus 21, No. 1*
    Variations on a Hungarian Theme, Opus 21, No. 2
    Chorale, Prelude and Fugue, "O Traurigkeit," for Organ
Bristow, George, *Overture, A Winter's Tale, Opus 70*
Bruch, Max, *String Quartet, Opus 9*
Cornelius, Peter, *Brautlieder* (song cycle)
    Weihnachtslieder, Opus 8
Dargomijsky, Alexander, *Russalka* (opera)
Dorn, Heinrich, *Ein Tag in Russland* (opera)
Flotow, Friedrich von, *Albin* (opera)
    Die Libelle (ballet)
Foster, Stephen, *Gentle Annie* (song)
Gade, Niels, *Symphony No. 6, Opus 32*
Gounod, Charles, *Jésus de Nazareth* (cantata)
Halévy, Jacques, *Valentine d'Aubigny* (opera)
Kalliwoda, Johann, *Concert Overture No. 14, Opus 206*
    Variations and Rondo, Opus 57, for Bassoon and Orchestra
Lecocq, Charles, *Le docteur Miracle* (operetta)
Liszt, Franz, *Dante Symphony*
    Concerto No. 1 in E-flat Major for Piano and Orchestra
Maillart, Louis, *Les dragons de Villars* (opera)
Massé, Victor, *La reine Topaze* (opera)
Mosonyi, Mihály, *Symphony No. 2 in A Minor*
Offenbach, Jacques, *Ba-ta-clan* (operetta)
    Le savetier et le Financier (operetta)
    La bonne d'enfants (operetta)
    Les bergers de Watteau (ballet)
Pedrotti, Carlo, *Tutti in maschera* (opera)
Ponchielli, Amilcare, *I promessi sposi* (opera)
Saint-Saëns, Camille, *Symphony in F Major, "Urbs Roma"*
    6 Bagatelles for Piano
Spohr, Louis, *String Quartet, Opus 155*
Wagner, Richard, *Die Walküre* (opera)

1857

World Events:
In the U.S., overspeculation results in a financial panic; the Dred Scott decision is handed down by the Supreme Court; Michigan State University becomes the first Land Grant College under the Department of Agriculture; the National Teacher's Association is formed; Omaha, Nebraska, and Minneapolis, Minnesota, are incorporated; future President William Henry Taft is born. Internationally, the Sepoy Rebellion against British rule begins in India; Persia surrenders to the British; the French take over in Algeria; the Italian National Association is formed by Garibaldi in an attempt to unify Italy; a new liberal constitution is drawn up for Mexico.

Cultural Highlights:
The Victoria and Albert Museum opens in London; the American Institute of Architects is formed; Currier and Ives' prints first appear in New York; James Russell Lowell become editor of *Atlantic Monthly*; Charles F. Daubigny is taken into the Legion of Honor, Eugène Delacroix into the French Institute. Births in the field of art include American sculptors Alexander Doyle and Edward C. Potter, artist Bruce Crane and German artist Max Klinger; deaths include American sculptor Thomas Crawford, German sculptor Christian Rauch and Norwegian artist Johan C. Dahl. Births in the literary world include Scottish poet John Davidson, Danish author Hendrik von Pontoppidan, Polish novelist Joseph Conrad, British author George Gissing, Norwegian dramatist Gunnar Heiberg and German novelist Hermann Sudermann; deaths include French poets Pierre de Béranger and Alfred de Musset, novelist Marie Joseph Sue, Spanish poet Manuel Quintana and German poet Joseph von Eichendorff. Other highlights include:

Art: Antoine-Louis Barye, *Napoleon Dominating History and the Arts*; George Bingham, *Jolly Flatboatmen in Port*; Arnold Böcklin, *Pan in the Bulrushes*; Gustave Courbet, *Hunting Party*; Thomas Crawford, *Armed Freedom*; George Inness, *Indian Pastoral Scene*; Ernest Meissonier, *The Blacksmith*; John Millais, *Escape of the Heretic*

Literature: Charles Baudelaire, *Les Fleurs du Mal*; Elizabeth Browning, *Aurora Leigh*; Charles Dickens, *Little Dorrit*; Alexander Dumas, fils, *La Question d'Argent*; Octave Feuillet, *La Petite Comtesse*; Gustave Flaubert, *Madame Bovary*; Thomas Hughes, *Tom Brown's Schooldays*; Charles de Lisle, *Poèmes et Poèsies*

MUSICAL EVENTS

A. Births:

Jan 5	David Bispham (Am-bar)	May 12	Lillian Nordica (Am-sop)
Jan 17	Wilhelm Kienzl (Aus-cm)	Jun 2	Edward Elgar (Br-cm)
Jan 20	Sam Franko (Am-vn-cd)	Aug 18	Eusebius Mandyczewski
Jan 31	James Huneker (Am-cri)		(Rom-mus)
Feb 2	Jan Drozdowski (Pol-mus)	Sep 6	Benjamin Cutter (Am-the)
Feb 21	Nicolai Figner (Rus-ten)	Oct 20	Leandro Campanari (It-vn)
Feb 25	Hermine Spies (Ger-alto)	Oct 24	Charles Hedmont (Am-ten)
Mar 3	Louis A. Bruneau (Fr-cm)	Oct 31	Julie Rivé-King (Am-pn)
Mar 4	Gustav Kobbé (Am-cri)	Nov 10	Waldo S. Pratt (Am-m.ed)
Mar 8	Ruggero Leoncavallo (It-cm)	Nov 17	Rose Lucille Caron (Fr-sop)
Apr 14	Edgar S. Kelley (Am-org)	Dec 27	Charles Manners (Ir-bs-imp)

B. Deaths:

Jan 20	Edward Fitzwilliam (Br-cm)	Sep 18	Karol Kurpinski (Pol-cm-cd)
Feb 14	Johannes van Bree (Hol-cm-cd)	Sep 23	John Sinclair (Scot-ten)
Feb 15	Mikhail Glinka (Rus-cm)	Nov 18	Clara Heinefetter (Ger-sop)
May 4	Jacob N. Ahlström (Swe-cm)	Nov 19	James Davie (Scot-cd)
Jul 15	Carl Czerny (Aus-pn)	Dec 11	François Blaze (Fr-mus)

C. Debuts:
U.S. -- Karl Johann Formes (N.Y.), Theodor Formes (tour), Erminia Frezzolini (N.Y.),

Other - Victoire Balfe (London), Bronislawa Dowiakowska-Klimowiczowa (Warsaw), Emil Fischer (Graz), Angelo Masini (Modena), Nicolini (Paris), Friedrich Niecks (Düsseldorf), Charles Santley (Paris), Teresa Stolz (Tiflis), Louise Wippern (Berlin)

D. New Positions:
Conductors: Daniel Auber (maître de chapelle, Napoleon), Jean J. Bott (kapellmeister, Meiningen), Gaetano Gaspari (maestro di cappella, S. Petronio, Bologna), Georg A. Schmitt (Schwerin Court), Karl Stör (Weimar)

Educational: Pascual Arriete y Corera (composition, Madrid Conservatory), Charles Dancla (violin, Paris Conservatory), Hermann Langer (music director, Leipzig University), Karel Miry (harmony, Ghent Conservatory), Ludwig Stark (theory, Stuttgart Conservatory)

Others: Alexandre Guilmant (organ, St. Nicholas, Boulogne), Hermann Küster (organ, Berlin Cathedral and Court), Camille Saint-Saëns (organ, Madeleine, Paris)

E. Prizes and Honors:
Prizes: Peter Benoit and George Bizet (Prix de Rome)

F. Biographical Highlights:
Leopold Auer enters the Vienna Conservatory for further music study with Dont; Charles Bataille's career is interrupted by serious throat problems; Dudley Buck goes to Leipzig to study at the Conservatory; Hans von Bülow marries Cosima Liszt; Edouard Colonne enters the Paris Conservatory; César Cui graduates from the Military Engineering Academy in St. Petersburg; Prosper Dérivis retires from the stage; Antonin Dvorák enters the Prague Organ School; Julius Eichberg emigrates to the U.S.; William S. Gilbert graduates from the University of London and begins working as a clerk; Antonio Giugliani makes his London debut; Louis Moreau Gottschalk tours South America; Vladimir Kashperov begins an eight-year Italian stay; Modest Mussorgsky, through Dargomijsky, meets Balakirev and Cui; Arthur Sullivan enters the Royal Academy in London; Giuseppe Verdi leaves Paris to return to Italy; Henri Vieuxtemps, along with Sigismond Thalberg, makes a second U.S. concert tour; Richard Wagner moves to the Asyl on the Wesendonck's property.

G. Institutional Openings:
Performing Groups: Adelaide Liedertafel (Australia); Brooklyn PO; Gürzenichkonzerte (Cologne); National Opera of Rio de Janeiro; Pine-Harrison English Opera Co. (London)

Festivals: Handel Festival (Crystal Palace)

Educational: American Academy of Music (Philadelphia); Imperial Academy of Music (Rio de Janeiro); Peabody Conservatory (Baltimore); Stuttgart Musikschule

Other: Friedrich Ehrbar Organ Factory (Vienna); Forsyth Brothers, Ltd., Music Publishers (Manchester); Gebethner and Spólka (and Wolff, 1860), Music Publishers (Warsaw); Hohner Harmonica Factory (Trossingen); Keller's Patent Steam Violin Manufactory (Philadelphia); W. W. Kimball Co., Music Publishers (Chicago); *La Maîtrise* (Paris); *Ruch Muzyczny* (Polish music magazine); Santiago Municipal Theater (Chile); George Steck and Co., Piano Makers (N.Y.); Charles Taphouse and Son, Ltd., Music Dealers (Oxford); Teatro Colón (Buenos Aires)

H. Musical Literature:
Balfe, Michael, *A New Universal Method of Singing*
Child, Francis J., *English and Scottish Popular Ballads*
Emerson, Luther, *The Golden Wreath*

Fodor-Mainvielle, Joséphine, *Reflexions et conseils sur l'art du chant*
Halévy, Jacques, *Leçons de lecture musicale*
Hering, Karl F., *Methodischer leitfaden für Violinlehrer*
Niedermeyer/d'Ortigue, *Méthode d'accompagnement du plain-chant*
Proksch, Josef, *Allgemeine musiklehre*
Rimbault, Edward, *The Organ, Its History and Construction*
Sowinski, Wojciech, *Les Musiciens polonais et slaves, anciens et modernes*
Viner, William, *The Chanter's Companion*

I. Musical Compositions:

Alkan, *12 Etudes in Minor Keys, Opus 39, for Piano*
Balakirev, Mily, *Overture on a Spanish March Theme*
Balfe, Michael, *The Rose of Castilla* (opera)
Bizet, Georges, *Doctor Miracle* (operetta)
  Cloris et Clothilde (cantata)
Brahms, Johannes, *Serenade No. 1 in D Major, Opus 11*
Cui, César, *2 Orchestral Scherzi, Opus 1 and 2*
David, Félicien, *6 Esquisses Symphoniques for Piano*
Dorn, Heinrich, *Ein tag in Russland* (opera)
Flotow, Friedrich von, *Johann Albrecht* (opera)
  Pianella (opera)
Fry, William H., *Overture, World's Own*
Genée, Richard, *Der Geiger aus Tirol* (operetta)
Hopkins, J. H., *We Three Kings of Orient Are* (carol)
Joachim, Joseph, *Concerto, Opus 11, "Hungarian," for Violin and Orchestra*
Liszt, Franz, *Die Ideale* (tone poem)
  The Battle of the Huns (tone poem)
  The Legend of St. Elizabeth (oratorio)
Mabellini, Teodulo, *Fiammetta* (opera)
Massé, Victor, *Le cousin de Marivaux* (operetta)
Mercadante, Saverio, *Pelagio* (opera)
Moniuszko, Stanislaw, *Military Overture*
Mosonyi, Mihály, *Kaiser Max auf der Martinswand* (opera)
Mussorgsky, Modest, *Souvenirs d'enfance* (piano)
Offenbach, Jacques, *Croquefer* (operetta)
  Dragonette (operetta)
  Une demoiselle en lôterie (operetta)
  Les deux pêcheurs (operetta)
Pacini, Giovanni, *Sant-Agnese* (oratorio)
Reinecke, Carl, *Dame Kobold Overture*
Root, George, *The Haymakers* (cantata)
Smetana, Bedrich, *Richard III, Opus 11* (symphonic poem)
Southard, Lucien, *Omano* (opera)
Spohr, Louis, *Symphony No. 10 in E-flat Major*
  String Quartet, Opus 157
  Requiem (unfinished)
Thomas, Ambroise, *Psyché* (opera)
  Le carnaval de Veniçe (opera)
  Messe Solennelle
Verdi, Giuseppe, *Simon Boccanegra* (opera)
Wagner, Richard, *Wesendonck Songs*

1858

World Events:
In the U.S., the Lincoln and Douglas debates take place all around Illinois; Minnesota becomes State No. 32; Denver, Colorado, is founded; a stagecoach line is established between St. Louis and San Francisco; the first American YWCA opens in New York; Squibb Phamaceutical Lab is founded; the Esterbrook Pen factory opens; future President Theodore Roosevelt is born. Internationally, the Sepoy Rebellion ends and the India Act passed by Parliament makes India a Crown Colony; Cyrus Field lays the first Atlantic Cable which soon breaks; the Treaties of Tientsin ends the British-Chinese war and opens China for exploitation by the European Powers; F. Carre introduces the refrigerator.

Cultural Highlights:
Weimar Art School opens its doors; János Arany is inducted into the Hungarian Academy, Pierre de Laprade into the French Academy and Richard Hubbard into the National Academy in Washington; Albert Bierstadt returns to the U.S. and joins a wagon train to the Pacific. In the art world, Russian artist Lovis Corinth is born and Dutch artist Ary Scheffer and American sculptor Hezekiah Augur die. Births in the literary field include American author Charles Chesnutt, Belgian poet Iwan Gilkin, French author Remy de Goncourt, Irish novelist Edith Somerville and Swedish novelist and poetess Selma Lagerlöf. Other highlights include:

Art: Albert Bierstadt, *Yosemite Valley*; Gustave Courbet, *The Polish Exile*; Charles Daubigny, *Le Printemps*; Eugène Delacroix, *Fording a Stream in Morocco*; William Frith, *Derby Day*; Edwin Landseer, *Trafalgar Square Lions*; Adolf von Menzel, *Bon Soir, Messieurs*; Erastus Palmer, *The White Captive*; James Whistler, *Self-Portrait*

Literature: Wilhelm Busch, *Max und Moritz*; Alphonse Daudet, *Les Amoreuses*; George Eliot, *Scenes from Clerical Life*; Octave Feuillet, *Roman d'un Jeune Homme Pauvre*; Oliver W. Holmes, *The Autocrat at the Breakfast Table*; Henry W. Longfellow, *The Courtship of Miles Standish*; Ivan Turgenev, *A Nest of Gentlefolk*

MUSICAL EVENTS

A. Births:

Jan 6	Ben Davies (Br-ten)	May 24	Camille Bellaigue (Fr-cri)
Feb 10	Karl Pohlig (Ger-cd)	Jun	Antonio Pini-Corsi (It-bar)
Feb 15	Marcella Sembrich (Pol-sop)	Jul 16	Eugène Ysaÿe (Bel-vn)
Feb 18	Max Hesse (Ger-pub)	Aug 15	Emma Calvé (Fr-sop)
Feb 19	Tobias Matthay (Br-pn)	Sep 8	Romualdo Sapio (It-cd)
Feb 24	Arnold Dolmetsch (Br-mus)	Sep 15	Jenö Hubay (Hun-vn)
Feb 24	Eugène Oudin (Am-bar)	Oct 12	Georges Servières (Fr-mus)
Mar 27	Peter C. Lutkin (Am-hymn)	Nov 7	Luigi Torchi (It-mus)
Apr 12	Michel Brenet (Fr-mus)	Nov 11	Alesandro Moreschi (It-cas)
Apr 16	Stanislaw Barcewicz (Pol-vn)	Dec 22	Giacomo Puccini (It-cm)
Apr 19	Siegfried Ochs (Ger-cd)	Dec 25	Hermann Devries (Am-bs)
Apr 23	Ethel Smyth (Br-cm)	Dec 25	Francis W. Galpin (Br-mus)
May 6	Georges A. Hüe (Fr-cm)		Guy d'Hardelot (Fr-cm)

B. Deaths:

Jan 23	Luigi Lablache (It-bs)	Apr 23	Pauline Duchambge (Fr-pt-cm)
Mar 8	William Ayrton (Br-cri)	May 31	Guillaume Gand (Fr-vn.m)
Apr 3	Sigismund v. Neukomm (Aus-pn)	Jun 3	Julius Reubke (Ger-pn)
Apr 7	Anton Diabelli (Aus-cm-pub)	Jun 12	William Horsley (Br-org)
Apr 12	Siegried W. Dehn (Ger-the)	Aug 24	Francis E. Bache (Br-pn)
Apr 13	Bernard Sarrette (Fr-cd)	Sep 11	Alexander Gurilyov (Rus-cm)
Apr 16	Johann B. Cramer (Ger-pub)	Sep 15	Johann Mosewius (Ger-ten)

Oct 26   Isaac Woodbury (Am-cm)
Nov 7   Carl Reissiger (Ger-cm)
Nov 9   Karl Holz (Aus-vn-cd)
Nov 27   Hermann G. Dorn (Ger-cm)

Dec 18   Joseph H. Mees (Hol-cm-cd)
Dec 27   Alexandre Boëly (Fr-org)
Dec 30   Kathinka Heinefetter (Ger-sop)

C. Debuts:
U.S. -- Benjamin Lang (Boston), Arthur Napoleão (tour)

Other - Carlo Andreoli (Milan), Georg E. Arlberg (Stockholm), Desirée Artôt (Paris), Gabrielle Krauss (Berlin), Sebastian Bach Mills (Leipzig), Franz Nachbaur (Meiningen), John Patey (London), Bernhard Pollini (Cologne), Raoul Pugno (Paris), Ludwig Schnorr von Carolsfeld (Karlsruhe), Carl Tausig (Berlin)

D. New Positions:
Conductors: Luigi Arditi (Her Majesty's Theatre, London), Leopold Damrosch (Breslau PO), Otto von Königslöw (Gürzenich Orchestra, Cologne), Ignaz Lachner (kapellmeister, Stockholm), Eduard Lassen (kapellmeister, Weimar), Stanislaw Moniuszko (Warsaw Conservatory), Anton Rubinstein (St. Petersburg Court)

Educational: Heinrich Döring (piano, Dresden Conservatory), Josef Krejci (director, Prague Organ School), Karl Mikuli (director, Lvov Conservatory)

Others: Franz Espagne (head, music division, Royal Library, Berlin), Filippo Filippi (editor, *Gazzetta Musicale*), César Franck (organ, Ste. Clothilde), Louis Lefébure-Wély (organ, St. Sulpice), Karl Reinthaler (organ, Bremen Cathedral)

E. Prizes and Honors:
Prizes: Samuel David (Prix de Rome)

Honors: Thomas Hastings (honorary doctorate, N.Y. University)

F. Biographical Highlights:
Luigi Arditi settles in London as conductor and voice teacher; Mily Balakirev suffers from encephalitis; Charles-Auguste de Bériot becomes completely blind; Alexander Borodin receives his doctorate in chemistry from the St. Petersburg Academy of Medicine; Max Bruch begins teaching violin in Cologne; Emanuel Chabrier begins studying law in Paris; Charles de Coussemaker, while gathering information on music, is appointed a judge in Lille; Edvard Grieg, on the advice of Ole Bull, is sent to the Leipzig Conservatory for further music study; Hermann Levi graduates from the Leipzig Conservatory; Barbara and Carlotta Marchisio make their joint debut at La Scala; Eugène Massol retires from the operatic stage; Pietro Mongini debuts at La Scala; Modest Mussorgsky resigns his cadet commission in order to concentrate on music; John Knowles Paine goes to Berlin for music study; Sigismond Thalberg buys a villa near Naples; Theodore Thomas, on a moment's notice, conducts Halévy's *La Juive*, sight unseen; Therese Tietjens makes her London debut; Richard Wagner goes to Venice as Minna leaves for Germany.

G. Institutional Openings:
Performing Groups: Edinburgh Royal Choral Union; Hallé Orchestra (Manchester); Metropolitan Choral Society of Toronto; Milwaukee Liedertafel; Popular Concerts of Chamber Music (London); Vienna Singverein

Festivals: Worcester Music Festival (Massachusetts)

Educational: Vienna Academy of Music

Other: Covent Garden Theater III; *Dalibor*; Matthias Gray Co., Music Publishers (San Francisco); Musical Society of London; Root and Cady, Music Publishers (Chicago), Russell and Tolman, Music Publishers (Boston), St. James Hall (London)

H. Musical Literature:

Bazin, François, *Cours d'harmonie théorique et pratique*
Bellermann, Heinrich, *Die Mensuralnoten und Taktzeichen*
Bradbury, William, *The Jubilee*
Fétis, François, *Memoire sur l'harmonie simultanée*
Gollmick, Karl, *Handlexicon der Tonkunst*
Köhler, Louis, *Systematische Lehrmethode für Klavierspiel und Musik*
Kosmaly, Carl, *Über die Anwendung des Programmes zur Erklärung musikalischen Compositionen*
Kullak, Adolph, *Das Musikalisch-Schöne*
L'vov, Alexei, *On Free or Non-Symmetrical Rhythm*
Sieber, Ferdinand, *Vollständiges Lehrbuch der Gesangkunst für Lehrer und Schüler*
Tuckerman, Samuel, *A Collection of Cathedral Chants*

I. Musical Compositions:

Balakirev, Mily, *Overture on Three Russian Themes*
Balfe, Michael, *Satanella* (opera)
Berlioz, Hector, *Les Troyens* (opera)
Berwald, Franz, *2 Piano Quintets*
Brahms, Johannes, *Ave Maria, Opus 12*
    Funeral Hymn, Opus 13
    8 Songs and Romances, Opus 14
    14 Folksongs, Books I and II
Bristow, George, *Symphony No. 3, Opus 26*
Bruch, Max, *Scherz, List und Rache* (opera)
Cornelius, Peter, *The Barber of Bagdad* (opera)
Cui, César, *The Prisoner of the Caucasus* (opera)
David, Félicien, *The Last Judgment* (oratorio)
David, Samuel, *Jephté* (cantata)
Franck, César, *Messe Solennelle*
    3 Motets
Gade, Niels, *Frühlings-Botschaft, Opus 35* (cantata)
    Baldur's Dream (cantata)
Gevaert, François, *Quentin Durward* (opera)
Gounod, Charles, *Le médecin malgré lui* (opera)
Halévy, Jacques, *La magicienne* (opera)
Hiller, Ferdinand, *Saul* (oratorio)
Kalliwoda, Johann, *Concert Overture No. 15, Opus 226*
Liszt, Franz, *Hamlet* (tone poem)
    Huldigungs Marsch
Marschner, Heinrich, *Sangeskönig Hiarne* (opera)
Moniuszko, Stanislaw, *The Raftsman* (opera)
Mussorgsky, Modeste, *Scherzo in C-sharp Minor for Piano*
    Scherzo in B-flat Major for Orchestra
Offenbach, Jacques, *Orpheus in the Underworld* (operetta)
    Mariage aux lanternes (operetta)
    Mesdames de la Halle (operetta)
Pacini, Giovanni, *Il saltimbanco* (opera)
    La distruzione di Gerusalemme (oratorio)
Raff, Joseph J., *Barnhard von Weimar* (incidental music)
Rubinstein, Anton, *Paradise Lost* (oratorio)
Saint-Saëns, Camille, *Concerto No. 1, Opus 17, for Piano and Orchestra*
Strauss, Johann, Jr., *Tritsch-Tratsch Polka*
    Champagne Polka
Vieuxtemps, Henri, *Concerto No. 5, Opus 37, for Violin and Orchestra*
Vogel, Charles, *Le nid de cigognes* (opera)
Wells, Marcus, *Holy Spirit, Faithful Guide* (hymn)

1859

World Events:

In the U.S., the first oil well is drilled in Titusville, Pennsylvania, by Edwin Drake; the Comstock Lode is discovered in Nevada, causing a new rush; a Gold Rush is also started in Colorado; Oregon becomes State No. 33; the Pawnee War takes place in the Nebraska Territory; John Brown raids Harper's Ferry. Internationally, the Franco-Italian War with Austria over the Sardinia territory closes with the Treaty of Zurich; the German National Association is formed for a Germany united under the leadership of Prussia; work begins in Egypt on the Suez Canal; Oscar I of Sweden dies and is succeeded by Charles XV.

Cultural Highlights:

The National Gallery of Scotland opens in Edinburgh; the National Gallery of Victoria opens in Melbourne, Australia; *Macmillian's Magazine* begins publication; Eduard Bendemann becomes director of the Dresden Academy of Art; Feodor Dostoyevsky, given amnesty, returns from Siberian exile. Births in the art world include American artists Childe Hassam, Maurice Prendergast and Henry O. Tanner and French artist Georges Seurat; deaths include British artist David Cox and German sculptor Konrad Eberhard. Births in the literary field include British poets Alfred E. Housman and Francis Thompson and novelist Arthur Conan Doyle, Italian poet Guido Mazzoni, Swedish poet Werner von Heidenstam, novelist Knut Hamsun and French novelist and poet Gustave Kahn; deaths include American author Washington Irving, French historian Alexis de Tocqueville and poet Marceline Desbordes-Valmores, German authors Bettina von Arnim and Wilhelm Grimm, British author Thomas Macaulay and poet Leigh Hunt and Russian novelist Sergei Aksakov. Other highlights include:

Art: Albert Bierstadt, *Thunderstorm in the Rockies*; Edward Burne-Jones, *Merlin and Nimue*; Jean-Baptiste Corot, *Macbeth*; Henri Fantin-Latour, *The Two Sisters*; Eastman Johnson, *My Old Kentucky Home*; Jean-François Millet, *The Angelus*; William Page, *Venus*; R. Spencer Stanhope, *Thoughts of the Past*; James Whistler, *Black Lion Wharf*

Literature: William Barnes, *Hwomely Rhymes*; Charles Darwin, *The Origin of Species*; Charles Dickens, *A Tale of Two Cities*; George Eliot, *Adam Bede*; Washington Irving, *The Life of George Washington*; George Meredith, *The Ordeal of Richard Feverel*; Alfred Lord Tennyson, *The Idylls of the King*; William Thackeray, *The Virginians*

MUSICAL EVENTS

A. Births:

Jan 15	Andrew Black (Scot-bar)	Sep 19	Hugo Goldschmidt (Ger-mus)
Jan 20	Rudolf Schwartz (Ger-cm)	Oct 14	Camille Chevillard (Fr-cd)
Jan 21	Karl Scheidemantel (Ger-bar)	Oct 22	Karl Muck (Ger-cd)
Feb 1	Victor Herbert (Am-cm-cd)	Oct 26	Arthur Friedheim (Ger-pn)
Feb 5	Jules Combarieu (Fr-mus)	Nov 1	William H. Flood (Ir-mus)
Feb 7	Emma Nevada (Am-sop)	Nov 19	M. Ippolitov-Ivanov (Rus-cm)
Feb 9	Robert Hope-Jones (Br-org.m)	Nov 22	Cecil Sharp (Br-folk-cm)
Mar 21	Henry W. Savage (Am-imp)	Nov 28	Winthrop Sterling (Am-org)
Apr 3	Reginald de Koven (Am-cm)	Nov 29	Charles Farnsworth (Am-org)
Apr 4	Medea Figner (It-sop)	Dec 27	William H. Hadow (Br-mus-cm)
Jul 14	Willy Hess (Ger-vn-cd)	Dec 30	Josef B. Foerster (Boh-cm)
Aug 8	Léon Escalaïs (Fr-ten)		Emilie Herzog (Ger-sop)

B. Deaths:

Feb 19	John Abbey (Br-org.m)	Apr 14	Ignaz Bösendorfer (Aus-pn.m)
Mar 14	Nicola Tacchinardi (It-ten)	Jun 18	Joseph H. Stuntz (Ger-cd)
Mar 30	Philippe Musard (Fr-cm-cd)	Jul 18	Anton Forti (Aus-bar)
Apr 13	Angiolina Bosio (It-sop)	Aug 18	Antonio d'Antoni (It-cd)

Aug 28 Edward Holmes (Br-cri)
Oct 22 Louis Spohr Ger-cm)
Nov 2 Charles Knyvett, Jr. (Br-org)

Nov 4 Christian Fischer (Ger-bs)
Nov 24 Henry Forbes (Br-pn)
Dec 31 Luigi Ricci (It-cm)

C. Debuts:
U.S. -- Sebastian Bach Mills, Adelina Patti (N.Y.)

Other - Célestine Galli-Marié (Strasbourg), Pauline Lucca (Olmütz), Angelo Neumann (Vienna), Francesco Pandolfini (Pisa), Georgine Schubert (Hamburg), Zélia Trebelli (Madrid)

D. New Positions:
Conductors: Johann Herbeck (Gesellschaft der Musikfreunde, Vienna), Hermann Levi (Saarbrücken), Ludvig Norman (Stockholm PO), Carl Reinecke (Breslau University)

Educational: Woldemar Bargiel (theory, Cologne Conservatory), Immanuel Faisst (head, Stuttgart Conservatory), Oskar Kolbe (theory, Stern Conservatory), Julius Leonhard (piano, Dresden Conservatory), Teodulo Mabellini (composition, Istituto Reale Musicale, Florence), Ernst Pauer (piano, Royal Academy, London), Joseph Rheinberger (piano, Munich Conservatory)

Others: Filippo Filippi (music critic, *Perseveranza*), Charles Kingsley (chaplain to Queen Victoria), Edwin G. Monk (organ, York Cathedral), Anton Rubinstein (director, Russian Musical Society), Peter I. Tchaikovsky (clerk, Ministry of Justice, St. Petersburg)

E. Prizes and Honors:
Prizes: Ernest Guiraud and Jean-Théodore Radoux (Prix de Rome)

F. Biographical Highlights:
Jean Becker begins his career as a violin virtuoso; Johannes Brahms is given a women's chorus to conduct in Hamburg, but is not successful in his endeavor; Peter Cornelius meets his idol Wagner and visits in Vienna; Enrico Delle Sedie and Nicolini make their La Scala debuts; Antonin Dvorák graduates and begins playing violin in various bands; Jean Baptiste Faure marries singer Constance Lefebvre; Jullien, returning to Paris, is arrested and imprisoned over his outstanding debts and dies shortly in an insane asylum; Gabrielle Krauss makes both her Vienna and Paris debuts; Pietro Mongini makes his London debut; Ebenezer Prout gives up teaching and devotes himself completely to music; Charles Santley makes his Covent Garden debut; Pablo Sarasate begins a concert tour of Europe; Alexander Serov, on a study trip to Germany, meets Wagner and becomes his ardent disciple; Peter Tchaikovsky graduates from the School of Jurisprudence in St. Petersburg and becomes a government clerk; Theodore Thomas begins his conducting career; Giuseppe Verdi finally marries singer Giuseppina Strepponi; Richard Wagner moves to Paris where he is rejoined by Minna.

G. Institutional Openings:
Performing Groups: Concerts Spirituales (Madrid); Gilmore's Grand Band (Boston); Imperial Russian Music Society (St. Petersburg)

Festivals: Welsh Music Festival (Aberdare)

Educational: Florentine Liceo Musicale

Other: Aberdeen Music Hall; John Church and Co. (Philadelphia); Elkan and Schildknecht, Music Publishers (Stockholm); Förster Piano Co. (Lobau, Germany); French Opera House (New Orleans); Gebauer Music Publishers (Bucharest); Giudici and Strada, Music Publishers (Turin); Göteborg Grand Theater; Gutheil Music House (Moscow); J. H. and C. S. Odell, Organ Builders (N.Y.); *Le Plain-Chant*; *Revue Fantaisiste*; *The Southern Musical Advocate and Singer's Friend*; Viktoria Theater

(Berlin)

H. Musical Literature:
Berlioz, Hector, *Les Grotesques de la musique*
Bertrand, Jean G., *Histoire ecclesiastique de l'orgue*
Dehn, Siegfried, *Lehre vom Kontrapunkt, dem Kanon und der Fuge*
Hohmann, Christian H., *Praktische Orgelschule*
Karasowski, Moritz, *History of Polish Opera*
Knorr, Julius, *Ausführliche Klaviermethode*
Liszt, Franz, *Des Bohemiens...en Hongrie*
Lobe, Johann C., *Aus dem Leben eines Musikers*
Richter, Ernst F., *Lehrbuch der Fuge*
Sobolewski, Eduard de, *Das Geheimmis der neuesten Schule der Musik*

I. Musical Compositions:
Alkan, *Funeral March on the Death of a Parrot* (piano)
Auber, Daniel, *Magenta* (opera)
Bizet, Georges, *Vasco da Gama* (symphonic poem)
    Don Procopio (opera)
Bradbury, William, *Sweet Hour of Prayer* (hymn)
Brahms, Johannes, *Serenade No. 2, Opus 16*
    Marienlieder, Opus 22, for Chorus
    Piano Trio, Opus 8
    5 Songs, Opus 19
Cui, César, *Tarantella for Orchestra, Opus 12*
    The Mandarin's Son (opera)
David, Félicien, *Herculanum* (opera)
David, Samuel, *Le Génie de la Terre*
Emmett, Daniel, *Dixie* (song)
Flotow, Friedrich von, *La veuve Grapin* (opera)
    Wintermärchen (incidental music)
Gade, Niels, *Judith* (operatic fragments)
Gevaert, François, *Le diable au moulin* (opera)
Gottschalk, Louis M., *Escenas Campestres* (opera)
    Symphony No. 1, "A Night in the Tropics"
    Souvenir de Porto Rico (piano)
Gounod, Charles, *Faust* (opera)
    Ave Maria (on Bach's *Prelude No. 1*)
Halévy, Jacques, *Les plages du Nil* (cantata)
    Italie (cantata)
Liszt, Franz, *The Beatitudes* (cantata)
Loewe, Carl, *Das hohe lied Salomonis* (oratorio)
Macfarren, George, *Christmas Cantata*
Meyerbeer, Giacomo, *Le pardon de Ploërmel* (opera)
    Schiller Centenary March
Offenbach, Jacques, *Geneviève de Brabant* (operetta)
    Un mari à la porte (operetta)
    Les vivandières de la grande armée (operetta)
Pedrotti, Carlo, *Isabella d'Aragona* (opera)
Saint-Saëns, Camille, *Concerto No. 1, Opus 20, for Violin and Orchestra*
Verdi, Giuseppe, *The Masked Ball* (opera)
Wagner, Richard, *Tristan und Isolde* (opera)

1860

World Events:
In the U.S., the Census shows a population of 31,443,000, a 35% increase in 10 years; Abraham Lincoln is elected as President No. 16; the first and only convention of the Constitutional Union Party is held; Pony Express service begins between St. Joseph, Missouri, and Sacramento, California. Internationally, the Second Maori War ushers in 10 years of strife in New Zealand; F. Walton introduces linoleum; Picinotti invents the first continuous current dynamo; the British Open Golf Tournament holds its first open; Vladivostok, Siberia, is founded.

Cultural Highlights:
The magazine *L'Artiste* begins publication in Canada; Nathaniel Hawthorne returns to Concord after 7 years in Europe. Births in the art field include American primitive painter, "Grandma" Moses and sculptor Thomas Clarke, British sculptor George Frampton, Belgian artist James Ensor and Swedish artist Anders L. Zorn; deaths include American artist Rembrandt Peale, British artist Alfred E. Chalon, German artist Johannes Riepenhausen and French artist Alexandre Decamps. Births in the literary field include Russian novelist Anton P. Chekhov, British novelist James Barrie, American author Hamlin Garland and poet Clinton Scollard; deaths include German philosopher Arthur Schopenhauer and poet Ernst M. Arndt, Dutch poet Isaäc DaCosta and Russian author Konstantin Aksakov. Other highlights include:

Art: Edgar Degas, *Spartan Girls and Boys Exercising*; Eugène Delacroix, *Horses Fighting*; William Dyce, *Pegwell Bay*; William Hunt, *The Boy Jesus in the Temple*; Eastman Johnson, *Cornhusking*; Édouard Manet, *Spanish Guitar Player*; John E. Millais, *The Black Brunswicker*; Jean-François Millet, *Woman Carrying Water*.

Literature: Elizabeth Browning, *Poems before Congress*; Wilkie Collings, *Woman in White*; George Eliot, *The Mill on the Floss*; Nathaniel Hawthorne, *The Marble Faun*; Oliver W. Holmes, *The Professor at the Breakfast Table*; Coventry Patmore, *Faithful Forever*; Algernon Swinburne, *The Queen Mother*; John Greenleaf Whittier, *Home Ballads*

MUSICAL EVENTS

A. Births:

Jan 9	Laura V. Aulin (Swe-pn)	Jun 25	Gustave Charpentier (Fr-cm)
Jan 18	Lillian Henschel (Am-sop)	Jul 3	Vilém Hes (Cz-bs)
Jan 31	James G. Huneker (Am-cri)	Jul 3	Théodore Reinach (Fr-mus)
Feb 23	Celeste Heckscher (Am-cm)	Jul 7	Gustav Mahler (Aus-cm-cd)
Feb 28	Mario Ancona (It-bar)	Jul 7	Arthur Prüfer (Ger-mus)
Mar 13	Hugo Wolf (Ger-cm)	Aug 6	Francesco Frontini (It-cm)
Mar 22	Otto Barblan (Swi-org)	Sep 1	Cleofonte Campanini (It-cd)
Mar 28	Josef Mantuani (Aus-mus)	Sep 18	Alberto Franchetti (It-cm)
Mar 30	Georges Houdard (Fr-mus)	Sep 22	Heinrich Rietsch (Aus-mus)
Apr 22	Alexander Bandrowski-Sas (Pol-ten)	Oct 11	Fernando de Lucia (It-ten)
May 4	Emil Reznicek (Aus-cm)	Oct 16	Emilio Pente (It-vn-cm)
May 5	Pietro Floridia (It-pn)	Oct 24	Luise Reuss-Belce (Aus-sop)
May 29	Isaac Albéniz (Sp-cm)	Nov 18	Ignace Jan Paderewski (Pol-pn)
			Hariclea Darclée (Rom-sop)

B. Deaths:

Jan 26	Wilhemine Schröder-Devrient (Ger-sop)	Mar 13	Guglielmo Andreoli (It-pn)
		Mar 14	Louis A. Jullien (Fr-cd)
Feb 29	George Bridgetower (Pol-vn)	Mar 28	Ludwig Böhner (Ger-pn-cm)
Mar 6	Friedrich Dotzauer (Ger-cel)	Apr 29	Nanette Schechner-Waagen (Ger-sop)

Aug 26	Friedrich Silcher (Ger-cm)	Oct 6	Stephen Elvey (Br-org)
Sep 25	Carl Zöllner (Ger-cd-cm)	Nov 5	Karl Binder (Aus-cm-cd)
Oct 2	Julius Cornet (Aus-ten)	Nov 27	Ludwig Rellstab (Ger-cri)

C. Debuts:
U.S. -- Inez Fabbri, Giovanni Sbriglia (N.Y.)

Other - Isabella Galleti-Gianoli (Brescia), Melitta Otto (Dresden), Guido Papini (Florence), Janet Patey (Birmingham), Angela Peralta (Mexico), Emil Scaria (Pest), Sophie Stehle (Munich)

D. New Positions:
Conductors: Hans Balatka (Chicago Philharmonic Society), Joaquim Casimiro Júnior (mestre de capela, Lisbon Cathedral), Felix Dessoff (Vienna Opera), Pierre-Louis Dietsch (Paris Opera), Karl Eckert (Stuttgart Opera), Julius O. Grimm (Münster SO), Eduard Lassen (Weimar Opera), Carl Reinecke (Leipzig Gewandhaus), Théophile Tilmant (Concerts du Conservatoire, Paris), Johannes Verhulst (Diligentia Concerts, The Hague)

Educational: Vilém Blodek (flute, Prague Conservatory), Pierre Chevillard (cello, Paris Conservatory), Carl Davidov (cello, Leipzig Conservatory), Immanuel Faisst (director, Stuttgart Conservatory), Daniel de Lange (cello, Lvov Conservatory), Franz von Lenbach (professor Weimar Academy), Ernst Naumann (music director, University of Jena), Eugène Sauzay (violin, Paris Conservatory), Otto Scherzer (music director, Tübingen University)

Others: Joseph Rheinberger (organ, St. Michael's, Munich), Charles Marie Widor (organ, St. François, Lyons)

E. Prizes and Honors:
Prizes: Emile Paladilhe (Prix de Rome)

F. Biographical Highlights:
George Bizet leaves Rome to return to Paris; Dudley Buck goes to Dresden to study music; Antonio Cotogni makes his La Scala debut; Jean Baptiste Faure makes his London debut; Edvard Grieg suffers a nervous breakdown and pleurisy which leaves him a cripple for life; Minnie Hauk moves with her family to New Orleans; George Macfarren becomes totally blind; Clara Novello gives her farewell performance in London and retires to Italy; Ede Reményi is given amnesty and returns to become court violinist in Vienna; Hans Richter studies at the Vienna Conservatory; Charlotte Sainton-Dolby marries Prosper Sainton; Ludwig Schnorr von Carolsfeld marries soprano Malvina Garriques; Giuseppe Verdi is elected a Deputy to the first Italian National Parliament; Richard Wagner is given amnesty in all of the German states except Saxony--he writes the Paris version of *Tannhauser*; Henryk Wieniawsi marries Isabella Hampton and settles in Russia.

G. Institutional Openings:
Performing Groups: Amateur Musical Society (Hawaii); Asociación Artistico-Musical de Socorros Mutuos (Madrid); Boulogne Philharmonic Society; Canterbury Vocal Union (New Zealand); Duitse Opera (Rotterdam); Märkischen Zentral-Sängerbund (Berlin); Musik-Dilettantenverein (Bayreuth); Newark Harmonic Society; St. Louis Philharmonic Society; Société des Concerts de Chant Classique (Paris); Vienna Orchesterverein

Educational: Frankfurt Musikschule; Istituto Musicale (Florence)

Other: *Deutsche Musikzeitung*; Heintzman and Co., Ltd., Piano Makers (Toronto); Hopwood and Crew, Music Publishers (London); Elias Howe Publishing Firm II (Boston); Mariinsky (Kirov) Theater (St. Petersburg); Russian Musical Society;

Zenészeti Lapok (Hungary)

H. Musical Literature:

Clément, Félix, *Histoire générale de la Musique religieuse*
Coussemaker, Charles, *Drames liturgiques de Moyen-Age*
Elwart, Antoine, *Histoire de la Société des concerts du Conservatoire*
Emerson, Luther, *The Golden Harp*
Knorr, Julius, *Ausführliche Klaviermethode: Schule der Mechanik*
Macfarren, George, *The Rudiments of Harmony*
Nisard, Théodore, *Le vrais principes de l'accompagnement du plain-chant*
Oliver, Henry, *Oliver's Collection of Hymn and Psalm Tunes*
Poisot, Charles, *History of Music in France*
Rimbault, Edward, *The Pianoforte: Its Origin, Progress and Construction*
Weitzmann, Carl, *Harmoniesystem*

I. Musical Compositions:

Auber, Daniel, *La circassienne* (opera)
Balfe, Michael, *Bianca* (opera)
Benoit, Peter, *Cantate de Noël*
Bizet, Georges, *Vasco da Gamba* (ode-symphony)
Brahms, Johannes, *String Sextet No. 1, Opus 18*
 4 Part-Songs, Opus 17 (women's voices)
 2 Motets, Opus 29 (a capella chorus)
 3 Duets, Opus 20
Bruch, Max, *String Quartet in E Major*
Foster, Stephen, *Old Black Joe* (song)
 Camptown Races (song)
 Virginia Belle (song)
Franck, César, *Mass, Opus 12*
Fry, William Henry, *Evangeline Overture*
Gevaert, François, *Le Chateau Trompette* (opera)
Goldmark, Karl, *Symphony in C Major*
 String Quartet In D Major, Opus 8
Gottschalk, Louis M., *Grand Tarentelle* (piano)
 Grand March for Orchestra
Gounod, Charles, *Philémon et Baucis* (opera)
Liszt, Franz, *2 Episodes from Lenau's Faust*
 Les Morts (orchestra)
Loewe, Carl, *Polus von Atella* (oratorio)
Macfarren, George, *Robin Hood* (opera)
Maillart, Louis, *Les pêcheurs de Catane* (opera)
Meyerbeer, Giacomo, *La Jeunesse de Goethe* (opera)
Moniuszko, Stanislaw, *Verbum nobile* (opera)
Mosonyi, Mihály, *Festival Music for Orchestra*
Offenbach, Jacques, *Le Papillon* (ballet)
 Daphnis et Chloé (operetta)
 Carnaval des revues (operetta)
Root, George, *Belshazzar's Feast* (cantata)
Saint-Saëns, Camille, *Macbeth* (opera)
 Scenes from Horace, Opus 10
Smetana, Bedrich, *Song of the Czechs* (cantata)
 Wallenstein's Camp, Opus 14 (symphonic poem)
Strauss, Johann, Jr., *Perpetual Motion* (orchestra)
Suppé, Franz von, *Tannhäuser* (operetta)
 Das Pensionat (operetta)
Thomas, Ambroise, *Le roman d'Elvire* (opera)
Vieuxtemps, Henri, *Concerto, Opus 37, "Grétry," for Violin and Orchestra*

1861

World Events:

In the U.S., the Civil War begins--the Battle of Bull Run takes place; West Virginia chooses to stay with the Union and secedes from Virginia; Kansas becomes State No. 34; the Dakota Territory is formed; Denver, Colorado, is incorporated; Yale University gives the first Ph.D. in America; Vassar College is chartered. Internationally, Czar Alexander II emancipates the Russian serfs; Victor Emmanuel II of Sardinia is crowned and Italian Unification begins; Pedro V of Portugal dies and is succeeded by Louis I; Abdul Aziz succeeds to the Turkish throne.

Cultural Highlights:

The Czech literary society, Kolo, is founded; Albert F. Bellows is inducted into the National Academy; Mark Twain begins his travels through the American west. Births in the literary field include American author John Luther Long, Irish poet Katherine Tynan, Indian poet Rabindranath Tagore, Canadian poet William Campbell and Swedish novelist Axel Lundegard; deaths include French dramatist Augustin Scribe, Russian poets Taras Shevchenko and Ivan Nikitin, British poets Elizabeth Browning and Arthur Clough, Italian poet Giovanni Niccolini and Scottish poet David Gray. Births in the art world include American Frederic Remington and sculptor Cyrus E. Dallin, French artists Émile Bourdelle, Louis Anquetin and sculptor Aristide Maillol; deaths include American artist Samuel Waldo and sculptor Benjamin Akers, German sculptor Ernst Rietschel and Irish artist Francis Danby. Other highlights include:

Art: Jean-Baptiste Carpeaux, *Ugolino and His Sons*; Jean-Baptiste Corot, *Le Lac de Terni*; Gustave Courbet, *The Stag Fight*; Eugène Delacroix, *The Lion Hunt*; Gustave Doré, *Dante's Inferno*; Ernest Meissonier, *The Emperor at Solferino*; Joseph Paton, *Luther at Erfurt*; William Rimmer, *The Falling Gladiator*.

Literature: Berthold Auerbach, *Edelweiss*; Charles Dickens, *Great Expectations*; Feodor Dostoyevsky, *The House of the Dead*; George Eliot, *Silas Marner*; Thomas Hughes, *Tom Brown at Oxford*; Henry Kingsley, *Ravenshoe*; Henry W. Longfellow, *Paul Revere's Ride*; Charles Reade, *The Cloister and the Hearth*; Alexei Tolstoy, *Don Juan*.

MUSICAL EVENTS

A. Births:

Jan 15	Vasily Andreyev (Rus-bal)	Jun 25	Theodor Gerlach (Ger-cd)
Jan 30	Charles M. Loeffler (Fr-cm)	Jun 27	Fanny Davies (Br-pn)
Mar 6	Karl Waack (Ger-cd)	Jul 6	Clifford Curzon (Br-pn)
Mar 20	Sigrid Arnoldson (Swe-sop)	Jul 12	Anton Arensky (Rus-cm)
Apr 2	Ernest Van Dyck (Bel-ten)	Jul 23	Nahan Franko (Am-vn-cd)
Apr 14	Jean François Delmas (Fr-bs)	Jul 24	Lionel de Laurencie (Fr-mus)
May 16	Albert Alvarez (Fr-ten)	Jul 24	Maurice Renaud (Fr-bar)
May 19	Nellie Melba (Aust-sop)	Aug 18	Selma Kronold (Pol-sop)
Jun 15	Ernestine Schumann-Heink	Sep 6	Frank T. Arnold (Br-mus)
	(Aus-sop)	Oct 8	Marie van Zandt (Am-sop)
Jun 20	Arthur Whiting (Am-pn)	Dec 18	Edward MacDowell (Am-pn-cm)
		Dec 29	Walter Alcock (Br-org)

B. Deaths:

Jan 22	Giovanni Velutti (It-cas)	Jun 6	Giuseppe Concone (It-voc-ed)
Feb 12	Hippolyte Chélard (Fr-vn-cm)	Jun 17	Julius Knorr (Ger-pn)
Mar 10	C. H. Eisenbrandt (Ger-inst.m)	Jul 17	Christian F. Barth (Den-ob)
Mar 14	Louis Niedermeyer (Swi-cm)	Jul 17	James Bland (Br-bs)
Mar 17	Petter Boman (Swe-mus)	Aug 9	Vincent Novello (Br-pub)
Mar 28	Joseph Staudigl, Sr. (Ger-bs)	Aug 11	Catherine Hayes (Ir-sop)
May 3	Anthony Heinrich (Cz-vn-cm)	Aug 29	Franz Glaser (Boh-cm)

Sep 14 Fortunato Santini (It-mus)	Dec 20 Carl Proske (Ger-mus)
Dec 14 Heinrich Marschner (Ger-cm)	Dec 29 Alexandre Boucher (Fr-vn)
Dec 16 Karl Lipiński (Pol-vn)	Horace Meacham (Am-pn.m)

C. Debuts:

U.S. -- William Castle (N.Y.), Clara Louise Kellogg (N.Y.), Carlotta Patti (N.Y.)

Other - John Francis Barnett (London), Joseph-Amédée Capoul (Paris), Jean Morère (Paris), Jean Baptiste Sbriglia (Naples), Jeannie Winston (Sydney)

D. New Positions:

Conductors: Niels Gade (kapellmeister, Danish Court), Hermann Levi (Rotterdam Opera), Matteo Salvi (Vienna Opera)

Educational: Charles-Aimable Battaille (voice, Paris Conservatory), Hermann Berens (composition, Stockholm Conservatory), Antoine L. Clapisson (harmony, Paris Conservatory), Joseph Dachs (piano, Vienna Conservatory), Eduard Hanslick (professor, University of Vienna), Apollinaire de Kontski (director, Warsaw Conservatory), Johann C. Lauterbach (violin, Dresden Conservatory), Ebenezer Prout (piano, Crystal Palace School of Art), Camille Saint-Saëns (piano, École Niedermeyer)

Others: Gustav E. Engel (music critic, *Vossiche Zeitung*), Johannes E. Habert (organ, Gmunden), William Rust (organ, St. Luke's, Leipzig), Arthur Sullivan (organ, St. Michael's, London)

E. Prizes and Honors:

Prizes: Théodore Dubois (Prix de Rome)

Honors: Robert Franz (honorary doctorate, Halle University), Jacques Offenbach (Legion of Honor), William Spark (honorary doctorate, Dublin University)

F. Biographical Highlights:

August Wilhelm Ambros begins 8 years of collecting archival materials for his history of music book; Emmanuel Chabrier graduates from law school and begins to work in the Ministry of the Interior; Robert Franz receives his masters degree from Halle University; Louis Moreau Gottschalk leaves the West Indies for the U.S. when the Civil War begins; Edvard Grieg returns to Leipzig for further music study; Franz Liszt goes to Rome to seek Vatican approval for his marriage to the Princes Sayn-Wittgenstein but is turned down; Jacques Offenbach resigns his position as manager of the Théâtre de la Gaîte; John Knowles Paine returns to Boston; Charles Parry enters Eton; Adelina Patti makes her Covent Garden debut; Bedrich Smetana resigns his Göteborg post and returns to Prague to lead the Nationalist movement in music; Arthur Sullivan returns to London; Peter Tchaikovsky travels through western Europe.

G. Institutional Openings:

Performing Groups: Akademischer Gesangverein (Munich); Biscacciante Opera Co. (San Francisco); Concerts Populaire de Musique Classique (Paris); Denver City Band; Heidelberg Kammerorchester; Hlahol Choral Society (Prague Male Chorus); Music Society of Victoria (Melbourne); Società del Quartetto di Firenze (Florence); Wuppertal Konzertgesellschaft

Educational: Brooklyn Academy of Music; Katski (Kontski) Music Conservatory (Warsaw); London Royal Academy of Music; University of Edinburgh Music Department

Other: Allgemeiner Deutscher Musikverein; American Cabinet Organ; Collection Litolff; Frankfurt Concert Hall; Harrison and Harrison, Organ Builders (Rochdale); P.I. Jurgensen, Music Publisher (Moscow); Morris and Co. (London); Prix Chartier (Paris); *Revue Musicale Suisse (Schweizerische Musikzeitung)*

H. Musical Literature:

Battaille, Charles, *Nouvelles recherches sur la phonation*
Bradbury, William, *Golden Chain of Sabbath School Melodies*
Eslava, Hilarión, *Escuela de armonía y composición*
Laurencin, Ferdinand, *Die Harmonik der Neuzeit*
Lobe, Johann C., *Vereinfachte harmonielehre*
d'Ortigue, Joseph, *La musique à l'eglise*
Palgrave, F., *Golden Treasury of Songs and Lyrical Poems I*
Reissmann, August, *Das deutsche Lied in seiner historischen Entwicklung*
Savard, Augustin, *Principes de la musique*
Weitzmann, Carl, *Die neue harmonielehre im Streit mit der Alten*

I. Musical Compositions:

Alkan, *Chants, Set III, for Piano*
Balakirev, Mily, *King Lear* (incidental music)
Balfe, Michael, *The Puritan's Daughter* (opera)
Becker, Albert, *Symphony in G Minor*
Benvenuti, Tommaso, *Guglielmo Shakespeare* (opera)
Bizet, Georges, *Overture, La chasse d'Ossian*
    Scherzo and Funeral March
Brahms, Johannes, *Variations on a Theme by Schumann, Opus 23*
    Variations and Fugue on a Theme by Handel, Opus 24
    Piano Quartets No. 1 and 2, Opus 25 and 26
    3 Songs for Male Voices, Opus 42
Bristow, George, *Columbus Overture, Opus 32*
    Praise to God (oratorio)
Bruckner, Anton, *Ave Maria* (a capella chorus)
    Fugue in D Minor or Organ
Chélard, Hippolyte, *L'Aquila romana* (opera)
Dubois, Théodore, *Atala* (cantata)
Dvoràk, Antonin, *String Quintet, Opus 1*
Dykes, John, *Nicaea* (hymn tune, "Holy, Holy, Holy")
Flotow, Friedrich von, *Der Tanzkönig* (ballet)
    Violin Sonata, Opus 14
Gade, Niels, *Hamlet Overture, Opus 37*
    Michelangelo Overture, Opus 39
    The Holy Night, Opus 40 (cantata)
Gevaert, François, *Les deux amours* (opera)
Gomes, Antonio C., *Noite do Castello* (opera)
Liszt, Franz, *12 Part Songs for Chorus*
Loewe, Carl, *Johannes der Täufer* (oratorio)
Mosonyi, Mihály, *Pretty Helen* (opera)
Offenbach, Jacques, *La chanson de Fortunio* (operetta)
    Apothécaire et perruquier (operetta)
    Le pont des soupirs (operetta)
Pedrotti, Carlo, *Mazeppa* (opera)
    Guerra in quattro (opera)
Ponchielli, Amilcare, *La savojarda* (opera)
Raff, Joseph, *Symphony No. 1, Opus 98, "An das Vaterland"*
Reyer, Louis, *La statue* (opera)
Rubinstein, Anton, *Die Kinder der Heide* (opera)
Sullivan, Arthur, *The Tempest* (incidental music)
Thomas, Ambroise, *Gille et Gillotin* (opera)
Wallace, Vincent, *The Amber Witch* (opera)
Wieniawski, Henryk, *Légende, Opus 17, for Violin and Orchestra*

1862

World Events:
In the U.S., the Civil War Battles of Shiloh and Antietam take place as does the second battle of Bull Run; on the seas, the *Monitor* and the *Merrimac* engage in the first battle between iron-clad boats; Slavery is abolished in the District of Columbia; the Congressional Medal of Honor is created; the Department of Agriculture is created; the Great Northern and the Union Pacific railroads are formed; former Presidents John Tyler and Martin Van Buren die. Internationally, Otto von Bismarck becomes Chancellor of Prussia; Otto I of Greece resigns after a revolution and is succeeded by George I; Richard Gatling patents the Gatling Gun; L. Foucault measures the speed of light; the London International Exposition is held.

Cultural Highlights:
Births in the art world include American artists Arthur B. Davies and Edmund C. Tarbell, Canadian sculptor Alexander Proctor and Austrian artist Gustav Klimt. Births in the literary field include American authors W.S. Porter, better known as O'Henry, and Edith Wharton, Belgian dramatist Maurice Maeterlinck, British novelist Eden Phillpotts and poet Henry Newbolt, German dramatist Wilhelm Meyer-Förster and author Gerhart Hauptmann, Swedish novelist Tor Hedberg and French novelist Marcel Prévost; deaths include Austrian poets Ignaz Castelli and Joseph von Zedlitz, German author Ludwig Fulda and poets Andreas Kerner and Johann Uhland, Danish novelist and poet Bernhard Ingemann, Russian poet Lev Alexandrovich Mei and American author Henry Thoreau. Other highlights include:

Art: Honoré Daumier, *Third-Class Carriage*; William Frith, *The Railway Station*; Robert Gifford, *Kauterskill Falls*; Jean-Auguste Ingres, *Bain Turque*; Wilhelm von Kaulbach, *Battle of Salamis*; Édouard Manet, *The Old Musician*; Jean-François Millet, *Planting Potatoes*; Pierre-Auguste Renoir, *Sleeping Cat*; Moritz von Schwind, *The Honeymoon*.

Literature: Ventura Aguilera, *Elegías*; Charles Browne, *Artemus Ward: His Book*; Elizabeth Browning, *Last Poems*; Gustave Flaubert, *Salammbó*; Victor Hugo, *Les Misérables*; Charles de Lisle, *Poèmes Barbares*; Christina Rosetti, *Goblin Markets*; William Thackeray, *The Adventures of Philip*; Ivan Turgenev, *Fathers and Sons*

MUSICAL EVENTS

A. Births:

Jan 6	Frances Saville (Am-sop)		Aug 11	Carrie Jacob Bond (Am-cm)
Jan 9	Guglielmo Andreoli II (It-pn)		Aug 22	Claude Debussy (Fr-cm)
Jan 29	Frederick Delius (Br-cm)		Sep 2	Alphons Diepenbrock (Hol-cm)
Jan 30	Walter Damrosch (Ger-cd)		Sep 25	Léon Boëllmann (Fr-org)
Feb 17	Edward German (Br-cm)		Oct 15	Conrad Ansorge (Ger-pn)
Mar 12	George Anthes (Ger-ten)		Nov 1	Johan Wagenaar (Hol-org)
Mar 13	Vassili Metallov (Rus-mus)		Nov 23	Alberto Williams (Arg-cm)
Apr 4	Wilhelm Altmann (Ger-mus)		Nov 25	Ethelbert Nevin (Am-cm)
Apr 5	Louis Ganne (Fr-cm-cd)		Dec 9	Karel Kovarovic (Cz-cd)
Apr 5	Leopold L. Stern (Br-cel)		Dec 18	Moriz Rosenthal (Pol-pn)
Jun 1	Alice Barbi (It-mez)		Dec 21	Zélie de Lussan (Am-sop)
Jun 11	Perry Averill (Am-bar)			

B. Deaths:

Jan 5	Joseph Fröhlich (Ger-cm)		Sep 29	Auguste Baumgartner (Ger-cm)
Feb 7	Franz Skroup (Cz-cd)		Nov 17	Alexei Vertovsky (Rus-cm)
Mar 4	George Perry (Br-cd)		Dec 25	Adolf Kullak (Ger-cri)
Mar 8	Juste de la Fage (Fr-mus)		Dec 28	J. Casimiro Júnior (Por-cm)
Mar 27	Jacques Halévy (Fr-cm)			Geltrude Righetti (It-alto)
Jul 2	Charles Mayer (Ger-pn)			

C. Debuts:

U.S. -- Nikodem Biernacki (tour), Teresa Carreño (N.Y.), Genevieve Ward

Other - Franz H. Celli (London), Carolina Ferni-Giraldoni (Turin), Daniel Filleborn (Warsaw), Wilhelm Fitzenhagen (Brunswick), Allen James (Signor) Foli (Catania), George Henschel (Berlin, as a pianist), Ilma di Murska (Florence), Louis Pabst (Königsberg), Anna Schimon-Regan (Siena), Eduard Strauss (Vienna), Vilma von Voggenhuber (Budapest), Sarah Edith Wynne (London)

D. New Positions:

Conductors: Carlo Barbieri (National Theater, Buda), Leopold Damrosch (Breslau)

Educational: Karl Davïdov (cello, St. Petersburg Conservatory), Alexander Dreyschock (piano, St. Petersburg Conservatory), Gustav Engel (voice, Kullak Academy, Berlin), Theodor Leschetizky (piano, St. Petersburg Conservatory), John Knowles Paine (Harvard Music School), Henri Reber (composition, Paris Conservatory), Anton Rubinstein (director, St. Petersburg Conservatory), Etienne-Joseph Soubre (director, Liège Conservatory), Henryk Wieniawski (violin, St. Petersburg Conservatory)

Others: Léo Delibes (organ, St. Jean-St. François, Paris), Adolphe Deslandres (organ, Ste. Marie, Paris), Marie-Auguste Durand (organ, St. Vincent de Paul, Paris), Filippo Filippi (critic, La Perseveranza), Edmund Kretschmer (organ, Dresden), James H. Mapleson (manager, Her Majesty's Theater)

E. Prizes and Honors:

Prizes: Louis Bourgault-Ducoudray (Prix de Rome)

Honors: Arrigo Boito (Government stipend), Léon Burbure de Wesembeck (Belgian Royal Academy), Félicien David, Théodore Labarre and Louis-Etienne Reyer (Legion of Honor), Octave Feuillet (French Academy), Joseph Mayseder (Order of Franz Joseph)

F. Biographical Highlights:

Charles Battaile retires from the stage; Alexander Borodin returns to Russia; Johannes Brahms, on tour, visits Vienna for the first time; Dudley Buck returns to the U.S. and begins teaching in Hartford; Enrico Delle Sedie and Theodor Wachtel make their Covent Garden debuts; Louis Moreau Gottschalk makes a second tour of the U.S.; Edvard Grieg graduates with honors and gives his first concert; Vincent d'Indy begins the study of harmony and piano; Barbara and Carlotta Marchisio make their joint London debut; Saverio Mercadante becomes totally blind; Nicolini makes his Paris debut; Jacques Offenbach becomes a naturalized French citizen; Adelina Patti makes her Paris Opera debut; Nicolai Rimsky-Korsakov begins a 3 year cruise around the world with the Russian Navy; Carl Tausig moves to Vienna and begins concertizing; Peter Tchaikovsky joins Anton Rubinstein's composition class; Zélia Trebelli makes her London debut; Richard Wagner is given amnesty by the Saxon government and makes a break with Minna.

G. Institutional Openings:

Performing Groups: Berliner Bachverein; Berne Caecilienverein; Breslau Orchestral Society; Brno Musikverein; Eidgenössicher Musikverein (Switzerland); Società del Quartetto (Turin); Theodore Thomas Orchestra; Zurich Male Chorus

Educational: Eduard Ganz Music School (Berlin); Harvard Music School; St. Petersburg Conservatory of Music

Other: Balakirev Circle; D.H. Baldwin Co. (Cincinnati); Elberfelder Kapelle; Robert Forberg Music Publishing Co. (Leipzig); Journal des Maîtrises (Paris); Musical Standard; Prague National Opera House; Ulster Hall (Belfast)

H. Musical Literature:

Ambros, August, *History of Music I*
Bellermann, Heinrich, *Der Kontrapunkt*
Chorley, Henry, *30 Year's Musical Recollections*
Edwards, Henry S., *History of the Opera from Its Origin in Italy to the Present Time*
Hogarth, George, *The Philharmonic Society of London*
Hullah, John, *History of Modern Music*
Köchel, Ludwig, *Chronologisch-thematisches Verzeichnis...Tonwerke...Mozarts*
Kothe, Bernhard, *Die Musik in der katholischen Kirche*
Reber, Henri, *Traité d'harmonie*
Vivier, Albert, *Traité complet d'harmonie*

I. Musical Compositions:

Benedict, Julius, *The Lily of Killarney* (opera)
    The Lake of Glenaston (opera)
Bennett, William S., *Overture-Fantasy, Paradise and the Peri*
Benoit, Peter, *Te Deum*
Berlioz, Hector, *Beatrice and Bénédict* (opera)
Berwald, Franz, *Estrella de Soria* (opera)
Bizet, Georges, *La guzla de l'emir* (opera)
Boito, Arrigo, *Le Sorelle d'Italia* (cantata)
Brahms, Johannes, *Soldatenlieder, Opus 41, for Male Voices*
    4 Duets, Opus 28
Bruckner, Anton, *Preiset den Herrn* (cantata)
    String Quartet in C Major
    Three Pieces for Orchestra
David, Félicien, *Lalla Rookh* (opera)
Delibes, Léo, *Mon ami Pierrot* (operetta)
Dvořák, Antonin, *String Quartet in A Major*
Flotow, Friedrich von, *Naida* (opera)
    Wilhelm von Oranien (incidental music)
Franck, César, *Fantasie in C Major, Opus 16* (organ)
    Grand Pièce Symphonique, Opus 17 (organ)
    Prélude, Fugue and Variations, Opus 18 (organ)
    Pastorale, Opus 19 (organ)
Franz, Robert, *Magelone Romance, Opus 33* (song cycle)
Fry, William, *Overture to MacBeth* (orchestra)
Gade, Niels, *Four Fantastic Pieces, Opus 41* (piano)
Goldmark, Karl, *String Quintet in A Minor, Opus 9*
Gottschalk, Louis M., *The Union* (piano)
Gounod, Charles, *La reine de Saba* (opera)
Grieg, Edvard, *Four Little Pieces, Opus 1*
Halévy, Jacques, *Noë* (opera--finished by Bizet)
Hiller, Ferdinand, *Die Katacomben* (opera)
Howe, Julia Ward, *Battle Hymn of the Republic* (song)
Massé, Victor, *Mariette la promisse*
Meyerbeer, Giacomo, *March Overture* (orchestra)
Offenbach, Jacques, *Jacqueline* (operetta)
    Monsieur et Madame Denis (operetta)
Smetana, Bedrich, *Hakon Jarl* (symphonic poem)
Suppé, Franz von, *Zehn Mädchen und kein Mann* (operetta)
    Die Kartenaufschlägerin (operetta)
    Voyage de Monsieur Dunanan (operetta)
Verdi, Giuseppe, *La forza del destino* (opera)
    Hymn of the Nations (tenor, chorus, orchestra)
Wieniawski, Henryk, *Concerto No. 2, Opus 22, for Violin and Orchestra*
Work, Henry C., *Kingdom Coming* (song)

1863

World Events:

In the U.S., the Civil War Battle of Gettysburg takes place in July; President Lincoln gives his Gettysburg Address in November; the Emancipation Proclamation is made public; Thanksgiving is made a National holiday; West Virginia becomes State No. 35; draft riots take place in New York; the National Bank Act is passed by Congress; Henry Ford is born. Internationally, Maximilian is made Emperor of a French Empire in Mexico; the first subway opens in London; an epidemic of Scarlet Fever breaks out in Europe; Ismail Pasha begins the modernization of Egypt; Frederick VII of Denmark dies and is succeeded by Christian IX.

Cultural Highlights:

Le Salon de Refusés opens in Paris; the Czech House of Art opens in Prague; the magazine *American Art Journal* begins publication; John Everett Millais is made a member of the Royal Academy. Births in the art field include American sculptors George Barnard, Henry Kitson, Frederick MacMonnies and artist Cecilia Beaux, Norwegian artist Edvard Munch and French artists Lucien Pissarro and Paul Signac; deaths include French artists Eugène Delacroix and Horace Vernet. Births in the literary world include the Germans Richard Dehmel, Gustav Frenssen and Arno Holz, Italian poet Gabriele d'Annunzio, French poet Adolphe Retté, Dutch novelist Louis Couperus, British novelist Anthony Hawkins and Spanish author George Santayana; deaths include American educator and poet Clement C. Moore, British novelist William Thackeray, Dutch author Florentius Kist, French poet Alfred de Vigny and German dramatist Christian Hebbel. Other highlights include:

Art: Albert Bierstadt, *The Bombardment of Fort Sumter*; Ford M. Brown, *Work*; Gustave Courbet, *The Trellis*; Honoré Daumier, *Crispin and Scapin*; Édouard Manet, *Dejeuner sur l'Herbe*; Jean-François Millet, *Man with the Hoe*; Dante Rosetti, *Beata Beatrix*; Elihu Vedder, *Questioner of the Sphinx*; James Whistler, *The White Girl*.

Literature: Louisa M. Alcott, *Hospital Sketches*; John Brown, *Marjorie Fleming*; Charles Dickens, *Our Mutual Friend*; Elizabeth Gaskell, *Sylvia's Lovers*; Edward E. Hale, *The Man without a Country*; Charles Kingsley, *The Water Babies*; Henry W. Longfellow, *Tales of a Wayside Inn*; Jules Verne, *Five Weeks in a Balloon*.

MUSICAL EVENTS

A. Births:

Jan 12	Willibald Nagel (Ger-mus)	Aug 16	Gabriel Pierné (Fr-cm)
Jan 18	Marie Renard (Aus-sop)	Sep 2	Isidore Philipp (Fr-pn)
Mar 4	Ellen Gulbranson (Swe-sop)	Sep 12	Benno Schönberger (Aus-pn)
Mar 12	Henry Expert (Fr-mus)	Sep 15	Horatio Parker (Am-cm-ed)
Mar 25	Alfred Kalisch (Br-cri)	Oct 9	Alexander Siloti (Rus-pn)
Apr 4	Ludwig Riemann (Ger-mus)	Oct 11	Xavier Leroux (Fr-cm)
Apr 21	Blanche Marchesi (Fr-sop)	Oct 24	Arnold Rosé (Rom-vn)
May 14	Paul H. Lebrun (Bel-cd-cm)	Nov 1	Alfred Reisemann (Ger-pn)
May 27	Franz Schalk (Aus-cd)	Dec 7	Pietro Macagni (It-cm)
Jun 2	Felix Weingartner (Aus-cd)	Dec 19	Milka Ternina (Yug-sop)
Jul 4	Emma Juch (Am-sop)	Dec 24	Enrique Arbós (Sps-cm-cd)
Jul 31	Richard Aldrich (Am-cri)		

B. Deaths:

Jan 28	Arthur T. Corfe (Br-org)	Mar 13	Emile Prudent (Fr-pn)
Feb 25	Laure Cinti-Damoreau (Fr-sop)	Jun 7	Franz Gruber (Aus-hymn)
Mar 8	Karl Albrecht (Ger-cm-cd)	Jun 12	Pietro Alfieri (It-mus-cm)
Mar 12	Edward Taylor (Br-m.ed)	Aug 5	Adolf F. Hesse (Ger-org)
May 6	Ferdinand Stegmeyer (Aus-cd)	Sep 18	Hermann Wollenhaupt (Ger-pn)

Nov 21   Joseph Mayseder (Aus-vn)   Dec 21   Désiré Beaulieu (Fr-cm)
Dec 19   Pierre I. Begrez (Fr-ten)

C. Debuts:

Other - Teresa Brambilla-Ponchielli (Odessa), Italo Campanini (Parma), John Carrodus (London), Edward Dannreuther (London), Clara Kathleen Rogers (Turin), Gustav Siehr (Neustrelitz), Agnes Zimmermann (London)

D. New Positions:

Conductors: Johannes Brahms (Vienna Singakademie), François Hainl (Paris Opera), Robert Radecke (Berlin Opera)

Educational: Marius P. Audran (director, Marseilles Conservatory), Michal Bergson (piano, Geneva Conservatory), Pablo Hernández (voice, Madrid Conservatory), Samuel de Lange (organ, Rotterdam Music School), Louis Lübeck (cello, Leipzig Conservatory)

Others: Yury Arnold (editor, *Neue Zeitschrift für Musik*), Joseph Barnby (organ, St. Andrews, London), Eugène Gigout (organ, St. Augustin, Paris), Edmund Kretschmer (organ, Dresden Court), Louis Lefébure-Wély (organ, St. Sulpice, Paris), Joseph Louis d'Ortigue (editor, *Le Ménestral*), George P. Upton (music critic, Chicago *Tribune*), Henry Clay Work (editor, *The Song Messenger*)

E. Prizes and Honors:

Prizes: Jules Massenet (Prix de Rome)

F. Biographical Highlights:

Leopold Auer studies violin with Joachim in Hanover; Charles-Aimable Battaille comes down with severe throat problems leading to his retirement from the opera stage; Alexander Borodin marries pianist Catherina Protopopova; Johannes Brahms fails to gain the Hamburg PO position he desires and meets Wagner; William S. Gilbert is called to the bar; Benjamin Godard enters the Paris Conservatory; Edvard Grieg spends time in Copenhagen and gets to meet Gade; Alexandre Guilmant inaugurates the new organ at St. Sulpice in Paris; Joseph Joachim marries contralto Amalie Weiss who gives up her career on the stage; Pauline Lucca makes her Covent Garden debut; Modest Mussorgsky begins a four-year stint as a clerk in the Russian Ministry of Communications; Carlotta Patti makes her London debut; Adelina Patti makes her first appearance in Vienna; Johann Strauss, Jr., is put in charge of all court balls in Vienna; Johan Svendsen enters the Leipzig Conservatory; Peter I. Tchaikovsky quits his government post in order to devote full time to music; Pauline Viardot-García retires from the stage.

G. Institutional Openings:

Performing Groups: Concerti Popolari a Grande Orchestra (Florence), Monte Carlo Opera Orchestra

Educational: Civica Scuola di Musica (Casale Monferrato), Giorgio Ronconi Vocal School (Granada)

Other: Albrecht and Co., Piano Makers (Philadelphia); *The Choir and Musical Record*; John Curwen and Sons, Ltd., Music Publishers (London); *Jahrbuch für Musikalische Wissenschaft*; Mathushek Piano Co. (N.Y.); Henry F. Miller and Sons Piano Co. (Boston); Philip Phillips, Music Publisher (Cincinnati); Player Piano (by Tourneaux in France); Société des Compositeurs de Musique (Paris)

H. Musical Literature:

Andries, Jean, *Précis de l'histoire de la musique...*
Battaille, Charles A., *De la physiologie appliquée au méchanisme du chant*
Daniel, Francisco S., *La musique arabe*

Emerson, Luther, *The Harp of Judah*
Gevaert, François, *Traité général d'instrumentation*
Hauff, Johann C., *Theorie der Tonsetskunst I*
Helmholtz, Hermann von, *On the Sensations of Tone...*
Köstlin, Karl R., *Aesthetik I*
Kunkel, Franz J., *Die neue Harmonielehre...*
Maier, Julius, *Auswahl englischer Madrigale*
Weitzmann, Carl, *Geschichte des Clavierspiele*

I. Musical Compositions:

Balfe, Michael, *Blanche de Nevers* (opera)
    The Armourer of Nantes (opera)
Benedict, Julius, *Richard the Lion-Hearted* (cantata)
Benoit, Peter, *Requiem*
Bizet, Georges, *The Pearl Fishers* (opera)
Brahms, Johannes, *Variations on a Theme of Paganini, Opus 35* (piano)
    12 Songs and Romances, Opus 44
    3 Vocal Quartets, Opus 31
    3 Sacred Choruses, Opus 37
Bruch, Max, *Die Loreley* (opera)
Bruckner, Anton, *Symphony in F Minor* (unpublished)
    Overture in G Minor (orchestra)
    Psalm CXII for Double Chorus and Orchestra
Delibes, Léo, *Le jardinier et son seigneur* (opera)
Dvorák, Antonin, *Scherzo Capriccioso, Opus 66, for Orchestra*
Fauré, Gabriel, *3 Romances sans Paroles, Opus 17* (piano)
Franck, César, *44 Little Pieces for Organ*
Fry, William, *Notre Dame de Paris* (opera)
Gade, Niels, *String Sextet in E-flat, Opus 44*
    Piano Trio in F Major, Opus 42
Goldmark, Karl, *Orchestral Scherzo, Opus 19*
Grieg, Edvard, *6 Poetic Tone Pictures, Opus 3* (piano)
    2 Symphonic Pieces, Opus 14, for Piano, 4 Hands
Liszt, Franz, *Variations, "Weinen, Klagen, Sorgen, Sagen"* (piano)
Loewe, Carl, *Die auferweckung des Lazarus* (oratorio)
Massé, Victor, *La mule de Pedro*
Massenet, Jules, *Ouverture de Concert, Opus 1* (orchestra)
Meyerbeer, Giacomo, *L'Africaine* (opera)
    Coronation March (orchestra)
Offenbach, Jacques, *Il Signor Fagotto* (operetta)
    Lischen et Fritzchen (operetta)
Ponchielli, Amilcare, *Roderico, re dei goti* (opera)
Root, George, *Battle Cry of Freedom* (song)
Rossini, Gioacchino, *Petite Messe Solennelle*
Rubinstein, Anton, *Feramors* (opera)
Saint-Saëns, Camille, *Oratorio de Noël*
Serov, Alexander, *Judith* (opera)
Sullivan, Arthur, *Procession March*
    Princess of Wales March
Suppé, Franz von, *Flotte bursche* (operetta)
    Das corps der rache (operetta)
Wallace, Vincent, *The Desert Flower* (opera)

1864

World Events:
In the U.S., Civil War events include Sherman's March to the Sea through Georgia and the appointing of U.S. Grant as Supreme Commander of the Northen Army; Abraham Lincoln is re-elected as President; Nevada becomes State No. 36; "In God We Trust" first appears on coins; the first railway sleeping car is put out by Pullman. Internationally, Otto Bismarck leads Prussia against Denmark over the question of Schleswig-Holstein; Karl Marx forms the first International Workingmen's Association; the International Red Cross is formed in Geneva; the Charlottetown Conference on the unification of Canada is held.

Cultural Highlights:
New openings include the National Gallery of Dublin and the Austrian Museum of Art and Industry; the Early English Text Society is formed and the German Shakespeare Society is founded; James R. Lowell becomes editor of the *North American Review* and Winslow Homer is inducted into the National Academy of Design. Births in the art field include French artist Henri Toulouse-Latrec and Russian artist Alexei von Jawlensky; deaths include British sculptor William Behnes and Scotch artist William Dyce. Births in the literary field include American novelist Thomas Dixon and poet Richard Hovey, British novelist Israel Zangwill and poet Stephen Phillips, Swedish poet Erick Karlfeldt, French poet and novelist Henri de Régnier and German dramatist Frank Wedekind; deaths include American poets Nathaniel Hawthorne and George Morris, British novelists Frank Smedley and Robert Surtees and poets John Clare and Walter S. Landor, Hungarian poet Andras Fáy and French author Jean Ampères. Other highlights include:

Art: Karl Becker, *The Doge in Counsel*; Henri Fantin-Latour, *Homage à Delacroix*; Édouard Manet, *The Battle of the Kearsarge and the Alabama*; Gustave Moreau, *Oedipus and the Sphinx*; Auguste Rodin, *Man with the Broken Nose*; Elihu Vedder, *Lair of the Sea Serpent*; John Quincy Adams Ward, *The Indian Hunter*.

Literature: Robert Browning, *Dramatis Personae*; William C. Bryant, *30 Poems*; Alexis Kivi, *Kullervo*; David Locke, *The Nasby Papers*; James R. Lowell, *Fireside Travels*; John Marston, *Donna Diana*; Alfred Lord Tennyson, *Enoch Arden*; Jules Verne, *Journey to the Center of the Earth*; John Greenleaf Whittier, *In Wartime and Other Poems*.

MUSICAL EVENTS

A. Births:

Jan 12	Anna Schoen-René (Ger-sop)		Jul 5	Stephen Krehl (Ger-the)
Jan 28	Thomas Tapper (Am-m.ed)		Jul 27	William Haynes (Am-fl.m)
Feb 10	Karl Pohlig (Boh-cd-pn)		Aug 3	Giorgio Bari (It-mus-cri)
Feb 16	Evgenia Mravina (Rus-sop)		Aug 18	Gemma Bellincioni (It-sop)
Mar 15	Johann Halvorsen (Nor-cm)		Oct 20	Elizabeth Coolidge (Am-pat)
Mar 25	Marie Soldat (Aus-vn)		Oct 23	Benjamin Whelpley (Am-org)
Mar 30	Ella Russell (Am-sop)		Oct 24	Franco Leoni (It-cm)
Apr 10	Eugen d'Albert (Scot-pn)		Oct 24	Charles S. Terry (Br-mus)
Apr 10	Godfrey Arkwright (Br-mus)		Oct 25	Alexander Gretchaninov (Rus-cm)
Jun 11	Richard Strauss (Ger-cm)		Dec 19	Adolf Sandberger (Ger-mus)
Jun 15	Joseph Guy Ropartz (Fr-cm-cd)		Dec 30	Alessandro Longo (It-pn)

B. Deaths:

Jan 4	Mateo Ferrer (Sp-org-cd)		Mar 16	Nathan Adams (Am-br.m)
Jan 8	Victor C. Dourlen (Fr-cm)		Mar 29	August K. Kahlert (Ger-mus)
Jan 13	Stephen Foster (Am-cm)		Mar 30	Ludwig Schindelmesser (Ger-cd)
Jan 15	Isaac Nathan (Br-cm-au)		Apr 13	Johann Schneider (Ger-org)
Jan 15	Anton Schindler (Aus-cd)		May 2	Giacomo Meyerbeer (Ger-cm)

May 21	William Knabe (Ger-pn.m)	Sep 30	Friedrich Hofmeister (Ger-pub)
Jul 21	Mary Anne Paton (Scot-sop)	Oct 14	Pierre Scudo (It-cri)
Jul 28	Johann Kufferath (Ger-vn-cd)	Oct 18	Jacques Gallay (Fr-hn)
Aug 27	Moritz Dietrichstein (Aus-cm)	Dec 11	Aloys Ander (Boh-ten)
Sep 10	John Firth (Am-pn.m)		Giovanni Davide (It-ten)
Sep 21	William S. Fry (Am-cm)		

C. Debuts:

U.S. -- Giorgio Stigelli (tour)

Other - Leopold von Auer (Leipzig), Armand de Castelmary (Paris), Julius Melgunov (St. Petersburg), Christine Nilsson (Paris), Hermann Winckelmann (Sonderhausen)

D. New Positions:

Conductors: Hans von Bülow (Royal Opera, Munich), Johann N. Fuchs (Bratislava Opera), Hermann Levi (Karlsruhe), Friedrich Marpurg (Sonderhausen), Karl Millöcker (Graz Theater), Holger Paulli (Copenhagen Court Orchestra), Joseph Rheinberger (Munich Oratorio Society), Franz Wüllner (kapellmeister, Munich)

Educational: Heinrich Ehrlich (piano, Stern Conservatory), Fritz Kirchner (piano, Kullak's Academy), Théodore Lack (piano, Paris Conservatory), Giovanni Rossi (director, Parma Musical Institute)

Others: Cornelius Gurlitt (organ, Altona Cathedral), Jacob Josephson (organ, Uppsala Cathedral), James C.D. Parker (organ, Trinity Church, Boston), Samuel Tuckerman (organ, Trinity Church, N.Y.)

E. Prizes and Honors:

Honors: Franz Adolf Berwald (Swedish Royal Academy), Hyacinthe Klosé (Legion of Honor)

F. Biographical Highlights:

Emma Albani moves with her family to New York; Isaac Albéniz appears as pianist at age 4; J. Lathrop Allen moves his brass shop to New York; Michael Balfe retires from active musical life; Antonio Bazzini makes a farewell tour of the Netherlands and retires from concert life to spend full time on composition; Johannes Brahms gives up his post with the Vienna Singakademie; Cesar Cui begins a writing career as critic and journalist; Alexander Dargomijsky makes his second European tour; Carlos Gomes begins study in Italy on a Brazilian government grant; Carl Loewe suffers a stroke; Wilma Neruda marries Swedish conductor Ludvig Norman (divorced 1869); Christine Nilssen debuts in London as well as Paris; Carl Tausig marries Seraphine von Vrabely; Felice Varesi makes his London debut; Richard Wagner is befriended by Ludwig II of Bavaria and begins an affair with Cosima von Bülow; August Wilhelmj goes to Frankfurt to study with Raff.

G. Institutional Openings:

Performing Groups: Barnby's Choir (London); Düsseldorf Municipal Orchestra; Irving Hall Symphonic Soirées (by Theodore Thomas); Montreal Mendelssohn Choir; Moscow PO; Portland (Oregon) Mechanics Band; Sheffield Amateur Musical Society; Società del Quartetto (Milan)

Educational: Bucharest Conservatory of Music; Eitner Piano School (Berlin); Royal College of Organists (London); Scuola Comunale di Musica ("Orazio Vecchi", Modena); Yale University Fine Arts Department (first in U.S.)

Other: J. Fischer and Brother, Music Publishers (Dayton); Kranich and Bach Piano Co. (N.Y.); Gustav Mollenhauer, Woodwind Manufacturer (Kassel); Music Hall (Academy of Music, Milwaukee); Thalia Theater (Graz); Ukrainian Theater (L'vov)

H. Musical Literature:

Arban, Jean-Baptiste, *Grande Méthode... pour Cornet à Pistons*
Elwart, Antoine, *Petit Manuel d'Instrumentation*
Engel, Carl, *Music of the Most Ancient Nations*
Gregoir, Edouard, *Les Artistes-Musiciens Néerlandais*
Haberl, Franz X., *Theoretisch-praktische Anweisung zum harmonischen Kirchengesang*
Hiller, Ferdinand, *Die Musik und das Publikum*
Hullah, John, *A Grammar of Counterpoint*
Köhler, Louis, *Die Neue Richtung in der Musik*
Meerens, Charles, *Instruction élémentaire de calcul musical*
Tuckerman, Samuel, *Trinity Collection of Church Music*

I. Musical Compositions:

Auber, Daniel, *La fiancée du Roi de Garbe* (opera)
Balfe, Michael, *The Sleeping Queen* (operetta)
Benedict, Julius, *The Bride of Song* (opera)
Benvenuti, Tommaso, *La Stella de Toledo* (opera)
Berwald, Franz, *The Queen of Golconda* (opera)
Bradbury, William, *Aughton* (hymn tune, "He Leadeth Me")
Brahms, Johannes, *Piano Quintet, Opus 34*
    String Sextet No. 2, Opus 36
    4 Songs, Opus 46 (voice and piano)
Bruch, Max, *Frithjof-Scenen, Opus 23*
Bruckner, Anton, *Symphony in D Minor, "Die Nullte"* (revised 1869)
    Mass No. 1 in D Minor (revised 1876)
Delibes, Léo, *Grande nouvelle* (operetta)
    Le serpent à plumes (operetta)
Flotow, Friedrich von, *Der Königsschuss* (ballet)
Foster, Stephen, *Beautiful Dreamer* (song)
Fry, William, *Kyrie and Mass in E-flat Major*
Gevaert, François, *Le Captaine Henriot*
Gilmore, Patrick, *When Johnny Comes Marching Home* (song)
Gottschalk, Louis M., *The Dying Poet* (piano)
Gounod, Charles, *Mireille* (opera)
Grieg, Edvard, *Symphony in C Minor*
    6 Songs, Opus 4 (voice and piano)
    The Heart's Melodies, Opus 5 (4 songs)
Guiraud, Ernest, *Sylvie* (opera)
    Bajazet et le joueur de flûte (cantata)
Joachim, Joseph, *Concerto No. 2 for Violin and Orchestra*
Lecocq, Charles, *Liliane et Valentin* (operetta)
    Le baiser à la porte (operetta)
Macfarren, George, *She Stoops to Conquer* (opera)
Offenbach, Jacques, *L'amour chanteur* (operetta)
    Das Rheinnixen
    Les Géorgiennes (operetta)
Root, George, *Tramp! Tramp! Tramp!* (song)
Rubinstein, Anton, *Faust, Opus 68* (musical picture)
Smetana, Bedrich, *Shakespearean Festival March*
    The Brandenburgers in Bohemia (opera)
Stebbins, George C., *Gordon* (hymn tune, "My Jesus, I Love Thee")
Strauss, Johann, Jr., *Morning Papers Waltz*
Sullivan, Arthur, *Kenilworth* (oratorio)
    The Sapphire Necklace (ballet)
Suppé, Franz von, *Pique Dame* (operetta)
    Franz Schubert (operetta)
Tchaikovsky, Peter I., *Overture to the Tempest*
Wagner, Richard, *Huldigungsmarsch*

1865

World Events:
In the U.S., President Lincoln is assassinated following the end of the Civil War; Andrew Johnson becomes President No. 17; the Thirteenth Ammendment ends slavery in the United States and territories; the Southern Pacific Railroad is chartered; work begins on the transcontinental line; Cornell and Purdue Universities are founded; future President Warren G. Harding is born. Internationally, the War of the Triple Alliance begins in South America with Argentina, Brazil and Uruguay lined up against Paraguay; Peru declares war on Spain; Leopold I of Belgium dies and is succeeded by Leopold II.

Cultural Highlights:
The Artistic Circle of Moscow is founded; the magazine *L'Art* begins publication as does the *Pall Mall Gazette*; Thomas Carlyle becomes rector of Edinburgh University; Alexander W. Thayer becomes U.S. Consul in Trieste; Rosa Bonheur is inducted into the Legion of Honor. Births in the art field include American artist Robert Henri and sculptor Paul Bartlett and British artist Robert Bevan; deaths include American artist John Neagle and Austrian artist Ferdinand Waldmüller. Births in the literary world include Irish poet William Yeats and British novelist Emmuska Orczy; deaths include German novelist Otto Ludwig, Finnish novelist Fredricka Bremer, Swedish author Bernhard Malmström and British novelist Elizabeth Gaskell. Other highlights include:

Art: David Blythe, *Dry Goods and Notions*; Jean-Baptiste Corot, *La Zingara*; Gustave Doré, *Bible Illustrations* Winslow Homer, *Prisoners from the Front*; Georges Inness, *Delaware Valley*; Édouard Manet, *Olympia*; William Orchardson, *Challenged*; Elihu Vedder, *The Lost Mind*; John Quincy Adams Ward, *Freedman*.

Literature: Charles Browne, *Artemus Ward, His Travels*; Lewis Carrol, *Alice's Adventures in Wonderland*; Mary E. Dodge, *Hans Brinker*; Elizabeth Gaskell, *Wives and Daughters*; David Locke, *Divers Opinions of Yours Truly, Petroleum V. Nasby*; Cardinal Newman, *The Dream of Gerontius*; Walt Whitman, *Drum-Taps*; John G. Whittier, *National Lyrics*.

MUSICAL EVENTS

A. Births:

Jan 2	William L. Phelps (Am-cri)		Jun 21	Herbert Brewer (Br-org)
Jan 3	Richard R. Terry (Br-org-mus)		Jun 24	H. Plunkett Greene (Ir-bar)
Jan 4	Peter C. Cornelius (Den-ten)		Jun 29	John Coates (Br-ten)
Feb 19	Ferdinand Löwe (Aus-cd)		Jul 6	Emile Jaques-Dalcroze (Swi-m.ed)
Feb 28	Margaret Glyn (Br-mus)		Aug 10	Alexander Glazunov (Rus-cm)
Feb 28	Arthur Symons (Br-pt-cri)		Aug 13	Emma Eames (Am-sop)
Mar 19	Vilhelm Herold (Den-ten)		Sep 9	Edwin H. Lemare (Br-org)
Mar 28	Leo Schulz (Ger-cel)		Oct 1	Paul Dukas (Fr-cm)
Mar 29	Stewart Macpherson (Br-the)		Oct 15	Charles W. Clark (Am-bar)
Apr 4	Frank Metcalf (Am-hymn)		Oct 20	Franz Navál (Aus-ten)
Apr 13	Heinrich Reinhardt (Ger-cm)		Oct 27	Giulio Rossi (It-bs)
Jun 7	Guido Gasperini (It-mus)		Dec 8	Jan Sibelius (Fin-cm)
Jun 9	Albéric Magnard (Fr-cm)		Dec 15	Joseph von Slivinski (Pol-pn)
Jun 9	Carl Nielsen (Den-cm)			Margaret Macintyre (Br-sop)

B. Deaths:

Jan 3	Gotthilf Körner (Ger-pub)		Feb 7	Johann H. Lübeck (Hol-vn-cm)
Jan 9	Elizabeth Masson (Br-mez)		Feb 14	Carlo A. Gambini (It-pn-cm)
Jan 17	Giuseppe Rocca (It-vn)		Feb 20	Louis Dietsch (Fr-org)
Jan 28	Felice Romani (It-lib)		Apr 1	Giuditta Pasta (It-sop)
Jan 28	Henri Valentino (Fr-cd)		Apr	Tommaso Barsotti (It-cm-au)

Jul 23 Jean Louis Tulou (Fr-fl)
Aug 17 Johann N. Poissl (Ger-cm)
Sep 7   Angelo Villanis (It-cm)
Oct 8   Heinrich Ernst (Cz-vn-cm)
Oct 12 Angonio Giuglini (It-ten)
Oct 12 W. Vincent Wallace (Ir-cm)

Oct 15 Maria Caradori-Allen (It-sop)
Nov 17 Cesare Badiali (It-bs)
Dec 18 Francisco da Silva (Bra-cm-cd)
Dec 24 Charles Eastlake (Br-art-cri)
Dec 24 Julian Fonatna (Pol-pn)
        Pierre Blondeau (Fr-cm)

C. Debuts:

U.S. -- Rose Hersee (tour), Euphrosyne Parepa-Rosa (tour), Ernst Perabo (Boston)

Other - Luigi Agnesi (London), Mathilde Bauermeister (London), Eugen Gura (Munich), Teodozja Jakowicka-Friderici (Warsaw), Francis A. Korbay (Budapest), Lilli Lehmann (Prague), Johann Leitert (Dresden), Amalie Materna (Graz), Pierre Melchessédec (Paris), Aglaja Orgeni (Berlin), Clara Rogers (Turin), Marie-Hippolyte Roze (Paris), Heinrich and Therese Vogl (Munich), Maria Waldmann (Pressburg), Marie Wilt (Graz)

D. New Positions:

Conductors: Emil Büchner (kappelmeister, Meiningen), Karl Doppler (kappelmeister, Stuttgart), Friedrich Hegar (Zurich Tonhalle SO), Alfred Mellon (Liverpool PO), Franz von Suppé (Leopoldstadt Theater, Vienna)

Educational: Max Bruch (director, Koblenz Concert-Institute), Ludwig Bussler (theory, Ganz School of Music, Berlin), Maurits Hagemann (director, Batavia Conservatory), Josef Krejci (director, Prague Conservatory), Henri-Marie Lavoix (librarian, Bibliothèque Nationale, Paris), Mathilde and Salvatore Marchesi (voice, Cologne Conservatory), Auguste Tolbecque (cello, Marseilles Conservatory)

Others: Frederick Bridge (organ, Holy Trinity, Windsor), Henry Frost (organ, Chapel Royal), Vincent d'Indy (organ, St. Leu-la Forêt), Samuel S. Wesley (Gloucester Cathedral)

E. Prizes and Honors:

Prizes: Gustave-Léon Huberti and Charles Lenepveu (Prix de Rome)

Honors: Friedrich Kiel (Prussian Academy), Halfdan Kjerulf (Swedish Royal Academy)

F. Biographical Highlights:

Johannes Brahms, after his mother dies, spends the summer with Clara Schumann; Zdenek Fibich leaves Prague and enters Leipzig Conservatory; Allan J. (Signor) Foli and Ilma di Murska make their London debuts; Antonietta Fricci makes her La Scala debut; Louis Moreau Gottschalk, in trouble over a young lady in California, flees to Brazil; Edvard Grieg visits Rome and writes his first orchestral work; Vincent d'Indy begins harmony lessons with Lavignac; Leoš Janácek sent to the "Queens" Monastery in Old Brno; Edouard Lalo marries contralto Mlle. Bernier de Malighy; Franz Liszt suffers his first serious bout with dipsomania; Nicolai Rimsky-Korsakov returns from the Navy world cruise and joins Balakirev's music circle; Carl Tausig settles in Berlin and opens his own school; Peter Tchaikovsky translates Gervaert's instrumentation treatise into Russian; Giuseppe Verdi gives up his post in the National Parliament; Richard Wagner is exiled to Switzerland by Ludwig II.

G. Institutional Openings:

Performing Groups: Christiania String Quartet; Concerts Populaires de Musique Classique (Brussels); Edinburgh University Musical Society; Euterpe Music Society (Denmark); Harvard Musical Association; Oberösterreichischer und Salzburgischer Sängerbund; Oxford Philharmonia Society; Quartetto Fiorentino (by Jean Becker); Städtisches Orchester (Augsburg)

Educational: London Organ School; Oberlin College Conservatory of Music; Ramann-

Volkmann Music School (Nuremberg)

Other: Crosby Opera House (Chicago); Charles Foetisch Music Co. (Lausanne); Hawkes and Co., Instrument Makers and Music Publishers (merges with Boosey and Co. in 1930); Tony Pastor's Opera House (N.Y.); Moses Slater, Brass Instruments (N.Y.); Staatstheater am Gärtnerplatz (Munich)

H. Musical Literature:

Brendel, Karl F., *Die Organisation des Musikwesens...*
Coussemaker, Charles, *Les Harmonistes des XIIe et XIIIe Siècles*
Emerson, Luther, *Merry Chimes*
Haberl, Franz, *Magister Choralis*
Kudelski, Karl, *Kurzgefasste Harmonielehre*
Mach, Ernst, *Über musikalische Akustik*
Marx, Adolf, *Erinnerungen: aus Meinem Leben*
Reissmann, August, *Grundriss der Musikgeschichte*
Thayer, Alexander, *Chronologisches Verzeichnis der Werke Ludwig von Beethoven*
Vesque von Püttlingen, Johann, *Das musikalische Autorrecht*

I. Musical Compositions:

Balakirev, Mily, *Overture No. 2 on Russian Themes, "Russia"*
Bizet, Georges, *Ivan, the Terrible* (unfinished opera)
Brahms, Johannes, *Trio in E-flat, Opus 40* (horn, violin, piano)
    16 Waltzes, Opus 39 (piano duet)
Cornelius, Peter, *Le Cid* (opera)
David, Ferdinand, *Le Saphir* (opera)
Dorn, Heinrich, *Der Botenläufer von Pirna* (opera)
    Gewitter bei Sonnenschein (operetta)
Dubois, Theodore, *Concerto Overture in D Major*
Dvorák, Antonin, *Symphony No. 1 in, Opus 31, "The Bells of Zlonice"*
    Symphony No. 2, Opus 41
Dykes, John, *Lux Benigna* (hymn tune, "Lead, Kindly Light")
Fibich, Zdenek, *Romeo and Juliet* (incidental music)
Flotow, Friedrich von, *La Châteleine* (opera)
Franck, César, *The Tower of Babel* (oratorio)
Gade, Niels, *Symphony No. 7, Opus 45*
Goldmark, Karl, *Sakuntala Overture, Opus 13*
Grieg, Edvard, *Sonata in E Minor, Opus 7, for Piano*
    Sonata No. 1, Opus 8, for Violin and Piano
    4 Songs, Opus 9 (contains "*I Love Thee*")
Liszt, Franz, *Missa Choralis*
    Rakoczy March
Massenet, Jules, *Suite No. 1 for Orchestra*
Moniuszko, Stanislaw, *The Haunted Castle* (opera)
Mussorgsky, Modest, *From Memories of Childhood* (piano)
Offenbach, Jacques, *La belle Hélène* (operetta)
    Rêve d'un nuit d'été (operetta)
    Cascoletto (operetta)
Pacini, Giovanni, *Dante Symphony*
Pedrotti, Carlo, *Marion Delorme* (opera)
Rimsky-Korsakov, Nikolai, *Symphony No. 1*
Saint-Saëns, Camille, *Piano Quintet, Opus 14*
Serov, Alexander, *Rogneda* (opera)
Suppé, Franz von, *Die schöne Galatea* (operetta)
Svendsen, Johan, *String Quartet No. 1, Opus 1*
Tchaikovsky, Peter, *Concert Overture in F Major*
    Piano Sonata in C-sharp Minor, Opus 37
Work, Henry C., *Marching Through Georgia* (song)

1866

World Events:
In the U.S., Congress passes the Civil Rights Act over President Johnson's veto; U.S. Grant becomes the first American General; the "Nickel" is approved for coining by the Treasury Department; the Society for the Prevention of Cruelty to Animals (SPCA) is formed; the Grand Army of the Republic (GAR) is founded. Internationally, Cyrus Field succeeds in laying a lasting Atlantic Cable; Alfred Nobel invents dynamite; the Seven Weeks War takes place between Prussia and Austria; Mendel publishes his laws of heredity; Carol I becomes ruler in Romania.

Cultural Highlights:
The Metropolitan Museum opens in New York; the American Society of Painters in Watercolors is founded; Francis Grant is knighted and becomes President of the Royal Academy of Art in London; Henrik Ibsen is given a government pension. Births in the field of art include American artist Robert MacCameron and sculptor Herman MacNeil, Russian artist Wassily Kandinsky and British artist and critic Roger E. Fry; deaths include American artist Chester Harding and British artist John Gibson. Births in the literary field include Americans George Ade and George McCutcheon, Spanish dramatist J. Benavente y Mártinez, Swiss novelist Heinrich Federer, German poet Paul Ernst and French dramatist Tristan Bernard; deaths include British poets Thomas Peacock and John Keble, German poet Friedrich Rückert, Austrian poet Johann Vogl, Swedish author Carl Almqvist and French poet and novelist Roger de Beauvoir. Other highlights include:

Art: Honoré Daumier, *Don Quixote and the Windmills*; Edward Hicks, *The Barbershop Musicale*; Winslow Homer, *Morning Bell*; Frederic Leighton, *The Syracusan Bride*; Édouard Manet, *The Fifer*; Claude Monet, *Camille*; Valentine Prinsep, *General Gordon in Chinese Dress*; Dante Rosetti, *Monna Vanna*; John Q. Ward, *The Good Samaritan*.

Literature: Thomas Carlyle, *Reminiscences*; Feodor Dostoyevsky, *Crime and Punishment*; William D. Howells, *Venetian Life*; Victor Hugo, *Toilers of the Sea*; Henry W. Shaw, *Josh Billings, His Sayings*; Algernon Swinburne, *Poems and Ballads*; Alexei Tolstoy, *Death of Ivan the Terrible*; Lev Tolstoy, *War and Peace*; John G. Whittier, *Snowbound*.

MUSICAL EVENTS

A. Births:

Jan 13	Vasily Kalinnikov (Rus-cm)		Jul 2	Karl Schaefer (Ger-acous)
Jan 25	Antonio Scotti (It-bar)		Jul 26	Francesco Cilea (It-cm)
Jan 29	Romain Rolland (Fr-mus)		Aug 27	Erik Schmedes (Den-ten)
Feb 1	Henri Albers (Hol-bar)		Sep 10	Tor Aulin (Swe-vn-cm)
Feb 16	David Mannes (Am-vn-cd)		Sep 20	Gustave Doret (Swi-cd-cm)
Apr 1	Ferruccio Busoni (It-cm)		Oct 26	Théodore Gérold (Fr-mus)
May 13	Ottokar Novácek (Hun-vn-cm)		Oct 31	Max Pauer (Aus-pn-ed)
May 17	Erik Satie (Fr-cm)		Nov 15	Gervase Elwes (Br-ten)
May 31	Vladimir Rebikoff (Rus-cm)		Nov 23	Fanny Moody (Br-sop)
Jun 3	Maria Mikhaylova (Rus-sop)		Nov 30	Andreas Dippel (Ger-ten)
Jun 15	Charles Wood (Ir-cm)		Dec 2	Harry T. Burleigh (Am-cm)
Jun 21	Paul Knüpfer (Ger-bs)			

B. Deaths:

Feb 20	Charles Richault (Fr-pub)		May 17	Adolph B. Marx (Ger-the)
Mar 4	Jean L.F. Danjou (Fr-org.m)		May 31	Prosper Simon (Fr-org)
Mar 10	Antonio Pacini (It-cm-pub)		Jul 25	Aloys Schmitt (Ger-pn-ed)
Mar 19	Antoine Clapisson (Fr-vn-cm)		Aug 4	Eduard F. Genast (Ger-bar)
Mar 20	Richard Nordraak (Nor-cm)		Aug 14	Nicola Benvenuti (It-org-cm)
Apr 1	Aimé A. Leborne (Bel-cm-the)		Aug 20	Charles Delyenne (Fr-acous)

Aug 27	Engelbert Aigner (Aus-cm)	Nov 23	Otto Kraushaar (Ger-the)
Sep 5	Angelo Catelani (It-org-mus)	Nov 26	Adrien F. Servais (Bel-cel)
Sep 14	John Brownsmith (Br-org)	Dec 3	Johann Kalliwoda (Boh-cm)
Nov 20	Joseph d'Ortigue (Fr-mus)		

C. Debuts:

U.S. -- Minnie Hauk (age 14, N.Y.), Carl Rosa (tour)

Other - Giuseppe Fancelli (Milan), Gustav Frieman (Dresden), George Henschel (Hirschberg, as bass), Leonard Labatt (Stockholm), Mathilde Mallinger (Munich), Anna Mehlig (London), Stanislaw Niedzielski (Krakow), Albert Niemann (Berlin), Eugenie Pappenheim (Linz), Emile Sauret (London), Sofia Scalci (Mantua)

D. New Positions:

Conductors: Adolf l'Arronge (Kroll Opera, Berlin), Théodore Dubois (maître de chapelle, Ste. Clothilde), Johann Gerbeck (kapellmeister, Vienna Cons.), Edvard Grieg (Christiana PO), Bedrich Smetana (Czech Opera), Arthur Sullivan (Royal Academy)

Educational: Heinrich Bellermann (musicology, Berlin University), Hilarión Eslava (director, Madrid Conservatory), Vladimir Kashperov (voice, Moscow Conservatory), Friedrich Kiel (composition, Stern Conservatory, Berlin), Ferdinand Laub (violin, Moscow Conservatory), Victor Massé (counterpoint, Paris Conservatory), Nicolai Rubinstein (director, Moscow Conservatory), Peter Tchaikovsky (harmony, Moscow Conservatory)

Others: Gabriel Fauré (organ, St. Sauveur, Rennes), Alphonse Goovaerts (archivist, Royal Archives, Brussels), Ernst Pauer (piano, Austrian court), Wilhelm Tappert (editor, *Allgemeine Deutsche Musikzeitung*)

E. Prizes and Honors:

Prizes: Edvard Grieg (Stockholm Academy Prize), Emile-Louis Pessard and Alexandre Regnault (Prix de Rome)

Honors: Charles Gounod (French Institute)

F. Biographical Highlights:

Arrigo Boito joins Garibaldi's forces for a short term of service; Johannes Brahms tours as accompanist to Joachim; Annie Louise Cary goes to Milan for further voice study; Carolina Ferni-Giraldoni makes her La Scala debut; Célestine Galli-Marié makes her London debut; Edvard Grieg visits Rome for the second time; Ruggero Leoncavallo is admitted to the Naples Conservatory of Music; Carl Loewe quits his Stettin post and settles in Kiel; Gustav Mahler begins music instruction; Jules Massenet marries his student Constance de Sainte-Maria; Nicolini and Oglaja Orgeni make their Covent Garden debuts; Arthur Nikisch enters the Vienna Conservatory of Music; Janet Patey marries baritone John Patey; Emil Paur enters the Vienna Conservatory; Pablo de Sarasate acquires his famous Stradivarius violin; Sergei Taneyev enters the Moscow Conservatory of Music; Theodore Thomas becomes sole conductor of the Brooklyn PO; Henri Vieuxtemps moves to Paris to escape political unrest.

G. Institutional Openings:

Performing Groups: Augsburger Oratorienverein; Bedford Music Society (England); Louisville Philharmonic Society; Mendelssohn Glee Club of New York; Muza (Kraków amateur music society); Philharmonic Music Society (Portland, Oregon); Sociedad Artístico-Musical de Socorros Mutuos (Madrid); Sociedad de Conciertos (Madrid); Sociedad de Música Clásica (Havana); Summer Terrace Garden Concerts (N.Y.); Union Musicale de Québec

Educational: Istituto Musicale Antonio Venturi (Brescia); Klavier-Schule Tausig

(Berlin); Liceo Musicale (Turin); Moscow Conservatory of Music

Other: Alsbach Music Publishers (Rotterdam); Continental Theatre (Boston); Domino Club (Bologna); *Fliegende Blätter für Katholische Kirchenmusik*; Greenlaw Opera House (Memphis); Georges Hartmann, Music Publisher (Paris); Instituto Filarmonico (Vicenza); Leypoldt and Holt, Book Publishers; *Musica Sacra*; G.P. Putnam and Son (N.Y.); St. Paul Opera House; G. Schirmer Publishing Co. (N.Y.); Schwartzer Zither Factory; *Il Secolo*; Tonhalle (Düsseldorf Concert Hall)

H. Musical Literature:

Bertini, Domenico, *Compendio de' principi di musica...*
Bertrand, Jean G., *Les origines de l'harmonie*
Engel, Carl, *An Introduction to the Study of National Music*
Jahn, Otto, *Gesammelte Aufsätze über Musik*
Krüger, Eduard, *System der Tonkunst*
Mach, Ernst, *Einleitung in die Helmholtz'sche musiktheorie*
Oettingen, Arthur von, *Harmoniesystem in dualer Entwickelung*
Tappert, Wilhelm, *Musik und musikalische Erziehung*
Vroye, Théodore de, *De la musique religieuse*
Walker, William, *The Christian Harmony*

I. Musical Compositions:

Balakirev, Mily, *Symphony No. 1 in C*
Barnard, Charlotte, *Come Back to Erin* (song)
Benedict, Julius, *St. Cecilia* (oratorio)
Bristow, George, *Daniel, Opus 42* (oratorio)
Bruckner, Anton, *Symphony No. 1* (revised 1890)
    Symphony No. 2 (revised 1882)
Butterfield, James A., *When You and I Were Young, Maggie* (song)
Delibes, Leo, *La source* (ballet)
Dubois, Théodore, *Les sept Paroles du Christ* (oratorio)
Dykes, John B., *St. Agnes* (hymn tune, "Jesus, the Very Thought of Thee")
Flotow, Friedrich von, *Zilda* (opera)
Gade, Niels, *Die Kreuzfahrer, Opus 50* (cantata)
Gounod, Charles, *Tobie* (cantata)
Grieg, Edvard, *Concert Overture, Opus 11, "In Autumn"*
Lalo, Edouard, *Fiesque* (opera)
Lecocq, Charles, *Le Myosotis* (operetta)
    Ondines au champagne (operetta)
Liszt, Franz, *Christus* (oratorio)
Mercadante, Saverio, *Virginia* (opera)
Moniuszko, Stanislaw, *Polonaise de Concert*
Mussorgsky, Modest, *Hopak* (song)
Offenbach, Jacques, *Barbe-bleue* (operetta)
    La vie parisienne (operetta)
Raff, Joseph J., *Symphony No. 2, Opus 140*
Rimsky-Korsakov, Nikolai, *Overture on 3 Russian Themes, Opus 28*
Saint-Saëns, Camille, *3 Organ Rhapsodies, Opus 7*
Sullivan, Arthur, *Symphony in E Minor, "Irish"*
    Overture, In Memoriam
    Concerto for Cello and Orchestra
Suppé, Franz von, *Light Cavalry* (operetta)
    Freigeister (operetta)
Tchaikovsky, Peter I., *Symphony No. 1, Opus 13, "Winter Dreams"*
    Festival Overture on Danish Hymn, Opus 15
    Concert Overture in C Minor
Thomas, Ambroise, *Mignon* (opera)

1867

World Events:

In the U.S., Seward's Folly takes the headlines as the U.S. buys Alaska from Russia; Nebraska becomes State No. 37; the Standard Oil Co. is founded by John D. Rockefeller; the first cattle drive is sent along the Chisholm Trail; John Hopkins University is founded. Internationally, the Austrian-Hungarian Empire is formed with Joseph I as emperor; the French Mexican Empire dream comes to an end with the execution of Maximilian; the North German Federation is formed by Bismarck; Canada becomes a sovereign state in the British Commonwealth; the typewriter is patented.

Cultural Highlights:

The Chicago Academy of Design is set up; Philip Calderon and George Watts are inducted into the Royal Academy. Births in the literary field include Spanish novelist Vincente Ibañez, British novelists Arnold Bennett and John Galsworthy, Russian poet Konstantin Balmont, Italian poet Luigi Pirandello, French philosopher Julien Benda and author Léon Daudet and Austrian dramatist Karl Schönherr; deaths include Scotch poet Alexander Scott, Spanish author Serafín Estébanez Calderon, American author Charles Browne and poet Fitz-Greene Halleck, French poets Charles Baudelaire and François Ponsard and German poet and novelist Julius Mosen. Births in the art world include American sculptors Karl Bitter and Bela Pratt and artist George Luks, German artists Käthe Kollwitz and Emil Nolde, British artist Frank Brangwyn and French artist Pierre Bonnard. Other highlights include:

Art: Lawrence Alma-Tadema, *Tarquinius Superbus*; Albert Bierstadt, *In the Mountains*; Edgar Degas, *Head of a Young Woman*; Édouard Manet, *Execution of Emperor Maximilian*; John Millais, *Jephthah*; Claude Monet, *Ladies in a Garden*; Edward Poynter, *Israel in Egypt*; Pierre-Auguste Renoir, *Diana*.

Literature: Michel Carré, *Mignon*; George Catlin, *Life among the Indians*; Francis Finch, *The Blue and the Grey*; Henrik Ibsen, *Peer Gynt*; Sydney Lanier, *Tiger Lilies*; David Locke, *Ekkoes from Kentucky*; Karl Marx, *Das Kapital*; Ivan Turgenev, *Smoke*; Mark Twain, *The Celebrated Jumping Frog of Calaveras County*; Émile Zola, *Thérèse Raquin*.

MUSICAL EVENTS

A. Births:

Jan 9	Jacques Urlus (Ger-ten)	Jul 29	Enrique Granados (Sp-cm)
Jan 20	Yvette Guilbert (Fr-sop)	Aug 10	Emil Oberhoffer (Ger-cd)
Feb 15	Charles Douglas (Am-org)	Aug 28	Umberto Giordano (It-cm)
Feb 27	Wilhelm Peterson-Berger	Sep 5	Mrs. H. H. A. Beach (Am-cm)
	(Swe-cm)	Sep 7	Harry E. Williams (Am-ten)
Mar 25	Arturo Toscanini (It-cd)	Sep 12	Herbert Clarke (Am-tpt-cd)
Mar 27	Edyth Walker (Am-mez)	Oct 16	Ferdinand Hoesick (Pol-mus)
Mar 28	Edmond Clément (Fr-ten)	Oct 27	Robert Blass (Am-bs)
Mar 29	Thomas Salignac (Fr-ten)	Nov 6	Eduard Bernoulli (Swi-mus)
Apr 3	Edward Maryon (Br-cm)	Nov 27	Charles Koechlin (Fr-cm)
Apr 29	Henry T. Parker (Am-cri)		John A. Lomax (Am-folk)
May 5	T. Terlius Noble (Br-org-cm)		

B. Deaths:

Feb 23	George T. Smart (Br-org-cd)	Jul 24	William L. Viner (Br-hymn)
Mar 18	Wiktor Kazynski (Pol-cm)	Sep 1	Edward Hodges (Br-org)
Mar 19	Jósef Stefani (Pol-cm-cd)	Sep 7	Henriette Lalande (Fr-sop)
May 3	Fanny Persiani (It-sop)	Sep 10	Simon Sechter (Boh-cm-cd)
May 6	Johann Aiblinger (Ger-cm-cd)	Sep 28	Carlo Barbieri (It-cd-cm)
Jul 18	Charles L. Triebert (Fr-ob)	Oct 6	Henry Timrod (Am-pt)

Oct 9 Ignace Dobrzynski (Pol-pn-cm)
Oct 26 John Fawcett (Br-cm)

Dec 4 Constance Nantier-Didiée
        (Fr-mez)
Dec 19 Jean G. Kastner (Fr-the-cm)

C. Debuts:
U.S. -- William Candidus (N.Y.)

Other - Marianne Brandt (Olmütz), Annie L. Cary (Copenhagen), Antonio Cotogni (London), Pierre Gailhard (Paris), Marie Hanfstängel (Paris), Elizaveta Lavrovskaya (St. Petersburg), Marie Lehmann (Leipzig), Angelo Masini (Italy), Ivan Mel'nikov (St. Petersburg), Sophie Menter (Leipzig), Luise Radecke (Cologne), Joseph Servais (Warsaw), Georg Unger (Leipzig)

D. New Positions:
Conductors: Johann J. Abert (kapellmeister, Stuttgart), Mily Balakirev (Musical Society Concerts, Moscow), Julius Benedict (Liverpool PO), George Bristow (N.Y. Mendelssohn Society), Max Bruch (kapellmeister, Schwarzburg-Sondershausen), William Cusins (Philharmonic Society, London), Franz von Dingelstedt (Vienna Opera), Karl Eckert (Baden-Baden), Eugenio Terziani (La Scala)

Educational: Hans von Bülow (director, Munich Conservatory), Enrico Delle Sedie (voice, Paris Conservatory), Stephen Albert Emery (New England Conservatory), Julius Epstein (piano, Vienna Conservatory), Niels Gade (director, Copenhagen Conservatory), Frédéric Louis Ritter (professor, Vassar), Eben Tourjée (director, New England Conservatory)

Others: Elfrida Andrée (organ, Göteborg Cathedral), Alexander Dargomijsky (President, Russian Musical Society), François Gevaert (music director, Paris Opera), Franz Haberl (organ, Santa Maria, Rome)

E. Prizes and Honors:
Prizes: Hendrik Waelput (Prix de Rome)

F. Biographical Highlights:
Hector Berlioz, on his last Russian tour, meets Balakirev and Tchaikovsky; Anton Bruckner suffers a nervous breakdown; Antonio Cotogni makes his Covent Garden debut; Friedrich von Flotow divorces his second wife; Robert Franz resigns his music positions because of deafness; Edvard Grieg, settling in Copenhagen to teach, marries Nina Hagerup; Georg Hellmesberger retires from active concert life; Victor Herbert enters Stuttgart Conservatory; Emma Juch moves to the U.S.; Clara Kellogg makes her London debut; Alexei L'vov, due to growing deafness, retires from active music life; Modest Mussorgsky is dismissed from his Ministry job; Franz Nachbaur begins a 23-year association with the Munich Opera; Euphrosyne Parepa-Rosa marries impresario Carl Rosa; Alexander Stasov, in an article, creates the "mighty handful"; Johann Strauss takes his orchestra on their only English visit; Arthur Sullivan, in Vienna with Charles Grove, helps discover Schubert's lost manuscripts; Johan Svendsen, leaving the Conservatory, tours the North Atlantic countries.

G. Institutional Openings:
Performing Groups: Bilseche Kapelle (Berlin); Denver Musical Union; Florentine String Quartet; Hamburg Tonkünstlerverein; Hungarian Singer's Association (Budapest); Kiev Opera Co.; Manchester Vocal Union; Pest Philharmonic Society; Società dei Concerti Benedetto Marcello (Venice); Società Romana del Quartetto (Rome); Uppsala Cathedral Choir

Educational: Basler Musikschule; Buda Music Academy; Chicago Musical College; Cincinnati Conservatory of Music; Flemish Music School (Antwerp); Free Music School (Vilnus); Melopea Accademia Filarmonica-Drammatica (Messina); New England Music Conservatory; Norwegian Academy of Music; Tonic Sol-Fa College

(Manchester)

Other: Augsburger Stadttheater; Clube Mozart (Rio de Janeiro); Colston Hall (Bristol); Enoch and Sons, Publishers (London); Ginn and Co., Publishers (Boston); Music Lover's Society of Pest; National Hungarian Association of Choral Societies; Pence Opera House (Minneapolis); Pernerstorfer Circle (Vienna Conservatory); Regio Teatro Nuovo (Pisa); St. George's Hall (London); Schreiber Cornet Co. (N.Y.); Working Men's Society of London

H. Musical Literature:

Allen/Ware/Garrison, *Slave Songs of the U.S.*
Bastiaans, Johannes, *Treatise on Harmony*
Bradbury, William, *Fresh Laurels for Sabbath School*
Bussler, Ludwig, *Musikalische elementarlehre*
Fourneaux, J.B., *Instrumentologie: traité théorique et practique*
Macfarren, George, *Six Lectures on Harmony*
Marx, Adolf, *Das ideal und die Gegenwart* (posthumous publication)
Mason, William, *A Method for the Piano*
Mathews, William, *Outlines of Music Form*
Tyndall, John, *Sound*

I. Musical Compositions:

Balakirev, Mily, *Overture on Czech Themes*
Bennett, William S., *The Woman of Samaria* (oratorio)
Benoit, Peter, *Isa* (opera)
Bizet, Georges, *The Fair Maid of Perth* (opera)
Borodin, Alexander, *Symphony No. 1 in E-flat Major*
    The Bogatyrs (opera)
Bruch, Max, *Schön Ellen, Opus 21* (chorus and orchestra)
Bruckner, Anton, *Mass No. 3 in F Minor* (revised 1876, 1881, 1890)
Dargomijsky, Alexander, *The Triumph of Bacchus* (opera-ballet)
Dubois, Théodore, *The Seven Last Words of Christ* (oratorio)
Gounod, Charles, *Romeo and Juliet* (opera)
Grieg, Edvard, *Lyric Pieces, Book I, Opus 12* (piano)
    Violin Sonata No. 2, Opus 13
Kashperov, Vladimir, *The Storm* (opera)
Liszt, Franz, *Hungarian Coronation Mass*
    Hungarian Crown March
Massenet, Jules, *La grand'tante* (opera)
Mussorgsky, Modest, *A Night on Bald Mountain* (symphonic poem)
    The Rout of Sennacherib (cantata)
Offenbach, Jacques, *Robinson Crusoé* (operetta)
    La Grande-Duchesse de Gérolstein (operetta)
Paine, John Knowles, *Mass in D, Opus 10*
Ponchielli, Amilcare, *La stella del Monte* (opera)
Reinecke, Carl, *König Manfred* (opera)
Rimsky-Korsakov, Nikolai, *Fantasy on Serbian Themes* (orchestra--revised 1888)
Rossi, Lauro, *Lo Zingaro rivale* (opera)
    Il maestro e la cantante (opera)
Saint-Saëns, Camille, *Les noces de Prométhée, Opus 19* (cantata)
Smetana, Bedrich, *Dalibor* (opera)
Strauss, Johann, Jr., *On the Beautiful Blue Danube*
Sullivan, Arthur, *Cox and Box* (operetta)
    Contrabandista (operetta)
Suppé, Friedrich von, *Banditenstreiche* (operetta)
Svendsen, Johan, *Symphony No. 1, Opus 4*
Verdi, Giuseppe, *Don Carlo* (opera)

1868

World Events:

In the U.S., the impeachment of President Andrew Johnson fails by one vote; Ulysses S. Grant is elected as President No. 18; the Fourteenth Amendment on the apportionment of Representatives is ratified; the first railway dining car service appears; Reno, Nevada, is founded; the Atlanta *Constitution* is founded. Internationally, the Burlingame Treaty opens uninhibited immigration of cheap labor from the Orient; Cuba attempts to win her freedom by war with Spain; William Gladstone becomes British Prime Minister; Isabella II is deposed in the Spanish Revolution.

Cultural Highlights:

The Chaucer Society is founded in London; the magazine *Literary Bulletin* begins publication; Jean Cazin becomes director of the École de Beaux-Arts; Antoine Barye is inducted into the Parisian Royal Academy of Fine Arts, George Inness into the National Academy of Design and Jean François Millet into the Legion of Honor. Births in the art field include French artists Émile Bernard and Édouard Vuillard, German artist Max Slevogt and British artist Charles Furse; deaths include American artist William S. Mount, German artist Emmanuel Leutze and French artist Charles Meryon. Births in the literary field include French poets and dramatists Paul Claudel and Edmond Rostand, Russian novelist Maxim Gorky, Polish novelist Wladyslaw Reymont, German poet Stefan George, British poet Stephen Phillips and Austrian novelist Norman Douglas; deaths include German dramatist Robert Griepenkerl and Irish novelist and artist Samuel Lover. Other highlights include:

Art: Lawrence Alma-Tadema, *The Visit*; Edgar Degas, *L'Orchestre*; Jean Falguière, *The Christian Martyr*; Martin Heade, *Thunderstorm over Narragansett Bay*; Claude Monet, *The River*; Pierre-Auguste Renoir, *The Skaters*; George Watts, *The Meeting of Jacob and Esau*; James Whistler, *Symphony in White and Red*; Albert Wolff, *Judith*.

Literature: Charles Aïdé, *The Marstons*; Horatio Alger, *Ragged Dick*; William Barnes, *Poems of Rural Life*; Alphonse Daudet, *Le Petite Chose*; Feodor Dostoyevsky, *The Idiot*; Ralph W. Emerson, *May Day and Other Poems*; Cincinnatus Miller, *Specimens*; William Morris, *Earthly Paradise I, II*; Alexei Tolstoy, *Czar Feodor Ivanovich*.

MUSICAL EVENTS

A. Births:

Jan 23	Paul Bergmans (Bel-mus)
Jan 28	Julián Aguirre (Arg-cm)
Jan 28	Frederic Lamond (Scot-pn)
Feb 9	Max Seiffert (Ger-mus)
Feb 26	Leonard Borwick (Br-pn)
Apr 19	Max von Schillings (Ger-cd)
May 27	Marie Wittich (Ger-sop)
Jun 1	Alfred M. Richardson (Br-org)
Jun 10	Heinrich Schenker (Ger-the)
Jul 11	Alfred O. Lorenz (Aus-mus)
Jul 24	Nikolai Findeisen (Rus-mus)
Aug 7	Granville Bantock (Br-cm)
Aug 14	Leone Sinigaglia (It-cm)
Aug 16	Charles Skilton (Am-org)
Aug 18	Ellison Van Hoose (Am-ten)
Aug 22	Maud Powell (Am-vn)
Sep 26	Henry F. Gilbert (Am-cm)
Nov 2	Vassily Sapelnikov (Rus-pn)
Nov 6	John Forsell (Swe-bar)
Nov 24	Scott Joplin (Am-cm)
Nov 28	Franz Drdla (Hun-vn-cm)
Nov 30	Ernest Newman (Br-cri)

B. Deaths:

Jan 3	Moritz Hauptmann (Ger-cm-the)
Jan 7	William Bradbury (Am-cm-ed)
Jan 20	Antoine Prumier (Fr-hp-cm)
Mar 2	Carl Eberwein (Ger-vn-cm)
Apr 3	Franz Berwald (Swe-cm)
Apr 11	Emma Romer (Br-sop)
Jun 5	Anselm Huttenbrenner (Aus-cm)
Jun 17	Alphonse Leduc (Fr-pub)
Jul 10	Carlo Conti (It-the-cm)
Aug 11	Halfdan Kjerulf (Nor-pn-cm)
Oct 6	Léon Kreutzer (Fr-cm-cri)
Nov 9	William Harrison (Br-ten-imp)

Nov 13   Gioacchino Rossini (It-cm)
Nov 25   Karl F. Brendel (Ger-cri)
Nov 26   Alexandre Vincent (Fr-the)
Dec 13   Peter J. Simrock (Ger-pub)

Dec 14   Mario Aspa (It-cm)
Dec 26   Karl Haslinger (Aus-pub)
Dec   Pierre Hédouin (Fr-mus)

C. Debuts:
U.S. -- Ferdinand von Inten (N.Y.)

Other - Alfred-Auguste Giraudet (Paris), Alma Haas (Leipzig), Natalia Janotha (Warsaw), Franz Krückl (Brünn), Jean Lassalle (Liège), Victor Maurel (Paris), Romilda Pantaleoni (Milan), Laura Rappoldi (Vienna), Franz Ries (Germany)

D. New Positions:
Conductors: Ernst Frank (Würzburg), Friedrich Marpurg (kapellmeister, Darmstadt), Carlo Pedrotti (Teatro Regio, Turin)

Educational: Leopold Auer (violin, St. Petersburg Conservatory), Mily Balakirev (director, Free School of Music), William S. Bennett (principal, Royal Academy of Music), Anton Bruckner (organ and theory, Vienna Conservatory), Carl D. Fuchs (piano, Kullak Academy), Joseph Joachim (director, Berlin Hochschule), Otto Kitzler (director, Brünn Music School and Music Society), Karl Klindworth (piano, Moscow Conservatory), Philipp Scharwenka (composition, Kullak Academy)

Others: Wilhelm Bergner (organ, Riga Cathedral), Ernst Grosjean (organ, Verdun Cathedral), Alexandre Guilmant (organ, Notre Dame), John R. Hassard (music critic, N.Y. *Tribune*), James H. Mapleson (manager, Drury lane), Jules Pasdeloup (manager, Théâtre Lyrique), Karl Riedel (president, Allgemeiner Deutscher Musikverein)

E. Prizes and Honors:
Honors: Edvard Grieg (government grant), Ferdinand Hiller (honorary doctorate, Bonn), Camille Saint-Saëns (Legion of Honor)

F. Biographical Highlights:
Emma Albani travels to Paris to study with Duprez; Arrigo Boito suffers a catastrophic premiere of his *Mephistopheles*; Anton Bruckner moves to Vienna; Michele Carafa suffers from paralysis; Friedrich von Flotow marries the sister of his first wife; Robert Franz, due to increasing deafness and nervous disorders, retires; Minnie Hauk goes to Europe and debuts at Covent Garden; Clara Kellogg makes her London debut; Hermann Kretzschmar enters Leipzig University to study musicology; Franz von Lenbach settles in Munich; Silas Pratt goes to Berlin for further music study; Hugo Riemann enters the University of Berlin; Sofia Scalchi, Therese Tietjens and Zélia Trebelli make their Covent Garden debuts; Heinrich Vogl marries soprano Therese Thomas; Richard Wagner begins a friendship with Nietzsche; Hugo Wolf observes with enthusiasm his first opera.

G. Institutional Openings:
Performing Groups: Allgemeine Deutsche Caeciliaenverein (Bamberg); Apollo Club of Boston; Chicago Oratorio Society; Church Music Association (N.Y.); Copenhagen Society of Chamber Music; Montevideo Philharmonic Society; Radecke Choral Society (Berlin); Societatea Filarmonica Româna (Filarmonica George Enescî); Société des Oratorios (Paris)

Educational: Academie de Musique (Quebec); Halle School of Music (Germany); Orleans Municipal Music School; Peabody Institute (Baltimore); Royal Danish Music Conservatory (Copenhagen)

Other: Belgrade National Theater; Edition Peters (Leipzig); Erben Organ (St. Patrick's, N.Y.); Fürstner Publishing Co. (Berlin); Gesellschaft für Musikforschung (Berlin); Grand (Pike's) Opera House (N.Y.); Gubrynowicz Publishing House (L'vov); Johann

C. Neupert, Piano and Harpsichord Maker; *New York Philharmonic Journal*; Powell Symphony Hall (St. Louis); Seyfarth Music Publishers (Lvov) Société Bourgault-Ducoudray (Paris); Society for the History of Netherlands' Music; Tonhalle-Gesellschaft (Zurich); *Zeitschrift für Katholische Kirchenmusik*

H. Musical Literature:

Clément, Félix, *Les musiciens célèbres depuis le 16ème siècle*
Hiller, Ferdinand, *Aus dem Tonleben unserer Zeit*
Lotze, Rudolf, *Geschichte der Aesthetik in Deutschland*
Meerens, Charles, *Phénomènes Musico-Physiologiques*
Ouseley, Frederick, *Treatise on Harmony*
Paul, Oscar, *Geschichte des Klaviers*
Schuré, Edouard, *Histoire du Lied*
Tappert, Wilhelm, *Musikalische Studien*
Tiersch, Otto, *System und Methode der Harmonielehre*
Weitzmann, Carl, *Der Letzte der Virtuosen*

I. Musical Compositions:

Auber,Daniel, *Le premier jour de bonheur* (opera)
Bendl, Karel, *Lejla* (opera)
Bizet, Georges, *Noé* (opera--with Halévy)
   Roma (symphony for orchestra)
Boito, Arrigo, *Mephistopheles* (opera-revised 1875)
Borodin, Alexander, *5 Songs* (includes *The Sea*)
Brahms, Johannes, *Ein Deutsches Requiem, Opus 45* (soloists, chorus, orchestra)
   "Magelone" Songs, Opus 33 (voice and piano)
   Rinaldo, Opus 50 (cantata)
   21 Songs, Opus 43, 47, 48, and 49
Bruch, Max, *Concerto No. 1 for Violin and Orchestra*
Converse, Charles, *Converse* (hymn tune, "What a Friend We Have in Jesus")
Goldmard, Karl, *12 Songs, Opus 18* (voice and piano)
Gottschalk, Louis, *Symphony No. 2, "A Montevideo"*
   Marche Solennelle (orchestra)
Grieg, Edvard, *Concerto in A Minor, Opus 16, for Piano and Orchestra*
Lecocq, Charles, *Fleur-de-thé* (operetta)
   L'amour et son carquois
Mussorgsky, Modest, *The Marriage* (opera)
Nápravník, Eduard, *The Inhabitants of Nishij Novgorod* (opera)
Offenbach, Jacques, *La Périchole* (operetta)
   L'île de Tulipatan (operetta)
Redner, Lewis H., *St. Louis* (hymn tune, "O Little Town of Bethlehem")
Rimsky-Korsakov, Nikolai, *Symphony No. 2, "Antar"*
Saint-Saëns, Camille, *Concerto No. 2, Opus 22, for Piano and Orchestra*
   Concerto No. 1 in A Major for Violin and Orchestra
Serov, Alexander, *Taras Bulba* (unfinished opera)
Smetana, Bedrich, *Festive Overture in C Major*
   Song of the Czechs II (cantata)
Strauss, Johann, Jr., *Tales from the Vienna Woods*
   Thunder and Lightning Polka
Suppé, Friedrich von, *Die Frau Meisterin* (operetta)
Tchaikovsky, Peter, *Fatum, Opus 7* (symphonic poem)
   Pan Voyevoda, Opus 3 (opera)
Thomas, Ambroise, *Hamlet* (opera)
Wagner, Richard, *Die Meistersinger von Nurnburg* (opera)
Wieniawski, Henryk, *Fantasy on Gounod's Faust, Opus 20* (violin and orchestra)

1869

World Events:
In the U.S., the transcontinental railroad is completed at Promontory Point, Utah; Black Friday on Wall Street begins a Panic; the American Women Suffrage Association is founded; the University of Nebraska is founded; the Knights of Labor are formed in Philadelphia; former President Franklin Pierce dies. Internationally, the Suez Canal officially opens to sea traffic; the British Debtor's Act abolishes mandatory imprisonment for debt; Dmitri Mendeleyev publishes the Periodic Table for Element Classification; Napoleon III gives France a parliamentary government.

Cultural Highlights:
The American Museum of Natural History opens in New York; Friedrich Nietzsche begins teaching classical philology in Basel; John Ruskin becomes the first Slade Professor at Oxford. Births in the literary field include American authors Edgar Masters and Booth Tarkington and poet Edwin A. Robinson, French novelist André Gide, Swedish poet Bo Hjalmar Bergman and author Hjalmar Söderberg and British poet Laurence Binyon; deaths include French author Charles Sainte-Beuve, poet Alphonse de Lamartine and Irish author William Carleton. Births in the art field include American architect Frank Lloyd Wright, sculptor Sergeant Kendall and French artist Henri Matisse; deaths include French artist Paul Huet and Scotch artist Robert Lauder. Other highlights include:

Art: Frédéric Bazille, *Scene d'été*; Eugène Boudin, *On the Beach at Deauville*; Jean-Baptiste Carpeaux, *The Dance*; Edgar Degas, *At the Race Track*; Frederic Leighton, *Electra at Agamemnon's Tomb*; Édouard Manet, *The Balcony*; Alexandre Regnault, *Judith*; Pierre-Auguste Renoir, *Woman with Bodice of Chantilly Lace*.

Literature: Louisa May Alcott, *Little Women*; Charles Baudelaire, *L'Art Romantique*; Richard Blackmore, *Lorna Doone*; Robert Browning, *The Ring and the Book*; Victor Hugo, *L'Homme qui rit*; James Thomson, *Sunday up the River*; Mark Twain, *Innocents Abroad*; Aubrey de Vere, *Irish Odes*; Paul Verlaine, *Fetes Galantes*.

MUSICAL EVENTS

A. Births:

Feb 2	Jean Périer (Fr-ten-act)	Jul 9	Arnold Volpe (Rus-vn-cd)
Feb 3	Giulio Gatti-Casazza (It-imp)	Jul 23	Susanne Dessoir (Ger-sop)
Feb 12	Theodore Bertram (Ger-bar)	Aug 14	Armas Järnefelt (Fin-cm)
Feb 12	André Pirro (Fr-mus)	Oct 9	Harry L. Freeman (Am-cm)
Mar 3	Henry Wood (Br-cd)	Oct 15	Alfred Andersen-Wingar (Nor-cm)
Mar 16	Juan B. Fuentes (Mex-cm-the)	Oct 19	Alexander Khessin (Rus-cd)
Apr 5	Albert Roussel (Fr-cm)	Nov 4	Lucienne Bréval (Swi-sop)
Apr 17	Johannes Wolf (Ger-mus)	Nov 29	Ivor Atkins (Br-org)
May 5	Hans Pfitzner (Ger-cm)	Dec 14	Fritz Feinhals (Ger-bar)
May 16	John Austin (Am-org.m)	Dec 23	Hugh P. Allen (Br-org)
Jun 6	Siegfried Wagner (Ger-cd)		
Jun 16	George W. Stebbins (Am-org)		

B. Deaths:

Jan 17	Alexander Dargomijsky (Rus-cm)	May 10	Bernhard Molique (Ger-vn)
		Jun 15	Albert Grisar (Bel-cm)
Feb 6	Raimund Dreyschock (Boh-vn)	Aug 14	Giuseppe Persiani (It-cm)
Mar 8	Hector Berlioz (Fr-cm)	Sep 9	Otto Jahn (Ger-mus)
Mar 12	Ernst Haberbier (Ger-pn)	Nov 13	August Berwald (Swe-vn)
Apr 1	Alexander Dreyschock (Boh-pn-cm)	Nov 29	Giulia Grisi (It-sop)
Apr 20	Carl G. Loewe (Ger-cm)	Dec 18	Louis Moreau Gottschalk (Am-pn-cm)

Dec 31   Jules Fontana (Pol-pn)   Dec 31   Louis Léfebure-Wély (Fr-org)
Dec 31   Anton Haizinger (Aus-ten)

C. Debuts:
U.S. -- Nahan Franko (N.Y.), Sam Franko (N.Y.), Walton Perkins (N.Y.), Hermine Rudersdorff (Boston)

Other - Francesco Benucci (Florence), Alexander Girardi (Rohitsch-Sauerbrunn), Giuseppe Kaschmann (Zagreb), Alexander Michalowski (Leipzig), Josef Mödlinger (Zürich), Vladimir de Pachmann (Odessa), Theodor Reichmann (Madgeburg)

D. New Positions:
Conductors: Karl Eckert (Berlin Opera), Karl Millöcker (Theater an der Wien), Eduard Nápravník (Russian Imperial Court)

Educational: August Ambros (music history, University of Prague), Jean Baptiste Arban (trumpet, Paris Conservatory), Louis Brassin (piano, Brussels Conservatory), Anton Door (piano, Vienna Conservatory), Louis Ehlert (piano, Tausig's School), Franz Krenn (harmony and counterpoint, Vienna Conservatory), Eduard Mertke (piano, Cologne Conservatory), Adolf Prosniz (piano, Vienna Conservatory), Ernst F. Rudorff (piano, Berlin Hochschule), Hendrik Waelput (director, Bruges Conservatory), Alexander Winterberger (piano, St. Petersberg Conservatory)

Others: Frederick Bridge (organ, Mancester Cathedral), Charles A. Chauvet (organ, Trinité, Paris), Robert Eitner (editor, *Monatschefte für Musikgeschichte*), Richard Hol (organ, Utrecht Cathedral), Heinrich Laube (director, Leipzig Stadttheater)

E. Prizes and Honors:
Prizes: Jan van den Eeden and Antoine Taudou (Prix de Rome)

Honors: Michael Costa (knighted), Félicien David (French Institute), Nicholas Levasseur (Legion of Honor), John Knowles Paine (honorary M.A., Harvard)

F. Biographical Highlights:
Isaac Albéniz enters Madrid Conservatory; Désirée Artôt marries baritone Mariano Padilla y Ramos; Georges Bizet marries Geneviève Halévy; Anton Bruckner appears as organ virtuoso in France; Dudley Buck moves to Chicago; Cosima von Bülow divorces Hans and bears Wagner's son, Siegfried; Claude Debussy begins piano lessons at age seven; Frederick Delius begins violin lessons; Patrick S. Gilmore stages a mammoth National Peace Jubilee in Boston; Edvard Grieg loses his only child; Lilli Lehman makes her Berlin debut; Franz Liszt returns to Weimar, meets Olga Janina; Edward MacDowell begins piano lessons; Mathilde Mallinger begins a long association with the Berlin Opera; Amalie Materna makes her Vienna Opera debut; André Messager gains admission to École Niedermeyer; Modest Mussorgsky re-enters government service as a clerk in the Ministry of State Property; Christine Nilsson makes her Covent Garden debut; Teresa Stolz makes her debut at La Scala; Theodore Thomas takes his orchestra on a national tour.

G. Institutional Openings:
Performing Groups: Beethoven Musical Society (Buffalo, N.Y.); Joachim String Quartet (Berlin); Portland Rossini Club (Maine); Société Sainte-Cécile (Quebec); Vienna Staatsoper; Washington Choral Society (D.C.)

Educational: College of Organists (London); Czech Teacher's Institute; Dijon Conservatory of Music; Liceo Musicale "G. Frescobaldi" (Ferrara); Philadelphia Musical Academy; Radecke Music School (Berlin); Schola Cantorum of San Salvatore (Lauro); Tonic Sol-Fa College (Curwen Institute); Wyman Music School (Claremont, N.Y.)

Other: Bessel and Co., Music Publishers (St. Petersburg); Concordia Publishing House

(St. Louis); Detroit Opera House; *L'Écho Musical*; German Theater (San Francisco); *Monatschefte für Musikgeschichte*; *Organist's Quarterly Journal* (London); *The Portfolio*; *Le Rappel*; Durand Schoenewerk and Cie. (A. Durand et Fils, 1891-- Paris); J. H. Willcox Co. (Hutchings, Plaisted and Co.), Organ Builders (Boston)

H. Musical Literature:
Alcedo, José, *Filosofía elemental de la música*
Coussemaker, Charles, *Les Harmonistes du XIV Siècle*
Engel, Carl, *Musical Instruments of All Countries*
Eslava, Hilarión, *Lira Sacra-Hispana*
Fétis, François-Joseph, *Histoire général de la Musique I*
Gumprecht, Otto, *Musikalische charakterbilder*
Hanslick, Eduard, *Geschichte des Concertwesens in Wien*
Krause, Emil, *Ergänzungen: Aufgabenbuch für die Harmonielehre*
Lobe, Johann C., *Consonanzen und Dissonanzen*
Wagner, Richard, *Über das Dirigieren*

I. Musical Compositions:
Auber, Daniel, *Rêve d'amour* (opera)
Balakirev, Mily, *Islamey* (tone poem)
Bendl, Karel, *Bretislav* (opera)
Bizet, Georges, *La mort Savance* (soloists, orchestra)
Brahms, Johannes, *Liebeslieder Waltzes, Opus 52*
    Alto Rhapsody, Opus 53
Converse, Charles, *American Concert Overture*
Cowell, Henry, *Symphony No. 1 in C Major*
Cui, César, *William Ratcliff* (opera)
Dargomijsky, Alexander, *The Stone Guest* (unfinished opera)
Gade, Niels, *Festsang* (chorus)
    Denderliedeken (song cycle)
Gottschalk, Louis Moreau, *Fantasy on Brazilian National Anthem* (piano)
Gounod, Charles, *Le temple de l'harmonie* (cantata)
Guiraud, Ernest, *En prison* (opera)
Hofmann, Heinrich, *Cartouche* (opera)
Lecocq, Alexandre, *Gandolfo* (operetta)
    Le rajah de Mysore (opera)
Loewe, Carl, *5 Songs for Low Voice, Opus 145*
Marchetti, Filippo, *Ruy Blas* (opera)
Moniuszko, Stanislaw, *Paria* (opera)
Morales, Melesio, *La Locomotiva* (orchestra)
Mussorgsky, Modest, *Boris Goudonov* (opera--revised 1872)
Offenbach, Jacques, *Vert-vert* (operetta)
    La diva (operetta)
    Les brigands (operetta)
Raff, Joseph, *Symphony No. 3, Opus 153, "Im Walde"*
Rheinberger, Josef, *Die sieben Raber* (opera)
Saint-Saëns, Camille, *Oratorio de Noël, Opus 12*
    Concerto No. 3, Opus 29, for Piano and Orchestra
    Piano Trio in F Major, Opus 18
Sherwin, William F., *Sound the Battle Cry* (hymn)
Strauss, Johann, Jr., *Wine, Women and Song*
    Pizzicato Polka
Sullivan, Arthur, *The Prodigal Son* (oratorio)
Suppé, Franz von, *Isabella* (operetta)
Svendsen, Johan, *Concerto, Opus 6, for Violin and Orchestra*
Tchaikovsky, Peter, *Romeo and Juliet Fantasy Overture*
    Undine (opera)
Wagner, Richard, *Siegfried* (opera)

1870

World Events:

The U.S. census shows a population of 39,818,000, a 26% increase in 10 years; the Fifteenth Ammendment on the right to vote is ratified; the first known use of the Democratic donkey symbol occurs; the Department of Justice is created; the U.S. Weather Bureau is authorized; Ohio State University is founded; Phoenix, Arizona, is founded; former Confederate General Robert E. Lee dies. Internationally, the Franco-Prussian War begins in July; Napoleon III is deposed and the Third French Republic is proclaimed; Heinrich Schliemann begins excavations on the supposed site of ancient Troy; Amadeo of Savoy becomes ruler of Spain; Papal Infallibility is proclaimed by Rome.

Cultural Highlights:

The Boston Museum of Fine Arts opens; the Metropolitan Museum of Art opens in New York City; the Society of Wandering Exhibitions is founded in Moscow; Charles W. Brooks becomes the editor of *Punch*. Births in the art world include American artists William Glackens and Maxfield Parish, sculptors Alexander Calder and Roland H. Perry, French artist Maurice Denis and German sculptor Ernst Barlach; deaths include American artist George Bingham, French artist Frédéric Bazille and Irish artist Daniel Maclise. Births in the literary field include American author Frank Norris, Russian novelists Ivan Bunin and Alexander Kuprin, French historian and poet Hilaire Belloc and poet Pierre Louijs; deaths include French authors Alexander Dumas, père, Jules de Goncourt, Prosper Mérimée and Charles de Montalembert, Scotch author George Hogarth, British novelists Frederick Chamier and Charles Dickens and Spanish poet Gustavo Bécquer. Other highlights include:

Art: Lawrence Alma-Tadema, *Un Jongleur*; Paul Cézanne, *The Black Clock*; Henri Chapu, *Jeanne d'Arc*; Jean-Baptiste Corot, *Interrupted Reading*; Gustave Courbet, *The Wave*; Jean Falguière, *Victor in the Cockfight*; George Inness, *Olive Groves near Rome*; William Page, *Head of Christ*; Alexandre Regnault, *Salome*; William Rinehart, *Antigone*

Literature: Louisa May Alcott, *An Old-Fashioned Girl*; Thomas Aldrich, *The Story of a Bad Boy*; Benjamin Disraeli, *Lothair*; Bret Harte, *The Luck of Roaring Camp*; Alexis Kivi, *The Seven Brothers*; Alexei Tolstoy, *Tsar Boris*; Paul Verlaine, *La Bonne Chanson*; Jules Verne, *Twenty Thousand Leagues under the Sea*; Émile Zola, *La Débacle*.

MUSICAL EVENTS

A. Births

Jan 12	Carl Burrian (Cz-ten)	Aug 14	Harry Lauder (Scot-cm)
Jan 13	Henryk Opienski (Pol-mus-cm)	Sep 2	R. Kennerley Rumford (Br-bar)
Jan 20	Guillaume Lekeu (Bel-cm)	Sep 28	Florent Schmitt (Fr-cm)
Jan 22	Charles Tournemire (Fr-cm)	Oct 3	Felix von Kraus (Aus-bs)
Feb 10	Alessandro Bonci (It-ten)	Oct 8	Louis Vierne (Fr-org)
Feb 13	Leopold Godowsky (Pol-pn)	Oct 25	Hector Dufranne (Fr-bar)
Feb 22	Albert Reiss (Ger-ten)	Nov 11	Edmund Fellowes (Br-mus)
Mar 6	Oscar Straus (Ger-cm)	Nov 26	Heinrich Knote (Ger-ten)
Mar 12	Mabel Wood Hill (Am-cm)	Nov 30	Cecil Forsyth (Br-cm-au)
Apr 30	Franz Lehár (Aus-cm)	Dec 5	Vitezslav Novák (Cz-cm)
Jun 29	Joseph C. Brell (Am-ten-cm)	Dec 7	Richard Specht (Am-cri)
Jul 15	August Schmid-Linder (Ger-pn)	Dec 28	Matja von Niessen-Stone
Jul 18	Emil Mlynarski (Pol-vn-cd)		(Rus-sop)

B. Deaths

Jan 18	Anton Berlijn (Hol-cm-cd)	Mar 9	Théodore Labarre (Fr-hp)
Jan 26	Cesare Pugni (It-cm)	Mar 10	Ignaz Moscheles (Pol-pn)

Apr 8	Charles de Bériot (Bel-vn)	Sep 9	Paul Jausions (Fr-mus)
May 14	Ramón Vilanova (Sp-cm)	Sep	Joseph A. Roeckel (Ger-ten)
May 30	Gustave Vogt (Fr-ob-cm)	Oct 20	Michael Balfe (Ir-cm)
Jun 8	Johann G. Töpfer (Ger-org)	Oct 31	Mihály Mosonyi (Hun-cm-au)
Jun 9	Erik Drake (Swe-cm)	Dec 17	Giuseppe Mercadante (It-cm)
Aug 14	Joséphine Fodor-Mainvielle (Fr-sop)	Dec 28	Alexei L'vov (Rus-vn-cm)
Aug 14	Franz Hauser (Boh-bar)		August H. Cranz (Ger-pn)

C. Debuts:

U.S. -- Annie Louise Cary (N.Y.), Christine Nilsson (tour)

Other - Emma Albani (Messina), Lucien Fugère (Paris), Anton Schott (Frankfurt), Francesco Tamagno (Turin), Georgina Weldon (London), Heinrich Wiegand (Zurich)

D. New Positions:

Conductors: Johann Herbeck (Vienna Opera), Isador Seiss (Cologne Conservatory Orchestra), Auguste Vianesi (Covent Garden)

Educational: Julius Eichberg (director, Boston Conservatory), Zdenek Fibich (teacher, Vilna, Poland), Nicolai Hubert (theory, Moscow Conservatory), Basil Köhner (director, Tiflis Conservatory), Lauro Rossi (director, Naples Conservatory), Wilhelm Rust (theory, composition, Stern Conservatory), Ludwig Scharwenka (composition, Kullak Academy, Berlin)

Others: Hermann Mendel (editor, *Deutsche Musiker-Zeitung*), Léon Vasseur (organist, Versailles Cathedral), Charles Widor (organ, St. Sulpice)

E. Prizes and Honors:

Prizes: Charles E. Lefebvre and Henri-Charles Maréchal (Prix de Rome)

Honors: William George Cusins (Master of the Queen's Music), William Sterndale Bennett (honorary doctorate, Oxford)

F. Biographical Highlights:

Claude Debussy takes further piano studies with Mme. de Fleurville; Gabriel Fauré returns to Paris and joins the light infantry; Arthur Foote enters Harvard; Charles Gounod visits London and forms his own choir; Edvard Grieg visits Rome, meets Liszt; Minnie Hauk makes her Vienna debut; Ferdinand Hiller conducts in St. Petersburg; Vincent d'Indy serves with the Army of Paris; Lilli Lehmann begins a fifteen-year association with the Berlin Opera; Anatol Liadov enters St. Petersburg Conservatory; Victor Maurel makes his La Scala debut; Hubert Parry receives his B.A. degree; Emil Paur graduates from Vienna Conservatory; Vladimir Stasov donates his music collection to the St. Petersburg library; Henri Vieuxtemps makes his first U.S.tour; Richard Wagner marries Cosima von Bülow; Hugo Wolf sent to school in Graz.

G. Institutional Openings:

Performing Groups: Berner Männerchor; Denver Männerchor; Gounod's Choir (London); Leeds Philharmonic Society; Société Chorale (Dijon); University Choral and Orchestral Society (Aberdeen); Worcester Musical (Festival Choral) Society; Zagreb Opera Co.

Festivals: Brighton Festival (England)

Educational: Conservatorio Nacional de Música (Quito); Free School of Music (St. Petersburg); Nancy Conservatory of Music; Philadelphia Musical Academy; Salzburg Mozarteum; Warnot's Music School (St. Josseten-Noode)

Other: Coates Opera House (Kansas City, Missouri); *Deutsche Musiker-Zeitung*; Durand and Schönewerk, Publishers (successor to Flaxland); Gewerbehaussaal (Dresden

Concert Hall); Internationale Mozart-Stiftung (Salzburg); Stanislaw Krzyzanowski, Bookseller and Music Publisher (Kraków); Merced Theater (Los Angeles); Scribner's Monthly; Société Nationale de Musique (France); Wagner Tubas; Warsaw Music Society

H. Musical Literature:

Berlioz, Hector, *Mémoires* (posthumous publication)
Brinsmead, Edgar, *History of the Pianoforte*
Eslava, Hilarión, *Escuela de contrapunto, fuga y composición*
Fechner, Gustavo, *Vorschule der Aesthetik*
Hanslick, Eduard, *Aus dem Concertsaal*
Kornmüller, Utto, *Lexikon der Kirchlichen Tonkunst*
Naumann, Emil, *Die Tonkunst in der Culturgeschichte*
Parker, James, *Theoretical and Practical Harmony*
Ritter, Frédéric, *History of Music I*
Stade, Friedrich, *Vom Musikalisch-Schönen*

I. Musical Compositions:

Balfe, Michael, *The Knight of the Leopard* (opera)
Barnby, Joseph, *Rebekah* (oratorio)
Benedict, Julius, *St. Peter* (cantata)
Bizet, Georges, *Clarissa Harlowe* (opera)
Bruch, Max, *Symphony No. 1, Opus 28*
    Symphony No. 2, Opus 36
Converse, Charles, *Fest-Ouverture*
Delibes, Léo, *Coppélia* (ballet)
Dubois, Théodore, *Solemn Mass*
Dvořák, Antonin, *String Quartet in E Minor, Opus 10*
    Alfred the Great (opera)
    Dramatic Overture
Flotow, Friedrich von, *L'ombre* (opera)
Franck, César, *Paris, a Patriotic Song* (tenor and orchestra)
Gomes, Antonio C., *Il Guaraný* (opera)
Gounod, Charles, *Messe des Orphéonistes*
    À la frontière (cantata)
Grieg, Edvard, *Norwegian Songs and Dances, Opus 17* (piano)
Guiraud, Ernest, *Le Kobold* (opera)
Liszt, Franz, *Élégie No. 2 for Piano*
Moniuszko, Stanislaw, *Mass in A Minor*
Offenbach, Jacques, *La romance de la rose* (operetta)
    Mam'zelle Moucheron
Pedrotti, Carlo, *Il Favorito* (opera)
    La vergine di Kermo (opera)
Raff, Joseph J., *Dame Kobold* (opera)
Reinecke, Carl, *Symphony No. 1, Opus 79*
Rubinstein, Anton, *The Tower of Babel* (opera)
    Don Quixote, Opus 87 (symphonic poem)
Saint-Saëns, Camille, *Introduction and Rondo Capriccioso, Opus 28*
Smetana, Bedrich, *The Bartered Bride* (opera)
Strauss, Johann, Jr., *Wiener Blut*
Suppé, Franz von, *Lohengelb* (operetta)
Svendsen, Johan, *Concerto, Opus 7, for Cello and Orchestra*
Tchaikovsky, Peter, *Nature and Love* (cantata)
Wagner, Richard, *Siegfried Idyll*
Wieniawski, Henryk, *Polonaise No. 2, Opus 21, for Violin and Orchestra*

1871

World Events:

In the U.S., the Great Chicago Fire destroys much of Chicago from October 8 to 11; the Treaty of Washington settles fishing disputes between the U.S. and Canada; the Civil Service Commission is formed; midwest cattle drives reach their peak; Minneapolis, Minnesota, and Birmingham, Alabama, are incorporated. Internationally, the Franco-Prussian War ends with the proclamation of the German Empire; labor unions in England are authorized by the Parliament; Henry Stanley finds David Livingston in Africa; the first luxury liner, the *S.S. Oceanic*, is launched.

Cultural Highlights:

The Slade School of Fine Arts opens in London; François Bazin is inducted into the French Academy of Fine Arts; Emily Dickinson becomes a recluse in her Amhurst home. Births in the literary field include American authors Stephen Crane, Theodore Dreiser and James Johnson, Russian author Leonid Andreyev, French novelist Marcel Proust and poet Paul Valéry and British dramatist J. M. Synge; deaths include American poets Alice and Phoebe Cary, British dramatist Thomas Robertson, French poet Émile Deschamps and novelist Paul de Kock, German authors Willibald Alexis, Friedrich Halm and Eduard Koch. Births in the art field include American artist James Johnson and sculptor Victor Brenner, French artists Auguste Delacroix and Georges Roualt, Irish artist Jack Yeats and Czech artist Frantisek Kupka; deaths include American artist Thomas Rossiter, French artist Alexandre Regnault, German artist Moritz von Schwind, British artist George Hayter and Czech artist Josef Mánes. Other highlights include:

Art: Reinhold Begas, *Schiller Memorial* (Berlin); Edgar Degas, *Father Listening to Pagans*; Vinnie Hoxie, *Abraham Lincoln* (Capitol Rotunda); Eastman Johnson, *The Hatch Family*; Édouard Manet, *Le Repos*; John Millais, *Chill October*; Dante Rosetti, *The Dream of Dante*; James Whistler, *The Artist's Mother*.

Literature: Louisa May Alcott, *Little Men*; Charles Darwin, *The Descent of Man*; Edward Eggleston, *The Hoosier Schoolmaster*; Ralph W. Emerson, *Essays*; John M. Hay, *Pike County Ballads*; Edward Lear, *Nonsense Songs, Stories...*; Arthur Rimbaud, *Les Illuminations*; Algernon Swinburne, *Songs before Sunrise*.

MUSICAL EVENTS

A. Births:

Jan 1	Charles Dalmorès (Fr-ten)	Apr 21	Leo Blech (Ger-cd-cm)
Jan 3	Daniel Robles (Peru-cm-mus)	Apr 30	Louise Homer (Am-alto)
Jan 5	Frederick Converse (Am-cm)	May 20	Eugenio Giraldoni (It-bar)
Jan 15	Bertram Shapleigh (Am-cm)	Jun 7	Leonid Sobinoff (Rus-ten)
Feb 7	Wilhelm Stenhammar (Swe-cm)	Jun 20	Halfdan Rode (Nor-bar)
Mar 5	Karl Grumsky (Ger-cri)	Jun 29	Luisa Tetrazzini (It-sop)
Mar 14	Olive Fremstad (Swe-mez)	Sep 29	William Kraft (Am-cm)
Mar 17	Giuseppe Borgatti (It-ten)	Nov 5	Clarence Whitehill (Am-bar)
Mar 25	Hermann Abert (Ger-mus)	Nov 28	J. G. Prud'homme (Fr-mus)
Mar 28	Willem Mengelberg (Hol-cd)	Dec 20	Henry Hadley (Am-cm)

B. Deaths:

Feb 1	Alexander Serov (Rus-cm)	Apr 9	John Chatterton (Br-hp-cm)
Feb 7	Henry Steinway (Ger-pn.m)	Apr 11	Jean J. Deruyts (Bel-cm)
Mar 12	Sylvanus B. Pond (Am-cm-pub)	Apr 15	Ferenc Bräuer (Hun-cd)
Mar 20	Antonio Buzzola (It-cm)	Apr 27	Sigismond Thalberg (Swi-pn)
Mar 26	François Fétis (Bel-the-mus)	May 12	Daniel Auber (Fr-cm)
Apr 5	Georg A. Henkel (Ger-cm)	May 24	Francisco Daniel (Fr-mus)

May 26 Louis Maillart (Fr-cm)
Jul 17   Carl Tausig (Pol-pn)
Sep 26 Philip Potter (Br-pn)
Dec 6   Nicholas P. Levasseur (Fr-bs)

Dec 12 Friedrich Müller (Ger-cd)
Dec 17 Alessandro Gandini (It-cm-cd)
Dec 21 Theodor Hagen (Ger-cri)

C. Debuts:

U.S. -- Leopold Damrosch (N.Y.), Tom Karl (N.Y.), Francis Korbay (N.Y.), Janet Patey (tour), Clara K. Rogers (N.Y.), Hermine Rudersdorff (Boston), Charles Santley (tour), Theodor Wachtel (tour)

Other - Numa Auguez (Paris), Walter Bache (London), Jacques-Joseph Bouhy (Paris), Italo Campanini (Bologna), Heinrich Gudehus (Berlin), Virginia Gungl (Munich), Adèle Isaac (Paris), Edward Lloyd (Gloucester), Joseph Maas (London), William F. Parker (London), Hedwig Reicher-Kindermann (Karlsruhe), Rosa Sucher (Munich), Alwina Valleria (London)

D. New Positions:

Conductors: Pietro Coppola (maestro di capella, Novara Cathedral), Michael Costa (Her Majesty's Opera), Max von Erdmannsdörfer (Sonderhausen), Franco Faccio (La Scala), Franz Haberl (kapellmeister, Regensburg Cathedral), Hans Richter (National Theater, Pest), Bernhard Scholz (Breslau SO), Franz Wüllner (kapellmeister, Munich court Opera)

Educational: Théodore Dubois (harmony, Paris Conservatory), François Gevaert (director, Brussels Conservatory), Salomon Jadassohn (theory, Leipzig Conservatory), Louis-Henri Obin (voice, Paris Conservatory), Nikolai Rimsky-Korsakov (composition, St. Petersburg Conservatory), Adolphe Samuel (director, Ghent Conservatory), Ambroise Thomas (director, Paris Conservatory), Henri Vieuxtemps (violin, Brussels Conservatory)

Others: Joseph Barnby (organ, St. Anne's, London), Alexandre Guilmant (organ, La Trinité), Silas Pratt (organ, Church of the Messiah, Chicago), Ebenezer Prout (editor, *Monthly Musical Record*)

E. Prizes and Honors:

Prizes: Gaston Serpette (Prix de Rome)

Honors: Julius Benedict, George Elvey and William Sterndale Bennett (knighted)

F. Biographical Highlights:

William Barrett receives his Bachelor degree from Oxford; Anton Bruckner appears as organ virtuoso in London; Dudley Buck, following the Chicago fire, moves to Boston; Leopold and Walter Damrosch move to the U.S.; Léo Delibes quits his job, gets married and devotes full time to music; Antonin Dvorák gives up his theater job; Pierre Gailhard makes his Paris Opera debut; William S. Gilbert begins his collaboration with Sullivan; Alexander Girardi makes his Vienna debut; Edvard Grieg begins choral conducting for the Norwegian Music Society; Francesco Pandolfini and Maria Waldmann make their La Scala debuts; Silas G. Pratt returns to the U.S.; Hugo Riemann enters Leipzig Conservatory; Root and Cady lose their publishing business to the Chicago fire; Camille Saint-Saëns gives organ recitals in London; Ira Sankey joins D. L. Moody in evangelism; Johann Svendsen marries American Sara Levett.

G. Institutional Openings:

Performing Groups: Boston Apollo Club; Fisk Jubilee Singers; Indianapolis PO; Musical Society of Christiana (Oslo Musikforenning, Norway); Oslo PO; Royal (Albert Hall) Choral Society; Schroeder String Quartet (Leipzig); Sociedad de Cuartetos Clásicos (Granada)

Educational: Athens Conservatory of Music; Minneapolis Academy of Music; Petersilea Academy of Music (Boston)

Other: Grand Opera House (Milwaukee); Hubebni Matice, Music Publishers (Czechoslovakia); *Monthly Musical Record*; Royal Albert Hall (London); Society for the Publication of Danish Music

H. Musical Literature:

Boucheron, Raimendo, *Esercizi d'Armonia*
Eitner, Robert, *Hilfsbuch beim Klavierunterricht*
Hiles, Henry, *The Harmony of Sounds*
Jacobsthal, Gustav, *Die Mensuralnotenschrift des 12. und 13. Jahrhunderts*
Kornmüller, Utto, *Die Musik beim liturgischen Hochamt*
Moniuszko, Stanislaw, *Textbook on Harmony*
Naumann, Emil, *Deutsche Tondichter*
Pohl, Carl, *Die Gesellschaft der Musikfreunde und ihr Conservatorium in Wien*
Stainer, John, *A Theory of Harmony*
Tchaikovsky, Peter, *Practical Study of Harmony*

I. Musical Compositions:

Benoit, Peter, *Drama Christi* (oratorio)
Bizet, Georges, *Djamileh* (opera)
Brahms, Johannes, *Schicksalslied, Opus 54*
    Triumphslied, Opus 55
    Eight Songs, Opus 57
    Eight Songs, Opus 58
Fibich, Zdenek, *Bukovin* (opera)
    Overture, Der Jude von Prag
Franck, César, *Panis Angelicus* (song)
Gade, Niels, *Symphony No. 8 in B-flat Minor*
    Kalanus (cantata)
Gilbert and Sullivan, *Thespis* (operetta)
Gould, J. E., *Jesus, Saviour, Pilot Me* (hymn)
Gounod, Charles, *Messe Brève*
    The Annunciation (oratorio)
    Messe des Anges Gardiens
Guiraud, Ernest, *Orchestral Suite No. 1*
Lecocq, Charles, *Le barbier de Trouville* (operetta)
    Le Testament de M. de Crac (operetta)
Liszt, Franz, *Mass for Male Voices*
    Psalm 114
Massenet, Jules, *Scènes hongroises* (orchestra)
Raff, Joseph J., *Symphony No. 4 in G Minor*
    Violin Concerto No. 7 in B Minor
Rossi, Giovanni, *La Contessa d'Alternberg* (operetta)
Rubinstein, Anton, *The Demon* (opera)
    String Quartet No. 2, Opus 90
Saint-Saëns, Camille, *March héroïque, Opus 34*
    Le Rouet d'Omphale (symphonic poem)
Strauss, Johann, Jr., *One Thousand and One Nights*
    Indigo und die Vierzig Rauber (operetta)
Sullivan, Arthur, *On the Shore and Sea* (oratorio)
    The Merchant of Venice (incidental music)
Tchaikovsky, Peter, *String Quartet No. 1, Opus 11*
    5 Piano Pieces, Opus 9 and 10
Verdi, Giuseppe, *Aïda* (opera)
Wagner, Richard, *Kaisermarsch* (orchestra)

1872

World Events:

In the U.S., President Ulysses S. Grant is re-elected for a second term; the Credit Mobilier scandal breaks out; the Amnesty Act clears all Confederate leaders of treason; Arbor Day is inaugurated in Nebraska; Yellowstone National Park is created; Montgomery Ward opens his first store in Chicago; Spokane, Washington, is founded; future President Calvin Coolidge is born; Horace Greeley, American journalist, dies. Internationally, the Spanish Civil War results in the defeat of the Carlists; Porfirio Diaz is elected President of the Mexican Republic (becomes dictator in 1876); the British Ballot Act introduces secret voting; Charles V of Sweden dies and is succeeded by Oscar II.

Cultural Highlights:

The Teatro della Commedia (Manzoni) opens in Milan. Births in the art world include American artists Charles W. Hawthorne, John Marin and sculptor Frederick Sievers, British artist and author Max Beerbohm, Dutch artist Piet Mondriaan and Russian sculptor Naoum Aronson; deaths include American inventor and artist Samuel Morse, artist George Catlin and poet and artist Thomas B. Read, British artist Thomas Sully and German artist Julius Schnorr von Carolsfeld. Births in the literary world include American authors Paul Dunbar, Rupert Hughes and Harold B. Wright, French poets Paul Fort and Félix Bataille and Canadian poet John McCrae; deaths include Austrian dramatist Franz Grillparzer, German philosopher Ludwig Feuerbach, French author Théophile Gautier, Polish poet Wincenty Pol and Finnish novelist Alexis Kivi. Other highlights include:

Art: Thomas Barker, *Wellington Crossing the Pyranees*; Arnold Böcklin, *Battle of the Centaurs*; Mary Cassatt, *On the Balcony*; Thomas J. Duveneck, *Whistling Boy*; Henri Fantin-Latour, *Un Coin du Table*; Max Liebermann, *Women Plucking Geese*; Claude Monet, *Impression: Sunrise*; Pierre-Auguste Renoir, *Pont Neuf.*

Literature: Samuel Butler, *Erewhon*; Lewis Carroll, *Through the Looking Glass*; Alphonse Daudet, *L'Arlesienne*; Feodor Dostoyevsky, *The Possessed*; George Eliot, *Middlemarch*; Oliver W. Holmes, *Poet at the Breakfast Table*; Victor Hugo, *L'Année Terrible*; David Locke, *Struggles of Petroleum V. Nasby*; Mark Twain, *Roughing It.*

MUSICAL EVENTS

A. Births:

Jan 6	Alexander Scriabin (Rus-pn-cm)		Jul 15	Alfred Hertz (Ger-cd)
Jan 16	Henri Büsser (Fr-cm-cd)		Aug 15	Rubin Goldmark (Am-cm)
Feb 1	Clara Butt (Br-alto)		Aug 16	Siegmund von Hausegger (Aus-cd)
Mar 4	Joaquin Malate (Sp-pn)		Sep 9	Edward B. Hill (Am-cm)
Mar 10	Felix Borowski (Br-cri)		Sep 18	Carl R. Friedberg (Ger-pn)
Mar 19	Sergei Diaghilev (Rus-bal)		Oct 4	Alexander Zemlinsky (Aus-cd-cm)
Mar 30	Frederic Austin (Br-bar)		Oct 7	Frank Ward (Am-cm)
Mar 30	Serge Vassilenko (Rus-cm)		Oct 12	Ralph Vaughan-Williams (Br-cm)
Apr 23	Arthur Farwell (Am-cm-pub)		Nov 11	Frederick Stock (Ger-cd)
May 1	Hugo Alfvén (Swe-cm)		Nov 27	Peter Raabe (Ger-mus)
May 8	Friedrich Ludwig (Ger-mus)		Nov 28	Suzanne Adams (Am-sop)
Jun 15	Johanna E. Gadski (Ger-sop)		Nov 28	Ethel Sharpe (Br-pn)
Jul 7	J. Lamote de Grignon (Sp-cm)		Nov 29	Anna von Mildenburg (Aus-sop)
Jul 14	Irene Abendroth (Aus-sop)			

B. Deaths:

Jan 21	Jean Andries (Bel-vn-mus)		Apr 30	Flodoard Geyer (Ger-cm)
Mar 12	Conrad Kocher (Ger-cm-au)		May 2	Charles Battaille (Fr-bs)

May 15	Thomas Hastings (Am-hymn)	Aug 4	Friedrich Wieprecht (Ger-inv)
May 17	Hans Schläger (Aus-cm)	Aug 6	Benedetta Pisaroni (It-alto)
May 18	Eduard de Sobolewski (Ger-cm)	Aug 11	Lowell Mason (Am-cm-ed)
May 23	Hugo Ulrich (Ger-cm)	Aug 19	Eugène P. Prévost (Fr-cd)
Jun 4	Stanislaw Moniuszko (Pol-cm)	Oct 2	Eberhard Walcker (Ger-org)
Jun 28	Carlotta Marchisio (It-sop)	Oct 6	Karl Liebig (Ger-cd)
Jul 11	Thomas Appleton (Am-org.m)	Nov 18	Sabina Heinefetter (Ger-sop)
Jul 26	Michele Carafa (It-cm)	Dec 18	Édouard Gassier (Fr-bar)

C. Debuts:

U.S. -- Pauline Lucca (N.Y.), Minna Peschka-Leutner (Boston), Anton Rubinstein (tour), Emile Sauret (tour), Henri Wieniawski (tour)

Other - Richard Andersson (Stockholm), Jacques Rensburg (Leipzig), Franz Rummel (Antwerp)

D. New Positions:

Conductors: Constanz Berneker (Königsberg Singakademie), Johannes Brahms (Gesellschaft der Musikfreunde, Vienna), Ernst Frank (kapellmeister, Mannheim), Andreas Hallén (Göteborg), Heinrich Laube (Vienna Stadttheater), Hermann Levi (Munich Court Theater), Karl Schröder (Kroll Opera, Berlin), Ernst von Schuch (Dresden Court Opera)

Educational: César Franck (organ, Paris Conservatory), Asger Hamerik (director, Peabody Conservatory), John Pyke Hullah (Inspector of schools, London), Gustav Jensen (composition, Cologne Conservatory), Hubert Kufferath (counterpoint, Brussels Conservatory), Alberto Mazzucato (director, Milan Conservatory), Jean-Théodore Radoux (director, Conservatoire Liège), Joseph Servais (cello, Brussels Conservatory)

Others: Vincent d'Indy (organ, St. Leu), John Stainer (organ, St. Paul's, London)

E. Prizes and Honors:

Prizes: Gaston Salvayre (Prix de Rome)

Honors: Edward Armitage (Royal Academy), François Bazin (French Academy), John Goss and Robert P. Stewart (knighted), Edvard Grieg (Swedish Academy), William Mason (honorary doctorate, Yale), Victor Massé (French Institute)

F. Biographical Highlights:

Emma Abbott goes to Europe to study voice; Franz Abt is well received on his U.S. conducting tour; Emma Albani and Marianne Brandt make their Covent Garden debuts; Isaac Albéniz runs away from home, stows away to South America; Giovanni Boldini settles in Paris; Tomás Bretón takes first prize in composition at Milan Conservatory; Italo Campanini makes his London debut; Claude Debussy studies with Lavignac; Adolphe M. Foerster enters Leipzig conservatory; Engelbert Humperdinck turns from architecture and enters Cologne Conservatory; Leoš Janácek graduates from Czech Teachers' Institute; Charles Lamoureux becomes assistant conductor of the Concerts du Conservatoire de Paris; Jean Louis Lassalle makes his Paris Opera debut; Ignace Jan Paderewski enters Warsaw Conservatory; Nicholas Rimsky-Korsakov marries Nadezhda Purgold; Anton Rubinstein tours the U.S. with Wieniawski; Charlotte Sainton-Dolby opens her own vocal school in London; Johann Stauss, Jr., visits the U.S. and conducts several "monster concerts"; Alwina Valleria makes her La Scala debut; Richard Wagner goes to Bayreuth for cornerstone ceremonies for his Festspielhaus.

G. Institutional Openings:

Performing Groups: Allgemeiner Deutscher Musikerverband (Berlin); Apollo Music Club (Chicago); Beau-Rivage Orchestra (Lausanne); Cincinnati SO; Concerti Populari

(Turin); Koblenz Verein der Musikfreunde; Royal Amateur Orchestral Society (London); St. Petersburg Society for Quartet (Chamber) Music; Symphonie- und Kurorchester (Baden-Baden)

Educational: Ducal Orchestral School (Liszt Hochschule, Weimar); St. Louis Conservatory of Music; Sainton-Dolby Vocal School (London); Scuola Gratuita de Canto (Turin); Trinity College of Music (London); Verein zur Erforschung alter Choralhandschriften

Other: Bösendorfer Saal (Vienna); Brisbane Musical Union (Australia); Carl Fischer, Inc. (New York); Moeller Organ Co. (Maryland); Monte Carlo Concert Hall; *Musical Leaflet*; Oxford University Musical Club; Staub's Opera House (Knoxville); Teatro dela Opera (Buenos Aires); Theater in der Guckengasse (Cologne); Turnverein Hall (Los Angeles); Franz A. Urbánek Music Publishing Co. (Prague); Wagner Society of London

H. Musical Literature:

Ambros, August, *Bunte Blätter: Skizzen und Studien für freunde der Musik...*
Bertrand, Jean, *Les Nationalities musicales étudiées du la Drame lyrique*
Kowalski, Henri, *A Travers l'Amerique*
Küster, Hermann, *Über die Formen in der Musik*
Langhans, Wilhelm, *Das musicalische Urteil und seine Ausbildung durch des Erziehung*
Lobe, Johann, *Katechismus der Compositionslehre*
Mach, Ernst, *Zur Theorie des Gehörorgans*
Nietzsche, Friedrich, *Die Geburt der Tragödie aus dem Geiste der Musik*
Pruckner, Karoline, *Theorie und Praxis der Gesangskunst*
Richter, Ernst, *Lehrbuch des einfachen und doppelten Kontrapunkts*

I. Musical Compositions:

Bizet, Georges, *L'Arlésienne* (incidental music)
    Jeux d'enfants (piano--four hands)
Bristow, George, *The Pioneer, Opus 49* (cantata)
Bruch, Max, *Hermione* (opera)
Bruckner, Anton, *Symphony No. 2 in C Minor* (revised 1876 and 1891)
Cowell, Henry, *Symphony No. 2 in F Minor*
Dvořák, Antonin, *Heirs of the White Mountain, Opus 30* (cantata)
    Piano Quintet in A Major
Fibich, Zdenek, *Concert Overture in E* (orchestra)
Franck, César, *Redemption* (oratorio)
Gounod, Charles, *The Nativity* (oratorio)
Grieg, Edvard, *Sigurd Jorsalfar, Opus 22* (incidental music)
d'Indy, Vincent, *Symphony No. 1 in A Major*
Lalo, Edouard, *Concerto in F Minor, Opus 20, for Violin and Orchestra*
Lecocq, Charles, *La fille de Madame Angot* (operetta)
Massenet, Jules, *Don César de Bazan* (opera)
Mussorgsky, Modest, *The Nursery* (song cycle)
Offenbach, Jacques, *Le Roi Carotte* (operetta)
    Le corsaire noir (operetta)
Raff, Joseph J., *Symphony No. 5, Opus 177, "Lenore"*
Rimsky-Korsakov, Nikolai, *Ivan, the Terrible* (opera)
Saint-Saëns, Camille, *La princesse Jaune* (opera)
Smetana, Bedrich, *Libuše* (opera)
Sullivan, Arthur, *Festival Te Deum*
    Onward, Christian Soldiers (hymn)
Tchaikovsky, Peter, *Symphony No. 2, Opus 17, "Little Russian"*
    Serenade for Small Orchestra
    The Oprichnik (opera)
Widor, Charles, *Organ Symphonies No. 1, 2, 3 and 4*

1873

World Events:
In the U.S., a financial panic ushers in a six-year depression; the first train robbery by Jesse James takes place; the San Francisco cable cars make their debut; Penny Post Cards make their appearance; P.T. Barnum's Greatest Show on Earth opens; Texas Christian University is founded; former President James Buchanan dies. Internationally, Buda, Óbuda and Pest unite to form the city of Budapest, Hungary; Spain begins a two-year experiment as a republic; the city of Zanzibar in Africa closes all slave markets and halts all slave trade in its territory; the first known color photographs are developed; Scottish missionary David Livingston dies.

Cultural Highlights:
The New Shakespeare Society is formed in London; Walt Whitman is stricken with paralysis; Charles Kingsley becomes canon of Westminster. Births in the art field include American artists Howard C. Christy, Ernest Lawson and sculptor Louis M. Potter and French artist André Bouchant; deaths include American sculptor Hiram Powers and British artist Edwin Landseer. Births in the literary world include American novelists Anne Sedgwick and George C. Cook and Russian poet Valery V. Bryusov; deaths include British novelist Edward Bulwer-Lytton, Italian poet Alessandro Manzoni, French dramatist Pierre Lebrun, German poet Wolfgang Müller, Spanish poet Manuel Bretón de los Herreros, Norwegian poet Johan Welhaven and Russian poet Feodor Tyutchev. Other highlights include:

Art: Paul Cézanne, *The Straw Hat*; Jean-Baptiste Corot, *Souvenir d'Italie*; Edgar Degas, *Cotton Market, New Orleans*; Thomas Eakins, *Rowers Turning the Stake*; Winslow Homer, *A Basket of Clams*; George Inness, *The Monk*; Édouard Manet, *The Railway*; Claude Monet, *Poppy Fields*; Camille Pissarro, *Self-Portrait*.

Literature: Thomas Aldrich, *Marjorie Daw*; Mathew Arnold, *Literature and Dogma*; Robert Browning, *Red Cotton Nightcap Country*; Thomas Hardy, *A Pair of Blue Eyes*; Paul von Heyse, *Kinder der Welt*; Arthur Rimbaud, *Une Saison en Enfer*; Charles Stoddard, *South Sea Idylls*; Jules Verne, *Around the World in Eighty Days*.

MUSICAL EVENTS

A. Births:

Jan 6	Karl Straube (Ger-org)	Aug 1	Henri Verbrugghen (Bel-cd)
Feb 11	Feodor Chaliapin (Rus-bs)	Aug 18	Leo Slezak (Aus-ten)
Feb 15	Modest Altschuler (Rus-cd)	Sep 6	Rosa Olitzka (Ger-alto)
Feb 25	Enrico Caruso (It-ten)	Sep 9	Theodor Kroyer (Ger-mus)
Mar 19	Amadée Gastoué (Fr-mus)	Oct 1	Max Graf (Aus-cri)
Mar 19	Max Reger (Ger-cm)	Oct 6	Oscar G. Sonneck (Am-mus)
Apr 1	Serge Rachmaninoff (Rus-pn)	Oct 9	Karl Flesch (Hun-vn-ped)
Apr 18	Jean Roger-Ducasse (Fr-cm)	Nov 8	Louise Kirkby Lunn (Br-mez)
May 7	Clarence Dickinson (Am-org)	Nov 10	Henri Rabaud (Fr-cm-cd)
May 14	Nicholai Tcherepnin (Rus-cd)	Nov 16	W.C. Handy (Am-pop)
Jun 8	Otto Goritz (Ger-bar)	Nov 20	Daniel H. Mason (Am-cm-ed)
Jul 8	Jane Osborn-Hannah (Am-sop)	Nov 25	Peter W. Dykema (Am-m.ed)
Jul 20	Joseph M. Sévérac (Fr-cm)	Dec 13	Mario Sammarco (It-bar)
Jul 21	Herbert Witherspoon (Am-bs)	Dec 14	Joseph Jongen (Bel-org-cm)
Jul 30	Anita Rio (Am-sop)	Dec 22	Karl Weinmann (Ger-mus)

B. Deaths:

Jan 10	Georges Chanot, Sr. (Fr-vn.m)	Mar 31	Domenico Donzelli (It-ten)
Feb 16	Jan K. Pišek (Boh-bar)	Apr 13	Carlo Cocchia (It-cm)
Mar 9	Thomas Oliphant (Br-cm-au)	Apr 17	Semyon Gulak-Artemovsky
Mar 12	Ludovicus Coenen (Mol-org.m)		(Rus-bar)

Apr 23	Wolfgang Menzel (Ger-cri)	Aug 16	Georg Hellmesberger (Aus-vn-cd)
Apr 29	Ignazio Marini (It-bs)		
May 26	August Conradi (Ger-cd-cm)	Sep 8	Louis F. Drouet (Fr-fl-cm)
Jun 13	Angelo Mariani (It-cd)	Oct 6	Friedrich Wieck (Ger-m.ed)
Jul 3	Josef Poniatowski (Pol-cm)	Oct 8	Albrecht Agthe (Ger-pn-ed)
Jul 18	Ferdinand David (Ger-vn-cm)	Oct 20	August Adelburg (Tur-cm-vn)
Jul 29	Théodore Devroye (Bel-mus)	Dec 7	Ernst J. Wiedemann (Ger-cm)

C. Debuts:

U.S. -- Arabella Goddard (tour), Joseph Maas (tour), Victor Maurel (N.Y.), Ilma di Murska (tour), Giuseppe del Puente (N.Y.), Enrico Tamberlik (N.Y.)

Other - Bianca Bianchi (Karlsruhe), Mary Davies (England), Julián Gayarre (Italy), Mieczyslaw A. Horbowski (Warsaw), Therese Malten (Dresden), Martin-Pierre Marsick (Paris), Moritz Moszkowski (Berlin), Arvid Odmann (Stockholm), Clementine Schuch-Proska (Dresden), Ottokar Ševcik (Vienna), Antoinette Sterling (London), Feodor Stravinsky (Kiev)

D. New Positions:

Conductors: Antonio Cagnoni (maestro di capella, Novarra Cathedral), Leoš Janácek (choirmaster, Svatopluk Choral Society), Johann A. Langert (kapellmeister, Gotha), Friedrich Marpurg (Laibach), Giovanni G. Rossi (Teatro Carlo Felice, Genoa)

Educational: Antonio Bazzini (composition, Milan Conservatory), Hans Bischoff (piano, Kullak's Academy, Berlin), Theodor Kirchner (director, Würzburg Conservatory), Emil Naumann (music history, Dresden Conservatory), Gustav Roguski (professor, Warsaw Conservatory)

Others: Constanz Berneker (organ, Königsberg Cathedral), Filippo Capocci (organ, St.John-Lateran, Rome), Théodore de Lajante (archivist, Paris Opera), William H. Longhurst (organ, Canterbury Cathedral), Charles Stanford (organ, Trinity College and conductor, Cambridge Musical Society)

E. Prizes and Honors:

Prizes: Paul-Charles Puget and François M. Servais (Prix de Rome)

Honors: Georges Bizet (Legion of Honor)

F. Biographical Highlights:

Teresa Carreño marries violinist Emile Sauret; Emmanuel Chabrier marries Marie Alice Dejean; Claude Debussy enters Paris Conservatory; Antonin Dvorák marries Anna Cermákova and meets with first compositional success; Charles Grove begins work on the *Dictionary*; Vincent d'Indy begins study at the Paris Conservatory with Franck and meets Liszt; Sidney Lanier becomes first flutist with the Peabody Orchestra; Melitta Otto makes her London debut; John Knowles Paine becomes assistant professor at Harvard; Giacomo Puccini begins his career as an organist; Giuseppe del Puente makes his Covent Garden debut; Hugo Riemann receives his Ph.D. from Göttingen; Nicholas Rimsky-Korsakov becomes inspector of Naval Bands in Russia; Antoinette Sterling leaves the U.S. for London and debuts at Covent Garden; Henri Vieuxtemps suffers a paralytic stroke causing him to temporarily retire from teaching; Hugo Wolf leaves the Benedictine school at St. Paul and is transferred to a school in Maribor, Yugoslavia.

G. Institutional Openings:

Performing Groups: Beethoven String Quartet (Boston), Colonne Concerts (Paris), Concerts Symphoniques Populaires (Lyons), English Opera Co., Finnish National Opera Co., Kellogg Opera Co. (N.Y.), Oratorio Society of New York, Orpheus Society of Springfield (Massachusetts), St. Cecilia Society of America, Société de l'Harmonie Sacrée (Paris), Stockley's Concerts (Birmingham)

Festivals: Bristol Music Festival (England), Cincinnati May Music Festival

Educational: Academy for the Higher Development of Pianoforte Playing, Augsburger Musikschule, Bernuth Music Conservatory (Hamburg), Hamburger Musikakademie, La Lira Conservatory (Montevideo), National Training School for Music (Royal College, London), Russian Musical Society Music School (Vilnius)

Other: Henry Holt and Co., Publishers

H. Musical Literature:

Bellermann, Heinrich, *Die Grösse der Intervalle als Grundlage der Harmonie*
Chouquet, Gustave, *Histoire de la musique dramatique en France...*
Dancla, Charles, *Les compositeur chefs d'orchestre*
Hallé, Charles, *Pianoforte School*
Kolbe, Oskar, *Handbuch der Harmonielehre*
Köstlin, Heinrich, *Geschichte der Musik im Umriss*
Lussy, Mathis, *Traité de l'expression musicale*
Meerens, Charles, *Le diapason et la notation musicale simplifiées*
Paul, Oscar, *Handlexicon der Tonkunst*
Sankey, Ira, *Sacred Songs and Solos*

I. Musical Compositions:

Bizet, Georges, *Patrie Overture* (orchestra)
Brahms, Johannes, *Variations on a Theme by Haydn, Opus 56a* (orchestra)
    String Quartet No. 1, Opus 51, No. 1
    String Quartet No. 2, Opus 51, No. 2
    8 Songs, Opus 59
Bruckner, Anton, *Symphony No. 3* (revised in 1877 and 1889)
Delibes, Léo, *Le roi l'a dit* (opera)
Dubois, Théodore, *La Guzla de l'Emir* (opera)
    Divertissement for Orchestra
Dvorák, Antonin, *Symphony No. 3, Opus 10*
Fibich, Zdenek, *Lustspiel Overture, Opus 3*
    Othello (symphonic poem)
Gade, Niels, *Zion, Opus 49* (cantata)
    The Mountain Thrall (cantata)
Gounod, Charles, *Funeral March of a Marionette*
    Jeanne d'Arc (incidental music)
    Requiem in F
Grieg, Edvard, *Olaf Trygvason, Opus 50* (cantata)
Lalo, Edouard, *Symphonie Espagnole, Opus 21, for Violin and Orchestra*
Massenet, Jules, *Phèdre Overture*
    Scènes dramatiques
Moniuszko, Stanislaw, *Mass in B flat Major*
Offenbach, Jacques, *Les braconniers*
Paine, John Knowles, *St. Peter, Opus 20* (oratorio)
Ponchielli, Amilcare, *Clarina* (ballet)
    Il parlatore eterno (opera)
Raff, Joseph J., *Symphony No. 6, Opus 189*
    Concerto in C Minor for Piano and Orchestra
Saint-Saëns, Camille, *Concerto, Opus 33, for Cello and Orchestra*
    Phaeton, Opus 34 (symphonic poem)
Sullivan, Arthur, *The Light of the World* (oratorio)
Tchaikovsky, Peter, *The Tempest, Opus 18* (symphonic fantasy)
    The Snow Maiden, Opus 12 (incidental music)
Verdi, Giuseppe, *String Quartet in A Minor*

1874

World Events:
>In the U.S., the first electric-powered streetcar is demonstrated in New York; the Women's Christian Temperance League is founded; the Republican elephant first appears in a Nast cartoon; barbed wire, a "revolution in ranching" is invented by J. F. Glidden; future President Herbert Hoover is born; former President Millard Fillmore dies. Internationally, Benjamin Disraeli becomes British Prime Minister; Great Britain annexes the Fiji Islands; Switzerland revises its constitution; Henry Stanley begins exploring the African Congo region; the British Factory Act sets a work week of 56 and a half hours; future Prime Minister Winston Churchill is born.

Cultural Highlights:
>First known exhibit of Impressionistic Art; Henry Ward Beecher is accused of adultery by his parishioners; Ignazio Ciampi teaches history at the University of Rome. Births in the literary world include American authors Gertrude Stein, Ellen Glasgow and poet Amy Lowell, Austrian poet Hugo von Hofmannsthal, British novelist W. Somerset Maugham and French novelist Jérome Tharaud; deaths include German authors Johann Burgmüller and Augustus Hoffmann, British poets Sidney Dobell and Bryan W. Proctor and Czech poet Vítezslav Hálek. Births in the art field include American artist Charles Knight and French sculptor Charles Despiau; deaths include American sculptor William Rinehart, German artist Wilhelm von Kaulbach and Irish sculptor John Henry Foley. Other highlights include:

Art: Thomas Barker, *Charge of the Light Brigade*; Jules Bastien-Lepage, *Spring Song*; Jean Louis Garnier, *Grand Staircase of the Paris Opera*; Édouard Manet, *Boating at Argenteuil*; John Millais, *The Northwest Passage*; Pierre-Auguste Renoir, *The Loge*; Dante Rossetti, *Proserine in Hades*; James Whistler, *Nocturne in Black and Gold*.

Literature: Pedro de Alarcón, *The Three Cornered Hat*; Berthold Auerbach, *Waldfried*; François Coppée, *Le Cahier Rouge*; Gustave Flaubert, *Temptation of St. Anthony*; Théophile Gautier, *Histoire du Romantisme*; Thomas Hardy, *Far from the Maddening Crowd*; Victor Hugo, *93*; Sydney Lanier, *Corn*; Paul Verlaine, *Romances sans Paroles*.

MUSICAL EVENTS

A. Births:

Jan 1	Hugo Leichtentritt (Ger-mus)	Aug 22	Edward Bairstow (Br-org)
Jan 4	Josef Suk (Cz-cm)	Sep 13	Arnold Schoenberg (Aus-cm)
Jan 29	Robert Lach (Aus-mus)	Sep 21	Gustav Holst (Br-cm)
Feb 10	Marie Gutheil-Schoder (Ger-sop)	Oct 15	Selma Kurz (Aus-sop)
Feb 14	Pierre Aubry (Fr-mus)	Oct 20	Charles Ives (Am-cm)
Mar 16	Lillian Blauvelt (Am-sop)	Nov 13	Charles H. Kitson (Br-the-org)
Mar 27	Andrés de Segurola (Sp-bs)	Nov 17	Charles van dem Borren (Bel-mus)
Mar 31	Henri Marteau (Fr-vn)	Nov 18	Riccardo Martin (Am-ten)
Apr 17	Rudolf Berger (Ger-bar)	Dec 13	Josef Lhévinne (Rus-pn)
May 29	Emilio de Gogorza (Am-bar)	Dec 22	Franz Schmidt (Aus-cm)
Jun 28	Oley Speaks (Am-bar-cm)	Dec 24	Adam Didur (Pol-bs)
Jul 21	Giuseppe Agostini (It-ten)	Dec 25	Lina Cavalieri (It-sop)
Jul 26	Serge Koussevitsky (Rus-cd)	Dec 26	Léon Rothier (Fr-bs)
Jul 29	Amadeo Bassi (It-ten)		

B. Deaths:

Jan 1	John F. Hart (Br-vn.m)	Feb 5	Johann Bellermann (Ger-mus)
Jan 7	Ernesto Carallini (It-cl-cm)	Mar 20	Hans C. Lumbye (Den-cm-cd)
Jan 21	Euphrosyne Parepa-Rosa (Scot-sop)	Apr 24	Jean de Méreaux (Fr-pn)
		Apr 27	Pietro Mongini (It-ten)
Jan 24	Francesco Caffi (It-mus)	May 1	Vilém Blodek (Cz-fl-cm)

May 3	William Hall (Am-pn.m)		Nov 24	Friedrich Grund (Ger-cm)
Jul 4	Edvard Mantius (Ger-ten)		Dec 10	Friedrich Belcke (Ger-trom)
Oct 6	Thomas Tellefsen (Nor-pn)		Dec 22	Johann P. Pixis (Ger-pn)
Oct 26	Peter Cornelius (Ger-cm)			Salvatore Agnelli (It-cm)
Nov 8	Justin Cadaux (Fr-pn-cm)			

C. Debuts:

U.S. -- Emma Albani (N.Y.), Emmy Fursch-Madi (tour), Giovanni Tagliapietra (N.Y.)

Other - Blanche Deschamps-Jehin (Brussels), Maurice Devries (Liège), Anna Essipova (London), Camille Gurickx (Paris), Luigi Mancinelli (Perugia, as conductor), Medea Mei-Figner (Sinaluga), Jean de Reszke (Venice, as baritone), Josephine de Reszke (Venice), Julie Rivé-King (Leipzig), Wladyslaw Seideman (Vienna), August Spanuth (Frankfurt), Edmund Vergnet (Paris)

D. New Positions:

Conductors: Otto Malling (Copenhagen Concert Society), Luigi Mancinelli (Teatro Apollo, Rome), J. Gustav Stehle (choir, St. Gall Cathedral)

Educational: Woldemar Bargiel (composition, Berlin Hochschule), Johann Hrimaly (violin, Moscow Conservatory), Gustave Huberti (director, Mons Conservatory of Music), Léon Jouret (voice, Brussels Conservatory), Samuel de Lange (cello, Basel Music School), Joseph Pembaur, Sr. (director, Innsbruck Music School)

Others: Henry Krehbiel (critic, *Cincinnati Gazette*), André Messager (organ, St. Sulpice)

E. Prizes and Honors:

Prizes: Antonin Dvorák (Austrian State Prize), Oskar Pasch (Meyerbeer)

Honors: Edvard Grieg (life stipend), Johan Svendsen (state grant), Samuel S. Wesley (civil pension)

F. Biographical Highlights:

Isaac Albéniz enters Leipzig Conservatory; Theodore Baker goes to Germany to study music; Teresa Brambilla marries composer Amilcare Ponchielli; Joseph Conrad begins a 20-year sea-faring career; Zdenek Fibich becomes second conductor at the National Theater of Prague; Charles Gounod returns to Paris; Leoš Janácek enters the Prague Organ School; Pauline Lucca joins the Vienna Opera; Arthur Nikisch joins the Vienna Court orchestra; Jacques Offenbach is forced into bankruptcy; Hubert Parry leaves the business world for full time in music; Nicholai Rimsky-Korsakov debuts as a conductor in his own *Third Symphony*; Bedrich Smetana becomes totally deaf in left ear and resigns his conducting position; Richard Strauss enters Ludwigsgymnasium in Munich; Francisco Tárrega enters Madrid Conservatory; Peter Tchaikovsky visits Italy; Giuseppe Verdi is elected to the Italian Senate as an honor member; Richard Wagner moves into his Villa Wahnfried in Bayreuth.

G. Institutional Openings:

Performing Groups: Association Artistique des Concerts du Châtelet (Paris); Barmer Orchesterverein; Belfast Philharmonic Society; Cecilia Society of Boston; Concerts Nationaux (Paris); Copenhagen Koncertforeningen; Darmstadt Stadtkirchenchor; Glasgow Choral Union Orchestra; Komische Oper am Schottentor (Vienna); Leipziger Bach-Verein; Mendelssohn Glee Club of Philadelphia; Musical Association of London; Philharmonic Club of Boston; Romanian Orchestral Society

Educational: Akademie der Tonkunst (Munich); Chatauqua Institute (N.Y.); Detroit Conservatory of Music; Kirchenburg Kirchenmusikschule; Milwaukee College of Music; Olivet Conservatory of Music (Michigan); Ratisbon School of Church Music (Regensburg)

Other: J. and W. Chester, Music Publishers (Brighton); *Deutsche Rundschau*; Ernst Eulenburg, Music Publisher (Leipzig); Künstler- und Dilettantenschule für Klavier (Stuttgart); William Lewis and Son, Violin Dealers and Publisher (Chicago); *Musica Sacra: Revue du Chant Liturgique et de la Musique Religieuse* (France); Sustaining Pedal for Piano (patented by Henry G. Hanchett); Toronto Grand Opera House

H. Musical Literature:

Abrányi, Kornél, *Harmony*
Ambros, August, *Bunte Blätter II*
Becker, Georges, *La musique en Suisse*
Crowest, Frederick, *The Great Tone Poets*
Kothe, Bernhard, *Abriss der Musikgeschichte für Lehrerseminare und Dilettanten*
Lunn, Charles, *Philosophy of Voice*
Lussy, Mathis, *Traité de l'expression musicale*
Mahillon, Victor C., *Les éléments d'acoustique musicale et instrumentale*
Paul, Oscar, *Musikalische Instrumente*
Tyndall, John, *On the Transmission of Sound by the Atmosphere*

I. Musical Compositions:

Brahms, Johannes, *Hungarian Dances* (complete publication)
    4 Duets, Opus 61
    7 Choral Songs, Opus 62
    9 Songs, Opus 63
Bristow, George, *Arcadian Symphony*
Bruckner, Anton, *Symphony No. 4, "Romantic"*
Chabrier, Emmanuel, *Lamento for Orchestra*
Dubois, Théodore, *Suite No. 1 for Orchestra*
Duparc, Henri, *Poème Nocturne, "Aux étoiles"*
Dvořák, Antonin, *Symphony No. 4, Opus 13*
    King and Collier, Opus 14 (opera)
    Rhapsody in A Minor, Opus 15, for Orchestra
    String Quartet, Opus 16
Flotow, Friedrich von, *La fleur de Harlem* (opera)
d'Indy, Vincent, *Max et Thecla* (symphonic poem)
Lecocq, Charles, *Giroflé-Girofla* (operetta)
    Les prés Saint-Gervais (operetta)
Liszt, Franz, *The Legend of Ste. Cecilia* (oratorio)
Massenet, Jules, *Scènes pittoresques*
Mussorgsky, Modeste, *Sunless* (song cycle)
    Pictures at an Exhibition (piano)
Ponchielli, Amilcare, *I lituani* (opera)
Raff, Joseph J., *Concerto No. 1 for Cello and Orchestra*
Reinecke, Carl, *Ein abenteur Händels* (opera)
Rimsky-Korsakov, Nicolai, *Symphony No. 3 in C Major*
Saint-Saëns, Camille, *Danse Macabre, Opus 40*
Sankey, Ira, *The Ninety and Nine* (hymn)
Smetana, Bedrich, *Vysehrad* (No. 1 of *Ma Vlast*)
    The Moldau (No. 2 of *Ma Vlast*)
    Sarka (No. 3 of *Ma Vlast*)
Strauss, Johann, Jr., *Die Fledermaus* (operetta)
Tchaikovsky, Peter I., *Valkula the Smith* (opera)
    String Quartet No. 2, Opus 22
    18 Songs, Opus 25, 27 and 28
Thomas, Ambroise, *Gille et Gillotin* (opera)
Verdi, Giuseppe, *Manzoni Requiem*
Wagner, Richard, *Götterdämmerung* (opera)

1875

World Events:
> In the U.S., the Civil Rights Act forbids racial discrimination in public facilities; the Specie Resumption Act permits the redeeming of paper money on demand; the Hebrew Union College is founded in New York; Brigham Young University is founded in Utah; former President Andrew Johnson dies. Internationally, the Socialist Democratic Party is founded in Germany; Verney Cameron becomes the first white man to cross the African continent east to west; Captain M. Webb becomes the first to swim the English Channel; Alphonso XII becomes King of Spain.

Cultural Highlights:
> The Association Artistique d'Angers is created; Alexandre Dumas, fils, is inducted into the French Academy; Henry Ward Beecher's adultery trial ends in a hung jury. Births in the art world include French artist Jacques Villon and sculptor Paul M. Landowski and Swedish sculptor Carl Milles; deaths include French sculptors Jean B. Carpeaux and Antoine Louis Barye and artists Jean François Millet and Jean-Baptiste Corot, Italian artist Francesco Coghetti, Belgian artist Alfred Stevens and American artist William J. Hays. Births in the literary world include American novelist Zane Grey and poet Robert Frost, Italian novelists Grazia Deledda and Rafael Sabatini, British poet George Ellis, German novelist Thomas Mann and poet Rainer Maria Rilke and Spanish poet Antonio Ruiz; deaths include British novelist Charles Kingsley, French author Edgar Quinet, Hungarian novelist Zsígmund Kemény, Russian novelist Alexei Tolstoy, Danish author Hans Christian Andersen, Portugese poet Antonio de Castilho and German novelist Edward Mörike. Other highlights include:

> **Art:** Thomas Eakins, *The Gross Clinic*; Daniel French, *The Minute Man* (Concord); George Inness, *Autumn Oaks*; Édouard Manet, *Washing Day*; Camille Pissarro, *Climbing Path at L'Hermitage*; Pierre-Auguste Renoir, *2 Little Circus Girls*; John Rogers, *Checkers Up at the Farm*; James Whistler, *Nocturne, Blue and Silver*.

> **Literature:** Ventura Aguilera, *La Arcadia Moderne*; Pedro de Alarcón, *Amores y Amoriós*; Holger Drachmann, *Muffled Melodies*; Bret Harte, *Tales of the Argonauts*; Paul von Heyse, *Im Paradiese*; Oliver W. Holmes, *Songs of Many Seasons*; Henry James, *Roderick Hudson*; Cincinnatus Miller, *The Ship in the Desert*.

MUSICAL EVENTS

A. Births:

Jan 11	Reinhold Glière (Rus-cm)	Jul 17	Donald Tovey (Br-mus)
Jan 14	Albert Schweitzer (Ger-org)	Jul 28	Paul Bender (Ger-bs)
Jan 28	Julián Carrillo (Mex-cm)	Aug 9	Albert Ketélby (Br-cm)
Feb 2	Fritz Kreisler (Ger-vn)	Aug 15	Samuel Coleridge-Taylor
Mar 7	Maurice Ravel (Fr-cm)		(Br-cm)
Mar 8	Franco Alfano (It-cm)	Sep 22	Mikolajus Ciurlionis (Lith-cm)
Apr 3	Marie Delna (Fr-alto)	Sep 25	Katherina Fleischer-Edel
Apr 4	Pierre Monteux (Fr-cd)		(Ger-sop)
Apr 26	Natalie Curtis (Am-folk)	Sep 28	Hermine Bosetti (Ger-sop)
Apr 29	Hans Volkmann (Ger-mus)	Oct 2	Henri Fevrier (Fr-cm)
Apr 30	Arthur H. Ryder (Am-org)	Dec 23	Griswold Putnam (Am-bs)
Jun 25	Pearl G. Curran (Am-cm)		Angelo Bada (It-ten)
Jun 26	Riccardo Stracciari (It-bar)		Josephine Jacoby (Am-alto)

B. Deaths:

Jan 30	Prosper Guéranger (Fr-mus)	Feb 19	Jean Vuillaume (Fr-vn.m)
Feb 1	William S. Bennett (Br-cm)	Mar	Alberico Curioni (It-ten)
Feb 2	Luigi Agnesi (Bel-bs)	Mar 3	Adolf Reubke (Ger-org.m)
Feb 16	Johannes Bastiaans (Hol-org)	Mar 4	Carlo Romani (It-cm)

Mar 18	Ferdinand Laub (Cz-vn)	Oct 12	Matthias Keller (Ger-vn)
Jun 3	Georges Bizet (Fr-cm)	Oct 15	Theodor Formes (Ger-ten)
Jun 9	Julius Schuberth (Ger-pub)	Nov 6	Marietta Brambilla (It-alto)
Jun 16	Evangelista Andreoli (It-pn)	Dec 22	Nikolai A. Titov (Rus-cm)
Sep 15	Jeanne L. Farrenc (Fr-pn)		Gustave A. Besson (Fr-inst.m)

C. Debuts:

U.S. -- Hans von Bülow (tour), Maud Morgan (N.Y.), Eugenie Pappenheim (N.Y.), Julie Rivé-King (N.Y.), Antoinette Sterling (tour), Therese Tietjens (N.Y.), Fannie Zeisler (Chicago)

Other - Elena Boccabadati-Varesi (London), Erminia Broghi (Bologna), Julia Gaylord (Dublin), Katharina Klafsky (Hungary--as a soprano), Maud Morgan (London), Edmund Straeten (Cologne), Sergei Taneyev (Moscow), Alexandre Taskin (Amiens), Zaré Thalberg (London), Hermann Winkelmann (Sondershausen)

D. New Positions:

Conductors: Felix Dessoff (Karlsruhe), Johann Herbeck (Gesellschaft der Musikfreunde, Vienna), Hans Richter (Vienna PO and Opera), Robert Volkmann (professor, Hungarian National Academy)

Educational: Joseph T. Barbot (voice, Paris Conservatory), Joseph Barnby (music director, Eton), Adolf Brodsky (violin, Moscow Conservatory), Anton Bruckner (theory, Vienna Conservatory), Ferenc Erkel (director, Budapest Academy), Robert Fuchs (harmony, Vienna Conservatory), Otto Klauswell (music history, Cologne Conservatory), George Macfarren (professor, Cambridge), John Knowles Paine (professor, Harvard), Otokar Sevcík (violin, Kiev Music School), Henryk Wieniawski (violin, Brussels Conservatory)

Others: Max Kalbeck (critic, *Schlesische Zeitung*)

E. Prizes and Honors:

Prizes: André Wormser (Prix de Rome)

Honors: Heinrich Bellermann (Academy of Arts, Berlin), Georges Bizet (Legion of Honor), Franz Liszt (Hungarian Academy), Carl Reinecke (Berlin Academy)

F. Biographical Highlights:

Johannes Brahms resigns as director of the Vienna Gesellschaft; Dudley Buck moves to New York where he becomes assistant to Theodore Thomas; Hans von Bülow makes a concert tour of the U.S.; Teresa Carreño marries baritone Giovanni Tagliapietra; Ernest Chausson enters law school; Vincent d'Indy becomes chorus master of the Colonne Concerts and marries his cousin Isabelle de Pampelonne; Mikhail Ippolitov-Ivanov enters St. Petersburg Conservatory; Leos Janácek returns to Brno; Charles M. Loeffler begins to study violin with Rappoldi in Berlin; Gustav Mahler enters the Vienna Conservatory; Angelo Masini makes his London and Paris debuts; Silas Pratt returns to Germany and studies with Liszt; Josephine de Reszke makes her Paris Opera debut; Camille Saint-Saëns takes a concert tour of Russia and marries Marie Truffot; Sergei Taneyev graduates from Moscow Conservatory; Therese Tietjens makes a concert tour of the U.S.; Hugo Wolf is sent to live with his aunt in Vienna in order to study at the Conservatory.

G. Institutional Openings:

Performing Groups: Bach Choir of London; Dublin Musical Society; Johaniterne (Norwegian Choral Society); Kärntner Quintet (vocal group); Ottawa Choral Union; Carl Rosa Opera Co.; Società Corale (Turin); Società del Quartetto Corale (Milan); Winterthur Stadtorchester

Festivals: Munich Opera Festival

Educational: Hershey School of Musical Art (Chicago); Istituto Musicale Livornese; Liszt Academy of Music (Hungary); National Hungarian Royal Academy of Music (Budapest); Potsdam Musikschule; Trinity College of Music (London); University of Washington Music Department

Other: A. B. Chase Co. (Ohio); C. G. Conn Co. (Elkhart); M. P. Möller, Organ Builder (Erie, PA.); New Paris Opera House; Palais Garnier (Paris); People's Theater (Budapest); *Siona*

H. Musical Literature:
Barrett/Stainer, *Dictionary of Music Terms*
Draeseke, Felix, *Anweisung zum kunstgerechten Modulieren*
Gevaert, François, *Histoire et théorie de la musique de l'antiquité I*
Hanslick, Eduard, *Die Moderne Oper I*
Hart, George, *The Violin: Its Famous Makers and Their Imitators*
Kashkin, Nicolai, *Elementary Music Theory*
Lavoix, Henri, *La musique dans l'imagerie du moyen-âge*
Leibrock, Joseph, *Musikalische Akkordenlehre*
Ouseley, Frederick, *Musical Form and General Composition*
Schuré, Edouard, *Le Drame Musical*

I. Musical Compositions:
Bizet, Georges, *Carmen* (opera)
Brahms, Johannes, *String Quartet No. 3, Opus 67*
　　Piano Quartet No. 3, Opus 60
Duparc, Henri, *Lenore* (symphonic poem)
Dvořák, Antonin, *Symphony No. 5, Opus 76*
　　Overture to Wanda, Opus 25
　　Serenade in E Major for Strings, Opus 22
Fauré, Gabriel, *Allegro Symphonique, Opus 68*
　　Les Djinns, Opus 12
　　Suite d'orchestre, Opus 20
Fibich, Zdenek, *Toman and the Wood Nymphs, Opus 49* (symphonic poem)
Gilbert and Sullivan, *Trial by Jury* (operetta)
Goldmark, Karl, *Die Königen von Saba* (opera)
Grieg, Edvard, *Peer Gynt, Opus 23* (incidental music)
Lalo, Edouard, *Allegro Symphonique for Orchestra*
Luigini, Alexandre, *Ballet Égyptien*
Massenet, Jules, *Notre Dame de Paris* (incidental music)
Offenbach, Jacques, *Voyage dans la lune* (operetta)
　　Whittington and his Cat (operetta)
Raff, Joseph J., *Symphony No. 7, Opus 201, "In den Alpen"*
Rubinstein, Anton, *Symphony No. 4, Opus 95*
　　Die Makkabäer (opera)
Saint-Saëns, Camille, *Concerto No. 4, Opus 44, for Piano and Orchestra*
Smetana, Bedrich, *From Bohemia's Wood and Meadows* (No. 4 of *Ma Vlast*)
Stainer, John, *Gideon* (oratorio)
Stanford, Charles V., *Symphony No. 1 in B-flat Major*
　　The Golden Legend (oratorio)
　　The Resurrection (oratorio)
Strauss, Joseph, Jr., *Cagliostro in Wien* (operetta)
Sullivan, Arthur, *The Zoo* (operetta)
Tchaikovsky, Peter, I., *Symphony No. 3, "Polish"*
　　Concerto No. 1, Opus 23, for Piano and Orchestra
　　Serenade Melancholique, Opus 26, for Violin and Orchestra
Work, Henry C., *Grandfather's Clock* (song)

1876

World Events:

In the U.S., Rutherford B. Hayes is elected as President No. 19; Colorado becomes State No. 38; the Battle of the Little Big Horn ends with the death of General Custer and all his troops; Alexander Bell patents the telephone--the first public message is sent on March 10; the International Centennial Exposition takes place. Internationally, Porfirio Diaz seizes the Mexican government by force (deposed in 1911); Korea receives its independence from Japan; Serbia and Montenegro declare war on Turkey; Abdul Aziz of Turkey dies and is succeeded first by Murad V, then by Abdul Hamid II.

Cultural Highlights:

The American Library Association is founded and the *Library Journal* begins publication; the Pennsylvania Academy of Fine Arts is created with Thomas Eakins as instructor in art. Births in the art world include American artist Everett Shinn and sculptor James E. Fraser, French sculptor Raymond Duchamp-Villon and artist Maurice de Vlaminck, Romanian sculptor Constantin Brancusi and Spanish sculptor Julio González. Births in the literary field include American authors Sherwood Anderson, Willa Cather, Irvin Cobb, Jack London and Mary Roberts Rinehart, Norwegian novelists Olav Duun and Ole Rölvaag, British author Arthur Hull, French dramatist Henri Bernstein and German poet Theodor Däubler; deaths include French authors Louis Colet and George Sand and Danish poet Frederik Paludan-Müller. Other highlights include:

Art: Edgar Degas, *The Absinthe Drinkers*; Thomas Eakins, *The Chess Players*; Winslow Homer, *Breezing Up*; Gustave Moreau, *L'Apparition*; Edward Poynter, *Atalanta's Race*; Valentine Prinsep, *The Linen Gatherers*; Pierre-Auguste Renoir, *The Swing*; Alfred Sisley, *The Flood at Port-Marly*; Willard, *The Spirit of '76*.

Literature: Lewis Carroll, *The Hunting of the Snark*; George Eliot, *Daniel Deronda*; Friedrich von Hackländer, *Verbotene Früchte*; Stéphane Mallarmé, *L'Après-midi d'un Faune*; William Morris, *Sigurd, the Volsung*; Alfred Lord Tennyson, *Harold*; Ivan Turgenev, *Virgin Soil*; Mark Twain, *The Adventures of Tom Sawyer*.

MUSICAL EVENTS

A. Births:

Jan 12	Ermanno Wolf-Ferrari (It-cm)		Aug 29	Lucien Muratore (Fr-ten)
Jan 20	Josef Hofmann (Pol-pn)		Sep 14	Terese Behr (Ger-alto)
Jan 29	Havergal Brian (Br-cm)		Sep 15	Bruno Walter (Ger-cd)
Feb 20	Feodor Akimenko (Rus-pn)		Oct 10	Walter Niemann (Ger-mus)
Feb 28	John Alden Carpenter (Am-cm)		Nov 16	Giuseppe Anselmi (It-ten)
Mar 11	Carl Ruggles (Am-cm)		Nov 23	Manuel de Falla (Sp-cm)
Mar 15	Horatio Connell (Am-bar)		Dec 7	Ludwig Schiedermair (Ger-mus)
Apr 23	Aïno Ackté (Fin-sop)		Dec 11	Mieczyslaw Karlowicz (Pol-cm)
May 19	Rosina Storchio (It-sop)		Dec 12	Marya Freund (Pol-sop)
Jul 26	Ernest Schelling (Am-cm)		Dec 25	Giuseppe de Luca (It-bar)
			Dec 29	Pablo Casals (Sp-cel)

B. Deaths:

Jan 12	Charles Coussemaker (Fr-mus)		Apr 2	Anton Mitterwurzer (Aus-bar)
Jan 22	John B. Dykes (Br-hymn)		Apr 19	Samuel S. Wesley (Br-org-cm)
Feb 28	Raimondo Boucheron (It-the)		Apr 28	Giovanni Bajetti (It-cm)
Feb 28	Charles Horsley (Br-org)		May 7	Franz Pocci (It-cm)
Mar 1	Giovanni Puzzi (It-hn)		Jun 18	August Röckel (Aus-cm)
Mar 18	Henri Rosellen (Fr-pn)		Jun 26	August W. Ambros (Aus-mus)
Mar 28	Joseph Boehm (Hun-vn-cd)		Jul 8	Josef Dessauer (Boh-cm)

Aug 10	Carl Bergmann (Ger-cd)	Oct 2	George Cooper (Br-org)
Aug 29	Félicien David (Fr-cm)	Nov 8	Henry Phillips (Br-bs)
Sep 9	Mary Shaw (Br-alto)	Nov 8	Antonio Tamburini (It-bar)
Sep 17	Ernst Lübeck (Hol-pn)	Nov 27	Henry R. Allen (Ir-bar)
Sep 26	Edward Rimbault (Br-mus)	Dec 3	Hermann Goetz (Ger-cm)
Oct 1	Henri J. Bertini (Fr-pn)	Dec 29	Philip P. Bliss (Am-hymn)

C. Debuts:

U.S. -- Anna Essipova , Amy Fay (N.Y.), Lilian Bailey Henschel (Boston), Lillian Nordica (Boston), Marie Selika, Jeannie Winston (San Francisco-?)

Other - Emma Abbott (London), Ada Adini (Varese), Eugénie Colonne (Paris), Johannes Elmblad, Etelka Gerster (Vienna), Ippolit Prianishnikov (Milan), Edouard de Reszke (Paris), Moriz Rosenthal (Vienna), Leo Schulz (Berlin), Ernestine Schumann-Heink (Graz)

D. New Positions:

Conductors: Léon Carvalho (Paris Opéra-Comique), George Matzka (New York PO), Emil Paur (Kassel), Gustav Schmidt (kapellmeister, Darmstadt)

Educational: Karl Davïdov (director, St. Petersburg Conservatory), Henry W. Dunham (organ, New England Conservatory), Percy Goetschius (harmony, Stuttgart Conservatory), Ernest Guiraud (composition, Paris Conservatory), Friedrich Hegar (director, Zurich Conservatory), Ebenezer Prout (harmony, National Training School), Jean Baptiste Weckerlin (librarian, Paris Conservatory)

Others: Samuel de Lange (organ, Cologne Cathedral), Charles H. Lloyd (organ, Gloucester Cathedral), Angelo Neumann (manager, Leipzig Opera)

E. Prizes and Honors:

Prizes: Paul Hillemacher (Prix de Rome)

Honors: Niels Gade (life stipend, Denmark), John Goss (honorary doctorate, Cambridge), Edward Hanslick (Austrian Imperial Council), Jules Massenet (Legion of Honor), Herbert Oakeley and John Steele (knighted), Louis-Etienne Reyer (French Institute)

F. Biographical Highlights:

Vincenzo Bellini's body is returned to his native Catania in Sicily; Carl Bergmann, in ill health, resigns from New York PO; George Chadwick quits his father's business and begins teaching at Olivet College in Michigan; Frederick Delius enters International College at Isleworth; Adolph Forster settles in Pittsburgh as teacher and conductor; Niels Gade visits England and conducts the Birmingham Festival; Victor Herbert enters the Stuttgart Conservatory; Lilli Lehmann makes her Bayreuth debut; Ruggero Leoncavallo moves to the University of Bologna; Anatol Liadov is expelled from St. Petersburg Conservatory for failure to attend classes; Edward MacDowell enters the Paris Conservatory; Amalie Materna is chosen by Wagner to be the first Bayreuth Brunnhilde; Felix Mottl becomes assistant to Wagner at Bayreuth; Jacques Offenbach visits the U.S.; Ede Reményi decides to settle in the U.S.; Peter Tchaikovsky begins correspondance with Mme. von Meck and meets Liszt and Tolstoy; Arturo Toscanini, age nine, enters the Parma Conservatory.

G. Institutional Openings:

Performing Groups: Basler Allgemeine Musikgesellschaft; Bernische Orchesterverein; Dresden Männergesangverein; Mainz Civic Orchestra; Music Society of Krakow; Prague Kammermusikverein; Purcell Society of London

Festivals: Silesian Music Festival; Wagner Festival (Bayreuth)

Educational: Conservatorio Benedetto Marcello (Venice); Music Teacher's National Association (NTNA); New York College of Music; Zurich Music School

Other: *Cäcilienkalender*; Evans Hall (Fort Worth); *Der Heimgarten* (Graz); Arthur P. Schmidt Music Co. (Boston); Sheffield Tonic Sol-Fa Association (Musical Union); Zimmermann Publishing Co. (St. Petersburg)

H. Musical Literature:
Aikin, Jesse B., *The Imperial Harmony*
Casamorata, Luigi F., *Manuale di Armonia*
Delle Sedie, Enrico, *L'art lyrique*
Engel, Carl, *Musical Myths and Facts*
Goovaerts, Alphonse, *La musique d'eglise...*
Hiller, Ferdinand, *Musikalisches und persönliches*
Horsley, Charles E., *Textbook of Harmony*
Inzenga, José, *Impresiones de un artista en Italia*
Prout, Ebenezer, *Instrumentation*
Rimsky-Korsakov, Nicolai, *Autobiography*

I. Musical Compositions:
Borodin, Alexander, *Symphony No. 2 in B Minor*
Brahms, Johannes, *Symphony No. 1, Opus 68*
Bruckner, Anton, *Symphony No. 5 in B-flat Major*
Buck, Dudley, *Centennial Meditation on Columbus*
Cui, César, *Angelo* (opera)
Delibes, Léo, *Sylvia* (ballet)
Dubois, Théodore, *Concerto Capriccio for Piano and Orchestra*
Dvořák, Antonin, *Concerto, Opus 33, for Piano and Orchestra*
    String Quartet, Opus 80
Fauré, Gabriel, *Violin Sonata No. 1, Opus 13*
Franck, César, *Les Eolides* (symphonic poem)
Godard, Benjamin, *Concerto Romantique for Violin and/or Orchestra*
Goldmark, Karl, *Rustic Wedding Symphony, Opus 26*
Gounod, Charles, *The Seven Last Words of Christ* (cantata)
d'Indy, Vincent, *Overture, Anthony and Cleopatra*
Lalo, Edouard, *Concerto in D Major for Cello and Orchestra*
Luigini, Alexandre, *Anges et Démons* (ballet)
Massenet, Jules, *Scènes Napolitaines*
    La Vie de Bohème (incidental music)
Offenbach, Jacques, *Pierette et Jacquet* (operetta)
Paine, John Knowles, *Symphony No. 1 in C Minor*
    Centennial Hymn
Ponchielli, Amilcare, *La Gioconda* (opera)
Pratt, Silas, *Centennial Overture*
Puccini, Giacomo, *Preludio Sinfonico*
Raff, Joseph J., *Symphony No. 8, Opus 205, "Frühlingsklänge"*
    Symphony No. 11, Opus 214, "Der Winter"
    Concerto No. 2 for Cello and Orchestra
Saint-Saëns, Camille, *Le Déluge, Opus 45* (oratorio)
Smetana, Bedrich, *The Kiss* (opera)
    String Quartet No. 1, "From My Life"
Suppé, Franz von, *Fatinitza* (operetta)
Tchaikovsky, Peter I., *Francesca da Rimini* (symphonic poem)
    Swan Lake, Opus 20 (ballet)
    Marche Slav, Opus 31
    String Quartet No. 3, Opus 30
    The Seasons, Opus 37b (piano)
Wagner, Richard, *Grosser Festmarsch* (for Philadelphia Centennial Celebration)

1877

World Events:

In the U.S., the Nez Perce Indian War occurs in the Northwest; the Desert Land Act provides up to 640 acres of land at 25 cents an acre; the Bell Telephone Co. is founded; Thomas Edison patents the phonograph; the United Labor Party begins a short career; Flag Day observance begins. Internationally, Romania gains its full independence, Russia joins in on the war against Turkey; Henry Stanley founds Leopoldville in the Belgian Congo; Emile Berliner introduces the microphone; discovery is made of the two moons, Deimas and Phobos, of the planet Mars.

Cultural Highlights:

The Society of American Artist is founded; the English magazine *Puck* begins publication; James Russell Lowell becomes U.S. Minister to Spain; William Orchardson is inducted into the Royal Academy and Victorien Sardou into the French Academy. Births in the literary field include American novelist Lloyd C. Douglas and French authors Paul Reboux and Jean Tharaud; deaths include American historian and novelist John Motley, Finnish poet Johan Runeberg, Swedish poet Carl Strandberg, Spanish novelist Fernán Caballero and German author Friedrich von Hackländer. Births in the art world include American artists Marsden Hartley and Joseph Stella, sculptor Gertrude Whitney, German sculptor George Kolbe, French artist Raoul Dufy and Dutch artist Kees van Dongen. Other highlights include:

Art: Albert Bierstadt, *Mount Corcoran*; Edward Burne-Jones, *Mirror of Venus*; Edgar Degas, *Dancers at the Bar*; William Hunt, *Gloucester Harbor*; John La Farge, *Murals, Trinity Church in Boston*; Édouard Manet, *Nana*; Claude Monet, *Gare Saint-Lazare*; Pierre-Auguste Renoir, *Bronze Age*; Alfred Sisley, *The Bridge at Sèvres*.

Literature: Rasmus Anderson, *Viking Tales of the North*; Michel Carré, *Paul et Virginie*; Alphonse Daudet, *The Nabob*; Henrik Ibsen, *Pillars of Society*; Henry James, *The American*; Sarah Orne Jewett, *Deephaven*; Sydney Lanier, *Poems*; Anna Sewell, *Black Beauty*; Lev Tolstoy, *Anna Karenina*; Émile Zola, *The Drunkard*.

MUSICAL EVENTS

A. Births:

Feb 20	Mary Garden (Scot-sop)	Jul 24	Percy A. Scholes (Br-cri)
Feb 24	Rudolph Ganz (Swi-pn-cd)	Jul 27	Ernst von Dohnányi (Hun-cm)
Feb 26	Celestina Boninsegna (It-sop)	Aug 26	Harriet Ware (Am-pn)
Mar 3	Alexander Goedicke (Rus-cm)	Sep 17	Jean Huré (Fr-org)
Apr 2	Arnold Schering (Ger-mus)	Sep 26	Alfred Cortot (Fr-pn-cd)
May 12	Emma Carelli (It-sop)	Oct	Jésus Aroca y Ortega (Sp-mus)
May 17	Jean Chantavoine (Fr-mus)	Oct 2	Michel Calvocoressi (Fr-mus)
May 29	Hermann Weil (Ger-bar)	Oct 31	Oscar Seagle (Am-bar)
Jun 9	Titta Ruffo (It-bar)	Nov 18	Richard Mayr (Aus-bs)
Jun 12	Vanni Marcoux (Fr-bar)	Nov 21	Sigfrid Karg-Elert (Ger-cm)
Jun 14	Jane Bathori (Fr-mez)	Nov 25	Morton Adkins (Am-bar)
Jul 13	Karl Erb (Ger-ten)	Dec 6	Jean Gerardy (Bel-cel)
Jul 14	Agnes Nicholls (Br-sop)	Dec 16	Artur Bodanzky (Aus-cd)

B. Deaths:

Jan 6	Pietro Romani (It-cm)	Apr 26	Louise Bertin (Fr-cm)
Mar 5	Julius Otto (Ger-cd)	Jun 3	Ludwig Köchel (Ger-mus)
Mar 15	Cristóbal Oudrid (Sp-cm)	Jun 20	Philipp Wackernagel (Ger-mus)
Mar 23	Caroline Unger (Aus-alto)	Aug 5	Luigi Legnani (It-gui)
Mar 30	Charles Neate (Br-pn)	Aug 7	Mary Ann Gabriel (Br-pn)
Apr 7	Errico Petrella (It-cm)	Sep 12	Julius Rietz (Ger-cd)
Apr 13	Johann A. Heckel (Ger-inst.m)	Sep 22	Elizabeth Rainforth (Br-sop)

Oct 3 Jenny Dingelstedt (Boh-sop)
Oct 3 Therese Tietjens (Ger-sop)
Oct 4 Eduard Devrient (Ger-bar)
Oct 14 Antoine Elwart (Fr-the)
Oct 28 Johann Herbeck (Aus-cd)

Nov 13 Pietro A. Coppola (It-cm)
Dec 3 Alexandre Debain (Fr-pn.m)
Dec 10 Federico Ricci (It-cm)
Dec 18 Pierre Chevillard (Fr-cd)

C. Debuts:
U.S. -- Emma Abbott (N.Y.), Marie-Hippolyte Roze (tour), Heinrich Wiegand (tour)

Other - Fanny Moran-Olden (Dresden), Pol Plançon (Lyons), Marcella Sembrich (Athens), Jullieta Simon-Girard (Paris)

D. New Positions:
Conductors: Jules Danbé (Paris Opéra-Comique), Henryk Jarecki (Lvov Opera), Charles Lamoureux (Paris Opera), Joseph Rheinberger (kapellmeister, Munich), Theodore Thomas (New York PO), Franz Wüllner (kapellmeister, Dresden)

Educational: Frans Coenen (director, Amsterdam Conservatory), Hermann Grädener (Conservatory of the Gesellschaft der Musikfreunde, Vienna), August Kretschmer (music director, Rostock University), Alexandre Luigini (harmony, Lyons Conservatory), Max Meyer-Olbersleben (piano, Würzburg Conservatory), Joseph Joachim Raff (director, Frankfurt Conservatory)

Others: William Barrett (editor, *Monthly Music Times*), Joseph Cox Bridge (organ, Chester Cathedral), Théodore Dubois (organ, Madeleine)

E. Prizes and Honors:
Prizes: Edgar Tinel (Prix de Rome)

Honors: Joseph Joachim (honorary doctorate, Cambridge)

F. Biographical Highlights:
Isaac Albéniz returns to Madrid after five years then goes to Belgium on a scholarship; Marietta Alboni marries her second husband Charles Ziéger; Tor Aulin enters the Stockholm Conservatory; Alexander Borodin travels in Europe and meets Liszt; Johannes Brahms refuses an honorary doctorate from Cambridge; George Chadwick leaves for Europe to study with Haupt and Jadassohn; Ernest Chausson is sworn in as a lawyer but never takes up the practice; Louis Elson leaves Leipzig and returns to the U.S.; Gabriel Fauré becomes second organist at the Madeleine; Julián Gayarre makes his Covent Garden debut; Etelka Gerster and George Henschel make their London debuts; Leos Janácek, on a walking tour of Bohemia, meets Dvorák; Adelina Patti makes her La Scala debut; Manuel Rosenthal begins piano study with Liszt; Camille Saint-Saëns resigns as organist of the Madeleine; Francesco Tamagno makes his La Scala debut; Peter Tchaikovsky marries Antonina Milyukov, attempts suicide after a week, but is given a yearly annuity by Mme. von Meck; Henri Vieuxtemps resumes limited activity after his stroke.

G. Institutional Openings:
Performing Groups: Helsinki Concert Society; Ladies (Indiana) Matinee Musical (Indianapolis); Montreal Philharmonic Society (revival); Nyack Symphonic Society; Romanian Opera Co.; Rostocker Konzertverein; Società dei Concerti Sinfonici Popolari (Milan); Württemberg Evangelical Kirchengesangverein

Festivals: Salzburg Festival; Württemberg Evangelical Festival

Educational: Academia de Belas Artas (Instituto de Música da Bahia); Instituto Nacional de Bellas Artes (Venezuela); Liceo Musicale (Rome); Philadelphia Conservatory of Music; Scuolo d'Arco (Verona)

Other: Francis, Day and Hunter, Music Publishers (London); I. K. Funk and Co. (Funk and Wagnalls), Publishers; Julien Hamelle, Music Publisher (Paris); *Journal de*

Musique; *Musical Opinion*

H. Musical Literature:
Ábrányi, Kornél, *Music Aesthetic*
Barrett, William A., *English Church Composers*
Cummings, W. H., *The Rudiments of Music*
Drobisch, Moritz, *Über reine Stimmung und Temperatur der Töne*
Grädener, Carl, *System der harmonielehre*
Hullah, John, *Music in the House*
Lamperti, Francesco, *Treatise on the Art of Singing*
Lavoix, Henri, *La Musique dans la Nature*
Naumann, Emil, *Zukunftsmusik und die Musik der Zukunft*
Pauer, Ernst, *Elements of the Beautiful in Music*

I. Musical Compositions:
Brahms, Johannes, *Symphony No. 2, Opus 73*
    23 Songs, Opus 69 - 72
Busoni, Ferruccio, *5 Pieces, Opus 3, for Piano*
Chabrier, Emmanuel, *L'étoile* (opera)
Clay, Frédéric, *Lalla Rookh* (cantata)
Dubois, Théodore, *Suite No. 2 for Orchestra*
Dvorák, Antonin, *Symphonic Variations, Opus 78*
    The Peasant as Rogue, Opus 37 (opera)
    Stabat Mater, Opus 58
    String Quartet, Opus 34
Fibich, Zdenek, *Blanik, Opus 50* (opera)
Gilbert and Sullian, *The Sorcerer* (operetta)
Goldmark, Karl, *Concerto, Opus 28, for Violin and Orchestra*
Gounod, Charles, *Cinq-Mars* (opera)
    Marche Religieuse
Hallström, Ivar, *The Viking's Voyage* (opera)
Janácek, Leos, *Suite for String Orchestra*
Lecocq, Charles, *La Marjolaine* (operetta)
Leoncavallo, Ruggero, *Chatterton* (opera)
Liszt, Franz, *Années de Pelerinage, Year III* (piano)
Luigini, Alexandre, *Les Caprices de Margot* (opera)
Mackenzie, Alexander, *Cervantes Overture*
Massenet, Jules, *Lahore* (opera)
Mussorgsky, Modeste, *Songs and Dances of Death*
Offenbach, Jacques, *Le Docteur Ox* (operetta)
    La Boite au Lait (operetta)
Planquette, Jean, *Les Cloches de Corneville* (opera)
Puccini, Giacomo, *I Figli d'Italia* (cantata)
Raff, Joseph J., *Concerto No. 2 for Violin and Orchestra*
Rossi, Lauro, *Biorn* (opera)
Saint-Saëns, Camille, *Samson and Delilah* (opera)
    Suite for Orchestra, Opus 49
    Le Timbre d'Argent (opera)
    La Jeunesse d'Hercule (symphonic poem)
Stanford, Charles V., *Festival Overture*
Strauss, Johann, Jr., *Prinz Methusalem* (operetta)
Sullivan, Arthur, *The Lost Chord* (song)
Suppé, Franz von, *Missa Dalmatica*
Tchaikovsky, Peter, *Symphony No. 4, Opus 36*
    Valse Scherzo, Opus 34, for Violin and Orchestra

1878

World Events:
In the U.S., the first telephone exchange is set up in New Haven, Connecticut and lists 50 names; the Bland-Allison Act on the coining of silver is passed by Congress; a gold strike in Arizona results in the founding of Tombstone; the St. Louis *Post-Dispatch* is bought by Joseph Pulitzer. Internationally, the Congress of Berlin divides the Ottoman Empire among the European Powers; Cuba is again defeated in an attempt at freedom from Spain; Victor Emmanuel II of Italy dies and Humbert becomes King; Pope Pius IX dies and is succeeded by Leo XIII.

Cultural Highlights:
The Duveneck School of Art opens in Munich; the magazine, *Der Sturm*, and the gallery are founded by Herwarth Walden; Frederic Leighton becomes President of the Royal Academy of Art; Bret Harte becomes U.S. Consul to Prussia. Births in the art field include American sculptor Robert Aitken, British artist Spencer Gore, German artist Otto Freundlich and Russian artist Kazimir Malevich; deaths include British architect Richard Upjohn, artist George Cruikshank and Charles-François Daubigny. Births in the literary world include Americans Grace W. Conkling, Donald Marquis, Carl Sandburg and Upton Sinclair, British poets Wilfred Gibson, John Masefield and Edward Thomas, Belgian poet Émile Cammaerts, Italian poet and critic Massimo Bontempelli and Hungarian author Ferenc Molnár; deaths include American poets William Cullen Bryant and Sarah H. Whitman. Other highlights include:

Art: Jules Bastien-Lepage, *The Haymakers*; Pierre de Chavannes, *The Story of Ste. Geneviève*; Edgar Degas, *The Cafe Singer*; Max Klinger, *The Glove*; Édouard Manet, *At the Cafe*; Hans von Marées, *The Ages of Man*; Ernest Meissonier, *Cuirassiers of 1805*; Pierre-Auguste Rodin, *The Walking Man*; John Twachtman, *Venetian Landscape*.

Literature: Rudolf Baumbach, *Lieder eines Fahrenden Gesellen*; Holger Drachmann, *On a Sailor's Word*; Thomas Hardy, *Return of the Native*; José Hernández, *La Vuelta de Martin Fierro*; Henry James, *Daisy Miller*; Sydney Lanier, *The Marshes of Glynn*; George Miller, *Flowers of Passion*; Margaret Oliphant, *The Primrose Path*.

MUSICAL EVENTS

A. Births:

Jan 1	Edwin F. Goldman (Am-cd)	May 27	Isadora Duncan (Am-bal)
Jan 27	Berta Morena (Ger-sop)	Jul 3	George M. Cohan (Am-cm)
Feb 7	Ossip Gabrilowitsch (Rus-pn)	Jul 5	Lawrence Gilman (Am-cri)
Feb 16	Selim Palmgren (Fin-cm)	Jul 8	E. Ferrari-Fontana (It-ten)
Feb 26	Emmy Destinn (Cz-sop)	Jul 17	Rita Fornia (Am-sop)
Mar 14	Paul Reimers (Ger-ten)	Jul 21	Ernest R. Ball (Am-pop)
Mar 21	Pasquale Amato (It-bar)	Sep 17	Vincenzo Tommasini (It-cm)
Mar 23	Franz Schreker (Aus-cm)	Oct 28	Conrado del Campo (Sp-cm)
Apr 2	Augusta Cottlow (Am-pn)	Nov 1	Eleanora de Cisneros (Am-mez)
Apr 28	Lionel Barrymore (Am-act-cm)	Nov 27	Otto Kinkeldey (Am-mus)
May 19	Adam Carse (Br-cm-au)	Dec 8	Tullio Serafin (It-cd)
May 24	Louis Fleury (Fr-fl)		

B. Deaths:

Jan 2	Oskar Kolbe (Ger-the)	Apr 3	Jean Gautier (Fr-cm)
Jan 15	Carlo Blasis (It-bal)	May 6	François Benoist (Fr-org)
Jan 28	Konstantin Decker (Ger-pn)	May 7	Josefine Fröhlich (Aus-sop)
Mar 4	Napoleone Moriani (It-ten)	May 7	Théophile Tilmant (Fr-cd)
Mar 12	Ossip A. Petrov (Rus-bs)	Jun 6	Gottfried Herrmann (Ger-vn)
Mar 17	Hermann Küster (Ger-mus)	Jul 2	Emmanuel Bazin (Fr-cm)

Jul 23	Hilarión Eslava (Sp-cm)	Oct 31	Heinrich Willmers (Ger-pn)
Aug 23	Adolf F. Lindblad (Swe-cm)	Dec 24	Lucy Anderson (Br-pn)
Aug 24	Rudolf Willmers (Den-pn)	Dec 26	Georgine Schubert (Ger-sop)
Oct 5	Louise Wippern (Ger-sop)	Dec 28	José Alcedo (Por-cm)
Oct 16	Ludwika Rivoli (Pol-sop)		John A. Latrobe (Br-cm)
Oct 25	Ludwig W. Maurer (Ger-vn)		

C. Debuts:

U.S. -- A. J. (Signor) Foli (tour), Etelka Gerster (N.Y.), Giuseppe del Puente (N.Y.), Franz Rummel (tour), Zélia Trebelli (tour), August Wilhelmj (tour)

Other - Mattia Battistini (Rome), Alma Fohstrom (Helsinki), Helen Hopekirk (Leipzig), Selma Kronold (Leipzig), Antonia Kufferath (Berlin), Julius Lieban (Leipzig), Barton M'Guckin (Dublin), Carl Nebe (Wiesbaden), Giovanni Battista de Negri (Bergamo), Antonio Pini-Corsi (Cremona), Karl Scheidemantel (Weimar), Gabriel Soulacroix (Brussels), Fernando Valero (Spain), Adolf Wallnöfer (Olmütz), Elly Warnots (Brussels)

D. New Positions:

Conductors: Joseph Mertens (Flemish Opera), Karl A. Raida (Viktoria Theater, Berlin)

Educational: Jan van den Eeden (director, Mons Musical Academy), Gyula Erkel (piano, Budapest Academy), Asger Hamerik (director, Peabody Institute), Joseph H. Hellmesberger, Jr. (violin, Vienna Conservatory), Anatol Liadov (theory, St. Petersburg Conservatory), Jules Massenet (composition, Paris Conservatory), Ignace Jan Paderewski (piano, Warsaw Conservatory), Hugo Riemann (lecturer, Leipzig University), Clara Schumann (piano, Frankfurt Conservatory), Sergei Taneyev (harmony, Moscow Conservatory)

Others: Francis Hueffer (music critic, *London Times*)

E. Prizes and Honors:

Prizes: Benjamin Godard and Samuel-Alexandre Rousseau (Prix de Rome)

Honors: Philip Calderon, Charles Lamoureux and Arthur Sullivan (Legion of Honor), Robert Franz (knighted by the King of Bavaria), Jules Massenet (French Academy)

F. Biographical Highlights:

Károly Aggházy and Jenö Hubay begins concertizing as a piano-violin duo; Isaac Albéniz begins piano study with Franz Liszt; Lillian Bailey goes to Paris to study with Pauline Viardot-García; Johannes Brahms visits Italy before settling in Vienna; Claude Debussy visits London and meets Gilbert and Sullivan; Riccardo Drigo goes to Russia for a forty-year stay; Antonin Dvorák enjoys his first publication, his *Slavonic Dances*; Antonietta Fricci retires from the stage; George Grove visits the U.S.; Minnie Hauk returns to the U.S. and sings the title role in the first American performance of *Carmen*; Ruggero Leoncavallo receives a literature degree from Bologna University; Theodor Leschetizky, for health reasons, moves to Vienna and begins teaching piano; Anatol Liadov is allowed to take tests in St. Petersburg and passes with honors; Edward MacDowell studies with Ehlert in Wiesbaden; Arthur Nikisch becomes second conductor at the Leipzig Opera; Ignace Jan Paderewski graduates from the Warsaw Music Institute; Hugo Wolf contracts venereal disease.

G. Institutional Openings:

Performing Groups: Emma Abbott Opera Co.; Los Angeles Philharmonic Society; Milwaukee Liederkranz; Moscow Choral Society; Munich Lehrergesangverein; New York SO; Oratorio Society of Newark; People's Concert Society (London); Unión Artístico-Musical (Madrid)

Educational: Cincinnati College of Music; Doppler School of Music; Escuela de Música de la Provincia (Buenos Aires); Hegar Music School (Zurich); Instituto Musicale (Padua); Milwaukee Conservatory of Music; Teodor Burada (Romanian Academy); Wellesley College School of Music

Other: Eugene Ascherberg and Co., Music Publishers; *Bayreuther Blätter; Boston Musical Record*; Cincinnati Music Hall; Dresden Opera House; *Der Klavierlehrer*; Mechanical Orguinette Co. (Aeolian Organ Co.); Monte Carlo Playhouse; Theodor Steingräber Publishing House (Hanover)

H. Musical Literature:

Hueffer, Francis, *The Troubadours*
Köstlin, Heinrich, *Die Tonkunst: einführung in die Aesthetik der Musik*
Langhans, Friedrich, *Musikgeschichte in zwölf Vorträgen*
Lavoix, Henri, *Histoire de l'instrumentation*
Marmontel, Antoine, *Les Pianistes célébres*
Mason, William, *Pianoforte Technics*
Moore, John, *The Sentimental Songbook*
Pauer, Ernst, *Musical Forms*
Riemann, Hugo, *Geschichte der Notenschrift*
Wasielewski, Wilhelm von, *Geschichte der Instrumental-Musik in XVI. Jahrhundert*

I. Musical Compositions:

Bland, James, *Carry Me Back to Old Virginny* (song)
Brahms, Johannes, *Concerto, Opus 77, for Violin and Orchestra*
    4 Ballades and Romances, Opus 75, for Piano
    8 Pieces, Opus 76, for Piano
    6 Songs, Opus 86
Bruch, Max, *Concerto No. 2 for Violin and Orchestra*
Debussy, Claude, *Beau Soir* (song)
Dvořák, Antonin, *Serenade, Opus 44*
    Slavonic Dances, Series I, Opus 46
    3 Slavonic Rhapsodies, Opus 45
    String Sextet, Opus 48
Fauré, Gabriel, *Concerto, Opus 14, for Violin and Orchestra*
Fibich, Zdenek, *Eternity* (symphonic poem)
Franck, César, *Fantasie in A Major* (organ)
    Pièce heroïque (organ)
    Cantabile in B Major (organ)
Gilbert and Sullivan, *H. M. S. Pinafore* (operetta)
Gounod, Charles, *Polyeucte* (opera)
Grieg, Edvard, *String Quartet in G Minor, Opus 27*
d'Indy, Vincent, *The Enchanted Forest, Opus 8* (symphonic poem)
Offenbach, Jacques, *Madame Favart* (operetta)
Raff, Joseph J., *Symphony No. 9, Opus 208, "In Summer"*
Rimsky-Korsakov, Nicolai, *Concerto for Trombone and Band*
    May Night (opera)
Rossi, Giovanni, *Overture, Saul*
Saint-Saëns, Camille, *Symphony No. 2, Opus 55*
    Requiem, Opus 54
Smetana, Bedrich, *The Secret* (opera)
    Tabor (No. 5 of *Ma Vlast*)
    14 Czech Dances for Piano
Tchaikovsky, Peter, *Eugene Onegin, Opus 24* (opera)
    Concerto, Opus 35, for Violin and Orchestra
    Liturgy of St. John Chrysostom, Opus 41
    Children's Album, Opus 39 (piano)
    12 Pieces, Opus 40, for Piano
Thomas, Ambroise, *Psyché* (opera)

1879

World Events:
In the U.S., the first Woolworth store opens in Lancaster, Pennsylvania; the first demonstration of the incandescent light bulb is given; the Archeological Institute of America is founded; Radcliffe College is founded; the Geological Survey Department is established. Internationally, the Belgian Congo is re-organized as the Congo Free State; the British fight the Zulu War in the Transvaal; in the War of the Pacific, in South America, Chile defeats Bolivia and Peru; Werner von Siemens sets up the first electric railway system; German scientist Albert Einstein and Russian dictator Joseph Stalin are born.

Cultural Highlights:
The Concord Summer School of Philosophy and Literature meets in Massachusetts; the magazines *New York Dramatic Mirror* and the *Deutscher Literatur-Kalendar* begin publication. Births in the literary field include American poets Vachel Lindsay and Wallace Stevens, British novelist E.M. Forster, French author René Dumesnil and German novelist Bernhard Kellermann; deaths include Swedish poet Heinrich Leuthold and Polish poet Ryszard Berwinski. Births in the art world include American artists Gifford Beal and Robert Spencer, British artist Vanessa Bell and sculptor John Gregory and Swiss artist Paul Klee; deaths include American artists George Bingham, William Hunt, William Powell and sculptor William Rimmer, French artists Thomas Couture, Honoré Daumier and sculptor Antoine Preault and German sculptor Emil Wolff. Other highlights include:

Art: Jules Bastian-Lepage, *Sarah Bernhardt*; Mary Cassatt, *Cup of Tea*; Benjamin Constant, *Favorite of the Emir*; Edgar Degas, *Awaiting the Cue*; Édouard Detaille, *Defense of Champigny*; Winslow Homer, *Girl and Laurel*; Édouard Manet, *In a Boat*; Camille Pissarro, *Le Fond de l'Hermitage*; Auguste Rodin, *John the Baptist Preaching*.

Literature: Edwin Arnold, *The Light of Asia*; Robert Browning, *Dramatic Idylls I*; George W. Cable, *Old Creole Days*; Feodor Dostoyevsky, *The Brothers Karamozov*; Giuseppe Giacosa, *The Husband in Love with His Wife*; Henrik Ibsen, *A Doll's House*; Henry James, *The Europeans*; George Meredith, *The Egoist*.

MUSICAL EVENTS

A. Births:

Jan 3	Lina Abarbanell (Ger-sop)	Jun 10	Maria Gay (Sp-alto)
Jan 7	Francis Maclennan (Am-ten)	Jun 11	Julia Claussen (Swe-mez)
Jan 16	Otto Ursprung (Ger-mus)	Jul 5	Volkmar Andreae (Swe-cm)
Feb 25	Otakar Ostrcil (Cz-cm)	Aug 13	John Ireland (Br-cm)
Feb 26	Frank Bridge (Br-cm)	Aug 30	Fritzi Scheff (Aus-sop)
Mar 17	Joseph Haas (Ger-cm)	Oct 13	Peter von Anrooy (Hol-cd-cm)
Apr 18	Maud Fay (Am-sop)	Oct 21	Marie Canteloube (Fr-cm)
Apr 29	Thomas Beecham (Br-cd)	Nov 25	Paul Stefan (Aus-mus)
May 4	Daniel Fryklund (Swe-mus)	Dec 2	Rudolf Friml (Cz-cm)
May 6	Tobias Norlind (Swe-mus)	Dec 4	Hamilton Hardy (Br-cd-cm)
May 22	Jean E. P. Cras (Fr-cm)	Dec 17	Fritz Stein (Ger-mus)

B. Deaths:

Feb 7	Pierre Varnay (Fr-cm)	Jul 4	Joseph Schad (Ger-pn-cm)
Mar 3	Karl Beck (Aus-ten)	Jul 25	Marie P. Hamel (Fr-org.m)
Apr	François de Villars (Fr-mus)	Aug 22	August Kummer (Ger-cel)
Apr 9	Ernst F. Richter (Ger-cm)	Aug 27	Henriette Nissen (Swe-sop)
May 15	Franz Diener (Ger-ten)	Sep 12	Peter Heise (Den-cm)
Jun 21	Melchiore Balbi (It-the)	Sep 12	Gustave H. Roger (Fr-ten)
Jun 30	Barbara Fröhlich (Aust-alto)	Oct 14	Karl A. Eckert (Ger-cd)

C. Debuts:

U.S. -- Timothée Adamowski (Boston), Mathilde Bauermeister (tour), Marie Litta, Zélie de Lussan (N.Y.), Melitta Otto (Cincinnati), Alwina Valleria (N.Y.)

Other - Max Alvary (Weimar), Hypolite Belhomme (Paris), Gemma Bellincioni (Naples), Armand Castelmary (Paris), Hermann Devries (Paris), Lillian Henschel (London), Pavel Khokhlov (Moscow), Adele Margulies (Vienna), Jean de Reszke (Madrid, as tenor), Arnold Rosé (Leipzig), Helena Theodorini (Cuneo), Giulia Valda (Paris), Marie van Zandt (Turin)

D. New Positions:

Conductors: Riccardo Drigo (Italian Opera, St. Petersburg), Ernst Frank (Hanover Opera), Anton Seidl (Leipzig Opera)

Educational: Ludwig Bussler (theory, Stern Conservatory), Joseph Callaerts (organ, Antwerp Music School), Gaetano Coronaro (harmony, Milan Conservatory), Carl Christian Müller (harmony, New York College of Music), Ebenezer Prout (Royal Academy, London), Hendrik Waelput (harmony, Antwerp Conservatory)

Others: Henri Dallier (organ, St. Eustache, Paris), Francis Hueffer (music critic, *London Times*), William Mathews (music critic, *Chicago Tribune*), Albert Peace (organ, Glasgow Cathedral)

E. Prizes and Honors:

Prizes: Georges Adolphe Hüe (Prix de Rome), Engelbert Humperdinck (Mendelssohn), Samuel-Alexandre Rousseau (Prix Cressent)

Honors: Johannes Brahms (honorary doctorate, Breslau), Arthur Sullivan (honorary doctorate, Oxford)

F. Biographical Highlights:

Timothée Adamowski visits the U.S. as violinist with Clara Kellogg and settles in Boston; Anton Arensky enters St. Petersburg Conservatory; Lillian Bailey marries George Henschel; Ernest Chausson begins music study with Massenet; Edward Elgar begins violin lessons and becomes bandmaster at Worcester Lunatic Asylum; Josef B. Foerster enters Prague Organ School; Emma Fursch-Madi and Alwina Valleria make their Covent Garden debuts; Niels Gade receives his Ph.D. from Copenhagen University; Alexander Glazunov begins music study with Rimsky-Korsakov; Engelbert Humperdinck meets Wagner in Berlin and becomes his disciple; Leos Janácek enrolls in Leipzig Conservatory; Franz Liszt becomes a Canon of Albano (honorary title only); Edward MacDowell enters Frankfurt Conservatory to study with Raff; Carl Nielsen finds employment in a military orchestra in Odensee; Lillian Nordica makes her opera debut in Milan; Fanny Olden marries tenor Karl Moran; Ernst Pauer becomes music examiner for Cambridge; Erik Satie enters the Paris Conservatory; Teresa Stolz gives her farewell performance at La Scala; Henri Vieuxtemps is forced to retire for health reasons.

G. Institutional Openings:

Performing Groups: Bloch'sche Verein (Berlin Opera Society); Boston Ideal Opera Co.; Brno Schubertbund; Ganz Orchestral Concerts (London); Mozart Club of Pittsburgh; Neuer Orchesterverein (Munich); Opéra de Monte Carlo; Oslo Cecilia Society; Palestrina Society; Sociedad de Música Clásica (Santiago); Società del Quartetto (Bologna); Società Orchestrale della Scala

Festivals: Pittsburgh Music Festival

Educational: Balatka Academy of Musical Art (Chicago); Choir School of Christchurch (New Zealand); Denver University School of Music; Lemmens Institute of Church Music (Mechelen); University of Michigan School of Music

Other: Antwerp Lassallekring; Geneva Grand Theater and Opera Co.; Krzyzanowski Concert Bureau (Krakow); *Music Trade Journal; La Nouvelle Revue* (Paris); Schroeder and Gunther, Music Publishers (N.Y.); Société des Quintettes pour Instruments à Vent (Paris); Teatro Politeama (Buenos Aires); Teatro San Felipe (Montevideo); *Zeitschrift für Instrumentenbau*

H. Musical Literature:

Engel, Carl, *The Literature of National Music*
Grove, George, *Dictionary of Music and Musicians I*
Hiles, Henry, *The Grammar of Music*
Hostinsky, Otakar, *Die Lehre von den musikalischen Klängen*
Kistler, Cyrill, *Harmonielehre*
Pole, William, *Philosophy of Music*
Reissmann, August, *Zur Aesthetik der Tonkunst*
Rockstro, William, *A History of Music*
Stainer, John, *Music of the Bible*
Wasielweski, Wilhelm von, *Musikalische Fürsten vom mittelalter...*

I. Musical Compositions:

Bland, James, *Oh, Dem Golden Slippers* (song)
Brahms, Johannes, *Violin Sonata, Opus 78*
    2 Rhapsodies, Opus 79 (piano)
Bristow, George, *The Great Republic* (cantata)
Chadwick, George, *Overture, Rip Van Winkle*
Dubois, Théodore, *Le Pain Bis* (opera)
    Overture in C Major
Dvořák, Antonin, *Orchestra Suite, Opus 39, "Czech"*
    Festival March, Opus 54
    String Quartet, Opus 51
Fauré, Gabriel, *Piano Quartet No. 1, Opus 15*
Franck, César, *The Beatitudes* (oratorio)
    Piano Quintet in F Minor
Gade, Niels, *A Summer Day in the Country, Opus 55*
Gilbert and Sullivan, *The Pirates of Penzance* (operetta)
Godard, Benjamin, *Scènes Poétiques for Orchestra*
Goldmark, Carl, *Penthesilea Overture, Opus 31*
Lecocq, Charles, *La petite Mademoiselle* (operetta)
Mascagni, Pietro, *Symphony in C Minor*
Massenet, Jules, *Scènes de Féerie*
    La Vierge (oratorio)
Mussorgsky, Modeste, *Song of the Flea*
Offenbach, Jacques, *La Fille du Tambour-Major* (operetta)
    La Marocaine (operetta)
Raff, Joseph J., *Symphony No. 10, Opus 213, "Zur Herbstzeit"*
Rubinstein, Anton, *Nero* (opera)
Saint-Saëns, Camille, *Suite Algierienne, Opus 60*
    Concerto No. 2, Opus 58, for Violin and Orchestra
    Étienne Marcel (opera)
    La Lyre et la Harpe, Opus 57
Smetana, Bedrich, *Blanik* (No. 6 of *Ma Vlast*)
    Evening Songs (song cycle)
Suppé, Franz von, *Boccaccio* (operetta)
Tchaikovsky, Peter, *The Maid of Orleans* (opera)
    Suite No. 2, Opus 43, for Orchestra
    7 Songs, Opus 47
Widor, Charles, *Organ Symphony No. 5*

1880

World Events:

In the U.S., James A. Garfield is elected as President No. 20; the census shows a population of 50,189,000, a 26% increase in ten years; New York City's population passes the one million mark; Cleveland, Ohio, becomes the first city to be lit by electricity; the first Salvation Army branch is founded in Pennsylvania. Internationally, William Gladstone begins his second term as British Prime Minister; the British Parliament votes to give free and compulsory education up to age 10; the Irish Insurrection begins against British rule; Pavlov runs his experiments on conditioning of dogs.

Cultural Highlights:

The National Gallery of Canada and the Royal Canadian Academy of Arts is founded in Ottawa; the Rhode Island School of Design opens. James Russell Lowell is appointed Minister to England and Gerard Brown becomes professor of art at Edinburgh. Births in the field of art include German artists Hans Hofmann, Ernst Kirchner and Franz Marc, French artist André Derain, American artists Arthur Dove and Walt Kuhn and sculptor Jacob Epstein; deaths include German artists Anselm Feuerbach and Karl Lessing. Births in the literary world include American novelists Kathleen Norris and Julia Peterkin, British poets John Freeman and Alfred Noyes, Russian poets Alexander Blok and Andrei Byely, French poet Guillaume Apollinaire and Spanish novelist Rámon Pérez de Ayala; deaths include French authors Gustave Flaubert and Eugéne Labiche, British novelist George Eliot and Italian poet and historian Ignazio Ciampi. Other highlights include:

Art: Arnold Böcklin, *Isle of the Dead*; Edgar Degas, *Dancer in a Rose Dress*; Paul Gauguin, *The Yellow Christ*; George Inness, *The Coming Storm*; Édouard Manet, *Woman Fixing Her Garter*; Claude Monet, *Banks of the Seine*; Pierre Renoir, *Sleeping Girl with Cat*; Auguste Rodin, *The Thinker*; George Watts, *Watchman, What of the Night?*; James Whistler, *La Petite Mephisto*

Literature: Robert Browning, *Dramatic Idylls II*; George Cable, *The Grandissimes*; Henri Chantavoine, *Satires Contemporaines*; Benjamin Disraeli, *Endymion*; Joel Chandler Harris, *Uncle Remus, His Songs and Sayings*; Henry W. Longfellow, *Ultima Thule*; Algernon Swinburne, *Songs of the Springtides*; Giovanni Verga, *Under the Shadow of Etna*; Lew Wallace, *Ben Hur*; Émile Zola, *Nana*

MUSICAL EVENTS

A. Births:

Jan 5	Nicolas Medtner (Rus-pn-cm)	Jul 24	Ernest Bloch (Swi-cm)
Jan 8	Melanie Kurt (Aus-sop)	Aug 3	Alberto Randegger (It-vn)
Feb 14	Maria Labia (It-sop)	Aug 3	Theodor Scheidl (Ger-bar)
Feb 19	Arthur Shepherd (Am-cm)	Aug 16	Marguerite Carré (Fr-sop)
Feb 23	Edgar Istel (Ger-mus)	Sep 17	D.E. Inghelbrecht (Fr-cd)
Feb 29	Oscar von Riesemann (Ger-mus)	Sep 20	Ildebrando Pizzetti (It-cm)
Mar 16	Albert von Doenhoff (Am-pn)	Sep 27	Jacques Thibaud (Fr-vn)
Apr 7	Elsa Alsen (Pol-alto)	Oct 2	George Russell (Am-org)
Apr 11	Bernardino Molinari (It-cd)	Oct 6	Julia Culp (Hol-sop)
Apr 26	Michel Fokine (Rus-bal)	Nov 3	Raffaele Casimiri (It-mus)
Apr 29	Adolf Chybinski (Pol-mus)	Dec 30	Alfred Einstein (Ger-mus)
Jul 5	Jan Kubelík (Cz-vn-cm)		

B. Deaths:

Jan 17	Michael Welte (Ger-inst.m)	Mar 11	Anna Fröhlich (Aus-sop)
Jan 22	James Coward (Br-org)	Mar 31	Henri Wieniawski (Pol-vn-cm)
Mar 5	Wojciech Sowinski (Pol-pn)	May 10	John Goss (Br-org)

May 16	Karl A. Krebs (Ger-cd-cm)	Oct 5	Jacques Offenbach (Fr-cm)
May 26	John Curwen (Br-m.ed)	Nov 7	Carl Weitzmann (Ger-the)
Jul 7	Nicola Ivanoff (Rus-ten)	Nov 24	Napoleon-Henri Reber (Fr-cm)
Jul 22	Anna Oury (Ger-pn)	Dec 2	Josephine Lang (Ger-cm)
Aug 17	Ole Bull (Nor-vn)	Dec 31	Franz J. Kunkel (Ger-the)

C. Debuts:
U.S. -- Árpád Doppler (N.Y.), Carl Valentine Lachmund (tour)

Other - Blanche Arral (Paris), Emilie Herzog (Munich), Vilém Hes (Brno), Antonio Magini-Coletti (Italy), Karl Muck (Leipzig), Francesco Navarrini (Treviso), Emma Nevada (London), Vasili Safonov (St. Petersburg), George Sieglitz (Hamburg), Alexander Siloti (Moscow), José Tragó (Paris)

D. New Positions:
Conductors: Max Bruch (Liverpool PO), Hans von Bülow (Meiningen), Felix Mottl (Karlsruhe Opera), Emil Paur (Mannheim), John Philip Sousa (U.S. Marine Band), Theodore Thomas (New York PO)

Educational: Henry Frost (organ, Guildhall School), Ernest Guiraud (composition, Paris Conservatory), Leoš Janácek (Brno Teacher's Training College), Giuseppe Martucci (piano, Naples Conservatory), Ilma di Murska (voice, National Conservatory, N.Y.), Amilcare Ponchielli (composition, Milan Conservatory)

Others: Hugh Allen (organ, St. Saviour's, Reading), Otto Floersheim (editor, *Musical Courier*), Henry Krehbiel (critic, N.Y. *Tribune*), Paul Piutti (organ, Thomaskirche, Leipzig)

E. Prizes and Honors:
Prizes: Lucien Hillemacher (Prix de Rome)

Honors: Leopold Damrosch (honorary doctorate, Columbia), Charles Gounod (Legion of Honor)

F. Biographical Highlights:
Guido Adler receives his doctorate in musicology; Emmanuel Chabrier resigns his post for full time in composition; George Chadwick returns to the U.S. and sets up a private studio in Boston; Ernest Chausson enters the Paris Conservatory to study with Massenet but soon leaves to study privately with Franck; Claude Debussy becomes accompanist and tutor for the von Meck family; Frederick Delius enters his father's wool merchandising business; Louis Elson becomes a lecturer on music history in the New England Conservatory; Edward German begins serious music study at the Royal Academy in London; Alexander Glazunov studies harmony and counterpoint with Rimsky-Korsakov; Karl Muck receives his Ph.D. degree; Modest Mussorgsky is permanently dismissed from government service; Giacomo Puccini enters Milan Conservatory; Marcella Sembrich makes her Covent Garden debut; Elena Teodorini makes her La Scala debut; Marie van Zandt makes her Paris Opera debut.

G. Institutional Openings:
Performing Groups: Archangelsky Chorus (Russia); Birmingham Musical Association (England); Dimitrescu String Quartet (Bucharest); Messina Società del Quartetto; Newcastle Chamber Music Society; St. Louis SO; Società del Quartetto (Naples); Società Orchestrale (Naples); Société Populaires des Concerts de Musique Classiques (Marseille)

Festivals: National Eisteddfod Association (Welsh Festival)

Educational: Ann Arbor School of Music (becomes part of the University of Michigan in 1892); Cardiff Choir School; Conservatorio Nacional de Música (Buenos Aires); Guildhall School of Music and Drama (London); Scuola Gregoriana (Rome);

University of Nebraska School of Music

Other: Enoch Frère et Costallat, Music Publishers (Paris); Haymarket Theatre II (London); Max Hesse Publishing House (Leipzig); *The Musical Courier; Neue Musikzeitung* (Stuttgart); Teatro Municipal (Caracas, Venezuela)

H. Musical Literature:

Cui, Cesar, *Music in Russia*
Culwick, James C., *The Rudiments of Music*
Gurney, Edmund, *The Power of Sound*
Hanslick, Eduard, *Musikalische Stationen*
Hueffer, Francis, *Musical Studies*
Kistler, Cyrill, *Musikalische elementarlehre*
Mathews, William, *How to Understand Music I*
Riemann, Hugo, *Skizze einer neuen Methode der Harmonielehre*
Upton, George, *Woman in Music*

I. Musical Compositions:

Bland, James, *In the Evening by the Moonlight* (song)
Borodin, Alexander, *In the Steppes of Central Asia*
Brahms, Johannes, *Academic Festival Overture, Opus 80*
Bruch, Max, *Scottish Rhapsody for Violin and Orchestra*
Debussy, Claude, *Symphony in G Minor*
Delibes, Léo, *Jean de Nivelle* (opera)
Denza, Luigi, *Funiculi Funiculà* (song)
Dvorák, Antonin, *Symphony No. 6, Opus 60*
    Concerto, Opus 53, for Violin and Orchestra
    Violin Sonata, Opus 57
    Gypsy Songs, Opus 55
Fauré, Gabriel, *Berceuse, Opus 16*
    3 Songs, Opus 18
Fibich, Zdenek, *The Tempest* (symphonic poem)
Gade, Niels, *Concerto, Opus 56, for Violin and Orchestra*
Godard, Benjamin, *Symphony*
Gounod, Charles, *The Redemption* (oratorio)
Grieg, Edvard, *12 Songs, Opus 18*
d'Indy, Vincent, *Wallenstein's Camp* (symphonic poem)
Ivanovici, Ion, *Waves of the Danube (Anniversary Waltz)*
Lalo, Edouard, *Norwegian Fantasy for Violin and Orchestra*
Mackenzie, Alexander, *Scottish Rhapsody No. 1*
Mahler, Gustav, *Das Klagende Lied*
Mussorgsky, Modest, *Khovantchina* (unfinished opera)
Offenbach, Jacques, *Tales of Hoffman* (opera)
Paine, John Knowles, *Symphony No. 2 in A Major, "In Spring"*
Ponchielli, Amilcare, *Il figliuol prodigo* (opera)
Puccini, Giacomo, *Mass in A-flat*
Rubinstein, Anton, *The Merchant Kalashnikov* (opera)
Saint-Saëns, Camille, *Concerto No. 3, Opus 61, for Violin and Orchestra*
    Morceau de Concert, Opus 62, for Violin and Orchestra
Strauss, Johann, Jr., *Roses from the South*
Strauss, Richard, *Serenade, Opus 7, for Winds*
Sullivan, Arthur, *The Martyr of Antioch* (oratorio)
Tchaikovsky, Peter, *Overture Solennelle 1812, Opus 49*
    Serenade for Strings, Opus 48
    Concerto No. 2, Opus 44, for Piano and Orchestra
Wolf, Hugo, *String Quartet in D Minor*

1881

World Events:

In the U.S., President James Garfield is assassinated and Chester Arthur becomes President No. 21; the Red Cross is founded by Clara Barton; the Federation of Organized Trades and Labor Unions is organized; Tuskegee Institute is founded; the Barnum and Bailey Circus takes to the road. Internationally, Alexander II of Russia is assassinated and Alexander III becomes czar; France takes over the North African port of Tunis; Louis Pasteur isolates the rabies virus; the British armed forces outlaws flogging as a punishment.

Cultural Highlights:

The American School of Classical Studies opens in Athens; the magazine *L'Art Moderne* begins publication in Brussels. Victor Cherbuliez and Sully Prudhomme are taken into the French Academy. Births in the art field include French artists George Braque, Fernand Léger and Albert Gleizes, German sculptor Wilhelm Lehmbruck, American sculptor Chester Beach and Russian-born artist Max Weber, Italian artist Carlo Carrà, and Spanish artist Pablo Picasso; dead are British artist Samuel Palmer and American sculptor Thomas Gould. Births in the literary field include American novelist Thomas Stribling and Austrian novelist Stefan Zweig; deaths include British author Benjamin Disraeli and Anna Marie Hall, Irish poet Arthur O'Shaughnessy, Scottish historian Thomas Carlyle, Russian novelist Feodor Dostoyevsky, American poet Alfred B. Street and Italian poets Tommaso Gherardi del Testa and Giovanni Ruffini. Other highlights include:

Art: Christian Krohg, *The Sick Girl*; Max Liebermann, *The Cobbler's Shop*; Wilhelm Leibl, *Three Women in Village Church*; Édouard Manet, *Emmanuel Chabrier*; Hans von Marées, *The Judgment of Paris*; Claude Monet, *Sunshine and Snow*; Pierre Renoir, *Luncheon of the Boating Party*; Ilya Repin, *Modeste Moussorgsky*; Auguste Rodin, *Adam* (bronze)

Literature: Carlo Collodi, *Pinocchio*; Henrik Ibsen, *Ghosts*; Henry James, *Portrait of a Lady*; Harriet Lothrop, *Five Little Peppers and How They Grew*; Guy de Maupassant, *La Maison Tellier*; Dante Rosetti, *The House of Life*; Johanna Spyri, *Heidi*; Mark Twain, *The Prince and the Pauper*; Paul Verlaine, *Sagesse*

MUSICAL EVENTS

A. Births:

Jan 4	Georgy Baklanov (Rus-bar)	Aug 14	Johann B. Beck (Fr-mus)
Feb 24	Paul A. Hirsch (Ger-mus)	Aug 19	George Enescu (Rom-cm)
Feb 26	Ferencz Hegedus (Hun-vn)	Aug 22	Edward Johnson (Am-ten)
Mar 16	Morgan Kingston (Br-ten)	Aug 24	Marthe Chenal (Fr-sop)
Mar 23	Egon Petri (Ger-pn)	Aug 25	Yvonne de Treville (Am-sop)
Mar 25	Béla Bártok (Hun-cm)	Sep 16	Clive Bell (Br-cri)
Apr 11	Harvey Gaul (Am-m.ed)	Nov 7	Nazzareno de Angelis (It-bs)
Apr 20	Nicholai Miaskovsky (Rus-cm)	Nov 16	Domenico Alaleona (It-mus)
May 10	Frank Mullings (Br-ten)	Dec 2	Henry Fillmore (Am-band)
Jun 1	Margarete Matzenauer (Hun-sop)	Dec 12	Barbara Kemp (Ger-sop)
Jun 29	Curt Sachs (Ger-mus)	Dec 14	Charles W. Cadman (Am-cm)

B. Deaths:

Jan 10	Lucien H. Southard (Am-cm)	Jun 6	Henri Vieuxtemps (Bel-vn-cm)
Mar 23	Nicholai Rubinstein (Rus-pn)	Jun 7	Augustin Savard (Fr-pn-cm)
Mar 28	Modest Mussorgsky (Rus-cm)	Jul 15	Karl von Bocklet (Cz-vn)
Mar 31	Gaetano Gaspari (It-mus-cm)	Jul 27	Johann C. Lobe (Ger-mus)
Apr 5	Julius Hesse (Ger-pn)	Aug 19	Joseph Labitzky (Ger-cm-cd)
Apr 22	Auguste F. Morel (Fr-cm)	Sep 21	François Durutte (Bel-the)

Sep 24	Luigi Casamorata (It-cm)	Oct 12	Paulina Rivoli (Pol-sop)
Oct 7	Wilhelm Fritze (Ger-pn)	Nov 2	Jan N. Bobrowicz (Pol-gui)
Oct 9	Richard Wuerst (Ger-cm)	Nov 25	Theobald Böhm (Ger-fl-inv)

C. Debuts:

U.S. -- Leandro Campanari (Boston), Emma Juch (N.Y.), Adele Margulies, (Ernest) Nicolini (tour)

Other - Eugen d'Albert (London), Alexander Bandrowski-Sas (Lvov), Emma Calvé (Brussels), Ben Davies (Birmingham), Wilhelm Grüning (Danzig), Alfred Reisenauer (Rome), Luise Reuss-Belce (Karlsruhe), Emily Shinner (London)

D. New Positions:

Conductors: Felix Dessoff (Frankfurt Opera), George Henschel (Boston SO), Wilhelm Jahn (Vienna Opera), Gustav Mahler (Laibach)

Educational: Károly Aggházy (piano, Budapest Conservatory), Alban Förster (violin, Dresden Conservatory), Nicolai Hubert (director, Moscow Conservatory), Leos Janácek (Brno Organ School), Edward MacDowell (piano, Darmstadt Conservatory), Emile-Louis Pessard (harmony, Paris Conservatory), Hugo Riemann (Hamburg Conservatory), Vasili Safonov (piano, St. Petersburg Conservatory)

Others: William F. Apthorp (critic, Boston *Transcript*), Léon Boëllmann (organ, St. Vincent de Paul, Paris), Enrico Bossi (organ, Como Cathedral), Henry T. Finck (critic, New York *Evening Post*)

E. Prizes and Honors:

Prizes: Eugen d'Albert (Mendelssohn), Alfred Bruneau and Sylvain Dupuis (Prix de Rome), Georges-Adolphe Hüe (Prix Crescent), Engelbert Humperdinck (Meyerbeer)

Honors: George Root (honorary doctorate, Chicago), Camille Saint-Saëns (French Institute)

F. Biographical Highlights:

Gustave Charpentier enters Paris Conservatory; Francesco Cilea, age 14, enters Naples Conservatory; Walter Damrosch leads a 250 piece orchestra and a 1200 member choir in a New York Festival; Claude Debussy visits Russia with the von Meck family; Alexander Gretchaninov enters Moscow Conservatory against his father's wishes; George Henschel marries the American soprano Lillian Bailey; Marie Lehmann makes her Vienna Opera debut; Charles M. Loeffler arrives in the U.S.; Mathilde Marchesi moves to Paris and opens her own singing school; Ignace Jan Paderewski, on his wife's death, goes to Berlin for further music study; Horatio Parker enters the Royal Conservatory in Munich; Josephine de Reszke makes her Covent Garden debut; Peter Tchaikovsky divorces his wife after the birth of her illegitimate child; Felix Weingartner begins the study of philosophy at Leipzig University.

G. Institutional Openings:

Performing Groups: Boston SO; Cleveland Philharmonic Society; Concerts Lamoureux (Paris); Heckmann String Quartet (Germany); Quintetto dell Regina (Rome); Royal Welsh Ladies' Choir; St. Gregorius Vereniging (Antwerp)

Educational: Kraków Conservatory of Music; Scharwenka Conservatory of Music (Berlin); Schumacher Conservatory of Music (Mainz)

Other: *Bulletin Critique de Littérature, d'Histoire et de Théologie*; Cincinati Musicians' Protective Union; Denver Grand Opera House; Harms Music Publishers (N.Y.); *La Jeune Belgique*; François Lorée, Woodwind Maker (Paris); National Theater of Prague; Ries and Erler, Music Publishers (Berlin); St. Louis Musical Union; Savoy Theatre (London); Società Artistico-Filarmonica (Modena); Hermann Wolff Concert Management (Berlin)

H. Musical Literature:

Adler, Guido, *Studie zur Geschichte der Harmonie*
Edwards, Henry S., *The Lyric Drama I, II*
Fay, Amy, *Music Study in Germany*
Gottschalk, Louis M., *Notes of a Pianist*
Hiller, Ferdinand, *Wie hören wir Musik?*
Kolbeck, M., *Wiener Opernabende*
Riemann, Hugo, *Die Entwickelung unserer Notenschrift*
Rockstro, William, *Practical Harmony*
Sevcík, Otakar, *Violin Method*

I. Musical Compositions:

Balakirev, Mily, *Thamar* (symphonic poem)
Barnby, Joseph, *Magnificat*
Brahms, Johannes, *Tragic Overture, Opus 81*
    Concerto No. 2, Opus 83, for Piano and Orchestra
    5 Songs and Romances, Opus 84
Bruch, Max, *Kol Nidrei* (cello and orchestra)
Bruckner, Anton, *Symphony No. 6 in A Major*
Busoni, Ferruccio, *String Quartet No. 1, Opus 19*
Chadwick, George W., *The Viking's Last Voyage*
Cui, César, *Marche Solennelle, Opus 18*
Dubois, Théodore, *Frithiof Overture*
Dvořák, Antonin, *The Pig-Headed Peasants* (opera)
    Overture, My Home, Opus 62
    String Quartet, Opus 61
    10 Legends for Piano, Four Hands, Opus 59
Elgar, Edward, *3 Little Pieces for Orchestra, Opus 10*
Fauré, Gabriel, *Ballade, Opus 19, for Piano and Orchestra*
Flotow, Friedrich von, *Sakuntala* (unfinished opera)
Gilbert and Sullivan, *Patience* (operetta)
Glazunov, Alexander, *Symphony No. 1, Opus 5*
Gounod, Charles, *Le tribut de Zamore* (opera)
    Mors et vita (oratorio)
Grieg, Edvard, *Norwegian Dances, Opus 35, for Piano Duet*
Lecocq, Charles, *Le jour et la nuit* (operetta)
Liszt, Franz, *Mephisto Waltz No. 2*
Massenet, Jules, *Scènes alsaciennes*
    Hérodiade (opera)
Mussorgsky, Modest, *The Fair at Sorochinsk* (unfinished opera)
Paine, John Knowles, *Oedipus Tyrannus, Opus 35* (incidental music)
Rimsky-Korsakov, Nicholai, *The Snow Maiden* (opera)
Saint-Saëns, Camille, *Concerto No. 3 for Violin and Orchestra*
    A Night in Lisbon, Opus 63
    Jota Aragonesa
    Septet, Opus 65 (trumpet, piano and strings)
Sgambati, Giovanni, *Symphony in D Major, Opus 16*
Smetana, Bedrich, *Libuse* (opera)
Stanford, Charles V., *The Veiled Prophet* (opera)
Strauss, Johann, Jr., *Der Lustige Krieg* (operetta)
Strauss, Richard, *Symphony in D Minor*
    Concert Overture in C Minor, Opus 4
Suppé, Franz von, *Der Gascogner* (operetta)
Verdi, Giuseppe, *Simon Boccanegra* (opera)
Widor, Charles, *Organ Symphony No. 6, Opus 42*

1882

World Events:
In the U.S., Labor Day observance begins with the New York Central Labor Union; the Chinese Exclusion Act is passed by Congress; the Knights of Columbus is chartered in Connecticut; Dow Jones and Co. is founded; the famous Hatfield and McCoy feud begins and continues until 1896; future president Franklin Delano Roosevelt is born. Internationally, the Triple Alliance is formed between Germany, Italy and the Austro-Hungarian Empire; Great Britain occupies Egypt and proclaims it a protectorate; the world's first hydroelectric plant is built in Appleton, Wisconsin, in the U.S; British evolutionist Charles Darwin dies.

Cultural Highlights:
James Barrie graduates from Edinburgh University; Thomas Eakins becomes director of the Pennsylvania Academy of Arts. Births in the literary field include American novelist Susan Glaspell, Norwegian novelist Sigrid Undset, Irish novelist and poet James Stephens, novelist James Joyce, British poet Alan A. Milne and author Virginia Woolf; deaths include American poets Ralph Waldo Emerson and Henry Wadsworth Longfellow, author Richard Dana, Jr., British novelists William Ainsworth and Anthony Trollope, poet James Thomson, German novelist Berthold Auerbach, Hungarian poet János Arany and Czech poet Karl Egon von Ebert. Births in the art world include American artists George Bellows and Edward Hopper, Polish sculptor Elie Nadelman, Italian artist Umberto Boccioni, French artist Georges Braque and sculptor Gaston Lachaise and British artist and novelist Wyndham Lewis; deaths include British poet and artist Dante Rosetti, artist Thomas Barker and Italian sculptor Giovanni Dupré. Other highlights include:

Art: Thomas Anschutz, *Steelworker's Noontime*; Mary Cassatt, *Reading "Le Figaro"*; Paul Cèzanne, *Fruit Bowl, Glass and Apple*; Benjamin Constant, *The Day after Victory*; Edgar Degas, *Waiting*; James Ensor, *Woman Eating Oysters*; Édouard Manet, *Bar at the Follies Bergere*; John S. Sargent, *El Jaleo*; Georges Seurat, *Farm Women at Work*

Literature: Charles Aïdé, *Songs without Music*; Mary Ames, *Poems of Life and Nature*; Robert Buchanan, *Ballads of Life, Love and Humor*; William Howells, *A Modern Instance*; Henrik Ibsen, *An Enemy of the People*; Robert L. Stevenson, *New Arabian Nights*; Frank Stockton, *The Lady or the Tiger?*; Walt Whitman, *Specimen Days*

MUSICAL EVENTS

A. Births:

Feb 2	Geoffrey O'Hara (Am-cm)		Jul 8	Percy Grainger (Aust-pn)
Feb 28	Geraldine Farrar (Am-sop)		Jul 14	Abraham Idelsohn (Ger-mus)
Mar 5	Pauline Donalda (Can-sop)		Aug 8	Olga Samaroff (Am-pn)
Mar 18	Gian F. Malipiero (It-cm)		Sep 6	John Powell (Am-cm)
Mar 26	Jeanne Gerville-Réache (Fr-alto)		Sep 11	Paul Bekker (Ger-mus)
Apr 16	Seth Bingham (Am-cm)		Sep 14	Claire Croiza (Fr-sop)
Apr 16	Luca Botta (It-ten)		Sep 27	Elly Ney (Ger-pn)
Apr 17	Arthur Schnabel (Aus-pn)		Oct 6	Karol Szymanowski (Pol-cm)
Apr 18	Leopold Stokowski (Am-cd)		Nov 2	Maurice d'Oisly (Br-ten)
Apr 23	Albert Coates (Br-cd)		Nov 18	Amelita Galli-Curci (It-sop)
May 2	Vladimir Cernikof (Fr-pn)		Dec 8	Manuel Ponce (Mex-cd)
May 25	Alfons Schützendorf (Hol-bar)		Dec 9	Joaquin Turina (Sp-cm)
Jun 17	Igor Stravinsky (Rus-cm)		Dec 16	Zoltán Kodály (Hun-cm)

B. Deaths:

Jan 21	Anton Emil Titl (Aus-cm-cd)		Feb 22	Catherine Stephens (Br-sop)
Feb 5	Hippolyte Seligmann (Fr-cel)		Feb 27	Alfred Jaëll (Aus-pn)
Feb 11	Gustav Schmidt (Ger-cm-cd)		Mar 1	Theodor Kullak (Pol-pn)

Mar 26 Italo Gardoni (It-ten)   Oct 29 Gustav Nottebohm (Ger-mus)
Jun 21 Joachim Raff (Ger-cm)   Nov 16 Karl Schelle (Ger-cri)
Sep 20 Maschinka Schneider (Ger-sop)   Nov 17 Carl Engel (Ger-mus)
Oct 3 Adelaide Phillipps (Br-alto)   Dec 12 Hermine Rudersdorff (Rus-sop)

C. Debuts:

U.S. -- Robert Philipp (tour), Sofia Scalchi (N.Y.)

Other - Agnes Adler (Copenhagen), Mary F. Allitsen (London), Francisco d'Andrade (San Remo), Alice Barbi (Milan), Lola Beeth (Berlin), Rose Lucille Caron (Brussels), Guerrina Fabbri (Viadana), Nicholai Figner (Naples), Franz Kniesel (Vienna), Selma Kronold (Leipzig), Victor Küzdö (Budapest), Charles Manners (London), Marie Renard (Graz), Francesco Signorini (Florence), Milka Ternina (Zagreb), Eva Tetrazzini (Florenc), Marie Wittich (Magdeburg)

D. New Positions:
Conductors: Richard Kleinmichel (Leipzig Municipal Theater), Gustav Mahler (Olmütz), Arthur Nikisch (Leipzig Opera)

Educational: Anton Arensky (harmony, Moscow Conservatory), Antonio Bazzini (director, Milan Conservatory), Antonin Bennewitz (director, Prague Conservatory), George W. Chadwick (harmony and composition, New England Conservatory), Michele Esposito (piano, Irish Academy, Dublin), George Grove (director, Royal College of Music), Jenö Hubay (violin, Brussels Conservatory), Mikhail Ippolitov-Ivanov (director, Tiflis Music School), Carlo Pedrotti (director, Liceo Musicale, Pesaro), Waldo S. Pratt (hymnology, Hartford Seminary), Martin Wegelius (director, Helsinki College of Music)

Others: John Fuller Maitland (critic, *Pall Mall Gazette*), Angelo Neumann (manager, Bremen Opera)

E. Prizes and Honors:
Prizes: Gabriel Pierné (Prix de Rome), Marie Soldat (Mendelssohn)

Honors: Peter Benoit (Belgian Royal Academy), Thomas Hovenden (National Academy), Karl Reinthaler (Berlin Academy)

F. Biographical Highlights:
Anton Arensky graduates from St. Petersburg Conservatory with a gold medal; Hans von Bülow marries the actress Marie Schanzer; Annie Louise Cary retires from the stage; Claude Debussy makes a second Russian visit; Paul Dukas enters Paris Conservatory; Engelbert Humperdinck moves to Paris; Mikhail Ippolitov-Ivanov graduates from St. Petersburg Conservatory; Fritz Kreisler, age 7, is admitted to the Vienna Conservatory; Edward MacDowell, at the invitation of Liszt, plays his *First Piano Concerto* at a Zurich music convention; Mathilde Mallinger retires from the stage; Pietro Mascagni enters Milan Conservatory; Lillian Nordica retires from the stage; Sergei Rachmaninoff, at his parent's separation, follows his mother to St. Petersburg and enters the Conservatory; Maurice Ravel begins study with Ghys; Erik Satie is dismissed from the conservatory for failing to reach required standard; Richard Strauss enters Munich University.

G. Institutional Openings:
Performing Groups: Berlin PO; Bethlehem Choral Union (Pennsylvania); Bohnscher Gesangverein (Breslau); Bradford St. Cecilia Society; Handel Society of London; Helsinki New Philharmonic Society; Siegfried Ochs Choral Union (Berlin); Oratorio Society of Baltimore; Rosé String Quartet (Vienna); St. Paul Schubert Club; Strolling Players Amateur Orchestral Society

Educational: Academia Nacional de Música (Bogota); Akademie für Dramatische Gesang (Berlin); Bengal Conservatory of Music (India); Brno Organ School; Helsinki College of Music (Sibelius Academy); Liceo Musicale (Pesaro); Prang Educational Co. (Boston); Seville Conservatory of Music

Other: Arena Peloro (Messina); Brno German Theater; *Grimaces*; Incorporated Society of Musicians (Manchester, England); Johannes Klais Organ Co. (Bonn); Ladies' Morning Musical Club (Montreal); Mason and Hamlin Piano Co. (Boston); *Notas Musicales y Literarias* (Barcelona); *Salterio Sacro-hispano* (Barcelona); Schwerin Landestheater; Teatro Nacional (Buenos Aires)

H. Musical Literature:
Albrecht, Eugen, *Orchestral Music in Russia*
Armingaud, Jules, *Consonances et dissonances*
Brenet, Michel, *Histoire de la Symphonie à Orchestre*
David/Lussy, *Histoire de la notation musicale*
Goetschius, Percy, *The Material Used in Musical Composition*
Krantz, Eugen, *Lehrgang im Klavierunterricht*
Langhans, Friedrich, *Die Geschichte der musik des 17., 18., und 19. Jahrhunderts I*
Lavignac, Albert, *Cours complet théorique de dictée musicale*
Riemann, Hugo, *Musiklexikon*
Rockstro, William, *Rules of Counterpoint*

I. Musical Compositions:
Brahms, Johannes, *Piano Trio, Opus 87*
    String Quintet No. 1, Opus 88
    Gesang der Parzen, Opus 89
Chadwick, George W., *Symphony No. 1*
Chausson, Ernest, *Vivianne, Opus 5* (symphonic poem)
    Les caprices de Marianne, Opus 4 (opera)
Debussy, Claude, *Printemps* (cantata)
    Le roi s'amuse
Dvorák, Antonin, *In Nature's Realm, Opus 63* (symphonic poem)
    Dimitri, Opus 64 (opera)
Fauré, Gabriel, *3 Songs, Opus 23*
    Romance, Opus 28, for Violin and Orchestra
Franck, César, *Le Chasseur Maudit* (symphonic poem)
Gilbert and Sullivan, *Iolanthe* (operetta)
Guiraud, Ernest, *Galante aventure* (opera)
    Overture Artevalde
d'Indy, Vincent, *La Mort de Wallenstein* (symphonic poem)
Lalo, Edouard, *Namouna* (ballet)
Paine, John Knowles, *Island Fantasy* (symphonic poem)
    The Realm of Fancy, Opus 36 (cantata)
Parry, Charles H., *Symphony No. 1*
Pugno, Raoul, *Ninetta* (opera)
Smetana, Bedrich, *The Devil's Wall* (opera)
Stanford, Charles V., *Symphony No. 2, "Elegiac"*
    Serenade for Orchestra, Opus 18
Strauss, Johann, Jr., *Voices of Spring Waltz*
Tchaikovsky, Peter I., *Russian Vesper Service, Opus 52*
    Piano Trio, Opus 50
Thomas, Ambroise, *Francesco de Rimini* (opera)
Wagner, Richard, *Parsifal* (opera)
Ward, S.A., *Materna* (tune for "America the Beautiful")

1883

World Events:
In the U.S., the Brooklyn Bridge opens in New York in May; the Pendleton Act establishes the second Civil Service Commission; William "Buffalo Bill" Cody opens his Wild West Show to eastern audiences; Vaudeville begins at the Gaiety Theater in Boston. Internationally, the South Pacific volcano, Krakatoa, erupts with great loss of life and causing world-wide weather problems; the French take over control of Tunis in North Africa; the famous Orient Express train makes its first run; Rayon is discovered as a synthetic fabric; German communist writer Karl Marx dies.

Cultural Highlights:
The Minneapolis Institute of Arts opens in Minnesota. Births in the literary field include American novelist Martin Flavin, poet William C. Williams, Russian novelist Alexei Tolstoy, Canadian poet Edwin Pratt, Spanish philosopher José Ortega, Austrian novelist Franz Kafka, British author Lord Berners, Swedish author Hjalmer Bergman and Norwegian poet Olaf Bull; deaths include British novelist Anna Eliza Bray, poet Edward Fitzgerald, French novelist Jules Sandeau, poet Pierre Laprade and Russian novelist Ivan Turgenev. Births in the art world include American sculptor Jo Davidson, artist Charles Demuth, Mexican artist José Orozco, British artist James McBey, German artist Erich Heckel and French artist Maurice Utrillo; deaths include American sculptor Clark Mills, artist Albert Bellows, French artists Paul Doré and Edouard Manet, German artist Oscar Begas and Irish sculptor Martin Milmore. Other highlights include:

Art: Arnold Böcklin, *Odysseus and Calypso*; William Chase, *In the Studio*; Thomas Eakins, *The Swimming Hole*; Winslow Homer, *Inside the Bar, Tynemouth*; George Inness, *Sunset in the Woods*; Édouard Manet, *White Lilacs and Roses*; William Orchardson, *Voltaire*; Pierre Renoir, *By the Seashore*

Literature: Joel C. Harris, *Nights with Uncle Remus*; Victor Hugo, *Legend of the Ages*; Friedrich Nietzsche, *Also Sprach Zarathustra*; James Whitcomb Riley, *The Old Swimming Hole and...More Poems*; Robert Louis Stevenson, *Treasure Island*; Mark Twain, *Life on the Mississippi*; Émile Zola, *Au Bonheur des Dames*

MUSICAL EVENTS

A. Births:

Jan 19	Hermann Abendroth (Ger-cd)	Jul 25	Alfredo Casella (It-cm)
Feb 7	Eubie Blake (Am-pop)	Sep 5	Otto E. Deutsch (Aus-mus)
Mar 19	Josef Hauer (Aus-cm-the)	Oct 1	Julius Kapp (Ger-mus)
Mar 27	Friedrich Gennrich (Ger-mus)	Oct 11	Archibald Davison (Am-cd)
Apr 1	Alexander Alexandrov (Rus-cm)	Oct 11	Fritz Stiedry (Aus-cd)
May 4	Nikolai Malko (Rus-cd)	Nov 6	Hubert Bath (Br-cm-cd)
May 28	Václav Talich (Cz-cd)	Nov 8	Arnold Bax (Br-cm)
May 28	Max Unger (Ger-mus)	Nov 11	Ernest Ansermet (Swi-cd)
May 28	Riccardo Zandonai (It-cm)	Nov 11	Elena Gerhardt (Ger-mez)
May 31	Frances Alda (N.Z.-sop)	Nov 28	Paul H. Allen (Am-cm)
Jun 20	Giannotto Bastianelli (It-pn)	Dec 3	Anton Webern (Aus-cm)
Jul 21	Carl Engel (Ger-mus)		Gustave Schützendorf (Ger-bar)

B. Deaths:

Jan 24	Friedrich von Flotow (Ger-cm)	Jun 2	H. Reicher-Kindermann
Jan 31	Wilhelm von Lenz (Rus-mus)		(Ger-sop)
Feb 13	Richard Wagner (Ger-cm)	Jul 25	Antonio H. Oury (Br-vn)
Feb 17	Napoléon Coste (Fr-gui)	Jul 27	Albert Doppler (Aus-fl-cm)
Apr 22	Pierre Louquet (Fr-mus)	Oct 15	Francesco Schira (It-cm-cd)

Oct 29 J. Vesque von Püttlingen
        (Aus-cm)
Oct 29 Carl G. Röder (Ger-pub)
Oct 30 Robert Volkman (Ger-cm)

Dec 11 Giovanni Mario (It-ten)
Dec 23 Jane Schirreff (Br-sop)
        Marie Litta (Am-sop)

C. Debuts:

Met --- Cleofonte (cd) and Italo (ten) Campanini, Joseph A. Capoul (ten), Baldassare Corsini (bs), Emmy Fursch-Madi (sop), Amadeo Grazzi (ten), Luigi Guadagnini (bar), Giuseppe Kaschmann (bar), Emily (mez) and Louise (mez) Lablache, Giovanni Mirabella (bs), Khristina Nilsson (sop), Franco Novara (bs), Sofia Scalchi (mez), Marcella Sembrich (sop), Roberto Stagno (ten), Zélia Trebelli (mez), Alwina Valleria (sop)

U.S. -- Antoine de Kontski (tour), Ovide Musin (tour)

Other - Vittorio Arimondi (Varese), Heinrich Bötel (Hamburg), Cleofonte Campanini (Parma), Léon Escalaïs (Paris), Félia Litvinne (Paris), Eugenia Mantelli (Treviso), Jean Noté (Ghent), Maurice Renaud (Brussels), Romualdo Sapio (Milan), Hermine Spies (Germany), Ernest Van Dyck (Paris), Hans Wessely (Vienna)

D. New Positions:

Conductors: Max Bruch (Breslau SO), Adolf Cech (Prague Opera), Charles Hallé (Liverpool PO), Wilhelm Kienzl (German Opera, Amsterdam), Anton Seidl (Bremen Opera), Johan Svendsen (Royal Theater, Copenhagen), Franz Wüllner (Berlin PO)

Educational: Adolf Brodsky (violin, Leipzig Conservatory), Charles Dennée (piano, New England Conservatory), Jenny Lind (voice, Royal Academy, London), Peter C. Lutkin (organ and piano, Northwestern University), Sophie Menter (piano, St. Petersburg Conservatory), Charles Parry (composition, Royal College)

Others: Henry Abbey (manager, Met), Ludwig Bussler (music critic, Berlin *National-Zeitung*), Max Kalbeck (critic, *Neue Freie Presse*)

E. Prizes and Honors:

Prizes: Paul Vidal (Prix de Rome)

Honors: Xavier van Elewyck (Belgian Royal Academy), Edvard Grieg (Leyden Musical Academy), George Grove, George Macfarren and Arthur Sullivan (knighted), Henry Oliver and Charles Parry (honorary doctorates, Cambridge)

F. Biographical Highlights:

Isaac Albéniz settles in Barcelona; Mattia Battistini makes his Covent Garden debut; Anna Bishop gives her farewell concert in New York; Max Bruch visits the U.S.; Walter Damrosch takes the New York SO on a tour of the western U.S.; Claude Debussy takes the second Prix de Rome; Mary Garden is brought to the U.S. by her family; Enrique Granados wins the first prize in piano from Barcelona Conservatory; Stephen Heller begins to go blind; Francesco Navarini and Fernando Valero make their La Scala debuts; Carl Nielsen enters the Royal Conservatory in Copenhagen; Pol Plançon makes his Paris Opera debut; Giacomo Puccini finishes his studies at the Milan Conservatory; Alwina Valleria becomes the first native American to appear at the Met; Felix Weingartner becomes an assistant to Liszt in Weimar; Arthur Whiting goes to Germany to study at the Munich Conservatory; Hugo Wolf meets Liszt.

G. Institutional Openings:

Performing Groups: Amsterdam Concertgebouw Society; Apollo Club of Portland, Oregon; Birmingham Choral and Orchestra Association; Clube Haydn (São Paulo); Darmstadt Instrumentalverein; Metropolitan Opera Association; Moscow Philharmonic Society; Sociedade de Concertos Clássicos (Rio de Janeiro); Stock Exchange Orchestral and Choral Society (London)

Educational: Adelaide College of Music (Australia); Christiania Organ School (Conservatory in 1894); Los Angeles Conservatory of Music; University of Southern California School of the Performing Arts

Other: Allgemeiner Richard-Wagner-Verband (Bayreuth); Buffalo Music Hall; Couesnon et Cie. (Paris, by merger); Crane Memorial Library (Boston); Dallas Opera House; Everett Piano Co. (Boston); Fort Worth Opera House; Fred Gretsch Mfg. Co. (Brooklyn); Emmons Howard, Organ Builder (Westfield); *Keynote*; New National Opera House (Prague); Theodore Presser, Music Publisher; Vienna Schubertbund

H. Musical Literature:
Bäumker, Wilhelm, *Das katholische deutsche Kirchenlied in seinen Singweisen*
Engel, Carl, *Early History of the Violin Family*
Gadsby, Henry, *Harmony*
Gumprecht, Otto, *Unsere Klassischen Meister I*
Jadassohn, Salomon, *Harmonielehre*
Köhler, Louis, *Allgemeine Musiklehre*
Ritter, Frédéric, *Music in America*
Stumpf, Carl, *Tonpsychologie I*
Tottmann, Albert, *Abriss der Musikgeschichte*

I. Musical Compositions:
Arensky, Anton, *Symphony No. 1*
Brahms, Johannes, *Symphony No. 3, Opus 90*
Bruckner, Anton, *Symphony No. 7 in E Major*
Chabrier, Emmanuel, *España Rhapsody*
Chadwick, George W., *Overture, Thalia*
Cui, Cesar, *Suite Concertante, Opus 25*
Debussy, Claude, *La belle au bois dormant*
Delibes, Leo, *Lakmé* (opera)
Dukas, Paul, *King Lear Overture*
Dvořák, Antonin, *Hussite Overture, Opus 67*
    Scherzo Capriccioso, Opus 66
Fauré, Gabriel, *3 Nocturnes, Opus 33, for Piano*
    3 Impromptus, Opus 25, 31 and 34
Fibich, Zdenek, *Symphony No. 1*
    The Water Sprite (symphonic poem)
Glazunov, Alexander, *Orchestra Serenade No. 1, Opus 7*
Grieg, Edvard, *Cello Sonata, Opus 36*
    Lyric Pieces, Book II, Opus 37
d'Indy, Vincent, *Le chant de la cloche, Opus 18* (dramatic legend)
Lalo, Edouard, *Concerto Russe for Violin and Orchestra*
Liszt, Franz, *From the Cradle to the Grave* (symphonic poem)
Mahler, Gustav, *Songs of a Wayfarer* (song cycle)
Parry, Charles, *Symphony No. 2, "Cambridge"*
Puccini, Giacomo, *String Quartet in D Major*
    Capriccio Sinfonico
Rimsky-Korsakov, Nicolai, *Concerto for Piano and Orchestra*
Rubinstein, Anton, *Sulamith* (opera)
Saint-Saëns, Camille, *Henry VIII* (opera)
Smetana, Bedrich, *Prague Carnival*
Strauss, Johann, Jr., *A Night in Venice* (operetta)
Strauss, Richard, *Concerto, Opus 8, for Violin and Orchestra*
Tchaikovsky, Peter I., *Orchestra Suite No. 2, Opus 53*
    Mazeppa (opera)

1884

World Events:
In the U.S., Grover Cleveland is elected for the first time as President No. 22; the American Historical Association is founded; the National Cash Register Co. is founded; the first practical fountain pen is introduced by L.E. Waterman; the first newspaper syndicate for news articles appears; future president Harry S. Truman is born. Internationally, the Berlin West German Conference meets while Germany begins annexing several South-West African states; Sir Hiram Maxim invents the Machine Gun, a weapon so terrible, it will wipe out warfare; the first modern bicycle appears in England; Royce, Ltd. (Rolls-Royce Co.), is founded.

Cultural Highlights:
Neo-Impressionism is introduced via the Salon des Indépendents in Paris; the Society of British Authors is formed; Alfred Lord Tennyson is given a baronet; Births in the art world include German artist Max Beckmann and Italian artist Amedeo Modigliani; deaths include American artist George Fuller and French artist Jules Bastien-Lepage. Births in the literary field include New Zealand-born novelist Hugh Walpole, Irish dramatist Sean O'Casey, Czech novelist Max Brod, Swiss novelist Lion Feuchtwanger, American author Damon Runyan and poet Sara Teasdale; deaths include British poet Charles Calverley and novelist Charles Reade, German poet Emmanuel Geibel and dramatist Heinrich Laube, Italian poet Giovanni Prati and Spanish dramatist Antonio Gutiérrez. Other highlights include:

Art: Paul Cézanne, *Blue Vase*; Pierre de Chavannes, *Humanistic and Christian Inspiration*; Winslow Homer, *The Life Line*; George Inness, *Mount Washington*; Pierre Renoir, *Girl with the Straw Hat*; Auguste Rodin, *The Burghers of Calais*; Albert Ryder, *Toilers of the Sea*; Georges Seurat, *Une Baignade, Asières*; Hamo Thornycroft, *Mower*

Literature: Gabriele d'Annunzio, *L'Intermezzo di Rime*; Alphonse Daudet, *Sapho*; Henrik Ibsen, *The Wild Duck*; Helen Jackson, *Ramona*; Sarah Orne Jewett, *A Country Doctor*; Lord Tennyson, *Becket*; Mark Twain, *The Adventures of Huckleberry Finn*; Giovanni Verga, *Cavalleria Rusticana*; Paul Verlaine, *Les Poétes Maudits*

MUSICAL EVENTS

A. Births:

Jan 1	John J. Williams (Am-pn)	May 13	Ernst Flade (Ger-mus)
Jan 19	Albert Wolff (Fr-cd-cm)	Jun 2	Lillian Granfelt (Fin-sop)
Feb 4	Marie Sundelius (Swe-sop)	Jun 14	John McCormack (Ir-ten)
Feb 17	Hans Lange (Ger-vn-cd)	Jun 29	Boris Asaf'yev (Rus-mus)
Mar 10	Maria Barrientos (Sp-sop)	Aug 2	Nanny Larsen-Todsen (Swe-sop)
Mar 11	Florence Austin (Am-vn)	Aug 3	Louis Gruenberg (Rus-cm)
Mar 18	Willem van Hoogstraten	Sep 1	Gertrude Kappel (Ger-sop)
	(Hol-cd)	Sep 17	Charles T. Griffes (Am-cm)
Mar 26	Wilhelm Backhaus (Ger-pn)	Oct 25	Florence Easton (Am-sop)
Apr 8	Marie Hall (Br-vn)	Nov 19	Norman Allin (Br-bs)
Apr 26	Eidé Norena (Nor-sop)	Nov 30	Ture Rangström (Swe-cm)
May 10	Lydia Lipkowska (Rus-sop)		Rafael Diaz (Am-ten)
May 11	Alma Gluck (Rom-sop)		

B. Deaths:

Jan 21	Auguste Franchomme (Fr-cel)	May 17	Louis Brassin (Bel-pn)
Mar 18	Anna Bishop (Br-sop)	Jun 8	Henry Clay Work (Am-cm)
Apr 29	Michael Costa (It-cm-cd)	Jul 5	Victor Massé (Fr-cm)
May 12	Bedrich Smetana (Boh-cm)	Jul 20	Karl Böhmer (Hol-vn-cm)

Sep 15   Joseph Rubinstein (Rus-pn)   Oct 30   Pasquale Brignoli (It-ten)
Oct 10   Jean Becker (Ger-vn)   Nov 5   Erminia Frezzolini (It-sop)

C. Debuts:

Met --- Carl Baumann (ten), Hermine Bely (sop), Marianne Brandt (alto), Leopold Damrosch (cd), Marie Hanfstängel (sop), Otto Kemlitz (ten), Joseph Kögel (bs), Isadora Martinez (mez), Joseph Miller (bs), Carrie Morse (mez), Martin Pache (bar), Anton Schott (ten), Joseph Staudigl, Jr. (bar)

U.S. -- Leopold Godowsky (Boston), Victor Küzdö (N.Y.), Zélie de Lussan (Boston), Michael Maybrick (tour), Emma Nevada (N.Y.), Emil Scaria (tour), Hermann Winkelmann (N.Y.)

Other - Teresa Arkel (Lemberg), Fritz Friedrichs (Nuremberg), Marie Goetze (Berlin), Pelagie Greef-Andriessen (Leipzig), Elisabeth Leisinger (Berlin), Henri Marteau (age 10, Vienna), Karl Perron (Leipzig), Richard Strauss (Meiningen), Felix Weingartner (Weimar)

D. New Positions:

Conductors: Giuseppe Galignani (maestro di cappella, Milan Cathedral), Wilhelm Gericke (Boston SO), Andreas Hallén (Stockholm PO), Franz Wüllner (Gurzenich Concerts, Cologne)

Educational: John C. Fillmore (director, Milwaukee School of Music), Hendrik Waelput (director, Ghent Conservatory), Franz Wüllner (director, Cologne Conservatory)

Others: Pierre Gailhard (co-manager with M. Ritt, Paris Opera), Frederick Gleason (critic, Chicago *Tribune*), John Fuller Maitland (critic, London *Guardian*), Hugo Wolf (critic, Vienna *Salonblatt*)

E. Prizes and Honors:

Prizes: Claude Debussy (Prix de Rome), Max Puchat (Mendelssohn)

Honors: Léo Delibes (French Institute), Charles H. Parry (honorary doctorate, Oxford)

F. Biographical Highlights:

Tor Aulin studies music in Berlin; Emma Calvé makes her Paris Opera debut; Frederick Delius leaves for his Florida orange plantation but meets Thomas Ward, Jacksonville organist; Antonin Dvorák visits England on a conducting trip; Alexander Glazunov, on European tour, meets Liszt; Enrique Granados studies composition at Madrid Conservatory; Vassily Kalinnikov enters Moscow Conservatory; Edward MacDowell returns to the U.S., marries Marian Nevins and goes again to Frankfurt; Gustav Mahler moves to Cassel; Pietro Mascagni is dismissed from Milan Conservatory for failure to apply himself to his studies; Ignace Jan Paderewski moves to Vienna and studies with Leschetizky; Theodor Reichmann, Karl Schiedemantel and Clementine Schuch-Proska make their Covent Garden debuts; Bedrich Smetana is committed to an insane asylum just before his death; Richard Strauss leaves Munich University to concentrate on music.

G. Institutional Openings:

Performing Groups: Beethoven String Quartet (N.Y.); Berliner Liedertafel; Boston Orchestral Club; Concerts Symphonique du Grand Theater (Lyons); Kunkel's Popular Concerts (St. Louis); Orquestra da Real Academia de Amadores de Música (Lisbon); Oxford Musical Union; Société des Concerts Populaires (Orleans); Treble Clef Club (Philadelphia)

Educational: American College of Musicians; Amsterdam Conservatorium; Charleston Conservatory of Music (South Carolina); Grand Ducal Conservatory (Badisches Konservatorium für Musik); Klindworth Klavierschule (Berlin); Krüss-Färber Konservatorium (Hamburg); Milwaukee School of Music

Other: Amsterdam Wagner-Vereniging; Brünn-Brno Opera House; Cercle des Vingts (Libre Esthétique, Brussels); Henry Distin, Instrument Maker (Philadelphia); John Friedrich and Brother, Violin Makers (N.Y.); John Spencer Murdoch, Piano Maker (London); Provisional Theater (National Theater, Brno); Royal Hungarian Opera House (Budapest); *Vierteljahrsschrift für Musikwissenschaft*

H. Musical Literature:
Banister, Henry, *Some Musical Ethics and Analogies*
Davenport, Francis, *Elements of Music*
Ehrlich, Heinrich, *Lebenskunst und Kunstleben*
Hiles, Henry, *Part-Writing or Modern Counterpoint*
Hiller, Ferdinand, *Erinnerungsblätter*
Jadassohn, Salomon, *Kontrapunkt*
Marmontel, Antoine, *Éléments d'aesthétique musicale*
Niecks, Friedrich, *Concise Dictionary of Musical Terms*
Riemann, Hugo, *Opernhandbuch*
Rimsky-Korsakov, Nicolai, *Textbook on Harmony*

I. Musical Compositions:
Brahms, Johannes, *6 Vocal Quartets, Opus 92*
    22 Songs, Opus 94, 95, 96 and 97
Chadwick, George W., *Overture, The Miller's Daughter*
Debussy, Claude, *L'enfant prodigue* (cantata)
    Claire de Lune (song)
Dubois, Théodore, *Aben-Hamlet* (opera)
Dukas, Paul, *Gotz von Berlichingen Overture*
Dvořák, Antonin, *From the Bohemian Forest, Opus 68* (symphonic poem)
    The Spectre's Bride, Opus 69 (opera)
Fauré, Gabriel, *Nocturne Nos. 4 and 5, Opus 36 and 37* (piano)
    Symphony in D Minor, Opus 40
Fibich, Zdenek, *The Bride of Messina, Opus 18* (opera)
Foerster, Josef B., *In the Mountains*
Franck, César, *Les Djinns* (symphonic poem)
    Prelude, Chorale and Fugue (piano)
Gade, Niels, *Holbergiana, Opus 61*
Gilbert and Sullivan, *Princess Ida* (operetta)
Glazunov, Alexander, *Overture No. 1 on Greek Themes, Opus 3*
    Serenade No. 2, Opus 11, for Small Orchestra
Godard, Benjamin, *Symphonie Orientale, Opus 84*
Grieg, Edvard, *Holberg Suite, Opus 40* (piano--also orchestral version)
Lalo, Édouard, *Scherzo for Orchestra*
Lecocq, Charles, *L'oiseau bleu*
MacDowell, Edward, *Forest Idyls, Opus 19* (piano)
Massenet, Jules, *Manon* (opera)
Puccini, Giacomo, *Le Villi* (opera)
Saint-Saëns, Camille, *Rhapsodie d'Aubergne, Opus 73, for Piano and Orchestra*
    Allegro Appassionata, Opus 70, for Piano and Orchestra
Stanford, Charles V., *Savonarola* (opera)
    The Canterbury Pilgrims (opera)
Strauss, Richard, *Concerto No. 1, Opus 11, for Horn and Orchestra*
    Symphony in F Minor, Opus 12
Tchaikovsky, Peter I., *Suite No. 3 in G Major*
    Concert Fantasy, Opus 56, for Piano and Orchestra
    6 songs, Opus 57
Weingartner, Felix, *Sakuntala* (opera)

1885

World Events:
In the U.S., the Washington Monument is dedicated in the nation's capitol; the American Telephone and Telegraph Co. is incorporated; the Sault-Ste. Marie Locks are opened between the Great Lakes; Stanford University is founded in California; the first commercial streetcar begins operation in Baltimore; General and former President Ulysses S. Grant dies. Internationally, William Gladstone is ousted as British Prime Minister by the Marquess of Salisbury; Louis Pasteur gives the first successful rabies innoculation; Belgium takes over control of the Congo region of Africa; Alfonso XII of Spain is succeeded by Maria Christina.

Cultural Highlights:
The Detroit Institute of Art opens its doors; the New English Art Club meets in London; the Rijksmuseum, the Royal Art Museum of Amsterdam, opens its doors; John Everett Millais is given a baronet. Births in the art world include American sculptor Paul Manship, French artist Robert Delaunay and Turkish-born artist Sonia Delaunay; deaths include American artist William Page, German artists Wilhelm Camphausen and Carl Spitzweg and sculptor Karl Cauer. Births in the literary field include Canadian novelists Thomas Costain and Mazo de la Roche, American authors Will Durant, Ring Lardner, Sinclair Lewis, Carl Van Doren and poets DuBose Heyward and Ezra Pound, French authors Sacha Guitry, André Mauriac and Jules Romains and British novelist David Lawrence; deaths include French novelist Victor Hugo, German author Alfred Meissner, Swedish poet Per Atterbom and American novelist Helen Jackson. Other highlights include:

Art: Ralph Blakelock, *Brook by Moonlight*; André Breton, *Song of the Lark*; Paul Cézanne, *Mont St. Victoire*; Benjamin Constant, *Vengeance of the Cherif*; Edgar Degas, *Jockeys*; William Harnett, *After the Hunt*; Winslow Homer, *Fog Warning*; Alfred Sisley, *Small Meadows in Spring*; Vincent Van Gogh, *The Potato Eaters*.

Literature: *Bible: Revised Version*; George W. Cable, *The Silent South*; Alphonse Daudet, *Tartarin on the Alps*; H. Rider Haggard, *King Solomon's Mines*; William Howells, *The Rise of Silas Lapham*; George Meredith, *Diana of the Crossways*; Walter Pater, *Marius the Epicurean*; Robert Lewis Stevenson, *A Child's Garden of Verse*.

MUSICAL EVENTS

A. Births:

Jan 14	Ludwig Hoffmann (Ger-bs)	Jun 26	Freida Hempel (Ger-sop)
Jan 27	Jerome Kern (Am-pop)	Jun 29	Pedro Allende (Chil-mus-cm)
Feb 9	Alban Berg (Aus-cm)	Jul 12	George Butterworth (Br-cm)
Apr 6	Carlos Salzédo (Fr-hp)	Aug 2	Claire Dux (Pol-sop)
Apr 10	Sigmund Spaeth (Am-cri)	Sep 5	Désiré Defauw (Bel-cd)
Apr 14	Carmen Melis (It-sop)	Sep 20	Eva Gauthier (Can-sop)
Apr 15	Margarethe Arndt-Ober	Oct 21	Egon Wellesz (Aus-cm-mus)
	(Ger-alto)	Oct 22	Giovanni Martinelli (It-ten)
Apr 17	Cecil Burleigh (Am-cm)	Nov 27	Rudolphe Reti (Serb-mus)
Apr 29	Wallingford Riegger (Am-cm)	Dec 22	Deems Taylor (Am-cm-cri)
May 14	Otto Klemperer (Ger-cd)	Dec 22	Edgar Varèse (Fr-cm)
Jun 12	Werner Josten (Ger-cd-cm)		

B. Deaths:

Jan 17	Michael Hermesdorff (Ger-mus)	Feb 18	Charlotte Sainton-Dolby
Jan 22	Félix Clément (Fr-mus-the)		(Br-alto)
Feb 15	Leopold Damrosch (Ger-cd)	Mar 14	Alexander Reichardt (Hun-ten)

Mar 24	James W. Davison (Br-cri)		May 23	Carl Baermann (Ger-cl)
Mar 28	Ludvig Norman (Swe-cd-cm)		May 23	Marie Cabel (Bel-sop)
Mar 31	Franz Abt (Ger-cm)		Jun 16	Eduard Krüger (Ger-the)
Apr 3	Julius Schneider (Ger-org)		Aug 12	Henry K. Oliver (Am-org-hymn)
May 1	Henry B. Richards (Br-pn)		Aug 26	August G. Ritter (Ger-org)
May 5	Lauro Rossi (It-cm)		Sep 12	Carl Hermann Bitter (Ger-mus)
May 11	Ferdinand Hiller (Ger-pn-cm)		Nov 25	Abramo Basevi (It-cri)
May 15	Lodovico Graziani (It-ten)		Dec 20	Karl Hubay (Hun-cm-cd)

C. Debuts:

Met --- Max Alvary (ten), Lola Beeth (sop), Helena Brandl (mez), Walter Damrosch (cd), Emil Fischer (bs), Anna Gutjar (sop), Carl Kaufmann (bar), Ida Klein (sop), Marie Krämer-Wiedl (sop), Lilli Lehmann (sop), Philip Lehmler (bs), John Lund (cd), Amalie Materna (sop), Emil Sänger (sbs), Anton Seidl (cd), Albert Stritt (ten)

U.S. -- Amy Beach (Boston), Alma Fohstrom (tour), August Hyllested (tour), Franz Kneisel (Boston), Félia Litvinne (N.Y.), Lillian Nordica (Boston), Maud Powell, Sophie Traubman, Edmund Vergnet (tour)

Other - Sigrid Arnoldson (Prague), Ramon Blanchart (Barcelona), Ellen Brandt-Forster (Danzig), Irene von Chavanne (Dresden), Fanny Davies (London), Laura Hilgermann (Prague), Paul Knüpfer (Sondershausen), Liza Lehmann (London), Fernando de Lucia (Naples), Juan Luria (Stuttgart), Fanny Moody (London), Ella Russell (London)

D. New Positions:

Conductors: Cosme Damián José de Benito (maestro de capilla, Royal Chapel, Madrid), Walter Damrosch (New York SO), Richard Henneberg (Stockholm Opera), Gustav Mahler (Prague Opera), Anton Seidl (Met)

Educational: Guido Adler (music history, Prague University), Jan Blockx (lecturer, Flemish Music School), Jacques-Joseph Bouhy (director, N.Y. Conservatory), Beniamino Cesi (piano, St. Petersburg Conservatory), Authur de Greef (piano, Brussells Conservatory), Heinrich von Herzogenberg (composition, Berlin Hochschule), Engelbert Humperdinck (theory, Barcelona Conservatory), Vasili Safonov (piano, Moscow Conservatory), Alexander Taneyev (director, Moscow Conservatory)

Others: Herbert Brewer (organ, Bristol Cathedral), Edward Elgar (organ, St. Georges, Worcester), Henry Hiles (editor, *Quarterly Musical Review*)

E. Prizes and Honors:

Prizes: Léon Dubois (Prix de Rome), Vincent d'Indy (City of Paris Prize), Lucien Lambert (Rossini), Xavier Leroux (Prix de Rome)

Honors: Cesar Franck (Legion of Honor), Vladimir de Pachmann (knighted, Denmark)

F. Biographical Highlights:

Claude Debussy visits Rome; Frederick Delius abandons his Florida orange farm and begins music teaching in Jacksonville; Ernst von Dohnányi begins music study with Karl Forstner; Henri Duparc suffers a general breakdown and retires from composition; Georges Enescu, age 4, begins violin study; Anna Essipova becomes pianist at the Russian court; Edvard Grieg builds his villa, Troldhaugen; Lillian Nordica, following her husband's death, re-debuts in Boston; Horatio Parker returns to New York and teaches at the Cathedral School; Sergei Rachmaninoff enters Moscow Conservatory; Josephina de Reszke, retiring from the stage, moves with her new husband to Poland; Jan Sibelius enters Helsinki University Law School but soon switches to music; Richard Strauss becomes assistant to von Bülow at Meiningen; Josef Suk enters Prague Conservatory; Francisco Tárrega settles in Barcelona; Arturo Toscanini graduates with highest grades from Parma Conservatory

G. Institutional Openings:

Performing Groups: Boston Pops Orchestra; Filharmoniska Sällskapet (Stockholm); Glauchau Konzertverein; Heidelberg Bachverein; Nice Opera; Russian Public Symphony Concerts (St. Petersburg)

Educational: Arizona Territorial College (Arizona State University) School of Music; Cleveland School of Music; Combs Conservatory (Philadelphia); Conservatorio Nacional (Havana); Forest Gate College of Music (London); Melbourne Academy of Music (Australia); National Conservatory of Music (N.Y.); Newark College of Music; Northwestern Conservatory of Music (Minneapolis)

Other: Belaiev Publishing House (St. Petersburg); Boston Music Co.; Estey Piano Co. (Vermont); *Die Gesellschaft*; *Kastner's Wiener Musikalische Zeitung*; Listemann Concert Co. (Boston); *The Metronome*; Musicians Mutual Benefit Association (St. Louis); *Revue Félibréanne*; *Russian Musical Review*; Schimmel Piano Factory (Leipzig); Ernst Hubertus Seifert, Organ Builder (Cologne); Henri Selmer et Cie. (Paris); Smetana Theater (Prague); Josef Weinberger, Music Publisher (Vienna); M. Witmark, Music Publisher (N.Y.)

H. Musical Literature:
Ábrányi, Kornél, *History of Music*
Clément, Félix, *Histoire de la musique*
Hausegger, Friedrich von, *Musik als ausdruck*
Hey, Julius, *Deutscher Gesangunterricht*
Marmontel, Antoine, *Histoire du piano et ses origines*
Paine, John Knowles, *Lecture Notes*
Stumph, Carl, *Tonpsychologie I*
Vincent, Heinrich, *Die Zwölfzahl in der Tonwelt*
Volckmar, Wilhelm, *Handbuch der Musik*

I. Musical Compositions:
Borodin, Alexander, *Scherzo for Orchestra*
Brahms, Johannes, *Symphony No. 4, Opus 98*
Busoni, Ferruccio, *Unter den Linden*
Cui, César, *7 Choral Works, Opus 28*
Dvořák, Antonin, *Symphony No. 7, Opus 70* (old No. 2)
    Ballad for Violin and Piano, Opus 15
Elgar, Edward, *Orchestra Suite No. 1, Opus 1a, "The Wand of Youth"*
Fauré, Gabriel, *Barcarolle Nos. 2 and 3* (piano)
Franck, César, *Hulda* (opera)
    Symphonic Variations for Piano and Orchestra
Gade, Niels, *Sonata No. 3, Opus 59, for Violin and Piano*
Gilbert and Sullivan, *The Mikado* (operetta)
Glazunov, Alexander, *Overture No. 2 on Greek Themes, Opus 6*
    Stenka Razin (symphonic poem)
Hubay, Jenö, *Symphony No. 1, Opus 26*
d'Indy, Vincent, *Sauge Fleurie, Opus 21* (symphonic poem)
Liszt, Franz, *Canticle of the Sun*
MacDowell, Edward, *Concerto No. 1, Opus 15, for Piano and Orchestra*
Mackenzie, Alexander, *Concerto for Violin and Orchestra*
Mascagni, Pietro, *Guglielmo Ratcliff* (opera)
Massenet, Jules, *Le Cid* (opera)
Stanford, Charles, *The Euminides* (incidental music)
Strauss, Johann, Jr., *The Gypsy Baron* (operetta)
Strauss, Richard, *Wanderer's Sturmlied, Opus 14*
Tchaikovsky, Peter I., *Manfred Symphony, Opus 58*

1886

World Events:
In the U.S., Samuel Gompers becomes the first President of the reorganized American Federation of Labor; the Haymarket Square Riots occur in Chicago; the Statue of Liberty is officially unveiled; the Presidential Succession Act is passed by Congress; Apache leader Geronimo is captured in the Arizona Territory; former President Chester Arthur dies. Internationally, Portugal claims the territory in Africa found between Angola and Mozambique; Vancouver, British Columbia, is incorporated in Canada; Ludwig II, the "Mad King" of Bavaria, dies; Alfonso XIII becomes king of Spain.

Cultural Highlights:
The New English Art Club is organized in London; the Philadelphia Art Student's League is founded; the magazine, *Le Symboliste*, begins publication; Frederic Leighton receives a baronet. Births in the art field include Austrian artist Oscar Kokoschka, German artist Ernst Kirchner, Mexican artist Diego Rivera, British sculptor Frank Dobson and Russian sculptor Antoine Pevsner; deaths include American architect Henry Richardson, sculptor Henry Brown and artist Asher Durand and French artist Paul Baudry. Births in the literary field include American authors Margaret Barnes and Wilbur Steele, poets John Fletcher and Alfred Joyce Kilmer, Russian poet Nikolai Gumilyov and German poet Gottfried Benn; deaths include American poet Emily Dickinson, German poet Josef von Scheffel, Russian dramatist Alexander Ostrovsky and British poet William Barnes. Other highlights include:

Art: Edward Burne-Jones, *The Depths of the Sea*; William Harnett, *The Old Violin*; Winslow Homer, *Eight Bells*; Charles Platt, *Three Fishermen*; Pierre Renoir, *Mother and Child*; Auguste Rodin, *The Kiss*; Henri Rousseau, *Un Soir de Carnaval*; Georges Seurat, *Sunday Afternoon, Grande Jatte*; Hamo Thornycroft, *A Sower*.

Literature: Frances Burnett, *Little Lord Fauntleroy*; William Howells, *Indian Summer*; Henrik Ibsen, *Rosmersholm*; Henry James, *The Bostonians*; James Lowell, *Democracy and Other Essays*; Arthur Rimbaud, *Les Illuminations*; Robert L. Stevenson, *Dr. Jekyll and Mr. Hyde*; Lev Tolstoy, *The Death of Ivan Ilyich*; Émile Zola, *L'oeuvre*.

MUSICAL EVENTS

A. Births:

Jan 22	John J. Becker (Am-cm)	May 24	Paul Paray (Fr-cd)
Jan 25	Wilhelm Furtwängler (Ger-cd)	May 24	Henry Prunières (Fr-mus)
Jan 27	Olin Downes (Am-cri)	Jun 1	Ernst Kurth (Aus-mus)
Jan 28	Artur Rubinstein (Pol-pn)	Aug 5	Oscar Esplá (Sp-cm)
Feb 12	Gustaf Nordquist (Swe-cm)	Aug 6	Edward Ballantine (Am-cm)
Mar 3	James Friskin (Scot-pn)	Aug 8	Daniel Ruyneman (Hol-cm)
Mar 28	Jaroslav Novotny (Cz-cm)	Aug 8	Pietro A. Yon (It-org-cm)
Mar 29	Gustav Bengtsson (Swe-cm)	Aug 14	Mignon Nevada (Br-sop)
Apr 19	Wilhelm Fischer (Aus-mus)	Aug 27	Eric Coates (Br-cd-cm)
Apr 24	Mabel Garrison (Am-sop)	Sep 1	Othmar Schoeck (Swi-cm-cd)
Apr 30	Frank Merrick (Br-pn-cm)	Oct 6	Edwin Fischer (Swi-pn-cd)
May 3	Marcel Dupré (Fr-org)	Nov 11	Mária Basilides (Hun-alto)
May 7	Armand Machabey (Fr-mus)	Dec 1	George Oldroyd (Br-org)
May 7	Leo Schützendorf (Ger-bs)		

B. Deaths:

Jan 16	Joseph Maas (Br-ten)	Feb 16	Louis Köhler (Ger-pn-cm)
Jan 16	Amilcare Ponchielli (It-cm)	Feb 18	Charlotte Cushman (Am-alto)
Jan 18	Joseph Tichatschek (Boh-ten)	Mar 30	Giovanni G. Rossi (It-cm)
Jan 30	Gustave Chouquet (Fr-mus)	Apr 30	Friedrich H. Truhn (Ger-cm)

May 2	Julian Dobrski (Pol-ten)	Jul 29	Adolf Müller, Sr. (Hun-cm-cd)
May 17	Jenny Bürde-Ney (Aus-sop)	Jul 31	Franz Liszt (Hun-pn-cm-cd)
May 26	Charles d'Albert (Fr-bal)	Aug 13	Adolf von Doss (Ger-cm)
Jul 2	John Templeton (Scot-ten)	Sep 14	Hubert Ries (Ger-vn)
Jul 5	August F. Riccius (Ger-cm-cd)	Nov 17	Louis Schlösser (Ger-vn)
Jul 22	Emil Scaria (Aus-bs)		

C. Debuts:

Met --- Wilhelm Basch (bar), Lenore Better (sop), Max Doerfler (bar), Jean Doré (bar), Silvia Franconi (mez), Max Heinrich (bar), Theresa Herbert-Förster (sop), Felix Krämer (ten), Wilhelmine Mayer (mez), Julius Meyer (ten), Georgine Neuendorff (sop), Albert Niemann (ten), Georg Sieglitz (bs)

U.S. -- Adele Aus der Ohe (tour), William C. MacFarlane (N.Y.), Ethelbert Nevin (Boston, as pianist), Eugène Oudin (N.Y.), August Spanuth (tour), Giulia Valda (N.Y.), Cornelia Van Zanten (tour), Benjamin Whelpley (Boston)

Other - Albert Alvarez (Ghent), Arthur Bird (Berlin), Olimpia Boronat (Naples), Jean-Francis Delmas (Paris), Ellen Gulbranson (Stockholm), Josef Hofmann (Berlin), Lawrence Kellie (London), Arturo Toscanini (Rio de Janeiro)

D. New Positions:

Conductors: Riccardo Drigo (Russian Imperial Ballet Orchestra), Antonio Gagnoni (maestro di cappella, S. Maria Maggiore), Wilhelm Kienzl (Steiermärkischer Musikverein, Graz), Felix Mottl (Bayreuth), Karl Muck (Deutsches Landestheater, Prague), Karl Schröder (Rotterdam German Opera), Fritz Steinbach (Meiningen)

Educational: Alfredo Catalani (composition, Milan Conservatory), George Henschel (voice, Royal College), Wilhelm Kuhe (piano, Royal Academy), Filippo Marchesi (director, Liceo Musicale, Rome), Giuseppe Martucci (director, Bologna Conservatory), Aglaja Orgeni (voice, Dresden Conservatory)

Others: Herbert Brewer (organ, St. Michael's, Coventry), Louis C. Elson (music critic, Boston *Advertiser*), Francis Hueffer (editor, *Musical World*), Max Kalbeck (critic, *Neues Wiener Tageblatt*), Max Reger (organ, Weiden Cathedral)

E. Prizes and Honors:

Prizes: Robert Fuchs (Vienna Conservatory Beethoven Prize), Marie-Emmanuel Savard (Prix de Rome)

Honors: Anton Bruckner (Order of Franz Josef and a government stipend), Niels Gade (Order of Daneborg), Pierre Gailhard and Ernesto C. Sivori (Legion of Honor)

F. Biographical Highlights:

Francisco d'Andrade and Lillian Nordica make their Covent Garden debuts; Gemma Bellincioni makes her La Scala debut and marries tenor Robert Stagno; Ferrucio Busoni goes to Leipzig for further music study; Claude Debussy deserts Rome but is talked into returning; Frederick Delius goes to Leipzig for study; Paul Dukas takes first prize in counterpoint at Paris Conservatory; Henry Gilbert enrolls in New England Conservatory; Victor Herbert marries Therese Förster and moves to New York; Hugo Kaun emigrates to the U.S. and settles in Milwaukee; Albéric Magnard enters Paris Conservatory; Gustav Mahler begins a two-year stint as assistant to Nikisch at Leipzig; Nellie Melba moves to Europe to study with Mathilde Marchesi and makes her London debut; Aglaja Orgeni, in poor health, quits the stage and begins teaching at the Dresden Conservatory; Adelina Patti marries Tomas Nicolini; Joseph Guy Ropartz leaves the Conservatory to study with Franck; Karl Schiedemantel and Rosa Sucher make their Bayreuth debuts; Frederick Stock enters Cologne Conservatory; Richard Strauss leaves Meiningen to become third conductor at the Munich Court Opera; Alwina Valleria retires from the stage.

G. Institutional Openings:

Performing Groups: Andreyev Balalaika Orchestra (St. Petersburg); Austin Musical Union; Berliner Lehrergesangverein; Church Choral Society (N.Y.); Concerts Classiques (Marseilles); Kneisel String Quartet (Boston); London Symphony Concerts; Sociedad del Cuarteto (Santiago); Società Orchestrale l'Avvenire (Messina)

Educational: American Conservatory of Music (Chicago); American Institute of Applied Music (Metropolitan Conservatory, N.Y.); Richard Anderssons Music School (Sweden); Minneapolis School of Fine Arts; Musikalische Akademie (Cologne); Toronto Royal Conservatory of Music; University of Oregon School of Music

Other: American Publisher's Copyright League; Berne Convention for the Protection of Literary and Artistic Works; Celeste (patented); *Het Orgal*; Slovak National Theater (Bratislava); *La Wallonie*

H. Musical Literature:

Christiani, Adolf, *Principles of Musical Expression in Piano Playing*
Curwen, Annie, *Mrs. Curwen's Pianoforte Method*
Davenport, Francis W., *Elements of Harmony, Counterpoint*
Hanslick, Eduard, *Konzerte, komponisten und virtuosen des letzten 15 Jahre*
Hartmann, Eduard von, *Philosophie des Schönen*
Nuitter/Thoinan, *Origines de l'Opèra français*
Rockstro, William, *General History of Music*
Stockhausen, Julius, *Gesangsmethode I*
Wallaschek, Richard, *Ästhetik der Tonkunst*

I. Musical Compositions:

Barnes, Edwin, *Southampton* (hymn tune, "O Worship the Lord")
    Morton (hymn tune, "O Let Me Walk With Thee")
Brahms, Johannes, *Sonata No. 2, Opus 99, for Cello and Piano*
    Sonata No. 2, Opus 100, for Violin and Piano
    Piano Trio No. 3, Opus 101
Busoni, Ferruccio, *String Quartet in C Minor*
Chabrier, Emmanuel, *Gwendoline* (opera)
Chadwick, George W., *Symphony No. 2*
Chausson, Ernest, *Hymne Védique, Opus 9*
Delius, Frederick, *Florida* (orchestral suite)
Fauré, Gabriel, *Piano Quartet No. 2, Opus 45*
Franchetti, Alberto, *Symphony*
Franck, Cesar, *Sonata in A Major for Violin and Piano*
Glazounov, Alexander, *Symphony No. 2, Opus 16*
    Brass Quartet, "In Modo Religioso"
Godard, Benjamin, *Symphonie Légendaire*
Grieg, Edvard, *Lyric Pieces, Book III, Opus 43* (piano)
d'Indy, Vincent, *Symphony on a French Mountain Air*
Lalo, Edouard, *Symphony in G Minor*
Liszt, Franz, *Missa Choralis*
Mackenzie, Alexander, *The Troubador* (opera)
Massenet, Jules, *La Terre Promise* (oratorio)
Nápravník, Eduard, *Harold* (opera)
Rimsky-Korsakov, Nikolai, *Fantasia on Russian Themes for Violin and Orchestra*
Saint-Saëns, Camilee, *Symphony No. 3, Opus 78, "Organ"*
    Carnival of the Animals (not performed till 1922)
Strauss, Richard, *Aus Italien, Opus 16* (tone poem)
Tchaikovsky, Peter I., *Dumka, Opus 59* (piano)
Widor, Charles, *Maître Ambros* (opera)

1887

World Events:

In the U.S., Congress passes the Hatch Act, the Interstate Commerce Act, the Electoral Count Act and the Dawes Severalty Act; Catholic University of America is incorporated; free mail delivery begins in the larger towns and cities. Internationally, the first World Colonial Conference opens in London; the southeast Asian states of Vietnam, Cambodia and Laos are combined to form French Indo-China; internal combustion cars are developed by both Gottlieb Daimler and Karl Benz; Ferdinand I becomes ruler of Bulgaria.

Cultural Highlights:

Births in the field of art include American sculptor Malvina Hoffman and artist Georgia O'Keeffe, Lithuanian artist William Zorach, Russian sculptor Alexander Archipenko and artist Marc Chagall, Spanish artist Juan Gris and French artists Jean (Hans) Arp and Marcel Duchamp; deaths include American architect Thomas Walter and German artist Hans von Marées. Births in the literary field include American poets Leonard Bacon, Robinson Jeffers and Marianne Moore and authors Edna Ferber and James N. Hall, British poets Rupert Brooke and Edith Sitwell and French poet and author Blaise Cendars; deaths include British poets Alfred Domett and John C. Hughes, French novelist Paul H. Féval, Canadian novelist Isabella Crawford and American poet Emma Lazarus. Other highlights include:

Art: Pierre de Chavannes, *Allegory: Arts and Sciences*; Childe Hassam, *Une Averse, Rue Bonaparte*; Max Klinger, *The Judgment of Paris*; John LaFarge, *Ascension*; Max Liebermann, *The Flax Spinners*; Hans von Marées, *The Hesperides*; Pierre Renoir, *The Bathers*; Henri Rousseau, *Landscape with Tree Trunks*

Literature: Charles Chesnutt, *The Goophered Grapevine*; Arthur C. Doyle, *A Study in Scarlet*; Thomas Hardy, *The Woodlanders*; Oliver W. Holmes, *Before the Curfew and Other Poems*; Stepháne Mallarmé, *Album de Vers et de Prose*; Victorien Sardou, *La Tosca*; August Strindberg, *Der Vater*; Oscar Wilde, *The Canterbury Ghost*

MUSICAL EVENTS

A. Births:

Jan 21	A.H. Ackley (Am-hymn)	Aug 25	Fartein Valen (Nor-cm)
Jan 27	Francesco Merli (It-ten)	Sep 1	Felice Lyne (Am-sop)
Mar 4	Josef Bartoš (Cz-mus)	Sep 16	Nadia Boulanger (Fr-cm-ed)
Mar 5	Heitor Villa-Lobos (Bra-cm)	Oct 6	Maria Jeritza (Cz-sop)
Mar 14	Lawrence Collingwood (Br-cd)	Oct 25	Willem Andriessen (Hol-cm)
Mar 23	Anthony von Hoboken (Hol-mus)	Nov 5	Paul Wittgenstein (Aus-pn)
Apr 18	Clara Edwards (Am-cm)	Nov 8	Youri Shaporin (Rus-cm)
May 2	Michael Bohnen (Ger-bar)	Nov 14	Bernhard Paumgartner (Aus-mus)
May 16	Florica Cristoforeanu (Rom-mez)	Nov 15	Elvira Casazza (It-mez)
Jun 2	Carmela Ponselle (Am-alto)	Nov 23	William Gustafson (Am-bs)
Jun 3	Roland Hayes (Am-ten)	Dec 7	Ernst Toch (Aus-cm)
Jun 23	John Williamson (Am-cd)	Dec 12	Kurt Atterberg (Swe-cm)
Jul 19	Walter Rummel (Ger-pn)	Dec 24	Lucrezia Bori (Sp-sop)
Jul 29	Sigmund Romberg (Hun-cm)		

B. Deaths:

Jan 9	Marcus P. Audran (Fr-ten)	May 12	Francesco Malipiero (It-cm)
Feb 2	Georg Unger (Ger-ten)	May 23	Gaetano Fraschini (It-ten)
Feb 27	Alexander Borodin (Rus-cm)	Jun 12	Karl G. Weber (Swi-cm)
Mar 18	Robert Schaab (Ger-org)	Jun 23	Filippo Filippi (It-cri)
Mar 25	Jean Desiré Artôt (Fr-bn)	Jun 24	Lindsay Sloper (Br-pn)
Apr 28	Carl F. Pohl (Ger-mus-org)	Aug 13	Jules Pasdeloup (Fr-cd)

Aug 17 Franz Commer (Ger-mus)
Oct 3 Therese Tietjens (Ger-sop)
Oct 30 Eugène E. Massol (Fr-bar)
Oct 31 George Macfarren (Br-cm-the)

Nov 2 Jenny Lind (Swe-sop)
Nov 18 Heinrich Panofka (Ger-voc)
Nov 27 Marianna Barbieri-Nini (It-sop)
Dec 2 Thomas P. Ryder (Am-org)

C. Debuts:

Met --- Biro DeMarions (sop), Minnie Dilthey (sop), Johannes Elmblad (bs), T. Ferenczy (ten), Lena (mez) and Hans (ten) Göttich, Louise Meisslinger (mez), Susan Strong (sop)

U.S. -- Arthur Hartmann (Philadelphia, age 6), Victor Herbert (N.Y.), Josef Hofmann (N.Y., age 11), Lawrence Kellie (N.Y.), Barton M'Guckin (tour), Sophie Sedlmair (N.Y.), Teresina Tua (N.Y.)

Other - Werner Alberti (Berlin), Andrew Black (London), Andreas Dippel (Bremen), Cesira Ferrani (Turin), Nicolai Figner (as tenor), Berta Foerster-Lauterer (Prague), Bruno Heydrich (Sondershausen), Ida Hiedler (Berlin), Nellie Melba (Brussels), Giulio Rossi (Parmi), Therese Rothauser (Leipzig), Anna Schoen-Rene (Altenburg)

D. New Positions:

Conductors: Auguste Charles Vianesi (Paris Opera), Felix Weingartner (Hamburg)

Educational: Charles W. Bériot (piano, Paris Conservatory), Pablo Berutti (piano, San Juan College, Argentina), Giovanni Bolzoni (director, Turin Conservatory), Louis Diémer (piano, Paris Conservatory), Alexis-Henri Fissot (piano, Paris Conservatory), Engelbert Humperdinck (Cologne Conservatory), Stewart Macpherson (composition, Royal Academy, London), Anton Rubinstein (director, St. Petersburg Conservatory), Charles Stanford (professor, Cambridge)

Others: Otto Barblan (organ, St. Peter's, Geneva), William Barrett (editor, *Musical Times*), Carl D. Fuchs (music critic, *Danziger Zeitung*), Basil Harwood (organ, Ely Cathedral), William J. Henderson (music critic, New York *Times*)

E. Prizes and Honors:

Prizes: Gustave Charpentier (Prix de Rome)

Honors: Stephen Heller and Charles Lenepveu (Legion of Honor), Salomon Jadassohn (honorary doctorate, Leipzig), John F. Murphy (National Academy), Joseph Rheinberger (Berlin Royal Academy), Charles Santley (Order of St. Gregory), Marcus Stone (Royal Academy, London)

F. Biographical Highlights:

Hugo Alfvén enters Stockholm Conservatory; Emil Berliner introduces the flat phono disc; Emma Calvé makes her La Scala debut; Claude Debussy joins Mallarmé's circle; Frederick Delius visits Norway and meets Grieg; Enrique Granados goes to Paris for further music study; Victor Herbert plays his own *Cello Concerto* with the New York PO; Leoš Janácek joins František Bartoš in investigating Moravian folk music; Clara Kellogg, after marrying her manager, retires from the stage; Fritz Kreisler graduates from Paris Conservatory; Albéric Magnard receives a degree from law school; Emma Nevada and Lillian Nordica make their Covent Garden debuts; Maurice Ravel begins studying harmony with René; Albert Roussel is admitted to the École Navale as a cadet; Richard Strauss meets Mahler and Pauline de Ahna; Peter Tchaikovsky debuts as a conductor; Alexander von Zemlinsky begins study at the Vienna Conservatory.

G. Institutional Openings:

Performing Groups: Aulin String Quartet (Sweden); Bostonian's Light Opera Group; Corale Rossini (Modena); Dallas Philharmonic Society; Fremantle Orchestral Society (Perth); Gesellschaft der Opernfreunde (Berlin); Shinner String Quartet (London); Marie Soldat String Quartet I (Vienna); South Place Sunday Concerts (London)

Festivals: Hovingham Music Festival

Educational: Denver Music Conservatory; Halifax Ladies' College Music Department; Liceo Musicale (Trieste); London College of Music; Maritime Conservatory of Music (Halifax); Tokyo Music School

Other: Carisch Music Publishers (Milan); Edinburgh Society of Musicians; North American Phonograph Co.; *Scribner's Magazine*; Società Wagneriana (Bologna); Théâtre Libre (Paris); Yamaha Co. (Japan)

H. Musical Literature:

Banister, Henry, *Lectures on Music Analysis*
Benoît, Camille, *Musiciens, poètes et philosophes*
Bulthaupt, Heinrich, *Dramaturgie der oper*
Hiller, Ferdinand, *Briefe an eine Ungenannte* (posthumous publication)
Kistler, Cyrill, *Volksschullehrer-Tonkünstlerlexicon*
Kretzschmar, August, *Führer durch den Konzert-Saal*
Malherbe/Soubies, *Précis d'histoire de l'Opéra-Comique*
Riaño, Juan F., *Critical & Bibliographical Notes on Early Spanish Music*
Riemann, Hugo, *Systematische Modulationslehre...*
Wegelius, Martin, *Foundations of General Music Science*

I. Musical Compositions:

Borodin, Alexander, *Symphony No. 3* (unfinished)
    Prince Igor (unfinished opera)
Brahms, Johannes, *Double Concerto, Opus 102 for Violin, Cello and Orchestra*
Bruch, Max, *Symphony No. 3, Opus 51*
Bruckner, Anton, *Symphony No. 8* (revised 1890)
Chabrier, Emmanuel, *Le roi malgré lui* (opera)
Cui, César, *Orchestral Suite No. 2, Opus 38*
    Orchestral Suite No. 4, Opus 40, "A Argenteau"
Debussy, Claude, *Printemps*
Dvořák, Antonin, *4 Romantic Pieces, Opus 75, for Violin and Piano*
    Mass in D, Opus 86
Fauré, Gabriel, *Requiem, Opus 48*
    Pavane, Opus 50
Glazounov, Alexander, *Der Walk*
Goldmark, Karl, *Symphony No. 2, Opus 35*
Grieg, Edvard, *Sonata No. 3, Opus 45, for Violin and Piano*
Ippolitov-Ivanov, Mikhail, *Ruth* (opera)
MacDowell, Edward, *6 Idyls after Goethe, Opus 28* (piano)
    6 Poems after Heine, Opus 31 (piano)
Pierné, Gabriel, *Concerto, Opus 12, for Piano and Orchestra*
    March of the Little Lead Soldiers, Opus 14
Reznicek, Emil von, *Die Jungfrau von Orleans* (opera)
Rimsky-Korsakov, Nikolai, *Capriccio Espagnole*
Saint-Saëns, Camille, *Proserpine* (opera)
Satie, Erik, *3 Sarabandes* (piano)
Stanford, Charles, *Symphony No. 3, Opus 28, "Irish"*
Strauss, Richard, *Sonata, Opus 18, for Violin and Piano*
    MacBeth, Opus 23 (tone poem)
Tchaikovsky, Peter I., *Orchestra Suite No. 4, "Mozartiana"*
    6 Songs, Opus 63
Verdi, Giuseppi, *Othello* (opera)

1888

World Events:
In the U.S., Benjamin Harrison is elected as President No. 23 despite his losing in the popular vote; Charles M. Hall introduces a cheaper method for the commercial production of aluminum; the Kodak Camera appears on the market; *Collier's Magazine* and the *National Geographic Magazine* begin publication. Internationally, Kaiser Wilhelm II of Prussia becomes Emperor of Austria as well; Cecil Rhodes becomes a virtual dictator in South Africa; the European powers declare the neutrality of the Suez Canal; France annexes the Island of Tahiti; the Institut Pasteur is established in France.

Cultural Highlights:
The magazine *Poet Lore* begins publication. Births in the literary world include American poets T. S. Eliot and Alan Seeger, dramatists Maxwell Anderson and Eugene O'Neill, author Anne Parrish, British novelist Katharine Mansfield and adventurer and author T. E. Lawrence and French dramatist Jean Bernard; deaths include American authors Louisa May Alcott and David Locke, British poet and artist Edward Lear, poet and critic Matthew Arnold, Russian author V. Mikhailovich Garshin and German poet Theodor Storm. Births in the art world include Russian artist Robert Falk, German artist Josef Albers, Greek artist Giorgio de Chirico, British sculptor Frank Dobson and French artist Roger Bissière; deaths include American artist Richard Hubbard and French sculptor Antoine Étex. Other highlights include:

Art: Frédéric Bartholdi, *Lion of Belfort*; Paul Cézanne, *L'estaque*; James Ensor, *Entry of Christ into Brussels*; Paul Gauguin, *The Swinherd, Brittany*; Vincent van Gogh, *L'Arlesienne*; Camille Pissarro, *River, Early Morning*; Pierre Renoir, *After the Bath*; Henri de Toulouse-Latrec, *Circus Fernando Ringmaster*

Literature: James Barrie, *Auld Licht Idylls*; William Henley, *Poems I*; Henrik Ibsen, *The Lady from the Sea*; Henry James, *Partial Portraits*; Rudyard Kipling, *The Phantom Rickshaw*; James R. Lowell, *Political Essays*; Robert L. Stevenson, *Master of Ballantrae*; Ernest Thayer, *Casey at the Bat*; Oscar Wilde, *The Happy Prince and Other Tales*

MUSICAL EVENTS

A. Births:

Jan 2	Tito Schipa (It-ten)	Jun 13	Marc Pincherle (Fr-mus)
Feb 6	Victor Belaiev (Rus-mus)	Jun 13	Elizabeth Schumann (Ger-sop)
Feb 8	Matthijs Vermeulen (Hol-cm)	Jun 30	Alice Gentle (Am-sop)
Feb 27	Lotte Lehmann (Ger-sop)	Aug 6	Heinrich Schlusnus (Ger-bar)
Mar 12	Hans Knappertsbusch (Ger-cd)	Aug 15	Albert Spalding (Am-vn)
Mar 18	Louis Graveure (Br-bar)	Aug 20	Eric Walter Blom (Br-cri)
Apr 9	Sol Hurok (Rus-imp)	Aug 22	Antoine Cherbuliez (Swi-mus)
Apr 17	Maggie Teyte (Br-sop)	Sep 2	Friedrich Schorr (Hun-bar)
Apr 18	Frida Leider (Ger-sop)	Sep 21	Rudolph Reuter (Am-pn)
Apr 30	John Ransom (Am-pt-cri)	Sep 22	Emil Ábrányi (Hun-cd-cm)
May 11	Irving Berlin (Am-pop)	Oct 11	Piero Coppola (It-cd-cm)
May 17	Elisabeth Ohms (Hol-sop)	Nov 16	Burnet Tuthill (Am-cm)
May 25	Anatol Alexandrov (Rus-cm)	Nov 20	Lillian Grenville (Am-sop)
May 27	Louis Durey (Fr-cm)	Dec 19	Fritz Reiner (Hun-cd)
Jun 9	Hugo Kauder (Aus-cm)		

B. Deaths:

Jan 5	Henri Herz (Ger-pn-cm)	Feb 22	Delphin Alard (Fr-vn-cm)
Jan 14	Stephen Heller (Hun-pn-cm)	Feb 29	Theódore Nisard (Fr-mus)
Jan 22	Giuseppe Fancelli (It-ten)	Mar 15	Henry Blaze (Fr-cri)

Mar 26	Walter Bache (Br-pn-cd)	Jul 31	Jean Vogt (Fr-pn-cm)
Mar 29	Charles Alkan (Fr-pn-cm)	Aug 8	Friedrich Jähns (Ger-ped)
Apr 2	Granz Götye (Ger-ten)	Aug 31	Blanche Cole (Br-sop)
Apr 15	Théophile Semet (Fr-cm)	Sep 7	Tito Ricordi (It-pub)
Jun 3	Karl Riedel (Ger-cd)	Oct 2	John Ella (Br-cri)
Jun 23	Emil Naumann (Ger-cm-au)	Dec 21	Oliver Ditson (Am-pub)
Jul 10	Rafael Hernándo (Sp-cm)		

C. Debuts:

Met --- Joseph Beck (bar), Alma Fohstrom (sop), Alois Grienauer (bar), Félice Kaschowska (sop), Emmy Miron (mez), Albert Mittelhauser (ten), Ludwig Mödlinger (bs), Karl Moran (ten), Fanny Moran-Olden (sop), Julius Perotti (ten), Hedwig Reil (mez), Wilhelm Sedlmayer (ten), Emil Steger (bar), Sophie Traubmann (sop)

U.S. -- Joseph Victor Capoul (N.Y.), Guerrina Fabbri (N.Y.), Sissieretta Jones (N.Y.), Leonard Labatt (tour), Edward Lloyd (Cincinnati), Fanny Moren-Olden (N.Y.), Leo Stern (tour), Eva Tetrazzini (N.Y.)

Other - Georg Anthes (Freiburg), Josephine von Artner (Leipzig), Pierre Cornubert (Paris), Hariclea Darclée (Paris), Marie Dietrich (Stuttgart), Harry Plunkett Greene (London), Lev Klementyev (Kiev), Margaret Macintyre (London), Luigi Mancinelli (London), Franz Navál (Frankfurt), Regina Pacini (Lisbon), Ignace Jan Paderewski (Vienna), Albert Saléza (Paris), Mario Sammarco (Palermo), Sybil Sanderson (The Hague), Vassily Sapelnikov (Hamburg), Francisco Vignas (Barcelona)

D. New Positions:

Conductors: Leopold Auer (Russian Imperial Music Society), Federic Cowen (London PO), Edward German (Globe Theater), Vilém Hes (Concertgebouw SO), Willy Hess (Hallé SO), Gustav Mahler (Budapest Opera), Luigi Mancinelli (Covent Garden), Josef Sucher (Berlin Opera)

Educational: George J. Bennett (professor, Royal Academy), Charles H. Farnsworth (music director, Colorado University), Vincenzo Ferroni (composition, Milan Conservatory), James Huneker, (piano, National Conservatory, N.Y.), Rafael Joseffy (piano, National Conservatory, N.Y.), Alexander C. Mackenzie (principal, Royal Academy), Alexander Siloti (piano, Moscow Conservatory)

Others: Augustus Harris (manager, Covent Garden), Horatio Parker (organ, Holy Trinity, Boston), Emil von Reznicek (military bandmaster, Prague), Hans Bronsort von Schellendorf (president, Allgemeiner Deutscher Musikverein)

E. Prizes and Honors:

Prizes: Camille Erlanger (Prix de Rome)

Honors: Louis Bourgault-Ducoudray and Edouard Lalo (Legion of Honor), Charles Hallé and John Stainer (knighted), Peter I. Tchaikovsky (government pension)

F. Biographical Highlights:

Sigrid Arnoldson makes her Covent Garden debut; Mattia Battistini makes her La Scala debut; Lola Beeth makes her Vienna debut; Johannes Brahms again tours Italy where he meets Tchaikovsky; Claude Debussy visits Bayreuth and begins liason with Gaby Dupont; Frederick Delius begins serious music study with father's permission; George Enescu enters Vienna Conservatory; Edvard Grieg meets Tchaikovsky and conducts at the Birmingham Festival; Gabrielle Krauss retires from the stage; Lilli Lehmann marries tenor Paul Kalisch; Edward MacDowell returns to the U.S. and settles in Boston; Albéric Magnard leaves the Conservatory with first prize in harmony; Nellie Melba debuts at both Covent Garden and the Paris Opera; Wilma Neruda marries her second husband, conductor Charles Hallé; Alexander Scriabin enters Moscow Conservatory; John Stainer resigns his organ post because of increasing blindness; Ernest Van Dyck makes both his Bayreuth and Vienna debuts.

G. Institutional Openings:

Performing Groups: Adamowski String Quartet (Boston); Amsterdam Concertgebouw (Concert Hall and Orchestra); Athens Philharmonic Society; Beethoven Club (Memphis); Ellis Club (Los Angeles); Newcastle & Gateshead Choral Union; Nouveaux Concerts Symphoniques (Belgium)

Educational: Artist-Artisan Institute (N.Y.); Des Moines Musical College; Karl Mikuli School of Music (Lvov); Toronto College of Music

Other: Ateneul Román (Bucharest Concert Hall); German Theater (Prague); Harlem Opera House; *Ilustración Musical Hispano-Americana*; Lessing Theater (Berlin); Mechanical Organette & Music Co. (N.Y.); Mozart Musical & Literary Society (Dayton, Ohio); *Music Review Weekly* (St. Petersburg); *Musica Romana*; Odd-Fellow Palace (Copenhagen Concert Hall); Plainsong & Medieval Music Society (London); Società Vincenzo Bellini (Ancona); Clayton F. Summy, Music Publisher (Chicago); Teatro Costanzi (Rome); Theater am Brausenwerth (Wuppertal)

H. Musical Literature:

Clarke, Hugh A., *Manual of Orchestration*
Edwards, Henry, *The Prima Donna I, II*
Elson, Louis C., *History of German Song*
Goodrich, Alfred, *The Art of Song*
Hanslick, Eduard, *Musikalisches Skizzenbuch*
Hipkins, Alfred, *Musical Instruments, Historic, Rare & Unique*
Nietzsche, Friedrich, *Der Fall Wagner*
Riemann, Hugo, *Lehrbuch des... Kontrapunkts*
Wegelius, Martin, *Treatise on General Musical Science & Analysis I*

I. Musical Compositions:

Brahms, Johannes, *Sonata No. 3, Opus 108, for Violin and Piano*
Busoni, Ferruccio, *Symphonic Suite, Opus 25*
Debussy, Claude, *Deux Arabesques for Piano*
Delius, Frederick, *Hiawatha* (tone poem)
Fibich, Zdenek, *Hákon* (symphonic poem)
Foerster, Josef B., *Symphony No. 1, Opus 9*
Foote, Arthur, *The Wreck of the Hesperus, Opus 17*
Franck, César, *Symphony in D Minor*
Gilbert and Sullivan, *Yeoman of the Guard* (operetta)
Godard, Benjamin, *Jocelyn* (opera)
Gounod, Charles, *Little Symphony* (woodwinds)
      Messe Solennelle No. 4
Grieg, Edvard, *Lyric Pieces, Book IV, Opus 47*
d'Indy, Vincent, *Piano Quartet in A Major, Opus 7*
Koven, Reginald de, *Oh, Promise Me* (song)
Mahler, Gustav, *Symphony No. 1, "Titan"*
Nielsen, Carl, *Little Suite, Opus 1* (string orchestra)
Paderewski, Ignace Jan, *Concerto, Opus 17, for Piano and Orchestra*
Rimsky-Korsakov, Nikolai, *Russian Easter Overture*
      Scheherazade
Satie, Erik, *Three Gymnopedies for Piano*
Sousa, John Phillip, *Semper Fidelis March*
Strauss, Johann, Jr., *Emperor Waltz*
Strauss, Richard, *Don Juan, Opus 20*
Tchaikovsky, Peter I., *Symphony No. 5, Opus 64*
      Hamlet, Opus 67a (overture-fantasy)

1889

World Events:

In the U.S., North and South Dakota becomes States No. 39 and 40, Montana No. 41 and Washington, No. 42; the Oklahoma Territory is opened and Oklahoma City is built up overnight; Hull House opens in Chicago; the Mayo Clinic is founded in Minnesota; the great Johnstown Flood occurs in Ohio; *Cosmopolitan Magazine* begins publication; Confederate President Jefferson Davis dies. Internationally, the first International American Conference is held; Parliamentary Government is introduced into Japan; the Eiffel Tower becomes a significant feature of the great Paris Exposition; British South Africa Co. is incorporated; Louis I of Portugal dies and is succeeded by Charles I.

Cultural Highlights:

Henry B. Adam's *History of the United States* is published. Births in the art world include Czech sculptor Otto Gutfreund, American artist Thomas Hart Benton and German artist Willi Baumeister; deaths include French artists Alexandre Cabanel and Jules Dupré. Births in the literary field include American humorist Robert Benchley, novelist Ben A. Williams and dramatist George Kaufman, French author Tristan Derème and British historian and author Arnold Toynbee; deaths include British poets Robert Browning, Eliza Cook, Gerard M. Hopkins and Frederick A. Ousley, novelist Wilkie Collins, Irish poet William Allingham, Romanian poet Mihail Eminescu and French novelist Champfleury. Other highlights include:

Art: Edgar Degas, *The Mante Family*; Thomas Eakins, *The Agnew Clinic*; Paul Gauguin, *La Belle Angèle*; Vincent van Gogh, *The Starry Night*; George Inness, *Niagara*; Max Liebermann, *Mending the Nets*; Frederick Macmonnies, *Diana*; Pierre Renoir, *Girl with Daisies*; Auguste Rodin, *The Thinker*; Georges Seurat, *Sideshow*

Literature: Gabriele d'Annunzio, *Il Piacere*; Eugene Field, *Little Book of Western Verse*; Verner von Heidenstram, *Endymion*; Emma Lazarus, *Collected Poems*; Maurice Maeterlinck, *La Princesse Maleine*; Friedrich Nietzsche, *Götzendämmerung*; Alfred Tennyson, *Crossing the Bar*; Mark Twain, *A Connecticut Yankee in King Arthur's Court*

MUSICAL EVENTS

A. Births:

Jan 1	Alexander Smallens (Rus-cd)	May 25	Hans J. Moser (Ger-mus)
Feb 6	Xeniya Derzhinskaya (Rus-sop)	Jun 1	Sigrid Onégin (Swe-alto)
Feb 7	Claudia Muzio (It-sop)	Jun 9	Alfred Jerger (Cz-bar)
Mar 4	Willibald Gurlitt (Ger-mus)	Jul 3	Alfred Orel (Aus-mus)
Mar 8	John S. Thompson (Am-pn-ped)	Jul 7	Franz Ludwig (Boh-mus)
Apr 3	Grigoras Dinicu (Rom-vn-cm)	Oct 15	Margaret Sheridan (Ir-sop)
Apr 8	Adrian Boult (Br-cd)	Oct 29	Anna Case (Am-sop)
Apr 9	Efrem Zimbalist (Rus-vn)	Nov 4	Charles Hackett (Am-ten)
Apr 15	Dom Anselm Hughes (Br-mus)		Juanita Caracciolo (It-sop)

B. Deaths:

Jan 14	Ilma di Murska (Yug-sop)	Apr 30	Carl Rosa (Ger-vn-imp)
Jan 19	Francis Hueffer (Br-cri)	Jun 12	Hans Bischoff (Ger-pn-ed)
Feb 6	Paul S. Althouse (Am-ten)	Jun 27	Carlotta Patti (It-sop)
Feb 26	Karl Davídov (Rus-cel-cm)	Jul 7	Giovanni Bottesini (It-cb)
Mar 1	William H. Monk (Br-org)	Aug 5	Carl Mangold (Ger-cm)
Mar 13	Enrico Tamberlik (It-ten)	Aug 17	Ernst Frank (Ger-cd)
Mar 13	Felice Varesi (It-bar)	Sep 17	Louis Maas (Ger-cm-pn)
Mar 25	Moritz Fürstenau (Ger-fl)	Oct 10	Adolph von Henselt (Ger-pn)
Apr 9	Jean Baptiste Arban (Fr-tpt)	Nov 24	Frédèric Clay (Br-cm)

Dec 3 Bastasar Saldoni (Sp-mus-cm) Dec 15 Karl J. Formes (Ger-bs)
Dec 8 Léon P. Burbure (Bel-mus) Dec 20 Konstancja Gladkowska (Pol-sop)

C. Debuts:

Met --- Joseph Arden (bar), Conrad Behrens (bs), Betty Frank (sop), Nina Hartmann (mez), Charlotte Huhn (mez), Paul Kalisch (ten), Karl Mühe (bs), Theodor Reichmann (bar), Edward Schlömann (bs), Emmy Sonntag Uhl (mez)

U.S. -- Eugen d'Albert (tour), Otto Hegner (tour, age 12), Fritz Kreisler (tour), Selma Kronold (N.Y.), Francesco Tamagno (Chicago)

Other - Irene Abendroth (Vienna), Henri Albers (Amsterdam), Maria Ancona (Trieste), Theodor Bertram (Ulm), Leonard Borwick (Frankfurt), Edmond Clément (Paris), Leopold Demuth (Halle), Emma Eames (Paris), George Enescu (Moldavia), Johanna Gadski (Berlin), Hermann Jadlowker (Cologne), Lise Landouzy (Paris), Antonio Scotti (Naples)

D. New Positions:

Conductors: Raoul Gunsbourg (Nice Opera), Arthur Nikisch (Boston SO), Richard Strauss (Weimar Opera)

Educational: Arrigo Boito (director, Parma Conservatory), Ferrucio Busoni (piano, Helsingfors Conservatory), Albert Fuchs (director, Wiesbaden Conservatory), Victor Herbert (National Conservatory), Stephan Krehl (piano & theory, Karlsruhe Conservatory), Andreas Moser (violin, Berlin Hochschule), Hans Müller (music history, Berlin Hochschule), Vasily Safonov (director, Moscow Conservatory), John Stainer (professor, Oxford)

Others: Richard Aldrich (music critic, Washington *Evening Star*), Ernest Chausson (secretary, Société Nationale de Musique), Henri de Curzon (music critic, *Gazette de France*), John Fuller-Maitland (music critic, London *Times*)

E. Prizes and Honors:

Prizes: Paul Gilson (Prix de Rome), August Schmnid-Lindner (Mendelssohn), Charles Smulders (Prix de Rome)

Honors: Johannes Brahms (Order of Leopold), Louis Diemer, Benjamin Godard and Jean Louis Meissonier (Legion of Honor), Franz Haberl (honorary doctorate, Würzburg)

F. Biographical Highlights:

Granville Bantock enters the Royal Academy; Giovanni Bottesini appointed director of Parma Conservatory six months before his death; Teresa Brambilla-Ponchielli retires from the stage; Claude Debussy makes his second Bayreuth pilgrimage, hears Javanese music at the Exposition and is introduced to Mussorgsky's *Boris*; Andreas Dippel makes his Bayreuth debut; Edward Elgar marries Caroline Alice Roberts; Henry Gilbert begins music study with MacDowell; Alexander Glazunov conducts his own works in Paris; Alexander Gretchaninov enters St. Petersburg Conservatory; Pauline Lucca retires from the stage; soprano Medea Mei marries tenor Nikolai Figner; Viteslav Novák begins the study of law and music in Prague; Eugène Oudin makes his London debut; Maurice Ravel enters Paris Conservatory; Jan Sibelius travels in Germany on a government grant; Richard Strauss leaves Munich and works summers in Bayreuth; Bruno Walter decides on a conducting career.

G. Institutional Openings:

Performing Groups: Bristol Choral Society; Church Choral Society of New York; Euterpe Choral Society of New York; Nahan Franko Orchestra; Heidelberg Stadtisches Orchester; Emma Juch Grand Opera Co.; Kansas City Apollo Club; Orpheus Club (Newark, N.J.); Marie Soldat String Quartet II; Treble Clef (later: Lyric Club, Los Angeles)

Educational: Associated Board of the Royal Schools of Music (London); Coblenz Music Conservatory; Metropolitan College of Music (London); Rauchenecker Music School (Elberfeld)

Other: Crosby Brown Instrumental Collection (Metropolitan Museum, New York); *Ethnographical Review*; Harold Flammer, Publisher; Freie Bühne (Theater Co.); Hamilton Organ Co. (Chicago); Manuscript Society of New York; *Le Monde Musical*; Károly Rozsnyai, Music Publisher (Budapest); Carlo Schmidl, Publisher (Trieste); Teatro Principal (Lima, Peru); Verein Beethovenhaus (Bonn)

H. Musical Literature:
Faelten, Carl/Reinhold, *Conservatory Course for Pianists*
Finck, Henry T., *Chopin & Other Musical Essays*
Goodrich, Alfred, *Complete Musical Analysis*
Hanslick, Eduard, *Musikalisches und Literarisches*
Hiles, Henry, *Harmony or Counterpoint?*
Hueffer, Francis, *Half a Century of Music in England*
Jadassohn, Salomon, *Die Formen in den Werken der Tonkunst*
    Lehrbuch der Instrumentation
Mathews, William, *100 Years of Music in America*
Prout, Ebenezer, *Harmony, Its Theory and Practice*

I. Musical Compositions:
Arensky, Anton, *Symphony No. 2*
Bristow, George, *Overture Jibbenainosay, Opus 64*
Chausson, Ernest, *Concerto for Piano, Violin and String Quartet, Opus 21*
Debussy, Claude, *Petite Suite* (piano)
    Fantasy for Piano and Orchestra
Delius, Frederick, *Petite Suite for Orchestra*
Dubois, Theodore, *Triumphant Fantasy for Organ and Orchestra*
Dvořák, Antonin, *Symphony No. 8, Opus 88*
    Piano Quartet in E-flat Major, Opus 87
Fauré, Gabriel, *Petite Pièce, Opus 49, for Cello and Piano*
    Shylock, Opus 57 (incidental music)
Foerster, Josef B., *Sonata No. 1 for Violin and Piano*
    Drei Ritter, Opus 21 (opera)
Foote, Arthur, *Suite for Strings, Opus 63*
Franck, Cesar, *String Quartet in D Major*
Gade, Niels, *String Quartet in D Major, Opus 63*
German, Edward, *Richard III* (incidental music)
Gilbert and Sullivan, *The Gondoliers* (operetta)
Glazunov, Alexander, *String Quartet No. 3, "Slavish"*
Goldmark, Karl, *Der gefesselte Prometheus Overture, Opus 38*
Lalo, Edouard, *Concerto for Piano and Orchestra*
MacDowell, Edward, *Concerto No. 2, Opus 23, for Piano and Orchestra*
Mackenzie, Alexander, *Scottish Concerto for Piano and Orchestra*
Nielsen, Carl, *Symphonic Rhapsody*
Sibelius, Jan, *String Quartet, Opus 4*
Sousa, John Phillip, *Washington Post March*
Stanford, Charles, *Symphony No. 4, Opus 31*
Strauss, Richard, *Death and Transfiguration, Opus 24*
Tchaikovsky, Peter I., *The Sleeping Beauty Ballet, Opus 66*
Wolf, Hugo, *Spanisches Liederbuch* (song cycle)
    Christnacht (cantata)

1890

World Events:
The U.S. Census shows a population of 62,980,000, a 25% increase in ten years; Idaho and Wyoming becomes States No. 43 and 44 respectively; the last major Indian War, the Ghost Dance War, is fought; Sitting Bull, chief of the Sioux Indians is killed in a skirmish with soldiers in South Dakota; the U.S. Weather Bureau is created by Congress; Sequoia and Yosemite National Parks are formed; the Sherman Antitrust Act and the Sherman Silver Purchase Act are passed; future General of the Armies and President Dwight D. Eisenhower is born. Internationally, Otto Bismarck is forced to resign as German Chancellor; the Duchy of Luxembourg becomes an independent state; the Daimler Motor Co. is founded; William III of the Netherlands dies and Wilhemina becomes Queen (rules until 1946); future French General and French President Charles de Gaulle is born.

Cultural Highlights:
The Société Nationale des Beaux-Arts (Salon de la Nationale) is formed in Paris; the Kelmscott Press is founded in London by William Morris; Vincent van Gogh commits suicide by shooting himself. The literary world witnesses the birth of American novelist Katherine Porter, Russian poet Boris Pasternak, Czech novelist Karel Capek and German novelist Franz Werfel; deaths include British author John H. Newman and poet John W. Marston, German archeologist and author Heinrich Schliemann and poet-novelist Gottfried Keller, French novelist Octave Feuillet and Austrian dramatist Eduard von Bauernfeld. Births in the art field include American sculptor Robert Laurent, British artist Gerald Brockhurst, Russian artist Naum Gabo, Italian artist Giorgio Morandi and Austrian Egon Schiele; deaths include Dutch artist Vincent van Gogh, British artist Charles W. Cope and French artist Louis E. Lami. Other highlights include:

Art: Mary Cassatt, *Woman Bathing*; Winslow Homer, *Summer Night*; Frederic Leighton, *Psyche's Bath*; Frederick Macmonnies, *Pan of Rohallion*; Edward Poynter, *The Queen of Sheba Visiting Solomon*; Pierre Renoir, *Girl Wiping Her Feet*; Albert Ryder, *Jonah*; Georges Seurat, *Le Chahut*; John H. Twachtman, *Along the River in Winter*

Literature: Stephen Crane, *Maggie: A Girl of the Streets*; Anatole France, *Thaïs*; Henrik Ibsen, *Hedda Gabler*; Henry James, *The Tragic Muse*; Sarah Orne Jewett, *Tales of New England*; Maurice Maeterlinck, *The Intruder*; George Moore, *Impressions and Opinions*; Lev Tolstoy, *The Kreutzer Sonata*; Oscar Wilde, *The Picture of Dorian Gray*

MUSICAL EVENTS

A. Births:

Jan 7	Antal Molnár (Hun-mus)	Jul 10	André Souris (Bel-mus)
Jan 15	George Wedge (Am-org-au)	Jul 31	André George (Fr-cri)
Jan 23	Vladimir Rosing (Rus-ten)	Aug 5	Hans Gál (Aus-mus-cm)
Feb 1	Germaine Lubin (Fr-sop)	Aug 5	Erich Kleiber (Ger-cd)
Feb 22	Benno Moiseiwitsch (Br-pn)	Aug 15	Jacques Ibert (Fr-cm)
Feb 25	Myra Hess (Br-pn)	Sep 15	Frank Martin (Swi-cm)
Feb 28	Vaclav Nijinsky (Rus-bal)	Oct 13	Gösta Nystroem (Swe-cm)
Mar 6	Fernand Ansseau (Bel-ten)	Oct 15	Arcady Dubensky (Rus-vn-cm)
Mar 13	Fritz Busch (Ger-cd)	Nov 30	John Tasker Howard
Mar 20	Beniamino Gigli (It-ten)		(Am-cm-au)
Mar 20	Lauritz Melchior (Den-ten)	Dec 8	Bohuslav Martinu (Boh-cm)
May 4	Paul Rosenfeld (Am-cri)	Dec 25	A. Zuckerman, "Mana-Zucca"
Jun 10	Powell Weaver (Am-cm)		(Am-cm)
Jun 20	Giannina Arangi-Lombardi		
	(It-sop)		

B. Deaths:

Jan 2 Julián Gayarré (Sp-ten)
Jan 8 Giorgio Ronconi (It-bar)
Jan 20 Franz Lachner (Ger-cd-cm)
Feb 5 Ferdinand Laurecin (Boh-mus)
Feb 14 Wilhelm Fitzenhagen (Ger-cel)
Feb 25 Karl von Schafhäutl (Ger-acous)
May 5 Emilio Naudin (Fr-ten)
May 6 Hubert Léonard (Bel-vn)
Jun 30 SamuelTuckerman(Am-org-cm)

Jul 6 Thomas Helmore (Br-the)
Jul 26 Otto Dreisel (Ger-pn)
Oct 17 Prosper Sainton (Fr-vn-cm)
Nov 8 César Franck (Fr-cm-org)
Nov 29 Emanuele Muzio (It-cd)
Dec 20 Joseph Goldberg (Aus-vn-ten)
Dec 21 Niels W. Gade (Den-cm)
Dec 27 Giovanni Belletti (It-bar)
Eugen d'Albert (Bel-w.w.m)

C. Debuts:

Met --- Heinrich Bartels (ten), Jennie Broch (sop), Andreas Dippel (ten), C. W. Ecklemann (ten), Nicolai Gorski (ten), Heinrich Gudehus (ten), Konrad Heim (bs), Olga Islar (sop), Marie Jahn (sop), Bruno Lurgenstein (bs), Juan Luria (bar), Antonia Mielke (sop), Edmund Müller (ten), Hannah Rothe (mez), Pauline Schöller-Haag (sop), Wilhelm Schuster (bs), Francesco Tamagno (ten), Heinrich Vogl (ten)

U.S. -- Andrew Black (N.Y.), Marie Goetze (N.Y.), Ignace Jan Paderewski (N.Y.), Gerhard Stehmann (St. Louis)

Other - Desider Aranyi (Brünn), Hermann Bachmann (Halle), Theodor Bohlmann (Berlin), Ben Davies (England), Annie Dirkens (Berlin), David T. Frangcon-Davies (Manchester), Enrique Granados (Barcelona), Hermann Gura (Weimar), Martha Leffler-Burckard (Strasbourg), Matja von Niessen-Stone (Dresden), Artur Schnabel (Vienna), Luisa Tetrazzini (Florence), Theodor Wiehmayer (Leipzig)

D. New Positions:

Conductors: Henry T. Fleck (Harlem Philharmonic Society), Joseph Hellmesberger, Jr. (Vienna Opera), Wilhelm Kienzl (Hamburg Opera)

Educational: Marco E. Bossi (organ and harmony, Naples Conservatory), Carl Faelten (director, New England Conservatory), Walter B. Haynes (organ, Royal Academy), Konrad Heubner (director, Koblenz Conservatory), Eugen Krantz (director, Dresden Conservatory), Hugo Riemann (theory, Wiesbaden Conservatory), Karl Schröder (director, Soderhausen Conservatory), Charles Widor (organ, Paris Conservatory)

Others: Philip Hale (music critic, Boston *Post*), Engelbert Humperdinck (music critic, *Frankfurter Zeitung*), Max Kalbeck (critic, *Wiener Monats-Revue*), Gabriel Pierné (organ, Ste. Clothilde)

E. Prizes and Honors:

Prizes: Ferruccio Busoni (Rubinstein), Michel-Gaston Carraud (Prix de Rome), Otto Findeisen (Magdeburg), Bernhard Stavenhagen (Mendelssohn)

Honors: Richard Andersson (Swedish Royal Academy), Anton Bruckner and Christian Sinding (government stipends), Edvard Grieg (French Academy), Alexander Mackenzie (honorary doctorate, Edinburgh), Pietro Mascagni (Knight of the Crown, Italy), John Knowles Paine (honorary doctorate, Yale)

F. Biographical Highlights:

Isaac Albéniz retires from active musical life; Mario Ancona, Hariclea Darclée, Félia Litvinne and Adelina Stehle make their La Scala debuts; Lèontine Bordes-Pène suffers a stroke and retires to teaching in Rouen; Leonard Borwick makes his London debut; Lucienne Bréval wins Conservatory Opera Prize; Clara Butt receives a scholarship to the Royal College of Music; Frederick Delius moves to Paris and meets Ravel, Schmitt and Gauguin; Alma Gluck's family leaves Romania for the U.S.; Percy Goetschius returns to the U.S. and teaches at Syracuse University; Harry Plunkett Green and Fernando Valero make their Covent Garden debuts; George Henschel becomes a British citizen; Franz Nachbaur retires from the stage; Carl Nielsen studies the Wagner operas in Germany; Max Reger takes further organ studies with Riemann; Franz Schmidt enters Vienna Conservatory; Wilhelm Stenhammar passes the organ exam on his own initiative; Peter Tchaikovsky loses the support of Mme. von Meck.

G. Institutional Openings:

Performing Groups: Amsterdam A Capella Choir; Capilla Catalana (Spain); Denver Choral Society; Harlem Philharmonic Society (N.Y.)

Educational: Athenaeum School (Royal Scottish Academy) of Music; Chicago National College of Music; Dublin Municipal School (College) of Music; Hanover Conservatory of Music; Hartford School of Music; North Texas State University Music Department; Spangenberg Music Conservatory (Wiesbaden); Sternberg School of Music (Philadelphia)

Other: Contrabass Clarinet; Curtis Publishing Co.; Annibale Fagnola, Violin Maker (Turin); Heckel-Clarina; Lorenz Publishing Co. (Dayton, Ohio); Magulies Trio; *Mercure de France*; Metzler und Söhne, Organ Builders (Switzerland); *Music Trades* (N.Y.); *Musikinstrumenten-Zeitung*; Netherlands Lyric Theater (Flemish Opera); *Paléographic Musicale*; Frederick A. Stokes Co., Publishers (N.Y.); Théâtre des Arts (Paris); Tivoli Opera House (San Francisco); Verdi Institute (Montevideo)

H. Musical Literature:

Elson, Louis, *The Theory of Music*
Gevaert, François-Auguste, *Cours méthodique d'orchestration*
Goldschmidt, Hugo, *Die italienische Gesangmethode des 17. Jahrhunderts*
Jadassohn, Salomon, *Die Kunst zu Modulieren...*
Krenn, Franz, *Musik- und Harmonielehre*
Mathews, William, *Primer of Musical Forms*
Meerens, Charles, *La gamme musicale majeure et mineure*
Prout, Ebenezer, *Counterpoint, Strict & Free*
Sousa, John Philip, *National, Patriotic & Typical Airs of all Countries*

I. Musical Compositions:

Brahms, Johannes, *String Quintet No. 2, Opus 111*
Busoni, Ferruccio, *Sonata No. 1 for Violin and Piano, Opus 29*
    Concertstücke for Piano and Orchestra, Opus 31a
Chadwick, George W., *Serenade for Strings*
Chausson, Ernest, *Symphony in B-flat, Opus 20*
Debussy, Claude, *Rêverie* (piano)
Dvořák, Antonin, *Requiem, Opus 89* (soloists, chorus, orchestra)
Foote, Arthur, *Sonata, Opus 20, for Violin and Piano*
German, Edward, *Symphony No. 1*
Glazunov, Alexander, *Symphony No. 3, Opus 33*
    The Sea, Opus 28 (symphonic poem)
    Oriental Rhapsody, Opus 29
Gounod, Charles, *Messe Brève*
Koven, Reginald de, *Robin Hood* (operetta)
Lecocq, Alexandre, *L'egyptienne* (operetta)
MacDowell, Edward, *12 Piano Studies, Opus 39*
Massenet, Jules, *Visions* (symphonic poem)
Pfitzner, Hans, *Sonata, Opus 1, for Cello and Piano*
Pierné, Gabriel, *Suite No. 1 for Orchestra*
Reyer, Ernest, *Salammbô* (opera)
Rimsky-Korsakov, Nikolai, *Mlada* (opera)
Vaughan-Williams, Ralph, *Organ Overture*
Widor, Charles, *Organ Symphonies No. 7 and 8*

1891

World Events:

In the U.S., the United States Court of Appeals is formed to relieve the pressure on the Supreme Court; the Populist party is formed by protesting farmers in Ohio; the International Copyright Law is passed by Congress; the Electric Car is developed by William Morrison; Yellowstone National Park is formed by the Forest Reserve Act; America's showman, P. T. Barnum, dies. Internationally, the United States of Brazil is established in South America; the Triple Alliance of Italy, Austria and Germany is renewed; the Duomintang is formed by Sun Yat-sen in promote Chinese democracy and reform; work begins on the Trans-Siberian Railway (finished in 1917)

Cultural Highlights:

The magazines *Bookman* and *Strand Magazine* begin publication; Edgar Cameron becomes art critic for the Chicago *Tribune.* Births in the art world include American artist Edwin Dickinson, German artists Otto Dix and Max Ernst, French sculptor Henri Gaudier-Brzeska and Lithuanian-born sculptor Jacques Lipschitz; deaths include French artists Jules E. Delaunay, Ernest Meissonier, Georges Seurat and sculptor Henri M. Chapu, Scottish sculptor John Steell, German artist Karl Oesterley and sculptor Ernst Hähnel. Births in the literary field include French novelist Jean Cocteau, German poet Nelly Sachs, Russian author Mikhail Bulgakov and Swedish poet and novelist Pär Lagerkvist; deaths include Americans James Russell Lowell and Hermann Melville, French poets Théodore de Banville and Arthur Rimbaud, Czech novelist and poet Jan Neruda, Spanish author Pedro de Alarcón and German poet Oskar von Redwitz. Other highlights include:

Art: Philip Calderon, *The Renunciation of St. Elizabeth*; Mary Cassatt, *La Toilette*; Paul Cézanne, *The Card Players*; Paul Gauguin, *Hail Mary*; Winslow Homer, *Huntsman and Dogs*; James Kelly, *Call to Arms*; Claude Monet, *Haystacks*; Albert Ryder, *Siegfried and the Rhinemaidens*; Henri de Toulouse-Latrec, *At the Moulin Rouge*

Literature: Edwin Arnold, *The Light of the World*; James Barrie, *The Little Minister*; Arthur C. Doyle, *The Adventures of Sherlock Holmes*; Hamlin Garland, *Main-Travelled Roads*; Thomas Hardy, *Tess of the d'Urbervilles*; Rudyard Kipling, *The Light That Failed*; George du Maurier, *Peter Ibbetson*; Herman Melville, *Billy Budd*

MUSICAL EVENTS

A. Births:

Jan 12	Florence Macbeth (Am-sop)	Jun 21	Hermann Scherchen (Ger-cd)
Jan 20	Emmanuel Bay (Rus-pn)	Aug 2	Arthur Bliss (Br-cm)
Jan 20	Mischa Elman (Rus-vn)	Aug 8	Adolph Busch (Ger-vn-cd)
Jan 25	Anthony Bernard (Br-cd)	Sep 3	Marcel Granjany (Fr-hp)
Jan 28	Karel B. Jirák (Cz-cm-cd)	Sep 6	John Charles Thomas (Am-bar)
Feb 1	Alexander Kipnis (Rus-bs)	Sep 12	Adolph Weiss (Am-bn-cm)
Feb 15	Dino Borgioli (It-ten)	Sep 24	Karin Branzell (Swe-alto)
Mar 28	Paul Whiteman (Am-pop)	Sep 26	Charles Munch (Fr-cd)
Apr 23	Serge Prokofiev (Rus-cm)	Oct 6	Hans Mersmann (Ger-mus)
May 4	Frederick Jacobi (Am-cm)	Oct 14	Joseph Maddy (Am-m.ed)
May 22	Lucien Calliet (Fr-cm-arr)	Oct 25	Karl Elmendorff (Ger-cd)
May 27	Claude Champagne (Can-cm)	Nov 18	Maria Ivogün (Hun-sop)
Jun 9	Cole Porter (Am-pop)	Dec 13	Samuel Dushkin (Pol-vn)
Jun 19	Michel Piastro (Rus-vn-cd)	Dec 25	Lotte Schöne (Aus-sop)

B. Deaths:

Jan 5	Emma Abbott (Am-sop)	Jan 16	Léo Delibes (Fr-cm)
Jan 7	Louis A. Vidal (Fr-cd)	Jan 17	Johannes Verhulst (Hol-cd-cm)

Feb 22	Josephine de Reszke (Pol-sop)	Jul 21	Franco Faccio (It-cd)
Apr 25	George Hart (Br-vn.m)	Aug 6	Henry C. Litoff (Br-pub)
Apr 30	Johann C. Hauff (Ger-the)	Aug 22	Livia Frege (Ger-sop)
Jun	Fanny Salvini-Donatelli (It-sop)	Dec 23	Holger S. Paulli (Den-cd)
Jul 4	Frédéric Ritter (Ger-cd)		

C. Debuts:

Met --- Emma Albani (sop), Mathilde Bauermeister (sop), Bella Baumann (sop), Eduardo Camera (bar), Emma Eames (sop), Adeline Epstein (sop), Anna Fields (mez), Oscar Gerber, (bar), Minnie Hauk (sop), Hermann Hoveman (bs), Selma Kronold (sop), Phillip Lellman (ten), Antonio Magini-Coletti (bar), Anna Mantel (mez), Lillian Nordica (sop), Maria Pettigiani (sop), Giulia (mez) and Sophia (sop) Ravogli, Edouard (bs) and Jean (ten) de Reszke, Enrico Serbolini, Antonio de Vascheti (bs), Jane de Vigne (mez), Marie van Zandt (sop)

U.S. -- Joseph Breil (N.Y.), Arthur Friedheim (N.Y.), Vladimir de Pachmann (tour), Edouard de Reszke (Chicago), Xavier Scharwenka (N.Y.)

Other - David Bispham (London), Marie Brema (London), Karl Burian (Brno), Francesco Daddi (Milan), Angelina DeLara (London), Arthur van Eweyk (Berlin), Edoardo Garbin (Vincenza), Eugenio Giraldoni (Barcelona), Fiorello Giraud (Vercelli), Marie Gutheil-Schoder (Weimar), Marcel Journet (Bézières), Adolphe Maréchal (Tournai), Joseph O'Mara (London), Selma von Scheidt (Elberfeld), Erik Schmedes (Wiesbaden, as baritone), Ethel Sharpe (London), Minnie Tracey (Geneva)

D. New Positions:

Conductors: Gustav Mahler (Hamburg Opera), Willem Mengelberg (Lucerne), Anton Seidl (New York PO), Theodore Thomas (Chicago SO), Felix Weingartner (Berlin Opera)

Educational: Max Bruch (composition, Berlin Hochschule), Ferruccio Busoni (New England Conservatory), Théodore Dubois (composition, Paris Conservatory), Antonin Dvorák (Prague Conservatory), Giuseppe Gallignani (director, Parma Cons.), Armand Gumprecht (organ, Georgetown University), Joseph Jongen (harmony and counterpoint, Liège Conservatory.), Edgar S. Kelley (piano, New York College of Music), Albert Lavignac (theory, Paris Conservatory), August Winding (director, Copenhagen Conservatory)

Others: Richard Aldrich (music critic, New York *Times*), Philip Hale (music critic, Boston *Journal*), James G. Huneker (music critic, New York *Recorder*)

E. Prizes and Honors:

Prizes: Paul Henri Lebrun (Prix de Rome), Charles Silver (Prix de Rome)

Honors: Anton Bruckner (honorary doctorate, Vienna), Victor Duvernoy (Legion of Honor), Antonin Dvorák (honorary doctorates, Cambridge and Prague), Augustus Harris (knighted), Gustave-Léon Huberti (Belgian Academy), Charles H. Parry (honorary doctorate, Dublin)

F. Biographical Highlights:

Teresa Arkel makes her La Scala debut; Béla Bartók makes his piano debut; Ramon Blanchart, Emma Eames, Pol Plançon and Ernest Van Dyck make their Covent Garden debuts; Adolf Brodsky moves to the U.S. and becomes concertmaster of the New York SO; Anton Bruckner retires from teaching at the Vienna Conservatory; Ferruccio Busoni moves to the U.S.; Edward Elgar settles at Malvern; Joseph Jongen becomes assistant professor at Liège Conservatory; Hugo Leichtentritt and Daniel G. Mason enter Harvard; Ethelbert Nevin travels to Europe as performer and teacher; Hubert Parry becomes examiner for the London University Music Department; Giacomo Puccini acquires a home on the lake at Torre del Lago; Sims Reeves retires; Maurice Renaud makes his Paris Opera debut; Ottorino Respighi enters the Bologna

Musical Lyceum; Joseph Suk graduates from Prague Conservatory; Peter Tchaikovsky visits the U.S. at the opening of Carnegie Hall; Theodore Thomas goes to work for G. Schirmer; Ermanno Wolf-Ferrari enters the Academy of Fine Arts in Rome.

G. Institutional Openings:

Performing Groups: Bellmanska Söllskapet (Stockholm choir); Chicago SO; Cleveland Singers' Club; Copenhagen Cecilia Society; Czech String Quartet; Lehrergesangverein (Zurich); Leipziger Männerchor; Scottish Orchestra (Glasgow); Zurich Opera and Opera House

Educational: Melbourne University Chair of Music; Scharwenka Conservatory, New York Branch; University of Kansas School of Fine Arts

Other: Carnegie Hall (New York); *Il Corriere di Napoli*; Independent Theatre Society (London); International Copyright Agreement; *Music*; *Nuevo Teatro Crítico* (Madrid); Orfeó Catalá (Barcelona); Palace Theatre (London); Vancouver Opera House

H. Musical Literature:

Aikin, Jesse B., *True Principles of the Science of Music*
Dubois, Théodore, *87 Leçons d'harmonie*
Ehrlich, Heinrich, *Musikstudium und Klavierspiel*
Jullien, Adolphe, *Musiciens d'Aujourd'hui I*
Kashkin, Nicolai, *First 25 Years of the Moscow Conservatory*
Pedrell, Felipe, *Por nuestra música*
Prout, Ebenezer, *Double Counterpoint, Canon & Fugue*
Ritter, Frédéric, *Music in Its Relation to Intellectual Life*
Wallaschek, Richard, *On the Origin of Music*

I. Musical Compositions:

Brahms, Johannes, *Trio, Opus 114, for Clarinet, Violin and Piano*
  Clarinet Quintet, Opus 115
Bruch, Max, *Concerto No. 3 for Violin and Orchestra*
Chabrier, Emmanuel, *Marche Joyeuse* (orchestra)
Chadwick, George, *Overture, Melpomene* (orchestra)
Dvořák, Antonin, *Piano Trio, Opus 90, "Dumky"*
  Overture, In Nature's Realm, Opus 91 (tone poem)
  Carnaval Overture, Opus 92
Fauré, Gabriel, *Valse-Caprice No. 3, Opus 59* (piano)
Foerster, Joseph B., *Deborah, Opus 41* (opera)
  Orchestral Suite in C Major
Foote, Arthur, *Francesca da Rimini, Opus 24* (symphonic prologue)
Grieg, Edvard, *Lyric Pieces, Book V, Opus 54* (piano)
d'Indy, Vincent, *Tableaux de voyage, Opus 36*
Lalo, Edouard, *Néron* (ballet)
Mascagni, Pietro, *L'amico Fritz* (opera)
Rachmaninoff, Sergei, *Concerto No. 1, Opus 1, for Piano and Orchestra*
Reinecke, Carl, *Der Gouverneur von Tours* (opera)
Saint-Saëns, Camille, *Africa Fantasy for Piano and Orchestra*
Scriabin, Alexander, *Symphony No. 1, Opus 26*
Sullivan, Arthur, *Ivanhoe* (opera)
Tchaikovsky, Peter I., *Hamlet, Opus 67b* (incidental music)
  Iolanthe, Opus 69 (opera)
  The Voyvoda, Opus 78 (symphonic ballad)
Wolf, Hugo, *Italianisches Liederbuch* (song cycle)

1892

World Events:

In the U.S., Grover Cleveland is elected for the second time, making him both President No. 22 and President No. 24; Charles Duryea and Henry Ford both enter the automobile manufacturing business; General Electric Co. is incorporated; W. S. Burroughs patents the adding machine. Internationally, William Gladstone begins his last term as Prime Minister of England; Rudolph Diesel patents the Diesel engine; the Gilbert and Ellis Islands become a protectorate of Great Britain; Abba II becomes Khedive of Egypt; an Old Age Pension is first set up in Denmark.

Cultural Highlights:

This is the year of the Munich Secession in art; Eugène Boudin and Jules Verne are inducted into the Legion of Honor. American artist Grant Wood is born; deaths include American artist William M. Harnett, sculptor Randolph Rogers, French artist Ernest A. Guys, sculptor Jean M. Bonnassieux and German sculptor Albert Wolff. Births in the literary field include American poets Archibald MacLeish and Edna St. Vincent-Millay, dramatist Elmer L. Rice, novelist Pearl S. Buck, British poets Richard Aldington, Osbert Sitwell and author J.R.R. Tolkien; deaths include American poets Thomas W. Parsons, Walt Whitman and John Greenleaf Whittier, British poet Alfred Lord Tennyson and German poet Friedrich von Bodenstedt. Other highlights include:

Art: Thomas Clarke, *Night Market, Morocco*; Thomas Eakins, *The Concert Singer*; Paul Gauguin, *Whispered Words*; William Harnett, *Old Models*; Winslow Homer, *After the Hunt*; Georges Rouault, *Job and His Friends*; Augustus Saint-Gaudens, *Diana*; Henri de Toulouse-Latrec, *Moulin Rouge 1892*; George Watts, *Sic Transit*.

Literature: Jane Barlow, *Irish Idylls*; Eugene Field, *With Trumpet and Drum*; Hamlin Garland, *A Spoil of Office*; Joel Chandler Harris, *Uncle Remus and His Friends*; Henrik Ibsen, *The Master Builder*; Rudyard Kipling, *The Naulakha*; Maurice Maeterlinck, *Pelléas et Mélisande*; Oscar Wilde, *Lady Windemere's Fan*; Émile Zola, *La Débacle*.

MUSICAL EVENTS

A. Births:

Jan 2	Artur Rodzinski (Pol-cd)	Jun 21	Hilding Rosenberg (Swe-cm)
Jan 8	Hans Kindler (Hol-cd)	Jul 1	Ruth Miller (Am-sop)
Jan 30	Charles Haubiel (Am-cm-ed)	Jul 11	Giorgio F. Ghedini (It-cm)
Mar 10	Arthur Honegger (Swi-cm)	Aug 3	Oscar van Hemel (Bel-cm)
Mar 27	Ferde Grofé (Am-cm-arr)	Aug 15	Knud Jeppesen (Den-mus)
Apr 10	Victor de Sabata (It-cd)	Aug 16	Sophie Braslau (Am-alto)
Apr 13	Gladys Moncrieff (Aus-sop)	Sep 4	Darius Milhaud (Fr-cm)
Apr 19	Germaine Tailleferre (Fr-cm)	Sep 5	Joseph Szigeti (Hun-vn)
Apr 26	Harold Gleason (Am-org-mus)	Sep 17	Hendrik Andriessen (Hol-cm)
Apr 28	John Jacob Niles (Am-folk)	Oct 2	Gilda Dalla Rizza (It-sop)
May 1	Howard Barlow (Am-cd)	Oct 11	Richard Burgin (Am-vn)
May 18	Ezio Pinza (It-bar)	Oct 17	Herbert Howells (Br-cm)
May 29	Mario Chamlee (Am-ten)	Oct 17	Otakar Jeremiáš (Cz-cm-cd)
May 30	Guido Maria Gatti (It-mus)	Nov 28	Robert Lachmann (Ger-mus)
Jun 13	Valeriya Barsova (Rus-sop)	Dec 11	Giacomo Lauri-Volpi (It-ten)

B. Deaths:

Jan 8	Baldassare Gamucci (It-cm-au)	Feb 27	Moritz Deutsch (Ger-ten)
Jan 10	Jean Baptiste Chollet (Fr-ten)	Mar 20	Ernst Pasqué (Ger-bar)
Jan 10	Heinrich Dorn (Ger-cm-cd)	Apr 22	Edouard Lalo (Fr-cm)
Jan 11	Arnold J. Blaes (Bel-cl)	May 6	Ernest Guiraud (Am-cm)
Feb 13	Lambert Massart (Bel-vn)	Jun 9	Friedrich Langhans (Ger-mus)
Feb 22	Catherine Stephens (Br-sop)	Jul 11	Rudolf Westphal (Ger-mus)

Aug 18	Zélia Trebelli (Fr-alto)	Nov 8	Alfred G. Badger (Am-fl.m)
Sep 24	Patrick Gilmore (Am-cd)	Nov 30	Anne Charton-Demeur (Fr-mez)
Oct 24	Robert Franz (Ger-cm)	Dec 25	Karl A. Fischer (Ger-org)
Nov 3	Hervé (Ger-cm-imp)		

C. Debuts:

Met --- Luigi Arditi (cd), Agostino Carbone (bs), Jean Louis Lassalle (bar), Sebastian Montariol (ten), Adelina Patti (sop), Margaret Reid (sop), Greta Risley (mez)

U.S. -- Martha Leffler-Burckhard (tour), Henri Marteau (tour)

Other - Robert Blass (Weimar), Lucienne Bréval (Paris), Clara Butt (London), Peter Cornelius (Copenhagen), Ada Crossley (Melbourne), Léon David (Paris), Marie Delna (Paris), Evangeline Florence (London), Carl Friedberg (Vienna), Ludwig Hess, Heinrich Knote (Munich), Salomea Krushelnytska (Lvov), Maria Mikhailova (St.Petersburg), Rosa Olitzka (Brünn), Jean Périer (Paris), Frances Saville (Brussels), Rosina Storchio (Milan)

D. New Positions:

Conductors: Edouard Colonne (Paris Opera), Léon Dubois (Théâtre de la Monnaie, Brussels), Andreas Hallén (Stockholm Opera), Alexander Mackenzie (London PO), Karl Muck (Berlin Opera)

Educational: Joseph Barnby (principal, Guildhall School), Alfred J. Caldicott (director, London College of Music), Antonin Dvorák (N.Y. Conservatory), Percy Goetschius (New England Conservatory), Gustaf Helsted (theory, Copenhagen Conservatory), Georges Humbert (music history, Geneva Conservatory), Emile Jaques-Dalcroze (harmony, Geneva Conservatory), Martin-Pierre Marsick (violin, Paris Conservatory), Raoul Pugno (harmony, Paris Conservatory), Martin Röder (voice, New England Conservatory), Otakar Ševčík (Prague Conservatory)

Others: Basil Harwood (organ, Christ Church, Oxford)

E. Prizes and Honors:

Prizes: Samuel-Alexandre Rousseau (City of Paris)

Honors: Joseph Barnby, William Cusins & Walter Parratt (knighted), Francisco A. Barbieri (Spanish Royal Academy), Hans Huber (honorary doctorate, Basle), Vincent d'Indy (Legion of Honor), William Leibl (Berlin Academy), Emile Paladilhe (French Institute), Camille Saint-Saëns (honorary doctorate, Cambridge)

F. Biographical Highlights:

Hugo Alfvén finally decides on a musical career; Max Alvary, David Bispham, Ernestine Schumann-Heink and Rosa Sucher all make their Covent Garden debuts; Granville Bantock graduates from the Royal Academy of Music; Ramon Blanchart and Karl Schiedemantel make their La Scala debuts; Arrigo Boito is made Inspector-General of the Italian conservatories; Henry Burleigh enters the National Conservatory in New York; Teresa Carreño marries her third husband, pianist Eugène d'Albert; Paul Dukas begins music criticism; Anna Essipova divorces Theodor Leschetizky; Gabriel Fauré accepts post as Inspector of Fine Arts; Johanna Gadski marries officer Hans Tauscher; Gustav Mahler conducts a German troupe in London; Carl Nebe debuts at Bayreuth; Nicholai Rimsky-Korsakov suffers a nervous breakdown; Arthur Shepherd enters the New England Conservatory; Jan Sibelius marries Aïno Järnefelt; John Phillip Sousa retires from the Marines to form his own band; Richard Strauss, seriously ill, spends the winter in Egypt; Ermanno Wolf-Ferrari transfers to Munich's Akademie der Tonkunst.

G. Institutional Openings:

Performing Groups: Association des Chanteurs de St. Gervais; Barcewicz String Quartet (Warsaw); Bohemian String Quartet (Prague); Orpheus Club of Oakland (California);

Parent String Quartet (Paris); People's Choral Union of New York; Societatea Simfonica "Buciumul" (Romania); Societatea Simfonica "Lyra" (Romania); John Phillip Sousa Band; Wellington Orchestra Society (New Zealand)

Festivals: Cardiff Triennial Festival

Educational: Ithaca Conservatory of Music; Kühner Music School (St. Petersburg); *School Music Review*

Other: Bibliographical Society of London; Bühnen der Stadt Essen; Circolo Scarlatti (Naples); Jakubowski Publishing House (Lvov); Manuscript Music Society (Philadelphia); New York Public Library; Semaines Saintes de St. Gervais (Paris); Slovene Regional Theater (Ljubljana); Union Gospel Tabernacle (Nashville)

H. Musical Literature:
Clarke, Hugh A., *Theory Explained*
Cummings, W.H., *Biographical Dictionary of Musicians*
Fleischer, Oskar, *Führer durch die Sammlung alter Musikinstrumente*
Gevaert, François-Auguste, *Abrégé du nouveau traité d'instrumentation*
Goetschius, Percy, *Theory and Practice of Tone Relations*
Hadow, W.H., *Studies in Modern Music I*
Hanslick, Eduard, *Aus dem Tagebuch eines Musikers*
Mach, Ernst, *Beitrag zur geschichte der Musik*
Meerens, Charles, *Acoustique musicale*
Stainer, John, *Music in Relation to the Intellect and Emotions*

I. Musical Compositions:
Brahms, Johannes, *Piano Intermezzi, Opus 117*
    6 Piano Pieces, Opus 118
    4 Piano Pieces, Opus 119
Bruckner, Anton, *Psalm 150* (chorus and orchestra)
Charpentier, Gustave, *La Vie du Poète* (cantata)
Chausson, Ernest, *Poème de l'Amour et de la Mer, Opus 19* (voice and orchestra)
Debussy, Claude, *Fêtes Galantes, Set I* (songs)
Delius, Frederick, *Irmelin* (opera)
Dukas, Paul, *Polyeucte Overture*
Dvořák, Antonin, *Othello, Opus 93* (symphonic poem)
Elgar, Edward, *Serenade, Opus 20, for String Orchestra*
Fauré, Gabriel, *La Bonne Chanson, Opus 61* (song cycle)
German, Edward, *Henry VIII* (incidental music)
Giordano, Umberto, *Mala Vita* (opera)
Glazounov, Alexander, *Le Printemps, Opus 34*
Leoncavallo, Ruggero, *I Pagliacci* (opera)
Massenet, Jules, *Werther* (opera)
Nevin, Ethelbert, *The Rosary* (song)
Parry, Hubert, *Job* (oratorio)
Rachmaninoff, Serge, *Aleko* (opera)
    5 Pieces for Piano, Opus 3
Scriabin, Alexander, *Piano Sonata No. 1*
Sibelius, Jan, *En Saga, Opus 9* (tone poem)
    Kullervo, Opus 7 (oratorio)
Suk, Josef, *Serenade for Strings*
Tchaikovsky, Peter I., *The Nutcracker, Opus 71* (ballet)
Vaughan-Williams, Ralph, *Super Flumina Babylonis*

1893

World Events:

In the U.S., a financial panic ushers in a four-year depression; the Cimarron Strip is opened in the Oklahoma Territory; Sears, Roebuck and Co. is founded in Chicago; Thomas Edison patents the kinetograph; the Columbian Exposition is held in Chicago where the Ferris Wheel is introduced; the Field Musuem of Natural History opens in Chicago; former President Rutherford B. Hayes dies. Internationally, Hawaii becomes a republic after the withdrawal of the first treaty for U.S. annexation; New Zealand becomes the first country to allow women's suffrage; France takes over Laos as a protectorate; Pope Leo VII dies and Pope Pius X is elected new Pope.

Cultural Highlights:

The Art Institute of Chicago opens its doors; the National Sculpture Society is formed in the U.S. Births in the literary field include American authors Anita Loos, Dorothy Parker, novelist John Marquand and dramatist Samuel N. Behrman and British poet Wilfred Owen; deaths include French novelist Guy de Maupassant and Russian poet Aleksei Plescheyev. Births in the art world include American artists Milton Avery and Charles Burchfield, German artist George Grosz and Spanish artist and sculptor Joan Miró; deaths include British artist Ford M. Brown and German sculptor Robert Cauer. Other highlights include:

Art: Henry Bush-Brown, *Indian Buffalo Hunt*; Daniel French, *Angel of Death and the Sculptor*; Paul Gauguin, *Annah, the Javanese Girl*; Hermann Knackfuss, *The Holy Family*; Constantin Meunier, *The Longshore-man*; Edvard Munch, *The Scream*; Georges Rouault, *The Ordeal of Samson*; Henry O. Tanner, *The Banjo Lesson*.

Literature: John Davidson, *Fleet Street Eclogues*; Arthur C. Doyle, *Memoirs of Sherlock Holmes*; Henry Fuller, *The Cliff-Dwellers*; Hamlin Garland, *Prairie Folk*; Henry James, *The Real Thing and Other Tales*; David Locke, *The Nasby Letters*; Stéphane Mallarmé, *Vers et Prose*; Robert L. Stevenson, *David Balfour*; Émile Zola, *Dr. Pascal*.

MUSICAL EVENTS

A. Births:

Jan 5	Friedrich Blume (Ger-mus)	Aug 15	Alexander Gauk (Rus-cd-cm)
Feb 4	Bernard Rogers (Am-cm)	Aug 18	Ernest C. Macmillan (Can-cm)
Feb 17	Andrés Segovia (Sp-gui)	Aug 21	Lili Boulanger (Fr-cm)
Mar 31	Clemens Krauss (Ger-cd)	Sep 3	Anthony Collins (Br-cd)
Apr 10	Astra Desmond (Br-alto)	Sep 18	Arthur Benjamin (Br-cm)
May 16	Paul Pisk (Aus-cm)	Sep 29	Fabian Sevitsky (Rus-cd)
May 20	Hans Nissen (Ger-bar)	Oct 4	Hans Schnoor (Ger-mus)
May 26	Eugene Goosens (Br-cd)	Oct 9	Mário de Andrade (Bra-mus)
May 30	Rosa Raisa (Pol-sop)	Oct 10	Willi Apel (Ger-mus)
Jun 10	Franz André (Bel-cd)	Oct 17	Jean Binet (Swi-cm)
Jun 21	Alois Hába (Cz-cm-the)	Oct 23	Jean Absil (Bel-cm)
Jun 27	Toti Dal Monte (It-sop)	Dec 7	Ilona Kabos (Hun-pn)
Jul 18	Willi Kahl (Ger-mus)	Dec 15	Edwin F. Kalmus (Am-pub)
Aug 2	Alfred Alessandrescu	Dec 16	Vladimir Golschman (Fr-cd)
	(Rom-cm-cd)	Dec 18	Josef Rufer (Ger-mus)
Aug 10	Douglas Moore (Am-cm)		Martha Graham (Am-bal)

B. Deaths:

Jan 13	Melitta Otto (Ger-sop)	Jun 15	Franz Erkel (Hun-cd-cm)
Jan 19	Julius Eichberg (Ger-vn)	Jul 8	Karl A. Riccius (Ger-vn)
Feb 26	Hermine Spies (Ger-alto)	Aug 5	Gustav Schirmer (Am-pub)
Mar 11	Georges Chanot, Jr. (Fr-vn.m)	Aug 7	Alfredo Catalani (It-cm)
Mar 31	Julius Melgunov (Rus-pn)	Aug 31	William Cusins (Br-pn-cm)

Sep 5 John S. Dwight (Br-cri)
Oct 16 Carlo Pedrotti (It-cm-cd)
Oct 18 Charles Gounod (Fr-cm)
Oct 24 Joseph Hellmesberger
(Aus-vn-cd)

Nov 6 Peter Tchaikovsky (Rus-cm)
Nov 14 Theodor Wachtel (Ger-ten)
Dec 1 Carl Kossmaly (Ger-mus)
Dec 9 George J. Elvey (Br-org)

C. Debuts:

Met --- Mario Ancona (bar), Sigrid Arnoldson (sop), Enrico Bevignani (cd), Emma Calvé (sop), Armand Castelmary (bs), Virginia Colombati (sop), Eugène Dufriche (bar), Pedro Guetary (ten), Elvira de Hidalgo (sop), Fernando de Lucia (ten), Luigi Mancinelli (cd), Georges Mauguière (ten), Nellie Melba (sop), Pol Plançon (bs)

U.S. -- Giuseppe Campanari (tour), Ben Davies (tour), Harry Plunkett Greene (tour), Alexandre Guilmant (tour), Vilhelm Herold (Chicago), Charles Manners (tour), Henri Marteau (tour), Alice Nielsen (St.Paul), Maurice Renaud (New Orleans), Joseph von Slivinski (tour)

Other - Harold Bauer (Paris), Lillian Blauvelt (Brussels), Alessandor Bonci (Parma), Giuseppe Borgatti (Castelfranco Veneto), Oto Briesemeister (Dessau), Alexander Davidov (Tiflis), Ivan Ershov (St. Petersburg), Vilhelm Herold (Copenhagen), Louise Kirkby-Lunn (London), Ernst Kraus (Munich), Adrienne von Kraus-Osborne (Leipzig), Lina Pasini (Milan), Aloys Pennarini (Pressburg), Thila Plaichinger (Hamburg), R. Kennerley Rumford (London), Thomas Salignac (Paris), Susan Strong (London), Rose Sutro (London) Egisto Tango (Venice)

D. New Positions:

Conductors: Raoul Gunsbourg (Monte Carlo Opera), George Henschel (Scottisch SO), Victor Herbert (Twenty Second Regiment Band), Felix Mottl (Karlsruhe Opera), Arthur Nikisch (Opera Royal, Budapest), Emil Paur (Boston SO)

Educational: Edward Dickinson (music history, Oberlin), Anna Essipova (piano, St. Petersburg Conservatory), Carl Friedberg (piano, Frankfurt Conservatory), Mikhail Ippolitov-Ivanov (composition, Moscow Conservatory), Isidore Philipp (piano, Paris Conservatory), Jan Sibelius (theory, Helsinki Conservatory)

Others: Granville Bantock (editor, *New Quarterly Musical Review*), Nikolai Findeisen (editor, *Russian Musical Gazette*), Edgar S. Kelley (music critic, San Francisco *Examiner*), Horatio Parker (choir and organ, Trinity Church, Boston), Heinrich Reimann (curator, Berlin Royal Library)

E. Prizes and Honors:

Prizes: Henri Büsser (Prix de Rome), Francesco Cilea (Crown of Italy), Lodewijk Mortelmans (Prix de Rome)

Honors: Arrigo Boito and Max Bruch (honorary doctorates, Cambridge), Walter Parratt (Master of the Queen's Music)

F. Biographical Highlights:

Isaac Albéniz settles permanently in Paris; Mario Ancona, Marie Brema, Nellie Melba and Milka Ternina all make their Covent Garden debuts; Vittorio Arimondi, Clotilde Bressler-Gianoli, Edoardo Garbin, Nellie Melba and Antonio Pini-Corsi all make their La Scala debuts; Irving Berlin is brought to the U.S.; Frederick Converse graduates from Harvard; Antonin Dvorák discovers the Bohemian colony at Spilsville, Iowa; Arthur Farwell graduates with an engineering degree; Joseph Forster moves to Hamburg and becomes a local music critic; Gustav Holst and John Ireland enter the Royal College of Music; Nicolai Miaskovsky is sent to military school; Horatio Parker resigns his posts in New York and moves to Boston; Fritz Scheel emigrates to the U.S.; Ernestine Schumann-Heink divorces her husband and marries Paul Schumann; Bruno Walter becomes a coach at Cologne Opera.

G. Institutional Openings:

Performing Groups: Brooklyn Oratorio Society; Capet String Quartet I (Paris); Kaim Orchestra (Munich); Popular Concerts (St. Petersburg); Munich PO; Newark SO; Royal Flemish Opera Company; Saint Louis Amateur (Philharmonic Society) Orchestra

Educational: Royal Manchester College of Music; Schweizerische Musikpädagogische Verband (Zurich); Alberto Williams Conservatory of Music (Argentina)

Other: Brockhaus Publishing Co. (Leipzig); Cape Town Opera House; *The Etude*; *Gazeta Musicale* (Brazil); Karl Gehrman, Music Publisher (Sweden); Gray's Armory (Cleveland); King Musical Instrument Co. (Cleveland); Lengnick Music Publishers (London); National Federation of Music Clubs; *The New Quarterly Musical Review* (England); Queen's Hall (London); Raimundtheater (Vienna); *Russian Musical Gazette*; Sociedad de Autores, Compositores y Editores de Música (Madrid); Tamburini Organ Co. (Crema); B.F. Wood, Music Publisher

H. Musical Literature:

Curzon, Henri de, *Musiciens du temps passé*
Dannreuther, Edward, *Musical Ornamentation I*
Ehrlich, Heinrich, *Celebrated Pianists, Past & Present*
Gade, Niels, *Aufzeichnen und Briefe* (posthumous publication)
Hausegger, Friedrich von, *Vom jenseits des Kunstlers*
Parry, Hubert, *Art of Music*
Prout, Ebenezer, *Musical Form*
Wallaschek, Richard, *Primitive Music*

I. Musical Compositions:

Bristow, George, *Symphony No. 5, "Niagara", Opus 62* (with voices)
Debussy, Claude, *String Quartet*
Delius, Frederick, *The Magic Fountain* (opera)
Dvořák, Antonin, *Symphony No. 9, "From the New World"*
Elgar, Edward, *The Black Knight, Opus 25* (cantata)
Fibich, Zdenek, *Symphony No. 2, Opus 38*
Foerster, Josef B., *Symphony No. 2, Opus 29*
Foote, Arthur, *The Skeleton in Armor, Opus 28*
German, Edward, *Symphony No. 2*
Gilbert and Sullivan, *Utopia Unlimited* (operetta)
Glazounov, Alexander, *Triumphal March, Opus 40*
Goldmark, Karl, *Sappho Overture, Opus 44*
Gounod, Charles, *Requiem* (chorus and orchestra)
Grieg, Edvard, *Lyric pieces, Book VI, Opus 57*
Humperdinck, Engelbert, *Hansel und Gretel* (opera)
MacDowell, Edward, *Orchestral Suite No. 1, Opus 42*
    Piano Sonata No. 1, "Tragica"
Paderewski, Ignaz Jan, *Polish Fantasy, Opus 19, for Piano and Orchestra*
Parker, Horatio, *Hora Novissimo* (oratorio)
Puccini, Giacomo, *Manon Lescaut* (opera)
Rachmaninoff, Serge, *12 Songs, Opus 4 and 8*
    Suite No. 1 for Two Pianos, Opus 5
    The Rock, Opus 7 (symphonic fantasy)
Sibelius, Jan, *Karelia Suite, Opus 11*
    The Swan of Tuonela, Opus 22 (symphonic legend)
Stenhammar, Wilhelm, *Concerto No. 1 for Piano and Orchestra*
Tchaikovsky, Peter, *Symphony No. 6, Opus 74, "Pathétique"*
    Concerto No. 3, Opus 75, for Piano and Orchestra
Verdi, Giuseppe, *Falstaff* (opera)

1894

World Events:
In the U.S., Jacob Coxey leads an "army" of unemployed in a march on Washington; a bitter Pullman Strike spreads; Labor Day is made an official government holiday; a graduated income tax law is passed by Congress; the United Daughters of the Confederacy is organized; the first sunday comics are printed; a Chinese Exclusion Treaty is signed with China. Internationally, the Sino-Japanese War begins; the Dreyfus Affair begins with the conviction of Captain Alfred Dreyfus of treason in France; the Turks begin the eradication of the Armenians; the Diesel engine is perfected; Alexander III of Russian dies and is succeeded by Nicholas II.

Cultural Highlights:
The Denver Art Museum opens; Eragny Press is founded in Bedford Park, London; the Ashendene Press is founded by C. H. St. John Hornby; Edward J. Poynter becomes director of the National Gallery of Art; Rosa Bonheur is given the Grand Cross of the Legion of Honor. Births in the literary field include American authors e. e. cummings, Mark Van Doren and James Thurber, British authors Aldous Huxley and J. B. Priestley and Swedish poet-novelist Frans Bengtsson; deaths include American poet Oliver Wendall Holmes, British poet Christina Rossetti and author Walter Pater, French poet Charles de Lisle, Scottish novelists Robert Ballantyne and Robert Louis Stevenson. Births in the art world include American artists Stuart Davis and Norman Rockwell and Finnish sculptor Wäinö Aaltonen; deaths include American artists Georges Inness and George Healy, French sculptor Pierre Cavelier and Irish sculptor Launt Thompson. Other highlights include:

Art: George Barnard, *The Struggle of Man's Two Natures*; Cyrus Dallin, *The Signal of Peace*; Paul Gauguin, *The Day of the God*; Winslow Homer, *Artist's Studio in the Fog*; Claude Monet, *Rouen Cathedral, Early Morning*; Boardman Robinson, *On the Tow Path*; Philip Steer, *Girls Running on Walberick Pier*; Édouard Vuillard, *Jardin de Paris*

Literature: Gabriele d'Annunzio, *The Triumph of Death*; Anthony Hawkins, *The Prisoner of Zenda*; William D. Howells, *Traveller from Altruria*; Kipling Rudyard, *Jungle Book*; Pierre Louijs, *Les Chansons de Bilitis*; George du Maurier, *Trilby*; George B. Shaw, *Arms and the Man*; Mark Twain, *The Tragedy of Pudd'nhead Wilson*

MUSICAL EVENTS

A. Births:

Jan 20	Walter Piston (Am-cm)
Feb 6	André Marchal (Fr-org)
Feb 27	Alexandrowitsch Dobrowen (Rus-cm)
Apr 26	Rosa Pauly (Hun-sop)
Apr 27	Florence Austral (Aust-sop)
May 7	Nicolas Slonimsky (Rus-cm-cd)
Jun 15	Edmond Appia (Swi-cd)
Jun 17	Robert R. Bennett (Am-cm-arr)
Jul 18	Pierre Luboshutz (Rus-pn)
Jul 25	Bernard Wagenaar (Hol-cm)
Aug 26	Kresimir Baranovic (Yug-cd-cm)
Aug 28	Arthur Loesser (Am-pn-au)
Aug 28	Karl Böhm (Aus-cd)
Sep 8	William Pijper (Hol-cm)
Sep 22	Elizabeth Rethburg (Ger-sop)
Oct 30	Peter Warlock (Br-cm)
Nov 5	Eugene Zador (Hun-cm)
Nov 6	Guy F. Harrison (Br-cd)
Nov 11	Aaron Avshalomov (Rus-cm)
Nov 28	Frank Black (Am-cd)
Dec 10	Paul Dessau (Ger-cd-cm)
Dec 17	Arthur Fiedler (Am-cd)
Dec 20	Hans Engel (Ger-mus)
Dec 22	Mihail Andrieu (Rom-cm)
Dec 31	Ernest J. Moeran (Br-cm)

B. Deaths:

Jan 21	Guillaume Lekeu (Bel-cm)
Feb 9	Adolphe Sax (Bel-inv)
Feb 12	Hans von Bülow (Ger-cd)
Feb 16	Thomas A. Cook (Br-bs)
Feb 17	Francisco Barbieri (Sp-mus)
Feb 19	Camillo Sivori (It-vn)
Feb 28	Janet Patey (Scot-alto)
Mar 21	Jacob Rosenhaim (Ger-pn)

Apr 12	Karl R. Köstlin (Ger-the)	Jul 8	Vladimir Kashperov (Rus-cm)
Apr 13	Julius A. Spitta (Ger-mus)	Sep 13	Emmanuel Chabrier (Fr-cm)
Jun 13	Filippo Coletti (It-bar)	Oct 27	Alphons Czibulka (Hun-cm)
Jun 23	Marietta Alboni (It-alto)	Nov 4	Eugène Oudin (Am-bar)
Jun 27	August G. Fricke (Ger-bs)	Nov 20	Anton Rubinstein (Rus-cm)

C. Debuts:

Met --- Maurizio Bensaude (bar), Giuseppe Campanari (bar), Alfred Guille (ten), Mira Heller (sop), Lucille Hill (sop), Fernando de Lucia (ten), Zélie de Lussan (sop), Catullo Maestri (ten), Eugenia Mantelli (mez), Alfonso Mariani (bs), Victor Maurel (bar), Ottavio Nouvelli (ten), Olga Pavny (sop)

U.S. -- Marie Brema (tour), Benno Schönberger (tour), Ottilie and Rose Sutro (N.Y.), Ellen Beach Yaw (St. Paul), Eugène Ysaÿe (tour)

Other - Lina Abarbanell (Berlin), Enrico Caruso (Naples), Feodor Chaliapin (St. Petersburg), John Coates (London), Ivan Erschov (Kharkov), Katharina Fleischer-Edel (Dresden), Theodor Lierhammer (Vienna), Max Lohfing (Metz), Vanni Marcoux (Turin), Angelica Pandolfini (Modena), Edouard Risler (Paris), Halfdan Rode (London), Mario Sammarco (Milan), Ottilie Sutro (London), Jacques Urlus (Amsterdam), Edyth Walker (Berlin), Erika Wedekind (Dresden)

D. New Positions:

Conductors: José Eibenschütz (Abo SO, Finland), Richard Strauss (Munich Opera)

Educational: Karel Bendl (composition, Prague Conservatory), Johann Fuchs (director, Vienna Conservatory), Josef Hofmann (director, Curtis Institute), Gustav Hollaender (director, Stern Conservatory), Korbay Edmundo Pallemaerts (director, Conservatorio Argentino), Horatio Parker (head, Yale Music Dept.), Charles H. Parry (director, Royal College, London), Guy Ropartz (director, Nancy Cons.)

Others: John C. Runciman (music critic, *Saturday Review*), Luigi Torchi (editor, *Rivista Musicale Italiana*)

E. Prizes and Honors:

Prizes: Ossip Gabrilowitsch (Rubinstein), Henri Rabaud (Prix de Rome), Carl Thiel (Mendelssohn)

Honors: Théodore Dubois (French Academy), Edvard Grieg (honorary doctorate, Cambridge), Walter Parratt (honorary doctorate, Oxford), Felipe Pedrell (Royal Academy, Madrid), Valentine Prinsep (Royal Academy)

F. Biographical Highlights:

Max Alvary is seriously injured in a fall during a Mannheim rehearsal; Mily Balakirev makes his last public recital appearance; Anton Bruckner retires from public life due to illness; Ferruccio Busoni leaves the U.S. and settles in Berlin; Italo Campanini retires from the stage; Feodor Chaliapin, missing the post in Berlin, moves back to Munich; Charles Gilibert, Rosa Olitzka and Antonio Pini-Corsi make their Covent Garden debuts; Reinhold Glière enters the Moscow Conservatory; Rubin Goldmark, for health reasons, leaves New York for Colorado; Percy Grainger begins music study in Frankfurt; Henry Hadley begins music study in Vienna; Edward Burlingame Hill graduates from Harvard with highest honors; Serge Koussevitsky graduates from Moscow Conservatory; Albert Roussel resigns his navy commission to devote full time to music; Ralph Vaughan-Williams receives his B.M. from Trinity College; Bruno Walter begins working under Mahler in Hamburg.

G. Institutional Openings:

Performing Groups: American SO; British Chamber Music Concerts; Cincinnati Orchestra Association; Czech PO; Czech Society of Chamber Music; Fitzner String Quartet (Austria); Goosens Male-Voice Choir (Liverpool); Ladies Choral Union of

Budapest; Musical Art Society of New York; New Haven SO; Nicodé Concerts (Dresden); Philharmonische Populäre Künstlerkonzerte (Dresden); Maud Powell String Quartet; Schola Cantorum of Paris; Societana Filarmonica Româna (II); Toronto Mendelssohn Choir

Festivals: Ann Arbor May Festival

Educational: Conservatorio Santa Cecilia (Buenos Aires); Dominion College of Music (Montreal); Heidelberg Conservatory of Music; Lawrence College Conservatory of Music (Wisconsin); Yale Universtiy School of Music

Other: Abbey Theatre (Ireland); *The Billboard*; Hope-Jones Organ Co. (Birkenhead); Kansas City Athenaeum; Lyric Theater (Baltimore); Massey Hall (Toronto); *The Organist and Choirmaster*; Peter's Music Library (Leipzig), *Revista Musicale Italiana*; *Weekblad voor Musiek* (Holland)

H. Musical Literature:
Conus, Georgi, *Manual of Harmony*
Expert, Henry, *Les maîtres-musiciens de la renaissance française I*
Fuller-Maitland, J.A., *Masters of German Music*
Hanslick, Eduard, *Aus meinem Leben*
Hiles, Henry, *Harmony, Chordal or Contrapuntal*
Kistler, Cyrill, *Über originalität in Tonkunst*
Macpherson, Stewart, *Practical Harmony*
Meerens, Charles, *L'avenir de la science musicale*

I. Musical Compositions:
Brahms, Johannes, *2 Clarinet Sonatas, Opus 120*
Bruckner, Anton, *Symphony No. 9*
Chadwick, George, *Tabasco* (opera)
Debussy, Claude, *Prélude à l'après-midi d'un faun*
Dvořák, Antonin, *10 Biblical Songs, Opus 99*
    Suite for Piano, "American Suite"
Fauré, Gabriel, *Dolly, Opus 56* (piano, four hands)
Foote, Arthur, *Concerto for Cello and Orchestra*
    String Quartet in E Major, Opus 32
Glazunov, Alexander, *Symphony No. 4, Opus 48*
    Carnaval Overture (organ and orchestra)
Grieg, Edvard, *Norway, Opus 58* (song cycle)
Hadley, Henry, *Hector and Andromache, Overture*
Herbert, Victor, *Concerto No. 2 for Cello and Orchestra*
Ives, Charles, *Circus Band March*
MacDowell, Edward, *12 Virtuoso Studies, Opus 46*
Magnard, Albéric, *Symphony No. 1, Opus 4*
    Yolande (opera)
Mahler, Gustav, *Symphony No. 2, "Resurrection"*
Massenet, Jules, *Thaïs* (opera)
Nielson, Carl, *Symphony No. 1*
Rachmaninoff, Serge, *7 Pieces for Piano, Opus 10*
    Caprice bohémien, Opus 12
Reznicek, Emil von, *Donna Diana* (opera)
Rubinstein, Anton, *Moses* (opera)
Sibelius, Jan, *Spring Song, Opus 16*
Stanford, Charles, *Symphony No. 5, Opus 56*
Suk, Josef, *A Winter's Tale, Opus 9*
Sullivan, Arthur, *The Chieftain* (operetta)
Wolf, Hugo, *Italian Serenade*

1895

World Events:

In the U.S., the Monroe Doctrine is given a test by the Venezuela-British dispute; the first auto race takes place between Chicago and Waukegan, Illinois--average speed of 7 and a half miles per hour; the Boston subway, first in the nation, opens for service; the Duryea Motor Wagon Co. is founded in Massachusetts. Internationally, the Sino-Japanese War comes to an end as Japan defeats China; Marconi sends the first telegraph message on a one-mile wire; the Lumiere Brothers, in Paris, present the first moving pictures; W. K. Roentgen discovers X-rays; French scientist Louis Pasteur dies.

Cultural Highlights:

The Museo Naciónal de Bellas Artes opens in Buenos Aires; the M. H. de Young Memorial Museum opens in San Francisco; the Montreal Literary School opens its doors. In the world of art, births include Hungarian artist László Moholy-Nagy and American sculptor William M. Story; deaths include American artist Peter Rothermel and sculptor Leonard W. Volk, British sculptor John Bell, Italian artist Silvestro Lega, Dutch artist Maurice de Haas, Irish artist Thomas Hovenden and French artist Berthe Morisot. Births in the world of literature include Irish poet Robert R. Graves and French poet Paul Éluard; deaths include American author Frederick Douglass and poet Eugene Field, British author Thomas Huxley and French novelist Alexander Dumas, fils. Other highlights include:

Art: Pierre de Chavannes, *Inspiring Muses and Genius*; Edgar Degas, *Dancer Looking at Her Foot*; Winslow Homer, *Northeaster*; Adolf von Hildebrand, *Wittelsbach Fountain, Munich*; Käthe Kollwitz, *Revolt of the Weavers*; Edvard Munch, *The Cry*; Frederic Remington, *The Bronco Buster*; Henri Rousseau, *Tiger Hunt*

Literature: James Allen, *Aftermath*; Hilary Belloc, *Verses and Sonnets*; Joseph Conrad, *Almayer's Folly*; Stephen Crane, *The Red Badge of Courage*; George Meredith, *The Amazing Marriage*; Coventry Patmore, *Rod, Root and Flower*; Lev Tolstoy, *Master and Man*; H.G. Wells, *The Time Machine*; Oscar Wilde, *The Importance of Being Ernest*

MUSICAL EVENTS

A. Births:

Jan 7	Clara Haskil (Rom-pn)	Jul 12	Kirsten Flagstad (Nor-sop)
Feb 7	André Schaeffner (Fr-mus)	Jul 22	Hans Rosbaud (Aus-cd)
Feb 28	Guiomar Novaës (Bra-pn)	Aug 31	Joseph Schillinger (Rus-cm)
Mar 9	Isobel Baillie (Br-sop)	Sep 22	Herbert Janssen (Ger-bar)
Apr 3	Misha Mischakoff (Rus-vn)	Oct 21	Shukichi Mitsukuri (Jap-cm)
Apr 29	Malcolm Sargent (Br-cd)	Nov 5	Walter Gieseking (Fr-pn)
May 1	Leo Sowerby (Am-org-cm)	Nov 16	Paul Hindemith (Ger-cm)
May 8	Edmund Wilson (Am-dri)	Nov 20	Alexander László (Hun-cm)
May 11	William Grant Still (Am-cm)	Nov 21	Ernest Charles (Am-cm)
May 19	Albert Hay Malotte (Am-cm)	Nov 24	Erné Maison (Fr-ten)
May 19	Cecil Gray (Br-mus)	Nov 25	Wilhelm Kempff (Ger-pn)
May 30	Jelly d'Aranyi (Hun-vn)	Nov 28	José Iturbi (Sp-pn-cd)
Jul 5	Gordon Jacob (Br-cm)	Nov 30	Johann N. David (Ger-org)
Jul 5	Mogens Wöldike (Den-cd)	Dec 15	David Guion (Am-cm)
Jul 6	Grete Stückgold (Ger-sop)		Sydney Rayner (Am-ten)
Jul 10	Carl Orff (Ger-cm)		

B. Deaths:

Jan 10	Benjamin Godard (Fr-cm)	May 21	Franz von Suppé (Aus-cm)
Feb 24	Ignaz Lachner (Ger-cm-cd)	Jun 15	Richard Genée (Ger-cm)
Mar 25	Elizabeth Sterling (Br-org)	Jul 6	Elias Howe (Am-pub)

Jul 13   John Carrodus (Br-vn-cd)
Jul 15   Teresa Brambilla (It-sop)
Aug 6   George Root (Am-cm)
Sep 7   August Gemünder (Ger-vn.m)
Sep 8   Herman von Helmholtz
        (Ger-acous)

Sep 10   Harrison Millard (Am-cm)
Oct 25   Charles Hallé (Br-cd)
Nov 11   Gustave Flaxland (Fr-pub)
Nov 11   Julius Tausch (Ger-cm-cd)
Nov 26   E. Van der Straeten (Bel-mus)

C. Debuts:

Met --- Vittorio Arimondi (bs), Lloyd d'Aubigné (ten), Lola Beeth (sop), Marie Brema (mez), Giuseppe Cremonini (ten), Maurice Devries (bar), Marie Engle (sop), Clara Hunt (sop), Avrelia Kitzu (mez), John Liverman (bar), Albert Lubert (ten), Julia Miramer (sop), Otto Mirsalis (ten), Rosa Olitzka (mez), Sybil Sanderson (sop), Frances Saville (sop), Rosa Sucher (sop)

U.S. -- Perry Averill (Boston), Johanna Gadski (N.Y.), Katherina Klafsky (tour), Elsa Kutschera (tour), Martin-Pierre Marsick (tour), Joseph Sheehan (Boston), Pietro Tirindelli (Boston), Minnie Tracey (Philadelphia), Herbert Witherspoon (New Haven)

Other - Suzanne Adams (Paris), Giuseppe Agostini (Nuovi Ligure), Ernesto Badini (Milan), Clotilde Bressler-Gianoli (Geneva), Adam Didur (Rio de Janeiro), Riza Eibenschütz (Leipzig), Fritz Feinhals (Essen), Karl Flesch (Vienna), Olive Fremstad (Cologne), Otto Goritz (Neustrelitz), Selma Kurz (Bamburg), Blanche Marchesi (Berlin), Frank Merrick (Bristol), Anna von Mildenburg (Bamburg), Agnes Nicholls (Manchester), Denis O'Sullivan (London), Emilio Pente (Florence), Hermann Schramm (Breslau)

D. New Positions:

Conductors: Frederick Archer (Pittsburgh SO), Anton Arensky (Russian Imperial Chapel), Johann H. Beck (Detroit SO), Alfred Hertz (Barmen-Elberfeld Opera), Willim Kes (Scottish SO), Ernst Kunwald (Rockstock Opera), Willem Mengelberg (Amsterdam Concertgebouw), Arthur Nikisch (Leipzig Gewandhaus), Fritz Scheel (San Francisco SO), Frank van der Stucken (Cincinnati SO), Arturo Toscanini (Turin Opera)

Educational: Beniamino Cesi (piano, Naples Conservatory), Leopold Godowsky (piano director, Chicago Conservatory), Henry Hadley (director, St. Paul's School, Garden City), Willy Hess (violin, Cologne Opera), Daniel de Lange (director, Amsterdam Conservatory), Peter Lutkin (Dean of Music, Northwestern University), Pietro Mascagni (director, Rossini Conservatory), Max Reger (Wiesbaden Conservatory)

Others: George J. Bennett (organ, Lincoln Cathedral)

E. Prizes and Honors:

Prizes: Omer Letorey and Martin Lunssens (Prix de Rome), Josef Lhevinne (Rubinstein)

Honors: Arrigo Boito (Legion of Honor), Edward German (Royal Academy), Alexander C. Mackenzie (knighted), Ebenezer Prout (honorary doctorate, Dublin, Edinburgh)

F. Biographical Highlights:

Louise Beatty marries composer Sidney Homer and travels to Paris; Gemma Bellincioni, Zélie de Lussan and Francesco Tamagno make their Covent Garden debuts; George Enescu goes for further violin study at the Paris Conservatory; Henry J. Gilbert travels in Europe; Percy Grainger enters the Conservatory of Frankfurt; Edward Hanslick retires from active music life; Hugo Leichtentritt enters the Berlin Hochchule; Willem Mengelberg returns to Holland; Nikolai Miaskovsky enters St. Petersburg Cadet School; Selim Palmgren enters Helsinki Conservatory; Ildebrando Pizzetti enters Parma Conservatory; Sergei Rachmaninoff tours Russia with violinist Teresina Tua; Maurice Ravel leaves Paris Conservatory; Frederick Stock moves to the U.S., begins playing in Thomas's orchestra; Ermanno Wolf-Ferrari leaves Munich without graduating and returns to Venice; Alexander Zemlinsky first meets Schoenberg.

G. Institutional Openings:

Performing Groups: Bournemouth SO; Bruges Concert Society; Cincinnati SO Association; Damrosch Opera Co.; Pittsburgh Orchestra; Promenade Concerts (N.Y.); Queen's Hall Promenade Concerts (London); San Francisco SO

Festivals: Sheffield Music Festival

Educational: American School of Classical Studies (Rome); Bendix Music Conservatory (San Francisco); Melbourne Memorial Conservatorium (Australia); Metropolitan School of Music; Northwestern Universtity School of Music; University of Illinois Department of Music

Other: Belfast Grand Opera House; Bobbs-Merrill Co., Publishers; Carnegie Music Hall (Pittsburgh); Museo Naciónal de Bellas Artes (Buenos Aires); Music Publisher's Association of the United States; *Musical Canada*; *The Musical Leader*; *Le Passetemps* (Canada); Shapiro, Bernstein & Co., Music Publishers (N.Y.); Société des Instruments Anciens (Paris); Société Moderne d'Instruments à Vent (Paris); M.H. de Young Memorial Museum (San Francisco); Zagreb Opera House

H. Musical Literature:

Baker, Theobald, *Dictionary of Musical Terms*
Davey, Henry, *History of English Music*
Flood, W.H., *History of Irish Music*
Gow, George, *The Structure of Music*
Lacombe, Louis, *Philosophie et Musique*
Lavignac, Albert, *La Musique et les Musiciens*
Prout, Ebenezer, *Applied Forms*
Weingartner, Felix, *Über das Dirigieren*

I. Musical Compositions:

Boëllmann, Léon, *Suite Gothique, Opus 25* (organ)
Busoni, Ferruccio, *Orchestral Suite No. 2, Opus 34a*
Delius, Frederick, *Over the Hills and Far Away* (tone poem)
Dvorák, Antonin, *Concerto, Opus 104, for Cello and Orchestra*
    Orchestral Suite, Opus 98
Enescu, Georges, *Tragic Overture*
    Triumphant Overture
Fibich, Zdenek, *The Tempest, Opus 40* (opera)
Foerster, Josef B., *Symphony No. 3, Opus 36*
Glazunov, Alexander, *Scènes de Ballet, Opus 52*
    Symphony No. 5, Opus 55
Grieg, Edvard, *Lyric Pieces, Book VII, Opus 62*
d'Indy, Vincent, *Fervaal* (opera)
Ippolitov-Ivanov, Mikhail, *Caucasian Sketches, Opus 10*
Kalinnikov, Vasily, *Symphony No. 1*
MacDowell, Edward, *Piano Sonata No. 2, "Eroica"*
Mascagni, Pietro, *Guglielmo Ratcliff* (opera)
Pfitzner, Hans, *Der Arme Heinrich* (opera)
Rachmaninoff, Sergei, *Symphony No. 1, Opus 13*
Rimsky-Korsakov, Nikolai, *Christmas Eve* (opera)
Scriabin, Alexander, *Piano Sonata No. 1, Opus 6*
    12 Etudes for Piano, Opus 8
Sibelius, Jan, *3 Legends for Orchestra, Opus 22*
Strauss, Richard, *Till Eulenspiegel's Merry Pranks, Opus 28*
Widor, Charles, *Symphonie Gothique, Opus 70* (organ)

1896

World Events:
> In the U.S., William McKinley is elected as President No. 25; Utah becomes State No. 25; Miami, Florida, is incorporated; William Cullen Bryant gives his "Cross of Gold" Speech; the electric stove and the flashlight are both introduced. Internationally, the Young Turks are formed to foster Turkish independence; the island of Madagascar is annexed by France; Italian troops, defeated by the Abyssinians, withdraw from their self-proclaimed protectorate; Octave Chanute begins his experiments with glider flight.

Cultural Highlights:
> The Syracuse Museum of Fine Arts opens; the Spenlove School of Modern Art (the Yellow Door School)opens; Vale Press opens in London; the magazine, *Collier's Weekly*, begins publication; Alfred Austin is made British Poet Laureate; Edward J. Poynter and Sourindro M. Tagore are knighted. Births in the field of art include American artist Louis Bouché and sculptor Allan Clark and French artist André Masson; deaths include American artists Wyatt Eaton, Theodore Robinson and Alfred W. Thompson, British artists Frederick Leighton, John-Everett Millais and Henry Moore. Births in the literary world include American authors Louis Bromfield, John Dos Passos, F. Scott Fitzgerald, Marjorie Rawlings and Robert Sherwood, Scottish novelist A. J. Cronin, Irish novelist Liam O'Flaherty and British poet and critic Edmund Blonden; deaths include French poet Paul Verlaine and author Edmond de Goncourt, American author Thomas Hughes, British novelists George du Maurier and William Morris. Other highlights include:

> **Art:** Paul Gauguin, *Nativity*; Frederic Leighton, *Clytie*; Gustave Moreau, *Jupiter and Séméle*; Camille Pissarro, *Boieldieu Bridge, Rouen*; Pierre Renoir, *Standing Bather*; Auguste Rodin, *The Kiss*; Henry O. Tanner, *Daniel in the Lion's Den*; Henri de Toulouse-Latrec, *Elles*; Anders Zorn, *Nymph and Faun* (bronze)

> **Literature:** James Barrie, *Sentimental Tommy*; Anton Chekhov, *The Sea Gull*; Thomas Hardy, *Jude, the Obscure*; A. E. Housman, *A Shropshire Lad*; Maurice Maeterlinck, *Twelve Chansons*; Marcel Proust, *Pleasures and Regrets*; Henryk Sienkiewicz, *Quo Vadis?*; H. G. Wells, *The Island of Dr. Moreau*; Oscar Wilde, *Salomé*

MUSICAL EVENTS

A. Births:

Jan 8	Jaromir Weinberger (Cz-cm)	Aug 7	Ernesto Lecuona (Cub-pn)
Feb 16	Alexander Brailowsky (Rus-pn)	Aug 16	Maria Kurenko (Rus-sop)
Feb 18	André Breton (Fr-pt-cri)	Aug 21	Queena Mario (Am-sop)
Feb 26	Tauno Hannikainen (Fin-cd)	Sep 25	Roberto Gerhard (Sp-cm)
Mar 1	Dmitri Mitropoulos (Gr-cd)	Oct 28	Howard Hanson (Am-cm-ed)
Mar 20	Serge Jaroff (Rus-cd)	Nov 16	Lawrence Tibbett (Am-bar)
Mar 26	Leonide Massine (Rus-bal)	Nov 25	Virgil Thomson (Am-cm-cri)
Jun 29	Matthieu Ahlersmeyer (Ger-bar)	Dec 1	Ray Henderson (Am-cm)
Jun 30	Wilfrid Pelletier (Can-cd)	Dec 9	Glen Haydon (Am-mus)
Jul 8	Richard Kountz (Am-cd)	Dec 12	Jenó Adám (Hun-cm-cd)
Jul 20	Rudolf Kolisch (Aus-vn)	Dec 21	Leroy Robertson (Am-cm)
Jul 27	Ivar Andrésen (Nor-bs)	Dec 28	Roger Sessions (Am-cm)

B. Deaths:

Jan 28	Joseph Barnby (Br-org-cm)	Apr 12	Alexander Ritter (Ger-cm-vn)
Feb 6	Julie Dorus-Gras (Bel-sop)	Apr 30	Antonio Cagnoni (It-cm)
Feb 6	Dar'ya M. Leonova (Rus-alto)	May 20	Clara Schumann (Ger-pn)
Feb 12	C. Ambroise Thomas (Fr-cm)	Jul 16	Alfred Novello (Br-pub)
Feb 13	Karl Reinthaler (Ger-cm-cd)	Jul 19	Achille Graffigna (It-cm)
Feb 21	Georg Arlberg (Swe-bar)	Aug 15	Rodolf J. Schachner (Ger-pn)

Aug 18	Frederick Crouch (Br-cel)	Oct 11	Anton Bruckner (Aus-cm)
Sep 16	A. Carlo Gomes (Bra-cm)	Nov 22	Italo Campanini (It-ten)
Sep 22	Katherina Klafski (Hun-sop)	Nov 26	Coventry Patmore (Br-cri)
Sep 23	Gilbert L. Duprez (Fr-ten)	Dec 17	Richard Pohl (Ger-cri)
Sep 30	Moritz W. Drobisch (Ger-mus)		

C. Debuts:

Met --- Suzanne Adams (sop), Johanna Bach (mez), Jacques Bars (ten), Maria Belina (sop), David Bispham (bar), Antonio Ceppi (ten), Igenio Corsi (ten), Jules Gogny (ten), Félia Litvinne (sop), Thomas Salignac (ten), Adolf Wallnöfer (ten)

U.S. -- David Ffrangcon-Davies (tour), Heinrich Gebhard (Boston), Charles Gregorovitch (tour), Yvette Guilbert (tour), Carl Halir (tour), Bronislaw Huberman (tour), Bruno Huhn (N.Y.), Oscar Seagle (N.Y.), Susan Strong (N.Y.), Milka Ternina (Boston), Pier A. Tirindelli (Cincinnati)

Other - Giuseppe Anselmi (Athens), Alessandro Bonci (Parma), Hans Breuer (Bayreuth), Alois Burgstaller (Bayreuth), Alfred Cortot (Paris), Hector Dufranne (Brussels), John Forsell (Stockholm), August Griebel (Heidelberg), Jeanne Marié Olenine d'Alheim (Paris), Fritzi Scheff (Frankfurt), Leo Slezak (Brünn), Friedrich Weidemann (Brieg), Harry E. Williams (Worcester)

D. New Positions:

Conductors: Frederic Cowen (Liverpool PO and Manchester Concerts), Oskar Nedbal (Czech PO), Emil von Reznicek (Mannheim Court)

Educational: Enrico Bossi (organ and hamony, Naples Conservatory), Francesco Cilea (harmony, Instituto Musicale, Florence), Théodore Dubois (director, Paris Conservatory), Gabriel Fauré and Charles Widor (composition, Paris Conservatory), Alexandre Guilmant (organ, Paris Conservatory), Hans Huber (director, Basel Conservatory), Xavier Leroux (harmony, Paris Conservatory), Edward MacDowell (head, Columbia University Music Department), Raoul Pugno (piano, Paris Conservatory)

Others: Herbert Brewer (organ and choir, Gloucester Cathedral), Walter Henry Hall (organ, St. James, N.Y.)

E. Prizes and Honors:

Prizes: Jules Mocquet (Prix de Rome)

Honors: Nikolai Afanas'yev (Russian Musical Society), Karl Goldmark (Order of Leopold), Louis Gouvy and Edvard Grieg (Legion of Honor), Charles Lenepveu (French Adacemy), Edward MacDowell (honorary doctorate)

F. Biographical Highlights:

Emma Albani retires from the stage; Alexander Bandrowski-Sas, Giuseppe Borgatti and Adam Didur make their La Scala debuts; Alfred Cortot wins first prize in piano at the Paris Conservatory; Antonin Dvořák makes his last journey to England; Alexander Glazunov travels to England on a conducting engagement; Percy Goetschius resigns his conservatory post and begins teaching privately in Boston; Ellen Gulbranson and Ernestine Schumann-Heink make their Bayreuth debuts; Engelbert Humperdinck, in ill health, retires from active music life; Sigfrid Karg-Elert enters the Leipzig Conservatory; Ernest Paur retires to Germany; Sofia Scalchi gives her farewell concert and retires; Alexander Scriabin, sponsored by Belaiev Publishing House, begins a grand concert tour.

G. Institutional Openings:

Performing Groups: Adamowski Trio; Catalunya Nova (Barcelona Choral Society); Nicodé Chorus (Dresden); Oregon SO (later - Portland SO); Oxford Bach Choir; Sociedade de Concertos Populares (Rio de Janeiro); Winderstein Orchestra (Leipzig); Women's String Orchestra of New York

Educational: University of Oregon Music Department

Other: American Federation of Musicians; American Guild of Organists; *La Cronaca Musical* (Italy); Editions Salabert (Paris); Genossenschaft Deutscher Tonsetzen (Munich); *Die Jugend*; Knudsen Piano Factory (Bergen); Joseph Koening, Piano Builder (Caen); *Monatschrift für Gottesdienst und Kirchliche Kunst*; Ignace Jan Paderewski Foundation; Russian Music Circle (Moscow); Steinert Hall (Boston); Theater des Westens (Berlin); Theatrical Syndicate (N.Y.)

H. Musical Literature:

Billroth, Theodor, *Wer ist musikalische?*
Gevaert, François-Auguste, *La Mélopée antique dans l'église latine*
Hennig, Carl, *Aesthetik der Tonkunst*
Hipkins, Alfred, *Description and History of the Pianoforte*
Kalbeck, Max, *Humoresken und Fantasien*
Krehbiel, Henry, *How to Listen to Music*
Mathews, William, *Dictionary of Music Terms*
Preobrazhensky, Anatoly, *Dictionary of Russian Church Chant*
Rimsky-Korsakov, Nikolai, *Principles of Orchestration*

I. Musical Compositions:

Brahms, Johannes, *4 Serious Songs, Opus 121*
    11 Chorale Preludes, Opus 122 (organ)
Chadwick, George, *Symphonic Sketches*
    Symphony No. 3
Chausson, Ernest, *Poème for Violin and Orchestra, Opus 25*
Coleridge-Taylor, Samuel, *Symphony in A Major*
Damrosch, Walter, *The Scarlet Letter* (opera)
Dukas, Paul, *Symphony in C Major*
Dvořák, Antonin, *The Water-Sprite, Opus 107* (symphonic poem)
    The Midday Witch, Opus 108 (symphonic poem)
    The Golden Spinning Wheel, Opus 109 (symphonic poem)
    The Wood Dove, Opus 110 (symphonic poem)
Elgar, Edward, *The Light of Life, Opus 29* (oratorio)
Enescu, Georges, *Piano Quintet*
Foote, Arthur, *Orchestral Suite, Opus 36*
Gilbert and Sullivan, *The Grand Duke* (operetta)
Giordano, Umberto, *Andrea Chenier* (opera)
Glazounov, Alexander, *Symphony No. 6, Opus 58*
Grieg, Edvard, *Lyric Pieces, Book VIII, Opus 65*
d'Indy, Vincent, *Ishtar Variations, Opus 42*
Ives, Charles, *String Quartet No. 1, "Revival Service"*
MacDowell, Edward, *Orchestral Suite No. 2, Opus 48, "Indian Suite"*
    Woodland Sketches, Opus 51
Mahler, Gustav, *Symphony No. 3*
Novák, Vitaslav, *Concerto for Piano and Orchestra*
Puccini, Giacomo, *La Bohème* (opera)
Rachmaninoff, Sergei, *24 Songs, Opus 14 and 15*
Rimsky-Korsakov, Nikolai, *Sadko* (opera)
Saint-Saëns, Camille, *Concerto No. 5, Opus 103, for Piano and Orchestra*
Sousa, John Philipp, *El Capitán* (operetta)
    Stars and Stripes Forever (march)
Stanford, Charles, *Shamus O'Brien, Opus 61* (opera)
Strauss, Richard, *Also Sprach Zarathustra, Opus 30*
Wolf, Hugo, *Der Corregidor* (opera)

1897

World Events:
In the U.S., the Klondike Gold Rush takes place in Alaska; the Dingley Tariff hits a new high in protectionism; the Kellogg Brothers introduce Corn Flakes to the public; C. W. Post introduces his Grape Nuts; the Katzenjammer Kids becomes the first American comic strip; the Boston Marathon begins. Internationally, the Peace of Constantinople marks the end of the Greek-Turkish War; Russia occupies Port Arthur in China while Germany occupies Kiao-Chow; the first Zionist Congress meets in Basle to seek ways to make Palestine a Jewish state; Marconi forms his own wireless company.

Cultural Highlights:
The Tate Gallery is opened in London by Sir Henry Tate; the *Saturday Evening Post* begins publication. Births in the art field include American artists Ivan L. Albright, John S. Curry and William Gropper, Dutch artist Charles Eyck and Belgian artist Paul Delvaux; deaths include American artists George W. Flagg and Homer Martin. Births in the literary field include American authors William Faulkner, Margaret Preston, Bernard de Voto and Thornton Wilder, French poet Louis Aragon and British poet Sacheverell Sitwell; deaths include French author Alphonse Daudet, Finnish novelist Minna Canth and Scottish novelist Margaret Oliphant. Other highlights include:

Art: Aimé-Jules Dalou, *Peasant*; Maurice Denis, *Spring*; Paul Gauguin, *Day-Dreaming*; Max Klinger, *Christ in Olympus*; Henri Matisse, *The Dinner Table*; Emil Nolde, *Mountain Giants*; Camille Pissarro, *Boulevard Montmartre*; Henri Rousseau, *The Sleeping Gypsy*; Henry O. Tanner, *The Raising of Lazarus*

Literature: Joseph Conrad, *Nigger of the Narcissus*; Fanny Crosby, *Bells at Evening and Other Poems*; Rudyard Kipling, *Captains Courageous*; Edward Robinson, *Children of the Night*; Edmond Rostand, *Cyrano de Bergerac*; George Bernard Shaw, *Candide*; Bram Stoker, *Dracula*; H. G. Wells, *The Invisible Man*

MUSICAL EVENTS

A. Births:

Jan 22	Rosa Ponselle (Am-sop)	Jun 25	Hans Barth (Ger-pn-cm)
Jan 29	Mary Lewis (Am-sop)	Jul 5	Paul Ben Haim (Ger-cm-cd)
Feb 7	Quincy Porter (Am-cm)	Jul 5	Wanda Landowska (Pol-hps)
Feb 12	Bretislav Bakala (Cz-cd)	Sep 15	Paul Schoeffler (Ger-bar)
Feb 14	Jørgen Bentzon (Den-cm)	Sep 30	Leone Giraldoni (Fr-bar)
Feb 19	Willi Fassbaender (Ger-bar)	Oct 13	Harrison Kerr (Am-cm)
Mar 6	Knudåge Riisager (Den-cm)	Oct 26	Tiana Luise Lemnitz (Ger-sop)
Mar 11	Henry Cowell (Am-cm)	Oct 29	Henry Swoboda (Cz-cd)
Mar 31	J. Murray Barboure (Am-mus)	Nov 4	Oscar L. Fernandez (Bra-cm)
May 29	Erich Korngold (Aus-cm)	Nov 14	Conchita Badia (Sp-sop)
Jun 7	George Szell (Hun-cd)	Nov 20	Margaret Sutherland (Aust-cm)
Jun 10	Frederich Jagel (Am-ten)	Dec 6	Gotthold Frotscher (Ger-mus)
Jun 11	Madelaine Gray (Fr-sop)	Dec 25	Carlo Morelli (Chil-bar)
Jun 12	Alexandre Tansman (Pol-cm)		

B. Deaths:

Jan 1	Joseph T. Barbot (Fr-ten)	Apr 30	Jan Pieter Land (Hol-mus)
Feb 10	Armand Castelmary (Fr-bs)	May 10	William T. Best (Br-org)
Feb 25	Marie-Cornélie Falcon (Fr-sop)	Jul 12	Félix Godefroid (Gel-hp)
Apr 3	Johannes Brahms (Ger-cm)	Jul 15	Alexander Thayer (Am-mus)
Apr 11	Hans Muller (Ger-mus)	Jul 25	Bernard Kothe (Ger-mus)

Sep 20   Karel Bendl (Cz-cm-cd)
Oct 5   Alexandre Taskin (Fr-bar)
Oct 11   Léon Boëllmann (Fr-org-cm)
Oct 17   Isodor Dannström (Swe-bar)
Oct 21   Paul Kuczynski (Ger-cm)
Nov 6   Édouard Delderez (Fr-cm-au)

Nov 14   Giuseppina Strepponi (It-sop)
Nov 20   Henry C. Banister (Br-the)
Dec 4   Adolf Neuendorff (Ger-cd)
Dec 29   Léon Carvalho (Fr-imp)
      Achille Errani (It-ten)

C. Debuts:

Met --- Clementine De Vere (sop), William Mertens (bar), Mina Schilling (sop)

U.S. -- Hans Breuer (tour), Riza Eibenschütz (tour), Maria Geistlinger (N.Y.), Emilio de Gogorza (N.Y.), Ellison von Goose (Philadelphia), Denis O'Sullivan (San Francisco)

Other - Aïno Ackté (Paris), Bella Alten (Leipzig), Celestina Boninsegna (Bari), Richard Breitenfeld (Cologne), Ernst von Dohnányi (Berlin), Katherine Goodson (London), Mizzi Günther (Hermannstadt), Heinrich Hensel (Freiburg), Hermann Jadlowker (Cologne), Giuseppe de Luca (Piacenza), Minnie Nast (Aachen), Albert Reiss (Königsberg), Aurelie Révy (Budapest), Anton van Rooy (Bayreuth), Leonid Sobinoff (Moscow), Joaquin Turina (Seville)

D. New Positions:

Conductors: Cleofonte Campanini (Covent Garden), Ferdinand Hummel (Kapell-meister, Berlin Court), Ernst Kunwald (Sondershausen), Alexander Luigini (Opéra-Comique), Hustav Mahler (Vienna Opera), Emil Mlynarski (Warsaw Opera), Hans Richter (Hallé Orchestra)

Educational: Felix Borowski (Chicago Musical College), George Chadwick (director, New England Conservatory), Carl Flesch (violin, Bucharest Conservatory), Giuseppe Gallignani (director, Milan Conservatory), Robert Kajanus (musicology, director, Helsinki University), Hans Pfitzner (composition, Stern Conservatory), Ebenezer Prout (composition, Royal Academy), Carl Reinecke (director, Leipzig Conservatory)

Others: Hugh Allen (organ, St. Asaph's Cathedral), Ivor Atkins (organ, Worcester Cathedral), Joseph-Amédée Capoul (manager, Paris Opera), Frederick Edwards (editor, *Musical Times*), William Fisher (editor, Oliver Ditson and Co.), Edwin Lemare (organ, St. Margaret's, London)

E. Prizes and Honors:

Prizes: Joseph Jongen and Max d'Ollone (Prix de Rome)

Honors: Frederick Bridge and George C. Martin (knighted), Emile Paladilhe (Legion of Honor), Jan Sibelius (life pension, Finland)

F. Biographical Highlights:

Max Alvary retires from the stage; Alessandro Bonci, Maria Giudice, Angelica Pandolfini and Francesco Signorini make their La Scala debuts; Ernest Bloch enters Brussels Conservatory; Nadia Boulanger enters Paris Conservatory; John Alden Carpenter graduates from Harvard and enters his father's business; Frank Damrosch becomes music supervisor of the New York public schools; Frederick Delius visits Florida and gets married; Andreas Dippel, Olive Fremstad, Marcel Journet and Maurice Renaud make their Covent Garden debuts; Ernst von Dohnányi begins his conducting career; Arthur Farwell goes to Germany to study with Humperdinck and Pfitzner; Charles Koechlin graduates from Paris Conservatory; Anna von Mildenburg, Thila Plaichinger and Anton Van Rooy make their debuts at Bayreuth; Moritz Moszkowski retires and settles in Paris; Maurice Ravel begins study of composition with Fauré; Alexander Scriabin marries Vera Isaakovich; Jan Sibelius is given a life pension by the Finnish government; Ralph Vaughan Williams travels to Berlin to study with Max Bruch; Hugo Wolf, suffering from recurring illness, finally goes mad.

G. Institutional Openings:

Performing Groups: Beethoven Society of Montevideo; Bournemouth Municipal Orchestra; Castle Square Opera Co. (Boston); Copenhagen Philharmonic Concerts; Hausermann Privatchor (Zürich); Kansas City Oratorio Society; Moody-Manners Opera Co.; Rostock Stadt- und Theaterorchester; Société Avignonase des Concerts Symphoniques; Teatro Massimo and Opera (Palermo)

Festivals: Feis Ceoil (Irish Festival); Maine Music Festival (Portland)

Educational: Adelaide University Chair of Music (endowed by Thomas Elder); Faelten Piano School (Boston); Library of Congress Division of Music; Sherwood Piano School (Chicago); Stierlin Music School (Münster)

Other: Doubleday and McClure Co., Publishers; Geibel and Lehmann, Music Publishers; Gesellschaft der Autoren, Komponisten und Musikverleger (Vienna); Museo Donizettiano (Bergamo); National Piano Manufacturer's Association; Providence Opera House; Théâtre Antoine (Paris)

H. Musical Literature:

Ábrányi, Kornél, *From My Life and Memories*
Banister, Henry, *The Harmonising of Melodies*
Chadwick, George, *Harmony, A Course of Study*
Maurel, Victor, *L'Art du Chant*
Nagel, Wilibald, *History of Music in England II*
Pfordten, Hermann von der, *Musikalische Essays I*
Preobrazhensky, Anatoly, *On Church Chant*
Wegelius, Martin, *Homophonic Writing*
Wolzogen, Hans von, *Grossmeister deutscher Musik*

I. Musical Compositions:

Alfvén, Hugo, *Symphony No. 1, Opus 7*
Busoni, Ferruccio, *A Comedy Overture*
    Concerto for Violin and Orchestra, Opus 35a
Chausson, Ernest, *Chant Funèbre*
Converse, Frederick, *Overture, Youth*
Debussy, Claude, *Chansons de Bilitis*
Delius, Frederick, *Concerto for Piano and Orchestra*
    Koanga (opera)
Dohnányi, Ernst von, *Symphony No. 1*
Dubois, François, *Concerto No. 2 for Piano and Orchestra*
Dukas, Paul, *The Sorcerer's Apprentice* (symphonic poem)
Dvorák, Antonin, *The Hero's Song, Opus 111* (symphonic poem)
Elgar, Edward, *Imperial March, Opus 32* (orchestra)
    The Banner of St. George, Opus 33 (cantata)
Fauré, Gabriel, *Theme and Variations, Opus 73, for Piano*
Fibich, Zdenek, *Sarka, Opus 51* (opera)
Foerster, Josef B., *Eva, Opus 50* (opera)
German, Edward, *Hamlet* (symphonic poem)
Humperdinck, Engelbert, *Königskinder* (incidental music)
Koven, Reginald de, *The Highwayman* (operetta)
Leoncavallo, Ruggero, *La Bohème* (opera)
Massenet, Jules, *Sapho* (opera)
Scriabin, Alexander, *Allegro de Concert, Opus 18, for Piano*
Strauss, Richard, *Don Quixote*
    9 Songs, Opus 31 and 32
Sullivan, Arthur, *Victoria and Merrie England* (ballet)
Vaughan-Williams, Ralph, *Serenade in A Major*

1898

World Events:

In the U.S., the Battleship *Maine* blows up in Havana harbor bringing on the beginning of the Spanish-American War; the Treaty of Paris gives Spain $20,000,000 for Guam, Hawaii, Puerto Rico and the Phillipines; discovery of the Kensington Stone proves the early visit of the Norsemen to the New World. Internationally, the Empress Elizabeth of Austria is murdered while on a visit to Geneva; the Paris subway, the "Metro" opens; Count von Zeppelin invents the motor driven airship named after him; the Curies discover the existence of radium (not isolated until 1902); the League of Human Rights is founded; the "Iron Chancellor," Otto Bismarck, dies.

Cultural Highlights:

The National Institute of Art and Letters is established in Washington, D.C.; the National Arts Club opens in New York; the Ten, a group of American painters, is formed; the Essex House Press is opened in London by C. R. Ashbee; Max Liebermann is admitted to the Berlin Academy. Births in the literary world include American poet Stephen Vincent Benét, German authors Bertold Brecht and Erich Remarque and Spanish author F. García-Lorca; deaths include American author Edward Bellamy, British author Lewis Carroll, French poet Stéphane Mallarmé, German poet Theodor Fontane, Russian poet Yakov Polonski and Swiss poet Conrad Meyer. Births in the art field include American artists Alexander Calder and Reginald Marsh, Belgian artist René Magritte, Dutch artist M. C. Escher, British sculptor Henry Moore and Lithuanian artist Ben Shaun; deaths include British artists William Beardsley, Edward Burne-Jones and Philip Calderon, French artists Eugène Boudin, Pierre de Chavannes and Gustave Moreau. Other highlights include:

Art: Arnold Böcklin, *The Pest*; Pierre Bonnard, *Palais de Glace*; Aurèle Coté, *Death of Archimedes*; Thomas Eakins, *Taking the Count*; Paul Gauguin, *The White Horse*; Wilhelm Leibl, *In the Kitchen*; Camille Pissarro, *Place du Théâtre Français*; Frederic Remington, *The Scalp*; Auguste Rodin, *The Hand of God*

Literature: Hilary Belloc, *The Modern Traveller*; Anton Chekhov, *Uncle Vanya*; Thomas Hardy, *Wessex Poems*; Henry James, *The Turn of the Screw*; Sidney Lanier, *Music and Poetry*; John Long, *Madame Butterfly*; George B. Shaw, *Plays Pleasant and Unpleasant*; H. G. Wells, *War of the Worlds*; Oscar Wilde, *The Ballad of Reading Gaol*

MUSICAL EVENTS

A. Births:

Jan 22	Alexander Abramsky (Rus-cm)	Aug 1	Giuseppina Cobelli (It-sop)
Jan 28	Vittorio Rieti (It-cm)	Aug 21	Hugh Ross (Br-cd)
Jan 29	Maria Müller (Cz-sop)	Aug 24	Malcolm Cowley (Am-au)
Feb 6	Erna Sack (Ger-sop)	Sep 12	Salvador Bacariesse (Sp-cm)
Feb 12	Roy Harris (Am-cm)	Sep 12	Benno Schönberger (Aus-pn)
Mar 5	Alessio de Paolis (It-ten)	Sep 13	Roger Désormière (Fr-cd-cm)
Mar 7	Wheeler Beckett (Am-cd)	Sep 14	Franco Abbiate (It-cri-mus)
Apr 9	Paul Robeson (Am-bar)	Oct 4	Maurice Martenot (Fr-inv)
May 26	Ernest Bacon (Am-cm)	Oct 7	Alfred Wallenstein (Am-cd)
May 27	Willi Reich (Am-mus)	Oct 18	Shin'ichi Suzuki (Jap-ped)
Jun 8	Robert Easton (Br-bs)	Nov 23	Dezso Ernster (Hun-bs)
Jun 19	Paul Müller (Swi-cd-cm)	Dec 26	Blythe Owen (Am-cm)
Jun 27	Tibor Harsányi (Hun-cm)		Augusta Oltrabella (It-sop)
Jul 15	Norman Demuth (Br-cm)		Iva Pacetti (It-sop)

B. Deaths:

Jan 11	Gaetano Capocci (It-org)		Jun 3	Nikolai Afanas'yev (Rus-vn-cm)
Jan 16	Antoine F. Marmontel (Fr-ped)		Aug 13	Grat-Norbert Barthe (Fr-cm)
Jan 19	(Ernest) Nicolini (Fr-ten)		Nov 4	Félix Delhasse (Bel-mus)
Mar 9	Michal Bergson (Pol-pn-cm)		Nov 4	Charles J. Hopkins (Am-cm)
Mar 13	Julius Schulhoff (Cz-pn)		Nov 7	Max Alvary (Ger-ten)
Mar 28	Anton Seidl (Hun-cd)		Dec 13	George Bristow (Am-cm)
Apr 18	Oscar Paul (Ger-the)		Dec 21	Sebastian Bach Mills (Br-pn)
May 15	Ede Reményi (Hun-vn)			

C. Debuts:

Met --- Henri Albert (bar), Rosalia Chalia (sop), Hermann Devries (bs), Hans Meffert (ten), Theodore Meux (bar), Minnie Molka-Kellog (mez), Adolph Mühlmann (bar), Lamprière Pringle (bs), Albert Saléza (ten), Ernest Van Dyck (ten), Anton Van Rooy (bar)

U.S. -- Giuseppe Agostini (Los Angeles), Yeatman Griffith (Cincinnati), Josephina Huguet (tour), Leon Rains (tour), Francis Rogers (Boston), Emil von Sauer (N.Y.), Ernestine Schumann-Heink (Chicago), Alexander Siloti (tour), Yvonne de Treville (N.Y.)

Other - Angelo Bada (Novara), Maria Barrientos (Barcelona), Therese Behr (Germany), Hermine Bosetti (Wiesbaden), Emmy Destinn (Berlin), Maria Farneti (Italy), Francesco Federici (Italy), George H. Fryer (London), Waldemar Henke (Posen), Louise Homer (Vichy), Gustav Huberdeau (Paris), Jan Kubelík (Vienna), Estelle Liebling (Dresden), Berta Morena (Munich), Titta Ruffo (Rome), Erik Schmedes (as tenor), Tullio Serafin (Ferrara), Riccardo Stracciari (Bologna), Clarence Whitehill (Brussels), Giovanni Zenatello (Vienna, as baritone)

D. New Positions:

Conductors: Filippo Capocci (maestro di cappella, St. John Lateran, Rome), Wilhelm Gericke (Boston SO), Victor Herbert (Pittsburgh SO), Willem Kes (Moscow PO), Ernst Kunwald (Essen), Ferdinand Löwe (Vienna Opera), André Messager (Opéra-Comique), Emil Paur (New York PO), Franz Schalk (Met), Josef Stransky (Landestheater, Prague), Richard Strauss (Berlin Opera), Arturo Toscanini (La Scala)

Educational: Guido Adler (musicology, University of Venice), Samuel Coleridge-Taylor (violin, Royal Academy), Luigi Denza (Voice, Royal Academy, London), Harold Randolph (director, Peabody), Alexander Scriabin (piano, Moscow Conservatory)

Others: Hugh Allen (organ, Ely Cathedral), Marcel Dupré (organ, St. Vivien, Rouen), John Freund (editor, *Musical America*), Giulio Gatti-Casazza (general manager, La Scala), Charles Tournemire (organ, Sainte Clotilde, Paris)

E. Prizes and Honors:

Prizes: Ernst von Dohnányi (Hungarian Millennium Prize), Emil Mlynarski (Paderewski)

Honors: Max Bruch (French Academy), Francesco Cilea (Royal Academy, Florence), Friedrich Niecks (honorary doctorate, Dublin University), Charles H. Parry (knighted)

F. Biographical Highlights:

Suzanne Adams, Johanna Gadski, Aurelie Révy, Milka Ternina and Anton Van Rooy make their Covent Garden debuts; Mily Balakirev makes his last conducting appearance; Frederick Converse graduates from the Royal Conservatory in Munich; Nina Grieg makes her final concert appearance in London; Charles Ives graduates from Yale; Anna von Mildenburg makes her Vienna Opera debut; Albert Roussel begins study with d'Indy; Erik Schmedes makes his Vienna debut; Antonio Scotti makes his La Scala debut; Josef Suk marries Dvorák's daughter, Otilie; Francesco Tamagno suffers a severe heart attack; Nicholai Tcherepnin graduates from St.

Petersburg Conservatory; Donald Tovey graduates with honors from Oxford; Felix Weingartner resigns his post at the Berlin Opera; Hugo Wolf, released from the asylum, tries to drown himself and is readmitted.

G. Institutional Openings:

Performing Groups: Euterpian Club (Fort Worth, TX); Los Angeles SO; New Brighton Choral Society; Società del Quartetto (Ferrara); Société Symphonique Lyonnaise; Vienna Volksoper; Worchestershire Philharmonic Society; York SO; Young People's Concerts (N.Y.)

Educational: Fox-Buonameci School (Boston); Mu Alpha Sinfonia Fraternity (Boston); Musikwissenschaftliches Institut (University of Vienna)

Other: Collection of Ancient Musical Instruments (Copenhagen); Deutsche Gramophon Gesellschaft; English Folk Song Society; Manhattan Opera House I; Metropol Theater (Berlin); Moscow Art Theater; *Musical America*; Royal Opera House (Stockholm)

H. Musical Literature:

Dechevrens, Antoine, *Études de Science Musicale*
Goetschius, Percy, *Homophonic Forms of Musical Composition*
d'Indy, Vincent, *Cours de Compositions Musicale I*
Jadassohn, Salomon, *Methodik des Musiktheoretisches Unterrichts*
Kalbeck, Max, *Opernabende I, II*
Kullak, Franz, *Der Vortrag in der Musik am Ende des 19 Jahrhunderts*
Prout, Ebenezer, *The Orchestra I*
Riemann, Hugo, *Geschichte der Musiktheorie*
Shaw, George Bernard, *The Perfect Wagnerite*

I. Musical Compositions:

Alfvén, Hugo, *Symphony No. 2, Opus 8*
Bristow, George, *Niagara* (opera)
Capua, Eduardo di, *O Sole Mio* (song)
Chausson, Ernest, *Soir de Fête, Opus 32*
Coleridge-Taylor, Samuel, *Hiawatha's Wedding Feast* (Canatata, Part I)
Converse, Frederick, *Symphony in D Minor*
Enescu, Georges, *Poème roumain, Opus 1*
Fauré, Gabriel, *Pelléas et Mélisande Suite, Opus 80*
Fibich, Zdenek, *Symphony No. 3*
Glazounov, Alexander, *Raymonda* (ballet)
Grieg, Edvard, *Symphonic Dances, Opus 64*
    Lyric Pieces, Book IX, Opus 68, for Piano
Herbert, Victor, *The Fortune Teller* (operetta)
Ives, Charles, *Symphony No. 1*
    Psalm 67 (chorus)
Kalinnikov, Vasily, *Symphony No. 2*
MacDowell, Edward, *Sea Pieces, Opus 55, for Piano*
Parker, Horatio, *The Legend of St. Christopher, Opus 43*
    Hora Novissima (oratorio)
Rimsky-Korsakov, Nikolai, *The Tsar's Bride* (opera)
    Mozart and Salieri (opera)
Saint-Saëns, Camille, *Dejanire* (incidental music)
Scriabin, Alexander, *Sonata No. 2 and 3, Opus 19 and 23, for Piano*
    Piano Concerto, Opus 20
Sibelius, Jan, *King Christian II, Opus 27* (incidental music)
Strauss, Richard, *15 Songs, Opus 36, 37, 39*
    Ein Heldenleben, Opus 40 (symphonic poem)
Vaughan-Williams, Ralph, *String Quartet in C Major*
Verdi, Giuseppe, *4 Sacred Pieces* (chorus and orchestra)

1899

World Events:

In the U.S., Cuba is made a protectorate of the U.S. as is Puerto Rico and Guam; the Philippines begins their revolt for independence from the U.S.; John Hay proclaims the Open Door Policy for trade with China; the first Packard automobile is built; the Vacuum Cleaner is patented; Mount Rainier National Park is established by Congress. Internationally, the First Hague Conference is held and sets up a Permanent Court of Arbitration to settle disputes between countries; the Boer War breaks out in South Africa; Friedrich Bayer and Co. introduces Aspirin.

Cultural Highlights:

The Berlin Secession takes place in Germany; the Irish Literary Theater is founded; the magazine *World of Art* begins publication; Lawrence Alma-Tadema is knighted; Frank Norris goes to work for Doubleday, Page and Co. Births in the literary field include American novelists Hart Crane and Ernest Hemingway and British novelist C. S. Forester and playwright Noel Coward; deaths include American author Horatio Alger, French dramatists Henri François Becque and Adolphe d'Ennery, German poet Klaus Groth, and Swiss novelist Victor Cherbuliez. Births in the art world include Russian artists Moses and Raphael Soyer, Italian artist Lucio Fontana and sculptor Ettore Colla and American artists Eugene Berman and Louise Nevelson; deaths include French artists Rosa Bonheur, Henri Delaborde and Alfred Sisley. Other highlights include:

Art: Pierre Bonnard, *At the Table*; Cyrus Dallin, *The Medicine Man*; Edgar Degas, *Three Dancers*; James Ensor, *Artist and Masks*; Paul Gauguin, *Tahitian Women and Mangoes*; Winslow Homer, *The Gulf Stream* and *After the Tornado*; Roland Perry, *The Valkyrie*; Maurice Prendergast, *Umbrellas in the Rain*; Pierre Renoir, *Gabrielle with a Rose*

Literature: Anton Chekhov, *The Three Sisters*; John Dewey, *School and Society*; John Galsworthy, *Jocelyn*; Henrik Ibsen, *When We Dead Awaken*; Henry James, *The Awkward Age*; Rudyard Kipling, *Stalky and Company*; Edwin Markham, *The Man with the Hoe and Other Poems*; Booth Tarkington, *The Gentleman from Indiana*

MUSICAL EVENTS

A. Births:

Jan 7	Francis Poulenc (Fr-cm)	Jul 20	Helen Traubel (Am-sop)
Jan 12	Pierre Bernac (Fr-bar)	Jul 9	Ania Dorfmann (Rus-pn)
Jan 21	Alexander Tcherepnin (Rus-cm)	Jul 27	Harl McDonald (Am-cm)
Feb 15	Georges Auric (Fr-cm)	Jul 30	Gerald Moore (Br-pn)
Apr 7	Robert Casadesus (Fr-pn)	Aug 1	William Steinberg (Ger-cd)
Apr 15	Rudolf Gerber (Ger-mus)	Sep 16	Hans Swarowsky (Hun-cd)
Apr 21	Randall Thompson (Am-cm)	Sep 23	William L. Dawson (Am-cm)
Apr 26	Karl Geiringer (Aus-mus)	Sep 25	Dennis Noble (Br-bar)
Apr 29	"Duke" Ellington (Am-pop)	Nov 18	Eugene Ormandy (Hun-cd)
May 6	Jascha Horenstein (Rus-cd)	Nov 29	Gustave Reese (Am-mus)
May 20	E. Bandrowska-Turska (Pol-sop)	Dec 2	Peter Adler (Cz-cd)
Jun 1	Werner Janssen (Am-cd)	Dec 2	John Barbirolli (Br-cd)
Jun 11	George McKay (Am-cm)	Dec 8	Conchita Supervía (Sp-mez)
Jun 13	Carlos Chávez (Mex-cd-cm)	Dec 31	Silvestre Revueltas (Mex-cm)
Jun 20	Anthon van der Horst (Hol-cm)		Kathryn Meisle (Am-alto)

B. Deaths:

Feb 3	Amalie Joachim (Aus-alto)	Apr 19	Hans Balatka (Cz-cd)
Feb 23	Friedrich v. Hausegger (Aus-the)	Apr 20	Luigi Valdrighi (It-mus)
Feb 25	Hans F. von Milde (Aus-bar)	May 14	Frederic Brandeis (Aus-pn)
Mar 2	Marie Luise Dustmann (Fr-sop)	May 28	Heinrich Wiegand (Ger-bs)

May 29 François Jehin (Bel-vn)
Jun 3 Johann Strauss, Jr. (Aus-cm)
Jun 10 Ernest Chausson (Fr-cm)
Sep 4 J. Decker-Schenk (Aus-imp)
Oct 5 Johann N. Fuchs (Aus-cd)

Oct 7 Stéphane Morelot (Fr-cri)
Oct 12 Oristide Caraille-Col (Fr-org)
Oct 20 A. J. (Signor) Foli (Am-bs)
Dec 21 Charles Lamoureux (Fr-cd)
Dec 23 Marietta Piccolomini (It-sop)

C. Debuts:

Met --Albert Alvarez (ten), Joseph Arden (bar), Johanna Gadski (sop), Emilie Herzog (sop), Emil Paur (cd), Antonio Pini-Corsi (bs), Ernestine Schumann-Heink (alto), Antonio Scotti (bar), Milka Ternina (sop)

U.S. -- Clara Butt (tour), Eleanora de Cisneros (Chicago), Katherine Heyman (Boston), William W. Hinshaw (St. Louis), Blanche Marchesi (tour), Wilma Neruda (tour)

Other - Amadeo Bassi (Florence), Johannes Bischoff (Cologne), Nicolai Bolshakov (St. Petersburg), Marguerite Carré (Nantes), Charles Dalmorès (Rouen), Gilly Dinh (Paris), Zdenka Fassbender (Karlsruhe), Jeanne Gerville-Réache (Paris), Hermann Jadlowker (Cologne), Heniot Lévy (Berlin), Otokar Marák (Brno), Antonio Paoli (Paris), Amelia Pinto (Brescia), Sergei Rachmaninoff (London), Robert Radford (Norwich), Léon Rothier (Paris), Domenico Viglione-Borghese (Lodi)

D. New Positions:

Conductors: Leo Blech (German Theater, Prague), Camille Chevillard (Lamoureaux Concerts), Jules Danbé (Theatre Lyrique, Paris), Michele Esposito (Dublin Orchestral Society), Johan Halvorsen (Oslo National Theater), Alfred Hertz (Breslau Opera), Peter Raabe (Netherlands Opera), Alexander Zemlinsky (Vienna Carltheater)

Educational: Frederick Converse (harmony, New England Conservatory), Alexander Glazunov (composition, St. Petersburg Conservatory), Otto Malling (director, Copenhagen Conservatory), Emil Paur (director, National Conservatory, N.Y.), Richard von Preger (director, Vienna Conservatory), Vassili Safonov (director, Moscow Conservatory)

Others: Oskar Fleischer (President, International Music Society)

E. Prizes and Honors:

Prizes: Charles Levadé, Léon Moreau and François Rasse (Prix de Rome), Benno Moiseiwitsch (Rubinstein)

Honors: Moritz Moszkowsky (Berlin Academy), Joseph Rheinberger (honorary doctorate, Munich University), Hugo Riemann (honorary doctorate, Edinburgh University)

F. Biographical Highlights:

Wilhelm Backhaus begins piano study with d'Albert in Frankfurt; Béla Bartók enters the Budapest Academy of Music; Lucienne Bréval, Johanna Gadski, Louise Homer, Félia Litvinne, Hermann Schramm and Antonio Scotti all make their Covent Garden debuts; Frank Bridge enters the Royal College of Music; Feodor Chaliapin becomes a member of the Bolshoi Opera; Claude Debussy marries Rosalie Texier; Geraldine Farrar goes to Paris for voice study; Arthur Farwell returns to the U.S. and begins lecturing at Cornell; Louise Kirkby-Lunn, following her marriage retires until 1901; Ernst Kraus and Felix von Kraus make their Bayreuth debuts; Fritz Kreisler resumes his concert career; Selma Kurz makes her Vienna Opera debut; Nicolas Miaskovsky enters the Academy of Military Engineering but also studies music; Léon Rothier graduates from the Paris Conservatory; Jan Sibelius visits Italy and Bayreuth where his anti-Wagner feelings begin to emerge.

G. Institutional Openings:

Performing Groups: Cambridge University Musical Club; Dublin Orchestral Society; Essen SO; Hartford PO; Kansas City Musical Club; Litchfield County Choral Union (Connecticut); Orpheus Choral Society of Dublin; Schola Cantorum d'Avignon; Washington Permanent Chorus (D.C.)

Educational: Conservatorio de Música y Declamación (Havana); Guilmant Organ School (N.Y.); Heidingsfeld Conservatory of Music (Danzig); Mokranjac (Serbian) Music School (Belgrad); University of Oklahoma School of Music; Vogt'sche Konservatorium (Hamburg); Wiest Conservatory of Music (Bucharest)

Other: Austin Organ Co. (Hartford); *Bollettino Bibliografico Musicale*; *Choir Journal*; *Die Fackel*; International Music Society (Berlin); Lyon and Healy Harp Co. (Chicago); Olympia Music Hall (N.Y.); Swiss Musicological Society; Willis Music Co. (Cincinnati)

H. Musical Literature:

Eitner, Robert, *Quellenlexicon der Musiker I*
Elson, Louis, *National Music of American and Its Sources*
Fuentes, Juan B., *Teoria de la Música*
Fuller-Maitland, J. A., *Musician's Pilgrimage*
Gasperini, Guido, *Storia della Musica*
Hanslick, Edouard, *Am ende des Jahrhunders*
Jadassohn, Salomon, *Das Wesen der melodie in der Tonkunst*
Lalo, Pierre, *La Musique*
Seiffert, Max, *Geschichte der Klaviermusik*

I. Musical Compositions:

Chadwick, George, *Overture, Adonais*
Coleridge-Taylor, Samuel, *The Death of Minnehaha* (cantata)
Debussy, Claude, *3 Nocturnes*
Delius, Frederick, *Paris: Song of a Great City*
Dvořák, Antonin, *The Devil and Kate, Opus 112* (opera)
Elgar, Edward, *Enigma Variations, Opus 36*
     Sea Pictures, Opus 37
Enescu, Georges, *Pastorale-Fantasie for Orchestra*
German, Edward, *The Seasons* (symphonic suite)
Glazunov, Alexander, *The Seasons* (ballet)
Herbert, Victor, *Cyrano de Bergerac* (operetta)
Ives, Charles, *The Celestial Country* (cantata)
Joplin, Scott, *The Maple Leaf Rag*
Magnard, Albéric, *Symphony No. 2, Opus 6*
Massenet, Jules, *Cendrillon* (opera)
     Overture, Brumaire
Ravel, Maurice, *Pavane for a Dead Princess* (orchestrated 1912)
Rimsky-Korsakov, Nicolai, *Song of Oleg, the Wise*
Schoenberg, Arnold, *Transfigured Night, Opus 4*
Scriabin, Alexander, *Reverie for Orchestra, Opus 24s*
Sibelius, Jan, *Symphony No. 1, Opus 39*
     Scènes Historiques I, Opus 25
     Finlandia, Opus 26 (tone poem)
     13 Songs, Opus 17 and 36
Stenhammar, Wilhelm, *Das Fest auf Solhaug* (opera)
Suk, Joseph, *Symphony In E Major, Opus 14*
Vaughan-Williams, Ralph, *Mass*
Vierne, Louis, *Organ Symphony No. 1*
Wolf-Ferrari, Ermanno, *La Sulamite* (oratorio)

General Musical Index

A

A = 440 vps- 1834g
Aachen Städtisches Orchester- 1852g
Abarbanell, Lina- 1879a, 1894c
Abba-Cornaglia, Pietro- 1851a
Abbey, Henry- 1883d
Abbey, John- 1859b
Abbey Glee Club- 1841g
Abbey Theatre- 1894g
Abbiati, Franco- 1898a
Abbott, Emma- 1850a, 1872f, 1876c,
    1877c, 1891b
Abbott, Emma, Opera Co.- 1878g
Abeille, Ludwig- 1801i, 1802f, 1809i,
    1815d, 1838b
Abendroth, Hermann- 1883a
Abendroth, Irene- 1872a, 1889c
Aberdeen:
    A. Choral Society- 1849g
    A. Euterpean Society- 1845g
    A. Harmonic Choir- 1847g
    A. Haydn Society- 1840g
    A. Music Hall- 1859g
    A. Place Opera House- 1847g
Abert, Hermann- 1871a
Abert, Johann J.- 1867d
Abramsky, Alexander- 1898a
Abrányi, Emil- 1888a
Abrányi, Kornél- 1822a, 1874h, 1877h,
    1885h, 1897h
Absil, Jean- 1893a
Abt, Franz W.- 1819a, 1837f, 1841d,
    1855d, 1872f, 1885b
Academia de Belas Artas- 1877g
Academia Melpomenense- 1846g
Academia Nacional de Música (Bogotá)-
    1882f
Academic Music Society- 1830g
Académie de Chant- 1827g
Academie de Musique- 1868g
Académie de Musique et de Chant- 1818g
Académie du Chant- 1842g
Academie für Dramatische Gesang- 1882g
Academy for the Higher Development of
    Pianoforte Playing- 1873g
Accademia dei Concordi- 1808g
Accademia Filarmonica (Cagliari)- 1824g
Accademia Filarmonica (Casale
    Monferrato)- 1827g

Accademia Filarmonica (Turin)- 1814g
Accademia Filo-Armonica di Messina-
    1833g
Accademia Peloritana- 1827g
Accademia Polimniaca- 1806g
Accademie di Revvivati- 1823g
Accademie Filarmonica Romana- 1821g
Accorimboni, Agostino- 1818b
Ackley, A.H.- 1887a
Ackté, Aïno- 1876a, 1897c
Adam, Adolphe- 1803a, 1824f, 1825f, 1829i,
    1830i, 1833i, 1834i, 1836i, 1838i,
    1839fi, 1841i, 1842i, 1844i, 1847f,
    1849di, 1850i, 1852i, 1853i, 1854i,
    1856bi
Adám, Jenó- 1896a
Adamberger, Valentin- 1804b
Adamowski, Timothée- 1879cf
Adamowski String Quartet- 1888g
Adamowski Trio- 1896g
Adams, Charles R.- 1834a, 1856c
Adams, Nathan- 1864b
Adams, Suzanne- 1872a, 1895c, 1896c,
    1898f
Adams, Thomas- 1802d, 1814d, 1824d
Addison, John- 1844b
Adelaide:
    A. Choral Society- 1843g
    A. College of Music- 1883g
    A. Liedertafel- 1857g
    A. University Chair of Music-
        1897g
Adelburg, August- 1830a, 1873b
Adelphi Glee Club- 1832g
Adelphi Theater- 1806g
Adini, Ada- 1876c
Adkins, Morton- 1877a
Adler, Agnes- 1882c
Adler, Guido- 1855a, 1880f, 1881h, 1885d,
    1898d
Adler, Peter- 1899a
Aerts, Egide- 1847d, 1853b
Afanas'yev, Nicolai- 1821a, 1836c, 1846f,
    1896e, 1898b
Aggházy, Károly- 1855a, 1878f, 1881d
Agnelli, Salvatore- 1874b
Agnesi, Luigi- 1833a, 1865c, 1875b
Agostini, Giuseppe- 1874a, 1895c, 1898c
Agthe, Albrecht- 1873b
Agthe Music Academy (Posen)- 1826g
Agthe Music Academy (Breslau)- 1831g

Berger, Rudolf- 1874a
Bergmann, Carl- 1821a, 1849f, 1855d,
    1876bf
Bergmans, Paul- 1868a
Bergner, Wilhelm- 1868d
Bergson, Michal- 1820a, 1840f, 1863d,
    1898b
Bergt, August- 1802d, 1837b, 1838h
Beringer, Oscar- 1844a
Bériot, Charles Auguste de- 1802a, 1821c,
    1829f, 1843d, 1852f, 1858f, 1870b
Bériot, Charles W.- 1833a, 1887d
Berlijn, Anton- 1817a, 1846e, 1870b
Berlin, Irving- 1888a, 1893f
Berlin:
    B. Kunstlerverein- 1844g
    B. Liedertafel- 1809g
    B. Männergesangverein- 1843g
    B. PO- 1882g
    B. Philharmonic Society- 1826g
    B. Symphoniekapelle- 1843g
    B.er Allgemeine Musikalische
        Zeitung- 1824g
    B.er Bachverein- 1862g
    B.er Lehrergesangverein- 1886g
    B.er Liedertafel- 1884g
    Neue B.er Musikzeitung- 1847g
    Neue Liedertafel von B.- 1819g
Berliner, Emil- 1887f
Berlioz, Hector- 1803a, 1815f, 1820f,
    1821f, 1822f, 1823i, 1825i, 1826fi,
    1827fi, 1828fi, 1829i, 1830efi,
    1831(f)i, 1832i, 1833f, 1834i, 1835d,
    1837i, 1838i, 1839i, 1840i, 1841fi,
    1843f, 1844(f)hi, 1846i, 1847f,
    1848hi, 1849i, 1850i, 1851di, 1853h,
    1854fi, 1855fi, 1856e, 1858i, 1859h,
    1862i, 1867f, 1869b, 1870h
Bern:
    B.e Caecilienverein- 1862g
    B.e Convention for the Protection
        of Literary and Artistic Works-
        1886g
    B.er Liedertafel- 1845g
    B.er Männerchor- 1870g
    B.ische Musikgesellschaft- 1815g
    B.ische Orchesterverein- 1876g
Bernard, Anthony- 1891a
Bernard, Emile- 1842a
Bernardel Violin Shop- 1826g
Bernat-Veri, Jorge- 1800b
Berneker, Constanz- 1872d, 1873d
Berner, Friedrich- 1827b
Bernoulli, Eduard- 1867a
Bernuth Music Conservatory- 1873g
Berr, Friedrich- 1833e, 1836h, 1838b
Berra, Marco, Publishing House and
    Music Shop- 1811g

Berry and Gordon, Music Publishers-
    1853g
Berteling Woodwind Co.- 1855g
Bertheaume, Isidore- 1802b
Bertin, Louise-Angélique- 1805a, 1827i,
    1831i, 1836i, 1877b
Bertini, Domenico- 1829a, 1866h
Bertini, Giuseppe- 1815h, 1852b
Bertini, Henri J.- 1876b
Bertinotti, Teresa- 1801f, 1810f, 1854b
Berton, Henri François- 1821d, 1826h,
    1832b
Berton, Henri Montan- 1803i, 1807d, 1809i,
    1811(f), 1815eh, 1816d, 1834e,
    1844b
Bertoni, Ferdinando- 1808f, 1813b
Bertram, Theodore- 1869a, 1889c
Bertrand, Aline- 1820c, 1835b
Bertrand, Jean G.- 1859h, 1866h, 1872h
Berutti, Pablo- 1887d
Berwald, August- 1869b
Berwald, Franz Adolf- 1812f, 1816i, 1817i,
    1820i, 1827i, 1829f, 1835f, 1841fi,
    1842i, 1845i, 1850f, 1855i, 1858i,
    1862i, 1864ei, 1868b
Berwald, Johann F.- 1819d, 1823d
Beseda, Umelecka- 1863c
Besozzi, Louis-Désiré- 1837e
Bessel, Vasily- 1843a
Bessel and Co., Music Publishers- 1869g
Besson, Gustave A.- 1820a, 1875b
Besson Instruments Co.- 1838g
Best, William T.- 1855d, 1897b
Bethlehem (Penn.):
    B. Choral Union- 1882g
    Philharmonic Society of B.- 1820g
Bethune, "Blind Tom"- 1849a
Better, Lenore- 1886c
Betts, John E.- 1823b
Betz, Franz- 1835a, 1856c
Bevignani, Enrico- 1841a, 1893c
Beyschlag, Adolf- 1845a
Bezekirsky, Vassili- 1835a
Bianchi, Bianca- 1855a, 1873c
Bianchi, Francesco- 1801i, 1809f, 1810b
Bianchi, Valentina- 1855c
Bibliographical Society of London- 1892g
Bibliographisches Institut- 1826g
Bierey, Gottlob B.- 1807i, 1840b
Biernacki, Nikodem- 1862c
Biese, Wilhelm- 1822b
Biese, Wilhelm, Piano Co.- 1853g
Bignami, Carlo- 1808a, 1827d, 1829d,
    1833d, 1848b
Bigot, Marie- 1809f, 1816(f), 1820b
Bihari, János- 1827b
The Billboard- 1894g
Billington, Elizabeth- 1809f, 1811f, 1818b

D

F

G

H

K

N

O

U